CONQUEST AND FUSION

THE SOCIAL EVOLUTION OF CAIRO
A.D. 642-1850

SOCIAL, ECONOMIC AND POLITICAL
STUDIES OF THE MIDDLE EAST

ÉTUDES SOCIALES, ÉCONOMIQUES ET
POLITIQUES DU MOYEN ORIENT

VOLUME XX

SUSAN JANE STAFFA

CONQUEST AND FUSION

THE SOCIAL EVOLUTION OF CAIRO
A.D. 642-1850

LEIDEN
E. J. BRILL
1977

The Bāb Zuwayla: Spiritual Node of the Traditional City.

CONQUEST AND FUSION

THE SOCIAL EVOLUTION OF CAIRO

A.D. 642-1850

BY

SUSAN JANE STAFFA

With a Frontispiece, 16 Illustrations and 3 Maps

LEIDEN
E. J. BRILL
1977

Le but de la collection est de faciliter la communication entre le grand public international et les spécialistes des sciences sociales étudiant le Moyen-Orient, et notamment ceux qui y résident. Les ouvrages sélectionnés porteront sur les phénomènes et problèmes contemporains: sociaux, culturels, économiques et administratifs. Leurs principales orientations relèveront de la théorie générale, des problématiques plus précises, et de la politologie: aménagement des institutions et administration des affaires publiques.

The series is designed to serve as a link between the international reading public and social scientists studying the contemporary Middle East, notably those living in the area. Works to be included will be characterized by their relevance to actual phenomena and problems: whether social, cultural, economic, political or administrative. They will be theory-oriented, problem-oriented or policy-oriented.

ISBN 90 04 04774 3

PRINTED IN THE NETHERLANDS

"What one can imagine always surpasses what one sees, because of the scope of the imagination, except Cairo, because it surpasses anything one can imagine"

(The *qāḍī* of Fez quoted by Ibn Khaldūn, *at-Ta^crīf*, edited by Muḥammad ibn Tāwīt aṭ-Ṭanjī, p. 248).

... and how should Cairo be otherwise when she is the Mother of the World?

("Tale of the Jewish Doctor," *The Book of a Thousand Nights and a Night*, translated by R. F. Burton, I, p. 290).

In loving memory of my mother

Susanne E. Staffa née *Heinz*

and to my father

George Staffa

TABLE OF CONTENTS

PART THREE

UNITY IN DIVERSITY IN TURKISH CAIRO (A.D. 1517-1850)

ILLUSTRATIONS

MAPS

PREFACE

At a time when so many social scientists are focusing their attention on urban studies, there should be little question that an understanding of the nature of urban life and development depends upon comparisons of diverse types of urban societies. Yet we find all too few works on the Near Eastern city, either historical or contemporary.

That an analysis of Cairo in the traditional period can contribute much to the study of urbanism cannot be denied, for the sources allow us to trace, better than for most European cities, the patterns of its growth and social life over a long and continuous period. As is the case with many towns of the Islamic world, Cairo's foundation and development was intimately connected with the rise and fall of dynasties and urban events figure importantly in the chronicles. Still, although the city passed through many crises, there was no radical change in its life and general organization until the nineteenth century. Let us note from the start that we are here concerned with the general character of urbanism and development associated with a cosmopolitan complex society, rather than the more specific problems of urbanization such as the circumstances surrounding ecological development or sociocultural problems related to rural-urban migration. What interests us is the structural continuity in the social fabric that persisted despite a number of transformations and necessary adaptations to historical contingencies.

Many of the recent historical works cited in this book are competent analyses of different aspects of Cairene society at various periods, but none of these writers has attempted a study of the city which provides an overall picture of its social development. The latest general history which contains many valuable insights is that of Stanley Lane-Poole, *The Story of Cairo* (1902). We can only lament the lack of method in the social sciences in his day! Marcel Clerget's geographical work, *Le Caire* (1934), deals primarily with the city of the early twentieth century, although it includes much material on the economic history of earlier periods, while the most recent book, Janet Abu-Lughod's *Cairo: 1001 Years of the City Victorious* (1971), focuses upon the origins of modern problems in ecology and town planning. Perhaps the work that most closely approximates our attempt is *Muslim Cities in the Later Middle Ages* (1967), by the historian Ira Lapidus, but that cogent volume deals with Syrian cities as well as Cairo during a much shorter span of time. There is no existing study then, that can be considered sociological, and the best historical interpretations fail to probe the underlying structure of the complex society upon which the urban manifestation rested as well as to comprehend its evolution.

It is worth noting that the sources upon which our analysis is based are not at variance with the forms of evidence that sociologists and anthropologists are wont to cite. There are four major kinds of primary sources useful for a study of medieval Cairo; chronicles and early travel reports, archaeological and architectural materials, contemporary commentaries and notes on urban life, and folklore. Of these, the first group provides the greatest mass of data and can be considered to be at least as reliable as reports of the early missionaries and travelers in the New World; more reliable in many cases, because by the period we are considering, the science of historiography was already well developed in the Arab world. One cannot wish a more spontaneous reflection of contemporary life than the letters, contracts, and notes found among the Geniza documents, while in recent years, extensive excavations of the medieval town of Fusṭāṭ which preceded and eventually blended with Cairo, have not only given us confirmation and elucidation of the written sources but have allowed us to perceive continuity between ancient and modern Egypt.

Of contemporary interpretations of the city and its social organization, that of Ibn Khaldūn is the most outstanding. Although social anthropologists frequently take into account the native philosopher's view of his society, few have the opportunity to utilize such penetrating observations as his. For not only was Ibn Khaldūn consciously involved in the search for general principles of development of human civilization and social organization, but he showed great interest in sedentary culture, specifically the life of towns and cities as centers of civilization. In the eyes of this philosopher, who wrote on anthropological subjects from human races to group solidarity and was the first to treat history as the proper object of a special science, the study of human civilization could not be separated from the study of urbanism or of Cairo.

If it is granted that folklore has any insights to offer the social anthropologist, then the one who studies medieval Cairo is one of the most favored of scholars. Who could ask for a more extensive or down-to-earth treasury of tales than *The Thousand and One Nights*? For it was in the coffee shops of Cairo that these stories were told and in that same city in the sixteenth century, that the latest manuscripts were written. Through these tales it is possible to glimpse the medieval city as it looked through the eyes of the Cairene who, although he often imagined many fantasies behind each unopened gate, never became separated, even in his wildest thoughts, from the life of the city itself. Such sources communicate something of the atmosphere of the city even today.

Historical data are basic but at least as essential to the conceptualization of this work was the experience of living in Cairo for eight years. The writer would like to thank the countless number of Egyptians who unconsciously not only stimulated many insights into the working of the social fabric but repeatedly confirmed her belief in the viability of a pattern developed over millennia of human experience. Especially in this regard she would like to thank ᶜAbd al-Jayyid as-Sayyid Thābit and Muḥammad ᶜAbd al-Mawjūd Fāyed, "middlemen *par excellence*," who revealed to her the intricacies of the "social knit."

The author is most grateful to the American Research Center in Egypt for its support of her initial year of research in Egypt. Also she will always remember with gratitude Drs. David Bidney and Wadie Jwaideh for their unfailing advice and encouragement during the initial stages of the preparation of this book, and Drs. Talal Asad, Heribert Adam, Ernest Gellner, and Ira Lapidus for their comments, support, and encouragement during its later stages. Thanks are also due to Estratia Patsalidis for her dedicated typing of the final manuscript, to Camille Caliendo Griffith for proof-reading, and especially to Elizabeth M. Rodenbeck for her sensitive rendering of maps and drawings and to Costa of Cairo for his special efforts in producing the photographic plates.

NOTE ON TRANSLITERATION

For the transliteration of Arabic words we use the following system:

أ	ب	ت	ث	ج	ح	خ	د	ذ	ر	ز	س	ش	ص	ض	ط
ʾ	b	t	th	j	ḥ	kh	d	dh	r	z	s	sh	ṣ	ḍ	ṭ

ظ	ع	غ	ف	ق	ك	ل	م	ن	ه	و	ى	ة
ẓ	ʿ	gh	f	q	k	l	m	n	h	w	y	-a (in the construct state, -at)

To approximate correct pronunciation more closely, the definite article (*al-*) is assimilated in the cases in which the initial letter of the word would be written with *shadda.* The letter *hamza* (ʾ) is omitted when it occurs initially.

For the Turkish terms which occur in Part III, we have in principle tried to use the Arabic variants appropriate to the Egyptian context. The consonants we use which do not have equivalents in the Arabic system are transcribed as ch (for چ), and g (for گ).

Titles, place names, and other words which have passed into common English usage are written in their English form. The name "al-Fusṭāṭ" is transcribed thus when it refers to the original camp city but is given as "Fusṭāṭ" when it refers to the subsequent agglomeration in the area. Similarly, "al-Qāhira" refers principally to the original military enclave, while "Cairo" indicates a more developed cosmopolitan urban center.

INTRODUCTION

1. Definition of the City

A study of the evolution of any urban center involves a consideration of the basic nature of urbanism. Just as civilization does not appear full-blown, apart from all of the folk culture which preceded it, so a city rarely appears in history with the characteristics of a developed town, even in rudimentary form. The evolution of the urban center, like that of civilization, does not proceed at a constant pace but rather comes about by fits and starts, affected always by the vicissitudes of fate and fortune to which all aspects of human existence are vulnerable.

The contribution of the city to civilization depends in large part upon its role as a communication center for the society it represents. To the city comes the wealth of the hinterland, material, intellectual, and spiritual. Thus the town serves as a focus for the interests which prevail in the cultural matrix and it becomes a symbol of that culture, giving rise to the strongest emotional attachments on the part of urban dwellers. Among people of the hinterland, residence in the city tends to become a symbol of ambition and accomplishment. The general question to which we are addressing ourselves, "What was the pattern of Cairene urbanism, socially, culturally, and physically?" can only be answered in terms of the kinds of interactions that prevailed between urban residents at various periods. It is also a question which has no answer unrelated to the mores of the society as a whole.

Consideration of the problem of the definition of the city reveals that the city cannot be understood as a geographic entity. It is true that it may be delimited by boundaries and even walls, just as it has a location and a certain size. These factors, however, have little significance in themselves and are important only in so far as they affect the social, economic, and cultural relations of urban residents. A city is a place of human activity, a place of clustering of human population. Traditional Cairo with a population of about 200,000-300,000, represented not only a clustering in terms of population but also a clustering in terms of interest, beginning with the juxtaposition of various ethnic groups with diverse cultural orientations and progressively organizing these elements and articulating their relations with one another. We cannot, however, rely on a particular social grouping or political organization to define our city. These are only part of the picture. *The only way to discuss the city is in terms of the influences upon it which resulted from its constituent systems of communication, whether these were internal or extended outside.* Geographically it is in the very nature of the city to have indispensable ties with its hinterland as well as with other urban centers of the world. The city *is* a nodal point of these interaction systems.

The patterns of human interaction which formed the basis of Cairene culture in the traditional period were profoundly affected by three major factors which continued to act as the given framework of all activity until modern times. These are the Near Eastern environment, Islamic culture, and the conditions of preindustrial technology.

A primary fact of life in the Near East which has had profound implications for the nature of settled life over the millennia is, of course, the scarcity of water. The traditional Near Eastern city was a fragile entity. From the beginning, the agricultural surplus upon which it subsisted depended upon canalization and storage of water as well as upon protection against nomadic incursions which always threatened settled territory. Historical accounts from ancient until modern times are full of periodic famines, disastrous to cities, which inevitably occurred upon the breaking down of authority. Cairo's strategic position, moreover, on the trade routes from east to west and north and south, together with its control of the vast resources of Egypt made it an enticing prize for those who sought to rule the world. Little wonder then, that the city has always been a center of government and the seat of military rule. Little wonder also that this rule did not stop at the confines of the city itself, but extended outward to organize and protect the resources that were its very life's blood.

The cultural matrix of Islam accounts in large part for the characteristic form of the traditional city. The very term "*madīna*" (city) means a place where justice is administered and the place where the seat of authority is located. Other places may have larger populations or be centers of economic activity, but these are not *madīna*s. Let us note too, that the city in Islam must be a religious capital, for ultimately there is no justice or authority except from God. Thus the congregational mosque (*jāmi*ᶜ) which carries importance for political activities is always found in the *madīna.*

The Islamic character of the city is nowhere so apparent as in the looseness of the urban structure. Authority was hierarchical, but within itself, Islam recognized no community but the community of believers (*umma*). It is therefore not surprising that the Islamic city, in contrast to the city of Western tradition, is not a corporate entity in the legal sense. [1] Nor indeed, did any corporate institutions exist within the urban center for two fundamental reasons. In the first place there is no concept of corporation in Islamic law to compare with the concept in Roman law. The only legal "persons" known to Islamic law are estates, endowments (*awqāf*), and the public treasury. [2] There is even some question as to whether all craft "guilds" which existed in Ottoman times were really corporate. The very spirit of Islam militated against the formation of permanent groups of limited membership that could potentially compete with the all-inclusive solidarity of the community of believers. In the second place it was implicit in the definition of the city as a *madīna* to have provisions within it for government and the

---

1 It is our view that the corporate city of Western tradition is as particular as the tradition of the legal outlook which gave rise to it. The Islamic city lies within a cultural matrix represented by another law. The proliferation of corporations in the narrow legal sense, moreover, is not at all characteristic of the majority of human societies. Indeed, ethnographically speaking, it appears that it is the autonomous municipality or city-state and the rather parochial mentality that goes with it that needs explaining. Moreover, it is not now unusual to hear Western urbanites of humanistic orientation proclaiming their "citizenship of the world" even as medieval Muslims felt some sense of unity with Muslims universally. Urban consciousness is thus not a necessary goal to be achieved in urban development.

It is important to note, however, that it has been in the tradition of social anthropology since the days of Sir Henry Maine to apply the concept of corporation to such institutions as had regularly recruited membership, leadership, were focused upon particular interests, rights and duties shared by members, and were "eternal" in the eyes of society. The family in most folk societies is a prime example. Various organizations might become corporate under certain conditions, *de facto* rather then *de jure*.

There is a kind of continuum, moreover, between the more or less temporary organization of factions and the "permanent" organization of corporations. Successful factions had success because they had corporate attributes. The existence of "corporate" institutions hung upon the interactions of persons who made up their membership; upon patterns of cooperation and competition within and without. Even as, except for a few instances, the semi-corporate groups which made up urban Islamic society tended not to be permanently institutionalized, so was their significance frequently of an *ad hoc* nature. Some factions lasted only a few months, but others lasted several generations. Alliances of persons from all sections of society gave rise to cliques and factions that directed the operation of legal institutions. One might say, in fact, that the legal institutions served the factions rather than the other way around. Cf. Jeremy Boissevain, "The Place of Non-groups in the Social Sciences," *Man*, 3 (1968), pp. 542-556; Eric R. Wolf, "Kinship, Friendship, and Patron-Client Relations in Complex Societies," *The Social Anthropology of Complex Societies*, edited by Michael Banton, A.S.A. Monograph, no. 4 (London: Tavistock Publications, 1966), p. 16.

2 S. M. Stern, "The Constitution of the Islamic City," *The Islamic City*, edited by A. H. Hourani and S. M. Stern (Oxford: Bruno Cassirer, 1970), p. 48.

regulation of social life, provisions which extended to the hinterland. Since the power of the state was already rooted in the city, there was no need for special municipal government to arise, and since the Islamic state already managed local social and economic affairs through a flexible chain of command, there was no reason for permanent autonomous institutions within the city to develop.

A number of writers have pointed out that in Islam, hierarchical personal authority is regarded as essential to the normal pattern of social existence. [3] Authority in large part is derived from status in the most general sense of the term. It is inseparable from the innumerable distinctions of kind as well as from the infinitesimal gradations of rank. [4] The patterns of deference which traditionally characterize social interaction testify to this fact. At each level the strata of urban society were tied together by networks characterized not only by reciprocity but by a relatively well-defined hierarchy which related directly to bases of power, formal and informal. In this connection we will devote considerable attention to patron-client ties.

The second characteristic which emerges from the orientation of Islam concerns the role of the urban notables and the middle orders of society. The fact that the religious law (*sharīʿa*) governed social and economic life encouraged a strong tie between religious notables (*ʿulamāʾ*) and the commercial sector. Religious men of learning married into rich bourgeois families and possessed a great degree of social and economic power through private investments as well as their control of endowments. These were able also to provide urban leadership both on the basis of the ideological resource that they controlled and their close connections with the society from which they sprang; for the scholars derived from all classes even as Islam applied to everyone without consideration of rank.

---

[3] See S. M. Stern, "The Constitution of the Islamic City," p. 34; Ronald Cohen, "Power and Authority and Personal Success in Islam and Bornu," *Political Anthropology*, edited by Marc J. Swartz et al. (Chicago: Aldine Publishing Co., 1966); and also Ibn Khaldūn, *The Muqaddimah*, translated by Franz Rosenthal (New York: Bollingen Foundation, 1958), I, p. 381.

[4] Thus C. A. O. van Nieuwenhuijze writes:

> "The true fixation of authority as an all-permeating feature of Middle Eastern society, and the completion of society as an authority system ... ensues from the fact that not merely absolute status results in authority but also relative status. Whenever a subject A encounters a subject B who belongs to a social category rated higher than his own, there is a potential element of authority inherent in B's dealing with A" *(Sociology of the Middle East* (Leiden: E. J. Brill, 1971), p. 731).

Within broad limits, Islam also recognizes the validity of cultural differences. Nowhere do we see Islamic tolerance for diversity so vividly expressed as in the explicit recognition of the right of other religious groups, "The People of the Book" (*Ahl al-Kitāb*), Jews, Christians, and Zoroastrians, to carry on their beliefs and practices. In addition, the practice of adopting traditional administrative routines when these did not conflict with Islamic law allowed a great deal of flexibility in the pattern of social interaction.

Thus the only social entities having separate legal status resembling that of corporations were non-Muslim religious communities. Within Islam there was no community but the entire community of believers (*umma*); there was only the *umma* on the one hand and private individuals on the other. Semi-corporate bodies such as families, residential units, or clienteles partially filled the gap, but generally these competed with others for control of resources. Some regulations had to keep people from treading too firmly on other's toes, but to a great extent, people were allowed to work out their existence in their own way.

This particularistic, individualistic emphasis together with the recognition of the validity of diversity accounts in large part for the intense factionalism that invariably resulted in the periodic weakening of central authority discussed at length by Ibn Khaldūn. Consideration of the events that shaped traditional Cairo is difficult in terms of well-defined groups and institutions. The outcome was much more dependent upon the vicissitudes of factions and alliances within the population which, though they often fell into a general pattern, were fluid, even as the fabric of the social structure within which they took place was loosely woven.

The third set of facts that gave urban life its shape were the conditions of life in the preindustrial period. Principally these facts had basis in the limitations of technology. Long-range communication of information and resources was slow and difficult. The power of the military elite was relatively limited by the short range of the instruments of control. The rulers like the ruled depended primarily upon personal ties, if not always face to face communication, to achieve their ends. Local leaders could be regarded, on the one hand, as emanations of the ruler's personality, acting on his behalf, on the other as representatives of their own clienteles. The urban complex was a vast network of such ties ranging from intimate friendships to less effective but more extended connections of persons who had only a second- or third-hand acquaintance with one another.

Relative autonomy of internal components, quarters, craft groups, and local associations was the keynote in the structure of the pre-industrial urban network. Since technology did not allow effective direct centralization in the modern sense, centralization was achieved indirectly through the formation of alliances and patron-client ties that extended throughout the fabric of society. In so far as the elite failed to accomplish these liaisons, the notables and bourgeoisie could control the city, temporarily asserting themselves as popular leaders *de facto* when the government was weak. Urban quarters thus were the most viable units of defense and organization. Even when there was no question of the power of the elite, the most efficient, in fact the only realistic method of administering the law and collecting taxes was through the recognition of local groups and of their leaders who were held personally responsible.

2. The Social Components and the Social Hierarchy

Our justification then, for treating the city from the point of view of continuity over so many centuries lies in the fact that the principal elements which formed the general framework of its social structure did not change. Muslim historians throughout the Middle Ages, as well as European travelers invariably outlined social classes of the same repeating pattern. They spoke of rank (*jāh*) and of the "layers" (*ṭabaqāt*) of society. The order was hierarchical:

> Ranks are widely distributed among the people, and there are various levels of rank among them. At the top, they extend to the rulers above whom there is nobody. At the bottom they extend to those who have nothing to gain or to lose among their fellow men. In between there are numerous classes. [5]

The most prominent groupings were the elite (*al-khāṣṣa*); [6] the notables (*al-aᶜyān*) including prominent and respected leaders whether in the field of religion (*al-ᶜulamāʾ*), commerce (the wealthy import-export merchants, *tujjār*), or local government (the leaders of religious minorities and/or urban quarters); respected men of lower rank (*an-*

---

[5] Ibn Khaldūn, *The Muqaddimah*, II, p. 328.

[6] The term "*al-khāṣṣa*," generally speaking, refers to the "upper crust" of cultured persons and to some extent overlapped "*al-aᶜyān*." Since political leadership tended to be seated primarily in the military elite, however, "*al-khāṣṣa*" proper came to refer in the Mamlūk period especially to the sultan and his retinue, the highest ranking *amīr*s and officials. Cf. Ira Lapidus, *Muslim Cities in the Later Middle Ages* (Cambridge, Mass.: Harvard University Press, 1967), p. 80.

nās) such as the less wealthy merchants, specialists in crafts or medicine, property owners, and so forth; and "the masses" (*al-ᶜāmma*) who were without education, property, wealth, or power. [7]

The dimensions of social inequality had reference in the main to three resources or bases of power, the hierarchy being generally arranged according to relative access thereto. First, there was military power, controlled almost exclusively by the elite; second, there were economic resources, largely controlled by the elite but many of which were in the hands of the *aᶜyān*, and third, there was religious or ideological power, formally the domain of the *ᶜulamāᵓ*, but in reality emanating from all levels of society. Let us note that these resources under the conditions of the traditional heritage, were communicated through channels that followed a very general pattern. They were, moreover, interdependent and exchangeable and this exchangeability is what led to the formation of reciprocal ties within the community. Everyone needed some access to each of the three to make his way. Thus although the elite owned land, they were chiefly occupied with military concerns and had to depend upon merchants and other agents to carry on their business activities. Without the backing of the *ᶜulamāᵓ* they could not govern effectively; having no moral or legal force, they could not rule. The merchants depended upon the elite to provide protection of trade routes and caravans, while the *ᶜulamāᵓ* needed not only protection, but access to the financial resources of the elite and commercial sectors for the endowment of their establishment. It would be useless to argue for the primacy of one or the other of these resources. The need for food seems paramount, but so is the protection of life and limb. The traditional Muslim would also argue that both are possible only through the will of God.

There is another more general marker of rank which should be mentioned, and perhaps this is even more diagnostic than the possession of any of the three resources although wealth, power, learning, and piety gave rise to it. We refer here to one's ability to command services and to provide services for others. Thus Ibn Khaldūn wrote:

---

[7] It is worth noting that there is considerable ambiguity in the way in which most of these terms were applied. Thus not only is there variation in the way in which "*al-khāṣṣa*" is used, but "*an-nās*" which means "people" sometimes included the rich merchants or even the elite. The vagueness of terminological reference tended to reflect the real fact that the society was by no means rigidly stratified and the social status of the individual was more seriously affected by his relationships in the power structure than by his technical classification.

> Each class among the inhabitants of a town ... has power over the classes lower than it. Each member of a lower class seeks the support of rank from members of the next higher class, and those who gain it become more active among the people under their control in proportion to the profit they get out of it. [8]

and

> A person of rank has the people approach him with their labor and property. (They do that) in order to obtain advantages. The labor and property through which they attempt to approach him is, in a way, given in exchange for the many good and bad things they may obtain (or avoid) with the aid of his rank. [9]

and again

> Rank means the power enabling human beings to be active among the fellow men under their control with permission and prohibition, and to have forceful superiority over them in order to make them avoid things harmful to them and to seize their advantages. [10]

He tells us too what the real difference is between merchants of high and low rank. Merchants of high rank are very wealthy but their wealth depends upon their having others work for them. A merchant of low rank may also be wealthy, but he has to involve himself in the conduct of his business affairs, not just direct them.

Rank then, is something that cannot be defined simply with reference to the control of resources, nor even necessarily by family ties. Family and resources help, but these are conducive to rather than diagnostic of rank. Persons of rank were hospitable and generous, cultivated in speech and manners, wise, urbane, and sophisticated. In short, they were those who were able to make the right alliances, become clients of the right people and patrons of others; they were those who managed to find a place in the hierarchy from which they could attain their ends.

Needless to say there was nothing resembling "class consciousness" that was shared by persons occupying the same layer of society. An exception may be made in the case of the elite, since for the most part these formed a relatively small group, were usually of the same or similar ethnic origin, and tended to reside together following the same occupation. The *ᶜulamāᵓ* may also have possessed a feeling of unity, since for most of the time we consider these were represented by a common establishment. The merchants, popular leaders, craftsmen,

---

[8] The *Muqaddimah*, II, p. 330.
[9] *Ibid.*, p. 328.
[10] *Ibid.*, p. 329.

and the masses, however, were divided into many units representing many different occupations and orientations. Common interest groups at lower levels of society did from time to time arise, but this banding together was usually with regard to specific issues and never became permanent.

Nevertheless there were some groups within Cairene society that were united by a sentiment resembling "class consciousness" stemming from the fact that they were either legally recognized as separate communities or socially recognized by society at large as sets of persons who shared certain bodies of tradition. These groups are what we will call "status groups." Generally they may be seen as segments occupying more or less specific positions in a system of segments. The term "status" refers to their orientation in society which was not necessarily "high" or "low" but was "special." Such categories resulted ultimately from the universally accepted ideological framework; they were considered as "part of the nature of things." Islamic society recognized a community of believers, therefore persons who were not Muslim fell outside this community. Since the *umma* was defined through shared belief in Islam, so were the "People of the Book," Jews and Christians, divided according to their religion.

The special status of ethnic communities is harder to derive from Islam, but we have already seen that differences were not only recognized but respected. No differences are so outstanding as those of ethnic origin that are marked by custom, dress, and language as well as by physical features. It is true that status groups defined by nationality were much less tightly knit than those defined by religion, since the latter involved legal status while the former did not. In both cases, however, a stereotyping prevailed in the ordering of public social relations. It was usual for people of special statuses to follow certain occupations, although this was far from a strict rule. Thus many Copts tended to be bureaucrats, gold, and silversmiths, and makers of alcoholic beverages. Jews often engaged in business of various kinds, many becoming prominent merchants, bureaucrats, or even advisors and ambassadors of the elite. Persons belonging to special ethnic groups frequently capitalized on their national origin by going into trades related to goods coming from foreign lands and tended to reside in their own quarters. In that case their unity was encouraged as the government looked upon commercial groupings and quarters as units for tax collecting and social control.

We should emphasize, nevertheless, that while people of the same status could have different professions, people of the same profession could have different statuses. *Members of all special status groups were represented at all levels of society*, with the single possible exception of the highest class. Thus social classes and status groups formed the warp and the weft of the social fabric. Special status guaranteed a degree of autonomy to a community and at the same time brought it into logical relation to other communities; hierarchy expressed the unity of society while connecting it to a universal conception of the nature of man.

PART ONE

THE EARLY CAPITALS AND THE FOUNDATION OF THE CAIRENE PATTERN (A.D. 642-1193)

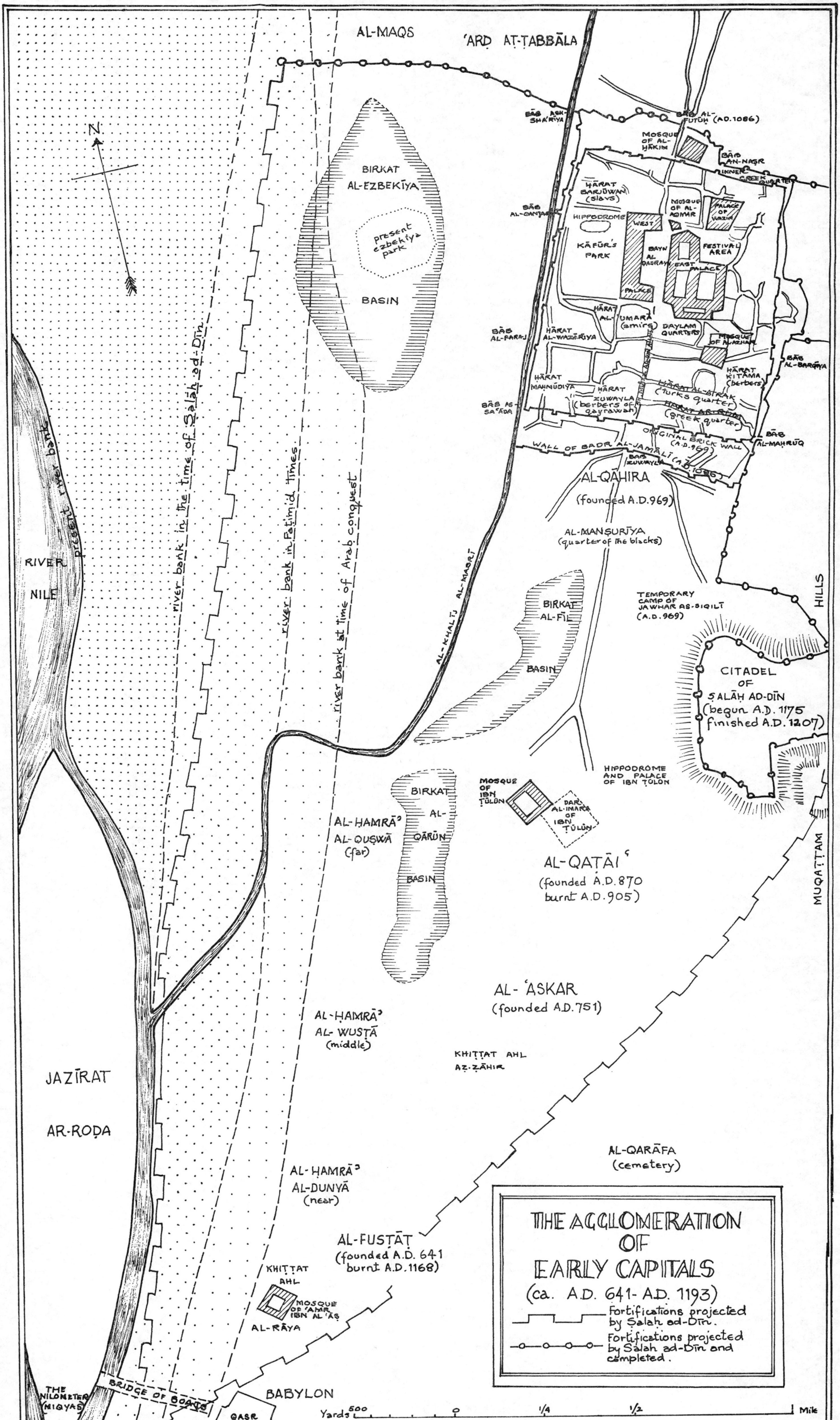

AL-MAQS
'ARḌ AT-ṬABBĀLA
N
BIRKAT AL-EZBEKĪYA
present ezbekīya park
BASIN
BĀB ASH-SHA'RĪYA
BĀB AL-FUTŪḤ (A.D. 1086)
MOSQUE OF AL-ḤĀKIM
BĀB AN-NAṢR
INNER GREEK QUARTER
ḤĀRAT BARJŪWAN (slavs)
BĀB AL-QANṬARA
HIPPODROME
MOSQUE OF AL-AQMAR
PALACE OF WAZIR
WEST
PALACE
KĀFŪR'S PARK
BAYN AL QASRAYN
FESTIVAL AREA
EAST PALACE
ḤĀRAT AL-'UMARĀ (amirs)
DAYLAM QUARTERS
BĀB AL-FARAJ
ḤĀRAT AL-WAZĪRĪYA
MOSQUE OF AL-AZHAR
BĀB AL-BARQĪYA
ḤĀRAT MAḤMŪDIYA
ḤĀRAT ZUWAYLA (berbers of qayrawan)
ḤĀRAT AL-ATRAK (turks quarter)
ḤĀRAT KITĀMA (berbers)
ḤĀRAT AR-RŪM (greek quarter)
BĀB AS-SA'ĀDA
ORIGINAL BRICK WALL (A.D. 969)
BĀB AL-MAḤRŪQ
WALL OF BADR AL-JAMĀLĪ (A.D. 1086)
BĀB ZUWAYLA
AL-QĀHIRA (founded A.D. 969)
AL-MANṢURĪYA (quarter of the blacks)
present river bank
river bank in the time of Ṣalāḥ ad-Dīn
river bank in Fāṭimid times
river bank at time of Arab conquest
AL-KHALĪJ AL-MAṢRĪ
RIVER NILE
BIRKAT AL-FĪL
BASIN
TEMPORARY CAMP OF JAWHAR AS-SIQILĪ (A.D. 969)
HILLS
CITADEL OF ṢALĀḤ AD-DĪN (begun A.D. 1175 finished A.D. 1207)
HIPPODROME AND PALACE OF IBN ṬŪLŪN
MOSQUE OF IBN ṬŪLŪN
DAR AL-IMARA OF IBN ṬŪLŪN
BIRKAT AL-QĀRŪN
BASIN
AL-ḤAMRĀ' AL-QUṢWĀ (far)
AL-QAṬĀI' (founded A.D. 870 burnt A.D. 905)
MUQATTAM
AL-'ASKAR (founded A.D. 751)
AL-ḤAMRĀ' AL-WUSṬĀ (middle)
KHIṬṬAT AHL AZ-ẒĀHIR
JAZĪRAT AR-RODA
AL-QARĀFA (cemetery)
AL-ḤAMRĀ' AL-DUNYĀ (near)
AL-FUSṬĀṬ (founded A.D. 641 burnt A.D. 1168)
KHIṬṬAT AHL AL-RĀYA
MOSQUE OF 'AMR IBN AL-'ĀṢ
THE AGGLOMERATION OF EARLY CAPITALS (ca. A.D. 641- A.D. 1193)
Fortifications projected by Ṣalāḥ ad-Dīn.
Fortifications projected by Ṣalāḥ ad-Dīn and completed.
THE NILOMETER (MIQYAS)
BRIDGE OF BOATS
BABYLON
QASR
Yards 500 0 1/4 1/2 1 Mile

INTRODUCTION

Cairo is at the point of the Delta, at the end of a funnel through which passed a continual flow of alien elements. Located not far from the ancient capital of Memphis, the old city lies on the route of an ancient canal which connected the Nile valley with the Red Sea. While foreigners contended for control of the richness of Egypt from the close of the Pharaonic period, the native part of the population played a passive but steady role in the political drama. At the crossing of two of the most important trade routes of the medieval world, one from Baghdad and Damascus to the Maghrib and the oases of the Sahara, and the other between Europe and the Mediterranean to the Sudan, Arabia and the Far East, the city became the most cosmopolitan commercial center of the Middle Ages; and yet it remained an essentially Egyptian city, depending upon the Nile for subsistence, influenced by the course of the river, and deriving most of its population from the villages of the hinterland.

The story of the origin of Cairo is the story of the juxtaposition and combination of diverse elements, of ancient Copts, Jews, and medieval Muslims, of native Egyptians and foreign governors and traders. Each group played its part in the growth of the urban center which came about not so much through specific choice or plan but by a special set of circumstances which gave the location significance economically and politically. During much of the time which we will consider, the city was not even thought to be a single unit, but a group of communities which happened to share the same location and a few common interests. It can be argued that the same conception has lasted until recent years but the story must have chronological limits. The Arab conquest began a new era in the history of Egypt, marking the real end of ancient culture and establishing the first Muslim settlement, while the reign of Ṣalāḥ ad-Dīn initiated the concept of Cairo as a group of united communities, at least in the physical sense. It was in this period that the basic aspects of urbanism first were realized. In many respects the transformations of later periods were based upon the patterns which took shape in the first few centuries of Cairo's history.

CHAPTER ONE

THE FOUNDATION OF FUSṬĀṬ: THE INITIAL CONFRONTATION (A.D. 642-750)

It is impossible to explain the social development of the Arab city without reference to the communities which ^{c}Amr ibn al-^{c}Āṣ and his followers found upon their arrival; for while they laid the foundations of the Muslim capital of Egypt, the Arabs were by no means the first to occupy the area. Archaeologists have found traces of settlements going back to prehistoric times, and continuity can be traced between medieval occupations and the ancient capital of Memphis only twelve miles to the south.

The fortress of Babylon, surviving even now under the name Qaṣr ash-Shama^{c}, takes its name from a fort built about 525 B.C. by the Persians on the cliff, ar-Raṣad, then on the river bank.[1] The present building was constructed early in the second century A.D. by the Roman emperor Trajan slightly to the north and on lower ground, the river by that time having retreated somewhat towards the west as it continued to do for several centuries. This fortress became a nucleus of Romano-Byzantine rule from which developed a rather disorganized proto-urban community. As difficulties arose in the relations between Egyptian Copts and Orthodox Greeks, the town came to be a center of hostility to Byzantine rule. When monophysites were declared heretics at the Council of Chalcedon in A.D. 451 many Copts felt more secure in inland Babylon than in Alexandria where the hand of Byzantium was more strongly felt.

The Coptic settlement at that time could be compared to cities of Europe at the beginning of the Middle Ages. Monasteries were very numerous, both within the precincts of the fortress and outside. Spreading northward to the southern suburbs of ancient Heliopolis lay the unfortified settlement of Miṣr,[2] probably consisting of monasteries,

---

[1] See *The Chronicle of John, Bishop of Nikiu*, translated from Zotenberg's Ethiopic text by R. H. Charles (Oxford, 1916), p. 55; al-Maqrīzī, *Kitāb al-Mawā^{c}iẓ wa al-I^{c}tibār bi-Dhikr al-Khiṭaṭ wa al-Āthār* (Cairo (Būlāq), 1853) (henceforth referred to as *Khiṭaṭ*), I, p. 296; and also a summary of the sources concerning the pre-Islamic occupation, *Babylon of Egypt*, by A. J. Butler (Oxford: The Clarendon Press, 1914).

[2] "Miṣr," the ancient name of Egypt, "Memphis," the name of the ancient capital, the Greek name "Letopolis," and "Fusṭāṭ," the name of the Arab camp, are all used

gardens, and vineyards scattered thinly over the plain between the river and the Muqaṭṭam Hills. [3] It is evident that most of the plain was unoccupied at the time of the conquest although gardens and farms covered the areas inundated by the annual flood as they have throughout known history. Until the last century the fortress remained a refuge for Copts whenever they were threatened by attack of a foreign power, internal upheavals, or intolerance on the part of Egyptian governments.

Babylon fell to the Arabs in April of A.D. 641 after a siege of seven months. Although it had been strongly defended, the local Copts were poorly disposed toward the Byzantines and offered them little assistance. After the fall of Alexandria in October, the commander ᶜAmr ibn al-ᶜĀṣ returned to the plain of Babylon to found his own capital, al-Fusṭāṭ, or "The Town of the Tent." While the general would have preferred to set up headquarters at Alexandria, the caliph ᶜUmar objected on the ground that the Nile's inundation would cut that city off from the Muslim capital at Madīna. [4] Accordingly al-Fusṭāṭ rose outside the walls of the fortress around the place where ᶜAmr had pitched his tent. [5] In order to maintain close relations with the caliph and provide a means of sending tribute and corn to Arabia, an ancient canal which connected Babylon with the Red Sea at Suez was reopened. [6]

There can be no doubt that the new capital was regarded primarily as a barrack rather than a center of economic and cultural significance, and we can point out the relationship between the Arabic word *fusṭāṭ*,

---

more or less interchangeably with "Babylon" by Coptic, Greek, or Arab writers in different periods. "Miṣr" generally refers to a less restricted area than the fortress and can thus refer to the whole agglomeration stretching between Heliopolis and the southernmost extension of the Coptic settlement. "Babylon" referred at first to the fortress only, but soon came to apply to the surrounding community as well. Following the establishment of the Arab camp, the term fell into disuse and was supplanted by "Fusṭāṭ" which was also extended progressively to include more than the military community. Curiously, some European writers of the medieval period continued to use "Babylon" to denote the whole country of Egypt (A. J. Butler, *Babylon of Egypt*, pp. 6, 39).

[3] Al-Maqrīzī, *Khiṭaṭ*, I, p. 286.

[4] See al-Yaᶜqūbī, *Livre de les pays* (a translation of *Kitāb al-Buldān* by Gaston Wiet) (Cairo, 1937), p. 185; also al-Maqrīzī, *Khiṭaṭ*, I, p. 296.

[5] For further information on the camp cities of early Islam, see Louis Massignon, "Explication du plan de Baṣra (Irak)," *Westöstliche Abhandlungen R. Tschudi* (Wiesbaden, 1954), pp. 155-174; by the same author, "Explication du plan de Qufa (Iraq)," *Mélanges Maspero*, III, Extraits de la *Mémoires de l'Institut Française d'Archéologie Orientale* (Cairo, 1935), pp. 337-360; and Else Reitemeyer, *Die Städtegründungen der Araber im Islām nach den arabischen Historikern und Geographen*, Munich, 1912.

[6] *The Chronicle of John, Bishop of Nikiu*, translated by R. H. Charles, p. 195.

the Greek *phossaton*, and the Latin, *fossatum*, all of which mean "entrenched camp." The location was chosen because of its obvious strategic advantages commanding the approach to Upper Egypt and the east-west routes by land and sea. The fact that ᶜAmr did not occupy the old town of Miṣr is an indication of the Arab attitude toward settlement; they simply did not think of themselves as colonists. The caliph's orders were that the Muslims should not acquire property and take root in Egypt. Their purpose was rather to stay in control of the resources of the land and to supervise shipment of tribute to Madīna. Moreover, it was felt that the comforts of an urban existence were incompatible with the retention of courage and strength necessary for success in battle.

We may note here that in the early years of the conquest, the fortress played a secondary role in Arab defense, as the true refuge for nomads is the desert. Al-Yaᶜqūbī speaks only of supervised guardposts (s. *maḥras*) apportioned among the tribal quarters. [7] During this period whole tribes migrated into Egypt, notably elements of the Rabīᶜa to become a factor to be reckoned with, even in later days. [8] Nevertheless the hundreds of thousands of soldiers coming to Egypt under the various Umayyad governors must have settled in the towns.

At first the Muslims wanted only a place to live and to pray. The mosque, constructed during the winter of A.D. 641-642, which came to bear ᶜAmr's name, was the only building of the early period of al-Fusṭāṭ that survived for any length of time. The original structure was made of rough unplastered brick, hardly more than an ordinary house, oblong in form with a low roof. [9] The mosque served also as a council chamber, a *qāḍī*'s court, and a place of lodging for strangers. The residence of ᶜAmr was hardly distinct from the houses of the other Arabs.

To the east and north of the mosque, around the place where the commander pitched his tent, were grouped the clans, more or less in the places which they had occupied during the siege. These were divided into three tracts called "*ḥamrā*ʾs" ("reds") possibly from the color of the standards set up in their midst. The quarter known as the Khiṭṭat Ahl al-Rāya or "Quarter of the People of the Flag," represented the

[7] *Kitāb al-Buldān, Bibliotheca Geographorum Arabicorum,* edited by M. J. DeGoeje, VII (Leiden: E. J. Brill, 1967), p. 331.

[8] S. Lane-Poole, *A History of Egypt in the Middle Ages, History of Egypt,* VI (London: Methuen & Co., 1901), p. 29.

[9] Al-Maqrīzī, *Khiṭaṭ,* II, p. 247.

nucleus of the army and was composed chiefly of *Muhājirūn* and *Anṣār*.[10] Other groups also became attached to this nucleus, retaining their tribal designations and places on the paylist in the official register (*dīwān*). A separate quarter outside, Khiṭṭat Ahl aẓ-Ẓāhir, was provided for people who could not find a place with kinsmen. Thus territorial arrangement followed political organization which was inseparable from religiously defined privilege. The Khiṭṭat Ahl al-Rāya was centrally located, around it were tribal groupings of others who had taken part in the conquest, and the late stragglers were on the periphery (see Map I).[11] The authority of ᶜAmr descended through his subordinates who were also heads of their respective tribal groups. The separation of clans was both conducive to the maintenance of army discipline and a safeguard against the outbreak of internal feuds but, if the Arab of Fusṭāṭ felt he had any obligation, it was to his clan and tribe or to "the Army of Islam" rather than the group of fellow "settlers" beside whom he was living in a foreign land.

As we have pointed out, the Egyptians had offered little resistance to the Muslim conquest and had even sided with the Arabs in procuring supplies and building bridges. The generous treaty granted them, as *dhimmīs*, or non-Muslim residents of a Muslim land, "security for themselves, their religion, their goods, and their churches and crosses, on land and sea" in return for payment of the poll tax. If the rise of the Nile was less than usual, the tax was to be reduced in proportion.[12]

The Arabs, having no experience in administrative matters aside from the rule of the clan and tribe, found it expedient to adopt the procedures already established in lands that they conquered. The law, which came in the next century to form the unitary framework of Islamic civilization, was yet undeveloped.[13] Although the legislation of the Qur'ān was the ideal, customary law (*ᶜurf*) prevailed in the many cases for which the former was not explicit or did not present direct contradiction to practice.

---

[10] The *Muhājirūn* were persons who had joined Muḥammad in his *Ḥijra* (flight) from Mecca. The *Anṣār* were those who took up the cause at Madīna.

[11] A. R. Guest, "The Foundation of Fustat and the Khittahs of that Town," *Journal of the Royal Asiatic Society*, 1907, pp. 49-83.

[12] A. J. Butler, *The Arab Conquest of Egypt* (Oxford: The Clarendon Press, 1902), p. 325.

[13] It appears that in the Umayyad period, the legal judgments made by tribal shaykhs or by the caliph or his representatives followed the principles of customary tradition modified to some extent by essential principles enunciated in the Qur'ān. See H. A. R. Gibb, *Mohammedanism* (London: Oxford University Press, 1949), p. 89.

Thus there was no abrupt breach of continuity in social institutions and it was some time before the older structures underwent essential transformation through penetration and development of the new ideology. In Egypt, Byzantine organization was taken over almost intact. The technical terminology found in papyri dating from the early caliphate is that of Byzantine rule. Under the Romans the administrative unit was the pagarchy, consisting of the metropolis under its curia, its contributory villages, and the notables of the district. The pagarchs and dukes were drawn from the more powerful members of the nobility. These had troops of their own, condottieri or bucellari, and were thus in a position to defy authority. While under the Arabs the pagarchs were still drawn from this same class, their force was greatly diminished and they came to be more in the nature of police. The regular army was exclusively Muslim: *Muhājirūn, Anṣār*, and *mawālī* (clients). [14]

The fiscal system of the Arabs was even more centralized than that of the Byzantines, the pagarchs being placed directly under the governor at Fusṭāṭ. The central government would set the amount of taxes to be collected from each pagarchy and send each pagarch an order for payment for each district within the pagarchy. Local assessors drew up schedules specifying who should pay each tax and in what proportion. In larger cities the quarter was the unit of taxation, separate assessments then being made for the taxpayers of each. [15]

For their part, the Arabs regarded Egypt as an especially valuable source of revenue. Their policy, like that of the Romans, was frankly exploitative, with little or no thought of the welfare of the inhabitants. It is known that in A.D. 715 the caliph Sulaymān commanded the finance minister Usāma ibn Zayd on his departure to Egypt to "milk the cow till she runs dry and drain the blood till it stops running." [16] ᶜAmr ibn al-ᶜĀṣ had collected £ 6,000,000 from a population of six to eight millions and it is said that on his death he left seventy sacks of dinars or ten tons of gold, which his sons declined to inherit. [17] In addition to taxes, there was a corvée for the upkeep of canals, a conscription for raiding fleets, and even compulsory transfer of skilled workers from one part of the empire to another. Egyptian conscriptees took part in the construction of the mosques of Jerusalem and Damascus.

[14] H. I. Bell, "The Administration of Egypt under the Umayyad Khalifs," *Byzantinische Zeitschrift*, 28 (1928), p. 280.

[15] L. Casson, "Tax Collection Problems in Early Arab Egypt," *Transactions and Proceedings of the American Philological Association*, 69 (1938), p. 275.

[16] H. I. Bell, "The Administration of Egypt," p. 286.

[17] S. Lane-Poole, *The Story of Cairo* (London: J. M. Dent & Co., 1902), p. 59.

The governor under the caliph al-Walīd, Qurra ibn Sharīq al-ᶜAbsī (A.D. 709-714) is generally represented in history as an infamous oppressor but the evidence of his own letters indicates that he was rather an efficient administrator of a system which emphasized revenue collection. It seems that in the first decade of the eighth century there was a considerable problem of tax arrears in Egypt that was growing continuously worse as time wore on. Under Qurra, a local agent, Basilius, is scolded for his tardiness in sending in two-thirds of the demanded sum. [18] A collection of letters from this period (the Aphrodite Papyri) refers to fugitives who had fled their homes under pressure of these burdens. [19] We should note, however, that the problem of refugees from governmental authority was acute long before Qurra's time and existed as well in the time of the Byzantines and even previous to that.

At first, because of the injunction against land ownership by Muslims, the tax on landed property (*kharāj*) applied principally to *dhimmī*s, but before long lands were held by Muslims as well. The feudal fief (*iqṭāᶜ*) moreover, came to be an important institution. Community lands leased hereditarily thus became a form of private property upon which, in theory, a tenth of the proceeds were due. Here patron-client ties afforded some relief from the exactions of the law. In Umayyad as in Byzantine times small landholders were wont to hold lands in the names of owners of large estates, thereby avoiding the payment of the land tax in place of the more favorable sum due from fiefs. In actual fact the owners were at liberty to sell or deal with them as they pleased. [20]

The Copts of Babylon lived next to their conquerors, probably regarding them with both respect and an eye for profit. For while the relations between the two groups were somewhat strained, many privileges were allowed to non-Muslims. From the very beginning Coptic merchants were attracted to the neighborhood of ᶜAmr's camp and set up dwellings there. Proselytizing on a large scale would have cut greatly into the profit of the caliph to say nothing of the earnings of successive governors who took their own share. [21] The Christians

---

18 L. Casson, "Tax Collection Problems," pp. 286-287.

19 Cf. Nabia Abbott, *The Ḳurrah Papyri from Aphrodite in the Oriental Institute* (Chicago, Ill.: University of Chicago Press, 1938).

20 Adam Mez, *Die Renaissance des Islams*, H. Rechendorf, ed. (Heidelberg: C. Winter, 1922), pp. 104-106.

21 The average governor held office for three and a half months and his livelihood depended upon his savings.

therefore for a long time remained in the majority. As the Arabs well realized that they themselves were not equipped to administer a complex society, they left all but the highest positions in the hands of the native inhabitants. Official documents in Egypt were written in Greek or Coptic for at least sixty years after the fall of Babylon, since written Arabic had not yet been developed for technical usage. With such dependence upon the subject people, the Arab community of al-Fusṭāṭ attracted a large Christian population including not only merchants and wives for the conquerors, but also clerks and officials. Even when Arabic became the language of administration, the Copts continued to manage nearly all of the governmental departments.

The Arabs, however, never allowed the distinction between ruler and ruled, Muslim and non-Muslim, to vanish. The great influence of the Copts in economic and administrative life necessitated checks on their power, or the Arab minority would have been overwhelmed. Throughout the history of Cairo, the influential *dhimmī*s are alternately favored and persecuted. While they fared pretty well during the first century of Muslim rule, during the second century governmental and social pressure drove the Copts into a ghetto-like existence. As one writer has said:

> The narrow streets of the Coptic quarters, the bare fortress-like walls of their churches, their hidden entrances, the fortifications of the desert monasteries with their towering keeps, bear witness to the necessity for defense, whether against the Muslim town-dweller or desert Beduin. [22]

By the end of the seventh century the pagarchs and the dukes were no longer drawn from the Christian aristocracy but were supplanted by Arabs. The first great Coptic revolt occurred in the year A.D. 725-726.

The Arabs could not do with non-Muslims and they could not do without them; for the bedouins looked down upon manual labor and the religion of Islam forbade the true believer from following certain occupations. At first the only really honorable profession was that of warrior and protector. Not even educated Christians found respect in the eyes of many fanatical pietists who, having no patience with monasticism, thought of the Coptic monks as despicable owners of secret hoards to be squeezed for the benefit of the faithful. [23] It is difficult to generalize on the treatment of non-Muslims but it is pro-

---

[22] Dorothea Russell, *Medieval Cairo and the Monasteries of the Wādi Natrūn* (London: Weidenfeld and Nicholson, 1962), p. 24.

[23] S. Lane-Poole, *The Story of Cairo*, p. 63.

bably safe to say that periods of security of the Arab rulers coincided with periods of comparative safety from persecution. The phenomenon of scapegoatism is most likely to appear in time of social and political anxiety. We should note however, that upon occasion Muslim rulers turned to Christians and Jews for support when support was lacking in their own ranks.

For a long time the bedouins retained the mentality of the desert, and numerous civil disorders interrupted the process of urbanization. There was even a lack of unity among the Muslims themselves. From the time of the caliph ᶜUthmān, many had supported the ᶜAlid cause. Resentments against the Umayyads, festering almost since the founding of al-Fusṭāṭ, broke out upon the accession of Marwān II. The replacement of the Egyptian governor Ḥafṣ ibn al-Walīd by Marwān's appointee Ḥassān ibn ᶜAṭāhiya was the immediate cause of a reaction on the part of the Egyptian Yemenite groups. The deposition of the caliph was proclaimed at the Mosque of ᶜAmr, the new governor driven out, and Ḥafṣ reinstated.[24] Although the latter sagely cooperated with Marwān in forbidding Yemenite fugitives from Syria entry into Egypt, he and his supporters were eventually arrested and executed.

The region of Ḥawf northeast of al-Fusṭāṭ was a chronic trouble spot. In A.D. 732 the treasurer ᶜUbaydallāh had imported 5,000 Arabs of the Rabīᶜa group (Qays tribe) to counteract the power of the Copts there.[25] From then on the roads were infested by robbers and every political crisis became more serious. At the time of the Umayyad disaster on the Great Zāb (A.D. 750), the caliph's support was derived from this tribe and, when Marwān II fled to Egypt as a last resort, ᶜAbbāsid troops in pursuit, the fighting that occurred in the region of the Ḥawf was especially bloody.

But although there was a tendency to assert themselves against central authority, the Arabs of al-Fusṭāṭ looked to the Islamic homeland for leadership. They felt intimately involved in the struggles over the caliphate and did not view their Egyptian residence as an opportunity to create a center of power. Putting little into the development of Egypt, they plundered her of what they could. Both merchants and craftsmen felt the heavy hand of the Umayyad governors and only a century after its founding, al-Fusṭāṭ was faced with severe economic problems. To add to the difficulty, a series of disastrous

---

24 Al-Kindī, *Kitāb al-Wulāh wa Kitāb al-Quḍāh*, edited by Rhuvon Guest (Leiden: E. J. Brill, 1912), p. 76.

25 Al-Kindī, *Kitāb al-Wulāh*, p. 76.

floods were followed by terrible famines. The water collected in low-lying areas, breeding mosquitos and epidemics. Thus environmental problems were added to political and economic ones. Many Arabs who probably did not at first realize the hazards of camping on low ground were compelled to move to drier and more healthy locations. The transition from the nomadic way of life to settled urban existence was not easy, either with respect to organization or environment.

Aside from the difficulties we have cited, the initial period was characterized by positive developments springing more from a set of fortunate circumstances than any special intentions on the part of either Arabs or Copts. It was only natural that sedentarization and contact with the luxuries of settled life should efface the primitive culture of the tribe. With the conclusion of the major stage of the Arab conquest of North Africa and the seizing of Egypt, the *raison d'etre* of the camp city began to disappear. Before many years had passed, the civilization of Egypt made a profound impression upon a second generation of Arabs who felt ill at ease in the dirt buildings of the first.[26]

The native people came in ever greater numbers to al-Fusṭāṭ to satisfy the constantly increasing demands of the political capital. As Alexandria fell into decline through the shift of the seat of power, the new city attracted to itself numerous native elements seeking a market for their services. Not only builders and tradesmen were in demand, but also producers of needed commodites. Among the first established industries were those connected with the most important products in the country: textiles, hides, oils, glass, and earthenware. In all of these the skill of craftsmen at Christian centers of Lower Egypt was well known.[27]

By A.D. 750, al-Fusṭāṭ had become the economic as well as the administrative capital of the region. As the two populations became more and more mixed, Miṣr and Babylon merged with the City of the

---

[26] Marcel Clerget, *Le Caire, Étude de géographie urbaine et d'histoire économique* (Cairo: E. and R. Schindler, 1934), I, p. 112.

[27] Recent excavations at Fusṭāṭ have yielded more evidence for the development of glass craftsmanship in Egypt before the time of the ᶜAbbāsid conquest. Dr. George Scanlon has found a superb goblet of lustre painted glass bearing the name of ᶜAbd aṣ-Ṣamad ibn ᶜAlī, who was governor for a short time in A.D. 773. It is one of the earliest pieces of Islamic glass with a datable inscription. The archaeologist notes that the find adds substance to the contention that lustre technique was imported into Sāmarrā from Egypt (George T. Scanlon, "Fustat Expedition: Preliminary Report 1965, Part I," *Journal of the American Research Center in Egypt*, V (1966), p. 105).

Tent. Early sources indicate that the names were used alternately, even during the first century after the conquest, making it nearly impossible to differentiate between Miṣr and al-Fusṭāṭ.

The physical growth of the town during the first stage of the Arab settlement is evidenced by the construction of some public buildings, warehouses, a treasury, and a luxurious residence of the governor. The Mosque of ᶜAmr was enlarged four times between A.D. 672 and 750 but still could not hold the crowd of worshippers within its sanctuary. As the rule was that a city had to have a single Friday service, [28] someone had to repeat the words of the *imām* in the surrounding shops. [29]

Although the nucleus of the urban expansion lay between the fortress of Qaṣr ash-Shamaᶜ and the Jabal Yashkūr near the present Ibn Ṭūlūn mosque, many of the factors in the city's growth pertained to the river. As the products of Upper Egypt came down the Nile, a numerous population of sailors and boat-builders were recruited from neighboring areas. Since the Arabs knew little of navigation, they utilized the skill of the native Egyptians in these matters also. The Island of Roḍa, then the only island in the area of the town, became the site of a dockyard by A.D. 673. The Arabs, having found a Byzantine fortress on this island, built a naval arsenal of their own there. [30] The Nilometer was first established at Roḍa in the year A.D. 715,

---

[28] The question of the number of mosques allowed in a single city has special relevance for the issue of urban unity. In the earliest days of Islam, tribal mosques were prone to become rallying points of various tribes, especially since the mosque was also a *majlis* where councils were held. The phrase "the people of your mosque" (*ahl masjidikum*) came to mean "your party." We must, however, draw the distinction between the *masjid* and the *masjid al-jāmi*ᶜ, the former being properly a "kneeling spot" and the latter the site of the congregational Friday service. The soldiers of the camp city usually prayed in their particular tribal mosques but assembled for Friday prayers in the chief mosque under the leadership of the general. At the time of the conquest there was, therefore, only one *masjid al-jāmi*ᶜ in each city in which the service was conducted by the governor of the province. As the religion of Islam gained adherents, however, the need for mosques became great. In some cases the rule was upheld by declaring separate communities of "quarters" to be cities unto themselves. Hence, as we shall see later, Ibn Ṭūlūn and others constructed separate mosques for their followers in new political capitals. Of the major schools of law, the Shāfiᶜīs permit more than one mosque in a city only if a single mosque is unable to hold the community. The Ḥanafīs, however, permit any number of mosques. Thus, following the former interpretation, Ṣalāḥ ad-Dīn moved the Friday service from al-Azhar to the Mosque of al-Ḥākim as that was the largest; but the Mamlūks, following the latter school, established many buildings throughout Cairo proper as Friday mosques. See John Pedersen, "Masdjid," *Encyclopaedia of Islam* (Leiden: E. J. Brill, 1913).

[29] M. Clerget, *Le Caire*, I, p. 113.

[30] C. H. Becker, "Cairo," *Encyclopaedia of Islam*, 1913.

superseding the ancient meter at Memphis for the prediction of the amount of rise of the Nile.

Thus although some individuals fled the unhealthy lowlands, others profited from the area along the river and settled on the land continually freed by the Nile as it shifted to the west. While these lands were at first considered public property, they came to be granted to particular people by the caliphs. [31] In the early part of the eighth century, the region of the Birkat al-Ḥabash ("Abyssinian Pond") south of Qaṣr ash-Shamaᶜ was made habitable by a project of a governor who instituted a system of canals in that area.

Considering as a whole the initial stage of Cairo's development, we can see the beginning of a number of general trends which are relevant to its subsequent history. In the first place, although the primary stimulus for urbanization was provided by the establishment of a military encampment, the real expansion was carried out by the drift of native population to the neighborhood. It was the local people who had industrial, mercantile, and administrative skills. The Arabs were responsible for management at the highest level, but by recognizing established traditions and by allowing equipped individuals to carry on administration of their own communities, commercial or industrial endeavors, they paved the way for a pattern of coexistence which allowed the community to grow, largely undisturbed by major political upheavals. [32]

Second, throughout this period the population was separated into Muslim and non-Muslim segments, corresponding generally to the rulers and the ruled, with subdivisions according to occupation and social status. Especially at the outset, the Muslim group was concerned primarily with defense and the chance to get fat on the produce of the Egyptian milch cow. The native population, on the other hand, were concerned primarily with maintaining their own security and religious privileges, and keeping as much of the profit for themselves as possible. Military functions were a Muslim prerogative and the law was Muslim law. Those outside the pale were responsible for the social control of their own group. Arabs were bound to defend the payers of the poll tax from attack, but that is all. If they were concerned with the

---

[31] M. Clerget, *Le Caire*, I, p. 113.

[32] It is interesting to compare, in this respect, developments in lands conquered by Arabs, with those of the West. The Western barbarians made nothing out of the financial and administrative systems of the Roman Empire and the whole organization disintegrated in the provinces which they conquered.

development of any community, it was the community of believers in the capital rather than the actual population of al-Fusṭāṭ.

Third, as the Arabs abandoned their nomadic ways, settled down, and married Egyptian women, and as the Copts sought to curry favor and profit with the new regime, a good deal of acculturation took place. In the area of language for instance, the Coptic tradition began to disappear. There is little doubt that during this period the majority of lower level administrators were Copts who spoke Arabic as well as the ancient tongue. A knowledge of Arabic would be necessary to deal with the ruling class, whereas the Arabs, on the whole, probably avoided using Coptic as the intimate association of Arabic with the Qur'ān gave it formally recognized value. Thus as far as language was concerned, if there was pressure for assimilation in any direction, it was for the conquered people to learn the language of the conquerors. The Arabs could take advantage of the wealth and comforts of Egypt in any case, and their limited goals with respect to the development of al-Fusṭāṭ only contributed to the lack of concern for real communication with other elements of the population. It was chiefly in the areas of daily life which were not directly associated with formal status in which acculturation took place most freely; that is, in areas which did not pertain to religion and political authority. In those areas the greatest division between Muslim rulers and subject populations lasted for centuries.

Fourth, there was a constant tension between the subject people and the group in power. The caliph ʿUmar had feared that the discipline of his settled army would disintegrate upon contact with civilized lands, and so it did. This thought seems always to have lurked in the minds of the rulers of al-Fusṭāṭ; they were defending themselves not so much from external threats as from the settled population. As *dhimmī*s waxed wealthy rising to high official positions, they became a threat to the maintenance of Muslim power and would be struck down with great severity, only to rise again a few years later. The segmentalization of society thus was in a delicate balance, each group trying to derive what it could from the situation, yet not intentionally cooperating in any real sense because of mutual suspicion and fear.

CHAPTER TWO

URBAN LIFE IN THE ᶜABBĀSID PERIOD (A.D. 750-969)

The subsequent period of Cairene history was no less shaped by events occurring outside of Egypt. As the Islamic empire submerged older Hellenistic and Sāsānian civilization, tensions of confrontation had to be resolved through the emergence of new social perspectives and the development of ideology. The birth pangs of the new order were most often expressed in sectarianism and heresy. Tribalism was still a force, and under the Umayyads non-Arab converts to Islam (*mawālī*) had often been unhappy with their status as "second class citizens." Under the ᶜAbbāsids, Persians and Turks came into prominence and frequently replaced the Arabs as rulers while the incorporation of ancient concepts of "universal empire" in Islamic theory and practice facilitated the development of cosmopolitanism. [1]

One of the greatest changes is seen in the emergence of social classes in a hitherto "democratic" society. The urban style of life with the luxuries it implied soon had its effect upon Muslims who, as ᶜUmar had feared, began to make distinctions within the *umma* according to concerns other than piety. Not only did an aristocracy arise, but out of the urban milieu emerged groups of notables and merchants, exploiting special resources and providing continuity in time of political tribulation. A series of new military capitals represented various divisions of the elite rather than the populace, but by virtue of the continued occupation of the popular center of habitation, some institutions and traditions became established that furthered the development of urban life.

1. *Fomentation and Fusion in al-ᶜAskar: Social Classes and Special Status* (A.D. 750-868)

With the fall of the Umayyads the capital of the empire moved from Damascus to Baghdad. Just so, a new encampment was established by the ᶜAbbāsid governors to the northeast of al-Fusṭāṭ on the part of the farther *ḥamrāʾ* which had been abandoned. The last Umayyad

---

[1] H. A. R. Gibb, "The Evolution of Government in Early Islam," *Studies on the Civilization of Islam* by H. A. R. Gibb, edited by S. J. Shaw and W. R. Polk (Boston: Beacon Press, 1962), pp. 44-45.

caliph, Marwān II, pursued to the death by his supplanters, had burnt much of the settlement in his attempt to escape to the opposite bank. According to a Christian source, Sāwīrus ibn al-Muqaffa^c (Severus of Ushmunayn), the whole of Fusṭāṭ was destroyed except the great mosque. [2] It is possible that this may have been the reason for the ^cAbbāsid rulers choosing a new site; on the other hand, the construction of barracks apart from the town was in the Arab tradition and here again, there would be reason to avoid the seditious atmosphere of the urban area populated by rebels of one sort or another.

For a hundred years al-^cAskar, "The Army," remained the seat of government. At first it was only a cantonment with houses of officers and soldiers surrounding the governor's palace and a mosque which was constructed in A.D. 785. About A.D. 810, for reasons of health and comfort, the rulers built a pleasure dome on a spur of the Muqaṭṭam where the Citadel now stands, Qubbat al-Hawā᾽ ("Dome of the Air"). In the beginning the official cantonment was not accessible to ordinary citizens but it was no easier to maintain segregation in this case than it had been in the case of al-Fusṭāṭ. Numerous and well-frequented markets became established in the quarter. Clerget points out that al-^cAskar did not go through the transitions which marked the beginning of the early capital. This settlement was better organized, and its streets were more thoughtfully laid out in an east-west direction. Toward the organization of urban life, it could boast of hospitals, a corps of police, night patrols, market inspectors, and a system of taxes on commerce. [3] Even so, despite the conflagration, Fusṭāṭ was still a center of activity. The old city expanded during this period. Either the fire of A.D. 750 had not completely destroyed the town, or the advantages of its position were incentive enough to bring it again to prosperity.

It is important that at this stage government had not yet evolved internally to differentiate between the ruling elite and the religious institution that supported them. Thus in the preceding period, the "interests of the state" were conceived of as inextricably tied to the interests of the Umayyad caliphs. [4] It was only natural that Arab tribesmen expressed their opposition and desire for independence in religious terms and if they did not tend toward political anarchy, sought

---

[2] *History of the Patriarchs of the Coptic Church of Alexandria*, translated by B. Evetts, *Patrologia Orientalis*, V (Paris, 1904), p. 168.

[3] M. Clerget, *Le Caire*, I, p. 114.

[4] H. A. R. Gibb, "The Evolution of Government in Early Islam," p. 32.

solution through the transference of the caliphate to other claimants. The young society, as yet lacking political institutions and only gradually becoming politically self-conscious, looked to the new line to initiate a transformation that would more successfully integrate the expanded, differentiated social order under the aegis of Islamic ideology. Given the magnitude of the task, it is not surprising that the ᶜAbbāsids, like the Umayyads, failed to make the caliphate an effective governing institution.

The early period of al-ᶜAskar was one of fomentation, experimentalization, and disorganization. To the Muslim—non-Muslim split were added tensions between Muslims of separate persuasions; between Umayyad supporters, ᶜAbbāsids, Khārijīs, ᶜAlids, and Muᶜtazilīs. In all of these the divisions fell along regional and tribal lines, each group making common cause with the others against what they regarded as a common enemy, the caliphal authority and the imposition of taxes. [5]

The years A.D. 750-860 are filled with uprisings not only of Copts but of Arabs and Muslim schizmatics. While most of the Umayyad partisans had been killed or driven out of the country, in A.D. 782 a pro-Umayyad revolt broke out in Upper Egypt with a simultaneous rebellion of the Yemenites and Qaysites in the Ḥawf. Rivalry between these Northern and Southern Arabian parties had contributed to the downfall of the Umayyads, but together they preferred the Umayyads to the ᶜAbbāsid regime. The governor sent a detachment against the rebels in the South and personally directed the campaign in the Delta, but his troops were defeated and he was killed on the field of battle. [6] This revolt was finally put down by another governor sent from Baghdad, and the head of the Umayyad pretender was sent to the caliph.

The Khārijīs too, very numerous in Egypt, added to the trouble of this period. These believers in the puritanical democratic principles of Islam were deadly opponents of all who maintained that the caliph should be one of the Quraysh. Allying themselves with Berbers and even with Umayyad supporters, they defeated the Egyptian army in A.D. 759. The ᶜAlids at one point (A.D. 764) nearly had their own caliph in Egypt. That year the insurrections became so violent that the pilgrimage to Mecca was forbidden. Order was eventually restored, however, and

---

[5] See Sāwīrus ibn al-Muqaffaᶜ (Severus of Ushmunayn), *History of the Patriarchs, Patrologia Orientalis*, X (Paris, 1915), p. 428.

[6] Al-Kindī, *Kitāb al-Wulāh*, p. 127.

> Fustát bore unpleasant witness to the revolts in the thousands of rebels' heads that were exhibited, and the courage of hesitating heretics was damped by the sight of their leader's skull hung up in the Mosque of ᶜAmr. [7]

The contest for the caliphate between the sons of Hārūn ar-Rashīd, al-Amīn and al-Maᵓmūn was partially carried on in Egypt. Al-Amīn nominated as governor the chief of the Qays tribe, thereby ensuring the support of these chronic trouble makers. With their help the representative of al-Maᵓmūn was seized and killed. With the death of al-Amīn in A.D. 813, the situation was reversed. Arab feeling in Egypt was intense against al-Maᵓmūn and his Persian supporters and when, in A.D. 826, the new caliph sent ᶜAbdallāh ibn Ṭāhir to Egypt with an army of soldiers from Khurāsān, violent fighting went on and Fusṭāṭ was besieged. The general succeeded in overcoming the opposition, however, and reorganized the local troops but no sooner did he leave when the Arabs of the Ḥawf arose again (A.D. 829).

Al-Maᵓmūn's attempt to enforce the Muᶜtazilī doctrine of the createdness of the Qurᵓān met with as much resistance in Egypt as elsewhere. When a *qāḍī* wrote on the walls of the mosques of Fusṭāṭ, "There is no God but God, the Master of the created Qurᵓān," the Mālikī and Shāfiᶜī jurists forbade all to enter these mosques. [8] Al-Mutawakkil in A.D. 849 reestablished orthodoxy and prohibited inflammatory philosophical discussions.

Thus most of the political difficulties of this period resulted not from conflict between Muslims and non-Muslims, but from differences among Muslims themselves. On the face of it, the rulers were defending their brand of Sunnī Islam against a local ᶜAlid faction and others who differed with them in interpretation of religious law. The resentments were often voiced in religious terms but the alignments were tribal and/or regional. As often as not the immediate cause of the trouble was merely the imposition of authority, in the shape of tax or tribute, upon groups who refused to forget their time-honored independence.

A new factor was added, moreover, as non-Arab Muslims came to play a prominent role in the political struggle. Many of these resented their status as clients (*mawālī*) of the Arabs under the Umayyads, especially in the light of the fact that they represented more ancient

---

7 S. Lane-Poole, *The Story of Cairo*, p. 66.
8 Al-Kindī, *Kitāb al-Quḍāh*, p. 451.

and more developed civilizations. First under the ᶜAbbāsids and more especially later under the Shīᶜī regime, Persians and Turks attain considerable influence and power.

The Copts too, continued to chafe against Muslim authority. Generally speaking, their rebellions were disorganized and confused, but in A.D. 829, the caliph thought the trouble serious enough to come himself to put down the revolt in the Delta. There the Bashmūrites, the last indigenous group to submit to the Arabs, rose against the fiscal impositions, even as they had under the Byzantines. A contemporary Arab doctor described them as "the most ferocious and ignorant people of Egypt, who eat course food and drink bad water." [9] Against these ruffians marched al-Maʾmūn, burning their villages, exiling their leaders, and taking prisoner their men, women, and children to be sold as slaves in Damascus. Others were taken to Baghdad. [10] Thus came to an end once and for all the national movement of the native people. After this the bilingual system disappeared through increasing acceptance of Islam by Egyptians and the settling of greater numbers of Arabs on the land.

The defects in ᶜAbbāsid rule gave impetus to the development of the law (*sharīᶜa*). The Qurʾān and tradition had gained acceptance as infallible sources, but their translation into social action depended upon skillful interpretation and elaboration. This period witnessed the emergence of the four major schools of law as well as some interpretations that did not take hold. The ᶜAbbāsids favored the Iraqi school founded by Abū Ḥanīfa (d. A.D. 767) while the Madīnan school of Mālik ibn Anas (d. A.D. 795) also gained many adherents, but the Muslims of Egypt by and large came to follow the system of their own *imām*, ash-Shāfiᶜī (d. A.D. 820). [11]

It is interesting that, although from the beginning, the formulation of religious law was independent of the secular authority, the rulers often did hold their own courts for the "redress of wrongs" (*maẓālim*). At the level of practice the line between the authority of the *qāḍī* and that of the ruler was not clearly drawn. Thus the office of the *qāḍī* in theory represented the sovereignty of the *umma* and was absolutely

---

9 See Gaston Wiet, *L'Égypte arabe, Histoire de la nation égyptienne*, edited by Gabriel Hanotaux (Paris, n.d.), IV, p. 73.

10 Sāwīrus ibn al-Muqaffaᶜ (Severus of Ushmunayn), *History of the Patriarchs, Patrologia Orientalis*, X, pp. 501-502.

11 The school of Aḥmad ibn Ḥanbal (d. A.D. 855) had a strong following in Iraq and Syria until the Ottoman conquest but was never popular in Egypt.

independent of the temporal power. Cases were conducted in public. Originally the *qāḍī* sat in the chief mosque leaning against a pillar, the court thus being open to the entire Muslim community. In A.D. 738 the *qāḍī* in Egypt heard cases in a room overlooking the street over the porch of his house.[12] There was, however, always some ambiguity concerning his jurisdiction, for the caliph was the supreme judge of the Muslim community. In the provinces like Egypt, the governor held this power on his behalf. In general the latter would act only if the *qāḍī* was too weak but sometimes he would set aside the *qāḍī*'s decisions. In two cases recorded by al-Kindī, the *qāḍī* was forced to suspend his work or resign.[13] Under the strong governor of the next century, Ibn Ṭūlūn, it was said that "people almost ceased to go to the *qāḍī*'s court." For seven years there was no *qāḍī* in Egypt and all matters were handled by the governor.[14]

The Umayyads have been accused of furthering the institution of "kingship" but it was the ᶜAbbāsids who developed the caliphate along the lines of a royal state. Historical records indicate too, the emergence of aristocracy and social classes in this period. We have already mentioned the fact that as the Arabs settled on the land, revenue was obtained from landed estates. It was only natural that inequities in wealth be accompanied by social stratification. Even in nomadic society certain families ranked more highly than others but now these divisions were emphasized. As illustrative of the winning out of the principle of aristocracy over Islamic-enjoined democracy we can cite the following happening recorded by al-Kindī: A suit was brought before a *qāḍī* regarding a marriage between a woman and one not her social equal. Her relatives demanded dissolution of the marriage on these grounds but the *qāḍī* refused to cancel the bond. The government, however, overrode his decision and parted the couple on its own authority.[15]

The bourgeoisie that became visible at the end of the second century of the Muslim era on the whole did not hesitate to amass capital. One was to serve God first with one's money, spending it on charity and for works of public utility but Islam, as popularly interpreted,[16]

[12] Al-Kindī, *Kitāb al-Quḍāh*, p. 351.

[13] *Ibid.*, pp. 367, 427.

[14] *Ibid.*, p. 512.

[15] *Ibid.*, p. 367.

[16] While the science of *ḥadīth* formed a basis for jurisprudence, the manufacture of spurious traditions reflected essential tendencies in the growth and development of Islamic society.

took a lenient view of luxury and the hoarding of riches. "When Allāh gives riches to a man, he wants them to be seen on him," went a saying attributed to the Prophet.[17] The ideal of the warrior saint predominent in the first century of Islam, is harder to find in the later periods. Certainly economic prosperity was an aid to spiritual independence. Traditional Islam, unlike Christianity, did not encourage the ascetic life. Abū Bakr, the first caliph, had been a cloth merchant. ᶜUthmān, the third caliph, had been an importer of cereals and the most pious ᶜUmar is reported to have said, "I prefer dying on my camel's saddle, while traveling on business, to being killed in the Holy War: has not Allāh himself mentioned those that travel on business before those that fight 'on the path of God'?"[18]

We are fortunate in having more than 13,000 biographies of members of the bourgeoisie in Egypt and the Eastern Islamic world from the early centuries. While these deal primarily with scholars and men of letters they attest to the fact that there was no real division between the religious life on the one hand and the secular life on the other.[19] The bourgeoisie could be defined not only by their relative affluence but by their knowledge of the art of writing. Reading and the elements of writing were taught systematically only at a higher stage of religious schooling. Thus some artisans could write and sign their names, but only such persons as physicians, merchants, government officials, and scholars could compose letters and documents.

Even as any Muslim could become literate, so the scholars and jurisprudents came from all divisions and levels of the society of the faithful. Women too became known for their piety and learning. Moreover these persons functioned for the most part as private individuals, without a license of any sort from the authorities. Receiving little or no formal salary, they subsisted partly on voluntary contributions

---

[17] See S. D. Goitein, "The Rise of the Middle Eastern Bourgeoisie in Early Islamic Times," in his *Studies in Islamic History and Institutions* (Leiden: E. J. Brill, 1966), p. 225.

[18] See S. D. Goitein, "The Rise of the Middle Eastern Bourgeoisie in Early Islamic Times," p. 222. Another apt anecdote is told of the same caliph. When seeing a group of pious men with downcast heads, these were described to him as the *mutawakkilūn* (people trusting in God and therefore not indulging in any trade). He replied, "No, these are *mutaʾakkilūn* (persons who live from other people's wealth). You had better lift up your heads and earn your own livelihood" (S. D. Goitein, "The Rise of the Middle Eastern Bourgeoisie in Early Islamic Times," p. 224).

[19] See Hayyim J. Cohen, "The Economic Background and the Secular Occupations of Muslim Jurisprudents and Traditionalists in the Classical Period of Islam," *Journal of the Economic and Social History of the Orient*, XIII (1970), pp. 16-61.

for their piety, teaching, and special services as well as a wide variety of economic endeavors.[20] Most acted as special agents of the government, as legal clerks, investigators, witnesses, market inspectors, and tax collectors, but many were virtually indistinguishable from merchants, being involved in businesses and industries of various kinds, especially those relating to foodstuffs, textiles, carpet making, and book copying and selling. Some others engaged in the import-export trade, an occupation that brought them into special relation with the elite as they often came to serve in this capacity as ambassadors.

Thus urbanized Islam itself gave rise to a class of educated notables: scholars (*ᶜulamāʾ*), judges (*quḍāh*), and theologians (*fuqahāʾ*) who were prominent leaders in the middle ranks of society. These did not at this time have an establishment of their own and did not even compose a coherent group with reference to common interests, origin, or orientation. Nevertheless, they did mold the legal framework of social relations, adapting it as circumstances demanded and they were all the better equipped to do so as they were not removed from secular pursuits but were intimately involved in them.[21] Without their backing the directives of the elite could never have been effective.

Despite the stamping out of the native Coptic movement, a large part of the Egyptian middle class remained Christian. Foreign to the state, they could not technically form part of it yet they came to play one of the greatest administrative roles through their domination of numerous public offices. Old and recurrent is the complaint that decisions concerning the lives and property of Muslims were in the hands of protected subjects. ᶜUmar I is supposed to have warned against making Christians and Jews state officers. As we have seen though, owing to the lack of administrative tradition among the Arabs, for a long time there was little choice in the matter. The Copts are said to have succeeded in introducing traditions of the Prophet favorable

---

[20] The question of whether the *qāḍī* should be salaried was debated in the early period and it was said that ᶜUmar I forbade the practice. Al-Kindī relates that in A.D. 709 a *qāḍī* served a guest a meal of a biscuit and water, saying that he could not afford bread (*Kitāb al-Quḍāh*, p. 331). In 736 another carried on the oil trade and when questioned about this, said, "Wait until you feel hunger through other stomachs than your own" (i.e., "have children to feed") (al-Kindī, *Kitāb al-Quḍāh*, p. 352). Under the ᶜAbbāsids, however, the *qāḍī* received a monthly salary of 30 dinars (al-Kindī, *Kitāb al-Quḍāh*, p. 378), an amount which was increased manyfold as time went on.

[21] Some practical and broad-minded legalists of this time even ruled that the construction of churches should be tolerated because it contributed to economic prosperity (al-Kindī, *Kitāb al-Quḍāh*, p. 131).

to themselves: "The Copts will help the faithful to the path of piety by removing worldly cares from them." [22] However this may be, in A.D. 849 the caliph decreed that only Muslims were to hold public office and even the task of recording the rise of the Nile was taken from the Christians. All to little avail; the administration ceased to work until the Copts returned. Ten years later these ordinances had to be reinstituted but again, in no time at all there were four Christians among the nine privy councilors.

In addition to their political resource, the protected non-Muslims had a potential economic advantage. As Islamic law forbade to the faithful usury and speculation in subsistence goods, Christians and Jews became money lenders. A Christian lawbook of the early ninth century A.D. allows a Christian to pay twenty-two per cent interest to another Christian. As much as one thousand per cent could be extracted as the result of advancing money to victims of governmental confiscations. [23]

But in spite of the fact that they played important roles in the urban center, *dhimmīs* were forever set apart by their special legal status. They had their own ecclesiastical courts whose jurisdiction extended over all matters of marriage and inheritance as well as disputes within the group. Muslim law was meant only for Muslims, and the state did not usually concern itself with the affairs of *dhimmīs*. [24] A disadvantage, however, was that they were not allowed to depose in a law court, a disability that they shared with slaves.

A number of regulations set up barriers between all groups having separate religious status. Regarding marriage, Muslim men could have Christian or Jewish wives but no Christian woman was allowed by her Church to marry a non-Christian. For all *dhimmīs*, mixed marriages were out of the question. A Christian man could only marry a non-Christian woman if she became Christian. Religious conversion, however, that did not involve acceptance of Islam was impossible. Christians could not become Jews and vice versa. Regarding inheritance, no person was allowed to inherit from one of a different faith.

---

[22] Adam Mez, *Renaissance*, pp. 48-51.

[23] *Ibid.*, p. 454.

[24] Evidently a number of Christians made use of the provision whereby a *dhimmī* could appeal to a Muslim court if he chose, although this was frowned upon by the Church. If he did submit to the jurisdiction of the Muslim court, he was bound to abide by its decision. In the year A.D. 738 the *qāḍī* of Fusṭāṭ sat in the mosque to deal first with the cases of the Muslims and then on the steps to deal with the Christians (al-Kindī, *Kitāb al-Quḍāh*, p. 351).

From time to time, actually throughout most of the traditional period, special legal status was given visual form through the institution of regulations on dress. This practice, of course, led to the stereotyping of these people in their public relations. In Egypt under the last Umayyads every Christian had to wear a signet in the shape of a lion on his hand. [25] Under the ᶜAbbāsids, Muslims had white turbans, the Christians blue, the Jews yellow, and the Zoroastrians red. [26] In A.D. 849 honey-colored headwear and girdles were assigned to *dhimmīs*. If caps were worn like Muslim caps they had to have different colored buttons. [27] An anecdote is repeated by al-Kindī that when, in the time of Hārūn ar-Rashīd, the people were abusing a *qāḍī* whom they hated, he stood at the door of the mosque and retaliated in kind calling out:

> "Where are the fellows in honey-colored mantles? Where are the sons of whores? Why doesn't one of them say what he wants to enable me to see and hear him?" [28]

Aside from the political, religious, and economic difficulties of the period, the populace was plagued by the erratic behavior of inexperienced governors. One in A.D. 779, Abū Ṣāliḥ ibn Mamdūd, was so enthusiastic about putting an end to crime in the city that:

> he ordered the people of Fustát to leave their doors and shops open all night, with no more protection than a net to keep the dogs out; abolished the office of the watchmen who used to guard the bathers' clothes at the public baths, and proclaimed that if anything were lost he would replace it himself. It is said that when a man went to the bath he would call out "O Abū-Sālih, take care of my clothes!" and no one would dare touch them. [29]

Such a system of security exemplified the "experimental" nature of the government of the period. The ruler's unwonted severity could only cause anxiety, as his strict laws of dress were an added irritation and nuisance. Another finance minister excelled at inventing new taxes, imposing duty on fodder and wine shops. So strained did nerves become that much blood was spilled at Alexandria, Giza, and the Fayyūm. The women of Fusṭāṭ were ordered to stay at home, not going out even to the bath. In the mosque no one was allowed to deviate from the

---

[25] Al-Maqrīzī, *Khiṭaṭ*, I, p. 492.

[26] Even as there are different colored fish in the sea. See Richard F. Burton, *The Book of the Thousand Nights and a Night* (Benares (= Stoke Newington), 1885), I, "The Tale of the Ensorcerelled Prince," p. 77.

[27] Adam Mez, *Renaissance*, p. 46.

[28] *Kitāb al-Quḍāh*, p. 390.

[29] Al-Kindī, *Kitāb al-Wulāh*, p. 122; quoted in S. Lane-Poole, *The Story of Cairo*, p. 66.

orderly rows of worshippers: a Turk stood by with a whip to marshal the congregation with military exactitude. [30]

That insecurity prevailed in Fusṭāṭ and al-ᶜAskar was only too well known to the ᶜAbbāsid caliphs. As their seat of authority was even farther away from the Egyptian capital than Damascus had been, they hesitated to permit any governor to remain long enough to gain local popularity. In the period of sixty years between the advent of the first ᶜAbbāsid caliph and the death of Hārūn ar-Rashīd, there were forty-two governors as opposed to twenty in the last sixty years of Umayyad administration. Moreover as a number of these men were themselves of the ᶜAbbāsid family, the caliphs were especially anxious to discourage possible aspirants to the caliphate.

Nevertheless the city had gained many attractions. Economically it was beginning to prosper. Although certain industries remained exclusively in the domain of non-believers, many of the social distinctions between Arabs and non-Arabs became effaced as the former lost some of his contempt for manual work. The disappearance of the Coptic majority and the absorption of many of its members into Muslim ranks contributed also to the creation of some social homogeneity.

We must not fail to mention here that in Egypt from ancient times the cemetery has been an important place for the living as well as the dead. Now in the southern burial ground, al-Qarāfa, were the tombs of ᶜAmr and many of the Companions of the Prophet to say nothing of the tomb-shrines of venerated persons like the Imām ash-Shāfiᶜī and popular "saints" such as Sayyida Nafīsa. Un-Islamic practices grew up in burials and the great even built mausoleums. By the year A.D. 804 the authorities attempted to forbid traditional practices like the blackening of faces, the tearing out of hair, and the employment of hired mourners. [31]

As the fortunes of the governmental center al-ᶜAskar depended more on political stability than economic factors, the settlement had little significance apart from the administration it housed. The real city again was the faubourg which was identical with the agglomeration of Fusṭāṭ and nothing could discourage the local people from trying to make a living regardless of the rise and fall of political fortunes which were outside their domain, and in spite of vexatious exactions of the government.

---

30 Al-Kindī, *Kitāb al-Wulāh*, p. 210.

31 Adam Mez, *Renaissance*, p. 370.

2. *The First Burgeoning: al-Qaṭāiᶜ and the Implications of Military Power* (A.D. 868-905)

As we pointed out in the preceding chapter, the ᶜAbbāsids lacked confidence in their Arab subjects, and came to depend more upon non-Arab elements, Persians, Khurāsānians, and Turks. Toward the end of the reign of al-Maᵓmūn, the latter began to play an important role in political affairs. Turkish slaves or *mamlūks*, prized for their courage, fidelity, and physical appearance, educated in Arabic, Qurᵓānic law, literature, science, and politics, would be manumitted to occupy important positions. The caliph al-Muᶜtaṣim thought so highly of these people, recruited from Farghāna and other parts of Central Asia, that he instituted a special Turkish bodyguard. From then on they played a decisive role in the government of the empire. The governor of Egypt appointed to the office by al-Muᶜtaṣim (A.D. 834) received explicit instructions to take control of the army from the Arabs. [32] Under al-Mutawakkil in 856, Egypt had its last Arab ruler.

In A.D. 868 a Turk, Aḥmad ibn Ṭūlūn, [33] was sent to govern Egypt as the caliph's representative. Having considerable diplomatic skill as well as military experience and energy, he soon created a center of power which rivaled the caliphate itself. After overcoming court intrigues and three rebellions at home, he rid himself of all but nominal allegiance to Baghdad, and marched through Syria, occupying territory to Ṭarsūs and the Euphrates.

It is understandable that Ibn Ṭūlūn wanted to make a real capital for his new empire. Finding al-ᶜAskar too small to hold his army and retinue, and probably reluctant to occupy the residence of the former governors, he founded a new quarter northeast of al-ᶜAskar on the Jabal Yashkūr.

Although al-Qaṭāiᶜ or "The Fiefs" was to symbolize a new regime, it differed from its predecessors chiefly in size and splendor. It was still primarily a military post, modeled after Sāmarrā in Mesopotamia where Ibn Ṭūlūn had grown up. Sāmarrā too had been divided into a certain number of quarters designated by this name. There special concessions were granted to officers and civil servants, while various

---

[32] G. Wiet, *L'Égypte arabe*, p. 77.

[33] Aḥmad ibn Ṭūlūn was the real or adopted son of a member of the Taghāzghān tribe who had been sent to Baghdad along with other youths by the governor of Bukhāra as a present to the caliph al-Maᵓmūn. As his father rose to a high rank in the court, Ibn Ṭūlūn received a fine education including military instruction at Sāmarrā, the caliph's new residence. See al-Maqrīzī, *Khiṭaṭ*, I, pp. 313-314.

General View.

Piers and Arches.

Detail in Wood.

Detail in Stucco.

1. The Mosque of Ibn Ṭūlūn.

corps of troops, Sūdānīs, Greeks, guards, policemen, camel drivers, and slaves were assigned to special areas. [34] Around the mosque were extensive markets, each dealing with a commercial specialty as the various groups of the population were separated one from the other.

A new mosque built by Ibn Ṭūlūn (A.D. 876-878) is said to have been constructed because the people of Fusṭāṭ complained that the Mosque of ᶜAmr could not hold all of the black soldiers at the Friday service. [35] Although no great ruler has failed to erect a mosque to perpetuate his name, there is little doubt that Aḥmad Ibn Ṭūlūn may also have wanted to reduce friction between his troops and local residents. [36]

The social significance of al-Qaṭāiᶜ was that it threw into relief the split between the Turkish elite and the populace, and underlined the luxury of the aristocracy. Everything was focused on fulfilling the needs of the ruler and his retinue. The bazaars were filled with the choicest of wares. Near the slopes of the eastern hills, on the site of the present park below the Citadel, a large area was set aside for military exercises, parades, horse racing, and polo. This became a favorite resort of the town, entered by a number of gates, restricted to special classes. The palace outshone anything over known to the inhabitants of Fusṭāṭ. It had not only great gardens, but a menagerie and an enclosed race course. A private passage led to the oratory of the *amīr* in the great mosque. Another palace held the *ḥarīm* with its own baths and markets. [37]

Nevertheless despite its great population, al-Qaṭāiᶜ was merely an addition of Fusṭāṭ and did not usurp the established importance of the older town. Most of the officials other than those connected with the palace resided in the main city.

From one point of view we can regard al-Qaṭāiᶜ as a foreign quarter. A large part of the army was of foreign origin as was the governor himself. During this period too, the black troops came into prominence. For while the son of Ibn Ṭūlūn, Khumārawayh, recruited his house-

---

[34] Al-Maqrīzī, *Khiṭaṭ*, I, pp. 315-317.

[35] D. S. Margoliouth, *Cairo, Jerusalem and Damascus* (London: Chatto and Windus, 1907), p. 8.

[36] The mosque, which can still be admired today, is often cited as an example of foreign architecture in Egypt (see E. Richmond, "The Significance of Cairo," *Journal of the Royal Asiatic Society*, 1913, p. 32). Its most noteworthy feature, however, is that the mosque is the third earliest and best preserved example of the use of the pointed each throughout a building, two centuries previous to any in England (D. Russell, *Medieval Cairo*, p. 119).

[37] Al-Maqrīzī, *Khiṭaṭ*, I, pp. 313-315.

hold from the Arabs of the Delta, he also instituted a special corps of robust Negroes, chosen for their impressive size. They wore black turbans, iron cuirasses, and black tunics, creating the effect, as they passed in review, of a "black ocean rolling by because of their complexions and their uniforms." [38]

Luxury and pomp reminiscent of the court in Mesopotamia was the keynote in the new quarter. Under Khumārawayh, the *maydān* was planted with rare trees and flowers, and a pigeon tower put in the middle, stocked with turtle doves, wood pigeons, and various kinds of birds of rich plumage. There horticultural experiments were carried on and apricots grafted onto almond trees. In the palace was a garden of gold and silver trees as well as sweet-smelling plants of many varieties, and a menagerie of lions, leopards, elephants and giraffes. Entire districts were set aside to grow fodder for the vast stables. One of the ruler's numerous pavilions, "The Golden House," was decorated with gold and ultramarine and had before its walls statues one and one-half times life-size of Khumārawayh and his wives, the heads of which were crowned with gold diadems and jeweled turbans.

It must not be thought that the Ṭūlūnids were uninterested in the public welfare. A large commercial street running from the palace was flanked by two parallel arteries cut by perpendicular streets. [39] Numerous waterworks benefited people living along the Nile, the ponds, and the canal, while an aqueduct which brought water from a spur of the Muqaṭṭam served a large segment of the population. [40] Perhaps the most remarkable of Ibn Ṭūlūn's institutions was the first large hospital of Muslim Egypt, founded A.D. 873. Located in al-ᶜAskar, the *māristān* like the aqueduct, was well endowed. According to al-Maqrīzī:

> He made one condition that no soldier or *mamlūk* would be treated there. (There were) two baths ... one for men and one for women ... and he made a condition that when the patient came, his clothes were taken from him and his money given to the supervisor who gave him new clothes and new linen, food, medicines, and treatment by physicians until he was well. And when it was found that he could eat a chicken and a whole loaf, he would be discharged and given his money and his clothes ... Ibn Ṭūlūn used to ride out himself every Friday and inspect the stores and physicians, and inquire as to the welfare of the ill and insane. [41]

---

38 *Ibid.*, p. 318.
39 M. Clerget, *Le Caire*, I, p. 117.
40 D. S. Margoliouth, *Cairo, Jerusalem and Damascus*, p. 8.
41 Al-Maqrīzī, *Khiṭaṭ*, II, p. 405.

The ruler continued these tours of inspection until a practical joke played by a lunatic caused him to discontinue his visits.

Thus the Muslim institution of *waqf* which put aside wealth and property for charitable purposes was extended considerably under the Ṭūlūnids. Mosques and pious foundations, staffed by government appointees, were more numerous and better supported by a more affluent state than had existed in the previous period. While it is said that Ibn Ṭūlūn paid for many of his projects through his remarkable power to discover buried treasure, there is little doubt that much of his wealth came from his foreign campaigns. For once revenue was flowing into the capital rather than out of it. Taxes were not increased, and some were even abolished. Following a far-sighted policy, he took pains to encourage cultivation and make the *fallāḥīn* more secure on their land.

After the reign of Ibn Ṭūlūn, Khumārawayh carried on the tradition of lavish building, even tearing down some of his father's buildings to reconstruct them more elaborately. [42] While interested primarily in beautifying the palace and its environs, he was also responsible for several canals and sewers.

Unfortunately, this dynasty remained in power for less than forty years. The sons of Khumārawayh were not able to defend the Syrian provinces or even the capital from the vengeful ᶜAbbāsids and, after a massacre of the black troops, al-Qaṭāiᶜ was leveled to the ground and its faubourg demolished (A.D. 905). After an orgy of plunder and devastation which lasted for four months, the only building left standing was the mosque. Henceforth the separateness of the quarter disappears altogether. Travelers of the next century rarely mention al-Qaṭāiᶜ at all but speak only of Miṣr. We can only assume that it, like al-ᶜAskar, became merged with the old town as the suburbs were contiguous and the borders ill-defined. Although al-ᶜAskar became once again the seat of government with the reinstatement of an ᶜAbbāsid governor, the name designating the official quarter had long since fallen out of use. [43] When al-Qaṭāiᶜ was destroyed, the markets around the Mosque of ᶜAmr regained some of the business that they had lost to the Ṭūlūnid suburb.

---

[42] C. H. Becker, "Cairo," *Encyclopaedia of Islam*, 1913.

[43] Al-Maqrīzī, *Khiṭaṭ*, I, p. 286.

3. *The Return to al-ᶜAskar: The Adjustment of the Social Fabric and the Emergence of Cosmopolitanism* (A.D. 905-969)

The next few years were a time of tribulation for Fusṭāṭ. Although still the capital of Egypt, it became again only the chief city of a province under the caliph's authority. Following the anarchy of the ᶜAbbāsid invasion, military despots acted more or less as they pleased. In the second decade of the tenth century A.D., the Fāṭimids of Qayrawān sent their Berber army through Egypt and even succeeded in attacking the camp at Giza across the river from the Egyptian capital. When the Berbers were driven out in A.D. 920, chaos reigned in the city. The army was clamoring for pay, the governor had died, and his son was forced to leave the country. Rivals for the governorship gathered their own troops, adding to the confusion.

Change in the power structure, however, was no new thing and many individuals had learned how to adapt themselves to sudden changes of the locus of authority. Some even benefited from them. Examples are the lords treasurers at this time, three men of the Persian family Mādharāʾī (so called from their place of origin, Mādharāya, near Basra in Iraq). These, possibly having come to Egypt on business, and also involved in the science of *ḥadīth*, attained the highest ranks of authority in the country.[44] One of them enjoyed the lucrative post of treasurer not only under the son of Ibn Ṭūlūn, but under some of the caliph's governors and two members of the following dynasty. It has been estimated that Muḥammad Mādharāʾī accumulated over £ 200,000 a year, not including rents.[45] It is significant that a Mādharāʾī treasurer went into hiding during the financial crisis mentioned above. In those turbulent times of political upheaval, the man of courage and foresight could often turn the tide to his advantage if he was cunning enough to win the favor of the right people. On their part, the governors must have borne the brunt of the blame for difficulties stemming from the actions of court officials and employees who could hide under the cloak of governmental protection.

---

[44] See H. Gottschalk, *Die Mādarāʾijjūn, Studien zur Geschichte und Kultur des islamischen Orients*, 6, Heft (Berlin and Leipzig: W. de Gruyter & Co., 1931).

[45] He was, however, reknowned for his charity and we should not underestimate the role such a man could play in the distribution of wealth. While making the pilgrimage to Mecca he spent from £ 60,000 to £ 80,000 each time. People said that in Mecca not a soul slept who was not enriched by his generosity. In Egypt he was wont to distribute every month a hundred thousand pounds weight of meal to the poor besides and to free thousands of slaves in addition to endowing charitable religious foundations (*waqf*) (S. Lane-Poole, *The Story of Cairo*, p. 92).

In August of A.D. 935, another capable Turk, a descendent of a noble family of Farghāna, sailed up the Nile with his warships and occupied the Island of Roḍa. Muḥammad ibn Ṭughj, "the Ikhshīd," [46] had, through the favor of the caliph's vizier, obtained an appointment as governor of Egypt.

Although he allowed his troops to plunder the capital for two days, it was soon evident that the anarchy that had reigned since the fall of al-Qaṭāiᶜ was over. The Ikhshīd concentrated his efforts on restoring order in Egypt and, while he waged war in Syria, did not try to extend his claims farther than Damascus. His rule, though severe, was a welcome change. An army of 400,000 men including 8,000 body guard discouraged the Fāṭimids temporarily from making any further attempts upon Egypt.

Upon the death of the Ikhshīd in A.D. 946, the Abyssinian eunuch Kāfūr acted as regent for his sons. This pleasure-loving but wily and capable statesman managed to retain his power for twenty-two years, eventually becoming titular prince of Egypt. The slave whom the Ikhshīd had bought from an oil man for less than ten pounds [47] became a competent general, a successful governor, and a noted patron of the arts.

Through the years since the founding of the original encampment, Fusṭāṭ had become an active and vital town, full of much potential for development though still a somewhat rough provincial city in which the most remarkable building was the Mosque of ᶜAmr. [48] Undaunted by earthquakes, floods, and famines, the inhabitants persisted in making the best of the situation. Only God knew the future, and the way was always open to the strong and cunning individual who could make the most of the opportunities which unpredictable fate presented.

Essentially Fusṭāṭ of the Ikhshīds did not differ much from what it had been in previous periods. [49] The Ikhshīd had a new dockyard

---

[46] He obtained permission to assume this title meaning "king" in Farghāna soon after his arrival in Egypt.

[47] S. Lane-Poole, *A History of Egypt*, p. 87.

[48] Ibn Ḥawqal, *Kitāb Ṣūrat al-Arḍ* (Leiden: E. J. Brill, 1938), p. 146. The mosque had been founded over three centuries before but was demolished and practically rebuilt by the ᶜAbbāsid governor ᶜAbdallāh ibn Ṭāhir in A.D. 827, when it attained its present dimensions.

[49] We should remember that the nucleus of the capital at this time was situated much farther to the south and east than its present position. The waters of the river which flowed under the walls of Qaṣr ash-Shamaᶜ covered the site of the present districts of Miṣr al-ᶜAtīqa, Qaṣr al-ᶜAynī, Qaṣr ad-Dubbāra, Būlāq, and most of the land west of the Ezbekīya. The capital's northern boundary did not extend far beyond

constructed at Miṣr to supersede the little shipyard at Roḍa. Few monuments or significant buildings were constructed with the exception of "Kāfūr's palace" probably located north of the Ṭūlūnid quarter near the site of the "Garden of Kāfūr." Another palace built by him near the Mosque of Ibn Ṭūlūn was deserted because of the miasma from the stagnant water nearby. The order and prosperity which reigned in all lands ruled from the Egyptian capital, from Damascus to the Holy Cities in Arabia, however, produced an atmosphere in which people could live, work, and travel with some security.

We have a few descriptions of the town dating from this period, most of which speak of a flourishing urban center. Ibn Ḥawqal, writing in A.D. 978, estimated that it was one-third the size of Baghdad. He speaks also of the city's pleasure gardens, "handsome markets, narrow streets, and brick houses of six or seven stories, large enough to accommodate two hundred people." [50]

The ninth and tenth centuries A.D. saw the efflorescence of Islamic civilization as Egyptians, North Africans, Syrians, and Persians contributed to the development of cosmopolitanism. In the tenth century the wealthy tradesman became the carrier of Islamic civilization and as he did so he had the greatest opportunity to gain not only wealth but also the most extensive experience of the world available until then. The Muslim empire in Ibn Ḥawqal's time was bounded on the east by India, on the west by countries on the shores of the Atlantic, on the north by the lands of the Romans, Turks, and Chinese, and on the south by the Persian Gulf (Baḥr al-Fāris). Within these borders caravans and cargo fleets moved in all directions. Wherever the true believer went he could find the same God, the same prayer, and even the same law. [51]

---

the Mosque of Ibn Ṭūlūn, while the palace of Kāfūr was the only significant building in that area.

Expansion toward the north, begun with the first settlement of al-Fusṭāṭ, continued during the periods of al-ᶜAskar, al-Qaṭāiᶜ, and the Ikhshīdid period. Successive rulers had seen the advantages of placing a military encampment in proximity to the apex of the Delta and the route of most invaders of Egyptian territory. Moreover, residence in the North allowed them to take advantage of the clean and fresh northerly breezes and avoid the dusty atmosphere of the town. The expansion toward the west allowed continuous profit from the resources of the river. Regions which were subject to inundations often gave way to neighboring areas on higher ground better adapted for building. Thus the ᶜAmāl Fawq east of Qaṣr ash-Shamaᶜ developed at the expense of the ᶜAmāl Asfal opposite the Island of Roḍa (al-Maqrīzī, *Khiṭaṭ*, I, pp. 5, 343).

[50] *Kitāb Ṣūrat al-Arḍ*, p. 146.

[51] The concept of the law thus supervened any territorial consideration. An individual was judged according to the school of his religious community, rather than that preferred by the territory in which he happened to be.

It is true that in this period Syria and Iraq attracted the greatest part of the traffic coming from the East, but Miṣr-Fusṭāṭ never lost the commercial importance it had from the very beginning. Despite the fact that, since the second century A.H., governors of Fusṭāṭ had neglected the canal to the Red Sea and in A.D. 761, the caliph al-Manṣūr had closed it to cut off supplies to ᶜAlid rebels and perhaps to turn traffic towards Baghdad,[52] there continued to pass through Miṣr the goods of Upper Egypt and beyond, especially wood, slaves, animals, and hides. Local industries such as wood carving, textiles, glass, ceramics, and metal working had continued uninterrupted from the Byzantine period. Indigenous Coptic techniques and motifs were modified by new stimuli from abroad. From the Ṭūlūnid period onward, Mesopotamian and Persian themes are increasingly utilized. Writing in A.D. 956, al-Masᶜūdī praised especially the markets of Miṣr, stating that:

> All the kingdoms located on the two seas which border the country bring to this commercial center all the most remarkable, the rarest, and best perfumes, spices, drugs, jewels, and slaves, as well as staples of food and drink, and cloth of all sorts. The merchandise of the entire universe flows to this market.[53]

The town was on its way to becoming a cosmopolitan city.

It is interesting to note, moreover, that the most prominent traders in the capital were foreigners. The genuine Egyptian had the reputation of rarely leaving his country.[54] The biographies of religious scholars who engaged in commerce do not include a single one who traveled to Europe to trade and few who migrated from Egypt to the eastern Muslim world. On the other hand, in the tenth century A.D. there seems to have been a relatively large influx of commercially minded jurisprudents from from Baghdad to Egypt, indicating the increasing importance of Fusṭāṭ as a center for international business.[55] For some time there had been a sizeable and influential Persian colony in the city.[56] We have already noted the important role played by the Mādharāʾī family in financial endeavors.

---

[52] M. Clerget, *Le Caire*, II, p. 78.

[53] *Kitāb at-Tanbīh, Bibliotheca Geographorum Arabicorum*, edited by M. J. DeGoeje, VIII (Leiden: E. J. Brill, 1893), p. 20.

[54] Adam Mez, *Renaissance*, p. 449.

[55] Hayyim J. Cohen, "The Economic Background and Secular Occupations of Muslim Jurisprudents," pp. 44-45.

[56] A *qāḍī* at the end of the eighth century had received thirty Persians into his exclusive list of witnesses (al-Kindī, *Kitāb al-Quḍāh*, p. 402). These officers recall

Rivaling the Persians were the Jews who specialized in the money trade. A Jew at this time controlled the whole pearl-fishery of the Persian Gulf, while others had exclusive access to territories usually closed to foreigners such as Kashmir. Towards the end of the ninth century A.D., their economic power in Egypt was such that they were able to buy religious estates and even part of the Muᶜallaqa church [57] from the Patriarch of Alexandria who had been put under heavy contribution by the government. [58]

It was not only in the field of commerce that the Egyptian capital was developing. With the decline of the ᶜAbbāsid caliphate and usurpation of authority by local governors, the law became all the more emphasized as a unitary framework for the social fabric. Since the focal point of learning was the interpretation of Qurʾānic law, the courts of all the mosques were continually filled with professors and students. The Mosque of ᶜAmr at this time provided special porticoes (*arwiqa*) for the various schools (*madhāhib*), fifteen each for Shāfiᶜīs and Mālikīs and three porticoes for Ḥanafīs. It has been recorded that the violence of their arguments forced the Ikhshīd to take away their rush mats and cushions and close the mosque except at the hours of prayer. Activity in letters and in science could not compare with that of al-Kūfa or Baghdad but the court of Kāfūr attracted such outstanding men as the poet al-Mutanabbī, the grammarian al-Bakhtarī, and the chronicler al-Kindī. [59]

For quite a while now the Christians had been in the minority and their language had dropped out of use except in ritual contexts. Sāwīrus ibn al-Muqaffaᶜ, at the end of the tenth century, noted that "the Arabic language (has) spread to such a point in Egypt today that most of the inhabitants do not know Greek or Coptic." [60] Being no longer a significantly dangerous faction, the Christians under the Ṭūlūnids and Ikhshīdids enjoyed considerable favor. The independent governors needed all the support that they could muster at home to face the Baghdad caliphate.

---

the "notaries" of the pre-Islamic empire. According to al-Kindī there was so much false swearing that the *qāḍī* compiled a permanent list of trustworthy men (*Kitāb al-Quḍāh*, pp. 361, 411).

[57] This church, built in the fourth or fifth century A.D., was the seat of the Coptic patriarch from the eleventh to the fourteenth century.

[58] Adam Mez, *Renaissance*, p. 449.

[59] S. Lane-Poole, *The Story of Cairo*, p. 100.

[60] *Historia Patriarcharum Alexandrinorum*, edited by C. F. Seybold (Beirut, 1904), p. 6.

Evidently good-feeling existed too at the popular level. Al-Masᶜūdī gives an account of a native Egyptian festival celebrated by Muslims, the "Night of the Bath" (*Laylat al-Ghiṭās*, Epiphany).

> It is one of the great ceremonies and the people all go to it on foot on the tenth of January ... (The) banks of Roḍa and Fusṭāṭ (are) illuminated with a thousand torches ... Muslims and Christians by hundreds of thousands thronged the Nile on boats or looked from kiosks over the river or from the banks, all emulous for pleasure and outdoing each other in their display and dress; gold and silver vessels and jewels. The sound of music was heard all about, with singing and dancing ... The doors of the separate quarters were left open (instead of barred as usual at sunset), and most people bathed in the Nile confident in its power (on that night) of preventing and curing all illnesses. [61]

The sharing of a common local culture and folk beliefs not strictly linked with religion must many times have helped to override the segmentation which was basic to social organization. Festivals such as the one described, or the one celebrating the Nile flood, were part of everyone's life, regardless of religion or social status. They marked a brief release from some of the rigorous restrictions of customary behavior as well as a welcome diversion from the dullness of everyday life.

The most vital part of the urban center since the beginning of the Arab period had been the agglomeration of Miṣr-Fusṭāṭ. There the majority of the population had carried on their indigenous trades and occupations with little interference in these concerns from the ruling element. The significance of Arab-Copt differentiation, moreover, became less and less as the local people accepted Islam and the army settled down. The first step had been taken as the clients were given a special place in Muslim society, and the second was taken as both clients and Arabs shared experiences as Egyptians. Now it was the Turks who were setting up administrative barracks, and many of the leading merchants were Persians or Jews. While there had been significant cultural achievements under the Ṭūlūnids and Ikhshīdids and Miṣr came to achieve considerable commercial importance, the capital still could not compete with Baghdad or Damascus in these respects; but ties were established with other regions of the Muslim empire, the way had been made, and the potential was there.

---

61 *Mūrūj adh-Dhahab* (Cairo, 1958), I, p. 343.

In contrast, the official quarters of al-ᶜAskar and especially of al-Qaṭāiᶜ fell by degrees into decay. By the eleventh century they had become a "quarry from which people took materials for building elsewhere." [62] A large part of the northern expansion had been the result of projects which had really involved only the ruling class. Al-Qaṭāiᶜ never recovered from the ravages of the ᶜAbbāsid troops and the only people left in the area were a few descendents of Ibn Ṭūlūn's soldiers. The policy of the early governors of building apart from the main town allowed the ruling faction to enjoy an especially luxurious environment while the dynasty lasted and gave the city a temporary stimulus, but with a political upheaval, the most ambitious survivors saw scant advantage in remaining on a site which had symbolized the old regime.

[62] Al-Maqrīzī, *Khiṭaṭ*, I, p. 305.

CHAPTER THREE

THE FĀṬIMID FLORESCENCE: COSMOPOLITAN ACHIEVEMENT AND CHALLENGE (A.D. 969-1169)

1. *The Fāṭimid Conquest*

It is not difficult to understand the success of the Fāṭimid conquest of Egypt in the light of the weakness of ᶜAbbāsid rule which had reached its most profound decadence by the middle of the tenth century. The capital had in fact been independent in all but name for most of the time since its foundation. If it remained orthodox on the whole, there had been pro-ᶜAlid leanings from the earliest days of Arab rule. The Fāṭimid offshoot of the Ismāᶜīlī movement which was so influential in the ninth and tenth centuries owed no small part of its success to a widespread underground propaganda network which had infiltrated both the elite and the common levels of society. Thus political purposes were accomplished by playing on the strings of religious sentiment and often rebellion against the orthodox regime took the form of allegiance to the ᶜAlid cause.

Throughout the Arab period, not only Muᶜtazilīs but Shīᶜīs had scribbled inscriptions on the gates of the Mosque of ᶜAmr. According to al-Kindī, the civilian population (or part of it) approved these formulas. [1] There was, therefore, considerable sympathy for the Fāṭimid cause within the city itself which, together with the Fāṭimid incursions into Egypt, continually plagued the Ikhshīdid governors. The army could erase the inscriptions but it was not so easy to deal with the raids of the *mahdī*'s troops.

By A.D. 909, the Fāṭimids had occupied Tunis, and sent the last Aghlabid in flight to Egypt. By A.D. 914, they had entered Egypt to occupy Alexandria and the Fayyūm, waging war with the harried governors for five years until they were finally repelled in 920. During this time, it is well to note, the *qāḍī* and Mādharāʾī the treasurer, as well as other leading persons, were discovered to be in communication with the Fāṭimid caliph. [2] The strength of the Ikhshīd, and that of Kāfūr after him held the movement at bay temporarily, but during the reign of the latter we hear of an official embassy from the Fāṭimid

---

[1] *Kitāb al-Wulāh*, p. 274.

[2] S. Lane-Poole, *History of Egypt*, p. 80.

inviting official recognition of the sovereignty of the caliph. Kāfūr received them kindly and in his court many were won to the cause. [3]

The Qarmaṭians, of whom the Fāṭimids were an offshoot, were frankly political in their intentions though they manipulated religious claims and arguments to gain adherents. As Lane-Poole says, "They used the claim of the family of ᶜAlī not because they believed in any divine right or any caliphate, but because some flag had to be flourished in order to rouse the people." [4] But masses cannot be seduced unless dissatisfaction is widespread. There must be a general belief that the newcomers have a genuine solution to offer and some means of coordinating isolated disaffected groups in an organized movement.

From one point of view, the tremendous success of Shīᶜī propaganda from the Atlantic to Central Asia, follows a period of continuous unrest and discontent with the conditions of life under the decaying ᶜAbbāsid regime. [5] Shīᶜī uprisings invariably voiced Messianic expectations of a ruler "who would fill the earth with justice and equity just as much as it is filled with injustice and oppression of one by the other." [6] Astrology was held in great esteem by the Qarmaṭians and Fāṭimids who made strong allusions to it in their propaganda. The cosmic significance of the new order of the *mahdī* was seen to be proclaimed by propitious conjunctions of the stars which set the date of the end of the old empire.

It was the superior organization of the Fāṭimid propaganda network however, that was the effective cause of the success of the "Shīᶜī revolution." The agents of the *imām* were his spiritual representatives to his followers; more like priests than the orthodox religious teachers, *mulla*s or *ṭālib*s, who are not ordained in any sense. For whereas the

---

[3] Marius Canard, "L'impérialisme des Fatimides et leur propagande," *Annales de l'Institut d'Études Orientales*, 6 (1942-1947), p. 176. Although Kāfūr withheld allegiance, most of his entourage and his chief officials gave promises of homage to the Fāṭimid. In the light of the ineffectiveness of ᶜAbbāsid authority at this time, it may well have been that Kāfūr thought of transferring the allegiance of Egypt to the Fāṭimid upon the next vacancy of the governorship (DeLacy O'Leary, *A Short History of the Fatimid Caliphate* (London: K. Paul, Trench, and Trubner, 1923), pp. 94-95).

[4] *History of Egypt*, p. 95.

[5] Generally, Shīᶜism, which grew up in Mesopotamia and Persia, found more fertile ground in cultures already imbued with Hellenistic philosophical ideas. Moreover the "legitimist" principle of hereditary descent, adhered to by the Shīᶜīs, as opposed to the Arab tribal theory whereby the caliph was chosen by the community, found many adherents in lands in which kingship was traditionally semi-divine in character.

[6] W. Ivanow, "The Organization of the Fatimid Propaganda," *Journal of the Bombay Branch of the Royal Asiatic Society*, N.S. 15 (1938), p. 2.

latter acquire their position by consent of the community, on account of their learning and piety, the former were accredited agents of the *imām*, by virtue of a commission received either directly from the leader or indirectly through others who had been selected by him personally. The *dāʿī*, or agent, was the leader of a *jazīra*, or religious cell in a region not under Fāṭimid sovereignty. A medieval manuscript sets forth the characteristics and personal qualities of the *dāʿī*. He was to be of good family, self-disciplined, well-studied in jurisprudence, an expert lawyer, of high moral character, a champion of the religious cause, and wise in the choice of subordinates. [7] Thus the organization both permitted the standardization of dogma and could function even in the absence of the *imām* himself. The decentralized organization of carefully selected agents who were given full authority for their "cells" and expected to act independently, strengthened the position of the caliph by allowing him to remain above the squabbles of his subjects and avoid responsibility for any occurrence that did not come up to expectations.

With matters as they were in Egypt after the death of Kāfūr, it would have been surprising if the Fāṭimids had not succeeded. In A.D. 967 the army was in revolt, the viziers palace had been plundered, and a terrible famine contributed to the misery of the country. Weakened by natural calamities and internal dissension, Egypt fell easily to a Fāṭimid force of 100,000 men led by Jawhar as-Siqilī. In Miṣr where more than half a million people had died of the plague and only some soldiers who had served under the Ikhshīd and Kāfūr defended the town, there was hardly an effort to resist. [8] A letter from Jawhar promised that the soldiers of the caliph al-Muʿizz had not come to conquer but simply

> "to deliver the Egyptians from the menace of the infidels who wanted to attack the country as they had attacked others in the East, and to conduct Holy War against them, and to reorganize the Pilgrimage and secure liberty, to reestablish security in commerce by a sound currency, abolish illegal taxes, and assure freedom of exercise of religion to all." [9]

Granting full amnesty for submission and forbidding pillage, Jawhar and his troops occupied Miṣr on the fifth of August, A.D. 969.

---

[7] W. Ivanow, "The Organization of the Fatimid Propaganda," pp. 18-35.

[8] S. Lane-Poole, *Story of Cairo*, p. 117.

[9] *Al-Maqrīzī, Ittiʿāẓ al-Hunafāʾ bi-Akhbār al-Aʿimma al-Fāṭimīyūn al-Khulafāʾ*, edited by H. Bunz (Jerusalem, 1909), pp. 67-70; also cited in M. Canard, "L'Impérialisme des Fatimides et leur propagande," p. 179.

The beginning of Fāṭimid rule marks a new epoch in the history of the Egyptian capital. Al-Qāhira (Cairo) was the first seat of a truly sovereign power in Egypt since the days of the Pharaohs. No longer was its government religiously subordinate to any foreign power. A direct break had been made with the orthodox caliphate and the new regime controlled a vast Mediterranean empire stretching from Fez, Corsica, Malta, Sardinia, and Sicily, to Damascus and the Holy Cities of Arabia. Connections with Europe through the development of naval power gave stimulus to commerce, while the capable leaders of the conquest brought order to the troubled land.

Three days after entering Miṣr, the Friday prayers at the Mosque of ᶜAmr were recited with the omission of the name of the ᶜAbbāsid caliph and the *khuṭba* was recited for the *imām*, al-Muᶜizz, *Amīr al-Muʾminīn* (Commander of the Faithful). The profession of the Shīᶜī faith was made through blessings of Alī, Fāṭima, and their sons.[10] That there was no outburst from the Egyptian public can perhaps be explained by the indifference of Egyptians to new rule on the assumption that profound changes were not going to take place in the religious sphere. On the face of it, the new regime may have appeared to many as "just another foreign dynasty." The majority regarded the new creed apathetically except when the celebration of the Shīᶜī Muḥarram festival aroused their indignation.[11] On the day following the announcement the markets which had been closed in anticipation of possible disturbance were opened in safety. Those who doubted the right of al-Muᶜizz to the caliphate and would withhold acceptance of his credentials were in no position to protest. To many Muslims, the residence of the *imām* among them was an unequalled honor. To non-Muslims, that the Fāṭimids were Shīᶜī meant little, on the contrary, most of them expected favors from the new regime which they had encouraged.

2. *Fāṭimid Culture and Society*

The beginning of a new era was signaled by the founding of a new city. On the very night of the capitulation of Miṣr, with due regard to astrological indications, Jawhar staked out a plan for a fortified palace enclosure north of Fusṭāṭ.[12] Named al-Qāhira, "the Victorious,"

---

[10] Ibn Khallikān, *Kitāb Wafayāt al-Aᶜyān*, translated into English by M. de Slane (Paris, 1843), I, p. 344.

[11] DeLacy O'Leary, *History of the Fatimid Caliphate*, p. 104.

[12] Al-Maqrīzī, *Khiṭat*, I, p. 377.

to commemorate the triumph of al-Muᶜizz, or some say to avert the sinister omen of the planet Mars which was on the ascendant, "The Conquering City" indeed became a seat of power rivaled by few before or since.

Twelve hundred yards each way and half a square mile in area, al-Qāhira lay on the road to Heliopolis between the canal and the Muqaṭṭam, about a mile from the river. Between it and Fusṭāṭ was a more or less uninhabited area surrounding the Birkat al-Fīl ("Pond of the Elephant") which was often flooded. The enclosure well deserved its epithet, *al-Maḥrūsa*, "The Guarded"; no one could pass through its gates without a permit and even ambassadors had to dismount and be led into the palace between guards. Like the preceding camp cities, it was intended only for the court of the ruler and his troops, but beyond the interests of military security, it represented the aura and mystery of the sacred person of the caliph.

The central portion of the town was occupied by the Great East Palace, the Palace of the Viziers, and an open space where the people could gather on feast days. A little later a West Palace for the *ḥarīm* was added on the eastern edge of Kāfūr's park. The space between the two palaces (Bayn al-Qaṣrayn) was so large that 10,000 guardsmen could parade within it. Part of this area, now the Sūq an-Naḥḥāsīn, still bears this name. A main street ran parallel to the canal, connecting the northern gates of Bāb al-Futūḥ and Bāb an-Naṣr with the Bāb Zuwayla on the south. The rest of the city was divided into quarters (*ḥārāt*) representing various ethnic groups and social classes as the *khiṭaṭ* of al-Fusṭāṭ once represented tribes. Jawhar settled his own people, the Greeks, near the main gates of the city, at the north and south. A small lane just inside the Bāb Zuwayla still bears the name, "Ḥārat ar-Rūm." Other divisions of the army, Kitāma Berbers, Berbers of Qayrawān, Kurds, Turks, Persians, and Masmūdī Blacks occupied their own areas. [13] To avoid racial disputes, al-Muᶜizz settled his Sūdānī forces at Heliopolis. They were not allowed to visit Fusṭāṭ at night although they could come and go freely in the daytime. [14]

The community of al-Qāhira prospered through the capable rule of al-Muᶜizz. The brick wall surrounding the city was finished in a year. To the west the caliph built a new dock at Maqs near the present

---

[13] Nāṣir-i Khusraw, *Sefer Nāmeh, Relation du voyage,* translated from the Persian by Charles Schefer (Paris: E. Leroux, 1881), pp. 144-145.

[14] DeLacy O'Leary, *History of the Fatimid Caliphate,* p. 113.

Ezbekīya to replace the port of Miṣr, and in a short time six hundred ships were constructed there. [15] As the years passed, a large unprotected city grew up outside the official enclosure. It is said that there were 20,000 houses and shops which belonged to the caliph and paid him rent. Caravanserais, baths, public buildings, markets, mosques, and gardens extended over what once had been a sandy waste. [16]

The luxury of the court of the Fāṭimids far surpassed that of Khumārawayh. The palace itself in the middle of the city was separated from all the other buildings in the enclosure by a large clearing. At night it was guarded by five hundred horsemen and five hundred footmen. [17] A report of a Frankish diplomat who visited Cairo in A.D. 1167 expresses fully the splendor and mystery which surrounded the caliph. The ambassadors, personally guided by the vizier Shāwar, were taken through long dark narrow passages and then a series of doors before each of which were numerous guards. They reached an outdoor court, completely paved with varicolored marble and set off with gold. Gold covered the rafters and beams and, through gold and silver pipes, a central fountain furnished water to canals and pools. Rare birds flitted here and there as they proceded through other more elaborate gardens, where animals unlike anything they had ever seen roamed the paths; then more doors more walks, and more wonders until they finally came to the Great Palace. Warriors in gold and silver armor guarded a throne room divided in two by a curtain on which were depicted animals, birds, and people embroidered with precious stones. The room was seemingly empty but the vizier prostrated himself three times as though before his God. Suddenly the tapestry was lifted and before the astonished eyes of the ambassadors the boy caliph appeared seated on a golden throne set with gems, his face covered by a veil. [18]

The chronicles refer to vast stores of treasure in the possession of the Fāṭimid caliphs and their families: sacks of emeralds and precious stones of all sorts, chased and inlaid silver vessels and Sicilian embroideries by the tens of thousands, and basins and ewers of pure

---

[15] The port flourished until the shifting of the Nile uncovered Būlāq in the thirteenth and fourteenth centuries.

[16] Nāṣir-i Khusraw *Sefer Nāmeh*, p. 127.

[17] *Ibid.*, pp. 127-128.

[18] See William of Tyre, *Historia rerum in partibus transmarinis gestarum*, book XIX, in *Recueil des historiens des croissades*: *historiens occidentaux* (Paris, 1844), I, chapters, 19, 20.

Musicians and Dancers.

A Lady Pouring a Drink.

A Christian Priest.

2. Some Fāṭimid Representations of People.

crystal. A silk map of the world done in gold and colored threads costing 22,000 dinars was made in Persia at the command of al-Muᶜizz.[19]

Even as al-Qāhira and Fusṭāṭ were separated by a distance of about two miles, so there was a gap between them socially. To be sure, some government officials who were civilians and other persons who served the court lived in the caliph's city but the formality of the capital contrasted strongly with the life of Fusṭāṭ which bustled with all kinds of urban activity. The population of al-Qāhira represented primarily the extremes of the upper crust and the menials who served them while that of Fusṭāṭ represented in the main an easy-going middle class.[20]

Yet despite the vast concentration of wealth in the new burg the wonders of Fusṭāṭ for a long time surpassed those of the capital. Writing in the year A.D. 985, the traveler al-Muqaddasī says little about the caliph's city, but describes Fusṭāṭ as "the most splendid and most populous city of the Muslim world" in which "living was cheap and the necessities of life continually flowed from all parts of the globe."[21] Travelers invariably praised the rare and costly wares available in the markets of Fusṭāṭ. Nāṣir-i Khusraw, a Persian who visited the city in the middle of the eleventh century mentions especially local products:

> All types of porcelain are made at Fusṭāṭ. It is so fine and transparent that a hand held outside a vase can be seen through it. Bowls, cups, dishes, and other utensils are made here. They are decorated with colors whose shades change with the positions of the object. A transparent and very pure glass which resembles the emerald is manufactured here, it is sold by weight.[22]

Druggists, grocers, and dealers in hardware sold their goods at fixed prices and even furnished containers and paper wrappings for

---

[19] Unfortunately few examples of these things have come down to us. We have only a single rock-crystal vase in the treasury of St. Mark's in Venice from the period of al-ᶜAzīz, some pottery and glass, mostly fragmentary, a few wood carvings, and textile fragments. We know from these few remains however, that the quality of the work produced does not fall short of what the historical record indicates.

[20] S. D. Goitein, "Cairo: An Islamic City in the Light of the Geniza Documents," *Middle Eastern Cities*, edited by Ira M. Lapidus (Berkeley, Calif.: University of California Press, 1969), pp. 84-85.

[21] *Kitāb Aḥsan at-Taqāsīm fī Maᶜrifat al-Aqālīm*, edited by M. J. De Goeje (Leiden: E. J. Brill, 1967), pp. 197-198.

[22] *Sefer Nāmeh*, pp. 151-152.

purchased items. Each shopkeeper had to keep a jar full of water in front of his shop to be used in case of fire; and well he might, considering the closeness of the streets and alleys! The picture these descriptions conjure up is one of intense bustling activity. Cookshops, caterers, and itinerant cooks too, were many, since few people prepared food at home but brought their meals from outside. During the reign of al-Ḥākim when an order was given that shops, doorways, streets, and dead-end lanes were to be lit up, the people kept lights burning all night. Markets and especially drinking establishments had crowds of customers, whose behavior scandalized the caliph. Subsequently a strict curfew was ordered. [23]

Physically, the popular center symbolized the spirit of enterprise and conservatism as well as the mobility and clannishness that characterized social life. Centuries had passed since the Arab conquest but the main quarters of the town still bore the names of the Arab tribal sections that originally settled them. By the twelfth century, however, the center of the first Muslim settlement was inhabited principally by Christians who were being displaced by Jews. [24] Although elements of these religious minorities predominated in the older sections of the city, there were no ghettos either residential or occupational. The Geniza documents so well analyzed by Professor Goitein show that Jewish dwellings bordered on Muslim and/or Christian properties. Many houses, moreover, were owned jointly by persons of different faith and origin. [25] The whole institution of holding property in partnership, as Goitein has cogently pointed out, reflected the polarity of social organization. People wanted the security of residing with or near their kin and branches of an extended family often occupied one house or adjacent houses, but they also felt the need of making ties with outsiders to secure various benefits. The right of preemption that served to exclude aliens was often waived or forgotten. [26]

What zoning there was was far from strict. Generally bazaars and industrial areas could be separated from residential districts. On the other hand numerous houses described in the Geniza documents were beside bazaars and had a place of business on the lower level, especially

---

[23] Al-Maqrīzī, *Khiṭāṭ*, II, p. 286.
[24] S. D. Goitein, "Cairo: An Islamic City," p. 86.
[25] *Ibid.*, p. 86.
[26] *Ibid.*, p. 88.

if they were those great multistoried edifices [27] described by Nāṣir-i Khusraw in A.D. 1046:

> When one looks at the city of Miṣr from a distance, it looks like a mountain. There are some houses which have fourteen floors, and others which have seven ... A well-known merchant told me that there are, in Miṣr, a large number of houses that have rooms for rent. [28]

Two or three hundred people could live in one house. Rents, according to the Geniza documents, were comparatively low. A modest apartment could be rented for a month for the price of the daily wage of a master mason. [29]

Despite evidence of considerable affluence in Fusṭāṭ, at all times the city's overall aspect seems to have been characterized by a peculiar juxtaposition of prosperity and decay. The grandest residences stood side by side with buildings in partial or total ruin. Although decay was more evident in some areas than in others, the presence of ruins did not indicate a lower class neighborhood. It is true that the institution of holding buildings in partnership (some had as many as twenty-four owners) militated against property restoration and upkeep, but the situation may also have reflected a cautious and realistic acceptance of the uncertainties of existence. The outside world could be the source of wealth and advancement but it was characterized by fluidity and irregulariarity. Households, in any case, were *interiors* even as the families who resided in them represented foci of honor, security, and pride.

Generally the offices of urban administration were directed at providing two things: security and justice. Provision of the other necessities of existence was left to individuals and the social communities to which they belonged. The government of the city was largely in the hands of the military commander (*amīr*), the chief of police (*wālī*), [30]

---

[27] It is tempting to describe in greater detail these houses which were provided not only with ordinary comforts but also with extensive hydraulic systems that furnished large roof gardens as well as the needs of sanitation. Nāṣir-i Khusraw describes a garden on a house of seven stories which sheltered an ox that had been raised there to operate the wheel of the *sāqiya* by which the water was drawn up. The terrace was planted with oranges and other fruit trees (*Sefer Nāmeh*, pp. 146-147). For information on the hydraulic and sanitation systems of Fusṭāṭ, see George T. Scanlon, "Housing and Sanitation: Some Aspects of Medieval Public Service," *The Islamic City*, edited by A. H. Hourani and S. M. Stern, pp. 179-194.

[28] *Sefer Nāmeh*, pp. 146-147.

[29] S. D. Goitein "Cairo: An Islamic City," pp. 88, 89.

[30] Although this term literally means "governor" it was used in this period to indicate the superintendent of police who in large cities assisted the *amīr*. Available

and the *qāḍī* who had extensive administrative as well as judicial duties. It was the last mentioned who controlled the collection of many taxes, oversaw the making of contracts, and even acted upon occasion as the legal representative for foreign merchants (*wakīl tujjār*).[31] There was, in reality, no clear division of duties between judicial and security officers. The chief *qāḍī*, because of his executive and economic powers, in actual fact often had more power than the governor. In any case people more frequently sought letters of recommendation to him. The *qāḍī*, however, could command only those policemen assigned to help him carry out his duties and governors and police officials upon occasion were known to deal with cases that normally came within the *qāḍī*'s sphere of influence.[32] Lesser urban officials were the *ṣāḥib ar-rub*ᶜ who supervised the quarter, regular police, and secret plain-clothesmen. The latter formed an extremely important governmental agency that utilized the "local grapevine" to police the town effectively and maintain internal security. We will meet them again in later periods. Through them the authorities kept track of suspicious persons of various kinds and foreigners who might get into difficulties. It is notable that although non-Muslims were not permitted to perform military service they frequently did serve as secret-servicemen.[33]

Sources of this period throw much light on economic and industrial life. There was much sophistication in the management of economic transactions. We should not fail to mention that charge accounts, checks,[34] and letters of credit were all familiar to the people of Fusṭāṭ. Evidence from the Geniza indicates that possibly more business was conducted on credit than in our own time.[35] We have many notes, properly dated and signed, indicating the quantity and price of items purchased. Thus grocers, for instance, would accumulate stacks of notes

---

records indicate that the office of the market inspector (*muḥtasib*) did not become important in Egypt until relatively late and his functions in Fāṭimid times may have been united with those of the *wālī*. See S. D. Goitein, "Cairo: An Islamic City," p. 91, and also his *A Mediterranean Society*, II: *The Community* (Berkeley, Calif.: University of California Press, 1971), p. 369.

[31] S. D. Goitein, *A Mediterranean Society*, I: *Economic Foundations*, p. 187.

[32] S. D. Goitein, *A Mediterranean Society*, II: *The Community* (Berkeley, Calif.: University of California Press, 1971), pp. 366, 368, 371.

[33] *Ibid.*, p. 379.

[34] It was common for orders of payment, or checks, to be written as follows: " 'May so-and-so (the issuing banker) pay to the bearer (not mentioned by name) such and such an amount (in words).' On the left lower corner the date (month and year, not the day) was indicated and on the lower edge of the note the name of the issuer" (S. D. Goitein, *A Mediterranean Society*, I, p. 241).

[35] S. D. Goitein, *A Mediterranean Society*, I, p. 197.

and bill their customers periodically by returning these to them in a bunch. [36] Bankers and merchants made special use of the letter of credit (*suftaja*) to avoid the risk of transporting money. These were of particular importance where long distances were involved and were honored wherever permanent business connections existed, from Baghdad to the Red Sea Coast, the Sudan, and the northern fringe of the Sahara. Payment would be received in exactly the form paid to the issuing banker. [37] Nāṣir-i Khusraw remarked that in Fusṭāṭ he was able to cash such a note received from an acquaintance in Aswān. [38]

The government made no attempt to impose strict control over the economy. True, the state was the greatest producer and consumer in the country and agricultural products were bought for the most part from or through government agencies. The government issued licenses and collected taxes on business. Still, much was left to private enterprise and we have few complaints about excessive taxation or impositions.

Although there was an attempt at centralization, a keystone in Fāṭimid administration was the tax farm which was granted to individuals. Most tax farmers were members of the middle class; businessmen who knew the social and economic situation of the district for which they stood security. They received their appointments from a local office or sometimes from a prominent person to whom the government had granted a certain revenue. Actual collection of taxes would often be done through assistants and the tax farmer had the right to send policemen to arrest those who did not pay. Tax farmers, however, at this time do not seem to have been very oppressive and there are few complaints about them. [39]

Thus individual capitalists played a central role in the state's fiscal activities. Even currency came into being not by being issued by the government but rather through being ordered from the state by private suppliers of gold and silver who would take their solid wealth to the mint and receive an equivalent in currency after a deduction for costs of production. These same individuals often headed the lists of donors to communal charities. [40]

Materials of the period reflect a rank conscious people who regarded

---

[36] S. D. Goitein, "Bankers' Accounts from the Eleventh Century A.D.," *Journal of the Economic and Social History of the Orient*, 9 (1966), p. 28.

[37] S. D. Goitein, *A Mediterranean Society*, I, p. 244.

[38] *Sefer Nāmeh*, p. 64.

[39] S. D. Goitein, *A Mediterranean Society*, II, p. 363.

[40] S. D. Goitein, *A Mediterranean Society*, I, p. 267.

social inequality as supernaturally pre-ordained and natural. This statement applies as well to special religious status or ethnicity. The broadest categories of urban social classes consisted of the *notables* connected to the government: high administrators, court physicians, chief judges and community leaders; a *bourgeoisie* of businessmen and professionals made up of two layers: first, the fairly well-off merchants and master craftsmen, and second, the petty merchants and shopkeepers; the *lower class* was made up chiefly of manual laborers and craftsmen. [41]

Generally, family affiliation assigned one's place in society and sons followed the profession of their fathers. Still, there was no set rule. Inequality of rank derived from heredity was a matter of fact rather than of law, and exceptions to the general pattern are not hard to find. Then too, economic hardships connected to class differences were somewhat mitigated by affiliation to particular religious or ethnic communities which split the society vertically, and every community had its members of high and low class. In fact, within the religious community, taking care of the poor of one's group was not just a duty, but generosity and providing for others was a major way of attaining rank (*jāh*).

Control of economic resources, occupation and wealth, served as a major, though by no means the only criterion of rank. With regard to this factor Egyptian society at this time was remarkably open. No automatic economic advantage pertained to membership in a class as such. Riches, moreover, seem to have been thought of as an *individual* blessing that came, like all forms of power, from God. Certainly the vast treasures of the Fāṭimids and of their advisors contrasted with the relative poverty of the masses. Strikingly they symbolized the gap between the rulers and the ruled. On the other hand, economic like political power could come and go with spectacular rapidity. With the exception of the dynasty itself, no single group or class monopolized either high office or the wealth it brought throughout the whole period.

In reality, the operation of economic institutions could not be separated from elements and attitudes pertaining to the sphere of social life. Security was achieved through personal links with others, through ties of partnership, clientage, and friendship.

In actual fact one's rank depended not so much upon one's occupation as upon *how* that occupation was undertaken. Manual labor in

---

[41] *Ibid.*, p. 79.

itself was not degrading. As we saw in the last chapter, many learned persons engaged in manual trades. What was degrading was having to work for wages. It was deemed much better to work *with* another than *for* him. Even a laborer or craftsman preferred to undertake his business by entering into contract. Thus the legal institution of partnership was pervasive, covering an economic field that in modern times comprises the institutions of employment and money lending.[42] Both borrowing money from and working for another was considered humiliating because these acts made one dependent without the ameliorating condition of mutual obligation based on common interest. Such an arrangement seems peculiar to us who are used to conducting economic affairs separate from personal interactions and who feel secure in an impersonal but fairly dependable economic environment. To these preindustrial people, however, security was found in the more personal relationship of partnership rather than in the cold outer world of universalistic institutions.

Partnerships too, reflected the polarity of social relations, for contractual conditions and social connections of partners varied widely. Frequently partners would be of diverse origin with respect to rank, ethnic derivation, and even religious status. [43] One factor encouraging family partnerships was the fact that the state regarded parents, children, and brothers and sisters to be mutually responsible in a legal sense. [44] In family partnerships, the transactions of one involved the others equally, and all profit achieved by the work of relatives was held in common. On the other hand, lifelong partnerships with persons outside the family could become stronger than family ties. The Geniza provides a case in which a man not only appointed his partner sole executor of his estate and guardian of his family but did so to the exclusion of his brother who was also a partner. [45]

---

[42] If a workman had no capital, he would affiliate himself with someone who could finance his activity and, in joint undertaking, contribute his labor. Profits and losses would be divided with consideration to a number of factors such as proportion of investment, responsibility, or imponderables such as the benefit accruing to the partnership from the social position of one of the partners. Sometimes daily payments would be taken out of the "purse of the partnership" but these were not considered wages (S. D. Goitein, *A Mediterranean Society*, I, p. 170). For a good discussion of the legal aspects of partnership see *Partnership and Profit in Medieval Islam* by Abraham L. Udovitch (Princeton, N.J.: Princeton University Press, 1970).

[43] S. D. Goitein, *A Mediterranean Society*, I, pp. 72, 170-174.

[44] An aspect of this relation is the fact that among *dhimmī*s members of one family were held responsible for each other's poll tax.

[45] S. D. Goitein, *A Mediterranean Society*, I, p. 89.

We have already seen the utility and importance of personal bonds for the achievement of political ends. Beyond the formal ties of partnership security lay in bonds of friendship.[46] Friends were essential in every undertaking of importance. People did not attempt long trips without two sources of personal help: both letters of safe conduct giving personal references and a trustworthy companion were indispensable.[47] If trouble befell a traveler, legal or otherwise, suspicion fell upon his companion. To let a friend or relative travel alone was considered a disgrace.[48]

Although there were some governmental institutions, like the office of the *wakīl tujjār* for instance, that merchants could utilize in the conduct of their business affairs away from home, it was thought advisable to depend upon friends to oversee one's interests. Friends helped one another through exchanging information, overseeing the sale of each other's goods and even carrying goods for each other. The chain of connection was often considerably extended both socially and spatially. The network of effective social bonds that one could manipulate to attain one's ends included not only close friends and relatives but second- and third-degree acquaintances.[49] Informal cooperation could last a lifetime and the debts involved could be claimed even after a generation or more had passed.[50]

Another factor which added to the utility of social connections was the very ambiguity of the relations involved. Not that there was a dearth of formal contractual arrangements or explicit statements of rights and duties, but simultaneous dependence upon friendship and mutual trust militated against the exact spelling out of what was expected, especially since one never knew what kind of eventuality might arise. Despite the development of formal commercial techniques, Geniza documents indicate that business associates were frequently unsure of the conditions of their collaboration.[51] Social sensitivity too, was

---

[46] Goitein states that friendship and mutual trust were the foundations of Mediterranean commerce during the High Middle Ages (*A Mediterranean Society* I, p. 186).

[47] An Arab proverb warns: "The neighbor before the house, the companion before the way" (*Al-jār qabl ad-dār wa ar-rafīq qabl aṭ-ṭarīq*).

[48] S. D. Goitein, *A Mediterranean Society*, I, p. 348.

[49] In one instance a merchant in Cairo owed a favor to a merchant in Fez. A friend of the latter sent via an Alexandrian friend a shipment to the Cairo merchant requesting him to oversee its sale and to purchase with its price a certain commodity (S. D. Goitein, *A Mediterranean Society*, I, p. 166).

[50] S. D. Goitein, *A Mediterranean Society*, I, p. 169.

[51] *Ibid.*, p. 186.

involved. We even find instances in which people reproved one another for requesting written accounts and formal apologies were sent for such behavior. Accounts of specific transactions and requests for them are numerous but these are often made indirectly: one person asks another to remind a third of his duty, or to ask a third to prod a fourth. [52]

The social system was relatively open in spite of and perhaps even because of the formal marking of differences in status. Not only were religious groups set apart, but masters were separate from slaves, and men from women. Still, in all of these cases by virtue of the fact that there was separateness, there also had to be some means of connection. In many cases the very restrictions of special status facilitated the development of personal liaisons.

With reference to women, for example, far from being excluded from economic life, many were economically active and owned considerable property of various kinds. Some were agents and brokers, for only women could enter the *ḥarīm*s of private houses to sell textiles and jewels. Similarly, educated *shaykha*s taught Qurʾān in private homes, while others, noted for their piety, were sought out by persons in need of a blessing. Prayers of old women were thought to be especially efficacious.

The social status of the slave is usually considered to be about as far removed from the attainment of high rank and as distantly removed from inclusion in respected social groups as it is possible to get. This assessment is true. The slave has no family. He has not even the legal status of a person. Yet there is no case in which we can see so clearly the importance of personal bonds in overcoming the influence of legal disadvantage. The legal disadvantage in fact generated such bonds. We have seen in an earlier chapter how caliphal masters *preferred to depend upon slaves rather than upon members of their own family who could be considered rivals.* The Middle Eastern situation in which slaves have more than once acquired the appurtenances of the highest rank even to become rulers [53] is not a paradox, it is the other side of the coin.

Slaves often acted not only in domestic capacities but as the business agents of their master, coming to occupy a *de facto* position similar

---

[52] *Ibid.*, pp. 204-205.

[53] Like Kāfūr previously and like the Mamlūks after him, Jawhar as-Siqilī was a liberated slave. The mothers of a number of Fāṭimid caliphs too, had been slaves.

to his. [54] A man was congratulated upon his acquisition of a male slave in the same way that he was congratulated on the birth of a son. [55] Moreover, in referring to the master-slave relationship the father-son simile was commonly used, and we also find the reverse simile referring to the son as a slave. [56] Although he was not supposed to inherit from his master, the slave did in fact perform many filial duties. The freeing of a slave was thought to be an act of special piety and to one manumitted it was like birth as through it he "joined the living." [57] In his new life he used the name of his former master. Little wonder then, that after manumission, the strongest sentimental ties remained between master and ex-slave which served to enhance the social standing of the latter. The tie was stronger even than that of alliance or partnership which depended only upon contract and could broken.

When people reached out to gain advantage they usually did so with the backing of their family and community, but they were bound to experience a widening of their social network that could not but transform their sphere of interaction. An example can be seen in travel which was viewed with mixed sentiments. When abroad, people from the same homeland stuck together. Expressions of homesickness are common and the fervor of attachment to one's homeland cannot be doubted. [58] On the other hand, the urge for travel was just as strong and for many travel was a necessity. Some would even commute. [59]

Reasons why individuals moved about were both positive and negative. The simple need to make a living contributed to the mobility

---

[54] Thus a scandal arose when the slave of the head of the Jewish academy in Old Cairo, known to be a trouble-maker, was flogged and jailed for publicly insulting a prominent person (S. D. Goitein, *A Mediterranean Society*, I, p. 133).

[55] S. D. Goitein, *A Mediterranean Society*, I, p. 133.

[56] Paul G. Forand, "The Relation of the Slave and Client to the Master or Patron in Medieval Islam," *International Journal of Middle East Studies*, 2 (1971), pp. 61-62.

[57] *Ibid.*, pp. 63-65.

[58] S. D. Goitein, "The Mentality of the Middle Class in Medieval Islam," in his *Studies in Islamic History and Institutions* (Leiden: E. J. Brill, 1966), p. 253.

[59] Nine tenths of the material in the Geniza records concerns international trade. From these documents we realize the extent of mobility in some cases:

> "A journey from Spain to Egypt or from Egypt to the Levant was a humdrum experience, about which a seasoned traveler would not waste a word. Commuting regularly between Tunisia or Sicily or even Spain and the eastern shores of the Mediterranean was nothing exceptional: 'I am astonished that he has not come around Passover (Easter), as he is accustomed to do,' says a letter from Alexandria with regard to a merchant from Tunisia, and there are numerous cases of persons from Qayrawān or Palermo or Seville of whom we read that they made similar journeys repeatedly" (S. D. Goitein, *A Mediterranean Society*, I, p. 42).

of scholars and intellectuals as well as of merchants. In fact, judges, teachers, and preachers were more often than not of foreign origin, [60] a condition as common among Muslims as among Jews. Many traveled to increase their erudition.

Nor should we forget the positive attraction of pilgrimage. To Muslims, pilgrimage was a duty and one who had completed the journey attained the respect and admiration of his associates as well as the honorific title of *Ḥājj* (Pilgrim). To Christians and Jews, making a trip to the Holy Land conveyed considerable social distinction. Pilgrimage was responsible for the regular movement of thousands of people from all parts of the known world.

Refugees from historic holocausts such as famines, plagues, fires, and invasions were many, while others fled from political or family pressures. Persons of the lower orders often traveled to avoid paying taxes which could become oppressive, even as they were known to travel to escape family duties or to get away from unpleasant spouses. [61] The invasions of Hilāl and Sulaym in the West and of the Crusaders in Palestine brought about mass movements into Egypt, while political upheavals were accompanied by upheavals in the social and economic spheres.

Casual contacts could turn into the most intimate bonds. International ties of friendship would be strengthened through marriage, although the families concerned were distant from each other in space. Goitein states that "the surest way for a young man to build himself a strong position in a foreign country was to marry a girl from an influential family." [62] Not only wealthy and influential persons would contract such unions but their agents as well. Such liaisons could be found which stretched from Spain to Egypt and Iraq and Arabia and were several generations deep. True, most if not all, marriages of this type took place between coreligionists or persons of common ethnic ancestry. However it was just such extended bonds that ultimately fed the community at home with new people as well as resources.

At least as important as economic and political power in establishing social position was ideological power. This had two aspects: first, there were the special institutions of different varieties of accepted religion that defined particular communities, and then there was religion and piety generally.

[60] S. D. Goitein, *A Mediterranean Society*, I, p. 53.
[61] *Ibid.*, pp. 58, 59.
[62] *Ibid.*, p. 48 .

In the formally institutionalized sphere boundaries were strict. One was a Muslim, or a *dhimmī* of Christian or Jewish persuasion, and within Islam he was Sunnī or Shīʿī. Yet there was considerable latitude. Despite the intense attempts of the Shīʿīs to gain followers, and the fact that the government gave all the best religious appointments to Shīʿīs, Mālikīs and Shāfiʿīs were numerous and still had their own *qāḍīs*. Celebration of anti-Shīʿī festivals was allowed to go on. [63] Nor was latitude absent at the popular level. For centuries holidays had been marked by common participation. Under the Fāṭimids a Christian festival celebrating the delivery of Joseph from prison in Giza was celebrated by Muslims, and in A.D. 1024 the government financed the festivities. During the same year the caliph patronized the Feast of the Epiphany. [64]

Knowledge of the art of writing, which in itself can be considered diagnostic of middle class membership, [65] was symbolic of religion and of its power. In medieval Islam, Judaism, and Christianity, scholarly proficiency gave access to the highest positions in religious and administrative officialdom. Instruction was open to everyone regardless of the rank of his family although family connections and economic resources helped in pursuing a scholarly career and in securing high positions. The art of writing, of course, was essential to a career as a merchant.

We only realize the full significance of spiritual power, however, through the appeals to it expressed in the correspondence of the period. Hardly an undertaking was initiated without invoking the Deity. [66] Moreover in personal and business dealings to invoke a person's religion (*dīn*) was to invoke his conscience and morality. We might say, in fact, that religion was considered an essential part of an individual's personality whatever persuasion he adhered to. As a rule one did not refer to a person by name without including a complimentary phrase referring to the Deity. As Professor Goitein has written:

---

63 Adam Mez, *Renaissance*, p. 62.

64 *Ibid.*, p. 54.

65 S. D. Goitein, "The Mentality of the Middle Class in Medieval Islam," p. 243.

66 One did not say "I bought this," but rather, "I let God choose for me the best and then bought." When partners entered into contract they said, "We let our Creator choose for us and concluded the partnership" (S. D. Goitein, "The Mentality of the Middle Class in Medieval Islam," p. 248). One of the things friends were supposed to do was pray for each other. Prayers were essential to success and safety. No journey was undertaken without them. No arrival was achieved without giving thanks to God.

> God was the most powerful reality in every man's life; therefore, even people of strong practical bent took him constantly into account and continuously attempted to be on good terms with him ... God was really in their hearts. [67]

Thus people established positions in the social network by making personal ties in the political and economic spheres and by appealing to conscience and honor in religious terms.

Unfortunately the efflorescence of ideas which took place in commerce and industry did not occur in the field of formal ideological culture. The mosque created by Jawhar, al-Azhar, became a center for the teaching of the Fāṭimid system of jurisprudence to replace the Sunnī codes. As one of its main functions was the training of agents to win proselytes to the Fāṭimid cause, it was the seat of heresy in the eyes of many Muslims. Most of the men of learning there were theologians, interested in refinements of the law rather than in history, literature, or poetry. Cairo, cut off from the intellectual currents of Baghdad and Damascus, attracted few of the literati who contributed so much to Islamic culture in the eleventh and twelfth centuries. [68]

Nevertheless, al-Azhar flourished as a center of Shīᶜī sectarianism. Under the expert direction of Yaᶜqūb ibn Killis, [69] a converted Jew

---

[67] "The Mentality of the Middle Class in Medieval Islam," pp. 247-248.

[68] In many respects, however, the influence of Shiᶜī free thinking contributed to progress in science and medicine. The caliph al-Ḥākim, in A.D. 1005, opened a "House of Learning" at which books from the palace libraries were made available to anyone to read or copy anything he desired. This collection, which grew to 200,000 volumes by the time of al-Mustanṣir, was said to have been the greatest that any prince had ever assembled. The books, stored in locked presses, with labels to indicate the contents of each press, included 2,400 illuminated Qurʾāns, thirty copies of a basic grammar book, twenty copies of aṭ-Ṭabarī's history with the author's autograph copy, and numerous rare manuscripts. It appears that the staff of the library consisted of one librarian, two copyists, and two servants (al-Maqrīzī, *Khiṭaṭ*, I, pp. 407-409). Paper, ink, and pens were provided to all on request. Curators, lecturers, grammarians, astronomers, and physicians were given yearly salaries by the caliph.

The development of science in the Fāṭimid period was graced by the names of such men as Ibn Yūnus the astronomer who was the first to discover a formula of spherical trigonometry, Ibn al-Haytham, a scientist responsible for works on many subjects including a notable treatise on optics which was of great use later to European physicists, ᶜAmmār ibn ᶜAlī, the author of a remarkable work on diseases of the eye, and Ibn Riḍwān, al-Ḥākim's own physician, who debated with the Christian doctor Ibn Buṭlān on the efficacy of written materials versus personal instruction in the training of physicians.

[69] Ibn Killis had become a convert to Islam in Baghdad and traveled to Egypt during the reign of Kāfūr. Obtaining considerable influence with the latter, he attained appointment to high office. When, after Kāfūr's death, a jealous superior forced him to leave the country, he fled to the court of al-Muᶜizz in Qayrawān where

who was advisor to al-Muᶜizz, regular classes were held and stipends given to scholars. [70] Living quarters were furnished for them beside the mosque. Thus was founded higher learning at al-Azhar and two years later Ibn Killis persuaded his master to make the classes "universal" which may have meant either the admission of students other than the original body, or the institution of a more complete program of studies to supplement the law course. [71]

The isolation from the mainstream of Muslim thought was somewhat compensated by the interaction with people of other faiths to whom the dynasty had to turn for support. Although experienced *dhimmīs* had made major contributions under the ᶜAbbāsids, under the Fāṭimids the Christians and Jews of North Africa and Spain played particularly prominent roles in fields of science and learning in which religious differences did not impose barriers to communication.

The *dhimmīs* as a class gained most from the change of regime. While their employment in the government had long been an established policy, under the Fāṭimids there was more than the usual degree of favor. Jews especially occupied important posts in the beginning of the period. In Fusṭāṭ the community was large and prosperous. Al-Muᶜizz and Jawhar probably regarded non-Muslims as less of a threat to their schizmatic religion than the orthodox of their own faith with whom they had to deal and *dhimmīs* were evidently regarded as being in league with the Shīᶜīs by most of the populace. It is no wonder, for the caliph al-Muᶜizz had a Christian wife and two of his brothers-in-law were the Malkite (Greek Catholic) patriarchs of Alexandria and Jerusalem. It was said that at his court nothing could be done without the help of some Jew or other. [72] Under al-ᶜAzīz, the vizierate was held by a Christian for a time, and the caliph himself provided troops to protect the restorers of a church from the wrath of Muslims who

---

he lost no time in becoming a great favorite of the caliph. Having notified the Fāṭimid that Egypt was ready for the taking and advising him as to conditions there, he was amply rewarded following the victory with control of the land administration. Under al-ᶜAzīz he became vizier (A.D. 978-979). It is said that he was always friendly and generous toward his former coreligionists, despite his conversion to Islam, even to the extent that some authorities maintain that he died a Jew and was only outwardly a Muslim. This contention is unjustified, however, if we consider his work in the founding of al-Azhar.

[70] Al-Maqrīzī, *Khiṭaṭ*, II, p. 273.

[71] Bayard Dodge, *Al-Azhar: A Millennium of Muslim Learning* (Washington, D.C.: The Middle East Institute, 1961), p. 13.

[72] Adam Mez, *Renaissance*, p. 52.

resented such concessions to "polytheists." [73] When the Christian vizier was ordered to prosecute dishonest Muslim officials, many influential persons lost their offices. [74]

Such a period of high favor only led to jealousy and hatred on the part of Muslims, many of whom could not bear to see unbelievers in authority over them. Sarcasm is plain in a quotation from a contemporary poet:

> "Become Christian, for Christianity is the true religion! Our time proves it so. Worry not about anything else: Yaᶜqūb, the Vizier, is the Father: al-ᶜAzīz, the Son, and Faḍl, the Holy Ghost." [75]

As the protestations had no force behind them, however, the palace had its way.

For their part, many of the Christians and Jews who had free rein with the collection of taxes took advantage of their unusually good fortune by succumbing to the temptation of filling their own purses in the traditional manner. Some of the resentment toward them was probably justified and confiscation of their property under the later rulers may have arisen from fiscal difficulties rather than resentment on religious grounds. Jewish money changers were very numerous in Fusṭāṭ in the year A.D. 973. As a consequence of their alleged acts of insubordination the governor ordered that none should appear without a Jewish badge. [76] Status differences that were being eroded by the intercourse of social and political life were periodically reasserted by formal proclamations.

It is probably not unreasonable to consider some of the outbreaks of religious intolerance and fanaticism of the period as attempts to restate group boundaries that were being eroded in the process of social life. People had a need to differentiate themselves as well as to relate themselves to others. Christian and Jewish communities flourished

---

[73] S. Lane-Poole, *Story of Cairo*, p. 112.

[74] Appendix to *Kitāb al-Quḍāh* by al-Kindī, derived mostly from Rafᶜ al-ᶜUṣr by Ibn Ḥajar, edited by Rhuvon Guest (Leiden: E. J. Brill, 1912), pp. 595-597.

[75] Ibn al-Athīr, *al-Kāmil fī at-Tārīkh*, edited by C. J. Tornberg, 12 vols. (Leiden: E. J. Brill, 1851-1876), IX, p. 117. As-Suyūṭī quotes a similar lampoon:

> " 'The Jews of our times have reached the goal of their desire and come to rule. Theirs is the dignity, theirs the money! Councillors of the state and princes are made from them. O people of Egypt! I give you advice: Become Jews, for Heaven has become Jewish!' " (*Ḥusn al-Muḥāḍara fī Tārīkh Miṣr wa al-Qāhira*, II (Cairo, 1968), p. 201).

[76] Al-Maqrīzī, *Ittiᶜāẓ al-Hunafāᵓ*, p. 87.

under their own leaders and there were strong personal ties between groups that extended all the way to the caliph's palace. [77]

The persecution of Jews and Christians under the later rule of al-Ḥākim can be regarded partly as the eccentric behavior of a fanatic who made life miserable not only for non-Muslims but for Muslims as well. It was probably also an attempt to restore the balance which had been upset by the previous periods of favoritism. According to al-Maqrīzī, restoration of the strict observance of old penal laws against religious minorities was due to the "arrogance and wealth of those Christians and Jews who had been unduly favored by the Fāṭimids." [78] Public opinion had managed to make itself heard and the caliph now

---

[77] It is important that by no means all, or even most, of the problems of *dhimmīs* originated in conflict with Muslims, and that the Muslim ruler indeed could ease tension between groups as the political keystone and ultimate mediator. Some of the letters among the Cairo Geniza documents are quite revealing as to the relationships within communities and the actual relation of the ruler to his subjects.

Intra-community rivalries and alliances even crossed the sea. In the Geniza material there is a letter of the eleventh century written by a Jewish weaver in Damascus to a friend in Cairo, requesting him to enlist the help of Abū Naṣr Faḍl ibn Sahl (Abū Naṣr at-Tustarī) one of two very powerful merchant-bankers and advisors to the caliph (S. D. Goitein, "Petitions to Fatimid Caliphs from the Cairo Geniza," *Jewish Quarterly Review*, N.S. 45 (1954-1955), pp. 30-38). These brothers, whose father came from Tustar in Persia, were of the Karaite sect of Judaism, the same sect to which the writer of the letter belonged. The unfortunate man had been denounced by the local Jews, Talmudists, to the supervisor of the imperial workshop so that he was forced to work there.

> " 'I had to suffer from them more than by gentiles, and was separated from our coreligionists, from participation in their joys and griefs, from the management of their affairs, and from leading their meetings ... our community met ... and wrote letters to his excellency my lord, the Sheikh Abū Naṣr at-Tustarī ... informing him to obtain an order from his Pure Majesty (The Fāṭimid caliph) to the effect that I should be exempted from all forced work' " (S. D. Goitein, "Petitions to the Fāṭimid Caliphs," p. 33).

Besides the addressee of the letter, the writer mentions two other Egyptian merchants who had witnessed his plight in Damascus. Thus from this document, we realize that the Jewish community of Cairo and Fusṭāṭ indeed had far-flung connections with sister communities all over the empire, and that difficulties arose between segments of this community itself, the repercussions of which were felt abroad. To add strength to his appeal, the writer asks that Abū Naṣr be reminded that his release from work would enable him to strengthen the local Karaite community.

Despite their ritual aloofness, the caliphs often took personal interest in their subjects and a master artisan in a distant city was not too insignificant a person to attract attention. It is true that the "People of the Book" were in theory special wards of the Prophet, and hence his successors, the caliphs, were supposed personally to look after the welfare of the "protected people" but we have here proof that the theoretical principle that any subject could apply to the Muslim ruler in person for aid, was not completely removed from the actual state of affairs, especially when the caliph was interested in winning the support of a local group.

[78] Quoted in DeLacy O'Leary, *History of the Fatimid Caliphate*, p. 143.

felt secure enough to reject the support which al-Muᶜizz and Jawhar had needed. On the one hand, the foolish and humiliating dress regulations and the monstrous persecutions were the work of a madman obsessed with his own power; on the other, they reflected a social tendency and a long period of popular resentment. Al-Ḥākim may have been asserting his own authority against that of the Christian *ḥarīm* which had produced him; but his reaction was a magnification of the reaction which was taking place throughout all levels of the social structure.

It was not long, however, before churches were restored under aẓ-Ẓāhir and in the twelfth century, we find not only a series of Armenian viziers, but the caliph al-Ḥāfiẓ receiving lectures in history twice a week from the Armenian patriarch. [79] Later caliphs are known to have made substantial contributions to the support of convents and churches and to have frequented monastery gardens to enjoy the hospitality and company of Coptic monks. [80]

The reorganization of the bureaucracy under the Fāṭimids was largely a "housecleaning" and expansion of the bureaucratic structure of the previous period. Administration of the state was patterned after the Persian-ᶜAbbāsid prototype and the same ethnic and religious groups in many cases continued to retain power. The restoration of security contributed in no small part to the general economic prosperity of which both the government and favored factions took their share.

The principal advance in the bureaucracy over the previous periods was that the structure was considerably more elaborate. There were viziers who supervised the army, and "men of the pen." Thousands of clerks were in the lower levels of administration. But despite the expansion of the administrative structure, there was no change in the basic pattern of obtaining and holding office. Positions were filled by bold and clever individuals who knew how to work their way into places of trust or who belonged to a segment of society which was riding the crest of caliphal favor. The success or failure of the whole system was determined by the ability of the ruler to keep factional jealousies from getting out of hand.

3. *Factionalism and Its Effects*

Many of the problems which beset the capital throughout the Fāṭimid period were the result of rapid growth in conjunction with sporadic

---

79 S. Lane-Poole, *Story of Cairo*, p. 122.

80 *Ibid.*, p. 123.

and uneven governmental control. At all times the population was fragmented not only physically but socially. Demographically and with respect to power the balance continually shifted. While Cairo depended upon Fusṭāṭ to a considerable extent for the necessities of existence, the two cities remained to a large degree independent, separated by a space of ground much of which was flooded at the time of inundation. Quarters and even houses had a fortified appearance proclaiming the uneasy security which was in constant danger of sudden interruption.

The residents of the commercial city at the time of the Fāṭimid conquest had numbered less than 100,000 [81] but before long the town regained the population it had lost through plague and economic decline. Several waves of immigrants from the West added another 100,000. By the eleventh century which marks the apogee of commercial and industrial prosperity, the total number of residents in the capital was at least 300,000. [82]

Factionalism within the official compound had the most immediate effect. According to Nāṣir-i Khusraw, the palace in the reign of al-Mustanṣir was the residence of 30,000 people including 12,000 servants, 1,000 horse and foot guards, and individuals belonging to the *ḥarīm.* [83] The residents of the official enclosure, the army of 235,000 men which marched in an official ceremony, consisted of 10,000 horsemen riding with the caliph at their head, followed by a cavalry of 15,000 Maghribīs, 50,000 Ḥijāzī bedouins, and an infantry of 20,000 Masmūdī blacks, 10,000 Egyptian-born Turks and Persians, 30,000 Sūdānī blacks, 30,000 slaves of mixed origin, 10,000 palace guards, and 30,000 black sabremen. [84]

Internal administration of the army reflected compartmentalization on the basis of ethnic affiliation. There were three principal ranks: the amīrs who were the highest officers and swordbearers of the caliph, officers of the guard, and separate regiments each of which bore a name that recalled a nationality or a caliph under whose authority the group had been instituted. Thus there were Ḥāfiẓīya, Juyūshīya, Rūmīya (Greeks), Ṣaqāliba (Slavs), and Sūdānīya troops. It was not unusual for disputes to arise between these corps or for the soldiers to make trouble in the town. We have already noted that to avoid unpleasant incidents, al-Muᶜizz settled his Sūdānī forces at Heliopolis.

---

81 M. Clerget, *Le Caire,* I, p. 239.
82 *Ibid.*, p. 239.
83 *Sefer Nāmeh*, p. 128.
84 *Ibid.*, p. 138.

A Man Holding a Drink.

Two Soldiers.

3. Some Fāṭimid Representations of People.

The effect of ethnic divisions within the army was soon felt. The power of the caliph, which had depended to a great extent upon the respect of his subjects for a holy *imām*, rapidly waned as it became apparent that the Fāṭimids could not even control their own court. The importation of Turkish and Negro mercenaries under al-ᶜAzīz only increased the resentment among the Berbers, especially the Kitāma, who felt that the fruits of conquest belonged to them as the conquerors of North Africa. Many of them who did not believe in the supernatural status of the *mahdī* formed a secular party. One Ibn ᶜAmmār, in A.D. 999, seized the office of chief minister. At this, the Turks threw their support to the caliph and street riots were the order of the day in Cairo.

By his fantastic acts of cruel and savage behavior, the mad caliph al-Ḥākim (A.D. 996-1021) soon lost all the regard and respect of the people. Under his rule, the city became like a place besieged or struck by a natural catastrophe. The lands of his unfortunate victims were bestowed at random to anyone, people began to leave the country, and the bazaars were closed. When the caliph was lampooned in the streets of the city, he sent his black troops to burn Fusṭāṭ. For three days the fighting went on and half the town was sacked or burnt. [85] By the time he announced his divinity, the people had had enough. When a preacher addressed the *qāḍī* "In the name of al-Ḥākim, the Compassionate, the Merciful," a near revolution occurred and black troops again looted and pillaged the old capital. Both Berbers and Turks then grasped the opportunity to suppress their common rivals. The mad caliph had lost complete control and a successful conspiracy resulted in his assassination in A.D. 1021.

With the crumbling of internal security, revolts and famines took their toll. By A.D. 1046 the Fāṭimid empire had shrunk to only the Nile valley in North Africa. The Berbers in the West had renounced the family they once so avidly supported and their governor accepted a fresh investiture from the ᶜAbbāsid caliph. Syria was held only uncertainly through force and the allegiance of the Arabian peninsula was nominal. Yet for a while capable viziers staved off collapse. Nāṣir-i Khusraw testifies to the popularity of the caliph al-Mustanṣir, remarking upon the security and calmness which prevailed under his rule [86] but since the terrible reign of al-Ḥākim, much of the real power lay with the viziers who all too often were but tools of various segments of the army. The ritualized status of the caliph was observed to the

---

[85] S. Lane-Poole, *History of Egypt*, p. 132.
[86] *Sefer Nāmeh*, p. 159.

end, but even in the guarded city, there were many to whom his sanctity was a myth. Mutinies occurred within the palace itself.

In Fusṭāṭ, where internal security was vital to urban life, everything depended upon governmental control of the military and upon foresight in economic matters involving basic subsistence. The old town was always the area most susceptible to epidemics and famine. The physician Ibn Riḍwān, writing in time of prosperity, drew attention to the utter lack of sanitation:

> "One of the practices of the people of Fusṭāṭ is to throw into the streets and alleys everything that dies in their house: cats, dogs, and other domestic animals of that kind. They rot there, and this putrescence spreads through the air. Another one of their habits is to throw into the Nile, whose water they drink, the remains and corpses of their animals. Their latrines empty into the Nile and sometimes obstruct the flow of water. They, thus, drink this putrid matter mixed with their water." [87]

Smoke from the bathhouses filled the air, making the dust so thick that "a troubled blackish vapor hung over the city" irritating the throats and soiling the faces of the inhabitants.

With governmental disintegration in the last half of the reign of al-Mustanṣir, Fusṭāṭ suffered a sharp decline. The vizier al-Yāzūrī, paralleling the Old Testament Joseph, had prepared for lean years by storing up the corn surplus of good harvests, but after he was poisoned in A.D. 1058, no one had the foresight or the power to follow his example. There were forty changes of viziers in nine months. The crux of the problem lay again in the army. When Turks and Berbers united to drive the Sūdānīs out of Cairo, the latter fled to Upper Egypt where they terrified the cultivators. Berbers overran the Delta, destroying irrigation systems, while the Turks went to work looting the capital and palace, dispersing its treasures, among them the priceless library. Everyone in Egypt paid dearly for the breakdown of authority.

For seven years a famine with no parallel in history ravaged the Nile valley. The *fallāḥīn*, so terrified and frustrated by the predations of the Sūdānīs and Berbers, had been unable to raise a crop or harvest it. A series of low Niles added to the difficulty. In the urban center a loaf of bread cost fifteen dinars. The situation became so bad that butchers sold not only the flesh of dogs and cats but that of human beings. The passerby on a narrow street was in danger of being captured

---

[87] Ibn Riḍwān quoted by al-Maqrīzī, *Khiṭaṭ*, I, pp. 339-340.

and eaten by his neighbors. While conditions were worse in Fusṭāṭ than in Cairo, the wife and daughters of the caliph fled to Baghdad and he himself was reduced to a ration of two loaves of bread a day. [88]

At last, in A.D. 1073, the suffering was alleviated by a good harvest. Al-Mustanṣir had had enough of Turkish despotism and sent an appeal for help to Badr al-Jamālī, who had become the most powerful general in Syria. Now the Armenians had their turn. Bringing with him his Syrian forces, he soon put an end to the Turkish oligarchy and became the first of a line of Armenian viziers who ruled with wisdom and liberality. He was given the title, *Amīr al-Juyūsh*, "Commander in Chief," and it is very probable that the Juyūshīya troops came then to be composed of Badr's Syrian Armenians. [89]

The subsequent revival of urban prosperity was largely the result of this man's hard work and intelligence. Badr, who had begun his political career as a slave, soon brought order to Egypt by thoroughly subduing the rampant military factions. As soon as the *fallāḥīn* could toil in peace, produce again began flowing to the capital.

The next thing the Armenian set about was restoring the fortifications of the town. The original brick wall had crumbled and disappeared through the long period of spoilation, while the town had gradually spread outside the original gates. In A.D. 1087 Badr rebuilt the wall and constructed the three gates which can still be seen in Cairo: the Bāb an-Naṣr, the Bāb al-Futūḥ, and the Bāb Zuwayla. [90] The northern and southern walls, from eleven to thirteen feet thick, were extended to enclose the Mosque of al-Ḥākim and the Quarter of the Greeks. Badr's own troops were quartered outside the ramparts.

Despite the valiant attempt of the Armenians to repair the damage, the Fāṭimid city had experienced too long a period of horror and

[88] Al-Maqrīzī, *Ighāthat al-Umma bi-Kashf al-Ghumma*, translated by Gaston Wiet, "Le traité des famines de Maqrīzī," *Journal of the Economic and Social History of the Orient*, V (1962), p. 25.

[89] Marius Canard, "Un vizir chretien à l'époque fâṭimite: L'Arménien Bahrâm," *Annales de l'Institut d'Études Orientales*, 12 (1954), p. 93.

[90] The architecture of these fortifications clearly reveals the influence of the Syrio-Byzantine school, the leading features of which are the square or oblong bastions with squared or rounded openings, in contrast to the round bastions and bent entrances of the later period of Ṣalāḥ ad-Dīn. The gates have vaulted passages between towers containing shooting floors and a cross passage above the arch with places for hurling stones and grenades upon the enemy. Al-Maqrīzī states that the architects were three brothers from Edessa. Since, according to Ibn al-Athīr, that city at the time was full of Armenians, it is not surprising that Badr imported his architects from there. See K. A. C. Creswell, "Fortification in Islam before A.D. 1250," *Proceedings of the British Academy*, 38 (1952), pp. 112-119.

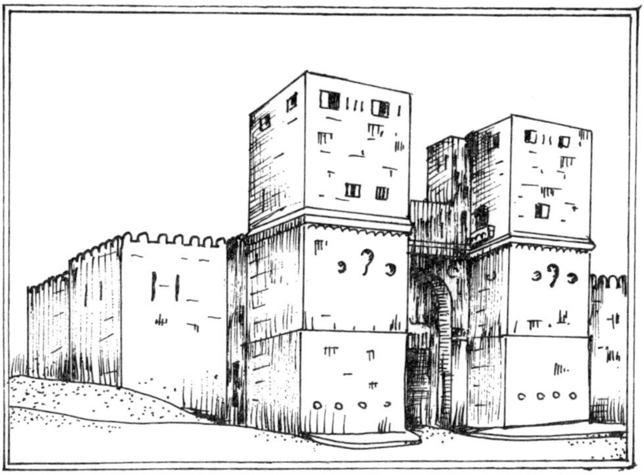

The Bāb an-Nāṣr.

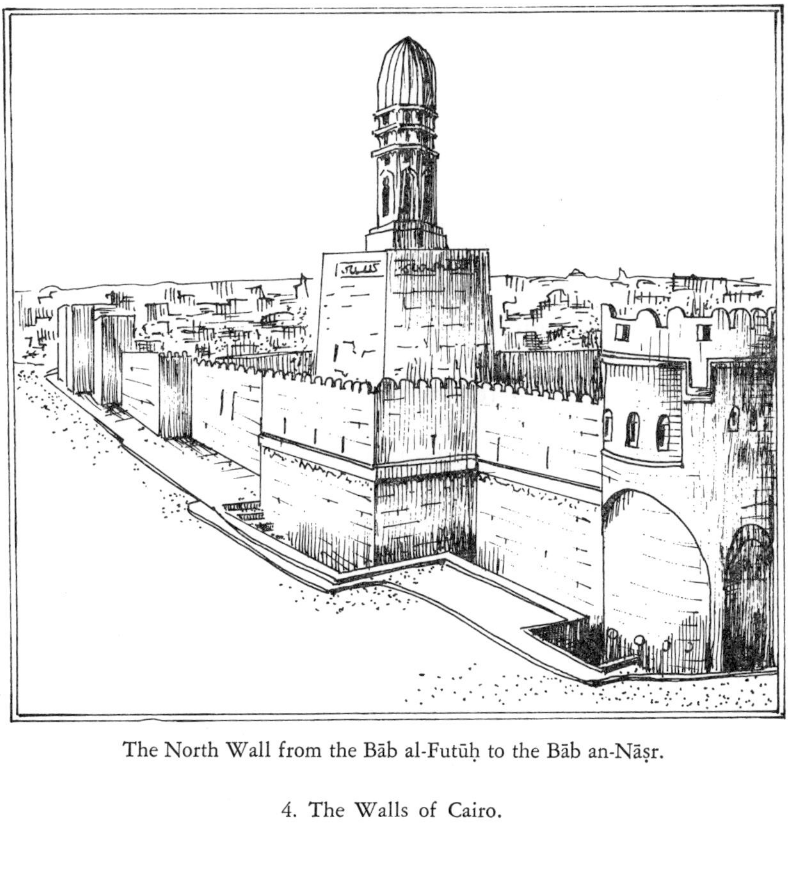

The North Wall from the Bāb al-Futūḥ to the Bāb an-Nāṣr.

4. The Walls of Cairo.

catastrophe. It never regained its former magnificence. Depopulation gave many parts of the town a deserted appearance. Often there were no heirs to the abandoned property. In the caliphate of al-Āmir (A.D. 1101-1131) the government attempted to encourage building by proclaiming that owners of structures in Cairo and Fusṭāṭ had to repair their ruined houses or sell them to someone who would do so, on pain of losing the property to the government. By this time, however, the political and commercial capitals were growing closer together. [91] The water that flooded the region of the Birkat al-Fīl south of Cairo had retreated enough for the establishment of markets nearby.

The revival was no solution to the problem of factional strife. By the fourth decade of the twelfth century the Armenians held all the important posts in every government department. [92] Despite their capability, it would have been surprising if a reaction had not taken place. When the vizier Bahrām and two thousand Armenians were expelled from Cairo in A.D. 1135, political chaos reigned again. At the death of al-Ḥāfiẓ in 1149, the power of the caliph barely extended beyond the palace walls. The memoirs of Usāma ibn Munqidh written between 1144 and 1154 record the intrigues and jealousies of the court. After the murder of the caliph aẓ-Ẓāfir in 1154 and a brutal palace massacre, the women of the court sent locks of their hair to the governor of Ushmunayn in Upper Egypt as an appeal. This gallant man restored order temporarily but was eventually murdered by the palace women who resented his austere morality. Power then fell into the hands of Shāwar, the Arab governor of Upper Egypt.

The situation of Cairo at the beginning of the Fāṭimid period was now reversed. The city which had once been a focal point of world power had become a prize for which its enemies, Christian and Muslim, contended. The next year, 1167, saw the involvement of the country in the wars of the Crusades. Both the Latin Kingdom of Jerusalem and the Turkish Sultanate of Damascus needed Egypt to win the fight. In the capital Shāwar struggled with another vizier for control. He sought an alliance with Nūr ad-Dīn the Turk who sent his lieutenant Shīrkūh, uncle of Ṣalāḥ ad-Dīn, with a Syrian army into Egypt. No sooner had the rival vizier been defeated when Shāwar, fearing to

---

[91] Goitein tells us that in the early part of the twelfth century rich merchants had two homes, one in Cairo and one in Fusṭāṭ. By the time the dynasty fell, most of them seemed to have moved into Cairo and to have abandoned their Fusṭāṭ residences (*A Mediterranean Society*, I, p. 148).

[92] S. Lane-Poole, *Story of Cairo*, p. 157.

be protected out of his command, called upon Amalric, leader of the Christian troops, to repel the Syrians. The conflict was settled by an uneasy armistice but conspiracy continued.

Now came the greatest blow that the old city had ever suffered. Shāwar felt as uncomfortable under the alliance with Amalric as he had in his dependence upon the Turks. The Franks had quartered a garrison in the Mosque of al-Ḥākim and were well aware of the weakness of the government. After a massacre of the civilian population at Bilbeys by the Crusaders in 1168, the vizier feared that they would succeed in taking Fusṭāṭ and set up a base of operations there. Knowing he could not defend both Cairo and old Miṣr, he ordered the immediate evacuation and burning of Fusṭāṭ. According to a contemporary account:

> The people left in great haste, abandoning their possessions and their goods, in order to save themselves and their children. There was an impetuous flow of human beings; it seemed as though they were leaving their tombs for the Last Judgment. Fathers neglected their children and brothers were not each other's keepers ... They camped in the mosques of Cairo, in the bathhouses, in the streets, and on the roads. There they were, thrown together pell-mell with their wives and children, having lost their possessions and waiting for the enemy to bear down on Cairo. [93]

Twenty thousand pots of naphtha and 10,000 fire-brands set off a conflagration which lasted for fifty-four days. Today we can still see its traces in the vast, uninhabited wilderness of rubble and sand heaps on the south of Cairo, stretching from near the Citadel to almost the Nile bank.

The population of Fusṭāṭ at its greatest prosperity had been approximately 300,000 and that of Cairo 225,000. By the end of the twelfth century, Fusṭāṭ had lost two-thirds of its inhabitants and Cairo about one-third. Clerget estimated that the total population at that time was between 150,000 and 200,000. [94] The center of habitation had shifted to Cairo, and although there was a partial revival of Fusṭāṭ under the Ayyūbids, the old city never regained its former significance. Cairo once meant to be only a royal residence, now became the commercial center. Under the late Fāṭimids, a new quarter of fashionable residence stretched to the south-east from the Bāb Zuwayla to a point

---

93 Quoted in G. Wiet, *Cairo: City of Art and Commerce* (Norman, Oklahoma: University of Oklahoma Press, 1964), pp. 41-42. See Ibn al-Athīr, *Al-Kāmil fī at-Tārīkh*, XI, p. 336 and al-Maqrīzī, *Khiṭaṭ*, I, pp. 285-286.

94 *Le Caire*, I, p. 239.

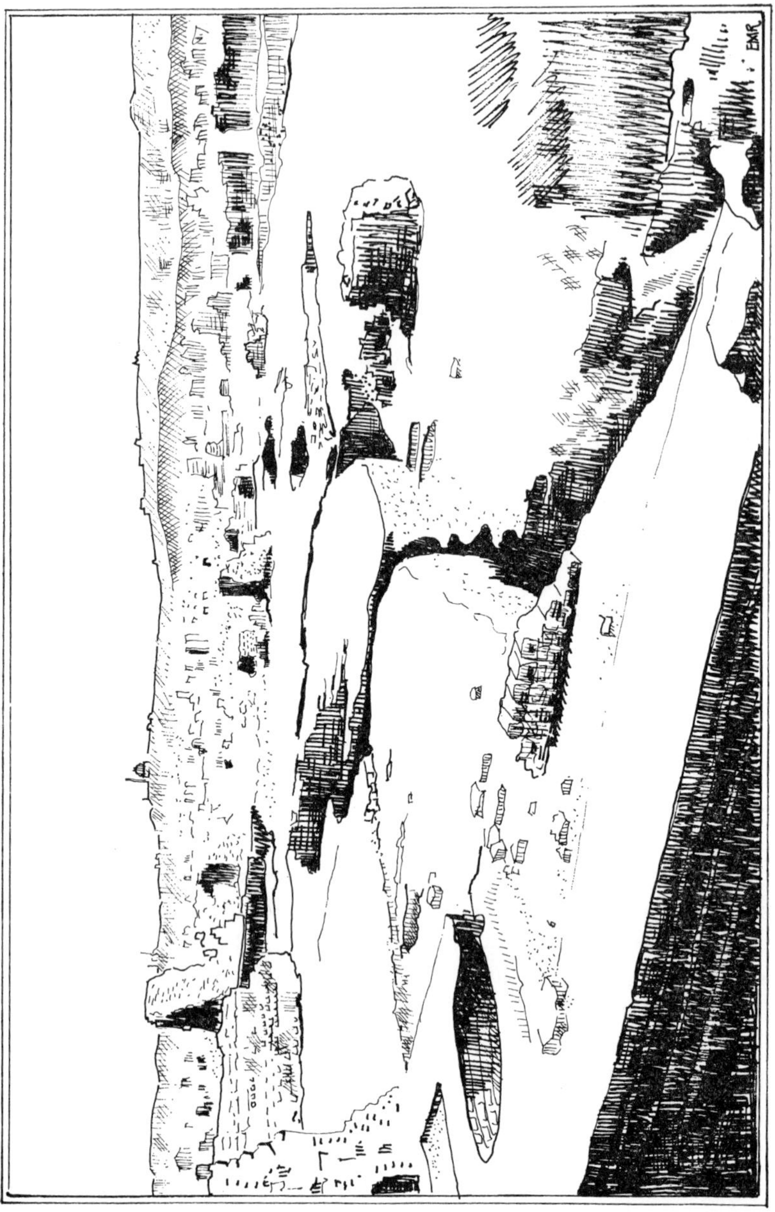

5. View of Fusṭāṭ.

opposite the present Citadel. The destruction of the greater part of the old city brought about the subsequent development of the long-neglected Ṭūlunid quarter. All that survived of Fusṭāṭ lay around the Mosque of ᶜAmr in the south and, as the new Cairene suburb was closer to the remains of al-Qaṭāiᶜ and al-ᶜAskar, these areas were incorporated into the Ayyūbid capital.

Unfortunately many of the artistic embellishments of the Fāṭimid enclosure did not survive the change in regime. Pious Muslims of later days were eager to efface all remnants of the schizmatic caliphs. Even al-Azhar fell out of use for a while, being the seat of heresy. It was as though no one wanted to be reminded of the dynasty that had begun in such splendor and ended so ignominiously.

CHAPTER FOUR

CAIRO IN THE TIME OF ṢALĀḤ AD-DĪN: THE AVOWAL OF UNITY (A.D. 1169-1193)

The city had decayed with the decay of the dynasty which had founded it. The task which faced Ṣalāḥ ad-Dīn was greater than that of any vizier who had preceded him. Whereas others had tried to infuse new life into the capital, he set out to revolutionize many aspects of the urban scene.

The first problem with which Ṣalāḥ ad-Dīn had to deal was a conspiracy in the great palace. The caliph, with his troops and dependents, was openly hostile and a plot was soon formed to destroy the vizier. He discovered it in time, however, and had the organizer, the chief eunuch, beheaded. At this, 50,000 of the caliph's troops, principally Sūdānīs infuriated at the death of their chief, rose in rebellion. There was a bloody struggle in the Bayn al-Qaṣrayn and many houses and streets were set on fire, but finally after two days of fighting, the blacks were overcome and banished. The Manṣūrīya quarter south of the city where their barracks were located was burned and gardens were planted in its place. Thus with the removal of a chronic source of disturbance, the major support of the caliph also disappeared.

Although he was technically the vizier of the Fāṭimid ruler, Ṣalāḥ ad-Dīn owed allegiance to the ᶜAbbāsid caliph as well. He realized too that the success of the Crusaders in Palestine was in large part due to the decline of the Fāṭimid empire and the resulting political weakness of the Muslim world. Hoping to restore the unity of the empire, and having no patience with heresy, he sought to place Egypt again under the direction of the ᶜAbbāsid caliphate. [1]

By A.D. 1171, Ṣalāḥ ad-Dīn's position had become much stronger. Following the removal of the black troops, the Fāṭimid caliph al-ᶜĀḍīd lost all vestige of power and remained confined to his quarters at the point of death. On the tenth of September, 1171, his name was omitted from the *khuṭba* and that of the ᶜAbbāsid substituted. The last Fāṭimid died three days later, unaware of his deposition. There was no reaction among the populace, not even a token of resistance. Evidently the

---

1 See H. A. R. Gibb, "The Achievement of Saladin," *Bulletin of the John Rylands Library*, 35 (Manchester, 1952), pp. 52-58.

people of the capital had remained basically Sunnī through the two centuries of Shīʿī rule. Most of those living in Fusṭāṭ probably never felt that they had much in common with those living in the *mahdī*'s enclosure and there must have been many among them who welcomed the return of official orthodoxy.

Additional measures, however, were needed to remove the ever-present threat from sympathizers with the fallen dynasty. In Cairo, there were still many Muslims who sincerely believed in the Shīʿī doctrine, as well as special groups of individuals who had profited greatly under the old regime.

Zealous Shīʿīs continued to press for the return of the holy dynasty and often the cry, "Long live the family of Alī!" was heard in the streets at night. Ṣalāḥ ad-Dīn met this opposition not with physical force, but with counter-propaganda. In the idea of state supported theological seminaries, he followed the example of Nūr ad-Dīn who had founded similar colleges in Damascus. The Nāṣirīya or Sharīfīya, and Qamḥīya colleges were founded by him near the Mosque of ʿAmr in 1170. In 1176, the first *madrasa* for the teaching of religious orthodoxy in Cairo was placed next to the shrine of Imām ash-Shāfiʿī. It was of enormous size and provision was made in it for teaching that great jurist's doctrine. [2] The second *madrasa* was strategically located next to the shrine of al-Ḥusayn, center of Shīʿī reverence. The palace of al-Maʾmūn became a Ḥanafī college. [3] While al-Azhar was not used for official services and the classes organized by the Fāṭimids were discontinued, some private classes were held there. The piety of Ṣalāḥ ad-Dīn attracted numerous pilgrims, mystics, and ascetics who began to use the mosque as a refuge. [4]

Thus new schools were established and old ones reoriented as the Sunnī creed became established. Before this time not a single orthodox college had existed in the Egyptian capital. Now all the accepted schools of law were represented. Muslims from all parts of the empire came to Cairo, reestablishing the intellectual connection with the outer world which had been broken two centuries before.

While Sunnī propaganda and the exemplary behavior of the ruler was effective upon Muslims, the Christian population was treated with a harder hand. Ṣalāḥ ad-Dīn's confiscation of Coptic property and

---

[2] Al-Maqrīzī, *Histoire d'Égypte* (a partial translation of *Sulūk*), translated by E. Blochet (Paris, 1908), p. 128.

[3] S. Lane-Poole, *Story of Cairo*, p. 185.

[4] Bayard Dodge, *Al-Azhar: A Millennium of Muslim Learning*, p. 36.

destruction of churches was an immediate expression of his rigid orthodoxy but these people had fared extremely well throughout most of the preceding period, through their association with the Fāṭimids. Then too, the Crusades had aroused Muslim ire against Christians in general and although the Copts of Cairo had played no significant part in the conflict, they bore the brunt of feeling which had been roused against the Christian powers.

The physical changes which took place in the town under Ṣalāḥ ad-Dīn were no less sweeping than the ideological revolution. No medieval ruler left a clearer imprint on the capital than he. It is his Citadel on the Muqaṭṭam that dominates the urban metropolis and he was the first to contemplate unification of all the earlier centers of habitation within a single enclosure.

Spurning the magnificance of the Fāṭimid palaces, the modest ruler installed himself temporarily in the house of the viziers and quartered his officers in the residence of the caliph. The palaces fell rapidly into decay. One of the doorkeepers is said to have remarked that "he had seen no wood brought in, and no rubbish thrown out, for a long time." [5] Thus the panelling was used for firewood, and new buildings, at first built against the walls, eventually spread into the palaces themselves as the walls crumbled. Of the Fāṭimid treasures, Ṣalāḥ ad-Dīn kept nothing for himself. Some he gave to Nūr ad-Dīn or to his followers, while the library of 120,000 volumes was presented to the learned chancellor, the *qāḍī* al-Fāḍil. The rest went to the public purse.

Like former governors he was ill at ease in the stronghold of the dynasty he had supplanted, but instead of establishing a new suburb, he built a fortress on a spur of the mountain from which he could command the metropolis below. The idea of the fortress was also Syrian, [6] for in the land of Ṣalāḥ ad-Dīn's origin, every city had its

[5] S. Lane-Poole, *Saladin and the Fall of the Kingdom of Jerusalem* (New York: G. P. Putnam's Sons, 1899), p. 115.

[6] Architecturally, the Citadel's round, truncated, and well-projecting bastions proclaim the influence of the Franco-Syrian School. Its masonry was executed chiefly by European prisoners with materials quarried from the mountain and the smaller pyramids of Giza (Ibn Jubayr, *Riḥlat Ibn Jubayr* (Beirut, 1959), p. 25). Since then the Citadel has been so often remodeled by Mamlūk sultans and by Muḥammad ᶜAlī that it is difficult to identify the original defenses; but about five and a half kilometers of Ṣalāḥ ad-Dīn's wall can still be seen between the southern side of the Citadel (*Bāb al-Qarāfa*) and the Mosque of Sayyida Nafīsa, while another portion of it is at the north-eastern corner of the Fāṭimid city. The work of Ṣalāḥ ad-Dīn is characterized by walls broken at intervals by half-round projecting towers with arrow-slits and bent entrances. For a good description, see Dorothea Russell, *Medieval Cairo*, pp. 195-210.

castle. Many times might a town be taken by besiegers and a citadel still remain impregnable.

The unification of the town as originally planned, meant the westward extension of Badr's fortifications to the Nile to take in the port of Maqs and their southern extension to include all the historic part of Miṣr. The project was never completed either because of the financial strain of the war against the Crusaders or because of the realization that it may not have been necessary to surround completely the dilapidated sections of Fusṭāṭ with two miles of fortifications. Nevertheless, the northern wall was extended to the river and the eastern wall was completed to a point near the Citadel. Thus secured from invasion, the land between the canal and the river could be developed in later years as the waters receded from that area. Whole suburbs between the old city and the southern cemetery, al-Qarāfa, were replaced by pleasure gardens. It is said that the Bāb Zuwayla could be seen from Ibn Ṭūlūn's mosque. [7]

Under the beneficent rule of Ṣalāḥ ad-Dīn, the city experienced not only an economic and cultural renaissance, but a renewal of governmental interest in the public welfare. The ruler established and took great interest in the *māristāns*, the splendid hospitals described in detail by Ibn Jubayr. There were two of these in Cairo and in Miṣr, the former having a separate building for women. Special care was provided for the insane. A dwelling place for pious strangers from the West was set aside in the Mosque of Ibn Ṭūlūn and the sultan provided rations for their livelihood. All religious foundations prospered through grants on the ruler's behalf just as learned and pious individuals found support and encouragement under his wing.

The visitor Ibn Jubayr records the rapid recovery of Cairo and its environs. Writing of his experience in A.D. 1183, he states:

> In Miṣr too are the remains of the destruction caused by the fire that occurred during the revolution at the time of the break-up of the ᶜUbaydīn (Fāṭimid) dynasty in the year 564 (1168). Most of the city has been restored and buildings now adjoin each other without intermission. It is a large city, and the ancient relics to be seen in and about it attest the size of its former boundaries. On the west bank of the Nile ... is a large and important burgh with fine buildings called al-Jīza (Giza). Every Sunday it holds a large market where many congregate. Between it and Miṣr is an island (Roḍa) with fine houses

[7] Al-Maqrīzī, *Khiṭaṭ*, II, p. 110.

> and commanding belvederes, which is a resort for entertainment and diversion. [8]

Thus we realize the extent of the expansion of the capital since the days of Arab rule. Despite fire, flood, and famine, it persistently grew, so that by the time of Ṣalāḥ ad-Dīn, not only Roḍa but Giza had to be considered part of the urban center. With the hazards of life in Cairo proper being what they were under the late Fāṭimids, numerous individuals must have sought residences in suburbs not so close to the scene of violence. The area now covered by the metropolis was extensive and the stage was set for renewed cultural development as well as population growth in a secure environment.

The wall of Ṣalāḥ ad-Dīn represents a conscious recognition that the city was a unified entity, at least in the sense of an area to be defended by a ruler who looked beyond his own immediate adherents for support. By the twelfth century, the city had expanded to a point from which there was no return to the establishment of a commanding barrack-enclave completely separated from the center of population. Unlike the earlier governors, Ṣalāḥ ad-Dīn was not defending himself against the local people, but sought rather to defend the whole urban agglomeration of which the Citadel was a part. In the greatest days of Baghdad, governors of Egypt, though acting in the name of the Sunnī caliph, did not have to think about creating the leading city of an empire; while *de facto* independents like Ibn Ṭūlūn did not have to contend with a counter-ideology or to retrieve the reputation of the Muslim world. The Crusades had focused attention upon the importance of Cairo remaining Muslim; Ṣalāḥ ad-Dīn wanted to make his Citadel impregnable from without, but he also wanted to establish a seat of Muslim power, undivided within.

---

[8] *Riḥla*, pp. 19-30; translation by R. J. C. Broadhurst, *The Travels of Ibn Jubayr*, pp. 46-47.

CHAPTER FIVE

THE CAIRENE PATTERN: SOME PRINCIPLES OF SOCIAL STRUCTURE

It is appropriate at this point to consider in some detail and to try to analyze more directly the social structure at this period. Of central importance was the nature of confrontation, a nature that underwent subtle transformations under the impact of shifts in the distribution of power, national and international.

While social boundaries demarcated by different religious systems remained paramount, ethnicity developed as a primary factor in group differentiation. Social classes with the exception of the elite, did not exist as identifiable communities. Rank, moreover, was attained for the most part within groups of persons who shared common traditions. At the very beginning, it was felt that Muslims should not mix with the settled people and should avoid sedentary pursuits to preserve both military discipline and a style of life suited to religious devotion. Therefore many offices and occupations were left to *dhimmīs*. Later, when the nomads settled down and when converts became numerous, such a division of duties was no longer practicable. New military elites, also Muslim but of varying *ethnic* origin, replaced one another even as civilian converts were of diverse origin. Compartmentalization of functions with reference to ethnicity was explicitly, if not always legally, recognized and developed as the principal framework of urban life, giving form and incentive to its productions.

But the problem of plurality in unity can only be understood with regard to the natures of the majority and the minorities and of their relationship. The domination of the whole by the majority was not a domination that tended to obliterate other components but rather provided a framework, a matrix, in which the disparate segments could be accommodated. Not only did the majority recognize the inevitability of minorities, but the minorities were enabled to retain a feeling of superiority to the majority. [1] By virtue of inhabiting the same sociocultural space, however, the majority and minorities shared the same underlying conception of a differentiated social reality even as

[1] The successful articulation of components does not presuppose shared perceptions of reality. Successful articulation merely calls for temporary overlooking of factors of potential conflict and recognition of common interest.

they faced common problems in the totality of existence. Thus all groups found themselves in a rather unstable situation created by the interplay of centripetal and centrifugal forces. Muslims as well as Jews and Christians and various ethnic components continually attempted to reassert their identities that were being eroded in the necessary conduct of social life.

Regarding the sway of the majority over the minorities, two cardinal points have relevance. In the first place the dominance of the majority in terms of political, economic, and ideological power, was never a complete dominance. We will deal with this factor a little farther on. In the second place the majority was but poorly institutionalized in the coalition of ruling elite and the notables who supported them. As it emerged in the early formative period, consensus (*ijmāᶜ*) upon which interpretation of the law (*sharīᶜa*) depended was institutionally ill-defined and the seat of authority hung ambivalently between the law and the secular power of the military elite who moved on their own to effectuate social cohesion. Given the fact that *the confrontation of major value systems was never fully resolved beyond immediate needs of accommodation* and the fact that the balance of power continually shifted, it should not be surprising that personalities should overshadow institutions and that accommodations should be preferred to formal resolutions. Institutionalization would have tended to rigidify a composite social structure that needed flexibility to exist. Members of each component needed the assurance of being able to reach out to resources which could sustain them, needed to make liaisons outside of their component as well as within it, for the very sake of the continuity of that component. Therefore inner limits were well-defined, but outer limits were left open-ended. In such a situation, the "core of the majority" emerges as a group of "middlemen *par excellence*." The ruler, as key piece in the social composite, himself is a middleman.

Even more important than the formal framework of administration were the groups of people for whom and through whom that framework existed and the means by which they manipulated the formal system to their advantage. For although society was structured through explicit and implicit rules regarding statuses, the exigencies of history frequently demanded spectacular readjustments which could only be effected through manipulation, reinterpretation, or even neglect of the rules. It seems paradoxical, but is really quite understandable, that people attained rank principally within their own community, but yet obtained the power upon which rank depended by developing connections outside this group. In any case the ideological framework normally permitted a number of alternatives to individuals in their social choices and the implications of personal relationships could purposely be left ambiguous and undefined. Partnerships, friendships, and the "debt structure" of favors necessarily stretched beyond community boundaries. Personal ties were essential for success in any undertaking, for it was through such ties that people gained access to and exchanged resources. Advantageous social position, not just in terms of status and rank, but in terms of *connections* was not only a help but requisite for survival. [2]

Ambiguity facilitated considerable interaction between different status groups. Since the government did not presuppose the allegiance of all groups in its territory and what is more, at times the military elite themselves could properly be considered but one group among many contenders, accommmodation and compliance became acceptable substitutes for allegiance. As Islam prescribed a system of coexistence with the "People of the Book" even Shīᶜī *imāms* felt justified in forming alliances with *dhimmīs*. Christians and Jews did not hesitate to rush to the side of the ruler to become his most trusted advisors, regardless of the formal religious cleavage. The cleavage, in fact, stimulated such behavior. Rulers preferred intimates who could not threaten their position, while minorities jumped at the chance to preserve their separate identities by exerting influence at the central point of coordination.

In terms of individual lives we see considerable mobility. Even the normal exigencies of day to day existence had the effect of altering possibilities. A favor done deserved another, social, economic, or political. The "debt structure" in conjunction with the social network created a vast range of transactional opportunities to be tapped. Capable individuals maneuvered themselves into key positions and often acted as intermediaries. We have seen some examples and we shall see more.

Power and rank then, depended upon the establishment of social bonds and mobility opened up new possibilities and enhanced one's field of action. The contrast of cosmopolitan and parochial attitudes, of restless adventure and of homesickness, reflects a basic truth about

---

[2] Goitein concludes from his vast acquaintance with the Geniza documents that "a man could really subsist only when he occupied a strong position or at least had connections with a person of high rank ... Even if a man had a very good case, his rights could rarely be secured without a letter of recommendation or the personal intervention of an influential dignitary or notable" ("The Mentality of the Middle Class in Medieval Islam," p. 254).

society at large. Special status was supported by sentiment and a framework of legal and ideological norms, but the maintenance of local communities in fact depended upon extensive ties outside the immediate group as well as upon formal recognition of religious and ethnic differences.

There is no doubt that in the political sphere divisiveness rather than unity prevailed. Certainly through key individuals diverse groups came to occupy positions of power, but even the most influential had their ups and downs, governed by public opinion as well as official favor.

It would be a mistake, however, to think of divisiveness and compartmentalization as primarily negative factors. Factionalism from the point of view of the whole is group solidarity from the point of view of the components. Moreover, within a syncretic framework, under conditions of security and optimism, the juxtaposition of cultural differences tends to stimulate sociocultural awareness and creativity. Thus faith in the coming *mahdī* can be viewed as a syncretic phenomenon claiming adherents among Berbers, Persians, Arabs, and Egyptians, and among Jews and Christians of various regions for whom its messianic message meant a return to justice, order, and a more acceptable position in Muslim-dominated society than was possible under the governorates of the decaying ᶜAbbāsid regime. During the Fāṭimid period Egyptian crafts came into their own, and Berbers, Turks, Armenians, and Persians played important roles in the culture of the city.

Especially if wealth flowed into Egypt as the power that emanated from the elite extended outward, resources continued to be accessible to local groups through channels of reciprocity and patronage. *Internationally extended factions could provide great support for the maintenance of the empire.* Let us note that members of effective factions were not necessarily coresident, as the letters of the Geniza show. Jews, Armenians, Persians, Berbers, and Greeks all owed some of their power to the fact that they had ties with sister communities in other parts of the empire, a feature as important for politics as it was for commerce. The contest for the caliphate between al-Amīn and al-Maʾmūn exemplifies the importance of "international" factional support to the ruler. Dynasties were successful only as long as they commanded the support of particular communities and it was the effective structure of the faction, most frequently based upon kinship and reinforced by ethnic ties, that was at the basis of the maintenance of authority in the extended empire. As personal loyalties owed the ruler became tenuous, and he became removed from his subjects, the empire disintegrated. The medieval communication system being what it was, the chain of personal relationships was all important.

Yet the negative side of factionalism always lurked close beneath the surface of the greatest efflorescence. As the independence of ethnic and religious groups was not negated they continued to agitate against imposition of authority; especially, as the fortunes of the whole declined with the power of the elite, the adverse effects of the competition between components were more strongly felt. As one such segment would become effectively extended, it would come into conflict with other segments challenging its control of resources. The ties of friendship, alliance, and patronage through which the elite ruled could easily be broken. Within two generations Muslims reasserted themselves against *dhimmīs* in high places and Berbers fought with Turks and Negroes to gain control of the caliph. Relations between components can best be described as symbiotic rather than integral.

It is of essential importance, however, that while the picture on higher levels was one of extreme fluctuation, there was more continuity in the bureaucratic and commercial spheres. Here broadly based local groups managed to survive political catastrophes and a succession of foreign invasions. Although they might experience considerable difficulty at initial shock, large segments in the population possessing needed skills or connections abroad would rise again to occupy their former positions in a few years. Notwithstanding the periodic depredations of the government, from the first days of Arab rule through the time of the Fāṭimids, the bureaucracy was largely filled with Copts.

Having reached a point in the history of Cairo at which the main lines of development have been drawn, let us now return to our concept of the city as a clustering of interaction systems through which resources are channeled. The basic dimensions of defense, political organization, economic growth, and ideology can all be discussed in terms of the decrease of isolation and the articulation of the interests of urban groups. As a cosmopolitan society emerged, it was the extension and multiplication of networks that gave the city access to vast resources, while the effectiveness of these chains of interaction made the system productive. Although some groups controlled particular resources to a greater extent than others, only the military power was in any sense monopolized; economic wealth and spiritual and ideological power were spread more evenly throughout the population. It was a significant fact that the Muslim "cultural majority" for a long time represented a demographic minority.

The acceptance of responsibility to defend an area and the people within it from external threats is one of the first proofs of a recognized community of interests and efforts. While it is true that individuals within the community may differ widely with respect to basic orientations and issues, if their very existence obviously depends upon security, desire to defend a common area may override these distinctions.

The first and often the only consideration of each new regime was defense, but extension of this responsibility to the entire agglommeration was slow to develop. The city as conceived by each governor until the Ayyūbid period was little more than his own military establishment. If there was already a settlement outside of the official enclosure, its existence was considered to be largely irrelevant to the political center which ruled a much larger territory than its immediate environs. Indeed, the defense of the capital meant defense from the local population as well as from foreign invaders. Especially in the early settlements, there was a deliberate intention of separating the military and civilian centers. It was only in the latest days of the Fāṭimid period and the beginning of Ayyūbid rule that there was any evidence of real intention to defend Fusṭāṭ. In fact, the popular center was burnt when its military significance vis-à-vis Cairo was realized. The primary concern was always for the political capital. For their part the people of Miṣr often had to defend themselves against the predations of uncontrolled military factions, as well as the animosities of their neighbors. Houses and quarters were barricaded as uneasy inhabitants sought security for themselves and their property.

Under the extreme extension of effective government, the existence of an empire, the city could flourish or fail depending upon whether or not it was the control center of the network. That is, if it was merely a provincial capital as in the time of the Umayyad or early ᶜAbbāsid governors, then revenue and even population would be drawn from it; laborers were sent to build the Mosque at Damascus, while "the last drop was extracted from the Egyptian milch cow." Even the people in the highest ranks sought leadership from abroad rather than locally. On the other hand, if, as in the time of the Ṭūlūnids and Fāṭimids, tribute was coming in, and people in factories at Damascus were toiling to produce luxuries for the Egyptian elite, then the city could utilize resources far beyond its immediate environs. In every instance, the major cultural innovations in the fields of art, architecture, literature, and science, took place when the city was the capital of an empire and not just a provincial town.

Taxation is a key to the knit of the complex social fabric. The fortunes of the city were directly related to its position in the fiscal organization of the empire. Taxes are inevitably a major cause of irritation among subject peoples, but the disturbance these impositions caused tended to be greater if, besides being levied on unsympathetic groups, the revenue was flowing to a distant power center. Much of the factional strife disappeared under strong rulers like Ibn Ṭūlūn who were not only able to remove irritating levies, but replace internal sources of revenue with external ones.

With reference to the resources upon which the efflorescence of social and cultural life depended, it is apparent that the security provided by the state and its authority was essential to development in all fields. The relationship between military and economic power is highlighted by the relationship of the political capital and its faubourg. Periods of political disorganization and chaos in Cairo were inevitably followed by severe economic problems in Fusṭāṭ. The prosperity described by Nāṣir-i Khusraw in A.D. 1046 lasted only until increasing factiousness in the court brought about forty changes of vizier in nine months. The famine and pestilence of 1069 was worse than any recorded to that time. Unable to take advantage of the products of the Nile valley, the old city suffered most. Although the development of industry and trade with the diversification of economic roles freed urban dwellers from the tilling of the soil, it made them all the more vulnerable to any break in the ties with the hinterland which was the source of their food supply.

Military power was the prerogative of a special division of the Muslim ruling group and with their overhelming force of arms, the elite could enforce their demands upon the civilian population, but even brute military power could seep away through the interstices that factionalism made in elite ranks. In the shifting balance notables and local leaders filled the gaps to avert chaos and preserve the social order. Confronted with a superior force from abroad, a regime limited to an official enclosure would be wiped out in a period of weeks or months, never to rise again. The vast sustaining economic and ideological networks which constituted the civilian metropolis, on the other hand, were enough to resurrect it even after disastrous conflagrations.

A more subtle situation pertained in the ideological sphere. As we have seen, separate religious communities within Islam and without were, for the most part, left to administer the spiritual needs of their own constituents. Spiritual power was both institutionalized within social groups and existed informally as an attribute of individual character. Yet the propagation of ideology by the state was recognized by many rulers as a primary factor in maintaining security. The first schools and universities were instituted for this reason. Al-Azhar was a Shīᶜī academy, while Ṣalāḥ ad-Dīn's founding of the *madrasa* was an attempt to create a firm support for the orthodox regime through the standardization of religious belief. [3] The Fāṭimid dynasty did not succeed in its attempt to make its Ismāᶜīlī persuasion universal and therein lay a primary cause of its downfall. The achievement of the Ayyūbids and Mamlūks who followed them was the institutional separation of military and ideological power; an arrangement that, together with the fact that spiritual resources were open to all, made possible a firmer and more important basis of urban unity.

The city that endures is the city which is not only a center of control and authority, but is also the focal point of the effective communication systems of the society of the time. The suburb, being the product of international ties as well as of connections with the countryside, was more enduring in nature than the official cantonment which was abandoned with the fall of the political regime. In the long run, it was the political capital which "fed" the popular suburb. In its decline and disappearance, the official compound gave its inhabitants to the cosmopolitan metropolis. Even groups "imported" to strengthen the support of a foreign ruler eventually blended with the local population until the distinction between Egyptian and Arab was obscured. So too, the craftsmen and merchants attached to the political capital were at first a class apart from their counterparts in Fusṭāṭ, for they earned their living through the patronage of the elite. Although these people made Cairo a truly cosmopolitan city and retained some foreign connections, the second and third generations were unfamiliar with the lands of their fathers and tended to be absorbed into the native population.

Thus conquest introduced new elements and initiated expansion, but once it had begun, the process of fusion took over to knit the social

---

[3] Ultimately Fāṭimid sectarianism limited variety and expansion in the intellectual field as the court and its associated intelligentsia remained aloof within its official enclosure. Ironically, the reestablishment of Sunnī orthodoxy had the same result, for in an attempt to standardize dogma, there came an end to the religious disputes so prevalent in the earlier periods. Extension of the ideological network may give rise to internal changes as new ideas are assimilated, but it can also hinder intellectual development if the immediate goal is an eradication of other points of view.

fabric. The fact of sharing a single physical and cultural environment encouraged not only accommodation and cooperation but unity in many aspects of life. But on the national as well as the international level, conquest bred contest. The chronic instability of the political situation, together with the need for securing local interests, necessitated the maintenance of identity of each community. Opportunely, local "corporations" consisting of families and special status groups filled defensive, economic, legal, and ideological functions. Thus a pattern of coexistence developed with a somewhat precarious balance of power, in which the keystone was the ability of the ruling body to control factional dissension. With the removal of this keystone, the stresses and strains which were released resulted in a condition of internal chaos, until a new regime appeared to reestablish order.

PART TWO

AYYŪBID AND MAMLŪK CAIRO AND THE EFFLORESCENCE OF URBAN CULTURE (A.D. 1193-1517)

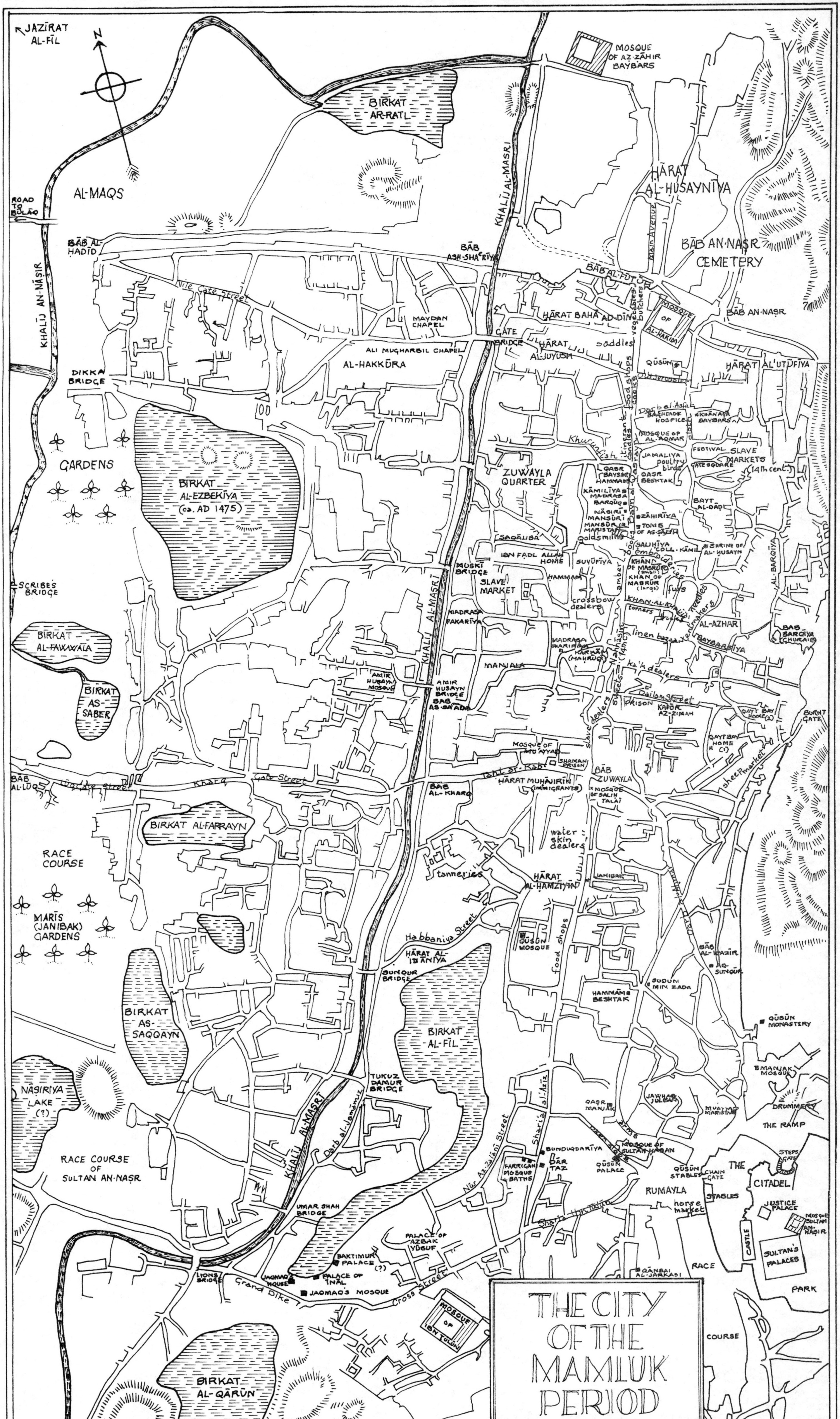

THE CITY OF THE MAMLUK PERIOD
N
JAZĪRAT AL-FĪL
MOSQUE OF AZ-ZĀHIR BAYBARS
BIRKAT AR-RATL
AL-MAQS
ROAD TO BŪLĀQ
KHALĪJ AL-MASRĪ
HĀRAT AL-HUSAYNĪYA
Main Avenue
BĀB AN-NASR CEMETERY
BĀB AL-HADĪD
BĀB ASH-SHAʿRĪYA
BĀB AL-FUTŪH
Nile Gate Street
HĀRAT BAHĀ AD-DĪN
MOSQUE OF AL-HĀKIM
BĀB AN-NASR
MAYDAN CHAPEL
GATE BRIDGE
HĀRAT AL-JUYŪSH
saddles
ALI MUGHARBIL CHAPEL
AL-HAKKŪRA
QŪSŪN
HĀRAT AL-ʿUTŪFĪYA
KHALĪJ AN-NĀSIR
DIKKA BRIDGE
food shops
Darb al-Asfar
BAGHDADI HOSPICE
KHĀNAQA BAYBARS
MOSQUE OF AL-AQMAR
Khurunfish
JAMALĪYA
poultry birds
FESTIVAL GATE SQUARE
SLAVE MARKETS (14th cent.)
GARDENS
BIRKAT AL-EZBEKĪYA (ca. AD 1475)
ZUWAYLA QUARTER
QASR BAYSARĪ
HAMMAM
QASR BESHTAK
KĀMILĪYA MADRASA
BARQŪQ
NĀSIRĪ
MANSŪRĪ
BAYT AL-QĀDĪ
ZĀHIRĪYA
TOMB OF AS-SĀLIH
goldsmiths
SAQĀLIBA
SĀLIHĪYA COLL.
KĀMIL
SHRINE OF AL-HUSAYN
IBN FADL ALLAH HOME
SUYŪFĪYA
KHĀN OF MASRŪR (small)
KHAN OF MASRŪR (large)
embroideries
furs
AL-BARQĪYA
MUSKI BRIDGE
SLAVE MARKET
HAMMAM
amber
crossbow dealers
SCRIBE'S BRIDGE
KHĀN AL-KHALĪLĪ
needles
MADRASA FAKARĪYA
turners
AL-AZHAR
BIRKAT AL-FAWWĀLA
MADRASA SHARIFĪYA
KARKAM (MAHRŪQ)
linen bazaar
BAYBARSĪYA
BĀB BARQĪYA (GHURAIB)
MANJALA
kaʿk dealers
sweets
BIRKAT AS-SABER
AMIR HUSAYN MOSQUE
AMIR HUSAYN BRIDGE
BĀB AS-SAʿĀDA
Dailam Street
PRISON
KAFŪR AZ-ZIMĀM
slave dealers
QAYT BAY HOME (2)
BURNT GATE
QAYT BAY HOME (1)
MOSQUE OF MUʿAYYAD
SHAMĀʾIL PRISON
sheep market
BĀB AL-LŪQ
Lūq Gate Street
Kharq Gate Street
BĀB AL-KHARQ
Taht ar-Rabʿ
HĀRAT MUHĀJIRĪN (IMMIGRANTS)
BĀB ZUWAYLA
MOSQUE OF SALIH TALĀʾI
BIRKAT AL-FARRAYN
RACE COURSE
water skin dealers
tanneries
HĀRAT AL-HAMZIYĪN
JANIBAK
MARĪS (JANIBAK) GARDENS
Habbaniya Street
QŪSŪN MOSQUE
food shops
HĀRAT AL-ʿIDĀNĪYA
SUNQUR BRIDGE
BĀB AL-WAZIR
AQ-SUNQUR
SUDŪN MIN ZADA
HAMMĀM BESHTAK
BIRKAT AS-SAQQAYN
BIRKAT AL-FĪL
QŪSŪN MONASTERY
MANJAK MOSQUE
NĀSIRĪYA LAKE (?)
TUKUZ DAMUR BRIDGE
Darb al-Jamāmīz
JAWHAR JULBAN
QASR MANJAK
MUʿAYYAD MARISTAN
DRUMMERY
THE RAMP
Shariʿ al-ʿAziz
Nūr Az-Zalānī Street
BUNDUQDARĪYA
FARRIGAN MOSQUE & BATHS
DAR TAZ
MOSQUE OF SULTAN HASAN
QŪSŪN PALACE
QŪSŪN STABLES
CHAIN GATE
THE CITADEL
STEPS GATE
RACE COURSE OF SULTAN AN-NASR
RUMAYLA
STABLES
JUSTICE PALACE
MOSQUE SULTAN AN-NĀSIR
horse market
CASTLE
SULTAN'S PALACES
Shariʿ Ibn Tulūn
UMAR SHAH BRIDGE
PALACE OF AZBAK YŪSUF
BAKTIMUR PALACE (?)
PALACE OF ĪNĀL
JAQMAQ'S HOUSE
JAQMAQ'S MOSQUE
LIONS BRIDGE
Grand Dike
Cross Street
QĀNBAI AL-JARKASI
RACE
PARK
MOSQUE OF IBN TULŪN
COURSE
BIRKAT AL-QĀRŪN

INTRODUCTION

A description of Cairene society and culture of the Mamlūk period must be prefaced by a discussion of the achievements of the successors of Ṣalāḥ ad-Dīn. As the elite are largely responsible for the control of the instruments of power and authority, the accomplishments of their organization must be appreciated before beginning a description of the city under their rule. The unification of Cairo in the physical sense was supplemented by reorganization in the upper echelons of society, the institution of a new elite group, and a reorientation of allegiance. Physically, the new elite were represented by the Citadel which symbolized their power and served as their communication center. Subsequent developments in the plan of the town, residences, public buildings, and markets reflected this new locus of authority and the policies of its ruling body, as well as environmental and cultural possibilities exploited by its inhabitants.

The achievements of the Ayyūbids and their immediate successors were threefold. First of all, they reversed the process of political deterioration which had brought about the gradual disintegration of the empire ruled from Cairo and finally made the city itself prey to foreign powers. Second, the Ayyūbids fitted Egypt to serve as the headquarters of Muslim orthodoxy during the centuries between the fall of Baghdad and the establishment of the Ottoman empire; and third, they established an efficient governmental organization of Turks and aliens which, though it continued the centuries-old tradition of foreign rule, was of a unique type not seen before in Egypt. We do not want to describe in detail the events which surround these transformations, but it is necessary to understand generally the status of Egypt in the world at the time.

In the last days of the Fāṭimids, the Franks had been in actual occupation of Cairo. Ṣalāḥ ad-Dīn secured the city, reconquered Jerusalem, and turned the tide against them in the Near East, while his descendants not only bore the brunt of the Crusades, but recovered the cities that the Crusaders had taken. These signal successes were followed by other victories under the late Ayyūbids and early Mamlūks. The defeat and capture of Louis IX at Damietta in A.D. 1250 ended Frankish designs on Egypt, while ten years later, the advance from the East under Hūlāgū was checked at ᶜAyn Jālūt by the efforts of the Mamlūks Quṭuz and Baybars. The victory over the Crusaders at Manṣūra had been accomplished by military forces of freed slaves acting as mercenaries of the Ayyūbid sultan, but Mamlūk victories over the Mongols as independent rulers increased tremendously their prestige at home and abroad. Baybars took many cities from the Franks including Caesarea and Antioch, and at the same time, established friendly relations with some of the Christian European powers, the emperor of Constantinople, and the kings of Naples and Castile. In the south, he made Nubia a tributary of Egypt.

As Ṣalāḥ ad-Dīn and his successors had restored and extended the sphere of Sunnī Islam, so the "second Ṣalāḥ ad-Dīn," Baybars I, made Cairo the new seat of the ᶜAbbāsid caliphate. The Mongol invasions of the thirteenth century which lay waste to the eastern lands of Islam left the rulers of Egypt with the burden of defending Muslim territories from the Mongol yoke. The fall of Baghdad and the murder of the caliph in 1258 was a terrible blow to the Muslim world, for even in the days of its greatest decline, the caliphate was a respected source of authority to the pious. It was only to be expected that the Mamlūk sultans should pay homage to the ᶜAbbāsid caliph. Recognizing as well that the investiture by the Commander of the Faithful would confer legitimacy upon his own position as ruler of Egypt, Baybars in 1260 brought an unassertive member of the ᶜAbbāsid line to Cairo and installed him in the Citadel with the title of al-Mustanṣir. Subsequently the caliph conferred upon him the title of sultan, with control of Islamic lands as well as any lands which might afterwards become Islamic through conquest. Henceforth the puppet caliph at Cairo existed solely to invest the Mamlūk sultans with the purple robe, black turban, and golden chain and spurs symbolic of recognition by the spiritual power.

The third achievement of the Ayyūbids, the institution and development of the Mamlūk organization to form an efficient elite, was not a wholly deliberate intention, but evolved from the time-honored practice of creating a class of emancipated slaves to act as bodyguards. The father of Ibn Ṭūlūn had been a mamlūk of the caliph as had many of the later governors of the early periods, but until the late Ayyūbid period the mamlūks of Egypt were neither independent nor organized. In the second chapter of this part we will deal with Mamlūk social structure in detail, but at this point, we must discuss generally the origin of these people and their subsequent history.

While Ṣalāḥ ad-Dīn had made use of the *ḥalqa*, or bodyguard of freedmen and white slaves, his grandnephew aṣ-Ṣāliḥ (A.D. 1240-1249) purchased slaves of various nationalities in great numbers and housed them in the Citadel. Like earlier rulers who followed a similar practice, he had little faith in local levies and chose to depend upon a perfectly trained army of personal slaves, the majority of whom were Turks. The *corps d'elite* of picked cavalry soon became a source of annoyance to the populace and they were subsequently installed in a fortress on the Island of Roḍa opposite Fusṭāṭ. From the site of these barracks, they were called "Baḥrī Mamlūks" or Mamlūks of the River." The murder of Tūrānshāh, the last Ayyūbid, in A.D. 1250 was largely the work of the Baḥrīs and until 1383, members of this regiment and their descendants were the sultans of Egypt. Baybars, the founder of Mamlūk power, reinforced this feudal system by the continual recruitment of fresh blood from abroad and the liberal distribution of fiefs. Although the principle of hereditary succession was not part of the Mamlūk system, and in fact, was opposed to it, at times a sort of hereditary succession was established. From A.D. 1279 to 1382 the power was in the hands of one family, the house of Qalāūn. One of his sons, an-Nāṣir Muḥammad, was temporarily deposed twice and restored to reign three times between A.D. 1293 and 1341.

Qalāūn, following Baybars, maintained the prestige of the empire abroad. In order to meet the danger of Mongol invasion, he entered into numerous political and commercial alliances and kept the army in a high state of efficiency. Twelve thousand strictly disciplined Mamlūks were quartered on the Island of Roḍa and also in the Citadel. The latter group, mostly Circassians or Mongols, came to be called "Burjīs" or "Men of the Tower," and constituted about a third of the troops. Following the feeble descendants of Mālik an-Nāṣir and the reign of a series of powerful amīrs, one of these, the amīr Barqūq, seized power in A.D. 1382. Although no important changes took place in the government of Egypt, what remained of the hereditary principle disappeared, for all practical purposes, for over three hundred years. We will discuss the principles of Mamlūk succession in the second chapter of this part, but suffice it to say that the Burjī or Circassian sultans were at the mercy of internal military factions far more than any of their predecessors had been.

Regardless of the fact that the Mamlūks were responsible for much disorder, literally fighting their way to the throne over the corpses of their rivals, plundering Cairo, carrying off women and children, and holding pitched battles in the streets, the city that was the capital of their empire owed much to the security that these hardy troops provided. To quote Gaston Wiet:

> The country was the personal property of the sultans; they ran it, with tireless vigor, like a private estate and did not try to tone things down with a hypocritical flow of liberal proclamations. [1]

The estate, protected from external threats and well-managed for the most part, grew considerably and prospered despite the bloody struggles which disrupted domestic politics. Local authorities under Qalāūn kept close watch of all quarters of the city. [2] While the character of many local officials left much to be desired, the sultans were usually supported by a capable bureaucracy and jurists of unusual ability. Ibn Khaldūn, a favorite of Barqūq, made his contribution to public life in the capacity of chief *qāḍī.*

Communication within Egypt and between Egypt and the lands abroad reached a peak scarcely paralleled even in the days of Fāṭimid glory. Baybars so well organized the provinces of his dominion that even the gross incapacity of many of his successors could not destroy it. Bridges were built, canals dug, and under an-Nāṣir, an important canal from the city of Fūwa in the Delta to the port of Alexandria permitted the country to receive maritime traffic direct from the sea. Ibn Baṭṭūṭa in the first half of the fourteenth century saw on the Nile thirty-six thousand ships belonging to the sultan and his subjects. [3] A great causeway along the east bank of the Nile afforded not only communication but also protection from the flood during the inundation. Transportation became so easy that the sultan could play polo in Damascus and Cairo within the same week [4] and more people undertook the pilgrimage than ever before.

Thus communication developed on sea, land, and even by way of

---

[1] *Cairo*: *City of Art and Commerce*, p. 68.

[2] In one set of instructions, they were ordered to
" 'keep special guard on such places of both cities as are likely to be rendezvous to evil-doers: such places are in particular the Nile-bank, the Cemeteries, and the Ponds, i.e. the Elephant's Pool, the Abyssinian's Pool and some others now dried up. At night both cities should be patrolled and the Dispensaries locked up; and especially certain public halls in the Husainiyyah quarter, called Halls of Chivalry (ka'ât al-futuwah) which were frequented by turbulent persons' " (quoted in D. S. Margoliouth, *Cairo, Jerusalem and Damascus* (London: Chatto and Windus, 1907), p. 79).

[3] *The Travels of Ibn Baṭṭūṭa* (A.D. 1325-1354), translated and selected by H. A. R. Gibb (Cambridge: Cambridge University Press, 1958), I, p. 42.

[4] S. Lane-Poole, *History of Egypt*, p. 264.

air. [5] Qalāūn organized the pigeon post to convey to the Citadel the first news of the rise of the Nile, and it was by this means that governors at the Euphrates were warned to bar the fords against the Mongols. When one of the royal pigeons arrived at the Citadel, no one was permitted to detach the message but the sultan himself, who, were he bathing or sleeping, would be informed at once of the event. Efficient communication was not restricted only to the elite, Baybars connected Cairo and Damascus with a postal service of four days, while Qalāūn started a system of passports which assisted foreign merchants in traveling through Muslim domains as far as India and China.

Responding to the favorable circumstances outlined above the population of Cairo regained and surpassed the highest point it had reached under Fāṭimids. It has been estimated that in the first half of the fourteenth century, there were at least 600,000 inhabitants in Mamlūk Cairo. [6] The political and economic decay which began at the end of the century, however, gradually took its toll. By A.D. 1550, following the defeat of the Mamlūks by the Ottoman forces, Cairo still had about 430,000 inhabitants. The subsequent period of economic distintegration brought the figure to 245,000 by the end of the eighteenth century.

The chapters which follow are only superficially chronological in arrangement. Their theses reflect rather a focus upon generalized groups in the population; the elite, middle, and lower classes with respect to their relationships in the power structure and to each other. Respective fields of influence will be outlined. It will be seen that not only the Mamlūk elite, but also merchants, religious officials, and members of the lower orders, played important roles in the peculiar structure of power and authority which maintained the culture and gave continuity to the agglomeration. The efflorescence of urban culture under the Mamlūks, which we see so vividly reflected in all its variety in *The Thousand and One Nights* and in the great architectural monuments of that time, was inseparable from the special constellation of urban networks that made up the society which produced it.

---

[5] The Qarmaṭians seem to have been the first to systematize the pigeon post on a large scale and the carrier pigeon had been used extensively, both officially and unofficially, in the Near East from the ninth century (Adam Mez, *Renaissance*, pp. 470-471). The Fāṭimids undoubtedly maintained contact with their agents in this way.

[6] M. Clerget, *Le Caire*, I, p. 240.

CHAPTER SIX

THE PHYSICAL EXPANSION OF CAIRO UNDER THE AYYŪBIDS AND EARLY MAMLŪKS

> He who has not seen Cairo does not know the grandeur of Islam. It is the metropolis of the universe, the garden of the world, the ant-hill of the human species, the throne of royalty, a city embellished with castles and palaces, its horizon decorated with monasteries and with schools, and lighted by the moons and stars of erudition ...... I went through the streets of this city which were choked with throngs of pedestrians and through its markets, which overflowed with all the delights of this life. One could talk forever of this city and of the extensive dimensions of its civilization. [1]

The foregoing description of Cairo by Ibn Khaldūn undoubtedly reflects an excess of enthusiasm for the capital that had welcomed him and had become a focus for his intensive and diversified social interests, yet there is little doubt that a city in its physical manifestation cannot but reflect the essential concerns and interactions of the society it represents. Cairo is no exception to this rule.

As in the case of the early centers, the locus of the military enclave had a profound effect upon the development of centers of commerce and habitation around it. The Citadel dominated the urban scene and was the focal point of urban authority as well as the chief residence of the elite from the time of Ṣalāḥ ad-Dīn until well into the nineteenth century. Following the death of its founder, work on the fortress was temporarily abandoned until the reign of al-Kāmil in A.D. 1207. At that time the sultan left the old vizier's palace in Cairo for a new palace in the southern enclosure.

The Citadel is our first example of the physical segmentation of the city during this period. Like the military enclosures of the preceding periods, it secured the inhabitants from external threats and kept the elite effectively isolated from social contact with the urban populace, but what was more important in time of Egypt's supremacy, it reinforced elite cohesion. Of all the rulers of Medieval Cairo, the Mamlūks were the most successful in maintaining their social distance from the

---

[1] Ibn Khaldūn, *At-Ta^c^rīf bi-Ibn Khaldūn wa Riḥlatuhu Gharban wa Sharqan*, edited by Muḥammad ibn Tāwīt aṭ-Ṭanjī (Cairo, 1951), pp. 246-247.

people whom they ruled. This separation was, for the most part, the result of their peculiar principles of recruitment and attainment of power, but we wish to point out here that the Citadel represented also the internal solidarity which characterized the highest ranks of the elite. The personal troops of the sultan who resided there formed not only the largest but the most cohesive group among the Mamlūks as a class. As in previous times residence in or near the official compound was an indisputable mark of rank and the compactness of elite residence helped to sustain close ties among members of the ruling group.

The establishment of Mamlūk supremacy permitted the fortress to become a more palatial residence. The most vivid description of the enclosure is given by the fifteenth century writer, Khalīl aẓ-Ẓāhirī.

> The royal residence, where the throne of the empire is located, is known today as the Castle of the Mountain. This palace has no equal in area, splendor, magnificence, and height. Around it are walls, moats, towers, and a number of iron gates which make it impregnable. It would take a long time to give a detailed description of the palaces, rooms, halls, belvederes, galleries, courts, squares, stables, mosques, schools, markets, and baths that are found in the palace; so we will limit ourselves to describing the most remarkable things and those which can best exemplify the greatness of the Empire. The Multicolored Palace is composed of three main buildings used for official ceremonies. These are inlaid with marble of different colors, and the ceilings are painted in blue and gold and are embellished with paintings. The Great Hall has no equal in the world; it stands apart, separated from the Multicolored Palace, surmounted by a very high, beautiful, green dome. This dome, a most beautiful structure inside and out, is supported by marble columns. The Great Mosque of the Citadel is equally wondrous; and I am told that it can hold five thousand worshippers. It is flanked by two minarets of striking design. In this castle are found small chambers for the sultan's private gatherings, which are of astonishing richness and elegance. A certain number of mansions are set aside for the sultan's wives. There are twelve Mamlūks barracks, each one of which is almost as long as a street and can hold up to a thousand Mamlūks. The interior court of the palace is enormous, and in it are a vast garden and a small pond. The stables in which the ruler's horses are kept are also very large and many in number. [2]

By the fifteenth century Cairo had attained the general dimensions which characterized it until the period of the Khedives. It spread out on all sides except on the east where the Muqaṭṭam stood in its way. In the north and west shifts in the river bed during the thirteenth

---

[2] *Kitāb Zubda Kashf al-Mamālik*, edited by P. Ravaisse (Paris, 1894), pp. 26-27.

century and the upheaval of the Jazīrat al-Fīl ("Island of the Elephant") were followed by the emergence of Būlāq a quarter of a century later. Cairo proper and what was left of Fusṭāṭ became one so that no uninhabited land lay between the two. The canal flowing through the town no longer demarcated its western boundary but passed through the center of the agglomeration. Under Sultan an-Nāṣir Cairo and Fusṭāṭ came to be one city and the whole area was covered with houses from the Nile bank opposite Giza to the Muqaṭṭam. [3] A contemporary traveler describing his view of Cairo from the Citadel communicates the following impressions:

6. View of Cairo from the Muqaṭṭam.

[3] See ʿAlī Pasha Mubārak, *Al-Khiṭaṭ at-Tawfīqīya al-Jadīda li-Miṣr al-Qāhira* (Cairo (Būlāq), 1888), Vol. II, pp. 117-119.

> I remember one of many times that I sat for more than a quarter of an hour on the rock outside the castle gate. Discovering Cairo from a height is one of the most agreeable sights. This pleasure comes from the multitude of white mosque towers, each of which has three or four rows of balusters. These towers seem to be interlaced with the beautiful green of the numerous palm trees growing in various city gardens; all of this joined together makes for a certain harmony and charming diversity which is greatly pleasing to the eye. The grandeur of the river, which during the flood season forms a lake larger than the eye can see, the multitude of islands which animate and diversify this silvery plain, and the haughty majesty of the mountains bordering this cheerful site, all give this scene unequaled nobility and variety. [4]

The area immediately adjoining the Citadel took on a military tone. The market place of special interest to Mamlūk cavaliers was that where horses were sold and, as we have seen, this was immediately transferred to the Rumayla near the stables of the sultan. Just on the other side of these stables was constructed, in the middle of the fourteenth century, one of the most striking monuments of the city to this day. This is the stupendous Madrasa of Sultan Ḥasan with its towering dome, for long nearly the highest in all of Islam, and 113-foot walls of stone quarried from the pyramids. Its importance, however, lies not in its significance as a great religious edifice, but rather in the fact that it served as a "counter citadel" until the time of Muḥammad ᶜAlī. As factionalism was rife among the Mamlūk elite for the whole period of their reign, it became the custom for any group challenging the Citadel to fortify themselves in this building. Cannon balls would be discharged across the Rumayla and we can see even now the remains of these attacks in the battered eastern wall of the mosque.

Most of the area between the Citadel and the Bāb Zuwayla was filled with gardens and parks covering the land that had been occupied by the Negro troops of the Fāṭimids. The region surrounding the Birkat al-Fīl also became a desirable residential area and many kiosks and villas were built along its banks as well as those of the canal. At night the amīrs would give parties on their terraces or in brilliantly illuminated vessels. It is said that in time of flood, the region resembled a "little Venice" and a poet of the period describing the pond wrote: "Round as the full moon, its pavilions encircle it like stars." [5] To serve the amīrs, markets and restaurants sprang up along the main street

[4] No citation given, quoted in Gaston Wiet, *Cairo*: *City of Art and Commerce*, p. 58.
[5] Al-Maqrīzī, *Khiṭaṭ*, I, p. 367.

coming from the Fāṭimid city and along the streets which entered upon it.

We must not forget, as part of the Citadel region, the great cemeteries, one to the north of the fortress next to the mountain and the other to the south, between it and the plain of Fusṭāṭ. The latter, al-Qarāfa, had been growing continuously from early times and contained still the respected shrines of numerous companions and relatives of the Prophet as well as of numerous local saints. [6] In the early fifteenth century, Ibn az-Zayyāt wrote a detailed guide of the cemetery for the use of visitors to the tombs. [7] In the cemetery north of the Citadel which stretched between the Fāṭimid city and the Muqaṭṭam were the tombs of the Mamlūks. It is there that many of the greatest rulers of the Middle Ages are buried and their tombs, notably those of Barqūq, Īnāl, and Qāyt-Bey represent the best in Mamlūk religious architecture.

Although the quarter demarcated by the Fāṭimid city lost all trace of importance as a special abode of the guarded elite, it remained an area of concentration of wealth and luxury. On the site of the Fāṭimid palaces rose one of the greatest business districts of the Middle Ages. The Bāb Zuwayla, coming now within the city, retained awe-inspiring significance as the spot where heads of rebels were displayed. How many of Cairo's elite ended their daring ventures at this point! Stimulated by the tremendous increase in the international traffic which flowed through Cairo at this time, large *sūqs*, *khāns*, and houses arose on both sides of the main street. In the reign of an-Nāṣir the area contained nearly 12,000 shops and the principal markets stretched along the Bayn al-Qaṣrayn and into the connecting streets and alleys. [8]

---

[6] This graveyard, now sometimes mistakenly called the "Tombs of the Mamlūks" is in fact the actual site of the "Tombs of the Caliphs," those pitiful remnants of the grand days of ᶜAbbāsid authority whom the Mamlūks had brought to Cairo. The phrase "Tombs of the Caliphs" is sometimes mistakenly applied to the Tombs of the Mamlūks in the eastern cemetery.

[7] See A. R. Guest, "Cairene Topography: El-Qarafa According to Ibn Ez-Zaiyat," *Journal of the Royal Asiatic Society*, 1926, pp. 57-61. The following description is of the early fifteenth century:

> "One mile away from Cairo is a city which is not walled, is as large as Venice, and has high buildings and low ones; in this city are buried all those who die in Cairo. Every Saracen and townsman has a building in this city. In the low ones they bury their dead, and in the high ones the Lords who own them give alms every Friday to the poor. On this day they have their feast, say their prayers, and prepare large meals of meat; and on this day all the poor of Cairo go there to eat and to receive the money that is given to them" (Piloti de Crete, *L'Égypte au commencement du quinzième siècle*, edited by P.-H. Dopp (Cairo, 1950), pp. 34-35).

[8] Al-Maqrīzī, *Khiṭaṭ*, II, p. 95.

The great Khān of Masrūr, so often referred to in *The Thousand and One Nights*, was on the site of the Fāṭimid palace kitchen. [9] The famous Khān al-Khalīlī, now the tourist bazaar, was built during the reign of Barqūq in A.D. 1400 on the site of the cemetery of the Fāṭimids whose remains were thrown on the rubbish mounds outside the eastern gate.

While many of the middle class flocked to the Fāṭimid city for business reasons, it was by no means neglected by the elite. Much stimulus was given to commerce by the numerous mosques and *madrasas* which were established there under the Mamlūks. Al-Azhar gradually regained its importance as the major center of learning and the Mosque of the Ḥasanayn [10] never ceased to be the central shrine of the area. The demolition of the Fāṭimid palaces came about largely through their use as a quarry in the construction of new buildings in the neighborhood. [11] The sultan al-Kāmil in A.D. 1225 was responsible for a school in the Naḥḥāsīn which was long known as the "Dār al-Ḥadīth" and an important center of orthodox teaching while Baybars was responsible for a school which had a rich library, the Ẓāhirīya, in the same street. Two prominent amīrs, Baysarī and Bashtāk, built imposing residences on the palace foundations.

Still one of the most beautiful and important monuments of the Bayn al-Qaṣrayn are the monuments of Qalāūn, [12] finished in 1285. This complex includes a tomb-mosque, a *māristān*, and a *madrasa*. It is said that all the artisans in Cairo and Fusṭāṭ were compelled to work on these buildings and to accept no other work until they were completed. The three buildings were finished in eleven months. [13] The hospital was open to anyone, native or foreign, slave or free, for any length of time and it is estimated that four thousand patients were treated in the clinic in a day. Separate wards were assigned to different maladies, treatments arranged for out-patients, and medical courses given to students who participated in its work. There was a large staff of paid officials including male and female attendants, while a special kitchen supplied food and pharmaceuticals. Also con-

---

[9] ᶜAlī Pasha Mubārak, *Khiṭaṭ at-Tawfīqīya al-Jadīda*, II, p. 23.

[10] This mosque, honoring the grandsons of the Prophet, Ḥasan and Ḥusayn, martyred at Karbala, was established by the Fāṭimids. From the tenth century it has sheltered the most important relic of Shīᶜī Islam, the head of Ḥusayn.

[11] All that remains of the carvings that decorated the palaces were found during restorations of mosques near the Bayn al-Qaṣrayn.

[12] Called Manṣūrīya from his name, Manṣūr ibn Qalāūn.

[13] Al-Maqrīzī, *Khiṭaṭ*, II, pp. 406-408.

nected to this complex were an orphanage and a library. One traveler noted that the furnishings rivaled those of the palaces of the amīrs.[14]

Later an-Nāṣir, Barqūq, al-Ghūrī, and others erected important mosques on this street and their amīrs emulated them in this respect. Some Mamlūks, as well as many of the rich merchants of the time, established luxurious living quarters in the area and it is into houses like these, hidden in the streets and alleys, that one often "stumbles" when reading *The Nights*. One powerful amīr who had a large following built his palace in the quarter and surrounded it with high walls which enclosed his private mosque, modeled in miniature after the Madrasa of Ḥasan, luxurious gardens, and a huge *ḥarīm*. To win the loyalty of his followers he constructed also fountains, baths, schools, and shops nearby.[15] Thus religious edifices, commercial establishments, and residences were all found in this important area and various institutions stimulated one another by their presence.

Despite the political significance of the Citadel, the main center of habitation was still what had been the Fāṭimid compound and so it remained until modern times. Retaining its former population and acquiring many persons who had fled the destruction of Fusṭāṭ, it came to shelter also numerous foreigners who were involved in business or special crafts. Especially during the first seventy or eighty years of the Mamlūk period, waves of immigrants seeking shelter from the Mongol invasions entered Egypt. These were called *wāfidīya* ("newcomers") and more will be said of them later. In the late thirteenth century a special suburb was set aside for the Mongols in the Ḥusaynīya quarter, just north of the old city, by the sultan Ketbughā who welcomed his countrymen to increase his support.[16] Wealthy families who had taken up residence near the Mosque of Baybars (Ẓāhirīya) to escape the plague and benefit from the dry north wind abandoned the area as it became populated by the lower class.[17] Al-Maqrīzī states that it expanded to become the greatest quarter in Cairo.[18]

On the other side of the canal, west of the Fāṭimid area, two major events influenced the development of the town. These were the natural retreat of the river with the rise of Būlāq in the thirteenth and early

---

14 One of the most remarkable examples of metalwork of the period, the Qurʾān table (*kursī*) bearing the name of Sultan Mālik an-Nāṣir ibn Qalāūn, now in the Museum of Islamic Art in Cairo, was found in this *māristān*.

15 Al-Maqrīzī, *Khiṭaṭ*, II, pp. 69-70, also M. Clerget, *Le Caire*, I, p. 157.

16 D. S. Margoliouth, *Cairo, Jerusalem and Damascus*, p. 83.

17 Even through the Ottoman period the quarter had a turbulent character.

18 *Khiṭaṭ*, II, p. 21.

fourteenth centuries, and the construction of a new canal by an-Nāṣir in 1324. Previous to this time there was nothing of importance in this region save the port of Maqs, which had decayed with the decline of the Fāṭimids, and a little to the north, a plot of land known as "Arḍ aṭ-Ṭabbāla" which had been given by the caliph al-Mustanṣir to a favorite singing girl.[19] The Ezbekīya, a pond dating from Fāṭimid times, had slowly dried up and was invaded by buildings. As the region gained a bad reputation, however, a vizier demolished these edifices and restored the pond. This however, again disappeared completely as under an-Nāṣir the canal which fed it was filled in. Only at the end of the fifteenth century, when the amīr Ezbek let some of the water again into the basin, did it become an area of elite residence. In the time of Qāyt-Bey (A.D. 1483) the traveler Breydenbach described it as a place of magnificent buildings, which adorned an area that had been desert fifteen years before.[20]

As the Nile retreated, the land uncovered was granted to various individuals who built houses upon it. Northwest Cairo did not become an important residential quarter, however, until the construction of the Nāṣirī Canal. This canal, linking the Nile with the old canal at a point near the Mosque of Baybars, aided in draining the tract and facilitated transportation of goods to the region. Like most bodies of water within the city, it was the site of numerous pleasure parties and processions. Persons of every class had dwellings in this area but until Napoleonic times, this portion of the city was never as crowded as the earlier town. European travelers of the fifteenth century reported seeing vast orchards, gardens, and fortress-like palaces as they approached Cairo from Maṭarīya and Būlāq.

On the land that emerged from the river, a new port was established to replace Maqs at Būlāq in A.D. 1313. Two main arteries connected it to Cairo. One, going to the Bāb al-Ḥadīd or "Maqs Gate" at the northwest corner of the agglomeration (now the site of the railroad station), became the chief route of commerce. Būlāq became the site not only of a maze of streets and markets but of baths, mosques, and palaces. Thus there arose a great suburb inhabited by grain, oil, and sugar merchants, millers, and artisans.

The area south of the main street connecting the Bāb al-Kharq, at the southwest corner of the Fāṭimid city (now the approximate site

[19] S. Lane-Poole, *The Story of Cairo*, p. 259.

[20] Bernard de Breydenbach, *Les saintes pérégrinations de Bernard de Breydenbach*, translated by F. Larrivaz (Cairo, 1904), p. 51.

of the Museum of Islamic Art) and the Bāb al-Lūq at the Nāṣirī Canal, reached its peak of development a little earlier than the region just discussed. On land freed earlier from the river opposite the barracks of Roḍa, a quarter of fashionable residence sprang up along the western bank of the Cairo canal. When a large group of Tatars, numbering about a thousand horsemen and their families, sought protection from the Mongols with the Egyptian sultan, they were welcomed by Baybars who gave them a public reception and ordered houses to be built for them in the vicinity of Bāb al-Lūq.[21] As many of them received speedy promotions, more refugees followed them.

At this time, the area of habitation extended to the part called Dayr at-Tīn, one and a half kilometers south of the Mosque of ᶜAmr, encroaching upon areas hitherto occupied by brick kilns and other heavy industries. As usual, land was set aside for the Mamlūk's favorite sport. Baybars had placed a stadium on the site of the recent Qaṣr an-Nīl barracks (now the region of the Nile Hilton Hotel) and after him, the sultan an-Nāṣir placed a racecourse between the Cairo canal and the one which he himself constructed. By the end of the thirteenth century, the recession of the river and the increase in population due to the immigration of Asiatics necessitated the extension of the canal past the old Sadd Bridge (Qanṭarat as-Sadd). In the time of al-Maqrīzī, the lands surrounding the Qārūn pond were covered with residences.

Although Fusṭāṭ never recovered from its devastation, the sections on the Nile bank had suffered least. Aside from some heavy industries in the interior near the Mosque of ᶜAmr, much of the economic significance of the area vanished as the majority of craftsmen migrated to the spaces between Fusṭāṭ and the center of Cairo along the southern prolongation of the main street, the Shāriᶜa al-ᶜAzīz. Sugar factories, warehouses, baths, and schools disappeared as Būlāq flourished and what was left of Fusṭāṭ came to be known as "Miṣr al-ᶜAtīqa," or "Old Cairo." We should mention, however, the pleasant surroundings of the Birkat al-Ḥabash ("Abyssinian Pond") one and a half kilometers south of the Mosque of ᶜAmr and the promontory, ar-Raṣad ("The Observatory"), nearby which attracted some of the elite to build pavilions there in the fourteenth century.

It is apparent from the foregoing description that the protection afforded to the city under the generally competent if erratic rule of the

---

[21] D. S. Margoliouth, *Cairo, Jerusalem and Damascus*, p. 72.

early Mamlūks, as well as the initiative taken by them in establishing new centers of habitation, provided the main stimulus for the city's expansion. Especially during the reign of an-Nāṣir, when security and prosperity led to an increase in the value of land, the heretofore separate sections of the agglomeration became contiguous as buildings proliferated. The increase in population was due in no small part to the resurgence of commerce which soon followed the reestablishment of authority. Likewise it was to the city protected by the only able army of the Islamic world, that the refugees from the Mongol invasions flocked, and these people played an important role in the life of the town from then onwards, even challenging for a time the power of the Mamlūks themselves.

It is worth noting too, that although the elite most often lived in the region of the Citadel, or on their grand estates in the new quarters, the old city was not abandoned by them. Since the principal concentration of the population remained in the area of the old walls and most of Fusṭāṭ between it and the Citadel had been destroyed, the sultans took measures to secure their authority in the old capital. The establishment of mosques, hospitals, and *madrasas* which stimulated the rise of markets and local commerce, attested to the power and efficiency of their administration. The tremendous and impressive buildings of the "dome builders," often constructed with the very stone of the pyramids, [22] overshadowed all others and dominated the scene long after shops of brick and wood had crumbled. Nearly the only remains of commercial establishments and houses are those *khāns* (caravanserais) and palaces built by sultans or amīrs. Thus there was a tendency for such landmarks to persist despite the waxing and waning of urban prosperity. In time of decline, it was against these sturdy walls that the struggling populace set up their dwellings. [23]

Thus in all districts from the most populous to the sparsely settled, social segregation, although to some extent present, was not strict. In the first place the greatest amīrs who were not in the Citadel, as well as the urban notables, simply could not live separated from the populace. They needed the services of the lower orders and they needed clients around them to maintain their rank. In the second place, as in

[22] The monuments of Giza were relatively well-preserved until the thirteenth century. From the writings of ᶜAbd al-Laṭīf (b. A.D. 1179) it would appear that the casing of the Great Pyramid was intact during his lifetime.

[23] Until two decades ago, the exterior of numerous Mamlūk monuments, as well as the northern wall of the Fāṭimid city and the Mosque of Ibn Ṭūlūn, were completely obscured by the lower class dwellings which crowded into every available space.

Fāṭimid days, there were no true ghettos and residential areas were only generally set apart from places of business. Certain ethnic groups were settled in certain areas but demographic changes and socioeconomic instability did not allow their restriction to these places even if it was ever intended. The commercial and religious establishments moreover, catered to persons of widely varied rank and status and provided an important common ground, perhaps the most important ground, for social and cultural interaction.

Physical and demographic expansion gave the city a new unity. New areas settled by the elite were immediately connected to the old agglomeration, the developing port, and the military installations of the Citadel and of Roḍa. The main arteries were so well traveled that one could scarcely venture upon them without being run over by carts or jostled by pedestrians. All European travelers were amazed at the size and density of the populace, the like of which they had never seen. One traveler in A.D. 1322 estimated the city to be twice the size of Paris and four times greater in population. [24]

Under such conditions we should wonder at the extent of land set aside for orchards, entertainment, and recreation. Despite the tremendous expansion of the area of habitation, there was a great congestion in some areas which was totally lacking in others. It was not only that the amīrs had a predilection for grand estates, but also that the less powerful urban residents conservatively clung to fortified quarters in which they felt secure. Each quarter, whether it represented an amīr and his following or a special status group, was a miniature power center and its efficiency depended upon the ability of the inhabitants to communicate with each other. Members of the middle and lower orders, even more than the elite, were dependent upon face-to-face contact in this respect, for they were unable to build and maintain widespread defenses and the arteries connecting them.

Thus the networks of urban groups varied widely as to their physical aspect and therein we see the polarity of society. While the Citadel enforced elite cohesion, at least among the forces of the sultan, the most powerful network did not need to be spatially central or physically well-defined if its communication channels to areas of military and economic significance were effective. On the other hand, it was to the advantage of merchants, craftsmen, and laborers to reside as close to their places of business, relatives, patrons, and associates as possible.

---

[24] Simon Simeonis quoted in G. Wiet, *Cairo: City of Art and Commerce*, p. 73.

CHAPTER SEVEN

THE MAMLŪK FEUDAL SYSTEM AND THE URBAN ELITE

As the fortunes of the city depended upon the military elite and their power, so now a study of the rulers of Cairo must address itself to the question: "What were the factors that maintained them as a class?" as well as "What were the mechanisms that linked them to the rest of society?" It will be seen that the elite were a most rigidly and narrowly delimited social category although a plural category in which competition was the characteristic mode of operation. The very success of their endeavor, however, depended upon their tapping roots in the society that they ruled, roots which were formed of personal liaisons as well as of formal claims to the resources that nourished them as a class.

1. *The Mamlūk Establishment*

The elite are typically urban and characteristically occupy the first place in the hierarchy of social power. While they do much to stimulate urban growth, on the other side of the coin, they can only achieve their ends in the urban milieu. Their position, dependent upon social complexity, is reinforced by secondary attributes relating to specialized occupation, recruitment patterns, speech, manners, and dress, all of which set them apart from members of other classes. The latter, constantly reminded of the special quality of those above them by visual and auditory symbols, come to recognize this patent sociocultural gap and tend all the more to accept the place assigned to them in the social hierarchy. In medieval Cairo, not only did the members of the elite hold the military power, but the greatest mass of wealth was in their hands. Only they had heraldic emblems, their dress was of a special kind, and they alone had the right to ride horses. Even their law was different. We do not wish to imply, however, that there were no individuals who were marginal to the class or that anything resembling a caste system [1] characterized the feudal order. In a very real sense

[1] There has been a tendency for some writers to refer to the Mamlūk elite as a "caste." See I. M. Lapidus, *Muslim Cities in the Later Middle Ages* (Cambridge, Mass.: Harvard University Press, 1967), p. vii; A. N. Poliak, *Feudalism in Egypt, Syria, Palestine, and the Lebanon, 1250-1900* (London: *The Royal Asiatic Society*, 1939), p. 1; and Gaston Wiet, *Cairo*: *City of Art and Commerce* (Norman, Oklahoma: The University of Oklahoma Press, 1964), p. 66. It is our contention that this use of the term does nothing to clarify the social structure. The existence of a

7. A Mamlūk in Arms.

the society was much more open than that of medieval Europe. [2] The question of mobility is an important one and we will deal with it. Rather we should say that, in their behavior among themselves and

---

caste, properly speaking, denotes not only stratification and ritual differentiation but a system of castes. The groups in Cairo that were ritually differentiated were special status groups which, except in the case of the Mamlūks, cut across the society vertically on the basis of ethnicity or religious persuasion, and were not stratified as a rule. Moreover, although the Mamlūks seem to have been preferentially endogamous, there are many indications that they did not hesitate to form intimate liaisons with the other orders of society in order to control the resources upon which their own status depended.

[2] Cf. I. M. Lapidus, *Muslim Cities in the Later Middle Ages*, p. 186.

with respect to other groups, the elite were markedly set apart by a number of features, some basic to their social role and others secondary to it.

As in the preceding periods, the elite were foreign in origin. In Mamlūk times, however, foreign derivation under the special system of slave service was not incidental to positions of power but virtually requisite for them. The rulers of Egypt, recognizing the importance of effective cavalry to their fighting force, esteemed the horsemen of the steppes over any other nation represented in their army. The migration of numbers of people from the south Russian steppes, Turks and Mongols seeking refuge from the advance of Hūlāgū, asylum from their overlords, or from internal conflicts in the western Mongol states, gave the Ayyūbids opportunities to purchase slaves on an extensive scale. We have seen how, during the reigns of Baybars I and Ketbughā, whole parts of tribes came to Egypt retaining their own organization.

The majority of mamlūks, however, were purchased from particular territories through special traders. Until the end of the fourteenth century, one of the most important sources of this type of slave was Kipchak on the Volga. Qalāūn, like Baybars, was from this region and he is known to have purchased Turks and Mongols in greater numbers than anyone before him. Under an-Nāṣir, the life of the mamlūk became so attractive, and so much money was offered by the sultan's agents, [3] that the people of Turkestan willingly sold their children to the Egyptian court. According to al-Maqrīzī:

> ... the traders would bring him many Mamlūks: and the Sultan's attitude towards his Mamlūks became well-known in their country of origin ..., and the Mongols gave their sons, daughters, and relatives to the traders, who bought them from them, wishing to enhance the glory and happiness of Egypt. The traders paid for every Mamlūk from 20,000 to 30,000 and even 40,000 dirhams; as a result, quarrels and disputes arose among the Mongols ..., and they came to Egypt. [4]

[3] Merchants bringing many Mamlūks to the sultan were especially honored for special service to the Muslim cause. According to a fifteenth century writer:

> "... The Sultan would dress these merchants in robes of cloth of gold and set them astride a horse to the sound of drums and trumpets, and he would go through the city, and the guards of the Sultan would say: 'These noble merchants have led three hundred souls, more or less as that may be, from Christian lands and (Christian) faith to the Sultan, and he bought them and they will live and die in the faith of Muḥammad, and so the faith of Muḥammad multiplies and increases and that of the Christian fails!" (Piloti de Crete, *L'Égypte au commencement du quinzième siècle*, edited by P.-H. Dopp (Cairo: Cairo University Press, 1950), p. 15).

[4] *Kitāb as-Sulūk li-Maᶜrifat Duwal al-Mulūk*, edited by Muṣṭafā Ziyāda (Cairo, 1934-58), II, p. 525; quoted by D. Ayalon "The Wafidiya in the Mamluk Kingdom," *Islamic Culture*, XXV (1951), p. 103.

Not only young males, but women and female slaves of the same races followed them. It is little wonder that the Turkish language became the tongue of the elite to the extent that to be a "Turk" meant that one did not know Arabic at all [5] and it was considered a degradation for a man in high office to have great familiarity with the language of the country.

Only with respect to religion did the Mamlūks become Egyptianized, and then not completely. Christian in the land of their birth, they had to become Muslim to be eligible to rule on behalf of the caliph. They did, however, adhere to the Ḥanafī code of jurisprudence as opposed to the Shāfiᶜī followed by the majority of native Cairenes. Instruction in Islam, therefore, formed the initial part of their training and the fact of their previous Christianity was erased from all records as well as from their minds. [6] Not only was their conversion necessary if they were to rule a Muslim polity, but importantly it served to acquaint them with the expectations and ways of those whom they governed. More especially, it formed the basis of ties with local notables who directly administered society.

Besides the barrier of language, another great element of differentiation between the rulers and the ruled stemmed from the foreign origin of the Mamlūks. Lawsuits relating to the status of amīrs, knights, and their estates were settled according to a special system of law called the *siyāsa* and not by *qāḍī*s according to Islamic law. The *siyāsa*, according to al-Maqrīzī, was founded upon the Great Yāsa or legal code of Chingiz-Khān. [7] It included not only criminal and civil law, but rules of communal organization, economic, social, and political. In character, the code was a military one and exclusively that of the elite. [8]

As Poliak has shown, the general outline of the Mamlūk organization

---

[5] A. N. Poliak, "Le charactère colonial de l'état mamelouk dans ses rapports avec la Horde d'or," *Revue des Études Islamiques*, 9 (1935), p. 237.

[6] See below p. 142. Curiously enough, there was a church in the Citadel itself for the use of their women who were not compelled to embrace Islam (A. N. Poliak, "The Influence of Chingiz-Khan's Yāsa upon the General Organization of the Mamluk State," *Bulletin of the School of Oriental and African Studies*, X (1942), p. 865).

[7] See A. N. Poliak, "Some Notes on the Feudal System of the Mamlūks," *Journal of the Royal Asiatic Society*, 1937, pp. 97-107.

[8] Among the Mongols it was thought to have a semi-magic power and was therefore concealed by the conquerors from the subject populations. No contemporary writer claimed to have seen the Mongol text although some were acquainted with a version written in the Turkish dialect (A. N. Poliak, "The Influence of Chingiz-Khan's Yāsa upon the General Organization of the Mamluk State," p. 863).

followed that of the Golden Horde. Beneath the sultan and his amīrs and beys, the Great Yāsa distributed the population among fixed divisions charged with special services within specified areas. While less strict than the Mongols, the Mamlūks of Egypt located their fiefs within separate provinces which were compelled to maintain their own troops. The amīrs received fiefs (*iqṭāʿ*s) of one to ten villages according to their rank. To help prevent coalitions against the sultan, moreover, the *iqṭāʿ*s of particular holders were not in one place but tended to be scattered over a large area. Every person was forbidden to pass from one division to another without permission. Transfers of troops between provinces were forbidden and peasants could not leave their villages without permission of their lords and then only temporarily. Townsmen, while not deprived by the code as were the *fallāḥīn*, lacked any means to deal with it and sometimes called for "justice" and a return to Islamic law. [9]

Having made their contributions to the military culture of the Mamlūk regime, the Mongols receded into the background to be replaced by Circassians. The population of Kipchak declined suddenly in the fourteenth century because of the Black Death, the wars of Tamurlane, and ironically enough because of the continual emigration of Turkish and Mongol youth which deprived the country of its best resources. The Circassians had been one of the prominent elements of the Mamlūk army in the Baḥrī period and they had been involved in racial strife as early as the reign of Ḥasan (A.D. 1347). At that time there had been an attempt at purging Circassians. Barqūq, overthrowing the last representative of the house of Qalāūn in A.D. 1382, successfully ousted the Turks and replaced them with his own countrymen. By A.D. 1412 al-Qalqashandī could write:

> In our time most of the amīrs and army have become Circassians ... The Turk Mamlūks of Egypt have become so few in number that all that is left of them are a few survivors and their children. [10]

The Circassians, like the Turks before them, never parted with the culture of their homeland. Even in matters of diet, they preferred horsemeat and mare's milk. [11]

---

[9] A. N. Poliak, "The Influence of Chingiz-Khan's Yāsa upon the General Organization of the Mamluk State," p. 875.

[10] *Aṣ-Ṣubḥ al-Aʿshā* (Cairo, 1914-1928), IV, p. 458.

[11] A. N. Poliak, "The Influence of Chingiz-Khan's Yāsa upon the General Organization of the Mamluk State," p. 865.

But foreign origin, Mongol, Turkish, or Circassian, did not alone suffice to fit one to join the ranks of the elite. While at first the Ayyūbids and Baḥrī Mamlūks welcomed free men into their army, it became increasingly difficult for a warrior who was not a freed slave to attain high rank. Even in the time of an-Nāṣir, we find the great amīr Qawṣūn the victim of snobbery because he had not passed through the crucible of slavery.

David Ayalon has drawn our attention to this curious situation in which freed slaves could rise to the highest positions of the empire while men who were born free and remained free invariably met with discrimination and were frustrated in their attempts to attain power. Many of the early immigrants from Turkestan, referred to as *wāfidīya* ("new arrivals"), entered as free men and were incorporated into the forces of the corps of the Royal Mamlūks. But although some intermarried with Mamlūks, the rank of the majority could never come up to that of the freed slaves. [12] There was a tendency for the rulers to suspect the loyalty of those who had not been bought in childhood and raised by themselves personally. Baybars I, at first welcoming numerous bands of Tatars, later expressed his distrust of such immigrants. "I fear there is something suspect in their coming from all sides," he is to have said. [13] After him, the Mamlūk Oirat Ketbughā attempted to raise the status of his countrymen but succeeded only in bringing about his own deposition. Out of 10,000 to 18,000 Oirats entering as free men, not one succeeded in attaining a position higher than the second rank of amīr, that of an amīr of forty. The son-in-law of Hūlāgū Khān, commander of the Oirats who had come in at the head of 10,000 horsemen, received this rank which permitted him to be in command of forty. Throughout the whole Baḥrī period, we hear echoes of this constant struggle between the Royal Mamlūks and the *wāfidīya.* The sultans, even those who were inclined to raise the latter to high positions, hesitated to promote them if they could gain a large following among the local population. We have already noted that the large quarter of Ḥusaynīya was populated by Oirats and difficult to control. It is during the years of declining migration that we find some amīrs of a thousand of *wāfidī* origin but the ruling body of Mamlūks was quick to sense any threat to its exclusive status. The Oirats were finally

---

[12] David Ayalon, "The Wafidiya in the Mamluk Kingdom," pp. 90-91.
[13] Al-Maqrīzī, *Sulūk*, I, p. 515.

dismissed by an-Nāṣir who, under pressure from the Royal Mamlūks, was readily persuaded that they could not be trusted. [14]

Of all the elements necessary for successful entry into the elite, the free immigrants lacked the most significant factor. Talented and efficient military men of foreign origin, handsome in appearance and often possessing powerful relations abroad, they simply were not united by the feeling of solidarity so strong among their opponents who shared the undisputable privilege of being the freed slaves of one master.

A study of the *esprit de corps* of the Mamlūk contingents reveals two principlies of loyalty, both of which have their origin in the system of training and promotion. Bought, given a liberal education, and set free by his purchaser (*ustādh*), the mamlūk owed everything to his lord. The support of the amīr, like that of the sultan, lay in his mamlūks. While there was competition between the mamlūks of one master for his favor, and promotion under him depended upon ability, all of them realized that, regardless of their individual accomplishments, they would be at a great disadvantage without the support of the house (*bayt*) to which they belonged. Thus the *khushdāshīya*, raised and liberated together, presented a united front to any external chal-

---

[14] The decline of the *ḥalqa* (originally a special escort of the sultan consisting primarily of free men) resulted also from the ascendancy of the Mamlūk corps. In Ayyūbid times some of its members even came to hold positions as foreign envoys or as escorts of foreign envoys, places usually reserved for the *khāṣṣakīya*, the highest division of the Royal Mamlūks (D. Ayalon, "Studies on the Structure of the Mamluk Army," *Bulletin of the School of Oriental and African Studies*, XV (1953), pp. 449-450). The *ḥalqa* at first ranked alongside the Baḥrīya and was occasionally mentioned before that elite division of the army in the sources. After the death of an-Nāṣir however, when the Mamlūk state was beginning to feel the cost of maintaining its huge army, the number of hired troops was greatly reduced. Members of the *ḥalqa* began to sell their feudal estates for payment or compensation. Subsequently the division came to be composed of common people, even peddlers and artisans in the time of al-Maqrīzī (D. Ayalon, "Studies on the Structure of the Mamluk Army," p. 453). Under the Circassians their chief task was the duty of guarding the gates of Cairo, the Citadel, and vital places in the old city and its suburbs. So the *ḥalqa* passed from being a corps of splendidly trained and equipped troops to an untrained rabble which had lost all possibility of regaining the esteemed position it once had. Ayalon writes that:

> "...it is very doubtful whether in the Mamluk regime, which opened the gates of the highest military society only to freed slaves, the *ḥalqa* would have been able to hold its ground for any length of time, even had its members been endowed with the finest military talents" ("Studies on the Structure of the Mamluk Army," p. 455).

Significantly the *ḥalqa* auxiliary corps came to be composed principally of the sons of mamlūks (*awlād an-nās*) who, owing to their status as free Egyptians, were not considered eligible to occupy positions in the highest ranks.

lenge. With the demise of their master, they often agitated against his successor or joined coalitions disputing the inheritance of feudal estates.

Everything in the experience of the mamlūk served to establish and reinforce the twofold loyalty to the *ustādh* and *khushdāshīya.* Obedience to his overlord and loyalty to his fellows was instilled over a long period of training. Together with others of his age the young mamlūk was first given instruction in the principles of the Qur'ān, writing, and Islamic law (*sharīʿa*). As he approached adulthood, in the company of these same fellows, he was given training in arms, the bow, and lance throughout which a harsh discipline was imposed and infractions severely punished. Upon completion of his studies at the military school, he had none of the property of a soldier, neither equipment, a horse, nor pay until he was freed. [15] Usually freedom, like training, was granted to a number of young mamlūks at once rather than individually, especially if their master was the sultan. The freed mamlūks of one master dined not with their own families but at the house of their lord and received from him pay, horses, equipment, and meat and fodder allotments twice a month.

The palatial residences of the amīrs were modeled after those of the sultan and every amīr of forty or higher was entitled to have a band playing in front of his house. Personal emblems decorated all of their properties from the doors of their palaces, factories, and warehouses to their military and household equipment. These devices, usually set upon circular shields, were often symbolic birds and animals, especially the eagle and lion which represented particular sultans (Eagle of Ṣalāḥ ad-Dīn, Lion of Baybars), or other motifs which symbolized certain court positions such as cupbearer (cup), polo master (polo sticks), secretary (writing box) and so on. It is little wonder that, in such an environment, the Mamlūks developed not only the strongest sentiments of loyalty to their house but a sense of competition with other establishments of its kind.

To functioning households, moreover, were attached not only mamlūks but vast numbers of other retainers, clients of various sorts, scribes, lawyers, merchants, tax collectors, and others needed to manage and administer its wealth. As we shall see, the role of the *bayt* as an urban center of power can hardly be overemphasized, whether military, economic, or bureaucratic factors are considered. On the one hand, it

---

[15] D. Ayalon, *L'Esclavage du Mamelouk* (Jerusalem: The Israel Oriental Society, 1951), p. 16.

a. Eagle of Ṣalāḥ ad-Dīn; b. Lion of Baybars; c. Cup of *Sāqī* (Cupbearer); d. Napkin of *Jamdār* (Master of the Robes); e. Polo Sticks of *Jūkandār* (Polo Master); f. Tray of *Jāshnigīr* (Food Taster); g. Pen case of *Dawādār* (Secretary); h. Sword of *Silāḥdār* (Armor Bearer).

8. Mamlūk Blazons.

represented the authority of the sultan, on the other, it was a node in a network of private power, managed by an amīr and his retainers, who sought factional support from all levels of society. The dialectic of elite social structure thus had a profound effect upon urban structure as a whole.

It has been stressed by a number of writers, Ayalon included, that the basic ties of the Mamlūk organization were analogous to those of the family that they replaced. Thus, certain aspects of the Mamlūk house (*bayt*) are seen to parallel the relationships of sentiment, association, and authority in the patriarchal relationship and the relationship between male siblings.[16] The fact that the mamlūk was frequently known by the name of his patron, and that this name was retained by his family long after the founder had passed away, can be offered in support of this analogy. The Ẓāhirīs, mamlūks of Baybars I, are a single example. Moreover, rarely did children reap the benefit of their father's estate. More often the property of the deceased, his house, wives, slaves, and goods would be seized by his strongest freedman or the sultan.

The *awlād an-nās* or "sons of the (best) people," the Mamlūks, present a noteworthy case for the weakness of the hereditary principle. These included also the sons of sultans and, especially under the regime of the Burjīs, constituted a peculiar problem. Fearing that the sons of his predecessors would be used by his adversaries as tools for their own ambition, the Circassian ruler was accustomed to treat them with strict severity. Of the *awlād an-nās*, Ayalon writes:

> Until the reign of Barsbāy, most of them were restricted to their quarters in the Cairo citadel; many had never even seen Cairo and had little notion of what a city looked like. They were ordered by Barsbāy ... to come down from the citadel and take up residence in the city. The tumultuous life of the metropolis soon corrupted them; many became impoverished, and all their former splendour left them.[17]

The sons of amīrs fared little better. When one of them came of age, his father would give him an allowance of pay, food, meat, and

---

[16] Remarks made by contemporary writers are often cited in evidence. Ayalon says, for instance:

> "In recounting that the sultan Lāgīn and his mamlūk Mungūtīmūr were assassinated because the former had given full power to the latter, which he abused, the historian remarked: 'As the proverb says: "The guilty child brings the curse upon his father"'" (*L'Esclavage du Mamelouk*, p. 35).

[17] "Studies on the Structure of the Mamluk Army," p. 458.

fodder until he became qualified to find a place in the free corps (*ḥalqa*). Thus the lowest division of the army came to have at its head these sons of the elite. Only occasionally did one, through connections with the sultan, ascend to the rank of an amīr of ten or of forty.

For a mamlūk to pass into the service of another master was an undoubted misfortune for, regardless of his abilities, such an individual had to face the united front of the mamlūks originally attached to that lord. The formal ranking of mamlūks, within the major divisions of mamlūks of the sultan and those of his amīrs, reflects this fact. Following Ayalon's succinct outline of the major divisions of the army, there were:

I. The Royal Mamlūks (*al-mamālīk as-sulṭānīya*)
   a. The mamlūks of the ruling sultan (*mushtarawāt, ajlāb*, or *julbān*)
   b. Mamlūks who passed into the service of the ruling sultan from the service of other masters (*mustakhdamūn*)
      1. Mamlūks who passed into the service of the reigning sultan from that of former sultans (*mamālīk as-salāṭīn al-mutaqaddima, qarānīṣ* or *qarāniṣa*)
      2. Mamlūks who passed into the service of the reigning sultan from that of the amīrs, because of the death or dismissal of their masters (*sayfīya*)

II. The Amīr's Mamlūks (*mamālīk al-umarā*ᵓ, *ajnād al-umarā*ᵓ)

III. The troops of the *ḥalqa* (*ajnād al-ḥalqa*) a corps of free men including the *awlād an-nās* who were the sons of the sultan, amīrs, and mamlūks. [18]

In the Baḥrī period the Royal Mamlūks were not less than 10,000 in number, although in later years they became fewer. Of these, those closest to the sultan were his bodyguards, the *khāṣṣakīya*, who were also the prospective amīrs. Under each new ruler, the hierarchy began with his special mamlūks whom he had bought, raised, freed, and then selected according to ability, while the mamlūks of the former sultan as well as those of deceased or deposed amīrs formed the lower ranks of the royal corps.

The usual pattern of patrilineal inheritance was bound to be effected by these principles of solidarity which tied together the Mamlūk house. From the sultanate to the feudal fief, there was a constant struggle between the rights of blood and those who had shared in its creation and reputation.

---

[18] D. Ayalon, "Studies on the Structure of the Mamluk Army," p. 204.

For a time, under the Baḥrīs, hereditary succession to the title of sultan was relatively strong. The house of Qalāūn reigned with hardly a break from A.D. 1279 to 1382. But it became the practice, especially in the Circassian period, for a weak son of the sultan, often a child, to be allowed to succeed him while his mamlūks fought for the prize. The unfortunate puppet would then conveniently be put away and the victorious amīr placed on the throne. In these proceedings, the *qarānīṣ* (mamlūks of former sultans) invariably played a significant role. Although they were not united as a class by the bonds of loyalty shared by *khushdāshīya*, they all hated the freedmen of the reigning sultan who were younger than they and in a position over them. Such coalitions, though temporary in nature, were a powerful and disturbing influence, especially when, because of a series of brief reigns, the corps of Royal Mamlūks was very large. [19]

The sultan, to establish his authority, often resorted to the most drastic means of shifting the balance of power to his favor. He would not only free his predecessor's young mamlūks, thereby making them his own, and would buy large numbers of slaves to be trained and freed later, but would throw the older mamlūks "bag and baggage" out of the Citadel barracks. Not infrequently under the Circassians, a wholesale purge would take place. While these procedures were in evidence generally from the beginning of the Mamlūk era, they were tempered somewhat by the tendency to adhere to the hereditary principle under the Baḥrīs. If, as during the earlier period, a son succeeded his father, his father's mamlūks were not foreign to him and their replacement was a gradual one. As the youthful mamlūks completed their long period of training they were freed to fill the positions left vacant by the older generation. During the later part of the period, the Mamlūk principle tended to replace the hereditary principle altogether where access to elite ranks was concerned.

2. *The Role of the Mamlūk Establishment in Urban Society*

The links which bound the elite to society as a whole had a dual nature. In the first place, there were the hard facts of their control of resources which stemmed from the might of their arms as well as legal claims. In the second place there were omnipresent personal bonds, for regardless of the narrowness of their social sphere in the strict sense, they could not manage their estate alone but depended upon

---

[19] D. Ayalon, "Studies on the Structure of the Mamluk Army," pp. 217-218.

subordinates who knew how to accomplish their ends on the local scene.

Mamlūk feudalism, which replaced the Fāṭimid system of tax farming with the allocation of military fiefs, was inseparable from the special organization which controlled it. In the pattern of feudal holding, we see a reflection of the tension between the sultan and his subordinates; the dialectic of state control and private ownership. The fiefs of the amīrs were fixed according to the number of knights they were allowed to maintain. Two-thirds of the revenue of the estate was to contribute to the support of the cavalry, while one-third was set aside for the lord's personal expenses (*khāṣṣa*). The feudal charter was a temporary grant by the state but the sultan always had to struggle to retain his control.[20] Under the Fāṭimids and Ayyūbids, fief holders had been hereditary holders and this right was recognized by the first Mamlūk sultans. There were, however, even in the early years, periodic redistributions of land (*rawk*s) between the ruler and his feudatories following every cadastral survey of cultivated land. The first *rawk* in Egypt under an-Nāṣir in 1298 was followed by another in Syria, Palestine, and the Lebanon in 1313, and another in Egypt in 1315. At the great redistributions which took place on the accession of the sultan or after a civil war, the factions of amīrs and their freedmen struggled for the spoils. In the Burjī period, the Circassians felt that they had prior right to the fiefs which was, of course, bitterly contested by the freedmen of the former sultans and their subordinates. The Nāṣirī *rawk* of A.D. 1315 influenced the financial administration of the state until the end of the fifteenth century. The 4/24 of the general tax revenues designated for the sultan was increased to 10/24. Nevertheless the amīrs maintained and increased their holdings.

Generally speaking, there were few if any branches of the economy over which the elite did not exercise direct or indirect control. Not only did the state monopolize strategic goods and materials like wood, metal, and stone needed for military purposes, but it participated in many economic endeavors that it did not monopolize through investment, taxation, confiscation, and forced purchase. The sultans and their amīrs were the greatest consumers, investors in commerce, and controlled by far the most urban property. They owned *khān*s, factories, granaries, baths, markets, and *qayṣarīya*s (bazaars) as well as the largest residential palaces in town. Lapidus describes the wealth of a single household:

---

20 A. N. Poliak, *Feudalism in Egypt, Syria, and the Lebanon 1250-1900,*" p. 24.

> The emirs and their households were enormously wealthy in comparison with the rest of the urban population. Whereas a worker or minor religious functionary might earn two dirhems a day, in the fourteenth century the income of emirs ran up to a half million and a million dirhems a year, the annual income of almost two thousand workers. An emir's household was as wealthy as the whole working population of small towns.[21]

The most important economic resource directly in their hands, however, was the vital urban grain supply; for the income from fiefs was paid in kind, for the most part, as was part of the salary intended to supply household needs. One amīr, Sayf ad-Dīn Salār, is said to have possessed 300,000 *irdabb*s (about 1,500,000 bushels) of grain, in addition to his other property when he died.[22] Naturally the Mamlūks did not hesitate to exploit their holdings by forcing townsmen to buy grain above the market price. Periodic famines gave opportunity for much manipulation. Sultans would try to secure the safety of the urban food supply but, owing to the insecurity of their own position, were often unable to keep the greed of the amīrs in check and dared only to announce price ceilings.

A large part of the grain coming to Cairo, moreover, was redistributed through elite households and never found its way to the market. Not only their subordinates and various "hangers-on" but Ṣūfīs and poor beggars could be provided for in this way. Sometimes the feeding of the poor was a duty assigned to amīrs by the sultan. The extent to which the populace benefited from such distribution, however, depended to a great extent upon the balance of power as well as the good will of the amīrs. Generosity, of course, was a principal means of creating a local following[23] and some became proverbial for their largess. It is said of Badr ad-Dīn Baysarī, possibly the most sumptuous figure of the thirteenth century who had an extremely palatial residence on the Bayn al-Qaṣrayn, that

> Hospitality was his foible, and his gifts to the poor ran in round sums of five hundred or a thousand dirhems ... to each applicant. He would daily distribute three thousand pounds of meat, and a single present consisted of a thousand pieces of gold, five thousand bushels of corn, and a thousand hundredweight of honey.[24]

---

[21] *Muslim Cities in the Later Middle Ages*, p. 50.

[22] *Ibid*., p. 51.

[23] The factions which competed in the contests between Mamlūk houses included elements of urban rabble that participated in street fights, as well as clients of the middle orders.

[24] S. Lane-Poole, *The Story of Cairo*, p. 274, from al-Maqrīzī, *Khiṭaṭ* II, pp. 69-70.

Such provision, however, like the functioning of the whole social organization, depended upon personal motivation rather than the establishment of an ordered distribution of responsibility. By the fifteenth century the sultans had become too weak to play a decisive part in the protection of urban resources, let alone compel the amīrs to feed the poor.

The social links of the elite with the lower echelons of society sprang from the prominent role their households played in urban administration, a role that could not have been played successfully without reliance upon personal bonds of kinship and association. A central bureaucracy administered the holdings of the sultan, but the greater part of urban concerns in fact came under the jurisdiction of the amīrs. While the city had a governor who was the leading administrator, other amīrs had independent duties coordinate with his that served to hold his power in check. [25] Some of these duties were official, but many others simply fell to them as a result of the fact of their economic power. For example, they were the only class capable of carrying out public works. (Not only materials but manpower was involved, for the army was the only organized body that could conveniently be called upon to provide unskilled labor). Waterworks, vital to urban life, received regular attention, although there was no planning to speak of, and streets and roads tended to be poorly looked after, while buildings were erected with more of an eye to the glory of their founders than to public welfare. Thus the fortunes of the town were in large part left to the discretion of these men who accepted or rejected traditional obligations as they chose. In managing their vast holdings, in governing and policing urban quarters, they enlisted the services of merchants, *ᶜulamāʾ*, and local leaders. No member of society lay outside the network that they manipulated through patronage. As Lapidus has written:

> The Mamluks governed not by administration, but by holding all of the vital social threads in their hands. [26]

In the above section we considered at some length the Mamlūk establishment as an institution that was, by very definition, separate from the rest of society. Many important aspects of the social structure are obscured however, if one concentrates upon this idealized view of the organization. True, recruitment depended upon restriction and

---

[25] I. M. Lapidus, *Muslim Cities in the Later Middle Ages*, p. 48.
[26] *Ibid.*, p. 187.

exclusiveness, but nourishment depended upon connections. In this respect family ties, despised where recruitment was concerned, were of utmost importance. In fact, it is hard to understand the working of the economy and the implications the economic system carried for Mamlūk social structure without reference to them.

Paralleling the attempts of sultans to secure the succession for their sons, Mamlūk feudatories found means to secure property for their descendants, means that frequently were not separate from family considerations, as many *ᶜulamāᵓ* themselves were sons of amīrs. For example, certain estates were classed not as lands granted by the state, but as "charity." This form of charity, a kind of pension (*ar-rizaq al-jayshīya*) could be received by old amīrs who could no longer perform their military functions, their wives, widows, and sons, the *awlād an-nās.* But as pensions could be taken by the state, feudatories who wished to help their offspring often succeeded in converting their fiefs to independent lands (*amlāk*) which could be passed on according to the patrilineal principle of inheritance outlined by the *sharīᶜa.* The *ᶜulamāᵓ* of the time abrogated the time-honored Islamic rule which forbade the transformation of tribute-paying lands which belonged to the state, into tithe-paying lands of independent ownership. Lands reverting to the state for any reason could be sold by the caliph and these were often purchased by the sultan and granted as gifts to his amīrs. These, as well as *waqf*s, or religious endowments, founded for the sake of mamlūks, remained in the family of the grantee. The manipulation of *waqf* was a key that gave access to vast amounts of wealth. All one needed was the consent of the *qāḍī* and the cooperation of professional witnesses to make good one's claims. [27] As the Mamlūk period drew to a close, the greater part of the lord's possessions came to be, through the above channels, independent estates rather than temporarily held military fiefs. [28]

While it is true that, even as a sultan secured power through and for his mamlūks, so the amīr could secure property by the agency of his force of freedmen, the factor of blood relationship provided a more subtle but not less effective means to power. It produced a vast network

---

[27] While the *ᶜulamāᵓ* might be reluctant to cooperate for moral reasons, often they would be persuaded to comply. In A.D. 1330 the amīr Qawṣūn obtained a bath that was in *waqf* by having adjacent properties torn down and then bringing in professional witnesses to testify that the bath had no value, and that the ruins were dangerous and should be removed (I. M. Lapidus, *Muslim Cities in the Later Middle Ages*, p. 61).

[28] A. N. Poliak, *Feudalism in Egypt, Syria, Palestine, and the Lebanon*, pp. 37-40.

of ties to be tapped not only at home but abroad. Patently, the continued existence of the Mamlūk house depended upon its foreign connections. It would be difficult indeed to understand why Mamlūks preferred to marry slave girls of their own stock if this were not the case. The Circassian supremacy was not separate from the preference of the sultans for their compatriots over Mamlūks of other nations and the advancement of this stock at the Egyptian court was accomplished partly through the practice of establishing marital ties. Ayalon says that the Circassian sultans secured their power not only through the appointments of their own brothers in slavery (*khushdāshīya*) and their mamlūks (*mushtarawāt*) to high positions, but by *appointing their blood relations as well.* [29] It is entirely possible that the struggles over the sultanate between the *mushtarawāt* and *qarānīṣ* (mamlūks of former sultans) were intensified by the fact that some of the latter had had kinship ties with the previous ruler but not with the incumbent, and therefore felt that the right to rule belonged to them. The overt attempts to adhere to the Mamlūk principles of recruitment and inheritance may well indicate a strong kinship principle lurking in the background. [30]

The Mamlūk elite group, like any other group, included marginal persons on its fringes, if only by virtue of the fact that the establishment could not expand, through natural population increase or other kinds of recruitment, beyond the point at which it was no longer able to control efficiently or be supported by the resources upon which it depended. The *awlād an-nās*, leading a life of luxury and ease in the

---

[29] See "Studies on the Structure of the Mamluk Army," p. 207. Elsewhere he writes:

> "... The immigration of relatives reached particularly large proportions from the middle of the fifteenth century onwards. The sources bearing on the period in question contain numerous references to relatives being brought over, sometimes singly, but usually in groups ... These older immigrants frequently attained high posts as amīrs, or at least as *khāṣṣakīya* without being slaves and without undergoing training in the military schools. Indeed, it would be no exaggeration to call the second half of the Circassian period 'the period of rule by brothers-in-law and relatives.' " ("The Circassians in the Mamluk Kingdom," *Journal of the American Oriental Society, LXIX* (1949), p. 144).

[30] Even Circassian sultans who were well aware that sons appointed by their fathers were regularly deposed by Mamlūks who disputed the succession, continued the practice of designating their sons as heirs. Ayalon notes that "this fact arouses the astonishment of Ibn Taghrībirdī who can find no explanation for it" ("The Circassians in the Mamluk Kingdom," p. 139, n. 32). Evidently the hereditary principle was stronger than the overt characteristics of political life would indicate. The fact that, in the Ottoman period, the kinship principle took little time to reassert itself reinforces this view. For further theoretical consideration of this point see below, p. 389, n. 2.

first generation, and softened by the deliberate withholding of any responsibilities which were the domain of the elite, in the second and third generations became merged with the Egyptian populace. [31]

Not all the *awlād an-nās*, however, were on the fringes of the lower orders. An important part of the middle class, bureaucrats, scholars, and intellectuals, were the sons of Mamlūks as we shall see later. Despite the preference for Circassian brides, the Mamlūks married the daughters of *qāḍī*s and wealthy merchants when it suited them. In the urban situation the elite, even though they represented the strongest military force, could not remain entirely disassociated with groups who controlled other kinds of authority and resources. In the next two chapters we will attempt to explore liaisons between these classes.

As a conclusion to this analysis of the Mamlūk establishment, it is interesting to refer to Ibn Khaldūn's contemporary discussion of *ᶜaṣabīya* (group solidarity). According to him:

> (Respect for) blood ties is something natural among men, with the rarest exceptions. It leads to affection for one's relations and blood relatives, (the feeling that) no harm ought to befall them nor any destruction come upon them. One feels shame when one's relatives are treated unjustly or attacked, and one wishes to intervene between them and whatever peril or destruction threatens them ... Clients and allies belong in the same category. The affection everybody has for his clients and allies results from the feeling of shame that comes to a person when one of his neighbors, relatives, or a blood relation in any degree (of kinship) is humiliated. *The reason for it is that a client (master) relationship leads to close contact exactly, or approximately in the same way, as does common descent* (italics mine). It is in that sense that one must understand Muḥammad's remark, "Learn as much of your pedigrees as is necessary to establish your ties of blood relationship." It means that pedigrees are useful only in so far as they imply the close contact that is a consequence of blood ties and that eventually leads to mutual help and affection. Anything beyond that is superfluous. [32]

Thus neither descent alone, nor any legal tie can establish solidarity in the absence of close contact between parties. Both the institution of the family and the Mamlūk *bayt* entered into group relations among

---

[31] Lacking, moreover, the status attached to the foreign born, they were called "*muwallad* (native born)," or nicknamed "*ᶜAbdallāwī*," i.e., degenerate or good-for-nothing as soldiers or administrators (Memorandum of Yacoub Artin Pasha in William Muir, *The Mameluke or Slave Dynasty of Egypt, 1260-1517* (London: Smith, Elder, and Co., (1896), p. 226).

[32] *The Muqaddimah*, I, pp. 264-265.

the elite. By a curious process of inversion, sentiments and functions normally assigned to relations of descent came to characterize the relation of client and patron, while sons often experienced harsh deprivation. Their very exclusion from the highest ranks forced them to find positions elsewhere. *Thus powerful kinship bonds that would otherwise have served only to consolidate the elite remained free to be exploited in the "infiltration" of society.*

But ties of kinship both reinforced the Mamlūk system and weakened it. As long as the sultan could utilize affinal and agnatic bonds to further his own interests, and secure control of the country's resources for his mamlūks, all was well. Following this generation however, the struggle arose between his mamlūks and his kinsmen. If the succeeding ruler, son or slave of his predecessor, did not assert himself with a strong hand on behalf of his own freed slaves, his authority, as well as the resources of the empire, slipped away to the descendants of former sultans and powerful amīrs. The last chapter of this section will deal with the subsequent development of the Mamlūk organization.

The extended, effective network established and maintained through the peculiar means of denying hereditary rights to native-born sons served to make the Mamlūk elite as unapproachable as the caliphs of the grand days of Fāṭimid rule. Their exclusiveness however, was sanctioned by the fact of their power and efficiency rather than their sacredness, and their system of servitude rather than their system of descent.

CHAPTER EIGHT

THE NOTABLES AND THE BUREAUCRACY: SOCIAL ASPECTS OF RELIGION AND ADMINISTRATION

The Ayyūbid and Mamlūk periods saw the emergence of new cadres of power, for with the fall of the Baghdad caliphate and the subsequent institutional split between military and spiritual domains [1] the notables were enabled to exploit the latter as they never had before. Since the caliph himself was a puppet, many learned shaykhs, out of regard for the moral order, aided the sultans in the administration of their "grand estate" and legitimacy in fact came to be conferred upon the Mamlūk regime by the *ᶜulamāᵓ* and scholars who represented the schools of law (*madhāhib*).

1. *The Notables*

The Mamlūks were in control, but their acceptance of caliphal authority through the sultan's *bayᶜa* (pledge of homage) indicated agreement not only to defend Islam but to sustain its traditions. In return for protection and for revenues essential to the maintenance of the religious establishment that supported the social order, the *ᶜulamāᵓ* recognized each new sultan, and generally enforced his rule, conferring upon it a kind of prestige he did not command.

The great resource of the notables lay principally in two factors. First, there was the honor and esteem that sprang from spirituality, an element which, as we have seen, was of profound consideration in all social relations in the medieval period. In its strongest, most tangible

---

[1] It can be noted that this division became greater under the Mamlūks than it had been under the Ayyūbids, for during the latter regime, notables not only influenced decision making but often played a direct role in creating and guiding state policy. Thus in A.D. 1284, Muᶜīn ad-Dīn a vizier of aṣ-Ṣāliḥ Ayyūb who sprang from a Khurāsānian family of Shāfiᶜī scholars and Ṣūfīs, had even been appointed commander in chief of the army and was sent to Damascus on behalf of his master, equipped in royal state. The background of Ayyūbid princes who were the most educated rulers in Islam encouraged such direct reliance upon the intelligentsia. The Mamlūks however, who had a more limited outlook on account of their more exclusively military background, tended to treat indigenous notables with more reservation (R. Stephen Humphreys, "The Political Role of the ᶜUlamā' in the Age of the Ayyūbids," A paper delivered at annual meeting of the Middle East Studies Association Toronto, Canada, November, 1969).

form, it was *baraka*, or "blessedness" which a holy man could communicate by touch as well as by will to those with whom he chose to associate. In its least form, it was simply the literacy acquired from religious education that fitted one to take part in "social management." Secondly, there was the inescapable fact that only the notables, who hailed from every social group, from every stratum of society, native and foreign, knew the labyrinths, the nooks and cranies of the governed society, and the ways of getting things done.

What the notables exploited was their pivotal roles as middlemen. Through liaisons with the elite, they enhanced and validated their local status, often acquiring official appointment to office. One omnipresent leading notable was the *shaykh al-ḥāra* or *ᶜarīf* who represented the quarter. Appointed by the governor and subject to removal by the central authority, his leadership in large part continued to depend upon his securing assistance for his local clientele. Not only these but *qāḍī*s, *muḥtasib*s (market inspectors), shaykhs, hospital administrators, preachers, and prayer leaders were confirmed in office by the ruler.

Thus the notables served as channels of service, wealth, and prestige, channels that for all their irregularity and informality, were none the less effective; perhaps more effective than a more organized system would have been, for as we have seen the elite establishment itself was in a continual state of flux and patronage was not as a rule extended to the community as a whole, but rather from one individual to another in accord with special objectives and interests. The keys to success could be found in the households, the centers of elite factions, around which social relations revolved. In this system of accommodations, understandably the notables tended to cooperate with the Mamlūks and on comparatively few occasions opposed them. They saw their interest as depending in the long term upon preservation of the safety of the community. Traditionally acquainted with the horrors in which a breakdown of authority could result, they were content to preserve the status-quo as long as the rapacity of the elite did not get out of hand.

Who were these notables (*al-aᶜyān*) who managed society, and how were they recruited? In brief, they did not form a distinct class but hailed from all of the vast numbers of classes and status groups that composed society in its totality. Even despised persons, entertainers and beggars, had their connections with Ṣūfī shaykhs, and sons of *fallāḥīn* were known to attain esteemed posts in the religious establish-

2 As in the earlier periods, through education the son of a poor man might come to attain official position. We should not fail to emphasize that in Cairo education

ment. [2] In fact the notables could be ranked according to their respective spheres of influence and connections, as well as the official offices that they held. Strictly speaking, *al-aᶜyān* were the high ranking *ᶜulamāʾ* and bureaucrats while *an-nās* were officials of lower rank and power. The point is, however, that while the social position of one's family strongly influenced one's chances of attainment of strategic position, recruitment to the ranks of notability was never closed to any by virtue of his descent. The whole viability of the managing establishment depended on this fact.

It is true that a middle class, especially working through a religious institution, can in many cases balance and counteract the ruling elite as a coexistent force of power. It is worthwhile, in this connection, to consider in some detail the relationship between society's managers and their patrons. Ibn Khaldūn gave his assessment of the situation:

> We, at this time, notice that science and scientific instruction exist in Cairo in Egypt, because the civilization (of Egypt) is greatly developed and its sedentary culture has been well established for thousands of years. Therefore, the crafts are firmly established there and exist in many varieties. One of them is scientific instruction. This (state of affairs) has been strengthened and preserved in Egypt by the events of the last two hundred years under the Turkish dynasty, from the days of Ṣalāḥ ad-dīn b. Ayyūb on. This is because the Turkish amirs under the Turkish dynasty were afraid that their ruler might proceed against the descendants they would leave behind, in as much as they were his slaves or clients, and because chicanery and confiscation were always to be feared from royal authority. Therefore, they built a great many colleges, hermitages, and monasteries, and endowed them with mortmain endowments that yielded income. They saw to it that their children would participate in these endowments, either as administrators or by having some other share in them. (This was their intention) in addition to the fact that they were inclined to do good deeds and hoped for (a heavenly) reward for their aspirations and actions. As a consequence mortmain endowments became numerous, and the profit (from them) increased. Students and teachers increased in numbers because a large

---

was not the basis of social disparity that it was in many preindustrial cities. Persons of the lower class were able to obtain basic literary skills and become versed in the religious tradition through mosques which had schools for the children of the poor. Three hundred children were killed in the school of the Madrasa of Sultan Ḥasan when one of the minarets fell in A.D. 1360. Higher education too, was available to all Muslim men regardless of class. As Lane-Poole wrote:

> "The poorest youth … will be immediately welcomed, and will be taught all that the professors know … which is synonymous with all Muslim learning. He will receive the highest education that a Muslim can receive, by Muslim methods, without being called upon to pay a single piastre" (*Cairo, Sketches of Its History, Monuments, and Social Life*, (London, 1895), p. 186).

> number of stipends became available from the endowments. People traveled to Egypt from the ᶜIrāq and the Maghrib in quest of knowledge. Thus, the sciences were very much in demand and greatly cultivated there. [3]

Thus patronage was at the root of the efflorescence of learning and of the fortunes of the notables who controlled the bureaucracy. As in medieval Europe sons of "feudal lords" unable to inherit gained livelihood and refuge in the religious institution, though these were disinherited not through primogeniture, but through their birth as free Egyptians.

Although the way was not closed for indigent scholars or men of low rank to attain positions of authority and respect, and by no means all of the intelligentsia came from wealthy families, many of the Cairene intellectuals had close connections with the Mamlūks and often powerful foreign families as well. The ambiguous position of the sons of the elite as non-mamlūks of Mamlūk origin, led them often to secure their rank through education. For while money and family provided numerous opportunities for a successful existence, the scholar was respected in his own right and his achievements were not subject to confiscation by the government. When the father of Ibn Taghrī-Birdī died, "the sultan confiscated all his wealth and took into his service his many hundreds of mamlūks." [4]

Not just the *awlād an-nās*, but even members of the notability who were not of Mamlūk descent, were by and large committed to the regime, being unable, even if they would, to stand against the monopoly of military power. They assisted the elite with tax collection and with the justification of new collections and impositions through *fatwā*s (legal decisions) that served to meet changing demands as new situations arose. [5] Importantly they served to marshal mass support for defense of the community when external danger threatened. For instance, when the Mongols stormed Damascus, the shaykhs declared a Holy War and a bureau was established below the Citadel for the collection of funds and military recruitment. The populace was urged to take up arms and even scholars and students were ordered to learn to shoot, preparing for the worst.

---

[3] *The Muqaddimah*, II, p. 435.

[4] William Popper, Introduction to *History of Egypt 1382-1469* A.D. by Ibn Taghrī-Birdī, translated by William Popper (Berkeley, California: University of California Press, 1960), p. xv.

[5] Not infrequently these decisions entailed extraordinary loans or gifts to the sultan from *waqf* funds set aside for charitable purposes.

Nor was it only external threats with which they concerned themselves. As a group it was to their advantage to preserve internal security as well, and in this respect the violence of the amīrs and the struggles between factions were of no small consideration. As Lapidus has written:

> Their political doctrine held that a military state was necessary for the good order of society, and that in cases of civil war or interregnum loyalty to any particular regime had to be sacrificed if recognition of the apparent victor would minimize conflict. In case of invasions as well, the religious community was prepared to repudiate the Mamluks if they were defeated, and accept the apparent victor as their new sovereign. [6]

Thus the notables could play a significant part, even a decisive part, in contests between elite factions. At most, rebels and contenders needed recognition of legitimacy, substantial backing in the urban quarters, and access to financial resources to augment and replenish the allotment granted to them by the state; at least, they felt the need of good reports of historians and biographers to add to their fame. It was not unknown for the *ᶜulamāᵓ* to issue a *fatwā* justifying rebellion. At the end of the fourteenth century the amīr Mintāsh, supported by Turks and Mongols in his rebellion against Barqūq, called upon the chief *qāḍī*s, the *ᶜulamāᵓ*, and other notables to give him official sanction. [7] When they did not avow a cause openly, it is only reasonable to suppose that they took sides informally in factional disputes and court intrigues. Their interest in security notwithstanding, middlemen could profit greatly by playing patrons off against one another.

To the people, the notables generally preached obedience, yet when the masses were shamefully exploited by the elite, the religious establishment could be an important source of support. Religious authorities were often the only individuals who dared to speak out against the sultan. When Qalāūn's contractor employed violent methods to hurry the building of his hospital, compelling all artisans in the city to work on that and nothing else, and even forcing passers-by to stop and carry stones, the jurists declared prayer in the new mosque unlawful and the chief authority spoke out in no uncertain terms against the sultan and the minister responsible for such actions. [8]

---

6 *Muslim Cities in the Later Middle Ages*, p. 131.

7 *Ibid*., p. 134.

8 Al-Maqrīzī, *Khiṭaṭ*, II, pp. 406-407.

2. *Al-Azhar: Center of Notability and Learning*

The role of the *ʿulamāʾ* as supporters of the people cannot be appreciated without consideration of al-Azhar which came at this time to represent their establishment. As al-Azhar was the central mosque of Cairo, it was also the most sacrosanct place of refuge. On occasions of civil disturbance, epidemics, and other holocausts, the people stampeded there to pray and find safety. [9] For centuries the greatest institution of Muslim learning served an important function as a place of lodging for the poor and for those who could not find lodging elsewhere; for pilgrims, lawyers, merchants, and soldiers, and for the pious who merely sought blessing through residence in the Mosque.

Generally speaking, the grand resurgence of al-Azhar which made Cairo the center of Muslim learning, like the development of other institutions in the Mamlūk period, was due in no small part to the devastations of the Mongols in the East and the decline and final fall of Arab civilization in Spain. Specifically, it was due to the efforts of Baybars and the following sultans who sought not only to reinforce their position by the creation of centers of legal authority, but also to embellish their capital and court with the intelligentsia of the Muslim world. [10]

The Ayyūbids had introduced *madrasas* into Egypt, endowed the *ʿulamāʾ* with *waqf* properties, and had begun creation of a structured hierarchy by appointing officials and a chief *qāḍī*. [11] Mamlūk rulers continued the process of development by appointing a *qāḍī* for each law school (*madhhab*) (A.D. 1262-63), appointing professors and shaykhs

---

[9] In A.D. 1348, during the reign of al-Ḥasan, when the bubonic plague carried off between ten and twenty thousand persons a day in Cairo, the mosque was crowded as the shaykhs read the traditions of the Prophet continuously and invoked the mercy of God. Their efforts were so appreciated by al-Ḥasan that he requested one of his amīrs to renovate some of the porticoes, repair the pavements, and rearrange the chests and boxes that cluttered the loggias.

[10] As we have seen, Ṣalāḥ ad-Dīn, in his attempt to further the cause of Sunnī Islam, had deprived the Fāṭimid university of its importance by placing Sunnī *madrasas* in strategic locations. He had also moved the single Friday service allowable in Shāfiʿī law to the Mosque of al-Ḥākim from al-Azhar rather than to allow this important function to be carried on in the major Fāṭimid center. By the time of Baybars, however, Shīʿism had lost its following and, as the founder of the new regime like most of the Turkish Mamlūks adopted the more relaxed Ḥanafī code, al-Azhar again became the site of the weekly congregational service.

[11] The Ayyūbids had formally recognized each of the four schools of law and had introduced that of the Ḥanbalīs who were without previous representation in Egypt. The Mamlūks, as a matter of policy, gave equal representation to all interpretations of Sunnī Islam.

of Ṣūfī orders, and by defining the jurisdiction of these and of their deputies. Under the Ayyūbids the chief *qāḍī* was always a Shāfiᶜī. Under the Mamlūks, the Shāfiᶜī *qāḍī*, as leader of the majority persuasion in the country, retained the most influence.

The schools of law became focal points of integration in the urban center, united by respect for the most prominent *qāḍīs* and professors and by international connections, for even as the various schools had reference to particular ethnic groups and regions of the Islamic world, so did they grow and prosper through the travels of students and scholars. They were, moreover, the most comprehensive intra-urban communities, standing between local quarters on the one hand, and the entire undivided *umma* on the other. The *madhāhib* had no power to tax or to govern in the strict sense, yet as they represented different interpretations of the law in ritual, commercial, and civil matters, their influence shaped the pattern of social relations. While it is doubtful that a great deal of social interaction took place on the ground of allegiance to separate persuasions, it is true that all Sunnī Muslims were members of one *madhhab* or another and looked to its leaders for authority and guidance.

For their part, the Mamlūks looked to al-Azhar and to education in general to justify their social order. In the first place, Islam was a new faith to them and religious training formed the initial part of the education of every Mamlūk. So essential was the Islamic faith to the elite, that biographers were not allowed to write about their Christian past or to mention the date of their conversion. [12] Moreover, as the Mamlūks retained their Turkish language and culture, al-Azhar formed an important function in preserving the study of the Arabic language as well as in making contributions to theology and law.

The internal organization of al-Azhar reflected the social divisions of the urban center. At the highest level, there were representatives of each of the four *madhāhib*. The Shāfiᶜīs and Ḥanafīs competed for the rectorship, the former representing the national interpretation, the latter representing the Tatars, Circassians, and Turks who were the government. The Mālikīs who lived chiefly in Upper Egypt and the Delta and had North African connections, held respected positions, while the Ḥanbalīs being insignificant in numbers, were represented but never presented a powerful front. [13]

---

[12] A. N. Poliak, "The Influence of Chingiz-Khan's Yāsa Upon the General Organization of the Mamluk State," p. 805.

[13] K. Vollers, "Al-Azhar," *Encyclopaedia of Islam*, 1913.

In terms of "personnel" the schools thus were organized as study groups centered on *ᶜulamāʾ*, their cadres of students and clients, their patrons and admirers, their followings of respectable people in the quarters, and of their deputies, notaries, clerks, and witnesses who served in bureaucratic capacities of law and management that stretched out into society at large. Among the student body in the mosque, there were territorial groups most of whom had their own *ḥārāt* (quarters) and *arwiqa* (porticoes). While some lived outside al-Azhar, others slept in the court or loggias. Special endowments often were set aside for the welfare of specific groups (*ṭawāʾif*). Thus al-Maqrīzī says that there were special porticoes for the Persians, people from districts of the Egyptian countryside, and from the Maghrib. [14] In the chronicles we often hear of "boorish Upper Egyptians," "restless Syrians," and "fanatic Maghribīs" becoming involved in brawls and quarrels over grants, gifts, sectarian disputes, or national differences. [15] As residents of al-Azhar who contributed to the unrest we should not fail to mention the beggars, loafers, and traveling men who took refuge there under cover of piety and were responsible for robberies and other disturbances especially on the nights of the great festivals. In A.D. 1415 there were seven hundred and fifty poor "students and Ṣūfīs living in al-Azhar whom the supervisor turned out with their boxes and book rests." [16]

The object of education at al-Azhar was, of course, not research but rather the transmission of acquired learning. The medieval curriculum was divided into two major parts: the linguistic and revealed sciences, and the rational sciences. [17] From the Mamlūk period onward, linguistic and revealed sciences formed the basis of formal education. To be sure, some courses in medicine were taught in hospitals, while astronomy and higher mathematics were taught to special students in some colleges. These fields, however, never had a place in the orthodox curriculum and progress in the natural sciences was usually the result of private instruction and personal effort. Thus the focal point of

[14] *Khiṭaṭ*, II, p. 276.

[15] K. Vollers, "Al-Azhar," *Encyclopaedia of Islam*, 1913.

[16] A. S. Tritton, *Materials on Muslim Education in the Middle Ages* (London: Luzac & Co., 1957), p. 120.

[17] Ibn Khaldūn speaks of the "sciences that are wanted *per se*," that is, interpretation of the Qurʾān, the science of *ḥadīth* (traditions), jurisprudence, speculative theology, and the physical and metaphysical sciences of philosophy. Philology, arithmetic, and logic were regarded as auxiliary to the first group. He states that "whenever the (auxiliary sciences) cease to be (auxiliary to the other sciences), they abandon their purpose and occupation with them becomes an idle pastime" (*The Muqaddimah*, III, p. 299).

teaching at al-Azhar was the law and the institution remained a bastion of legal authority and a center of conservatism.

Many persons who were critical of the prevailing moral order expressed their grievances in non-orthodox associations. For instance, another type of religious organization which we are to consider in detail in the next section of this book first became a political force during this period. This was the dervish order or Ṣūfī brotherhood, which attained special popularity among the lower classes. Ṣūfī shaykhs, many of whom were associated with al-Azhar, were particularly adept at acquiring local followings. In Mamlūk times the "priors" of many brotherhoods were foreigners and all were appointed by the sultan so that he could maintain authority over them. Even then, however, there were incidents, and in A.D. 1496 the Ṣūfīs of one establishment revolted against their leader. Often, under the aegis of religion, these leaders, sincere or otherwise, tried to stir up the masses and initiate popular uprisings. Things were not so different from ᶜAbbāṣid and Fāṭimid times after all.

Cairo's attraction for intellectuals the world over was well known. The Ayyūbids had recruited professors from all over the Muslim world to teach in the *madrasa*s of the city. From Spain and the Maghrib they came, from Jerusalem, Mosul, Ḥamāh, and from the countries of the East. [18] Library facilities and the opportunity to meet and study under the leading authorities in all fields drew scholars from the farthest reaches of the Muslim world. As Ibn Khaldūn wrote:

> Traveling in quest of knowledge is absolutely necessary for the acquisition of useful knowledge and perfection, through meeting authoritative teachers (shaykhs) and having contact with (scholarly) personalities. [19]

As in commercial endeavors, the richness of intellectual contribution depended considerably upon experience in foreign parts as well as upon connections with centers of political power. Sons of mamlūks or

---

[18] I. M. Lapidus, "Ayyūbid Religious Policy and the Development of the Schools of Law in Cairo," *Colloque international sur l'histoire du Caire* (Cairo: General Egyptian Book Organization, 1974), p. 284. Research on 4,600 biographies of *ᶜulamā*ᵓ who were resident in Cairo during the fifteenth century indicates that most of those who originated outside the city came from the central Delta (Gharbīya and Minūf) or districts of Damascus, Jerusalem, and Aleppo. The majority of foreign-born bureaucrats were Syrians, while many Ṣūfīs were Iranians and Anatolians (Carl Petry, "The Geographic Origins and Residence Patterns of the ᶜUlemaᵓ of Cairo during the Fifteenth Century," A paper delivered at the annual meeting of the Middle East Studies Association, Milwaukee, Wisconsin, November, 1973).

[19] *The Muqaddimah*, III, p. 308.

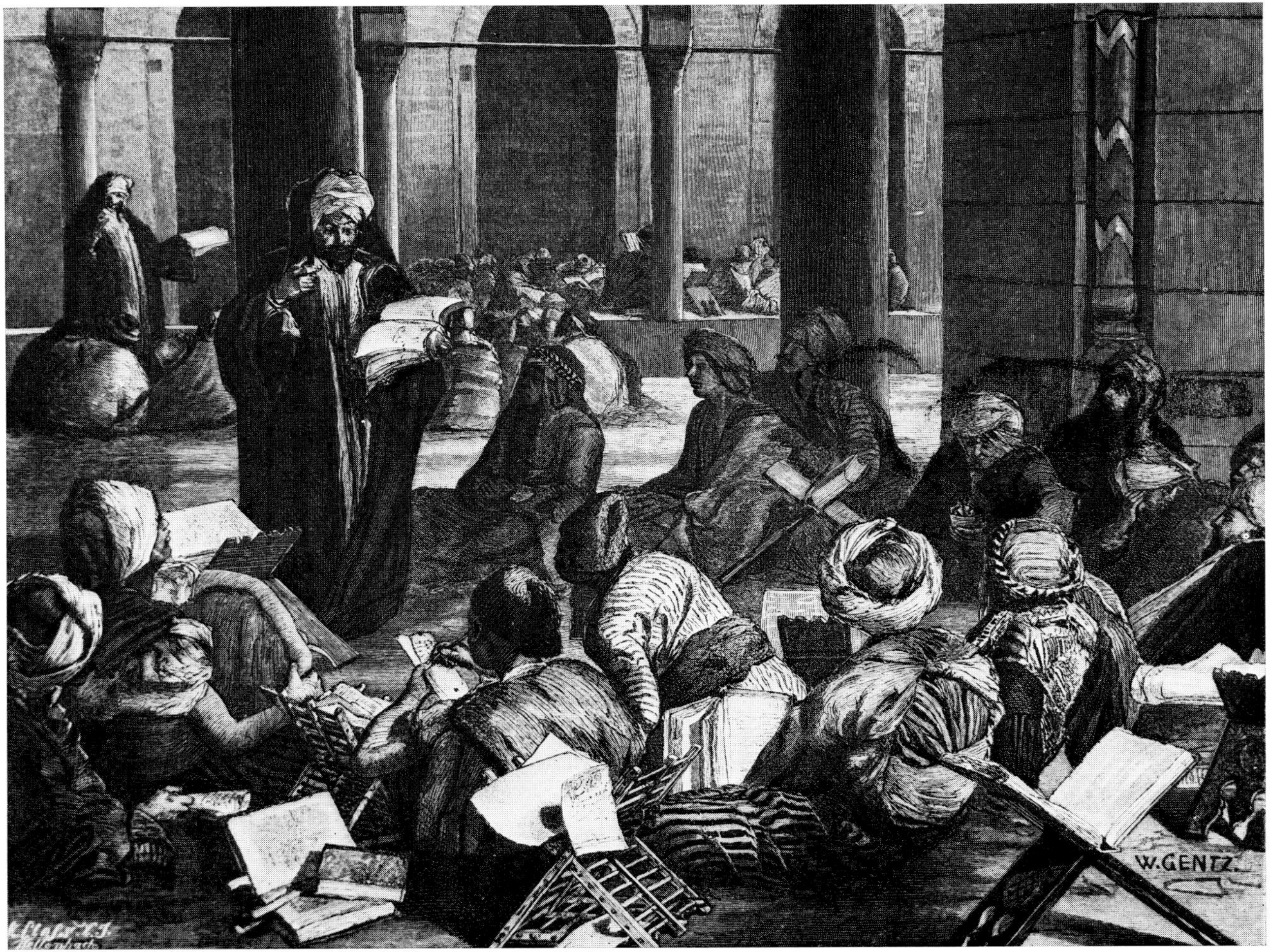

9. A Lecture at al-Azhar.

rich merchants were most able to benefit from travel. Those who came to study at the colleges and libraries of Cairo could not help but contribute to the culture of the town, adding vastly to the store of knowledge. The careers of the intellectuals of the period illustrate the importance of international connections as well as patronage, and remind us of the cosmopolitan character of this society.

Ibn Khaldūn himself, springing from a worthy family of scientists and scholars in Muslim Spain, spent most of his life in North Africa before coming to Cairo. Fleeing from an unpleasant political situation in Tunis, he left for Egypt in A.D. 1382, at the age of fifty, to build up a position for himself there and devote himself exclusively to scholarship. He soon came to the attention of Sultan Barqūq who had just begun his reign and was anxious to add the illustrious author of *The Muqaddima* to his entourage. "From the time of my arrival in Egypt on," wrote Ibn Khaldūn, "I enjoyed the favor of the Sultan. He let me forget my separation and remoteness from my native land." [20] He had many private audiences with Barqūq and enjoyed the latter's confidence to the extent that he twice occupied the post of chief *qāḍī* of the Mālikī school. Ibn Taghrī-Birdī said of him:

> Ibn Khaldūn was exceedingly strict. He ignored the intercession of high-ranking people of the country and refused to hear the appeals of the rich. For that reason they began to speak against him before the Sultan until he was dismissed as judge. [21]

The house of Ibn Khaldūn became a center for visitors from the Maghrib and his connections with the West made his services invaluable to the rulers who granted him hospitality, including Tamurlane, for whom he wrote a geography of North Africa.

Al-Maqrīzī too, (b. A.D. 1364), though a native Cairene, began his career as a deputy *qāḍī* and later became the leader of tradition at the Muʾayyadīya *madrasa.* He was transferred to posts in Damascus for ten years, but later returned to Cairo were he devoted himself to his studies. His pupil, Ibn Taghrī-Birdī (b. A.D. 1411) was the son of a Turkish slave of Barqūq. Besides making copious contributions to the history of Egypt, he served as governor of Aleppo and Damascus. Ibn Iyās (b. A.D. 1448) was the grandson of a Turkish mamlūk of Barqūq who reached the rank of second *dawādār.* His great-grandfather on

---

[20] Quoted by Walter J. Fischel, "Ibn Khaldūn's Activities in Mamlūk Egypt (1382-1406)." *Semitic and Oriental Studies*, edited by Walter J. Fischel (Berkeley, Calif.: University of California Press, 1951), p. 108.

[21] *Ibid.*, p. 112.

his mother's side had governed Tripolis, Aleppo, and Damascus under Sultan Ḥasan. His father was one of the *awlād an-nās* who managed to maintain a substantial fief and allowance under Qāyt-Bey and Ibn Iyās himself was related by birth and by marriage to many of the elite of Egypt.

3. *The Economic Rewards of Notability*

It is suitable at this point to take into account sources from which notables derived their income, for economic realities influenced in large part not only recruitment and performance but the extent to which they, as middlemen, could effectively maneuver. Generally speaking the economic power of the *ᶜulamāᵓ* had roots as diverse as their social connections.

We saw in the first part of this book that an early ideal of Islam was the independence of the *ᶜulamāᵓ* from state support and that a number of *qāḍī*s even refused to accept such "tainted money" as salaries. This attitude never disappeared entirely but religious officials progressively enriched themselves through their offices. In A.D. 1325 a *qāḍī* was paid a salary of 198,000 dirhams annually, nearly three hundred times that of a worker or minor functionary. A preacher received 60,000 and professors from 30,000 to 60,000 dirhams a year, while lesser scholars, shaykhs, reciters, and prayer leaders would earn only from twenty to one hundred dirhams monthly.[22]

Thus with regard to salary, they ranged from the very rich to the very poor.[23] In actuality, however, salary in many cases was but a fraction of total income. Much could be derived from fees customarily attached to functions they performed, to say nothing of "gifts in payment for services rendered." Their functions in tax collection were also an important source of revenue. *Muḥtasib*s (market inspectors)

---

[22] I. M. Lapidus, *Muslim Cities in the Later Middle Ages*, pp. 138-139.

[23] Ibn Khaldūn made his own investigation into this matter and emerged with an idealistic impression of the state of affairs. He wrote:

> "Persons who are in charge of offices dealing with religious matters, such as judge, mufti, teacher, prayer leader, preacher, muezzin, and the like, are not as a rule very wealthy ... Furthermore, because the things (the religious officials) have to offer are so noble, they feel superior to the people and are proud of themselves. Therefore, they are not obsequious to persons of rank, in order to obtain something to improve their sustenance. In fact, they would not have time for that. They are occupied with those noble things they have to offer and which tax both the mind and the body. Indeed, the noble character of the things they have to offer does not permit them to prostitute themselves openly. They would not do such a thing. As a consequence, they do not, as a rule, become very wealthy" (*The Muqaddimah*, II, pp. 334-335).

collected taxes, *qāḍīs* took oaths in certification of payment, and professional witnesses recorded contracts and transactions.

Nor should we fail to mention the numerous donations they received on account of their piety and the spiritual power (*baraka*) that they possessed. Some especially adept divines were said to subsist exclusively by this means and even affluent *ᶜulamāʾ* were given gifts of clothing and food on the occasion of festivals. [24]

Their most important source of wealth, however, which they controlled independently, was the administration of *awqāf*. Some *waqf* properties (*waqf khayrī*) were endowments for charitable purposes such as the upkeep of mosques, shrines, and hospitals, and wealth set aside for the support of widows, orphans, and the indigent; while others (*waqf ahlī*) were set aside for the benefit of the descendants of the founder although usually a percentage of such revenues went to charitable causes. *ᶜUlamāʾ* could and did benefit either as recipients or administrators, since often the terms of the *waqf* allowed distribution of revenues at their discretion, especially if the beneficiaries specified originally had died out. Through control of *waqf*, moreover, they derived extra benefits from their Mamlūk patrons who not only provided for their descendants by this means, but were wont to appropriate *waqf* holdings for themselves through the agency of the *qāḍī*. We saw in the previous chapter how the amīrs solicited favors from the notables in this regard.

In the manipulation of the office of *qāḍī* we can see the implications of appointment to a high post. The *qāḍī* had not only to decide cases of civil and criminal law and of inheritance, and to administer the *awqāf*, but held guardianships of minors, unmarried women, and persons who were held to be legally incompetent. The chief *qāḍī* was

---

[24] In a much later period Edward Lane was to write:

"(Before the Napoleonic invasion) a sheykh who had studied in the Azhar, if he had only two boys, sons of a moderately rich fellâḥ to educate, lived in luxury: his two pupils served him, cleaned his house, prepared his food, ... followed him whenever he went out ... and in every case treated him with the honour due to a prince ... and as he passed along the street ... passengers often pressed towards him to implore a short ejaculatory prayer on their behalf; and he who succeeded in obtaining this wish believed himself especially blessed: if he passed by a Frank riding, the latter was obliged to dismount: if he went to a butcher, to procure some meat (for he found it best to do so, and not to send another), the butcher refused to make any charge; but kissed his hand, and received as an honour and a blessing whatever he close to give" (*An Account of the Manners and Customs of the Modern Egyptians* (London, Everyman's Library, 1908), pp. 218-219).

required, according to Muslim law, to be a scholar and of blameless reputation. Since, however, he was frequently caught between his moral obligations and the demands and expectations of the elite, the office of *qāḍī* was avoided by many capable men who refused to compromise their principles. Judges posts became venal offices by the latter part of the fifteenth century.[25] Many judges were ignorant and corrupt and Muslim society chronically suffered from their unscrupulous behavior.[26]

Appointed to office by the sultan, the *qāḍī* himself was responsible for appointing his subordinates within his school to manage its properties and to serve in its courts. The sultans periodically intervened to curb unwarranted expansion as the practice of making appointments was subject to rank abuse.[27] The institution of selection of professional witnesses in particular led to much corruption. Limits were imposed on the number of witnesses that could occupy a shop in the market and the regime decreed that *qāḍī*s should select them only from their own schools but little could be done to change the ways of getting things done. The office of *wakīl*, the agent who was in charge of access to the *qāḍī*'s chambers was abolished because of the prevalence of bribe-taking.[28]

The *qāḍī*s, like the great merchants, often belonged to families specializing in their occupation, and relative freedom from confiscation permitted the establishment of dynasties. Thus the learned *imām* Badr ad-Dīn ibn Jamāᶜa was followed by his son, and the pious Taqī ad-Dīn al-Akhnāᵓī was descended from a long line of *qāḍī*s.[29]

As in the early periods the *ᶜulamāᵓ* did not hesitate to play the market. Possessing much capital, they made substantial investments in commercial endeavors, even coming partially to fill the gap when the great merchant families declined in the fourteenth and fifteenth centuries owing to taxation, forced loans, and confiscations. As in former

---

[25] I. M. Lapidus, *Muslim Cities in the Later Middle Ages*, p. 136.

[26] On the other hand, we must point out that many notable and worthy men were *qāḍī*s under the Mamlūks; for the administration of justice at height of Cairo's cultural splendor could not but profit from the presence of the intellectuals connected with its seat of religious learning. Ibn Baṭṭūṭa remarks specifically upon the nobility of the *qāḍī*s of his time (*The Travels of Ibn Baṭṭūṭa*, I, pp. 55-56).

[27] In A.D. 1380, the number of deputies for each *qāḍī* was set at a maximum of four, but thirty-six years later the number had risen to 200! The sultan then again limited them drastically, permitting the Shāfiᶜī and Ḥanāfī *qaḍī*s to have ten each, the Mālikī *qāḍī* five, and the Ḥanbalī, four (I. M. Lapidus, *Muslim Cities in the Later Middle Ages*, p. 137).

[28] *Ibid.*, p. 137.

[29] Ibn Baṭṭūṭa, *The Travels of Ibn Baṭṭūṭa*, I, p. 55.

times there was considerable overlap between the *ᶜulamāᵓ* and the merchants. In a sample of about 600 merchants, 225 were practicing shaykhs, *qāḍī*s, *muḥtasib*s witnesses, preachers, and prayer leaders. The most common combination of roles was that of merchant-teacher. [30] As formerly, a number of biographies of notables mention occupations in the crafts, from stoneworking to soap making and pharmacology.

For economic considerations and in principle, the notables usually stood against all forms of arbitrary governmental interference in economic life, notwithstanding their readiness to play the potentialities of their offices for what they were worth. Basically, many even resisted the time-honored contention of the military elite that all property belonged to the sultan who governed in the name of the *umma* and denied to him the right of eminent domain. Thus they managed to curb to some extent the power of the elite, both through the independent source of relatively inviolable power that they controlled and their breadth and foresight of viewpoint, shaped through the economic challenge and experience of every rank and division of society.

4. *The Bureaucracy*

Aside from the religious authorities and intellectuals, a large bureaucracy formed part of the upper middle class. No single administrative body dealt with urban concerns but rather the jurisdiction was divided between the deputies of the sultan and those of amīrs. Some of these bore the title of *qāḍī*, perhaps because in their supervisory capacities, they were responsible for maintaining conformity with the *sharīᶜa*. Here again, there seems to have been a considerable degree of overlap between the executive, administrative, and the judicial, religious spheres. In a number of cases the post of *qāḍī* (as judge) was attained after a career of secular administrative experience rather than legal experience of a more strictly religious nature. [31]

In the long run, the bureaucratic class served to guard the populace against the depredations of alien rulers whose primary, if not sole, interest was self-aggrandisement. It also served to mitigate somewhat the effects of competition among the elite, for while the rulers owned the products of the land, they did not have direct access to its resources and their administration. The bureaucrats, however, were more dependent upon the favor of their Mamlūk employers than the religious notables.

---

30 I. M. Lapidus, *Muslim Cities in the Later Middle Ages*, p. 109.
31 *Ibid.*, p. 138.

Although some offices remained the province of "Lords of the Sword" (*aṣḥāb as-suyūf*) who were trained exclusively to fill military functions, the important posts of private secretary (*kātib as-sirr*) and the head of the chancellory (*ṣāḥib dīwān al-inshāʾ*) were never given to mamlūks, Arabs, or sons of mamlūks, but were reserved for civilians, often Christians or Jews, or converts from these religions to Islam.[32] Thus as in former times the rulers of Cairo placed the primary offices of state in the hands of capable individuals who, because of their status as non-Muslims, could not pose a threat to the military. Thousands of clerks and technicians in the bureaus of the sultans and the households of amīrs were scribes whose families had been for generations employed in government service. The key organizational factor, here again, was not an overarching institutional structure, but patronage which gave flexibility and enabled individuals to exploit their positions in society at large.

The bureaucracy was, of course, the place for those whom the Mamlūks favored and thus the occupants of official positions tended to be from varied backgrounds depending upon the preferences of the rulers of the time and the distribution of power between factions. Sometimes they were of the commercial class and we have already noted the attempts on the part of merchants to establish ties with governmental authorities. Qāyt-Bey rewarded the son of the slave dealer who had sold him to a high official for fifty gold pieces by appointing him to superintend the building of his mosque.

5. *The Dhimmīs in the Mamlūk Regime*

While the control of the major institutions of notability and bureaucracy was in Muslim hands, it is well known that many important scholars and bureaucrats were Christian or Jewish. Some families are known to have retained authority for three or four generations and, as among Muslims, training was gained through apprenticeship or frequently by serving as a deputy for a relative. Education among *dhimmī*s followed a similar pattern to that of Muslims.[33]

---

[32] M. Soberneim, "Mamlūks," *Encyclopaedia of Islam*, 1913.

[33] Muslim writers do not say much about education among the religious minorities, but Joseph ibn Judah ibn ʿAqnīn, who died in 1226, described the Jewish system of basic education which was like that of orthodox Islam in general outline. We can assume that a school was often attached to the synagogue which served as a focal point for the Jewish community. Pupils began with the study of letters, the reading of the law, the Prophets, and moral poetry. Later boys read the Talmud, studied its meaning, and learned to refute the opinions of the gentiles. Those who did well went

Not only did *dhimmīs* serve the leading amīrs but they filled the important chancery posts assigned to them in the *dīwān* of the sultan. The former commonly served as a means to the latter, for usually the sultan did not ask a fallen minister to designate a successor, but would assemble the secretaries of his amīrs and choose one of them. [34]

Their patrons depended on them greatly. Ibn Taghrī-Birdī, writing in the fifteenth century about a bureaucratic family of Coptic converts, indicates the extent of their political influence:

> Their family is well-known in the secretariat, and they now are the authorities inside the state, although others have the glory, they are the real ones and (are responsible for) the welfare and deciding the needs of the people. [35]

An important thesis of Part I was the waxing and waning of the influence of religious minorities in response to the policies of the ruling faction and to political and economic events. The situation is no different in the Ayyūbid and Mamlūk periods. In his written advice (*waṣīya*) to Tūrānshāh, Sultan aṣ-Ṣāliḥ Ayyūb had warned that the Coptic clerks intended to weaken the army and ruin the country. [36] The spirit of *jihād* aroused against the Crusaders quite naturally stimulated animosities against all Christians, as did later fears of an anti-Muslim Mongol-Christian alliance and a realization of the fate of Muslim communities in the Christian reconquest of Spain. Certainly the state was concerned about the non-Muslim communities within it and was apprehensive about their potential connections with foreign powers. [37]

---

on from dialectics to logic, arithmetic, geometry, optics, astronomy, music, mechanics, natural science, medicine, and metaphysics (A. S. Tritton, *Materials on Muslim Education in the Middle Ages*, p. 146). Among Jews as among Muslims, the religious law had priority to all other fields of study and each scholar of account had a firm ground in religious studies.

[34] D. Richards, "The Coptic Bureaucracy under the Mamlūks," *Colloque international sur l'histoire du Caire* (Cairo: General Egyptian Book Organization, 1974), p. 374.

[35] *Al-Manhal aṣ-Ṣāfī* quoted by D. Richards, "The Coptic Bureaucracy," p. 377.

[36] Hassanein Rabie, "The Size and Value of the *Iqṭā*ᶜ in Egypt, 564-741 A.H. 1169-1341 A.D.," *Studies in the Economic History of the Middle East*, edited by M. A. Cook (London: Oxford University Press, 1970), p. 130.

[37] Leaders of religious minorities were recommended by their communities but confirmed by state appointment. Qalqashandī cites an official *waṣīya* (warning) concerning the Patriarch's private comportment:

> " 'Let the Patriarch take special care not to shelter in his ecclesiastical foundations any suspicious stranger who may turn up, and let him not omit to inform us about any doubtful matter which comes to his notice, whether from close at hand

Fatwās were even issued to unite the people against the Copts holding office. M. Perlmann quotes a pamphlet, written by a Muslim law student and *muḥtasib*, issued under aṣ-Ṣāliḥ ibn Nāṣir in 1351:

> "The Copts declare that this country still belongs to them, and that the Muslims evicted them from it unlawfully. Then they often steal as much as they can from the state treasury in the belief that they are not doing wrong. As to the possibility of confiscation and punishment, torture, they hold that the chances of these happening to them are about equal to that of falling sick, that is to say, sickness does sometimes come upon a man, but is not likely to be frequent.
>
> They will deposit those funds in churches and monasteries and other such institutions of the unbelievers, for they are more entitled to these funds than are the Muslims ...." [38]

Here again is the economic motive of persecution and the same "frantic" behavior on the part of some Christians to take what they can to compensate for the large scale confiscations that periodically threaten their community. There can be no doubt that the custom of giving high office to non-Muslims irked pious Muslims a great deal, especially since, in the Eastern fashion, even commerce and law were carried on with the "personal touch." A little farther on we read that:

> "For (activity against Christians) is one of the greatest things to the glory of God, as the employment of these Christians in the bureaux of the Egyptian state is one of the greatest calamities. It causes the Christian religion to be exalted. Most Muslims have to apply to and stand before the gates of the dignitaries of state for decisions in their affairs. When a man has some business which is in the hands of the diwan of a certain chief, he is compelled to abase himself and ingratiate himself with the official in charge of that particular diwan, whether he be a Christian or a Jew or a Samaritan ... Thus, a man has to stand before a Christian, whilst the latter may remain seated for many hours,

---

or from afar. Equally, let him be very careful not to conceal any letter reaching him from an external ruler (sc. from the Christian monarchs), and not to correspond with external rulers or behave at all in a dangerous manner like this. Let him avoid the ocean and let him take care not to rush blindly into it; for he will be drowned; and let him take care not to accept anything which the raven's wing may bring to him from across the sea, for the raven croaks, announcing separation' " (quoted by C. E. Bosworth, "Christian and Jewish Religious Dignitaries in Mamlūk Egypt and Syria: Qalqashandī's Information on their Hierarchy, Titulature, and Appointment," *International Journal of Middle East Studies*, 3 (1972), p. 202).

[38] Asnawī quoted in M. Perlmann, "Notes on Anti-Christian Propaganda in the Mamlūk Empire," *Bulletin of the School of Oriental and African Studies*, X (1940-1942), p. 847.

> until he has come to a decision regarding the matter in hand, the Muslim blessing him, and being more polite towards him than he would be toward a learned shaykh." [39]

Opportunities for graft were extensive and the distinction between public and private wealth, between the wealth of the minister and that of the sultan, was not always observed. [40]

Moreover, the fact that non-Muslims were not prevented, as were Muslims, from taking interest gave the former a tremendous advantage economically. Asnawī points also to the alleged moral laxity of Christians, namely their wine-drinking and seduction of Muslim women; "Their influence starts when they are in the retinue of an amīr. They gradually worm their way into his household ..." [41] In A.D. 1314-1315 a shaykh who led one demonstration before the Citadel directly attacked the sultan accusing him of empowering the Christians in a way that enabled them to waste the wealth of the public treasury on expenses not sanctioned by the *sharīᶜa*. [42]

Demonstrations against Christians, probably led by lesser *ᶜulamāʾ* and leaders of popular orders, created considerable disturbance. In A.D. 1320 a number of churches were destroyed and anti-Christian demonstrations accompanied extensive incendiarism of buildings both in the city and the Citadel. Christians did not dare to venture into the streets in Christian attire and disguised themselves as Jews. When demonstrators clashed with the police, a *qāḍī* who was defending the Christians was stoned. The sultan, an-Nāṣir, who favored them also, decided to let the persecutors have their way until feeling died down, rather than to risk anarchy by antagonizing the masses. [43] Other rulers had less sympathy with minorities who held the purse strings. On learning of the tremendous wealth of churches and monasteries, and the extent

---

[39] Quoted in M. Perlmann, "Notes on Anti-Christian Propaganda," pp. 860-861.

[40] D. Richards, "The Coptic Bureaucracy under the Mamlūks," p. 375.

[41] Cited in M. Perlmann, "Notes on Anti-Christian Propaganda," p. 851. While the writer speaks out primarily against the Copts, and it was they who were traditionally the bureaucrats, we may speculate that some of these Christians may have been unconverted relatives and associates of Mamlūks who had followed their more fortunate countrymen to Egypt. It has been suggested that complaints against Christians were expressive of the social distress of a population chafing under a largely unsympathetic and alien rule.

[42] D. Richards, "The Coptic Bureaucracy under the Mamlūks," p. 378.

[43] D. S. Margoliouth, *Cairo, Jerusalem and Damascus*, pp. 92-93. Thus in 1321 the Zuhrī church in Old Cairo was destroyed when excavations around it ordered by an-Nāṣir left it exposed and the mob took the opportunity to demolish it (al-Maqrīzī, *Khiṭaṭ*, II, p. 512).

of their feudal holdings, Ṣarghitmish flew into a rage and decreed that the land be taken from them and bestowed upon his mamlūks. Christians were again accused of exerting an evil influence on Muslims. Steps were taken to humiliate them and their churches were demolished.

It is small wonder that a large number of Christians became Muslim during the Mamlūk period. The fourteenth century especially saw numbers of conversions. As one writer has put it:

> Conversions to Islam, always a steady trickle, now became a flood, and even regions like Upper Egypt, which adjoined the Christian region of Nubia and had long been a Coptic stronghold, became in majority Muslim. [44]

But let us note that conversion did not erase the stigma of Coptic descent or membership in Coptic society. Wives and daughters often retained their Christianity and important families continued to be linked by marriage ties. [45] After all, the animosities toward them did not spring from religious feeling *per se* but from political and economic motives and religious conversion was easier to accomplish than ethnic submersion. If the same families remained in authority, the feeling against them was not diminished. [46] In the words of al-Maqrīzī:

> The unbelievers turned Muslim at the point of the sword
> If left alone they are transgressors
> They saved their skin and goods,
> They are safe, *sālimūn*, but no *Muslimūn* [47]

It is difficult to discern, in conclusion, any well defined networks of interaction among the notables based upon religion *per se.* An investigation into the constitution of the bureaucracy, and the connections and careers of some of the individuals who made up the intelligentsia reveals the fact that a loose interplay of prestige, influence and

[44] C. E. Bosworth, "Christian and Jewish Religious Dignitaries in Mamlūk Egypt and Syria," pp. 65-66.

[45] It is true, nevertheless, that many made marriage ties with ᶜ*ulamā*ᵓ and with Mamlūk families (D. Richards, "The Coptic Bureaucracy under the Mamlūks," p. 378).

[46] As Perlmann has written:

> "Conversion ... (created) a hotbed of suspicion, distrust, and mockery. As a rule the Muslim Copt still adhered closely to his own people, and in many ways kept apart from the Muslims; whilst to the Muslim he remained what he had been, "al-Ḳibṭī al-miṣrī," for the change had been imposed upon him from without, and had in it little of personal conviction ... And such are more antagonistic towards Muslims than are the other Copts ... 'The contemptible amongst them, would with malice humiliate the Muslims to an extent impossible to him whilst he was a Christian' " ("Notes on Anti-Christian Propaganda," p. 858).

[47] *Khiṭaṭ*, II, p. 498.

authority, a generally tolerant attitude of "give and take," to some extent mitigated the importance of distinctions of class and status. Notables who represented local groupings based on religion or ethnicity played major roles in the factional drama basic to the total pattern of life.[48]

While in the case of Muslims, the influence of al-Azhar acted to some extent as a unifying principle, we have seen how there were basic popular factions within the mosque organization itself, often based upon ethnic interests. Although the religious establishment usually cooperated with the sultan, smaller popular associations were frequently less amenable to manipulation. In the case of non-Muslims, ethnic derivation seemed to be more relevant to status than religion itself. Although conversion opened the door to advancement, the ethnic correlates of religion tended to persist for a longer time.

Solidarity among groups which constituted the upper middle class was therefore largely dependent upon ethnic and kinship ties. It is no accident that the *awlād an-nās* produced some of the most important scholars of the time. Elite fathers provided for their sons with the help of the religious institution. Nor is it surprising that, in the face of confiscation, marriages were contracted between scholars, officials, and rich merchants.

There is little doubt that religion in the broad sense favored the existence of social mobility. The ideals of Islam in particular tended to override the influence of descent, and piety in general, whether Muslim, Christian, or Jewish, was associated in everyone's mind with trustworthy character. On the other hand, the fact that there was a considerable amount of friendly interaction between persons of different faiths did not mean that differences were ever obscured to the point of obliteration; the government, even in patronizing *dhimmī*s, never ceased to treat them in a frame of reference other than non-Muslim, while the populace continued to voice every grievance against Coptic and Jewish bureaucrats in religious terms.

[48] The marginality of these middlemen deserves some comment for the diversity of their experience served to encourage a unified framework for the social order. Capable individuals who were sons of Mamlūks and sons of *fallāḥīn*, native Cairenes and foreigners, Muslims and non-Muslims, played pivotal roles in the debt-structure of favors and services that tied together the disparate ranks of society. Yet understandably, when society exhibited a tendency to fractionate, to reassert group boundaries, and carefully built up alliances and chains of patronage were torn asunder, their marginality could be the cause of pain and frustration. International figures like Ibn Khaldūn experienced periods of rejection as well as appreciation for their services at the sultan's court while the favor shown to *dhimmī*s had its chronic ebb and flow.

CHAPTER NINE

THE DEVELOPMENT OF CRAFTS, COMMERCE, AND THE ROLE OF MERCHANTS

The city of the Mamlūk period, no less than the city of the preceding eras, owed many of its cultural achievements to the efforts of persons of the middle and lower orders. Despite the important role of the elite in the control of resources and major channels of communication, without merchants and craftsmen, the vigorous efflorescence of Islamic culture in the fourteenth and fifteenth centuries would never have taken place. For the Mamlūk Age was the age of commercial, artistic, and intellectual splendor as well as of ruthless and sanguine contests for power.

It is a curious contrast that the very men who were so prone to shed each other's blood and tyrannize over their subjects, at the same time delighted not only in luxurious opulence and the endowment of pious foundations but in delicately refined arts. But while the commercial and industrial ventures which formed an important part of economic prosperity were initially a response to the policies and demands of the elite, they also gave stimulus and encouragement to another class which became powerful in its own way, that of merchants and entrepreneurs.

For the elite, encapsulated as they were by rigid principles of military training and slave status, often did not have at their fingertips as much wealth as the "merchant princes" who were their contemporaries. Nor did they have their experience and connections. Medieval Cairo, as well as its military guardians, owed much of its well-being to the many individuals who so efficiently conducted its economic relations with foreign parts. Considering the magnitude of their achievement, it is little wonder that we have derived not only the word "check" from their vocabulary (*ṣakk*) but also the basic terms "traffic" and "tariff" which come from the Arabic words *tafrīq* and *taʿrīf* meaning respectively "distribution" and "information."

The fourteenth century in particular saw an efflorescence of commerce and the arts. Long-term fiscal stability led to relative constancy in the value of gold and silver and the price of wheat and other basic food products, [1] while the international spice trade bloomed at this

[1] There were about twenty dirhams to the gold dinar. The secular price of wheat ranged from fifteen to twenty dirhams per *irdabb* (one *irdabb* being equal to about five bushels) (I. M. Lapidus, *Muslim Cities in the Later Middle Ages*, p. 16).

time through the security which generally prevailed and the conclusion of commercial treaties. The period also saw an interdependence of Mamlūks and merchants that favored both parties. The regime could tax and it controlled the urban food supply, but did not itself manage these matters. Merchants like religious notables served as agents of the government not just in taxation but in buying and selling the holdings of the state.

1. *The Organization of the Market*

Official economic policy was shaped not just by the immediate interests of the elite or even the principles of religious law, but through broad considerations of the potentialities of the market and the relative contributions of different groups to the total picture. For the most part the commercial class was given a free hand and allowed to amass wealth as an incentive for their endeavors although the state, in return for the military protection and diplomatic advantages it afforded them, did not hesitate to tap their resources in time of need.

Control of urban markets was exercised through the office of the *muḥtasib* [2] and the *arīf*s and shaykhs whom he appointed from the crafts and trades. The tax farmer, (*ḍāmin*, guarantor), the scribe, [3] the witness, and the broker all had their parts to play. The office of the *muḥtasib* was conceived as having moral as well as legal functions. He was broadly empowered to see that fairness and honesty prevailed and could mete out punishment on the spot. He was to uphold the quality of manufactures, control prices, and collect a large part of the market taxes. The shaykhs and *ᶜarīf*s served informally to mediate state policy by advising the *muḥtasib*s about the condition of the market and the problems of the tradesmen and workers they represented. Although they assisted the *muḥtasib* in collecting taxes and were assigned certain local duties such as the transmission of the instructions of the governor (*wālī*) and the preparation of the markets for celebrations and public events, their responsibilities do not at this time seem to have been outlined very strictly.

What was the physical appearance of the Cairene *sūq*? An under-

[2] The *muḥtasib* (market inspector) seems originally to have been a Byzantine official. He does not appear in Egypt, however, until the Ayyūbid period.

[3] The scribe, a person of critical importance in a largely illiterate society, is frequently described as "a man worth consulting." With his ink pots, books, paper, and pens the scribe sat in certain places in the market, collecting taxes, advising clients, and transcribing documents official and unofficial.

standing of the conduct of business can be enhanced by an attempt to visaualize the environment of business activity. It was said that one could find 12,000 shops on the street leading from the northern edge of the Ḥusaynīya quarter to the tomb of Sayyida Nafīsa in the southern cemetery. [4] In this space, as we have seen, the greatest concentration of commercial enterprise occupied the part once enclosed by the walls of the Fāṭimid city, still protected by a heavy door that was closed at night. [5] One writer of the time said that the trash thrown into the rubbish heaps of the city every day was worth a thousand dinars. Another said that the wealth of Rome, Milan, Padua, Florence and four other cities like them would not measure up to half the wealth of Cairo. [6] Here, near the Khān al-Khalīlī, was the slave market, and farther up the street were the shops of butchers, grain and vegetable dealers. Thousands of itinerant cooks wandered in the streets of the city to supply the meals of residents as well as foreign visitors and many dishes were prepared by specialist cooks in the bazaar, for few people were equipped to prepare meals at home. [7]

The commercial city of the Mamlūk period is the city of *The Thousand and One Nights.* Every merchant's son who came to Cairo seeking his fortune stayed first at a *khān.* The Nazarene broker, coming from Baghdad with the merchandise of his city and of Mosul stays at the Khān of Masrūr. He conducts his business in the Qayṣarīya of Jahārkas, [8] an elegant *sūq* near the center of town. *The Nights* gives a realistic portrayal of the ways and means of doing business. The young man is advised by the shaykh of the brokers in the Qayṣarīya who says to him:

> "O my lord, I will tell thee how thou mayest make a profit of thy goods. Thou shouldst do as the merchants do and sell thy merchandise at credit for a fixed period, on a contract drawn up by a notary and duly witnessed; and employ a shroff to take thy dues every Monday

[4] Al-Maqrīzī, *Khiṭaṭ*, II, p. 95.

[5] See "The First Constable's History," *Supplemental Nights to the Book of the Thousand Nights and a Night*, translated and edited by Richard F. Burton (Benares = Stoke Newington, 1886-1888), II, p. 8.

[6] Gaston Wiet, *Cairo: City of Art and Commerce*, p. 93; Meshullam Ben R. Menahem in *Jewish Travelers*, edited by Elkan N. Adler (London: George Routledge & Sons, 1930), p. 166.

[7] Thus in *The Nights*, people most frequently send out for the meals that form an essential part of their diversion as well as their sustenance.

[8] Ibn Khallikān, quoted by al-Maqrīzī, says of this market:

> "I have seen a number of merchants who have visited various countries and who say, 'We have not seen in any country its equal in greatness and compactness of construction' " (*Khiṭaṭ*, II, p. 87).

and Thursday. So shalt thou gain two dirhams and more, for every one; and thou shalt solace and divert thyself by seeing Cairo and the Nile." [9]

The commercial city outwardly reflected the respective roles of various merchant groups in the placement and organization of its commercial establishments. Often a *khān* or *wakāla* would be established by a Mamlūk amīr for his own profit or for the benefit of the poor, [10] but as frequently as not these institutions were established by foreigners for their own use. Typically these were buildings with "hotel" rooms above the larger rooms below used for storage of goods. The Syrians occupied one of the busiest and noisiest *wakāla*s near the Mosque of al-Ḥākim where they stored oil, soap, preserves, nuts, and syrups. [11] The splendor of the foreign *khān*s depended upon the maintenance of connections between Egypt and the countries for which they had been founded. When the Mongols devastated Syria, and the supply of goods was cut off, the *khān*s used by Syrians, such as the above mentioned and the Khān of Masrūr, were ruined too. As with the political quarters, the departure of occupants brought about an abrupt decline of the locus of their authority. The abandoned *khān*s would be utilized by other merchants but they seldom regained their original splendor.

2. *Crafts and Industries*

While we wish to concentrate in this chapter upon the significance of commerce and the special role of merchants in the urban milieu, it is fitting to consider at the outset the important contributions of Cairene craftsmen to the culture of the old city. Magnificent products of urban workshops remain to testify to the high standard of artistry and skill during this period and these things, as well as raw materials and items of the transit trade, formed an important part of the stock handled by the Cairene merchants.

---

9 R. F. Burton, *Nights*, I, p. 266.

10 The present tourist bazaar takes its name from a *khān* constructed there by Jahārkas al-Khalīlī, Master of Horse under Barqūq. According to Leo Africanus, writing in the sixteenth century:

> " 'Near (the street leading to the Bab Zuwayla is) a fonduk called Khan al-Khalili, where the Persian merchants stay. This fonduk looks like a great lord's palace; it is very high, very solid, and has three floors. On the ground floor are the rooms where merchants receive their customers and sell merchandise of great value. Only merchants who are very wealthy have a counter in this fonduk. Their merchandise consists of spices, precious stones, and cloth from India, such as crepe' " (quoted in Gaston Wiet, *Cairo: City of Art and Commerce*, p. 104).

11 S. Lane-Poole, *The Story of Cairo*, p. 270.

The city produced much of the finest work in metal, wood, and ceramic of the age. The craft shops which supplied the Mamlūk court continued in the fine tradition of the Fāṭimid period, many of them occupying nearly the same locations as they had during the former era. Although styles changed considerably, some of the finest wares were turned out in or near the Bayn al-Qaṣrayn. The peak of the art of metalworking and inlay was reached in the reign of Mālik an-Nāṣir. Damascening, or inlaying graven copper with silver, gold, and black mastic, was practiced in Cairo as well as in Damascus and in Mosul where it had originated a few centuries earlier. Al-Maqrīzī in the fifteenth century speaks of it as a declining art which no longer matched the quality of the old days:

> We have seen inlaid work in such abundance that it could not be counted, there was hardly a house in Cairo or Miṣr that had not many pieces of inlaid copper. [12]

This school of metal working was, of course, greatly nourished by the thirteenth century immigrants from Mongol territory who brought to Cairo the techniques of Mosul and regions to the north and east. [13]

During the thirteenth century, a characteristically Egyptian style of woodworking developed out of both practical and decorative considerations. As wood was liable to shrink and warp and was scarce as well, small pieces were fitted together in elaborate geometric patterns, often curious in design and fascinatingly intricate in decoration and inlay. It is this type of work which is seen almost without exception on doors, windows, ceilings, and furnishings of the Mamlūk period.

Enameled glassware, the best pieces of which were produced by Syrian craftsmen, and glazed pottery became such popular items with European traders that the arts soon passed from the Mamlūk world to Venice and other European centers. While designs resembled the Persian-derived curvilinear figures of Fāṭimid times in many respects, the new orthodoxy brought about the disappearance of human figures in favor of geometric and calligraphic designs or complicated patterns of leaves and flowers.

Stimulated by the presence of al-Azhar and numerous colleges, the art of book production reached its peak in Cairo in the fifteenth century.

---

[12] Quoted in S. Lane-Poole, *The Story of Cairo*, p. 279.

[13] A. H. Christie, "Islamic Minor Arts and Their Influence Upon European Work," *The Legacy of Islam*, edited by Sir Thomas Arnold and Alfred Guillaume (London: Oxford University Press, 1931), p. 119.

Tooled leather covers, with flaps folded over to protect the front pages, often carried designs reminiscent of textiles and carpets and were embellished with gold leaf. Marbled and glazed paper was another product of Cairo which was much in demand throughout the educated world in the late Middle Ages. [14]

There is little doubt that medieval artists and artisans took great pride in their work and strove to make their productions second to none. Leo Africanus records a noteworthy custom in this connection:

> When it happens that one of the artisans turns out a beautiful, ingenious piece of work which has never before been seen, he is dressed in a brocaded coat, taken from shop to shop, accompanied by musicians in a sort of triumphal walk, and everyone gives him money. [15]

Regarding the organization of crafts, there was probably a loose structure involving the requirements of specialization, apprenticeship, and interdependence of facilities and functions. There were not at this time any corporate groups comparable to European guilds. [16] As in earlier periods, the relations between employers and employees were largely regulated through the institutions of partnership, mutual service, commission, and commenda, an arrangement whereby one party supplied the capital or goods and the other did the actual business. Such arrangements would be concluded between members of different ethnic and religious groups as well as within the same family or close-knit circle of friends. On many occasions Muslims would act as agents for Christians and Jews and vice-versa. Partnerships between members of different status groups could be found in workshops [17] and this pattern seems to have persisted into the Ottoman period.

In the absence of any overarching institutional framework, the coherence of the system depended in large part upon the ties of kinship and ethnicity that it utilized. As we have indicated, many of the important crafts and trades were associated with workmen of foreign derivation and this was one basis for the virtual monopoly of certain crafts among particular families and the national groups to which they belonged. Moreover to prevent tax evasion and assure greater

---

[14] A. H. Christie, "Islamic Minor Arts," pp. 145-147.

[15] Quoted in Gaston Wiet, *Cairo: City of Art and Commerce*, p. 105.

[16] Nor were there such groups in Ottoman times, for that matter, but guilds are the subject of a later chapter.

[17] Despite the problems which arose on account of religious restrictions regarding working days and profits gained on "days of rest" (S. D. Goitein, *A Mediterranean Society*, II, pp. 295-296).

control of the markets the state often required all those who practiced a certain trade to occupy one place (*taḥkīr*), a rule that reinforced bonds that sprang naturally from the requirements of communication and the tendency to establish common residence. [18]

3. *The Dimensions of Political Economy: National and International*

Who were these merchants, these entrepreneurs who added so much wealth, so much color, excitement, and interest to the urban milieu? They ranged from itinerant traders and small shopkeepers to the most experienced and sophisticated dealers in international commerce. They came, like the notables with whom they shared many roles, from all walks of life. There were retailers and wholesalers, there were "the beggars" or small businessmen and "the sons of houses" who were members of well-known business firms, [19] and there were brokers, auctioneers, and other middlemen. Not a few were peregrinators and of these a significant proportion were of foreign origin or non-Muslim; native Egyptians were not prone to travel while the Mamlūks themselves lacked the experience and connections needed for the successful conduct of business and for diplomacy which was a correlate of commercial endeavor. Moreover the elite tended to view all dealings with outsiders as a distasteful task for those who were not only true believers but the most powerful rulers of the world. The men who served them as ambassadors needed knowledge of diplomatic niceties, and they had to be conversant in several languages: Greek, Latin, Armenian, and Amharic as well as Arabic, Turkish, Hindi, and Mongol tongues. [20]

---

[18] The reconstruction of the social organization of crafts and industries in this period relies more upon "the educated guess" than upon concrete evidence. Most of the Geniza documents relate to an earlier period, while the material on Ottoman guilds is centuries later. Thus Lapidus writes:

> "... workmen *must have had* a more highly organized social life than our sources reveal. Apprenticeship arrangements for the perpetuation of craft skill and long training under close personal supervision of master-workers *must have been necessary* ... Informal traditions *must have created* uniform employment conditions. ... Moreover, *it seems probable* in some cases that solidarity of workers in a particular craft or trade was based on the broader social life of the quarters. Some quarters ... were economically specialized and in these cases workers' solidarities *may have been due* to communal as well as occupational bonds (italics mine)" (*Muslim Cities in the Later Middle Ages*, p. 101).

[19] S. D. Goitein, *A Mediterranean Society*, I, p. 152.

[20] A figure who comes to mind is one Taghrī-Birdī, dragoman and ambassador of Sultan al-Ghūrī to Venice in A.D. 1507. Though not a merchant, he has been described as a polyglot who, owing to his "experience gained from frequent contacts with the cosmopolitan world of diplomats, merchants, and travelers, probably (could) pass as a national of any group he might choose within the medieval Mediter-

Those who knew best the formal and informal intricacies of international relations were naturally the merchants. The Jews who traded freely in the West and East as a group had the most extensive connections. The businessmen concerning whom we have the most information, however incomplete though it may be, were the Kārimīs, [21] the major handlers of the Indian spice trade for three centuries. Professor Goitein and others have extensively investigated the Geniza documents concerning this group and from these reports we will take much of the following illustrative material.

In the first section of this work we emphasized the importance of commerce for urban culture, especially the development of international trade. Nearly all visitors to Cairo in the Mamlūk period drew attention to this fact. [22] The fourteenth century in particular saw a

---

ranean world." He seems to have been a Spanish Jew who became a sailor and left Europe in search of religious toleration. Subsequently converted to Islam, his career in Egypt began when he was captured by pirates and sold into slavery (John Wansbrough, "A Mamluk Ambassador to Venice in 913/1507," *Bulletin of the School of Oriental and African Studies*, XXVI (1963), p. 504).

[21] The first year in which the presence of Kārimīs is mentioned is A.D. 1181, but although al-Maqrīzī says they paid a tax at that time, in all probability their activities began at an earlier date. Goitein writes that:

> "By the beginning of the twelfth century, al-Kārim had become a household word in Cairo: any woman, whose husband was out in the Indian Ocean knew that she could expect sendings forwarded by him 'in the Kārim' " ("New Light on the Beginnings of the Kārim Merchants," *Journal of the Economic and Social History of the Orient*, I (1958), pp. 180-181).

The name "Kārimī" is not Arabic but foreign to the language, appearing in the first sources without the definite article. Thus in a letter dated A.D. 1140 the writer states:

> " 'We expected all the time that you would arrive in (!) Kārim this year. Instead, there came your letter (*wamā kunna quᶜūd nantaḍirak bi* (!) *Kārim al-sana waqad wāṣala kitābak*)' " (S. D. Goitein, "New Light on the beginnings of the Kārim Merchants," p. 184).

It has been pointed out too, that Tamil has a word *karyam*, which in many contexts means "business" or "affairs." This is as plausible a derivation as any, considering that most of the Kārimī trade was related to India.

Thus it may well be that the Kārimī trade was not a company at first but rather a convoy in which goods were transported under personal supervision of their owners. A survey of available sources shows that the traders were not of a single origin. Some were from Syria, others from Mesopotamia, Yemen, and Abyssinia. As the economic power of Cairo reached its peak in the fourteenth and fifteenth centuries, the small traders who had participated in the original convoys were most probably squeezed out by the system of taxes and monopolies as the sultans began to realize what a tremendous source of revenue the Indian trade could be (E. Ashtor, "The Kārimī Merchants," *Journal of the Royal Asiatic Society*, 1956, p. 52).

[22] Thus Piloti de Crete who was active in Egypt and the Levant from A.D. 1396 to 1438 wrote:

> "The aforesaid city is the most prosperous of the world in all the things that one could say; this prosperity comes from two principal causes: first because of the

resuscitation of Mediterranean trade which had declined with the disappearance of the ancient empires. In part this was, of course, due to the resurgence of European power. Until the period of the Crusades, the Mediterranean was almost exclusively the domain of Islamic navigation but Muslim relations with the Christian ports tended on the whole to be of a military and predatory nature.[23] As a matter of policy, many early rulers like the caliph ᶜUmar had seen the sphere of peaceful interaction as primarily an Islamic sphere and had tended to discourage commercial connections with Christian lands. (*Dār al-Islām* vs. *Dār al-Ḥarb*, "Muslim lands vs. the Territories of War"). Thus had the port of Alexandria declined from the first days of Arab rule.[24]

While the Crusades temporarily interferred with peaceful communication and, for considerable periods, papal bans on trade between Christians and Muslims were enforced, in the long run the contact engendered by war stimulated the establishment of economic liaisons. On one side, the West began intensively to feel needs for the products of the East and on the other, Ṣalāḥ ad-Dīn and his successors became aware of the vast profits to be made from trade. Even more to the point, they became aware that the rising powers to the north could not be ignored, that they had at least to be coped with and, if possible, manipulated. Subsequently, a two-pronged policy dictated ruthless warfare against Christian states in the Levant with the simultaneous development of commercial and political relations with European states and with Byzantium.

In this general picture, Egypt became the focal point of the transit trade. The fall of the ᶜAbbāsid empire and the protectionist policy of Ṣalāḥ ad-Dīn which excluded foreign traders from the Red Sea, Cairo, and the interior paved the way for pioneering merchants to exploit the Far Eastern trade as they never had before. Offered for export were grain, sugar, fruits, fish, dates, oil, leather, and alum, as well as fine manufactured products, textiles and carpets, paper, and metal goods. It was the transit trade, however, that realized the greatest

country, which is splendidly fertile all around ... (and) the second cause of that great prosperity is the great flow of traffic which comes from all the world to Cairo, by land and sea ..." (*L'Égypte au commencement du quinzième siècle*, edited by P.-H. Dopp, pp. 4-8).

[23] Although from the eighth century, Muslim traders were found in Italian towns and in Byzantium, raiding was more typical than peaceful intercourse.

[24] See p. 16 above.

profits. Slaves and spices especially were of paramount importance.[25] The Indian Ocean, for centuries the chief field of Islamic navigation, was the scene of lively traffic with the ports of China, Sumatra, Ceylon, India, and Madagascar. All of these places had their Arab colonies.

Without doubt the most widely traveled merchants and the most active were the Kārimīs. Although they are called "spice merchants" their sphere of activity was broader than that. The Yemen was their major supply center for goods of Indian origin and so it was natural also that they should include in their cargoes other products from that region such as textiles, wheat, weapons, armor, and silk.[26] Ibn Kathīr and al-Qalqashandī note that Kārimīs were present in Damascus, while al-Maqrīzī says that one of them, Nāṣir ad-Dīn ibn Musallam, perhaps dealing in the slave trade, sent employees to the Atlantic coast of Africa, Abyssinia, and some other places. It is recorded that another, ᶜAbd al-ᶜAzīz ibn Manṣūr, went to Malabar and made five voyages to China returning with great quantities of silk.[27] For the most part, however, their business involved the transportation of goods from the Yemen to Egypt, beginning at Aden, and going from there through the Red Sea to the Sudanese coast at ᶜAidhab, or sometimes aṭ-Ṭūr or Suez, to Cairo.[28] At the terminal their merchandise would be stored in *khān*s until it could be sold or shipped to European markets. The Kārimīs had their own *khān*s or *funduq*s in Aden, Jidda, Fusṭāṭ and Alexandria besides other cities in which they operated. Some of these buildings, to avoid taxes, were established as *waqf*, and some had mosques within their walls.

Before the discovery of the Cape Route, the Venetians imported an average of 1,500,000 pounds of pepper and nearly an equal amount of other spices from Alexandria annually.[29] As the Christian nations developed naval power on the Mediterranean, the Italian seaports of

---

[25] The significance of spices for the national economy can be seen in al-Maqrīzī's comment that out of the ten dirhams daily income of a member of the middle class, two were spent on spices (*Ighāthat al-Umma bi-Kashf al-Ghumma*, translated by Gaston Wiet, "Le traité des famines de Maqrīzī," p. 93).

[26] Ibn Taghrī-Birdī, *Nujūm az-Zāhira fī Mulūk Miṣr wa al-Qāhira*, edited by William Popper (Berkeley: University of California Press, 1915-1960), V, pp. 117-122, 571.

[27] E. Ashtor, "The Kārimī Merchants," p. 55.

[28] W. J. Fischel, "The Spice Trade in Mamluk Egypt," *Journal of the Economic and Social History of the Orient*, I (1958), p. 162.

[29] F. C. Lane, "Venetian Shipping During the Commercial Revolution," *American Historical Review*, XXXVIII (1933), p. 228; and by the same author, "The Mediterranean Spice Trade," *American Historical Review*, XLV (1940), p. 587.

Pisa and Genoa became important centers and there were many Venetians present both in Alexandria and in Cairo. The Italians indeed were intensely involved in Egyptian commerce.[30] Many of them persisted in carrying on their business despite the papal bans on trade with Muslim lands that accompanied attempts at Crusade.[31] From A.D. 1208 they were given special trading privileges by the government in Cairo. Before the last Latin establishments in Syria fell, Pisans, Genoese, and later the Venetians obtained permission to travel in the Egyptian interior and in Cairo.[32] In the fourteenth century similar commercial privileges were extended to the merchants of France and those of the kingdoms of Spain. Many European trading cities maintained consular missions in Egypt. Arrangements were made for separate living quarters[33] as well as for customs duties and special terms of trade. The Venetians in particular became the agents of Egyptian traders and were granted a number of privileges. A Frank could be arrested only on order of the sultan and his deputies. A claim against him on the part of any lower authority could never prevent his leaving the country. A *qāḍī* lost his office on account of illegal action taken against a Frank.[34]

The fortunes of the commercial class were inextricably linked with those of the state or states within which they worked. On the international scene, political and commercial matters were closely interwoven and we have seen that not infrequently merchants served as ambassadors. In the absence of formal treaties, their welfare depended at least upon the establishment of friendly relations. Governmental initiative could also encourage commercial undertakings. In A.D. 1288

---

[30] Cf. Subḥī Labīb, *Handelsgeschichte Ägyptens im Spätmittelalter 1171-1517* (Wiesbaden, 1965), p. 29.

[31] Even to the point of braving the danger of excommunication. See W. Heyd, *Histoire du commerce du Levant au moyen-âge*, translated by F. Reynaud, II (Amsterdam: Adolph M. Hakkert, 1959), p. 25 and passim.

[32] C. Cahen, "Les marchands étrangers au Caire sous les Fāṭimides et les Ayyūbides," *Colloque international sur l'histoire du Caire* (Cairo: General Egyptian Book Organization, 1974), p. 100.

[33] It appears that before this time there were no permanent European business establishments either in Alexandria or in Cairo. In the Ayyūbid and early Mamlūk periods the center of concentration of commercial representatives of Christian lands was Alexandria. Since they were fewer in Cairo, they had no *funduq* of their own there but lived in native *funduq*s or in private houses (C. Cahen, "Les marchands étrangers au Caire," p. 100).

[34] Subḥī Labīb, "Egyptian Commercial Policy in the Middle Ages," *Studies in the Economic History of the Middle East*, edited by M. A. Cook (London: Oxford University Press, 1970), pp. 71-72.

Qalāūn addressed an invitation to notables in India, China, and the Yemen promising them safe conduct in Egypt and Syria:

> "They will find security for their persons and their goods, as well as happiness which will adorn their situation and will surpass their hopes ... Whoever imports merchandise such as spices or other commodities habitually carried by the Kārimī merchants will have no fear of losing his rights. He will not be constrained to perform any disagreeable obligation ... Those who import Mamlūks or young female slaves will sell them at a price higher than that which they can hope ...." [35]

The government provided a regular convoy of three to five vessels to protect Kārimī ships from pirates in the Red Sea. Every merchant who carried a passport of the Egyptian sultan was guaranteed safety for himself and his goods as far as sovereignty extended.

Although the navigation of the Indian Ocean made the wares of China and the East more available than ever before, a great quantity of goods continued to be transported by the "ship of the desert." While India was most easily accessible by the ocean route, important overland routes led through Africa west and south, and through southern and central Russia and to China. The Mongol empire of the thirteenth century stimulated a great revival of commercial activity in the latter areas, diverting some traffic from Cairo, but one of the most important parts of the overland trade of Egypt was connected with the Meccan pilgrimage. The annual caravan not only provided opportunities for commerce but developed among Muslims a fairly good knowledge of other parts of the world. All those going to Mecca from the West passed through the Egyptian capital, while believers from the eastern reaches of Islam visited Cairo, only thirty days journey from Mecca, to see the "Paris" of the Near East. Piloti de Crete remarks on the size of the caravans going to the Holy City: "A tremendous number of camels carrying great loads, and as many merchants as pilgrims." [36]

The transit trade was a tremendous source of revenue for the Egyptian government. Customs authorities were meticulous book-keepers and had an accurate picture of the details concerning exports and imports (*taᶜrīf*). All goods passing through the country were liable to the *zakāt*, a tax of 2½ per cent which, when levied at five or six places, totalled ten to fifteen per cent of the value. [37] According to al-Maqrīzī, in 1426,

---

[35] Quoted by Gaston Wiet, "Les marchands d'épices sous les sultans mamlouks," *Cahiers d'histoire Égyptienne*, VII (1955), p. 91.

[36] *L'Égypte au commencement du quinzième siècle*, p. 44.

[37] C. H. Becker, "Egypt," *Encyclopaedia of Islam*, 1913.

when the merchants were prohibited from going directly from Mecca to Syria, they had to go to Egypt with the pilgrimage caravan and pay the duty on all objects they carried with them from Arabia and beyond. Nor were pilgrims exempt from this tax. When the caravan came near to Cairo, the chiefs and their soldiers carefully searched the packages of all arrivals, merchants and pilgrims, and took duty on all objects without exception, even taking from a poor woman ten dirhams for a little leather carpet. [38] The sultan's officials were at every port in the empire and until the end of the fifteenth century, Cairo controlled the entire volume of trade going between India and the Levant. Each year, at the time when the Indian vessels would come to Jidda, an officer from Cairo would levy duty on the merchandise and exact for the treasury as much as 70,000 dinars. [39]

Realizing the financial benefits which accrued from Kārimī business, the sultans appointed agents to supervise the sale of wares to European merchants. All taxes and customs derived from the Kārimīs were reserved for the sultan. According to Piloti:

> From there comes a very great part of the funds beyond measure that is in the hands of the sultan and all his officials. [40]

But while the government heavily taxed the international trade and had a virtual monopoly on some important commodities, throughout most of the period commerce was left largely in the hands of local and foreign businessmen. Until the fifteenth century when the process of decline had set in, it was possible for merchants to accumulate fortunes that rivaled those of the amīrs. [41] Some biographies cite fortunes of between 100,000 and 400,000 dinars besides other holdings. [42] The wealth of the Kārimīs became proverbial throughout the whole Orient. Often in the Geniza it is said about one of them

---

[38] Quoted by Gaston Wiet, "Les marchands d'épices sous les sultans mamlouks," p. 98.

[39] *Ibid.*, p. 99.

[40] *L'Égypte au commencement du quinzième siècle*, p. 8.

[41] As late as A.D. 1512 Jean Thenaud stated that there were 200 merchants who had over two million pieces of gold each and that they hid much of their wealth from the officials. (The latter fact may cast some doubt on the veracity of his information but if merchants did indeed control that much wealth, they would probably not have advertized their affluence). Cf. Subḥī Labīb, "Egyptian Commercial Policy," p. 77; I. M. Lapidus, *Muslim Cities in the Later Middle Ages*, p. 118.

[42] I. M. Lapidus, *Muslim Cities in the Later Middle Ages*, p. 118. The five sons of Nāṣir ad-Dīn ibn Musallam al-Bālisī, received an inheritance of 200,000 dinars apiece on the death of their father (G. Wiet, "Les marchands d'épices sous les sultans mamlouks," p. 113).

10. "The Venetian Embassy to Cairo" (ca. A.D. 1480?). The Venetians are wearing black caps. Those in high fur hats are the Mamlūks, while the men wearing turbans are probably Egyptian administrators and notables. The blazon on the palace is that of Sultan Qayt-Bey. This painting, by an artist of the school of Bellini, may also reflect similar scenes in Damascus.

10. The Venetian Embassy to Cairo (ca. A.D. 1500?). The Venetians are wearing black caps. Those in high fur hats are the Mamluks, while the men wearing turbans are probably Egyptian administrators and notables. The blazon on the palace is that of Sultan Qayt-bay. This painting by an artist of the school of Bellini may also reflect similar scenes in Damascus.

that "his wealth could not be counted" or, "no one surpassed him as far as money is concerned." One, ᶜAṭīya ibn Khalīfa, in the first part of the fifteenth century, said that every dirham he invested returned six. [43] With an income of such magnitude, they soon became bankers and were in a position to make sizeable loans to governments under whose protection they operated.

Their style of life may perhaps be taken as a good indication of their resources. Palatial residences of merchants were not uncommon as both *The Thousand and One Nights* and historical records attest. One especially prominent Kārimī, Burhān ad-Dīn al-Maḥallī, had a splendid residence on the banks of the Nile decorated with inlaid marbles and fine woodwork and spent as much money building a *madrasa* beside it as Sultan al-Muʾayyad Shaykh spent on his own tomb mosque beside the Bāb Zuwayla. [44] Some merchants were known to have had as many as two hundred armed mamlūk retainers for they did not always sell their slaves to amīrs. [45] Slaves contributed to social power as did the number of servants, agents, and employees. The greatest did not actually conduct their business themselves but directed it from Cairo, sending representatives to foreign ports. Ownership of land, orchards, and vineyards also was a source of social power and through subsidizing pious foundations [46] and marrying into families of Mamlūks and *ᶜulamāʾ* the merchant could consolidate his position. In the long run, however, his ships had to come in and misfortune through natural or political causes could strike at any time. The merchants experienced their ups and downs. Relatively few families retained their wealth over three generations. [47]

[43] W. J. Fischel, "The Spice Trade in Mamluk Egypt," p. 162. We are reminded of a trader in *The Thousand and One Nights* who describes how he and his brothers

> " 'got ready suitable goods and hired a ship and, having embarked our merchandise, proceeded on our voyage, day following day, a full month, after which we arrived at a city, where we sold our venture; and for every piece of gold we gained ten' " (R. F. Burton, *Nights*, I, p. 34).

[44] R. Lopez et al., "England to Egypt, 1350-1500: Long-term Trends and Long-distance Trade," *Studies in the Economic History of the Middle East*, edited by M. A. Cook (London: Oxford University Press, 1970), p. 123.

[45] In describing the households of "merchant princes" *The Thousand and One Nights* mentions mamlūk retainers as a matter of course.

[46] Through their lavish generosity, the Kārimīs caused hospitals, *madrasas*, mosques, and other institutions to flourish to the benefit of the public. Nāṣir ad-Dīn ibn Musallam founded a *madrasa* for Shāfiᶜīs and Mālikīs with a school for boys (E. Ashtor, "The Kārimī Merchants," p. 30).

[47] S. D. Goitein has remarked that "these people did not get excited overduly either by large profits or by heavy losses," an interesting observation especially in the light of the fact that many of the authors of the letters of the Geniza were involved in commerce ("The Mentality of the Middle Class," p. 252).

It is important to understand that organizationally, the import-export merchants seem to have been, on the whole, an open and flexible group. Indeed, even with respect to the Kārimīs who were united in formal association, there appear to be few if any traits that all members shared in common or strict rules that they observed.

There is considerable question as to whether the Kārimī organization can be called a "guild" or even a "corporation." While Fischel believes that

> we have every reason to assume that all Kārimī merchants were part of a closely organized corporation, Genossenschaft, or even guild dedicated to the spice trade [48]

he bases this conclusion chiefly upon the evidence of statements and expressions such as "he belonged to the Kārimī merchants" or "so-and-so was 'chief of the Kārimīs'." It can be pointed out, however, that Arabs habitually bestowed such lavish titles upon outstanding people of any social group and such references need not necessarily be indicative of formal leadership in an organization. [49] Nevertheless authorities generally agree that there was a special group of great businessmen who cooperated in some way or other in pursuit of a common commercial goal which centered around trade in pepper and spices. In all probability it was a loose confederation of merchants informally united under the leadership of the richest and most esteemed Kārimī who worked in close connection with other prominent members of the group deciding upon issues which arose within the group and dealing on behalf of them all with the government. The very nature of commerce on the scale of that conducted by the Kārimīs would make it imperative that an individual merchant unite with others to cope with the difficulties and risks of far-flung sea and land traffic. Mutual help and assistance too was needed as all of them bore the impositions of the government and were called upon frequently for loans and contributions.

There is some disagreement also among scholars as to the recruitment of Kārimīs. That is, Clerget and Ashtor say that they were Jewish, while Fischel believes that:

> It is certain ... that the Kārimī were confessionally a homogeneous group, that the bearers of the title Kārimī were devout and pious Muslims being unified through the common bond of Islam—and spices. [50]

---

[48] "The Spice Trade in Mamluk Egypt," pp. 164-165.

[49] E. Ashtor, "The Kārimī Merchants," p. 51.

[50] "The Spice Trade in Mamluk Eg pt," p. 166.

He states that only two are mentioned in the sources who were of non-Muslim origin, but even these were converted to Islam when they became traders. Judeo-Arabic literature however, and especially the Geniza, refutes this opinion. In one document cited by Ashtor, there is an outright statement: "There departed among the Kārimīs our comrades the Jews." [51] Goitein, after a thorough analysis of the available literature, concludes that:

> In any case, the Geniza papers show clearly that, at least in Fāṭimid times, Hindus, Muslims, Jews, and Christians, worked closely together in the pursuit of trade between India and the West. As we have seen, the Kārim carried both Jewish passengers and goods and there is no reason why the same should not apply to the members of any other denomination ... [52]

Although their religious unity was extremely questionable, it seems that there were some ties between individual Kārimīs on the basis of agnatic and affinal relationship. Leadership as well as ownership passed from father to son. Fischel speaks of a "dynastic" structure in which children of the leading Kārimīs were trained to fill the role of their fathers by being sent away on commercial missions at an early age. [53] There were, between the end of the twelfth century and the end of the fifteenth, a few really important families among them, the Musallams, Kharrūbīs, Maḥallīs, Damāmimīs, etc. Among these were at least three pairs of brothers who were both known to be Kārimīs. [54] A considerable number of marriages united these major families as a group. The Kharrūbīs were related to the Musallams through the marriage of Sirāj ad-Dīn al-Kharrūbī to a daughter of Nāṣir ad-Dīn ibn Musallam, whose mother was a daughter of another Kārimī, Shams ad-Dīn Muḥammad ibn Aḥmad al-Bālisī. Of course, it is not surprising that a certain amount of endogamy was the case, since even the marriage of parallel cousins is preferred in Muslim society; but it should be remembered too that no group in Cairo could compete with the spice merchants as to wealth excepting the Mamlūks.

It should be noted that some Kārimīs married into Mamlūk families and others into the bureaucratic class. Thus Shihāb ad-Dīn al-Maḥallī, the greatest merchant of his time, was the father-in-law of the Shāfiᶜī *qāḍī*, ᶜAbd ar-Raḥmān ibn ᶜAlī at-Tafahnī (d. 1432). [55] Jews, of

[51] "The Kārimī Merchants," p. 55.
[52] "New Light on the Beginnings of the Kārim Merchants," p. 183.
[53] "The Spice Trade in Mamluk Egypt," p. 165.
[54] See Gaston Wiet, "Les marchands d'épices sous les sultans mamlouks," passim.
[55] E. Ashtor, "The Kārimī Merchants," p. 49.

course, married within their own faith but often marriage ties extended to Jewish communities in other parts of the globe as we have seen earlier. No group in the city could afford to remain in total isolation from other families of its kind, or even from other families who controlled the ideological and political networks of the city. In the case of the Kārimīs religious boundaries were often crossed through conversion and the preferential rule of endogamy could be put aside with a view toward maintaining economic cooperation or establishing connections in high places. According to Gaston Wiet's list of major Kārimīs, not a few of them married their daughters to *qāḍī*s or professors.

As in the cases of kinship and religion, there seem to have been no rigid economic standards for recruitment into the Kārimī society. Many were parvenus. Nāṣir ad-Dīn ibn Musallam al-Bālisī, said to be the richest man of his time, was the son of a poor man even as, it seems, was Burhān ad-Dīn al-Maḥallī, often called "the greatest of the Kārimīs," whom the sultan charged with his affairs. [56] One ᶜIzz ad-Dīn ᶜAbd al-ᶜAzīz ibn Qayṣur began as a tailor, while two others of great repute are known to have built up their fortunes through their own efforts. On the whole, however, they were well educated. Some were respected scholars and others attained the post of *qāḍī*.

If there was any factor that united the Kārimīs it was their shared responsibility in relation to the government. Patronage led to liaisons between merchants and the elite even as it did in the case of the notables. One of the most spectacular examples of individual achievement is that of a foreign merchant Abū al-Majd as-Sallāmī who succeeded in negotiating a peace between the Mongols and Mamlūks in Iran (A.D. 1323). For his pains the sultan entertained him in Cairo and presented him with a license to trade to the value of 50,000 dirhams annually. He was also granted the privilege of conducting half his business tax-free. [57] Less spectacularly, many merchants served as agents and brokers for the elite. The fact that the sultan and his amīrs controlled so much wealth led naturally to their dependence upon the merchant class.

Thus also the Kārimīs did not add to the revenue of the state only through the taxes that they paid, but also through lending money to the elite who were militarily capable but often lacked the resources

[56] See G. Wiet, "Les marchands d'épices sous les sultans mamlouks," p. 112; also E. Ashtor, "The Kārimī Merchants," p. 47, quoting Ibn Hajar al-ᶜAsqalānī.

[57] Subḥī Labīb, "Egyptian Commercial Policy," p. 75.

to equip their troops. When Barqūq marched to Syria to repel Tamurlane in A.D. 1394, Burhān ad-Dīn al-Maḥallī, Shihāb ad-Dīn ibn Musallam, and Nūr ad-Dīn al-Kharrūbī were summoned to collect funds for a loan to the sultan of one million dirhams. But because it was to their interest also to maintain political security in the Yemen, in the fourteenth century they made a sizeable loan to the ruler of that country who was imprisoned in Cairo. [58] Their connections throughout the known world made the Kārimīs invaluable as ambassadors. They frequently acted as willing mediators in the field of international affairs, for any breach of the peace was immediately detrimental to their activities as well as those of the state. On the whole, they were on good terms with the elite and, while they were expected to make magnificent presents to the sultan and amīrs for special consideration, they were frequently requited with tremendous sums in return for their services.

The liaison with the elite, however, had both positive and negative effects upon merchants. The Mamlūks were the primary consumers of luxury goods even as they sought outlets for their excess supplies and assistance in managing the distribution of these in the urban center. When affluent, the elite invested thousands of dinars in commercial expeditions, but when they needed ready cash, either for defense against an external threat or to meet internal challenges to their power, it was to the merchants that they turned. All too often the sale of excess supplies became an extortionate forced purchase (*ṭarḥ*) and heavy loans demanded by the rulers were scantily repaid or not repaid at all.

We should not wonder that many traders officially entered government service especially as monopolies increased as time went on. *Khawājā* (now a word applied colloquially to foreigners) was a special rank held by traders in the sultan's service. Some, especially slave traders, had places at court as agents of the privy purse, while in the town others staffed the trading bureaus that normally formed part of the sultan's private treasury and controlled the outlet of strategic supplies. [59] *Ṣayrafīs* (money changers) who worked in the bureaus as paymasters and assisted in the collection of revenues derived a 3½ per cent commission on transactions. [60]

Despite the hardships and inconveniences merchants could suffer at the hands of the elite, and partly because of them, many found

---

[58] Ibn Taghrī-Birdī, *Nujūm*, edited by William Popper, V, p. 562.
[59] I. M. Lapidus, *Muslim Cities in the Later Middle Ages*, p. 122.
[60] *Ibid.*, p. 120 .

places in the regime itself. After all, if a forced loan was not repaid it might have the effect of a bribe. Not only did they enter the secretariat but in some cases they entered the military by buying negotiable pay tickets! In the fifteenth century a few even purchased the rank of amīr. Although many of the elite viewed such infiltration of their ranks with horror, others possibly saw it as a way to pack their households with clients. In this case as in others there were conflicting demands of internal solidarity and external support.

Not unlike the ruling elite, all the merchants failed to establish a dynasty which could maintain for long the control of resources so disputed among political and economic factions. Although a few families came to control the greatest volume of trade, none retained their envied position for more than two or three generations. Even the Kharrūbīs were impoverished through the system of contributions and outright confiscations of inheritance. Like the Mamlūks, despite the "eternality" of their organization in the abstract, they fell prey to the general decline of the Egyptian economy as well as to conflicting principles of inheritance and personal association.

The economic networks of Cairo extended far beyond the lands of Mamlūk authority. Economically and culturally the welfare of the city depended upon events taking place far removed from the locality with which most of the inhabitants were familiar. The wares of the richest merchants, like the techniques of local craftsmen were derived in large part from abroad. It was Cairo's privileged position on the crossroads of the known world that was responsible for the efflorescence of arts, building, and style of life which springs to mind when we think of the city of *The Thousand and One Nights*. The men who exploited this situation were from varied backgrounds, some Egyptian, some foreign, some rich, some poor. Their social networks, like those which unified the Kārimī association, were generally characterized by solidarity based on ethnic, religious, or kinship ties, but retained enough flexibility to accommodate changes in the economic environment and in the power structure. Although for a time certain families could virtually monopolize certain areas of trade or production, the exigencies of circumstance did not permit total recruitment from the same family or even the same social group in every case.

The Kārimīs exploited the accumulated geographical knowledge of the Muslim world and a period of non-interference from foreign governments, to become the forerunners of the Portuguese, English, French, and Dutch East India companies two centuries later, Not only did they supply Egypt and the West with the products of the East, but they contributed substantially to the maintenance of security in the Mamlūk empire. By willingly or unwillingly making payments to the government, they enabled their rulers to stave off the westward advance of Tamurlane and contributed over a long period to the survival of the Mamlūk regime.

CHAPTER TEN

THE LOWER ORDERS AND THE URBAN MILIEU

Even more than the elite, notables, and merchants, the lower orders formed part of the urban milieu. If the elite were the head, the notables were the nerves, and the merchants were the circulatory system of the city, the common people were its very flesh and blood. From the Citadel and the houses of the amīrs to the Bāb Zuwayla, al-Azhar, and the cemeteries, there was scarcely a place where they could not be found. Not only geographically, but historically they were pervasive. Although their role in the drama is far from easy to define, scarcely an important event occurred without their participation and the streets of Cairo bore witness to their involvement in factional strife and to their sufferings in time of hardship. Yet despite their obvious, extreme vulnerability to economic crises, they were not totally without resources. Persistant and prevalent, they not only survived but found ways of succeeding in their spectacularly unstable environment.

1. *The Urban Milieu*

Just as a population is not simply a set of demographic facts, so an urban environment is not simply a geographical space. The city is a place where an individual can make his fortune or meet his doom. As so compellingly portrayed in *The Thousand and One Nights*, Cairo was not only crowded but was a conglomeration of cosmopolitan of elements, all converging upon its centers of wealth and of power. One never knew what consequences might evolve from an innocent trip out of one's quarter into the squares and *sūq*s where one could encounter every sort of stranger. In the crowded throughfares, poor beggars and blacks, professors of the law, veiled women, Mamlūks, and ignorant *fallāḥīn* disputed the way with merchants, coarse entertainers and prostitutes, Maghribīs, Persians, Copts, Mongols, Franks, and Jews. Despite the existence of rules and preferences for separation, there could be no true isolation or insulation.

It is not easy to reconstruct the everyday life of the common people. Serious chronicles do not dwell on the commonplace and the lower orders are peripheral to the central political drama. Yet from historical and literary sources and even present day traditions, we can derive some idea of what their existence was like.

The places where one particularly notices the common people are certainly not without interest. Typically they are crowd scenes. Even today in Cairo, such regular events as marriages, funerals, and minor accidents do not happen without attracting a crowd. But today life is tame; with reference to physical things, perhaps, and with reference to scale, everything is more extensive, but with reference to the human drama, life is tame. In those days one could witness processions and events such as we cannot imagine. There were victory parades that would proceed along gorgeously bedecked routes heralded by musicians blowing copper trumpets and singers beating on drums. Companies of soldiers would march in procession while pages dressed in yellow silk carried the symbols of the sultanate encrusted with gold, an unsubtle reminder of the sovereignty of the sultan, who would appear in his most elaborate robes riding a white horse and carrying a sabre. As an even less subtle reminder of the sultan's power would come the prisoners, not infrequently defeated rival amīrs, in chains and iron collars, their disgraceful humiliation contrasting sharply with their former arrogance and glory. The whole performance would often end when the unfortunate rebels, stripped and nailed to camels, were finally executed at the Bāb Zuwayla where their remains would be left hanging as long as anyone cared to watch.

Less morbid but no less exciting was the annual procession of the *maḥmil* [1] that took place when the pilgrim caravan set out. Gaston Wiet, quoting a contemporary source, gives us a good idea of what it was like:

> "A large crowd of spectators always gathers the day that the mahmal is brought out. Here is how the day is celebrated. Four important cadis, the treasury minister, and the provost of the markets, all on horseback, are accompanied by the most learned jurists, the syndics of the corporations, and the greatest men of the empire. They all go together to the gate of the Citadel. The mahmal is brought out upon their arrival; it is carried on a camel and is preceeded by the emir who is designated to make the trip to Hejaz that year. The emir is accompanied by his men and by water-carriers mounted on camels. All classes of the population, men as well as women, gather for this purpose; then they accompany the mahmal through the two cities of Cairo and Fostat. The camel drivers precede them, shouting at their camels to make them move on."

---

1 From Fāṭimid times Egypt had provided the covering for the Holy Kaaba but the *maḥmil* (colloq. *maḥmal*) is copied from the palanquin in which Queen Shagar ad-Durr who ruled Egypt at the beginning of the Mamlūk period, rode when she first made the pilgrimage. It served as a symbol of Cairene power. The greatest chieftains in Ḥijāz had to bow before it.

> The procession soon degenerated into a bacchanalian orgy. The soldiers, dressed in frightening burlesque costumes, demanded money of the laughing crowd. The devils of the mahmal, as they were called, committed such excesses that the government decided to forbid these manifestations. After many years, toward the end of the fifteenth century, the mahmal was preceded by a cavalcade of lancers dressed in scarlet who simulated battle as they rode by. [2]

Then, as now, weddings and funerals were semi-public occurrences that necessitated processions. One category of lower class persons, the performers, hired themselves out on such ooccasions to publicly mourn or celebrate as the case might be. (Today the automobile has spoiled the whole effect.) On happy occasions people were invited to enjoy the display of lights, music, perfumes, and banqueting.

Nor should we fail to recall fairs and *mawlid*s (birthdays of popular saints), at which the animal trainers, storytellers, snake charmers, and reciters, types who still regale the inhabitants of quarters and patrons of coffee houses, drew large crowds. (Even now scarcely a day goes by in Cairo without a *mawlid* taking place on some street). That old Pharaonic custom, the Nile festival, always provided extensive opportunity for diversion. People would celebrate by setting up tents and sailing, while the entertainers, prostitutes, and gangs of thieves made the most of the occasion to ply their trades. International performers too, cashed in on the receptivity of the Cairene populace. One European gymnast in the middle of the fifteenth century had the intrepidity to stretch a tightrope from the Citadel to a minaret of the Madrasa of Sultan Ḥasan and perform with flaming torches to the gaping crowds below.

To the medieval Cairene the urban milieu juxtaposed spiritual elements on human ones. The Bāb Zuwayla, the site of so many executions, has had from time immemorial, a supernatural aura. It was supposed to be haunted and the favorite seat of the *quṭb*, or chief of the *walī*s (spirits of holy men who roamed the world). This being was thought to appear upon occasion in humble demeanor and mean dress to reprove the impious, but was seldom visible and always unrecognized. [3]

---

[2] *Cairo: City of Art and Commerce*, pp. 111-112.

[3] According to Lane, in the nineteenth century, the beggars who were seated near the Bāb Zuwayla were regarded as servants of the *quṭb* and

> "some curious individuals often try to peep behind the door, in the vain hope of catching a glimpse of (him), should be happen to be there, and not at the moment invisible" (*Manners and Customs*, p. 237).

Mamlūk Prisoners.

Dervishes and Others.

11. Some Characters in the Urban Milieu.

The juxtaposition of diversity, wealth, and power encouraged violence but generally people were good natured and made an effort to accommodate. Many tales in *The Nights* portray Cairenes as sharpers, for the challenge of the milieu had the effect of sharpening one's wits as well as whetting one's appetite for gain. The Nazarene Broker, a relatively honest young man from Mosul, is tempted when passing through the crowded street to snatch a trooper's purse. He is apprehended and has his hand cut off outside the Bāb Zuwayla but eventually comes into his fortune as a result of the misadventure.

The urban milieu had a vast potential. In its fluid drama it could offer violent death and destruction but it could also offer a life beyond a villager's wildest dreams. One's future was only partly a matter of luck. It also depended upon how one succeeded in maneuvering in the vast network of alliance and patronage that constituted the reality of social relations.

2. *The Definition of the Lower Orders and the Resources of the Resourceless*

The general term used for the lower classes, *al-ᶜāmma*, is usually translated "the masses," or "the common people." Often it is opposed to *al-khāṣṣa*, "the elite." Certainly *al-ᶜāmma* included many different kinds of people, some moderately well-off, others extremely poor, some respectable and others not. By and large they had little to bargain with, neither military, nor material, nor spiritual power. Yet it would not be proper to say that they were down-trodden as a class by the law or by tradition. In fact their condition and prospects tended to depend primarily upon respectability and social ties rather than upon origin.

There was ranking within *al-ᶜāmma* taken as a whole. At the top there were respectable shopkeepers and artisans, at the bottom were the desperate dregs of society: as Ibn Khaldūn put it, "those who have nothing to gain or to lose among their fellow men." [4] The foremost among them were the *nās min al-ᶜāmma*, known and capable persons who were often delegated by the government to collect taxes, transmit instructions, and to assist in maintenance of law and order in the quarters. Such turned honesty and dependability to profit and frequently reinforced their positions as middlemen through a tie to the religious institution.

---

4 *The Muqaddimah*, II, p. 329.

The tradesmen were ideally ranked according to a Muslim standard of respectability, aside from any consideration of practical importance. The best were generally those who held in their hands the physical and spiritual well-being of others. Barbers, surgeons, dealers in spices and drugs, doctors, and book sellers were in this category. Wealth was not of much consideration in the theoretical ranking: userers, brokers, and slave dealers were among the disreputable. The worst were those defiled by wastes: scavengers, butchers, tanners, donkey and dog handlers, and persons of questionable morality: prostitutes, professional entertainers, mourners, cockfighters, and wine sellers. In the middle ranks were tailors, carpenters, dyers, fishermen, and porters among others. The rank of cooks and dealers in food varied with the nature of the product in which they dealt.

Al-Maqrīzī gives us a general idea of the income of the lower classes. At the beginning of the fifteenth century a worker might receive two dirhams a day while a member of the lower middle class might earn about ten. He suggests a distribution of expenses: two dirhams for three *raṭls* (in Cairo, three pounds) of lamb, two dirhams for spices, and four dirhams for the expenses of children, family, and servants. [5] This was very little to get along on, especially when compared with the income of the elite and notables. Yet salary was not the only or even the primary source of income in every case. A considerable amount of subsistence goods reached the populace through redistribution. Not only was grain and meat channelled through elite households on special occasions but there were regular hand-outs to maintain local followings and informal payments for special services rendered. Moreover, as we have shown in the previous part, the most respectable hesitated to work for regular wages. In any case wages were usually supplemented by a food ration, a meal or two, and sometimes by lodging. Employers of *dhimmīs* sometimes paid their poll tax which was a considerable burden for the poor. [6]

The resources of the resourceless were the potentials of ability, respectability, and connections. As Lapidus has written:

> Skilled workers and even common laborers had ... opportunities. Positions in the bureaus and sometimes strikingly brilliant careers were accessible through patronage and purchase. A faithful and competent miller, furrier, or butcher might persuade his patron to give him a secretarial job. Market people attached to military expeditions may have

[5] *Khiṭaṭ*, II, p. 168; *Ighātha*, translated by Gaston Wiet, p. 83.

[6] S. D. Goitein, *A Mediterranean Society*, I, p. 97.

> had good chances too. Once the skills were learned, the former worker was on his way to a career limited only by his own abilities, his talent for flattery and intrigue, and, above all, by the prestige and fortunes of his original patron. Many men had the good luck to transfer their allegiance to the Sultan, and thus to reach very high posts in the government ... These opportunities differed, however, from the chances of the merchants in one decisive way ... Instances of upward mobility among craftsmen ... do not reveal a normal career pattern so much as good fortune in patrons or business. [7]

Another category among *al-ᶜāmma* were those who did not maintain their independence but had a more personal and permanent relationship with those whom they served. These included both slaves and hirelings (*ghilmān*, s. *ghulām*, "young man"; and *ṣabī*, "boy"). Apprentices in workshops, errand boys, and helpers could be included in the latter group. Slaves could be sold and free men might move from the service of one to another, but most saw it to their advantage to maintain a good relationship with the establishment that they served.

The institution of slavery itself bears special consideration. By far the greatest number of slaves were domestics. Fields were tended by the *fallāḥīn* while industry largely was served also by free men. The only other place besides households where slaves were found in numbers was the army, but there slavery was a special thing and a special kind of slave was involved. Unlike ancient Rome, where three quarters of society was constituted of slaves, in medieval Cairo they formed only a minority of the lower class. While some had been captured in war (many Crusaders had met this fate) most were imported and purchased at a high price. The term "*al-ᶜabd*" (pl. *al-ᶜabīd*, "slave") came to refer to black slaves whose origin was Nubia or West Africa. The source of by far the most domestic slaves was Nubia, but European slave girls were also common and prices ranged from fifteen to eighty dinars, the standard price being about twenty dinars in the High Middle Ages. [8] In the fourteenth and fifteenth centuries the price was considerably higher. The polite words to use when referring to slaves or addressing them were "*waṣīf*" ("servant"), "*ghulām*," or "*ṣabī*." In the case of female slaves, "*waṣīfa*" ("servant"), or "*jāriya*" ("errand girl") were commonly used.

Slaves and servants formed part of well-to-do households, it being generally beyond the means of a person of the lower middle class to

---

[7] *Muslim Cities in the Later Middle Ages*, pp. 129-130.

[8] S. D. Goitein, *A Mediterranean Society*, I, pp. 137-139.

keep a servant.[9] Male slaves were not usually used as menials but tended to be utilized as agents in positions of trust. Most domestic tasks, housecleaning and nursing of children, were done by female slaves; free women disdained employment as servants, especially because of the prevalence of slave girls in this occupational category.[10]

Because of their value and indispensability, slaves on the whole were well treated. In Part I we noted the close bond with their masters that was characteristic. They could also contract business on their own. Slaves were protected by rules as well as the ethical injunctions of Islam,[11] Judaism, and Christianity. Debt slavery did not exist and it was allowed, even encouraged, for a slave to purchase his freedom.[12] There is no evidence that any stigma attached to free men who had been slaves. They married free women and concluded contracts of considerable consequence while continuing to benefit in various ways from the social tie which remained after the dissolution of the legal bond.[13]

The slaves of the sultan and his amīrs did not fit into the regular life of the quarters. Attached to the great households many of them behaved in public as they pleased. Stable hands, huntsmen, falconers, and attendants attached to the palaces were responsible for some of the turbulence which chronically blotted the pages of urban history. The sultan in particular kept a large work force of prisoners for his own use, many of whom had been captured in war. These he would lend out from time to time to amīrs. Some were skilled workers and it was said that the Christian carpenters, laborers, and craftsmen who were slaves of the sultan were relatively well off and decently treated. A group in a Cairo prison, *al-khizānat al-bunūd*, were known for their production of wine from which the ruler obtained a good profit.[14]

The lowest of the low were persons who had no permanent attachments or serious business in town, drifters, criminals, and beggars;

---

[9] *Ibid.*, p. 130.

[10] S. D. Goitein, *A Mediterranean Society*, I, p. 129.

[11] A child born of a Muslim from his slave girl was immediately free and the mother, after producing such a child, could neither be alienated nor sold and became free on the death of her master. Manumission was held to be a meritorious act. The Qurʾān says:

> "And those of your slaves who desire a deed of manumission, write it for them, if ye have a good opinion of them, and give them of the wealth of God, which he has given you" (Sūra XXIV, 33).

[12] A. Mez, *Renaissance*, p. 159.

[13] S. D. Goitein, *A Mediterranean Society*, I, pp. 145-146.

[14] I. M. Lapidus, *Muslim Cities in the Later Middle Ages*, p. 173.

those who did not belong to families or households or have any visible means of support. These unassimilated persons were referred to by various terms: *awbāsh al-ʿāmma* (riff-raff), *ghawghāʾ* (trouble makers), *zuʿar* (scoundrels) and *ḥarāfīsh* (beggars). Not all were lawless by nature, however. They tended rather to get into trouble by virtue of their desperation or sheer lack of urban experience. Cairo always had a population of rootless foreigners, refugees, and poverty stricken *fallāḥīn* who slept in the streets when there was no other place to go. Feared as an underworld of thieves, spies, and assassins, at least they threatened pillage when things got too bad. When hands were needed for public works, it was this class and not the slaves who provided the unskilled labor. Corvées were used for the construction of canal works and fortifications, and the urban rabble would be impressed and even occasionally seized in the mosques. It was said that in A.D. 1322-23 so many of them were taken for labor on the canals that they could no longer be found in Cairo. [15] Whatever distasteful task had to be done fell to them. In times of plague and famine it was they who were charged with the collections and burial of the dead. [16] Sometimes a small wage was paid them, but other times it was not. Usually, at least, bread rations were distributed.

Their employment, in any case, was irregular. For the most part they were beggars, scavengers, and common entertainers who hung around the Citadel and disreputable quarters of the city, living off the largess of the sultan and amīrs and picking up a dirham or two in whatever way they could. The *ḥarāfīsh* in particular were considered a barbarous lot. Many were hashish addicts and scandalous in appearance and behavior. When grain crises touched off popular riots they were often responsible for considerable destruction and pillage. Once, when some of the Cairo *ḥarāfīsh* accompanied the army to fight the Mongols in 1281, they even plundered the soldiers food and belongings that had been left behind when the latter went out to engage the enemy. [17] On other occasions when urban authorities were preoccupied with crises in the city, some officials with foresight rounded up the *ḥarāfīsh* to prevent trouble. [18] Still, even they had certain talents that were worth something on the local market. True, they lived principally

[15] I. M. Lapidus, *Muslim Cities in the Later Middle Ages*, p. 178.

[16] Al-Jazarī, Jawāhir as-Sulūk fī Khulafāʾi wa al-Mulūk, MS Dār al-Kutub al-Miṣrīya, Cairo, no. 7575, pp. 317, 318.

[17] I. M. Lapidus, *Muslim Cities in the Later Middle Ages*, p. 179.

[18] Al-Maqrīzī, *Khiṭaṭ*, II, p. 32.

from hand-outs and were even assigned in groups to the amīrs who were to provide for them in time of famine. But it was not entirely a one-sided relationship. Amīrs wanted local followings and the *ḥarāfīsh* were people who could be most useful to them in this respect. The criminal elements had an indispensible knowledge of the ins and outs of the popular quarters combined with a desperation that made them willing tools in the hands of their employers. In fact, for the same reason many became watchmen, guards, police, and executioners, whose very degradation gave respectable people pause when tempted to run afoul of the law.

3. *The Organization of the Lower Orders*

It does not suffice merely to enumerate and describe in detail the groups making up the lower ranks of society. We must also ask, "What were the factors that gave cohesion to these groups?" and "What kind of solidarity did they have, if any?" It is obvious that they were not united as a whole in any way, if only because of their exceedingly divergent origins and orientations. Their appearances in the historical records are usually in connection with sporadic or impulsive actions and the crowds disperse as easily as they are formed. In fact, to use the rabble effectively, amīrs had to appoint leaders and make lists of names, creating units where none existed previously. [19] The most prevalent form of organization was the gang. Cairo was chronically plagued by the depredations of criminal gangs of *zuᶜar*, professional thieves, [20] and renegade black slaves. The latter even entered into serious street fights with the Mamlūks whose authority they dared to challenge. They raided shops and broke into women's baths in broad daylight. Such gangs might include as many as forty men who knew the urban locale. *The Nights* includes a tale in which seven men systematically mug unsuspecting victims with the help of their female hooker who lures them to various ruined houses in the city. [21] Toward

---

[19] The Cairo *zuᶜar* were definitely a criminal element made up of rabble, renegade slaves, and servants, much less organized than in Damascus where many *zuᶜar* were respectable young men with good connections. There is much less evidence of a tie with the Ṣūfī orders in Cairo. See William M. Brinner, "The Significance of the *Ḥarāfīsh* and Their 'Sultan'," *Journal of the Economic and Social History of the Orient*, 6 (1963), pp. 190-215.

[20] Mufaḍḍal ibn Abī al-Faḍāᵓil, *An-Najh as-Sadīd wa ad-Darr al-Farīd*, edited and translated by E. Blochet, "Histoire des Sultans Mamlouks," *Patrologia Orientalis*, XII (Paris, 1919), p. 472.

[21] "The Eighth Constable's History," *Supplemental Nights*, translated by R. F. Burton, II, pp. 34-41.

the end of the Mamlūk period especially, the activity of these gangs increased.[22] Yet there never seemed to be a clearly cut organization behind crime or civil disturbance. Rather it seemed to be a matter of fluid alliances for the purpose of taking advantage of particular situations. As Lapidus has written:

> Apart from the Ṣūfīs, these lower class gangs were powerful, but remained by and large at a rudimentary organizational level. Their forms of association were borrowed from Islamic high society which itself was singularly lacking in collective experience, and the paucity of social models in the high culture was matched by a lack of creativity in the alienated minority.[23]

On the occasions on which the rabble did organize, there are indications that their social forms pertained to popular religious movements, the life of the quarters, or to ethnic origin.[24] The common people were especially attracted to popular cults, often disapproved of by respectable shaykhs and *ᶜulamāᵓ* as being heretical.[25] Although some Ṣūfīs tended more toward orthodoxy, others practiced magic, used hashish, and scandalized honest and God-fearing men with their behavior. By the beginning of the Mamlūk period local branches of international orders had developed institutionally to the extent that there were many *zāwiya*s (saints tombs with hospices for dervishes attached), *khānqāh*s (monasteries) and *ribāṭ*s (hospices for the Ṣūfīs and the poor) in Cairo.

The *ḥarāfīsh* appear also to have developed some sort of organization on a popular religious framework.[26] Out of a loose organization of gangs, occasionally uniting under patrons, groups (*ṭawāᵓif*) emerged under shaykhs and a "sultan of *ḥarāfīsh*," introduced in 1389 on the

---

[22] Ibn Iyās, *Badāᵓiᶜ az-Zuhūr fī Waqāᵓiᶜ ad-Duhūr*, edited by P. Kahle, M. Muṣṭafā, and M. Soberneim (Istanbul, 1936), III, p. 200; translation by G. Wiet, *Histoire des mamlouks circassiens* (Cairo, 1945), II, p. 227.

[23] *Muslim Cities in the Later Middle Ages*, p. 107.

[24] The only times that black slave gangs of the city organized, religion seems to have offered inspiration. In A.D. 1260, they rebelled as Shīᶜīs against a Sunnī majority under the leadership of an ascetic, al-Kūrānī. Rioting Negro stable hands and pages terrified the populace and stole weapons and horses. In the fifteenth century fugitive slaves even set up their own government and chose a "sultan" to rule over them. Although their ranks swelled to as many as two thousand men, the organization actually succeeded for a time until it was split by rival claimants to the "throne" and order could no longer be maintained. The turbulent renegades were captured, sold, and exported to Turkey (I. M. Lapidus, *Muslim Cities in the Later Middle Ages*, pp. 171-172).

[25] As-Sakhāwī, *Aḍ-Ḍawᶜ al-Lāmiᶜ* (Cairo, 1934-35), V, p. 20.

[26] *Ibid.*, p. 20.

initiative of the Mamlūk sultan who jokingly sent their leader with the army in Syria since it had vowed not to march without the sultan. Not a serious office at first, the utility of organizing the *ḥarāfīsh* was obvious and the post was maintained to facilitate distribution of alms and maintenance of order. By the sixteenth century we see the sultan of the *ḥarāfīsh* and fraternities of Ṣūfī beggars marching in military parades. [27]

The factor of locality had perhaps the greatest relevance for the organization of the lower classes, such as it was, especially since locality in many cases was associated with ethnic origin. While the lower orders were absent from no area, there were certain quarters in which they were most prevalent. The Ḥusaynīya, populated by refugees and bordering on the cemetery was one of these, as was the Bāb al-Lūq (the vicinity of the American University in Cairo, at present) where could be found shadow plays, fortune tellers, wrestlers, prostitutes, magicians, and trained animals. The chiefs of the gangs were so well established in the Ḥusaynīya and the Ṣāliḥīya (a street of shops of uncertain location) that the local authorities in those places were held responsible for their arrest. In the middle of the fifteenth century the government did not even attempt to keep statistics on deaths in Ḥusaynīya. [28] Still, even this turbulent place came under the protection of a local amīr.

To some extent a quarter might take on the tone of an occupational group that inhabited it according to the ranking of occupations, but quarters, as in the Fāṭimid period, were not always easy to define. Al-Maqrīzī lists thirty-seven *ḥārāt* (usually signifying alleys which could be closed off) but these did not necessarily indicate unities of social organization. In actuality the urban whole was a conglomeration of small neighborhoods, some blending into others or into larger urban areas such as *sūq*s. As in earlier centuries particular ethnic or religious groups tended to have their own enclaves but there was no strict rule and just as often the property of a member of one group adjoined that of a member of another. Distinction as to class was hardly evident, partly because of the prevalence of ties of partnership and patronage and partly because special status distinctions tended to eclipse the significance of class. Dilapidated ruins still interspersed palatial dwellings, mirroring the transience of fortune, and the difficulty of establishing social boundaries.

[27] I. M. Lapidus, *Muslim Cities in the Later Middle Ages*, pp. 182-183.
[28] *Ibid.*, p. 176.

To visualize the life of the quarters we must turn again to folklore. The tale of Ma^{c}arūf the Cobbler in *The Nights* has a passage worth quoting. Ma^{c}arūf has met a merchant in Damascus and is discussing Cairo with him:

> "My name is Ma^{c}aruf and I am a cobbler by trade and patch old shoes." "What countryman are thou?" "I am from Cairo." "What quarter?" "Dost thou know Cairo?" "I am of its children. I come from the Red Street." "And whom dost thou know in the Red Street?" "I know such an one and such an one," answered Ma^{c}aruf and named several people to him. Quoth the other, "Knowest thou Shaykh Ahmad the druggist?" "He was my next neighbor, wall to wall." "Is he well?" "Yes." "How many sons hath he?" "Three, Mustafà, Mohammed, and Ali." "And what hath Allah done with them?" "As for Mustafà, he is well and he is a learned man, a professor: Mohammed is a druggist and opened him a shop beside that of his father, after he had married, and his wife hath borne him a son named Hasan." "Allah gladden thee with good news!" said the merchant; and Ma^{c}aruf continued, "As for Ali, he was my friend, when we were boys, and we always played together, I and he. We used to go in the guize of the children of the Nazarenes and enter the church and steal the books of the Christians and sell them and buy food with the price. It chanced once that the Nazarenes caught us with a book; whereupon they complained of us to our folk and said to Ali's father: — An thou hinder not thy son from troubling us, we will complain of thee to the King. So he appeased them and gave Ali a thrashing; ..." [29]

Origin in the quarter, like Cairene origin itself, was a means of identification. Social unities tended to be formed by people who hailed from the same place, the same village in the case of immigrant *fallāḥīn*, and the same country in the case of foreign nationals. The proximity of different groups could result in friction as well as cooperation. The tone of everyday social relationships was set by the stereotypes that prevailed. Although there were no ghettos, physical quasi-isolation contributed to group solidarity and reinforced the attitudes of the populace at large. Not only Jews and Christians were viewed with mistrust. Following the Fāṭimid period Shī^{c}īs seem likewise to have been disliked. In *The Nights* black slaves, Persians, and Maghribīs appear in the worst light as ghouls, scoundrels, and evil magicians.

Within the quarters were places for congregation. Baths, wine shops, hashish dens, and, by the sixteenth century, coffee houses were nodes of the local communications network. The role of "rumor mongers" in the political drama would be worth investigating if the

[29] R. F. Burton, *Nights*, X, pp. 8-9.

data were available. Some establishments catered to certain classes while others did not. Slaves, servants, and notably old women [30] transmitted messages when it would have been awkward or impossible for the principals to speak directly.

Local groups of common people generally rallied to the support of their own. Naturally, much of their activity was focused upon the households of the elite and the notables in their midst. When in the riots of A.D. 1389, an angry populace attacked a *qāḍī* and tried to pillage his house, both his household and the people of his quarter defended him. [31] Although there is no evidence of regular organization for defense, and some degree of systematization had to be imposed by the regime, in times of trouble barricades would be put up, the door of the quarter would be locked, and the people would be led by their shaykhs to prevent looting. *The Nights* certainly indicate that in normal everyday affairs, a needy resident could turn to his neighbors for material and moral support.

4. *The Lower Orders and the Elite*: *Conflict and Containment*

The life of the common people is best understood through examination of their behavior in urban crises. By far the most serious problem that chronically touched off demonstrations was the shortage of bread. [32] Taxes were a close second. Cairo was often the scene of rioting and plunder.

The lower middle class of shopkeepers frequently resorted to strikes, [33] closing the markets in defense against oppressive taxation,

[30] Old women are especially marked out in the literature as being active in this regard:

"'So summon Umm Rashīd, the marriage agent *(khāṭiba)*, even though she is one who goes out by night into the bush (*ḥāṭiba*). But she knows every honourable woman and every adultress and every beauty in Miṣr and al-Qāhira. For she lets them go out from the baths, disguised in servants' clothes, and guarantees the prostitutes for whom the police are looking in secret places, providing them with clothes and jewellery without fee ...

Mostly she goes round the houses of the women of rank and sells balls of material, raw and bleached, and all kinds of spices and incense. She sells on credit and makes appointments for Thursdays and Mondays. And she does not haggle over a price. And she keeps her appointments even if it is the night of fate (*lailat al-qadr*)' " (quoted from a shadow play of Ibn Dāniyāl by P. Kahle, "The Arabic Shadow Play in Egypt," in his *Opera Minora* (Leiden: E. J. Brill, 1956), p. 305).

[31] I. M. Lapidus, *Muslim Cities in the Later Middle Ages*, pp. 91-92.

[32] As-Sakhāwī, *At-Tibr al-Masbūk fī Dhayl as-Sulūk* (Cairo (Būlāq), 1896), pp. 259-260.

[33] Al-Muʾminī, Futūḥ an-Naṣr fī Tārīkh Mulūk Miṣr, DS Dār al-Kutub al-Miṣrīya, Cairo, No. 2399, pp. 247, 248.

arbitrary coinage manipulation, or outright Mamlūk depredations. These protests were largely spontaneous expressions of persons in common straits, not well planned or organized, but simply undertaken under the informal leadership of the most respected among them and perhaps the moral support of a few sympathetic notables. Nor can it even be said that such strikes were always an expression of the lower classes of society against the elite who oppressed them. The elite themselves were not well organized and amīrs sometimes deliberately encouraged protests in the market to embarrass their rivals or the sultan's government. The motives behind market closure were characteristically protective and there was not any thought of changing society in major ways or advancing new claims. [34]

On the whole, strikes and popular demonstrations in Cairo lacked effectiveness. In the first place, the military, even when divided, was strong and the presence of the sultan and his garrison especially militated against any possibility of the masses getting the upper hand, even when backed by the *ᶜulamāʾ*. [35] The crowds hesitated to move directly against the regime itself but rather would plead with the sultan to redress their grievances and chastize his deputies whom they held responsible. Their desperation and numbers gave them a certain amount of leverage, however, and even sultans feared them. During the famine of A.D. 1295 Ketbughā built a new stadium near the Citadel so he could avoid the populace when going to military reviews. Armed with sticks and stones the people would repair to the Citadel demanding to be heard. Sometimes they achieved their ends, but if, for political reasons, the sultan feared to take action against those they accused they might suffer a severe response. On one occasion in 1368-69, the mob gathered and demanded that the governor of Cairo and the head of the bureaus be turned over to them. The sultan sent an amīr to hear them but the situation got out of hand and they began to stone the guards at the gate. At this the Mamlūks retaliated horribly, even pursuing the people inside the Madrasa of Sultan Ḥasan where many of them had sought sanctuary and slaughtering them there. [36]

Another factor that tended to deprive popular demonstrations of

---

[34] I. M. Lapidus, *Muslim Cities in the Later Middle Ages*, p. 144.

[35] The situation differed from that of Damascus where the crowds were better able to organize. Protests there were much more violent and bloody and on a number of occasions the sultan's agents met their death at the hands of the mob.

[36] I. M. Lapidus, *Muslim Cities in the Later Middle Ages*, p. 148. Cf. al-ᶜIrāqī, adh-Dhayl ᶜala Kitāb al-ᶜIbar, MS Dār al-Kutub al-Miṣrīya, Cairo, no. 5615, p. 105, for a similar massacre in the Mosque of al-Ḥākim.

any real significance was the character of the notables. While they sometimes supported the people in their claims, as we have seen, the *ᶜulamā*ᵓ tended in the long run to preserve order, which usually meant siding with the military authorities.

On the other hand, grievances directed at notables tended to be more effective than those directed against amīrs. The middlemen were not so insulated from popular opinion. While the people did not have a direct voice in appointment to office, they could and did side with one claimant or another. When in 1419, Cairo *qāḍī*s disagreed about the appointment of a *muḥtasib*, the mobs supported their favorite. [37] Local magistrates bore the brunt of popular resentment [38] and often it was deserved. Al-Maqrīzī cites their venality as a major cause of economic crises, saying that many posts were filled by ignorant, unscrupulous, and cynical individuals who had obtained these responsible offices through court intrigue and bribery. [39] If abuses became too flagrant the people's most usual, most effective means of remedying the situation was direct retaliation through mob violence. Actual attacks were common enough to cause thinking officials to exercise care and restraint.

Ultimately the nature of urban life also militated against coherent expression of grievances by the lower orders and certainly ruled out the possibility of any large scale movement directed at revolutionizing society in major respects. In the first place there was little unity or organization in the causes of their discontent. Nature, greedy and unthinking amīrs, unscrupulous or careless officials all lay behind their troubles. The tax system, for instance, like the distribution of sustenance, was not well coordinated. There was variation not only in the manner of assessment, rates of assessment, and products taxed but also as to methods and individuals responsible for collection. Some people succeeded in securing favors and immunities, others did not. Decentralization and personalization resulted in particularistic complaints; issues never rose above immediate consideration. On the other side of the coin, the masses themselves were atomized; the common people did not conceive of themselves in any way as a class but rather as members of loose intra-urban communities that were united internally to some degree by kinship and ethnic ties and by

---

[37] I. M. Lapidus, *Muslim Cities in the Later Middle Ages*, p. 113.
[38] Al-Maqrīzī, *as-Sulūk*, II (Cairo, 1942), pp. 394-395.
[39] Al-Maqrīzī, *Ighātha*, tr. by G. Wiet, p. 45.

common experience in certain quarters. From the inside and the outside the prospect of real confrontation of classes was negated.

In this situation, the alternative was the chanelling of mob violence into the structure of factional disputes [40] that crystalized around elite interests. After all, the fortunes of the Mamlūk houses were played out on the streets of Cairo as well as in the palaces of the amīrs. Conflicts between factions in the higher ranks of society occupy the pages of history far more than the conflict between social classes and the turbulent elements of the populace more often chose to affiliate themselves with the Mamlūks than to stand alone or to affiliate themselves with respectable members of the middle class who did not offer much in the way of immediate gain.

While the mobs in general lacked effectiveness on their own, their capabilities, especially under Mamlūk leadership, were not to be denied. A considerable number had extensive military experience in foreign campaigns and Mamlūk civil wars, for the cavaliers could not do without infantry to bear the brunt of attacks and provide siege labor. Even *ḥarāfīsh* had taken part in the battles against the Crusaders in Syria and against the Mongols at the instigation of Ṣūfī shaykhs and *ᶜulamāʾ* who called for volunteers in Holy War. Their desperation and experience made them natural allies of the amīrs in the ruthless struggle for ascendancy in the quarters. As auxiliaries fighting with clubs, stones, and arrows they would back up their patrons, retrieve weapons, and harass the enemy.

In the struggle between Circassians and Turks in the latter part of the fourteenth century, the mobs played a significant, though undecisive, role, siding first with one party and then with another. At first Barqūq seemed to command their loyalty, but when the rebels Yalbughā an-Nāṣirī and Mintāsh gained the upper hand, the fickle auxiliaries joined the Turkomans in attacking the houses and stables of amīrs and plundering the quarters. [41] Barqūq, who had repealed all taxes and had seen to the arming of the people and the barricading of the streets, is said to have lost presence of mind, burst into tears, and taken refuge in a tailor's shop. [42] The gangs seized the opportunity to free desperados and assassins from the prisons who considerably

[40] B. Schäfer, *Beiträge zur Mamlukischen Historiographie nach dem Tode al-Malik an-Nasirs mit einem Teiledition der Chronik Šams ad-Dīn aš-Šugais* (Freiburg im Breisgau, 1971), pp. 156, 157.

[41] I. M. Lapidus, *Muslim Cities in the Later Middle Ages*, p. 174.

[42] S. Lane-Poole, *History of Egypt*, p. 330.

added to disorder in the city. Not only amīrs but persons of the middle class were attacked. Then the rebels themselves fell out. Yalbughā occupied the Citadel and encouraged the mobs to pillage his rival who entrenched himself in the Madrasa of Sultan Ḥasan. The two bombarded each other across the *maydān*, but Mintāsh made the mistake of neglecting the masses and Barqūq stepped into the breach to buy their favor. In A.D. 1391 the governor of Cairo led the *qāḍī*s in systematically organizing the quarters and markets to fight against Mintāsh. Although some, like the residents of Ṣāliḥīya, were torn by conflicting loyalties, the attempt succeeded. After much bloodshed in Cairo and in Syria, the rebels were finally overcome, humiliated, nailed to camel saddles, and paraded through the streets until they died. The head of Mintāsh was displayed on a lance in the main towns of Syria and finally exposed on the Bāb Zuwayla. [43]

The inducements the Mamlūks offered the rabble were many and ranged from outright payment to employment in official capacity. In an unsuccessful attempt to control the gangs Mintāsh had appointed *ᶜarīf*s over them and distributed 60,000 dirhams; but support of the masses was needed not only in times of conflict but to maintain regular followings. Clienteles included rumor mongers and rabble rousers to organize "spontaneous" demonstrations. Assistance would be bought by regular hand-outs and tax remissions, but in the case of the dregs of society, one of the strongest incentives was the right to plunder.

In the hope of spoils many of the lower orders clung to the strongest amīrs who by very virtue of their followings were enabled to keep the upper hand. The *ḥarāfīsh* and *zuᶜar* did not hesitate to pillage the houses of the elite when invited to do so by rival amīrs [44] and many of the more respectable of the common people grasped the opportunity when "lawful plunder" was declared, a custom that traditionally formed a regular part of punishment for capital offenses committed by members of the upper classes. Thus the most violent expressions of the masses were made to fit in with the balance of power that prevailed and never really got out of hand. On the whole, aside from the looting of bread in time of famine, and sporadic and temperamental acts of vengeance, [45] the Cairene mobs were remarkably controlled. Ibn Iyās

[43] S. Lane-Poole, *History of Egypt*, p. 326.

[44] B. Schäfer, *Beiträge zur Mamlukischen Historiographie*, pp. 196, 197.

[45] Upon occasion the people would revenge themselves upon persons whom they particularly hated. Thus the amīr Qawṣūn was plundered because he had executed a number of men for trying to rob his property and Christians, Jews, and foreigners

says that the *zu*ᶜ*ar* who dominated the streets during the coup of Barqūq in 1390 contented themselves with pillaging the houses of the amīrs and did not take a dirham from the civilian population. [46]

The kind of payoff that really "clinched" the unholy alliance between the lowest ranks of society and the elite was the appointment of the former as law enforcement officers. The crime stories in *The Nights* in which the plodding police officers are in league with criminals are not entirely fantasies of fiction. [47] Looters would be saved from arrest by their friends and in 1327-28 the governor of Cairo sold "deputyships" for a hundred dirhams a day giving a free hand to the purchasers in the name of the law. Wine parlors, hashish dens, and houses of prostitution were all illegal but flourished under government control. Tax farms on these existed despite periodic moralistic cancellations and were worth a thousand dinars a day. [48] We have seen also that the sultan himself profited from wine making, pork sales, and prostitution organized by prisoners of the state.

Yet the main reason for such alliances was not primarily venality, but a sensible utility and practicality. Criminality and violence were there to stay. If it could not be done away with it could be controlled and channelled along what seemed to be the least harmful and most profitable lines. The government itself organized the underworld to collect its taxes, enforce popular allegiance and, through threats and embarrassment, to coerce the middle ranks of society to fall into line.

5. *The Lower Orders in the Urban Milieu: the Nature and Consequences of Deprivation*

One of the most difficult problems we face in trying to reconstruct the life of the common people lies in comprehending the calamities

---

too frequently suffered from this kind of behavior that resulted not so much from desire for pillage as from other motives (I. M. Lapidus, *Muslim Cities in the Later Middle Ages*, pp. 168-169.) Intergroup animosities, however, were controlled to some extent by state approved extortions and official confiscations.

46 *Badā*ʾ*i*ᶜ *az-Zuhūr fī Waqā*ʾ*i*ᶜ *ad-Duhūr* (Cairo (Būlāq), 1892), I, p. 286.

47 As one police chief writes to a gang leader in Cairo:

" 'Thou knowest that I tormented Salah al-Din the Cairene and befooled him till I buried him alive and reduced his lads to obey me ... I am now become town-captain of Baghdad in the Divan of the Caliph who hath made me overseer of the suburbs. An thou be still mindful of our convenant, come to me; haply thou shalt play some trick in Baghdad which may promote thee to the Caliph's service, so he may appoint thee stipends and allowances and assign thee a lodging, which is what thou wouldst see and so peace be on thee' " (R. F. Burton, *Nights*, VII, p. 176.)

48 I. M. Lapidus, *Muslim Cities in the Later Middle Ages*, pp. 172-173.

that befell the urban center as a whole. Our milieu is relatively safe, stable, and predictable. Theirs literally hung between life and death in ways that we cannot imagine. Despite long term stability, the economy in the short run was far from stable. Low Niles, [49] delays in distribution, civil wars, hoarding, and fluctuations in the value of copper coin could be borne fairly well by the upper classes but for the lower orders who operated on a much slimmer margin, they could be disastrous. To the medieval Cairene these problems were normal but their significance went beyond stimulation of social conflict. In their most horrendous manifestations they were capable of resolving social differences in a classless amalgam of human frailty.

Al-Maqrīzī describes the chronic vulnerability of the urban populace to the effects of famine. Prices of wheat would rise from the normal fifteen or twenty dirhams per *irdabb* to thirty, forty, sixty, and as much as four hundred dirhams. The *fallāḥīn*, driven by hunger, would fall upon Cairo. People would steal bread from the shops and bakeries and would even pillage the dough on its way to the oven. Companies of guards armed with clubs attempted to defend it, but to no avail; the famished ones would throw themselves on the loaves not feeling the blows that rained down upon them. The government often sincerely tried to ameliorate the situation by taking measures against hoarders and dividing the task of feeding the poor between the sultan and his amīrs. An amīr of a hundred might be charged to feed a hundred, an amīr of fifty would get fifty, and an amīr of ten, ten. [50] But all too often nothing could be done when the Nile did not rise. At the beginning of the Ayyūbid period, in the year 1200, the river was so low that the channel between the Nilometer and Old Cairo and part of the Giza bank were uncovered and the taste and smell of the water were affected. Many people died from epidemics and the living turned to cannibalism:

> the father devoured his son, roasted or boiled, and the mother ate her child: the practice was strongly condemned but the crime became so widespread that the authorities did not interfere. Men and women carried in their robes shoulders and legs of infants or pieces of flesh. People would enter a neighboring house where the kettle was on the fire, and they would wait until the dish was done in order to ascertain

[49] See ᶜAli Pasha Mubārak, *al-Khiṭaṭ at-Tawfīqīya al-Jadīda li Miṣr al-Qāhira* (Cairo, 1888), XVIII, for a table giving information on rises in food prices correlated with failures of the Nile to rise from the Arab through Turkish periods, especially pp. 57, 58, 60.

[50] Al-Maqrīzī, *Ighātha*, tr. by Gaston Wiet, pp. 35-36.

> whether it was human flesh and often they encountered it in the best families. In the markets and in the streets one would jostle men and women who secretly carried the flesh of infants and, in less than two months, they burned thirty women caught in the act. This custom assumed such proportions and so many people dined on human flesh, finally becoming accustomed to it, that rarely were they prosecuted since no one could find food; all the grain was gone as were beans and other produce.[51]

Although the situation after a while returned to normal, scarcity was a common occurrence and the spectre of famine invariably reappeared. Two hundred years later in 1403 few animals could be found and nearly half the people of Egypt died of cold and hunger.[52]

Outbreaks of plague too were common and as in Europe, the epidemic of A.D. 1348-49 surpassed in horror anything previously known. People were terrified at the great number of deaths and the streets, quarters, and markets exuded a fetid odor. No one could keep track of the bodies in public places where they were piled up so they simply threw them into pits. In October 1348 the deaths in the city rose from 300 daily to 3,000 near the end of the month. Streets and houses became deserted. It was said that if a man inherited anything it would go in the same day to a fourth and a fifth party. So much property remained ownerless and survivors were so few that people helped themselves to furniture and money with little interference. In Cairo and its suburbs from 200,000 to 300,000 died.[53] While the Black Death of 1348 was the most virulent epidemic, there were at least eighteen outbreaks of plague during the following century and a half.

The terrors of the Death are beyond our comprehension and perhaps for this reason modern social scientists have for the most part failed to appreciate its full significance for the pattern of social relations. Psychologically, demographically, and economically, the plague was a great leveler.

With regard to the attitudes it engendered it has been noted that in Europe two psychological responses were common and the responses

---

[51] Al-Maqrīzī, *Ighātha*, tr. by Gaston Wiet, p. 30.

[52] *Ibid.*, p. 45.

[53] Al-Maqrīzī in his account of the plague (*Sulūk*, II, pp. 772-782) reports that the figure was 900,000, but this estimate reflects psychological rather than demographic reality. The mortality was very high in Egypt, however. In Europe where the ravages were less strong than in the East, nearly one quarter of the population was wiped out between 1348 and 1350. It is now estimated that in the following fifty years the total mortality rose to over a third of the population (W. L. Sanger, "The Black Death," *Scientific American*, 210 (1964), p. 114).

of Egyptian humanity almost certainly were no different.[54] Some people typically reacted with expressions of piety and guilt, believing that God was punishing mankind for its sins; others, noting that the Death punished all alike, rich and poor, young and old, good and bad, resolved to satisfy their desires as soon as possible with no fear of God or man. Both attitudes tended to deny distinctions of rank and class.

Demographically no stratum or division of society was spared, although some groups were more decimated than others. Deaths were highest among foreigners who were not biologically well adapted to the Egyptian milieu, "Mamlūks, children, black slaves, slave girls, and foreigners" the highest and lowest classes, the chroniclers say.[55] Craftsmen and artisans too, were hard hit. Al-Maqrīzī, speaking of economic problems some fifty years later describes eloquently the situation:

> As for the sixth category, these are the artisans, wage workers, porters, servants, grooms, weavers, builders, laborers, and their like. Their wages multiplied many times over; however, not many remain since most of them died.[56]

Indeed, one gets the impression that the lower classes nearly disappeared. Laborers, porters, and domestics were so scarce that their wages practically tripled. A stable boy who had been paid thirty dirhams a month was paid eighty.[57]

To say that no family monopolies lasting more than two or three generations were possible is a gross understatement. It was not simply a matter of "free-wheeling" social mobility but of major upheavals in which firm restrictions would have broken had they existed. Even under normal conditions changes of government and migration currents discouraged maintenance of a balanced equilibrium through careful

---

[54] See M. Dols, "Ibn al-Wardī's *Risālah al-Nabaʾ ʿan al-Wabaʾ*, a Translation of a Major Source for the History of the Black Death in the Middle East," *Near Eastern Numismatics, Iconography, Epigraphy, and History: Studies in Honor of George C. Miles*, edited by Dickran K. Kouymjian (Beirut: American University of Beirut Press, 1974), pp. 443-455.

[55] See D. Neustadt (Ayalon), "The Plague and Its Effects upon the Mamlūk Army," *Journal of the Royal Asiatic Society* 1946, p. 70; Cf. Ibn Iyās, *Badāʾiʿ az-Zuhūr fī Waqāʾiʿ ad-Duhūr*, edited by P. Kahle et al., III, pp. 378, 380; translation by G. Wiet, *Histoire des mamlouks circassiens*, pp. 426, 430.

[56] *Ighātha*, p. 75.

[57] R. Lopez, et al., "England to Egypt, 1350-1500: Long-term Trends and Long-distance Trade," p. 122; al-Maqrīzī, *Sulūk*, II, p. 786.

observance of distinctions of rank and class. Recurrent famines and plagues made a strictly regulated social structure impossible.

It is an ill wind that blows no good and even these catastrophic whirlwinds benefited the survivors by blowing away obstacles in their paths. Not only did persons of the lower orders come into unexpected windfalls through inheritance and looting but inflation worked in their favor. From the end of the thirteenth century to the beginning of the fifteenth, the price of bread rose sixty-six per cent while the typical wages of an urban laborer rose one hundred and twenty-two per cent. [58] Thousands of positions vacated in the higher ranks of society were filled by anyone who was reasonably respectable and could do the job. Although specific cases scattered throughout the chronicles have not been collected to give us a statistical concept of the degree of mobility, some of the evidence is intriguing. A number of the elite were called "Ibn Ḥarfūsh." In the urban milieu not only did *awlād an-nās* become rabble, but Mamlūk rules or no, beggars sons could become amīrs.

It is little wonder that popular uprisings lacked ideology and coherent expression, little wonder that the crowds of people dispersed as soon as they were formed; for the position of the lower orders, like the meaning of the terms "*an-nās*" and "*al-ᶜāmma*" was ambiguous. The common people as individuals were affiliated with every other class and yet were not part of any. That was why they fitted so easily into clienteles. The breadth of their experience made them invaluable while their deprivation made alliances with them a safe bargain.

Social mobility was partly a function of the vicissitudes of political fortune and partly a function of demographic and economic instability. However strict the rules of inheritance, implicit or explicit, with a change in state policy, national economy, or population size, the positions of individuals and groups could rise or fall overnight. The stakes were tremendous. Political purges were no less spectacular than natural calamities. Both the rich and poor, noble and ignoble, interacted as equal beings in the environment to which they were subject. Ibn Khaldūn's statement that the lower orders "had nothing to gain or to lose among their fellow men" was not exactly true. The real truth of the matter was that everyone had everything to gain and everything to lose.

---

[58] R. Lopez, et al., "England to Egypt, 1350-1500: Long-term Trends and Long-distance Trade," p. 121.

CHAPTER ELEVEN

THE MAMLŪK DECLINE AND ITS SOCIOECONOMIC CONSEQUENCES

From the preceding discussion of Mamlūk Cairo, it is obvious that the city's prosperity depended in no small part upon the efficiency of the Mamlūk organization, the sound management of the estate by the notables, and the exploitation of Egypt's economic and cultural advantages by the middle and lower classes. The successfully managed estate, in brief, was characterized by the exploitation of a certain set of circumstances by groups of persons united in formal and informal liaisons that gave access to the goods and services which they needed, military, economic, legal, and even ideological. The maintenance of prosperity also depended upon security and the capacity to adapt to changes in circumstance. We have seen that, while the military elite and persons of other classes cooperated in many situations critical to the security of Cairo, with possibly a few exceptions there was a large gulf between the elite and the rest of society socially and with respect to their control of resources, basic orientations, and culture.

The society of interdependent groups, moreover, did not exist in a vacuum. Its evolution took place in a national environment that was sensitive to changes on the international scene. As natural catastrophes could cause severe repercussions in the city, so shifts in the balance of economic and military power had profound effects on ways of life that had existed for centuries. The defeat of the Mamlūks by the Ottomans in 1516 was but the culmination of a process of decline that had set in over a century and a half before. Plague, famine, international competition, and internal forces of social disintegration all contributed to Cairo's loss of supremacy.

A total recovery from the effects of the Black Death was impossible and the demographic decline triggered declines in other areas. Epidemics recurred at intervals of ten and twenty years during the following century, seriously effecting the agricultural sector upon which urban life ultimately depended. So few were left to cultivate and to harvest that fief holders, finding that even offers of half the crop brought them no assistance, had to gather the grain themselves. [1] In-

[1] R. Lopez et al., "England to Egypt, 1350-1500: Long-term Trends and Long-distance Trade," p. 119.

flation brought about what Eli Ashtor has termed "a price revolution." [2] As we have seen, the salaries of urban laborers increased many fold. By the middle of the fifteenth century the price of bread in the city rose 66 per cent while the price of wheat rose 20 per cent and so it was with all processed food products. The prices of manufactured goods increased by as much as 500 per cent. [3]

Ultimately everyone suffered. The urban masses were confronted by chronically high food prices as well as shortages in meat, rice, and other staples. The middle classes also found many luxuries to which they had become accustomed beyond their means; textiles, clothing, and carpets that were traditionally important forms of wealth and important markers of rank all rose three to ten times in price. [4] Stipends upon which many middle class and lower class persons depended lagged terribly behind the inflation. The Mamlūks themselves were hard hit, and perhaps for them the disparity between income and expenses was the greatest. The cost of maintaining their establishment, from purchase and training of new recruits to the furnishing of households and payment of clienteles, rose many times over while their principal resources, the agricultural products that they received from their estates, were worth proportionately less on the urban market. [5]

The loose interdependence of different groups, with the maintenance of their relative independence, had allowed the development of efficient management in many areas of life through occupational concentration. The economic "squeeze," however, interfered with the balance as various parties struggled for resources to maintain themselves. Especially in the case of the elite, the struggle to maintain status as a class was inseparable from the inability to cope with demographic changes and the economic repercussions these engendered. Developments on the international scene severely aggravated their situation. Under the strain of circumstances, the Mamlūk establishment was all the more vulnerable to deterioration through the progressive evolution of the conflicting forces which we have already seen at work within it.

The decline of Mamlūk power, the gradual shrinkage of their

---

[2] "L'évolution des prix dans le Proche-Orient à la basse-époque," *Journal of the Economic and Social History of the Orient*, IV (1961), pp. 15-46.

[3] Subḥī Labīb, "Egyptian Commercial Policy in the Middle Ages," p. 76.

[4] I. M. Lapidus, *Muslim Cities in the Later Middle Ages*, p. 31.

[5] R. Lopez, et al., "England to Egypt, 1350-1500: Long-term Trends and Long-distance Trade," p. 120.

effective network and final defeat at the hands of the Ottomans, was only partially a result of external forces. Ironically, their military effectiveness, the bastion of state security, was impaired by factors implicit in the organization itself, elements which formed the very bases of Mamlūk solidarity. The *esprit de corps*, the feeling of fellowship between *khushdāshīya* and their loyalty to their *ustādh*, fostered the strongest competition between groups organized on the same principles. The various Mamlūk units, Ashrafīs. Nāṣirīs, Muʾayyadīs, and Ẓāhirīs struggled with one another for control of the army. Some units made payments to the sultan for exemption from participation in military expeditions to be on hand in Cairo to defend their interest. Preoccupation with internal politics eventually led to the neglect of military discipline and training.

The rapid changes of sultan in the Circassian period went hand in hand with the increase in factionalism. Of twenty-three sultans, the reigns of six extend over 103 of the total 134 years. [6] Nine Circassians, among them Barqūq, Faraj, Muʾayyad, and Qānṣūh al-Ghūrī, displayed extraordinary ability in managing the difficult segments of the army. Few, however, led their troops far afield but spent their greatest efforts contending with the constantly unsettled conditions at home. Not only sultans, but amīrs also, rapidly replaced one another. Under the Baḥrīs promotions had come at a slow rate and only after a long period of intensive military training. According to Ibn Taghrī-Birdī, however, at the time of the deposition of al-Ashraf Shaʿbān in 1376, many of those who suddenly rose to high positions had previously attained no higher standing than the rank of an amīr of ten. [7]

Military experience and extensive training thus came to be lacking in the corps closest to the sultan. The *qarānīṣ*, being the mamlūks of former sultans and therefore a chronic source of trouble in Cairo, were constantly sent forth to war if the occasion arose. These veteran units became the most effective fighting force through both training and experience. Ibn Taghrī-Birdī states that one hundred *qarānīṣ* could rout over one thousand *julbān* and even the lowest black slaves could put the latter to flight if it were not for the respect they held for the sultan. [8] Indeed, a large number of *julbān* were unable to overcome a small force led by an amīr on one occasion, and their ignorance of the arts of war even made them unable to resist a Cairo mob on

[6] S. Lane-Poole, *History of Egypt*, p. 325.
[7] *Nujūm*, edited by W. Popper, V, pp. 305-306.
[8] *Nujūm*, edited by W. Popper, VI, p. 641.

another. [9] The *qarānīṣ*, however, belonging to various Mamlūk houses, could not displace the united mamlūks of the sultan. Wily rulers like Khūshqadam would play off one faction against another. Yet even the sultan himself often lost control of his own men who were allowed the terrorize the populace and pillage as they pleased. David Ayalon describes vividly the breakdown of authority:

> From the middle of the 9th century onward, Mamlūk sources are permeated with the terror of the *ajlāb*, and a very great number of pages are devoted to its description. There are whole years in which little would remain in the chronicles if the description of these nefarious activities were removed. Hundreds of stories are told of the expulsion of high state officials (mostly those connected with payments to the army) the burning of their houses, the pillaging of the markets and shops of the capital, the burning down of the townspeople's houses, the abduction of women without any voice being raised in protest, the amirs' fear of the *ajlāb*, from whom they hide their treasures, etc. The sultan completely loses control of the *ajlāb*, who stone him and put him to shame in public. Whenever they wish to extort something from the sultan, they prohibit his going up to the citadel. They intervene in questions of appointments and depositions of sultans, and they have their way in the appointment of the king of Cyprus and that of the highest amirs of the kingdom. This situation had the effect of terrorizing the population, for it was known in advance that 'whatever they do will be permitted them, and the sultan will not protect those oppressed by them'. In such an anarchical state of affairs, the law courts lost all their value, and whoever desired anything addressed himself not to the tribunals, but to the *ajlāb*. One of the main reasons for the Circassian sultans' infrequent departures from the capital was the constant state of upheaval into which the city was thrown by the activities of the *julbān* ...
>
> For all their misdeeds the *julbān* were given surprisingly light penalties. When the sultan has one of them soundly trounced his act is described as being in opposition to accepted usage. [10]

The disappearance of discipline led to chaotic conditions reminiscent of Cairo under the late Fāṭimids. The effects of political anarchy had repercussions in every part of society. Even under Bars-Bey, the strongest of the Circassian sultans, the peasants hesitated to bring their produce to Cairo lest it be seized by predatory mamlūks. The infamy of the government included the open sale of official positions including the governorships of Tripolis and Damascus. Religious officials and administrators were every bit as corrupt as those of this class depicted in *The Thousand and One Nights*. Under al-Muʾayyad, the

---

[9] *Nujūm*, edited by W. Popper, VI, p. 693; VII, p. 25.

[10] D. Ayalon, "Studies on the Structure of the Mamluk Army," pp. 212-213.

Shaykh al-Islām himself, an ignorant Persian who could not speak Arabic, stole trust money and was exposed in public disputation and dismissed. Rarely, however, were such unsavory individuals removed from office.

The plague was responsible for seriously weakening the Mamlūk corps. Losses under the Burjīs were much higher than they had been under the Baḥrīs. Between A.D. 1416 and 1513 there were no less than fourteen epidemics of major proportions. The Royal Mamlūks suffered most. As the greatest number of deaths were among newly arrived foreigners and children, the *julbān* who had developed the least degree of immunity of all groups within the army suffered the greatest losses; substantially greater than the losses among the *qarānīṣ* who had built up some resistance as survivors of previous epidemics. In the outbreak of A.D. 1460, during the reign of Īnāl, more than a third of the Mamlūks of all classes died but the *julbān* lost more than half their number. In 1476, two thousand of Qāyt-Bey's *ajlāb* were wiped out. It was said that "the barracks in the Citadel were emptied of the Royal Mamlūks because of their death." [11] Such sudden changes in the size of the competing factions were bound to effect the sensitive political balance. The sultan and the *julbān* would try to weaken their opponents, the *qarānīṣ* by enlisting the aid of the *sayfīya* (mamlūks who had entered the service of the sultan from that of various amīrs) as these were not bound by the feeling of solidarity shared by the *qarānīṣ* as chief opponents of the *julbān*. The *sayfīya*, for their part, grasped the opportunity to achieve a higher rank. Thus it is easy to see how the plague contributed to the breakdown of discipline and the rapid turn-over of sultans and amīrs. Wholesale redistributions of property followed the ravages of the epidemic. In 1491 and 1513, each man of the *julbān* and *qarānīṣ* was given a horse, arms, and armor, from the effects of the deceased of the corps. One fief was known to change hands as many as nine times. Untrained and undisciplined troops acquired fiefs even before their graduation from the military schools, and artisans, tailors, and shoemakers replaced members of the *ḥalqa* as feudal lords. [12]

It is often said that a major cause of the economic decline of Egypt was the Portuguese discovery of the Cape Route in 1479 and the

---

[11] D. Neustadt (Ayalon), "The Plague and Its Effects upon the Mamlūk Army," pp. 70-71.

[12] *Ibid.*, p. 73.

subsequent diversion of the European-Eastern trade from the Red Sea. This is a large part of the story, but by no means the only part. In the inflation that beset the economy, gold dinars and silver dirhams became increasingly scarce. Al-Maqrīzī attributes the breakdown of the monetary system to the state's fiscal policy but, in fact, for a long time there had been serious drains on the country's gold reserves. Many of the luxury goods enjoyed by the upper classes were imports: porcelains from China, furs from the Black Sea, [13] and above all, slaves. Ultimately much wealth flowed to India, for while the transit trade in spices persisted as a major source of income, Cairenes themselves consumed a large amount of spices and aromatics. [14]

Meanwhile nature and changes in the international balance of power conspired to deprive Egypt of economic advantage. Nubian gold mines were nearly exhausted by the end of the thirteenth century, and although an energetic trade with the western Sudan kept gold coming in until the latter part of the next century, diversion of trade to Europe eventually closed that source as well. A number of important exports seriously declined. Sugar, for instance, had been exported in great quantities during the High Middle Ages, but following the Crusades sugar cane was introduced to Europe, and by the fifteenth century produced on a large scale in Madiera, Azores, and Cape Verde. Alum exports met a similar fate. In the thirteenth century between 5,000 and 13,000 *qinṭār*s were exported but in the middle of the next century large deposits were discovered in Italy and the Egyptian mines dried up. Even Egyptian textiles succumbed to foreign competition. Even in Cairo people preferred high quality, low cost Italian silks, and because of the decline in all industries and their development abroad, exports of linen and other materials likewise fell off. [15]

In these distressing economic circumstances the maintenance of the army became an even worse drain on the country's resources. While the *nafaqa*, or pay was considerably higher under the Baḥrīs than it had been under the Ayyūbids, under the Burjīs it was higher still. With the general decline of the Egyptian economy there was a constant struggle

---

[13] Furs came to be an indispensible part of attire for upper class males. One merchant alone arrived in Cairo with 300,000 furs worth hundreds of thousands of dinars (R. Lopez, "England to Egypt, 1350-1500: Long-term Trends and Long-distance Trade," p. 126).

[14] See above page 165 n. 25; R. Lopez, et al., "England to Egypt, 1350-1500: Long-term Trends and Long-distance Trade," pp. 126-128.

[15] C. Issawi, "The Decline of Middle Eastern Trade, 1100-1850," *Islam and the Trade of Asia*, edited by D. S. Richards (Oxford: Bruno Cassirer, 1970), pp. 254-256.

between the army and the treasury over salaries. For one thing the amīrs at this time were forced to spend an even greater amount on their personal troops. Owing to the decline of the *ḥalqa* and the disappearance of the *wāfidīya* in the last part of the fourteenth century, they were no longer able to purchase the relatively cheap services of Turkoman, Kurdish, and Mongol free horsemen but had to recruit their supporters from among the mamlūks and go to a considerable expense to rear and train them. One may ask how it was that the army could be three times smaller than formerly and yet be so much more expensive to maintain. One of the reasons for the rise of Mamlūk power was that the mamlūk corps had been less expensive to support than the *wāfidīya.* Ibn Taghrī-Birdī attributes the decline in the size of the army not only to plague but to the greed of the amīrs. According to him they would not only buy up fiefs but obtain monthly salaries from the sultan for their mamlūks, thereby making each man simultaneously an amīr's mamlūk, a member of the *ḥalqa*, and a Royal Mamlūk. [16] The loss of fiefs through their conversion to allodial lands has already been discussed. Thus the feudal revenues controlled by the sultan became substantially less than they had been while the expense of the army proportionately increased. The amīrs and their factions, on the other hand, had access to economic resources they had not controlled previously, and they used them with little consideration for the good of the army as a whole but only to further their own particular cause in factional strife.

The contraction of the power structure and exhaustion of Egypt's resources through the predations of the elite greatly exaggerated the effects of the general slump in the economy described above. As Ibn Taghrī-Birdī wrote:

> Were it not for the ... devastation which has befallen some of the regions of the realm, because of continuous oppression, increased taxation, and the ruler's neglect of the country's welfare, there should be no adversary capable of resisting the Egyptian forces, and no army worthy of comparison with them. [17]

The continual and desperate confiscation of the estates of amīrs and the wealth of merchants and entrepreneurs discouraged investment of all kinds. People hid their gold and silver in the ground or put it with trusted persons who, unknown to government officials, would keep it safely for them. The sultan, threatened always by an imminent

---

[16] *Nujūm*, VI, p. 387.
[17] *Ibid.*, VI, p. 387 .

coup d'état, felt only the urgent need of collecting payment for his troops. As the hereditary principle which governed succession to the sultanate was weakened and the Mamlūk "generations" became shorter through plague and rapid replacement, it became all the more difficult for any concentration of capital to develop within one group. To be sure, the amīrs did succeed in having some of their wealth set aside as *waqf*, but it became increasingly hazardous to invest in the most productive of endeavors, and those who attempted to do so were soon ruined.

A prime example of the extent of commercial disintegration is the decline of the spice trade and of the Kārimīs who had managed it so well. We have noted many times that international trade depended upon a high degree of political stability, and that while the government always did claim a share of the profits in the form of tax, it also performed certain services to facilitate the conduct of business on a large scale. The sultan Bars-Bey (A.D. 1422-1435) however, interfered directly with the Kārimī trade not only by increasing taxation but also by imposing a state monopoly upon all imported articles, spices, sugar, metal, wood, etc. The shipments were diverted from Syria and channelled through Egypt while prices of sale to European merchants were fixed by the government. The Kārimīs were likewise compelled to buy from the government at fixed prices. When pepper that cost 50 dinars in Cairo was sold to the Venetians in Alexandria for 130 dinars, [18] the latter broke off relations in protest and sent a fleet to Alexandria to remove their merchants, and the kings of Aragon and Castile set about capturing Egypt's cargo ships on the Syrian coast. Although Bars-Bey finally removed the monopoly from all goods but pepper and relations were restored, he then tempered with the coinage, putting foreign money out of currency and readmitting it. Duties were heavier than ever.

Of course the system of monopolies discouraged private enterprise in the very areas from which Egypt had previously derived the most revenue. The most esteemed Kārimīs became only agents of the government (*tujjār khawājā as-sulṭān, wukalāʾ as-sulṭān*). All of these were men of only moderate wealth compared to their illustrious predecessors. Private fortunes that had reached hundreds of thousands of dinars rapidly dwindled. It is notable that in 1430, when Bars-Bey inquired about the causes of an epidemic which ravaged the country, the leading theologians mentioned the pressures put upon the Kārimīs. [19]

[18] S. Lane-Poole, *History of Egypt*, p. 340.

[19] E. Ashtor, "The Kārimī Merchants," p. 54.

Although some of the successors of Bars-Bey tried to repair the damage, most were too busy satisfying their followers and contending with their enemies to give the merchants a freer hand. The notoriously corrupt Khūshqadam also followed a monopolistic policy, and by A.D. 1498 and the advent of the Portuguese on the scene, the revenue coming to Cairo from the Indian trade was but a fraction of what it had been a century before. The sultans had long neglected to make any serious investment in the businesses they now managed or to renew and replace markets and craftshops which fell into decay.

The populace as a whole suffered from the failing of Mamlūk investment, the keystone of the urban economy. Caught in inflation and the price squeeze, the Mamlūks could no longer satisfy large clienteles, they could no longer make substantial contributions to charitable foundations, and above all, they could no longer patronize the local crafts and industries that had flourished principally through the high consumption of luxury goods by the elite and upper classes. [20] Fewer and fewer public works were undertaken. By the time of al-Maqrīzī, scant evidence remained of the 12,000 shops that had once bustled with activity along the main street; by the middle of the fifteenth century two thirds of the city was in ruins. Only the port of Būlāq continued to flourish, being concerned not so much with urban fortunes as with foreign trade.

Events and conditions of the last years of the fifteenth century and the beginning of the sixteenth show how desperate the situation had become. Dislocations in the organization of the market produced not only high prices but unexpected shortages in staples. Sources of income that formerly met the needs of the regime no longer sufficed, so much had revenues from agriculture and trade [21] fallen off. When upon the accession of Qānṣūh al-Ghūrī to the sultanate in A.D. 1501, the Mamlūks clamored for their traditional "payment of fealty," the sultan at first considered outright confiscation of *waqf* endowments but, under advisement, he decided finally to levy eleven months taxes in advance upon urban properties, houses, shops, fields, and boats, even including *waqf* holdings.

Popular unrest in the city reached a peak in the latter part of the

[20] I. M. Lapidus, *Muslim Cities in the Later Middle Ages*, p. 29.

[21] The customs from Qaṭyā, on the main artery of Syrian-Egyptian trade fell from 350,000 dinars a year in A.D. 1326 to 96,000 dinars a year in 1395/6 and 8,000 dinars a year by the end of the fifteenth century (R. Lopez et al., "England to Egypt, 1350-1500: Long-term Trends and Long-distance Trade," p. 116).

fourteenth century. The agricultural decline was further precipitated by bedouin attacks on villages. No longer controlled effectively by the army, they did not hesitate to raid caravans and interfere with the transport of grain to Cairo. The *fallāḥīn*, unable to evade the increasingly unbearable pressures of serfdom, would migrate to Cairo and attempt to seize what grain they could and burn the rest before it reached Būlāq in the hope of avoiding payment of tax.[22] This continual rural-urban migration, especially heavy in years of famine, created a mass of permanently unemployed who, in their search for livelihood, became chronic trouble-makers.

Dissatisfied migrants and aligned slaves, workers, artisans, and peddlers had always constituted an urban problem, but gang activity increased with the decline. The factional wars and Ottoman incursions led to even greater enrollment of the *zuᶜar* and the rabble as auxiliaries to Mamlūk ranks and, as the masses became increasingly involved in struggles over food and pay, it became more and more difficult to maintain order in the city. Ultimately their intervention in the affairs of the elite was discouraged, for the later Circassians, weakened by the lack of discipline, came to fear the power of the rabble who were often led by settled bedouins never reconciled to taxation and military conscription. Pillage often took place independently, without the invitation of the elite. When in 1449-1450, famine drove the people to pillage the shops of bread, they stoned the *muḥtasib* and wounded the *qāḍī* who had told the sultan that "the people who have money to buy hashish and sweets can buy bread at the highest price."[23]

The corrupt *qāḍī*s, of course, saw scant advantage in opposing the Mamlūks who were in fact their masters, while the shaykhs of al-Azhar who might have spoken out on behalf of the people, were conservative to the highest degree and lacked the physical means to do anything to remedy the situation, even if they would. The rebels themselves came from various groups, urban and rural, and often had no goal beyond the immediate satisfaction of subsistence needs.

As was to be expected, the decline of discipline in the Mamlūk army went hand in hand with the deterioration of Mamlūk authority abroad.

---

[22] Ibn Taghrī-Birdī, *Ḥawādith ad-Duhūr fī Madā al-Ayyām wa ash-Shuhūr*, edited by Wm. Popper (Berkeley: University of California Press, 1932), pp. 109, 110, 696; Cf. A. N. Poliak, "Les révoltes populaires en Égypte à l'époque des mamelouks et leurs causes économiques," *Revue des Études Islamiques*, VIII (1934), p. 261.

[23] Ibn Taghrī-Birdī, *Nujūm*, VII, pp. 175, 176, 179, 195; *History of Egypt, 1382-1469 A.D.*, translated by W. Popper, V, pp. 118-119; Cf. A. N. Poliak, "Les révoltes populaires," p. 268.

The initial challenge in Syria was provided by the Tatars who, under Tamurlane, sacked and burned Damascus. The Egyptians under an-Nāṣir Faraj, son of Barqūq, attempted to check the advance but owed success in this endeavor to no military prowess of their own, but rather to the defeat of Tamurlane's army at the hands of the Ottomans at the Battle of Angora (A.D. 1402). Thus the Tatar came to terms with Faraj and the latter surrendered prisoners and even agreed to strike coins in the name of Tamurlane. Although no such coins have ever been found,[24] the sultan's reputation was considerable blackened by these proceedings and his Mamlūks fought among themselves for control of Syria.

In 1418, the sultan al-Muʾayyad attempted to restore Egyptian authority but upon his departure from Syria the Turks reoccupied the territory he had taken and the subsequent successes on the part of his son Ibrāḥīm came to an end when the father, afraid of being supplanted by a son so able, poisoned him. Governors were appointed from among the leading Turkoman families and these from then on became a continual source of annoyance on Syria's northern border. Every agitation became a pretext for Ottoman intervention. Bars-Bey, Jaqmaq, and Īnāl tried to appease these vassals by pursuing a conciliatory policy and even married their daughters, but the rupture could not be put off for long. By the 1460's the Turkomans set about capturing cities on their own and, in token of a fictitious vassalage, sending the keys to Cairo.

The Ottoman Porte, in control of Constantinople since 1453, entered the situation more and more, putting forth their own Turkoman contestants to rule Syrian principalities technically Egyptian. Qāyt-Bey, seizing a supposed opportunity to strike at the heart of Ottoman power, welcomed the sultan's exiled brother, Jem, and treated him royally in Cairo. Later, when the pretender repaired to Rome, the ruler of Egypt entered into negotiations with the Christians for his return. Failing in the endeavor, Qāyt-Bey then tried to repair relations with the Porte, but only after long and expensive campaigns did he restore peace and cause the keys of Syrian fortresses to be returned to Cairo. For the remainder of the century the situation deteriorated. Bedouin raids made international trade increasingly difficult. Between A.D. 1494/5 and 1513 the pilgrimage was nearly impossible.[25]

---

[24] S. Lane-Poole, *History of Egypt*, p. 334.

[25] I. M. Lapidus, *Muslim Cities in the Later Middle Ages*, p. 39.

With the accession of Selīm I to the throne of Turkey in 1512, and the Ottoman victory over the Ṣafavid Shāh Ismāʿīl at the Battle of Chaldirān in 1514, the Ottomans felt secure enough to turn their forces against Egypt. The Mamlūk sultan Qānṣūh al-Ghūrī was accused of harboring enemies of the Osmānlī house, of allowing them to take refuge in his territory, and of secretly supporting Ismāʿīl. His mistake, however, was in not joining openly with the Persians in 1514. Two years later, struggling alone against the Ottomans, both he and the Mamlūk empire were obliterated at Marj Dābiq. [26] His successor Ṭūmān-Bey was hanged by Selīm the Grim at the Bāb Zuwayla.

The story of the decline of Mamlūk power is not complete without special consideration of the immediate factor to which the Turks owed their victory, a technical achievement utilized by them but never assimilated by the Egyptian forces although they understood and had access to it. This factor is the use of firearms for which the Mamlūk case is as remarkable an example of cultural values and rules of social organization standing in the way of survival, as any in human history. As we shall see, an analysis of the Mamlūk treatment of firearms leads us back to many of the features of their social structure described above.

It is well known that the use of artillery on a large scale on the battlefield was the crucial factor in the Ottoman victories over all their opponents within Islam. When, during the last years of the fifteenth century, the Mamlūks began to realize that their empire was really in danger, Sultan al-Ghūrī undertook drastic measures to revive the army in plenty of time to have reversed the outcome of Marj Dābiq. His program included an increase in the number of cannon cast, the renewal of the *furūsīya* (cavalry) exercises, and the institution of a unit of arquebusiers.

To evaluate this program we must first consider the role of firearms until this time. We know that cannon were being used in battles near the Citadel after the middle of the fourteenth century, some sixty years earlier than their utilization by the Ottomans. From that time onward, the use of cannon increases steadily and firearms become primary weapons of siege in the many assaults on the fortresses of the elite. Al-Ghūrī established a foundry for cannon near his new hippodrome and undertook the casting of cannon on a scale unmatched in any

---

[26] Al-Ghūrī fell from his horse on the field of battle and his body was never recovered.

former time. These arms came to protect the Citadel and the Mediterranean and Red Sea coasts against the Ottomans and Portuguese, but none of them ever reached Marj Dābiq.

The renewal of the *furūsīya* exercises was a reaffirmation of the belief that the most powerful army was that with the best trained cavalry. In Chapter VII we emphasized the importance of horsemanship to the Mamlūks from their recruitment and training to their military service. From the days of Mongol glory it was axiomatic that the knight knew not only how to fight on horseback but also how to breed horses. The exercises which formed the main part of military training which produced the finest cavalry in the world included the correct use of the bridle and spurs, racing, knowledge of pedigrees of horses, wrestling, lance exercises, preparation and use of bows and arrows, etc. [27] In the days of the Baḥrīs there had been many race courses (*maydāns*) and racing fields in Cairo and its environs. With this discipline went a supporting ideology: "*fāris*" (rider) became synonymous with "Mamlūk" and skill in the equestrian arts stood for the upper class, its honor, pride, and superiority. No one but a Mamlūk was allowed to ride a horse.

With the decline of discipline under the Circassians, the great hippodromes fell into decay through disuse and the military elite became notoriously deficient in the very exacting profession which defined them as a class. [28] The cavalry was not what it had been in former times yet the ideology remained: the horseman was a horseman, however badly he was trained. The free cavalry (*ḥalqa*) which had once given the Mamlūk cavalry some competition had long since disappeared and, preoccupied with internal squabbles, the latter by A.D. 1483 had become so deficient in equestrian military skills that none of the amīrs of a thousand wanted to accept the honor of being appointed Leader of the Games. A man finally chosen was not picked for his competence but because he was the only one who volunteered! [29] In A.D., 1503 Sultan al-Ghūrī began construction of a great *maydān*

---

[27] A. M. Poliak, *Feudalism in Egypt, Syria, Palestine and the Lebanon*, 1250-1900, p. 15.

[28] The contemporary historian Ibn Taghrī-Birdī who was not a mamlūk but of Mamlūk descent and very conversant with equestrian arts wrote that he himself developed several new exercises but declined to show them to anyone because of the stagnant condition of horsemanship in his time and the attitude of envious persons who were stronger in their ignorant pretentions than their knowledge of methods and ability to perform (*Nujūm*, edited by W. Popper, VII, p. 312).

[29] Ibn Taghri-Birdī, *Ḥawādith*, p. 180.

which became the site of intensive *furūsīya* exercises. Despite the decline in equestrian arts, the program succeeded in producing a cavalry far superior to that of the Ottomans at Marj Dābiq. According to Ibn Iyās, the envoy of the Ottoman sultan, witnessing an official exhibition of skills, "studied the spectacles with great attention and did not hide his astonishment." [30] So ingrained was the idea that the cavalry was superior to every other fighting force that not a single contemporary writer singles out the use of firearms as a major cause of the defeat. [31]

We have seen, however, that al-Ghūrī planned also to employ cannon in siege and made provision for the institution of a unit of arquebusiers. The adoption of the former followed naturally the use of the catapult siege engine and was therefore not at odds with any Mamlūk military tradition. The use of the arquebus on the field of battle was an entirely different matter, however. A basic principle of military organization was opposed to its adoption. There was something not quite honorable about the use of artillery on the battlefield: for the Mamlūks to take up the arquebus (*bunduq ar-raṣāṣ*), they would have had to dismount and become foot soldiers beside the auxiliaries or be taken to battle in an oxcart. The pride that went with skill in horsemanship and the use of the lance and the bow stood unalterably in the way of such a revolution. Where the arquebus was employed, therefore, it became a weapon of the inferior groups in the army, first of the black slaves (A.D. 1498-1510) [32] and then of the *awlād an-nās* (A.D. 1510-1516). Considering the military ideology described above, it is not surprising that many regarded the payment and training of these corps as a waste of resources and money.

It is indeed ironic to contrast the military engagements on the north against the Ottomans in 1516 with those of the south against the Portuguese in 1513. In the latter case the Egyptian forces had consisted

---

[30] Ibn Iyās, *Badaʾiʿ az-Zuhūr*, IV, p. 391; translation by G. Wiet, *Journal d'un bourgeois du Caire, chronique d'Ibn Iyās* (Paris, 1960), p. 363.

[31] Cf. D. Ayalon, *Gunpowder and Firearms in the Mamluk Kingdom*, (London: Vallentine, Mitchell, 1956), p. 77.

[32] The attitude of the Mamlūk elite toward the black slave arquebusiers is well illustrated by an incident that took place in 1498. The son of Qāyt-Bey, an-Nāṣir Abū Saʿādāt Muḥammad, tried to equip a large number of slaves with firearms and raise their status. In an open ceremony he married one of them to a Circassian slave girl and bestowed on him a short-sleeved tunic symbolic of rank. At this the Royal Mamlūks became infuriated, donned full armor and attacked the five hundred black slaves, killing fifty of them and causing the rest to flee, Under threat of deposition, the sultan agreed to sell the blacks to the Turkomans (D. Ayalon, *Gunpowder and Firearms*, p. 70).

primarily of black arquebusiers, Maghribīs, Turkomans, and *awlād an-nās* led by a few Royal Mamlūks. Not a single amīr of a thousand was among them. The outcome was the capture of many towns and much booty from the Portuguese, and the historian singles out for special mention the prominent part played by the contingent of arquebusiers in relation to their numbers. As the Portuguese war was primarily a naval war, the cavalry was not expected to enter it. *The Portuguese front, moreover, was not considered as important as the Ottoman front and in the former conflict the forces which were thought to be the most effective were held in reserve.*

Following Marj Dābiq, Ṭūmān-Bey frantically attempted to increase the strength and size of his artillery units adopting, among other things, ox-drawn carts to carry arquebusiers and light cannon. The awkwardness of his achievements in this direction, however, is exemplified in the use of camels for carrying light guns which were fixed from above their humps. The time had long passed for such experiments to be of use and for a military organization to become accustomed to the effective management of the critical weapon. As long as the Mamlūk army retained its identity as an army of cavalry, it was impossible, especially in a time of decline of military discipline, for the ruling class to create a unit stronger than itself. To equip an army of foot soldiers with a weapon intrinsically superior to bows and lances would have invited their own downfall at the hands of what we have seen to be the most dissatisfied elements of society. [33]

---

[33] We may ask how it was that the Ottoman's had, in contrast, so little trouble in adapting their army to the use of firearms. It would seem that not only the ideological principle that constrained the Mamlūks, but also the organizational principles, were lacking in their case. Ayalon has a most illuminating discussion of this matter (*Gunpowder and Firearms*, pp. 97-107). When, in the middle of the fourteenth century, the Mamlūks first became acquainted with firearms, the structure of their military society had long been established and it had already met its greatest challenge in the shape of the Crusader and Mongol conquests. While their experience with firearms came somewhat earlier, the weapons involved were less developed and comparatively disappointing. The Ottomans, on the other hand, did not use firearms until 1425 when artillery had already proved to be of value and, gradually acquiring experience with it in conflict with the European powers, they used it to advantage in the capture of Constantinople. Thus firearms became an integral part of their expansion and the military structure which developed simultaneously readily accommodated the new weapon.

The factors which divided the Egyptian army were absent in the Ottoman case. The Ottoman Mamlūk was a slave until his death and never had a chance of becoming sultan whereas each Royal Mamlūk in Egypt legally had the right to become sultan on the demise of his predecessor. The Ottoman sultan was the only master of his mamlūks and the same group belonged to his heir even as they had to him. There

An analysis of the immediate cause of the final Mamlūk defeat has led us to see that a combination of attitudes, social and economic conditions, and historic accidents surrounding the introduction of firearms was responsible for the disaster at Marj Dābiq. The solidarity of the elite and the ideology which upheld it resulted in a condition so inflexible that the adjustment necessary to prevent obliteration of the organization could not be made. What meant solidarity and strength in one respect meant weakness in another. Every Mamlūk faction was opposed to every other and the elite as a whole so feared those on their fringes that they would brook no change in the status quo. Even when the fate of the empire was at stake, they did not dare to equip their infantry with firearms on a large scale.

The Mamlūk city in its period of decline was a city, the political, economic, and social networks of which had contracted to a great degree. The contraction was set off by a demographic decline and subsequent loss of productive power and aggravated by the impingement of foreign networks upon the resources and territories that Cairo once controlled; by the extension of Ottoman suzerainty and of European economic interest. These external pressures intensified the effect of internal forces of conflict both within elite ranks and within the urban society as a whole that ultimately brought about collapse.

Ironically, but not unpredictably, the forces of conflict arose from the forces of solidarity; the pattern of social cooperation bore the seeds of disintegration, even as the cultural efflorescence contained the

---

was no special personal relationship involved as designated the *julbān* apart from the *qarānīṣ*. The ruler therefore had much less difficulty in imposing his will on the army. The Egyptians, moreover, had to institute a new infantry corps with their adoption of the arquebus but the Ottoman Janissaries were easily converted from infantry archers to infantry arquebusiers. It was primarily a matter of the substitution of one weapon for another. Finally, the economic decline we have traced in Egypt came just at a time when firearms were being introduced, and their utilization and employment would have created an additional financial strain on a government already desperate to finance its army. The metals, especially copper, required for the casting of cannon were plentiful in the Ottoman territories but the Mamlūk empire was limited to only one major source, an iron mine near Beirut.

The extension of Ottoman power was the result of a happy coincidence of technological development, appropriate social structure, and economic situation. While strangely enough the Ottomans admired Mamlūk military achievements and even appeared to believe in their superiority in a sense they were not bound by an equestrian ideology that hampered them in other fields of technique. While the most idealistic of them might shake their heads at their own use of artillery against Muslims on the honorable field of battle, the fact that their social status was not linked unalterably with their mode of combat allowed considerable room for experimentation and the adoption of various means to achieve their ends.

decline. The unity within the Mamlūk houses and of their establishment as a whole brought the military elite to their highest degree of achievement, but when allowed to go to extremes, made them prey to every weakness and challenge they had to face. The gradual disintegration of the solidarity of the elite establishment destroyed the relationship of the upper class to the "managers" and lower orders of society, and to the "estate" which they controlled. The absorption of wealth in the maintenance of an incompetent army and its internal struggles caused an immediate and drastic decline in capital investment, entrepreneurship, and general attitude of confidence among the mercantile and popular elements of society. But arrogantly facing inward, the Mamlūks continued to shut their eyes to important developments at home and abroad. Their establishment was an overspecialized structure based on the ideology of horsemanship and the exclusiveness of slave status. It could not adapt to the evolution of its external environment and naturally had to succumb.

Thus the fortune of the Mamlūk city in its later days depended upon the capabilities and the fortune of its ruling class. Although a few families managed to maintain some of their wealth and culture, and Cairo's role as a commercial center did not come to an end, the fate of the economic network was immediately dependent upon the security provided by an effective political network as well as the existence of a degree of freedom within and outside of the political framework to adjust to changing conditions of political economy. The lower orders of society were further incapacitated by the fact that the effectiveness of urban institutions ultimately depended on the structure of patronage. There was no alternative to patronage.

The Mamlūks had a strangle-hold on a society already gasping for breath. The confiscation of wealth and the economic burdens placed upon the middle and lower classes with the destruction of their initiative and confidence, were not only detrimental to the activities that these people had carried out so admirably, but destroyed principal sources of revenue. The problems of the government already driven to seek new means of support for its military establishment, were increased. The army outgrew its usefulness and, unable to come to terms with changes in technology and society, turned back upon itself and consumed the very resources it was supposed to protect.

CHAPTER TWELVE

THE URBAN DIALECTIC

Taking a broad view of the efflorescence of Cairo under the Mamlūks, we can see at once that it resulted from an extension of the general patterns of urbanism developed in previous periods. A new set of fortuitous circumstances enabled the further extension of its effective interaction systems and their mutual reinforcement. It is also evident that as diversity increased and its validity was repeatedly reaffirmed, urban society became all the more accustomed to the accommodation of change and even of conflict. Diverse social components, assuming conflict and change to be part of the nature of things, manipulated them to their own benefit, but as such manipulation took place, it had the ultimate effect of knitting the total social fabric in an ever more complex pattern.

The greatest transformation arising from the conceptual unification of the city instituted by Ṣalāḥ ad-Dīn was a change in scale. A single city, so much less awkward than the earlier arrangement of separate popular and administrative centers, grew up and flourished as the land between Cairo proper, the new Citadel, and the river port gradually became filled with houses and places of business. As elite residences sprang up in the Fāṭimid city and on the banks of ponds and canals, security extended far beyond the Citadel. The rulers became part of the city in a way that they never had before. Socially isolated from the population, they were, nevertheless, far from a palace coterie living within their own fortification. With the construction of mosques, hospitals, colleges, and *khān*s throughout Cairo, the Mamlūk sultans and their amīrs, in providing for their descendants and for the poor whom it was their duty to support, encouraged urban growth far beyond anything the earlier agglomeration had experienced. Merchants, craftsmen, administrators, and scholars flourished in this new environment giving the elite a firmer support both economically and ideologically. The Mamlūks thus became an inseparable part of the urban center which they ruled, the city which increased year by year as their dominion extended and as people flocked to Cairo seeking security, profit, and culture under their wing.

Nor was the efflorescence of the city separate from international events taking place, from the fortunes of war and of peace, and from Cairo's role as the economic, religious, and cultural capital of the Islamic world. Its prosperity was linked with the development of the ports of Jidda and ᶜAidhab on the Red Sea coast, with a resurgence of Damascus, and even with the rise of cities like Pisa and Genoa, outside of the empire but economically tied to it. Merchants acted as ambassadors and, on the whole, tended to support the regime under which they could profitably conduct their business. As the population increased through the influx of foreigners, international ties were established that further broadened the capital's economic base. The presence of skilled refugees meant not just a transfer of techniques to Cairo but also an important stimulus to local innovation through the presentation of contrasts.

It is important that in this situation of expansion and change, that the "culture-core" which directed the orientation and arrangement of the composite was no well-defined entity but rather represented a dialectic of interests. The military elite possessed undisputed power but only the *ᶜulamāʾ* and notables who represented all ranks and divisions of society could confer legitimacy. From time immemorial Egyptian tradition had known a bureaucracy that mediated the interests of an exclusivist elite and those of the people and now, as the elite became all the more specialized militarily, tending to abandon direct religious pretensions, this class gained in importance. Within the orthodox Islamic frame of reference, the concept of the authoritative community (*ahl as-sunna wa al-jamāᶜa*) was never clear-cut but the *ᶜulamāʾ*, as constituted through the interplay of the ideal and the real demands of circumstance, came to fill this important role. Ambiguity may have been the enemy of standardization, but it was the friend of accommodation.

Religiously the elite were in quite a different position than their counterparts of former times. Under the Ṭūlūnids, the governor had not been opposed to the caliph at Baghdad in the religious sense but had declared himself independent politically, thereby losing support for his rule. Under the Fāṭimids, the ruler and the caliph had been one and the same. In both cases the whole administrative organization was destroyed with the destruction of the ruler and his forces. The Mamlūks, however, were supported by the shaykhs of al-Azhar who stood firmly behind the administration even if they did not control it, and this support did not come to an end with the victory of the Ottomans. The latter, being good Sunnīs, took the caliph for themselves but did not dare to challenge the legalists of Cairo on any basic matter. By their support of a separate religious establishment and by enabling their descendants to attain important positions in the religious field, the Mamlūks had gained some insurance against total annihilation.

With the change in scale, there came not only increasing diversity but the acceleration of changes in all spheres of life and the stimulation of cooperation and of competition. The Ayyūbid conquest of Cairo and its consolidation by the Mamlūks resulted in a kind of fusion but it was a rather brittle amalgam of separate and often quite heterogeneous segments of urban society which tended to lend one another support for reasons of mutual but not necessarily identical interests. Large scale cooperation by and large was limited to dealing with serious threats, as when Mamlūks, shaykhs of al-Azhar, Kārimīs, and rabble joined in turning back the Mongols in Syria. Group interests were only generally similar and no truly urban institutions existed to coordinate them.

Social change was related to social mobility. The social classes for the most part were not strictly defined. Only the elite were truly restricted and their restrictions were self-imposed. Persons of the other orders could not, except in rare circumstances, become Mamlūks, but all other occupations were certainly open to them in theory. A large number of notables and merchants were of lower class origin. Feudalism in Egypt was of a different order than European feudalism. Nothing comparable to a system of estates existed. The elite had rights to revenues but had no manorial jurisdiction and, except in rare cases, did not carry out administrative functions. Moreover their grants were limited and revokable. By and large the bureaucratic class, many of them Copts, continued their role of social management. In Europe the feudal nobility had close ties with the Church but the Church itself kept apart from secular life and there was no basis for development of any real ties with the bourgeoisie. [1] The religious notables in Islam, however, entered directly into commercial endeavors. Families of *ᶜulamāʾ* were one and the same as merchant families. One interest or the other would predominate but it was not possible to differentiate between them in terms of class since so much overlap of roles and intermarriage took place. While family ties were of great advantage in obtaining the highest bureaucratic and official positions, even the poorest boy could achieve the same through education and fortunate patronage.

---

[1] Cf. I. M. Lapidus, *Muslim Cities in the Later Middle Ages*, p. 186.

Class membership depended upon access to resources but not even the elite controlled all resources directly. Their estates and their vast wealth were managed by others and the whole fabric of society came thereby to be constituted in fact by ties of alliance and patronage. Ultimately, class was not as important as rank; rank that was defined by the ability to obtain favors and perform favors for others. As such, rank was primarily an individual and not a group matter. It was achieved through attachment to elite households and every household had clients of all classes, many occupations, and social divisions.

With the exception of military power the distribution of resources was characterized by fluidity if not equity, but even the Mamlūks could not do without auxiliaries in street fights and on the battlefield. In a deeply religious Islamic society the right of all to the highest spiritual attainments could never be denied. To the lowest levels of society, piety, respectability, honesty, capability, dependability, and above all, learning could generate the social bonds upon which the achievement of rank depended. Through the institution of the elite household wealth was siphoned off to notables, bureaucrats, craftsmen, laborers, and lower class clientele of the quarters. Natural catastrophes saw to it that wealth never remained in the same hands for long.

The weakness of class organization throws into relief the individualization of rank and the importance of ethnic ties and special status where attainment of rank was concerned. The complaints of the lower orders were never directed against the elite or the class of managers as such but invariably named individuals. When groups were blamed for an unfortunate turn of events these were *dhimmī*s or foreign communities. Group solidarity where it existed had two major foci: ethnic derivation and the Mamlūk household, both of which types of units cross-cut social classes in the fabric of society. The elite establishment as a whole was restricted ethnically even as competitive Mamlūk houses within it tended to be consolidated by ethnic ties, Turk or Circassian. Many, though not all, occupations held by persons of the middle and lower social orders had ethnic reference.

The pursuit of individual goals without controlling influences would tend to create chaos and disunity rather than unity. This is why we have tried to emphasize solidarity throughout this section. Two kinds of forces encouraged solidarity: formal legal rules and less formal personal bonds. In general, solidarity pertained to the components rather than to the composite although through the development of law and growth of social sophistication, unity of the latter sort tended to emerge.

It has been shown many times that religion and ideology serve as powerful reinforcements to solidarity. The formal development of the law schools (*madhāhib*) had a profound effect upon the regularity and uniformity of application of the *sharīʿa* and religious tradition. Al-Azhar became an important focus of ideological unity for Sunnī Muslims the world over. Yet the *madhāhib* related to regional persuasions and ethnic and territorial referents lay behind the organization of al-Azhar. For *dhimmīs*, the special legal status conferred on them at the time of the Arab conquest continued to form the basis of solidarity. It is impossible to over-emphasize badges of special status, ethnic, religious, social, and economic, in reinforcing solidarity through setting the framework of interaction. All communication between members of the designated groups was put into a specialized context that gave color and tone to the relationship even if the matter at hand did not immediately concern group interests.

The major religious divisions, however, were really too large to be a meaningful basis of solidarity in everyday affairs. Personal bonds were an effective means of complementing as well as implementing the formal system. Thus the formal solidarity that was at the basis of the efficient system of the Mamlūk period was the result of relatively intensive and frequent communication, usually face-to-face, between members of a group united by common experiences, goals, and interests. While rules and values were important, they only remained effective as long as the individuals saw advantage in adhering to them or were content with the relationships they established.

Kinship was an essential factor in both intragroup and intergroup solidarity. The great virtue of the kinship system is that recruitment and inheritance are built into the family organization as one generation follows another, giving automatic continuity to the group concerned. If no provision is made for regular recruitment and systematic inheritance of resources and function, solidarity based upon personal relationships may last no longer than the association of particular individuals involved. The Kārimīs, forming a large organization consisting of a number of families, married within their professional group except for occasions upon which they made alliances with notables and Mamlūks for political or economic reasons. Endogamy prevailed among the Mamlūks and with them it tended to exclude marriages with even the wealthiest native-born Egyptians although a number of such marriages did take place. Where rights of heredity were tenuous at best, the marriage of a daughter to a merchant or *qāḍī* served a good purpose if it gave the Mamlūk a powerful ally. The Mamlūk structure was itself patterned after the kinship structure. The elite corporation, however, was especially deficient in coping with the relationship of one generation to another. Identification was felt with the master (*ustādh*) but not with the master of the master.

Residence was a crucial factor in the creation of group feeling. Individuals living beside one another were, almost without exception, united by a set of multiple considerations, and this internal solidarity was based upon communication relating to many areas of life. It is significant that there was no true territorial segregation as to class or special status group, although the physical manifestation of the city reflected emphasis upon social components rather than the composite.

Although the elite had no single place of residence, the significance of the Mamlūk *bayt* was not to be denied. For every mamlūk, dining at the house of the *ustādh* was a sign of allegiance to him over all others. Each *bayt* owed no small part of its solidarity to the existence of other houses with which it competed. Although the Citadel symbolized the power of the elite, as a class they were divided residentially, their palaces being scattered throughout the capital. The elite could afford to be scattered, since as a group, their military power and control of communication channels gave them an advantage over the lower orders; but this same power and control encouraged their infiltration by outsiders: the dispersed and competing *bayt*s became packed with clients of all classes.

Coresidence was a virtual necessity for the organization of units within the lower social orders. Craftsmen continued to live in the specialized quarters their families had long occupied and, as new areas were settled, these came to be called by the names of the ethnic, religious, or occupational groups that resided in them. The localization of particular crafts was, of course, linked to the order of technological development. Rudimentary means of transport and communication necessitated physical clustering so that producers, middlemen, retailers, and consumers had ready access to each other's goods and services. Sociocultural values became inextricably interwoven not only with physical locations but with economic pursuits in complex fashion. It is revealing to trace the interplay of different factors that sustained the various residential segments of society.

Even more basic than the major formalized religious divisions were the localized followings of holy men and saints, the spiritual guardians of the quarters. We will see in the next part how popular religious movements, by virtue of localized foci, overcame the boundaries of orthodox religion in many cases and provided the most effective means of articulating the real with the ideal. The most effective and immediate source of moral support for the individual was not found in the abstract or generalized religious allegiances that separated large groups in the population, but rather corresponded to spiritual manifestations in his local community. There was, for example, a special quality of communication that pertained between residents of a quarter and their spiritual guardian that could not be duplicated by nonlocalized, nonpersonalized manifestations. His presence among his followers, like that of the Shīᶜī *dāᶜī* and the leader of the Ṣūfī order, served to bolster the group feeling that existed among them on the basis of other interests and activities.

The unity of urban groups, however, was more ideal than real. Even in the most well organized establishments, solidarity lasted no more than three or four generations. The Kharrūbīs, Maḥallīs, and Musallams dropped out of sight and became dispersed as their capital disintegrated with the economic decline of Egypt. Both the organization of the elite and the organization of merchants were dependent upon continued access to the resources upon which they depended. When the feudal system lost its efficiency through the uncontrolled extension of hereditary holdings and through the misuse of *waqf*, and when the rapid replacement of generations consumed the resources needed to nourish the group as a whole, the Mamlūk institution, like that of the Kārimīs, soon fell apart.

Pressures to remain separate reflected the magnitude of the pressures that assailed group boundaries. The effect of plague which upset the balance between factions of the elite had a tremendous effect upon the "normal" conservative pattern of social relations throughout the entire population. The spectacular transfer of resources and authority, occurring on a large scale, created new liaisons and interests but did little to reinforce the remains of original groups.

Endurance was dependent not only upon the efficient internal operation of a social unit but upon retention of a degree of flexibility in the segment to allow for adjustment to changes in ecology. The survival of each group in the urban situation was dependent upon preservation of its boundaries but no group was able to control directly all of the resources it needed to carry out its primary activities. Thus every unit experienced polarity in its social relations. Religious, social, and occupational restrictions in themselves led to necessary liaisons with other groups in the world outside. Artisans needed the services of merchants and bureaucrats and they all needed the patronage and protection of the military elite. The governing class could not do without merchants and other educated travelers in the efficient management of their foreign affairs and could not even do without the rabble in maintaining the supremacy of their houses. Thus with the expansion of the urban center and multiplication of constituent social segments, the strains springing from contradictory functional requirements of solidarity and external liaisons became greater rather than less.

It is interesting that even the most necessary liaisons, while contributing to the continuity and prosperity of a group, frequently were regarded as a threat. Small wonder that the most influential businessmen experienced periodic confiscation of their wealth and that the relationship of the elite and the masses was far from easy, for the rulers feared the gradual undermining of their power by those whom they had to enlist as allies at home, perhaps even more than any external challenge to their supremacy.

Marginal individuals, that is, those possessing certain of the most highly valued criteria of rank but not others, were always a threat to solidarity. The institution of the elite household itself made for the marginality of persons involved in its maintenance, for the rank of patrons gave prestige to clients and satisfaction of immediate interests through patronage and the growth of personal loyalties nipped in the bud the growth of any solidarities that might have developed on the basis of class. Since so much of the social order crystalized around elite households, the ties of interdependence so created had the potentiality of weakening both the solidarity of the elite and that of the lower orders who served them.

It is significant that in the contemporary texts Muslim writers do not speak of *ʿaṣabīya* or "solidarity" in the singular but rather use the plural, *ʿaṣabīyāt.*[2] Based upon personal relationships and nearly always associated with residence, *solidarity* was inseparable from *factionalism.* For the majority of the population, it is safe to say that kinship, ethnic ties, and patronage were not only primary elements in the establishment of group feeling but fostered competition with other groups organized on like principles. The Mamlūk case serves to highlight the rise of factionalism and its causes. The divisiveness that brought about the disintegration of the elite establishment resulted both from the weak-

[2] Cf. Claude Cahen, "Mouvements populaires et autonomisme urbain dans l'Asie musulmane de moyen âge," *Arabica*, VI (1959), p. 251.

ening of internal bonds through competition for and involvement with clienteles, and the working out of the Mamlūk principle of solidarity itself which made each man loyal to the house of his master and brothers in slavery. The word "solidarity" has a positive connotation, but "factionalism" was the unavoidable opposite side of the coin.

The urban dialectic developed upon patterns established in previous periods; a separatist military elite ruled local groups themselves divided on the basis of religion, ethnicity, and occupation. Restricted by formal rules they yet succeeded in managing society through personal bonds. For persons of the middle and lower orders the tie with the elite was all-important. Key administrative positions undoubtedly went to those who had a personal interest in Mamlūk affairs. Since the Mamlūks were the keystone in the composite structure, survival hung upon some degree of incorporation in the elite establishment. It also depended upon maintaining enough independence to avoid being engulfed when the deluge came.

Class was not the major characteristic or urban life any more than "feudalism" was. The developed traditional city was rather characterized by a *vast number* of effective associations or network clusters, each directed at the attainment of its own ends, but *coordinated* with others in a complex web of interactions serving the manifold needs of urban existence, military, economic, social, and cultural. Conversely, the gradual decline of Cairo at the end of the period came about with the contraction of its interaction systems. Mamlūk extortions seemed arbitrary but they were not more arbitrary than the forces of nature that initiated the process. Resources and energy, already scarce, were wasted and production declined in every area of culture as specialized urban networks, often working at cross purposes with one another, shrank through the evolution of internal deficiencies, the unfolding of inherent contradictions, and progressive maladjustment to the historico-cultural environment.

Factionalism and conflict, however, while inherent in social plurality, were not totally negative in their result. Even the experience of disintegration and decline gave birth to new social sophistication in accommodation of change: and "accommodation" is the word to use *for affirmation of the validity of ever-increasing diversity,* that is, *the discovery of new modes of perception to comprehend and successfully deal with more plurality, is a sine qua non of successful conflict manipulation.* [3]

---

[3] Thus C. A. O. van Nieuwenhuijze has pointed out that:

From this view the very opposite of social sophistication is the overwhelming drive to overcome and obliterate pluralism in a "melting pot" dominated rather than *mediated* by the culture core. It is but the result of ideological ethnocentrism backed by economic and political power.

Viewing in this light the advance of Ayyūbid-Mamlūk Cairo over the city of preceding epochs, we can focus upon three major developments, a tremendous change in scale, the progressive evolution of political, ideological, and economic institutions leading to a more efficient coordination of interests, and an efflorescence of urban culture which, though marred by conflict, dissonance, and contradictions, was never before equalled. The decline made obvious the need for order, for while ambiguous aspects of rank and social status gave flexibility to social relations, encouraging social mobility, these factors intensified the scramble for shrinking resources. The further articulation of social relations is a major theme of the following part of this book.

The fact that the social system crystalized around the elite resulted in chaos at their downfall; yet the populace as a whole did not lament their passing and replacement by another group of guardians. The need for regulation was obvious but upon the arrival of the Ottomans a basis of order was already there. The growth of the moral order with the development of social consciousness was not unrelated to the expansion of the city in other ways. It was no accident that universal religious institutions provided secure and respected positions for many individuals marginal to the elite and others drawn from diverse sections of the population. The continuity of Cairo as one of the greatest cities of a new empire under the Ottomans was due in no small part to the

---

"To Western man, the simultaneous occurrence of plural socio-cultural entities ... signals primarily a difference. Difference is contrast. As such it is a loaded phenomenon ... it must be, virtually if not actually, either some form of cooperation or some form of conflict. The distinction is vitally important ... because cooperation is good and conflict is bad.

The Middle Easterner, by comparison, takes the same basic distinctions of plural socio-cultural entities in his stride, so to speak. The consequence is that in observing traditional Middle Eastern society the Western observer will find, not without surprise, that not merely is contrast the cement of society but indeed it is highly and positively effective as such" (*Sociology of the Middle East*, p. 35).

and also:

"The Westerner's ... automatic response to conflict was supposedly to be creative conflict resolution, this is not the Middle Easterner's perception and inclination ... the proper term is conflict manipulation, or ... manipulation of antagonism; the affirming acceptance of diversity and diffraction" (*Sociology of the Middle East*, p. 697).

enduring respect that both rulers and ruled held for the religious law; a law which had become inseparable from the city that had supplanted Baghdad as the seat of orthodox authority and which had permeated the whole framework of its culture and social organization. The change in ideological ecology originating with Ṣalāḥ ad-Dīn and developing under the Mamlūks with the continued building and endowment of mosques, schools, and colleges made the integrity of the city inviolable. Rather than attempting to introduce a new ideology of control, the new Ottoman governors sought an effective means of relating themselves to the conquered capital and its existant social structure. They too were bound by the system of morality which had emanated from Cairo for so many centuries.

PART THREE

UNITY IN DIVERSITY IN TURKISH CAIRO
(A.D. 1517-1850)

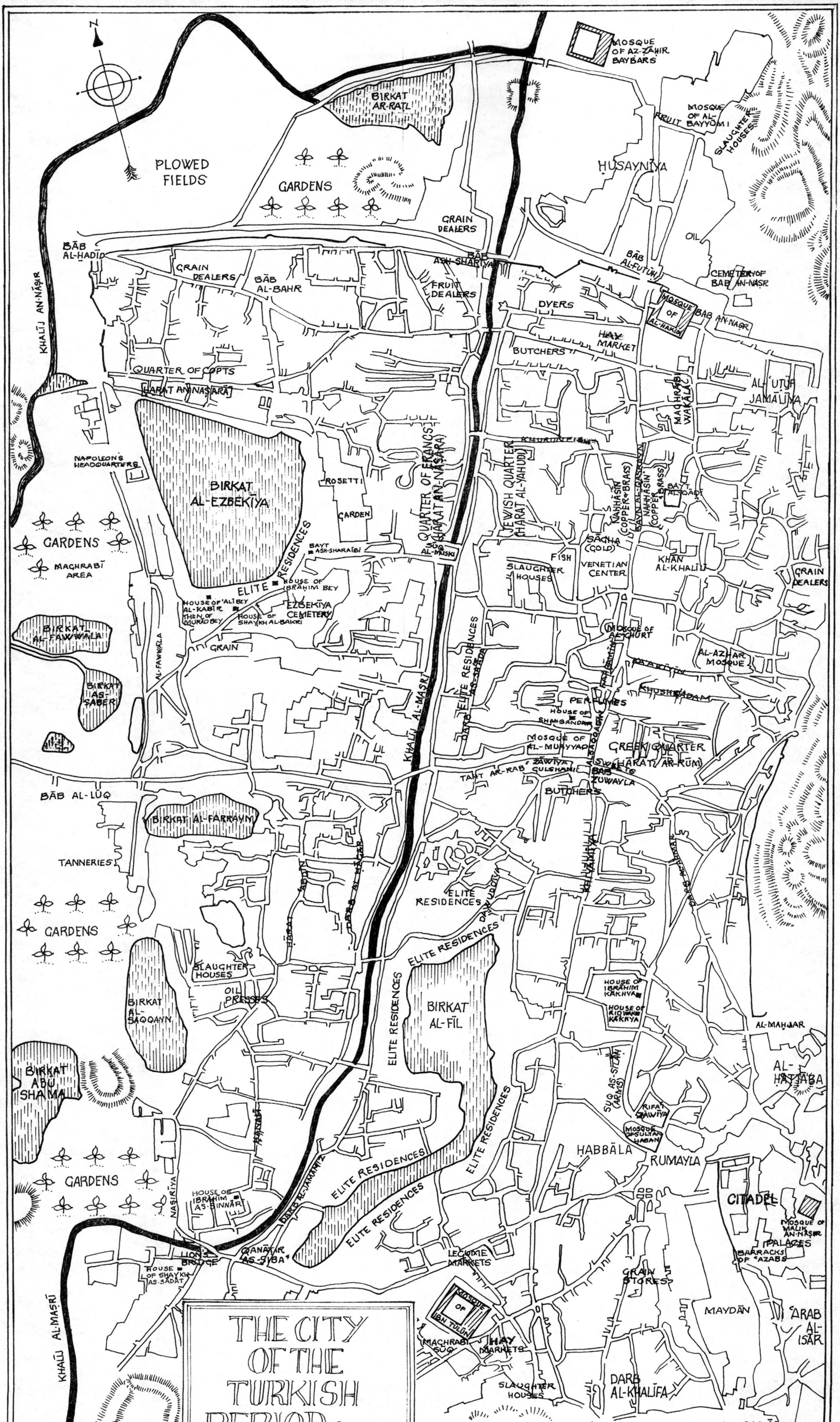
THE CITY OF THE TURKISH PERIOD
N
PLOWED FIELDS
GARDENS
BIRKAT AR-RATL
MOSQUE OF AZ-ZAHIR BAYBARS
MOSQUE OF AL-BAYYUMI
FRUIT
SLAUGHTER HOUSES
HUSAYNIYA
GRAIN DEALERS
OIL
BĀB AL-HADĪD
BĀB ASH-SHARIYA
BĀB AL-FUTŪH
CEMETERY OF BAB AN-NASR
GRAIN DEALERS
BĀB AL-BAHR
FRUIT DEALERS
DYERS
MOSQUE OF AL-HAKIM
BAB AN-NASR
KHALĪJ AN-NĀṢIR
HAY MARKET
BUTCHERS
QUARTER OF COPTS
HARAT AN-NASARA
AL-UTUF
JAMALIYA
MAGHRABI WAKALA
NAPOLEON'S HEADQUARTERS
BIRKAT AL-EZBEKĪYA
ROSETTI GARDEN
QUARTER OF FRANCS (HARAT AN-NASARA)
JEWISH QUARTER (HARAT AL-YAHUD)
KHURUNFISH
NAHHASIN (COPPER & BRASS)
BAYN AL-QASRAYN
BAYT AL-QADI
GARDENS
MAGHRABI AREA
ELITE RESIDENCES
BAYT ASH-SHARAIBI
SŪQ AL-MUSKI
SAGHA (GOLD)
FISH
VENETIAN CENTER
KHAN AL-KHALILI
SLAUGHTER HOUSES
GRAIN DEALERS
HOUSE OF IBRAHIM BEY
HOUSE OF 'ALI BEY AL-KABIR THEN OF MURAD BEY
HOUSE OF SHAYKH AL-BAKRI
EZBEKIYA CEMETERY
BIRKAT AL-FAWWALA
GRAIN
AL-FAWWALA
MOSQUE OF AL-GHURI
AL-AZHAR MOSQUE
BIRKAT AS-SABER
KHALIJ AL-MASRI
ELITE RESIDENCES
DARB AS-SA'ADA
KHOSHQADAM
PERFUMES
HOUSE OF SHAHBANDAR
MOSQUE OF AL-MU'AYYAD
GREEK QUARTER (HARAT AR-RŪM)
BĀB AL-LŪQ
TAHT AR-RAB
ZAWIYA GULSHANI
SWEETS
BAB ZUWAYLA
BUTCHERS
BIRKAT AL-FARRAYN
TANNERIES
ELITE RESIDENCES
DARB AL-AHMAR
GARDENS
SLAUGHTER HOUSES
OIL PRESSES
ELITE RESIDENCES
BIRKAT AL-SAQQAYN
BIRKAT AL-FĪL
HOUSE OF IBRAHIM KAKHYA
HOUSE OF RIDWAN KAKHYA
AL-MAHJAR
BIRKAT ABŪ SHAMA
AL-HATTABA
SUQ AS-SILAH (ARMS)
RIFAT ZAWIYA
MOSQUE OF SULTAN HASAN
HABBĀLA
RUMAYLA
GARDENS
NASIRIYA
HOUSE OF IBRAHIM AS-SINNAR
DARB AL-JAMAMIZ
ELITE RESIDENCES
ELITE RESIDENCES
CITADEL
MOSQUE OF MALIK AN-NASIR
PALACES
BARRACKS OF 'AZABS
LIONS BRIDGE
QANATIR AS-SIBA'
LEGUME MARKETS
HOUSE OF SHAYKH AS-SADAT
GRAIN STORES
MOSQUE OF IBN TULUN
MAYDĀN
'ARAB AL-YASAR
KHALĪJ AL-MAṢRĪ
MAGHRABI SUQ
HAY MARKETS
SLAUGHTER HOUSES
DARB AL-KHALIFA

INTRODUCTION: CONTINUITY IN CHANGE

The period initiated by the Ottoman conquest of Egypt is illustrative of the continuity which characterized the main features of urban life in the traditional period. It is true that the time span of "the Turkish period" covers three significantly different types of political regimes during which the seeds of change were sown but these did not really come to fruition until the latter part of the nineteenth century. Shifts in the political structure, however, do throw light upon patterns of social relations and the responses of the urban complex to varying conditions. There is no situation like one of change to reveal recurring patterns of structural stability as opposed to alterations which, however obvious, do not really interfere with the basic design.

The very term "Turkish" as applied to this period is illustrative of continuity in change. The culture of the Mamlūks and that of the Ottomans was not fundamentally dissimilar and their language was the same, standing in contrast to the Arabic of the native Egyptians. Muḥammad ᶜAlī was an Albanian and made himself independent in fact but, even as Egypt was formally still an Ottoman province, so he behaved as much as possible like an Ottoman sultan. His mosque in the Citadel imitates the mosques of Istanbul, and most of his retainers and subordinates were Turks. Indeed, Arabic was not spoken at court until the time of Fārūq and only by the end of the century did Arabic replace Turkish as the language of officialdom. Not until the 1870's were even the lower ranks of the administration Egyptianized.

The single most important factor which eventually brought about the modern transformation of the traditional way of life was, of course, the introduction of Western culture. The French occupation under Bonaparte saw numerous abrupt changes but made little lasting impression. The doors of the quarters that were taken down were replaced, street cleaning was given up, and attempts to keep accurate vital statistics were not made again for several decades. It has been estimated that at the end of the eighteenth century there were no more than a few hundred Europeans in all of Egypt. During the time of Muḥammad ᶜAlī their numbers grew to 10,000; but it was later in the 1860's under Ismāᶜīl that they started to come by tens of thousands. Only then did traditional industries, markets, modes of administration, and ultimately political control fall before the onslaught of European competition.

Up to now we have emphasized the segmentation of the city, the typical differentiation of its functions, and the heterogeneity of its population. Although unity has been a general concern, less has been said of the cement which held the pieces together.

Diversity has long been regarded as an outstanding feature of Near Eastern society for the brilliant facets of the mosaic stand out by reason of their uniqueness. It would be a mistake, however, to argue that diversity was more prevalent than unity or vice versa. The direct contrast of the Middle Eastern case with that of the West has caused the cultural aspects of urban life which united the constituent segments, as well as the social mechanisms of union, to fall into the background.

The following chapters will deal with some previously discussed topics and some new ones. Pursuing our study of urban groups with reference to more detailed data, we hope to arrive at a more accurate conception of the nature of political, economic, and spiritual power in urban society and of their distribution; of the ways in which particular groups manipulated these resources and of recurring patterns of alliance. While we have gone a long way toward establishing the importance of residence for group solidarity, and we have indicated the importance of the *bayt*s of the elite in the formation of clienteles, it is most difficult at this point to comprehend the life of the popular quarters of the city. Certainly, however, strong solidarity pertained within the quarter and we will give ample evidence to show that the individual did identify in many aspects of his existence with his neighborhood and coresidents.

The social fabric with which we have been concerned was, after all, interwoven in various contexts and at various levels of social organization: the law which served as a universal framework of unity was subject, in interpretation and application, to less formal patterns of social interaction; individuals shared some values and interests with large numbers of persons, and held others in common with only a few. Shifts in the foci of power, moreover, continually gave rise to the emergence of new clienteles and factions, transformations of basic patterns of alliance. What we have called the moral order in the last section is the result of the evolution of such complex relationships in a common historico-cultural environment.

In the last analysis the city, evolved over so many centuries, can be viewed from the standpoint of the individuals who made up its social network. Ultimately, it was their actions and the conscious and unconscious choices that lay behind them that made the city as it was. For individuals whose fields of interaction involved a number of networks, contradictory functional requirements often demanded the choice of one consideration over another. Family loyalty and personal allegiance, usually accepted as having priority in the preindustrial society, did upon many occasions, come into conflict with the execution of professional duties; differences might often arise between social and religious obligation, between family considerations and obligations to patrons, between private considerations and those of the religious community. [1] Thus the urban dialectic was manifest at the lowest level of social organization and inherent conflicts were resolved through individual perceptions of the situation and subsequent courses of action.

The ambiguity in the social position of the individual, his involvement in a number of overlapping but not necessarily congruous networks, was also a chief clue to social mobility which will be one of our concerns in the next part. Even when belonging to a social segment united by the coincidence of a number of principles of organization, sentiments and values, the individual was always faced with the necessity of constant adjustment to new conditions. There is a contrast between the social system in its ideal aspect and the social system in fact. A person's relative position in the field of interaction constantly shifted with changes in his environment and in the set of persons with whom he interacted. Thus his conceptions of the implications of group membership were not constant but tended to shift, even though his performance of specific roles played a basic part in orienting him to his community and enabling him to contribute to its cultural achievement. Urban life was patterned but the very flexibility of this pattern is what allowed it to survive.

Historical Background

With the execution of Ṭūmān-Bey at the Bāb Zuwayla the Mamlūk regime officially came to an end. The new regime, however, differed from the old in degree rather than in kind. The army of occupation numbered about 20,000 but no significantly new elements were introduced culturally or racially as they had been under the Arabs, Fāṭimids, and Ayyūbids. The major change was that Cairo became only the capital city of one of thirty provinces of a new empire. Resources began

[1] With reference to the Mamlūk period one wonders, for instance, if the decision of the legalists to facilitate the transfer of inalienable state property from fathers to sons resulted from their conscientious desire to interpret the law to the best interests of the community of believers or from the fact that they themselves were *awlād an-nās*.

to flow from Cairo and Egypt to a foreign capital rather than vice versa. The last ᶜAbbāsid caliph, Mutawakkil, was taken to Istanbul and imprisoned for a time but freed on the death of Selīm. He then returned to Cairo where he bequeathed his title to the sultan of Turkey. The transfer, however, was not generally recognized by the majority of Muslims as it is held by most that the caliph must belong to the Prophet's tribe of Quraysh. As the Ottomans were good Sunnīs they never dared to challenge the Cairene *ᶜulamāᵓ* on any basic issue. The Egyptian religious establishment, far from collapsing, came into its golden age during the Turkish regime.

Stanley Lane-Poole wrote that "no one has had the heart to write the history of Egypt during the three centuries of its subjection to the Sultans of Turkey." [2] It can be argued that traditional historians have too darkly portrayed the state of economic affairs throughout the period, but it is true that initially the conquered capital suffered great shocks. Cairo had been occupied by foreign troops before, but now experienced looting on a scale not equalled previously. For four days severe fighting went on in the city and 10,000 people lost their lives. Ibn Iyās tells us that in the area west of the Citadel and later in other quarters, people were forced to abandon their homes to make room for Ottoman troops who "spread out like locusts." [3] An immediate consequence of the defeat was the exportation of resources, material and human. The buildings of the Citadel itself were stripped of marble slabs and huge granite columns which were taken to Istanbul. Libraries lost many manuscripts as plundering extended even to the seats of learning. A large number of persons were conscripted to labor on the construction of colleges and public works in Istanbul. These included engineers, masons, carpenters, smiths, and porters, Muslims, Christians, and Jews. Other convoys of civil servants, merchants, and arsenal workers left Cairo subsequent to this bringing the total of deportees to some thousands. [4] Over fifty crafts disappeared from Cairo through their transfer to Turkey and the decline in the demand for luxury goods in Egypt. [5] While a number of exiles were repatriated after

---

[2] *Story of Cairo*, p. 287.

[3] *Badāᵓiᶜ az-Zuhūr*, V, pp. 157-158; cf. G. Wiet, "Personnes déplacées," *Revue des Études Islamiques*, 27 (1959), pp. 11-13.

[4] G. Wiet, "Personnes déplacées," p. 21.

[5] Al-Jabartī, *ᶜAjāᵓib al-Āthār fī Tarājim wa al-Akhbār* (Cairo (Būlāq): Imprimerie Nationale, 1880), I, 20; *Merveilles biographiques et historiques ou chroniques du cheikh Abd-el-Rahman el-Djabarti*, translated by Chefik Mansour Bey et al. (Cairo (Būlāq): Imprimerie Nationale, 1888-1896), I, p. 48.

1521, and the sixteenth century in general saw an increase in prosperity on account of the restoration of authority and effective centralization, Egypt continued to remain but the leading province of an empire controlled from Istanbul. During the seventeenth and eighteenth centuries, when the old economic stresses resulting from internal political competition again set in, a large amount of wealth that was not consumed in political rivalry continued to flow abroad.

Although Selīm massacred a large number of amīrs and deported seven hundred others to Istanbul, the government he instituted differed from the previous one formally rather than actually. The policy of the Ottoman rulers was not to revolutionize society but rather to control their vast empire by granting a large degree of autonomy to the subject peoples. Their major concern in Egypt was the extraction of tribute in the form of money, food, drugs, and spices. To act as the sultan's viceroy, a Turkish pasha was installed in the Citadel at the head of a force of Janissaries, ᶜAzabs, and five other corps. The first of these viceroys, significantly enough, was Khāʾir-Bey, former Mamlūk governor of Aleppo, who emerged as leader of a collaborationist faction after Marj Dābiq. By deciding to rule through a Mamlūk, Selīm committed himself to the maintenance of the Mamlūk elite as such. At the withdrawal of the sultan, many fugitives returned and even found shelter with the new regime. Importation of mamlūks continued for nearly another three centuries. [6]

From the Ottoman point of view the arrangement was a means of securing tribute through the assistance of a quasi-indigenous group that was already experienced in such matters. [7] True, there was obvious

---

[6] Russian victories over the Ottomans in the second half of the eighteenth century finally made the procurement of slaves much more difficult. After the 1770's the places of origin of *mamlūks* became much less dependent upon the Ottoman government for support. See D. Ayalon, "Studies in al-Jabartī I: Notes on the Transformation of Mamlūk Society in Egypt under the Ottomans," *Journal of the Economic and Social History of the Orient*, III (1960), pp. 162-164.

[7] The treatment of the Egyptian capital by the Ottomans, when contrasted with that of former conquerors, throws into relief the great change that had taken place over more than three centuries of Ayyūbid and Mamlūk rule. There was no point in destroying the Citadel since the authority of the Mamlūks, emanating from palace-fortresses spread throughout the town, extended far beyond its immediate environs. To be sure, the Citadel was the symbol of Mamlūk rule, to some extent, and was always occupied by the incumbent faction, but it never pretended to be a whole city in any sense. Selīm the Grim had no real intention of doing away with the Mamlūks, but in any case he had to content himself with executing or deporting as many of them as he could catch. It was impossible to do away completely with an elite so entrenched in the capital and even in the provinces which they governed.

risk in relying upon an indigenous elite but various attempts at accomplishing the task of ruling Egypt through officers sent from Istanbul usually failed miserably. The Ottoman network itself was somewhat overextended and, in the light of conditions on the European and eastern military fronts, the Porte considered the expense of a military expedition to Cairo too great. It therefore attempted to retain control by playing the Mamlūk factions off against one another and in this, it was generally successful. From the point of view of the Mamlūks, the arrangement was a means of survival, even a means of recovering power. It was hardly any time before they regained *de facto* political control. Other Turks, Circassians, and Georgians rose from the lower echelons of the old elite to occupy the positions of the amīrs removed by Selīm and newly instituted offices. By the middle of the sixteenth century Ottoman rule was extended by a Circassian Mamlūk who established a province on the Red Sea coast and conquered Lower Nubia. For a time though, the Porte held the upper hand. Khāʾir-Bey was followed by a viceroy sent from Turkey and the last insurrection was put down in 1523-1524. In 1529 the *qānūnnāme* ("regulation" of Egypt) which set forth the relations between Egypt and Turkey, including the question of taxes, was promulgated.

In the Ottoman policy toward landholding we see the clearest and most significant case of real continuity in spite of formal change. At first the feudal system was explicitly abandoned; all fiefs were confiscated and became the property of the sultan. The Mamlūks were thus deprived of direct control and became salaried officials of the new regime. Although the Mamlūk *iqṭāʿ*s (fiefs) were retained as basic units of organization, these were assigned to agents who were to administer them, collect taxes, and send the funds to the treasury. As such the holdings came to be called *muqāṭaʿāt*.

Initially the Porte tried to administer the *muqāṭaʿāt* through its own agents (the *amīn*s), usually Ottomans from other places in the empire or Copts or Jews, and avoided relying on Mamlūks. This, however, proved unworkable as the *amīn*s did not have the incentive or the means to be efficient. As a result they came to rely on *ʿāmil*s or agents who were in fact Mamlūk amīrs. These then acted as tax farmers, paying what was due to the treasury to the *amīn*s and keeping the balance for themselves. At first the tax farm (*iltizām*) was sold at auction to the highest bidder. Ownership was temporary and it was impossible to acquire any permanent property rights in it. During the eighteenth century, however, the situation changed. Whenever a *muqāṭaʿa* was vacant Mamlūk leaders simply named new holders from the members of their own faction and paid the fees of transfer (*ḥulwān*) to the treasury. Actually the vacated positions were removed from the auctions and were awarded directly to the new owners. The final step of reversion to the feudal pattern came when the tax farm became inheritable. As long as the owner still paid taxes and transfer fees he could sell it or bequeath it as he wished. Thus the beys built up huge estates and the system of landholding was both a cause and a consequence of their return to power. [8]

The beylicate [9] which emerged was an order of the highest ranking military men who were not included in the cadre of officers of the seven corps under the command of the viceroy. Most of the members were Mamlūks, but in time the membership came to include some Turkish officers as well. The latter, however, never succeeded in attaining the highest title, that of *shaykh al-balad*, which during the eighteenth century was conferred upon the bey who held the *riʾāsa* or "supremacy." There emerged three great houses, each of which had its own ethnic affiliation, recalling the pattern of the *bayt*s of the earlier period. These were the Faqārīya, chiefly composed of Mamlūks of Circassian origin; the Qāsimīya, chiefly composed of Circassians but including a Bosniak element which became assimilated by the middle of the seventeenth century; and the Qāzdughlīya, a house founded by a Turkish officer but patterned after and becoming indistinguishable structurally from the Mamlūk houses during the eighteenth century.

The offices of state were held by both Turkish officers and Mamlūks, those apportioned to Mamlūks becoming more and more important as time wore on. From the beginning offices held by the beys were the *amīr al-ḥajj* (commander of the pilgrimage), *qāʾim-maqām* (acting viceroy), and the *defterdār* (register keeper). Mamlūks were later

[8] By the late seventeenth century the *fallāḥīn* who had been able previously to buy and sell their right to cultivate were subjected to numerous burdens. Not only were they forced to assume large debts at usurious rates of interest and subjected to forced labor without pay, but they could no longer buy and sell their right of usufruct.

[9] The beylicate was not a formal institution in the sense of having a structure outlined by explicit rules and principles as the Ottoman administration might be so characterized. The title of "bey" in Egypt signified a rank rather than a specific office, although the Porte traditionally granted it to Mamlūks holding particular positions. P. M. Holt has noted, in fact, that the very ambiguity of the title, with its absence of specialized functions, greatly facilitated the maneuvering of the Mamlūks in making good their claims to the resources and administrative offices of Egypt (*Egypt and the Fertile Crescent 1516-1922* (London: Longmans Green & Co., 1966), p. 73).

appointed *sanjaq-beys* or provincial governors. As this happened the Ottoman officers who were governors of sub-provinces (*kāshifs*) declined in rank.

In 1630 the pasha was deposed by the beys and from then on they occupied the center of the stage. The pasha had never been given the opportunity to compete. To prevent his governors from gaining a personal following in the country, the sultan recalled them after only a few years or even months. [10] While this procedure guarded against the rise of independent governors as had happened under the ᶜAbbāsids, it eventually rendered the representatives of the Porte incapable of controlling the Mamlūks and the military with whom they had to deal. Their own batallions of Janissaries and ᶜAzabs, in charge of policing the town and quartered in the Citadel, differed little from the unruly troops who had preceded them there. Disputes between the viceroy and his army gave the old elite additional advantage. The troops, moreover, possessed the legal right to veto the pasha's orders. As some became powerful amīrs, their mutual jealousies gave rise to civil wars and street fights as occurred in the age of the Circassians. Nor were the pashas permitted to attend the advisory councils, the Greater and Lesser Dīwāns, but had to send their deputies *kitkhudā*s or *kākhya*s [11] in their stead. The members of these councils included all the powerful groups in Cairo, the Mamlūk amīrs, leading administrators, heads of the schools of Muslim law, and important religious authorities who generally supported the Mamlūks rather than the Porte.

Structurally, the split between the houses of Faqārīya and Qāsimīya became far more important where politics were concerned than the division between Mamlūk beys and Turkish officers. On numerous occasions the latter sided with one faction or the other, these alliances being essential to the outcome. [12] The factions indeed, were wide and permanent, claiming ties in lower orders of the native population. The Faqārīs identified with the Niṣf Saᶜd and the Qāsimīs with the Niṣf Ḥaram, older groupings among the artisans and bedouins of Egypt. [13] The picture on the political scene that we see is con-

[10] Between 1517 and 1798 there were 100 pashas in Cairo.

[11] Both of these terms designated also an official attached to each regiment.

[12] Thus at the end of the seventeenth century, when Ibrāḥīm-Bey al-Faqārī sought the *riʾāsa,* he was allied not only with the Qāzdughlī household but also with the leader of the Janissaries, Küchük Muḥammad. The latter's support included popular elements and proved instrumental to Ibrāḥīm-Bey's success. See P. M. Holt, "The Career of Küçük Muḥammad (1676-94)," *Bulletin of the School of Oriental and African Studies, XXVI* (1963), pp. 269-287.

[13] P. M. Holt, "Dhuʾl-Faḳāriyya," *Encyclopaedia of Islam*, second edition (1960).

fusing. All contend for power while the pasha attempts to play one house against another. Yet through it all there emerges a typical Mamlūk pattern: major factions cross-cut by opportunist alliances and tied together by patronage. [14]

As the years progressed some capable individuals appeared among the beys to maintain order in the city and establish courts reminiscent of the former time. The great Faqārī amīr ᶜUthmān-Bey, *amīr al-ḥajj*, in 1739 deposed the pasha and took over the administration of the country to the extent that he himself held a court in his house, deciding cases and severely punishing extortion and injustice, fixing tariffs for bread, and seeing to it that *waqf* monies were properly administered. He was renowned as a severe and incorruptible judge and earned the high regard of all through his honesty, ability, and pride. He was replaced by Ibrāḥīm-Kākhya, deputy of the Janissaries and head of the Qāzdughlīya, who shared the *riʾāsa* with Riḍwān-Kākhya al-Julfī, deputy of the ᶜAzabs. Under these two Cairo is said to have enjoyed prosperity not seen for many years. Food was readily available to all classes and the amīrs were wont to keep open house every noon and evening. On feast days, special distributions of rice, milk, and honey were made to the poor. Some, like Riḍwān-Bey al-Faqārī in the seventeenth century and ᶜAlī-Bey in the eighteenth, dreamed of restoring the Circassian sultanate but these schemes proved premature. However they might try to pack the beylicate with their own mamlūks and clients, factionalism and rivalry never permitted them to prevail against the Ottoman power. ᶜAlī-Bey invaded Syria, but his own follower Abū adh-Dhahab, having taken Damascus, then challenged him in a struggle for the *riʾāsa.*

On the whole, as the eighteenth century progressed, Mamlūk depredations became worse. The "tax collections" of each house often resembled a raiding expedition, especially when wealth was needed to supply the immediate cause of survival against another group. As financial difficulties became more and more oppressive, it is not surprising that civil disorders and demonstrations became more and more frequent but the people, for the most part, were still disorganized so these movements had no lasting effect. Often temporary relief was achieved, however, through the intervention of the *ᶜulamāʾ* who emerged at this time as popular leaders. Until Bonaparte's invasion

[14] For a more detailed account of the factional struggles see P. M. Holt, *Egypt and the Fertile Crescent*, Chs. 5 and 6 and also his article, "The Beylicate in Ottoman Egypt during the Seventeenth Century," *Bulletin of the School of Oriental and African Studies*, XXIV (1961), pp. 214-248.

in 1798, the rule of the beys continued, and although for a time, the most powerful of them, Murād and Ibrāḥīm, fled to Upper Egypt before the Turkish forces sent to restore Ottoman authority, they soon returned to resume their offices. As in earlier days no great changes were made in the system of government and the religious authorities prevented many atrocities which could have resulted from the unbridled aggression and ruthlessness of the elite.

The capture of the capital by a power not only foreign but also non-Muslim was accompanied by much suffering and chaos. The artillery of Napoleon, more ruinous to the city than that of Selīm, destroyed the Ḥusaynīya quarter where the fiercest resistance had been made. Al-Azhar itself was used as a stable [15] by the French cavalry until complete submission was guaranteed by the most esteemed shaykhs. Realizing the authority of the *ᶜulamāᵓ* however, Napoleon sought to rule through them. Many notables felt embittered against the Mamlūks, blaming them for the occupation, and there was little choice but to capitulate. Therefore a collaborationist group supported the French, although other *ᶜulamāᵓ* led the people in armed revolts from time to time.

Before the French left two years later, Cairo experienced many horrors. Irate Muslims massacred the Christian population, native and foreign. General Kléber, left in command by Bonaparte, was faced with an insurrection led by the beys, shaykhs, Janissaries, and Mamlūks who battled the French troops in the Ezbekīya. Streets were barricaded while the cannon of the Citadel and the forts bombarded the city. In April 1800, Kléber stormed Būlāq and put the area to pillage and conflagration. The Ezbekīya also was nearly destroyed by fire and it is said that lighted torches were flung right and left and women and children threw themselves off walls and roofs to avoid the flames.

Although the French tried to initiate a number of changes in urban government and organization, most of these made little impression; the old ways appeared again at their departure. Nevertheless the occupation marked a reorientation of the Egyptian capital to the world outside. European travelers visited Cairo in greater numbers than ever before, seeking not only profit and adventure but knowledge about the East, so long guarded by the suzerain power of the Porte. In the last years of the eighteenth century, Sonnini, Savary, and Volney had written descriptions of Muslim society on the basis of extensive

[15] As was the Mosque of al-Ḥakīm, even as it had been occupied by Franks some six and a half centuries before.

travels in Egypt and the Levant but with the scholars of Napoleon came the first coordinated research. Their famous *Description de l'Égypte* provides much of the information utilized in this section of the book. Following the occupation, Egypt was visited by people like Edward W. Lane, his nephew Stanley Lane-Poole, and Sir John Gardner Wilkinson who even more particularly concerned themselves with the customs and cultural achievements of the East not understood or appreciated in Europe before this time.

The place vacated by the French was soon filled by the English who from 1800 on, became progressively involved in Egyptian affairs. Even before Napoleon left Egypt, Ibrāḥīm-Bey secured the assistance of an English general while his rival Murād had been confirmed by Kléber in the government of Upper Egypt. Internal factions sought help from contending foreign powers in curious parallel to the situation which prevailed in the last days of the Fāṭimid regime.

The Khedival period which begins with the rule of Muḥammad ᶜAlī marks the final end of Mamlūk authority and the beginning of a new era. The leader of the Albanian corps of the Ottoman forces soon came to play an important part in the struggles between the Turks and Mamlūks. Unlike ᶜAlī-Bey, he was unhindered by factionalism among his followers; moreover as a result of the French occupation, Mamlūk authority had become debilitated. At first joining forces with ᶜUthmān al-Bardisī and Ibrāḥīm-Bey, Muḥammad ᶜAlī forced the pasha to capitulate.

Order was restored for a time but soon problems arose as the new governor of Cairo, Khurshīd Pasha, was unable to cope either with the Mamlūks or the Albanian troops. In 1805 internal dissension and chaos had brought urban government to such a pass that the leading shaykhs, led by ᶜUmar Makram and popular leaders such as the shaykh of the green-grocers and the shaykh of the butchers, urged Muḥammad ᶜAlī to undertake administration of the city. As in the old days, the incumbent bombarded his opponent from the Citadel and the challenger employed the Madrasa of Sultan Ḥasan as a counter-fortress. Muḥammad ᶜAlī, however, also strengthened his position by placing cannon on the mountain to command the Citadel from behind. While such measures would probably have been sufficient to secure for him the governorship, the sultan in Istanbul confirmed the choice of the shaykhs and declared Khurshīd deposed. The Albanian entered the Citadel as legal governor and representative of the Porte on August 3, 1805.

Unlike the Ottoman pashas who had preceded him, he was in possession of much more real power than they had enjoyed. No military force could compare with his, and there was no prospect of his removal in the near future. The brief alliance with the *ᶜulamāᵓ* and popular elements lasted only until stability was reestablished. After consolidating his rule, Muḥammad ᶜAlī taxed the *ᶜulamāᵓ* and confiscated their tax farms.[16] ᶜUmar Makram had to disband his men. The *ᶜulamāᵓ*, after all, were unused to handling any form of power other than ideological. During the reign of Muḥammad ᶜAlī their influence was largely moral.

The necessity of alliance with the Mamlūks also had long since passed. In fact the quarreling factions were a hindrance to the effective centralization of authority. In two massacres all but a few of them were wiped out. The first of these took place not a month after Muḥammad ᶜAlī's assumption of the governorship. A number of Mamlūks, under the impression that the Pasha was away, were persuaded to enter Cairo by the northern gate. Soldiers on the roofs of the houses of the narrow street that runs from the Bāb al-Futūḥ to the Bāb Zuwayla fired upon the cavalry as it passed, killing both men and horses. A few men who took refuge in the school of Barqūq in the Naḥḥāsīn were captured and executed. Six years later when the Pasha invited all Mamlūks to a reception in the Citadel, the second perfidious trick was more effective than the first. The Bāb al-ᶜAzab was closed and four hundred and sixty perished in the gorge cut out of rock leading down from the Citadel to the Rumayla. A few not attending the party fled to Upper Egypt but the power of the Mamlūks was broken and their property was confiscated. In later years when some ventured to return to Cairo, the Pasha and his descendants, in undisputed control, wooed the support of the remnants of the former elite with the granting of amnesty and the return of some of the lands that had been taken.

There is no doubt that through this difficult period Cairene society, adapted to the uncertainties of the medieval environment, was able to absorb many shocks and survive numerous crises. Muḥammad ᶜAlī's success in establishing himself as uncontested ruler of Egypt, while putting an end to the chaos, resulted in the destruction of channels

[16] An interesting historic parallel can be seen in these developments. When the Ayyūbid dynasty fell in A.D. 1250, the *ᶜulamāᵓ* rose to prominence. Baybars submitted to their wishes only until he had consolidated his rule. When he felt secure, he controlled them by curtailing their finances (A. Lutfi al-Sayyid Marsot, "The Ulema of Cairo in the Eighteenth and Nineteenth Centuries," *Scholars, Saints and Sufis*, edited by Nikki R. Keddi (Los Angeles: University of California Press, 1972), p. 159).

12. The Citadel and the Rumayla in A.D. 1798.

of political power traditionally controlled by the middle orders of society. Certainly this was a serious alteration in the age-old pattern, but how basic really was the resultant transformation? From one angle, the regime of Muḥammad ᶜAlī can be seen as yet another attempt to set up an unchallenged "Mamlūk" household filled with Kurds, Turks, Albanians, Circassians, and others who owed loyalty only to their master. [17] Even his blood bath of Mamlūks in the Citadel was a resounding echo of the blood baths that blotted Mamlūk history, for the beys and pashas had, time and again, used the very same ruse to lure their rivals to destruction. [18]

Thus, while granting that during this period forces were set in motion that ultimately produced a new order, we will here treat the developments that surrounded the imposition of Ottoman rule, the challenges of the French occupation, and the eventful career of Muḥammad ᶜAlī as these illustrate the essential and continuous structure of social life rather than as they heralded social change. Muḥammad ᶜAlī may have given his followers a European-style education and certainly he had them instructed in modern military and administrative methods but still, it was many decades before most of the seeds he planted became established and bore fruit. The essential style of life remained unaltered. Administratively, the Turkish regime continued to function with the assistance of local officials. The urban quarter was still headed by the *shaykh al-ḥāra* who carried out police and tax collecting functions. [19]

Despite the fact that Muḥammad ᶜAlī attempted to create large-scale industries employing salaried workers, this experiment failed utterly. His monopolies were liquidated by ᶜAbbās and Saᶜīd who sold or gave his factories to private individuals. Guilds only declined in the second half of the nineteenth century as a result of European competition in the economic sphere. For the most part no sharp economic differentiation existed between guild members and it was relatively easy to become a master. Class struggle as such was unknown; the creation of modern-style labor unions only came about in the twentieth century.

17 A. Hourani, "Ottoman Reform and the Politics of Notables," *Beginnings of Modernization in the Middle East: The Nineteenth Century*, edited by William R. Polk and Richard L. Chambers (Chicago, Ill.: The University of Chicago Press, 1968), p. 56.

18 D. Ayalon, "Studies in al-Jabartī," p. 302.

19 This same official, even until after the First World War, kept records of births and deaths. Guilds also continued to operate. Until 1860 the shaykhs were responsible not only for payment of taxes but also for advising the authorities on fixing prices.

Observations of the rules regarding special statuses remained in effect throughout the first half of the last century. While Muḥammad ᶜAlī removed the restrictions on dress which marked non-Muslim minorities, only in 1855 was the *jizya* tax levied on non-Muslims abolished. This latter move finally deprived religious leaders of non-Muslim communities of their most important administrative functions, although they continued to administer their people in such matters as inheritance, adoption, and marriage which relate to personal status. During the first half of the last century, many members of religious minorities still tended to live in their own quarters, although after 1850 residences of Christians and Jews became much more scattered in the urban center.

Also essential to the organization of urban life in the traditional city was religious orientation. While the political power of the *ᶜulamāᵓ* declined under Muḥammad ᶜAlī, the popular aspects of religious life continued to flourish. Thus the religious orders (*ṭuruq*, s. *ṭarīqa*) were not superseded until modern times by any kind of secular organization. Persons of all classes belonged to the orders which served as the main outlet for expression of social consciousness. Likewise, in their administrative and ideological functions, the *ᶜulamāᵓ* were not really displaced until a new cadre of civil servants and lawyers appeared who were educated abroad or otherwise exposed to Western modes of thought and procedures. During the first part of the nineteenth century there was little if any secular education, learning being still largely a function of the religious establishment. [20]

Social classes remained essentially as they were: a military elite composed of Turks, [21] religious notables, rich merchants, respected men of lower rank, and "the masses." Slaves and rabble occupied the bottom of the scale until nearly the end of the century. There were over eleven thousand slaves in Cairo in 1850. (Official edicts forbidding the slave trade were proclaimed only in 1877 and 1895). Thus basic changes in the class structure, like the changes in economic and political life, only came about under stimulation of external influences, but these

---

[20] Although a few scholars went to Europe to study, it is estimated that during the time of Muḥammad ᶜAlī, not more than five per cent of the children between the ages of six and twelve received formal education of any kind (G. Baer, "Social Change in Egypt: 1800-1914," *Political and Social Change in Modern Egypt*, edited by P. M. Holt (London: Oxford University Press, 1968), p. 159).

[21] During the first couple of decades of the nineteenth century all army officers of high rank and local officials ranking above *shaykh al-balad* (village mayor) were "Turks."

changes did not appear until later. Generally the ruling class remained separate from the urban notables, traders, craftsmen, and laborers. Alliances were formed from time to time, but normally persons of each class followed their proper sort of occupation.

By 1850 there were indications that medieval characteristics were disappearing, and yet on the whole, the style of life in the town had undergone little change. There must, therefore, have not only been stability borne of a stubborn conservatism, but also a basic cement founded upon social, economic, political, and religious mechanisms. What these mechanisms were we may not be able to explain completely. Yet it is hoped that we have enough information to indicate the direction in which the answers are most likely to lie.

CHAPTER THIRTEEN

THE DEMOGRAPHIC FACTOR: THE PEOPLE

It is evident from the material presented in the preceding sections that the city's vulnerability to political, economic, and natural disasters had a profound effect upon the social relations of urban groups and the maintenance of their way of life. The hardships suffered by urban residents, though in many ways less than those which peasants had to bear, produced an atmosphere of insecurity which no formal provisions for defense could dispel. Demographic data, far from being dry and colorless, gives much evidence of the sharp vicissitudes of fortune experienced by urbanites. The relative size of groups, as well as the bases of their solidarity, strongly influenced the degree of social mobility which is one of the keys to the unity of the urban center.

Up to now we have been able to cite few statistics on the size of the population and its constitutent groups. Medieval travelers did sometimes attempt to estimate total population but they frequently based their estimates upon no more than general impressions and comparison with European towns. Although some utilized censuses made for purposes of taxation, considering the behavior and methods of administrators in those days, the context of these figures alone is enough to make them suspect. The first censuses of the late eighteenth and early nineteenth centuries, while leaving much to be desired, are somewhat more reliable.

According to available estimates, it appears that there was a good deal of fluctuation over this period. Volney in 1787 stated 250,000 as a maximum. [1] The authors of the *Description de l'Égypte* state that, in 1797, Cairo had a population of 263,000 including Mamlūks and foreigners, although a previous estimate had indicated 300,000. [2] Another census in 1821 recorded only 218,560 inhabitants. [3] Lane, who visited the city some fifteen years later, says that the plague of

---

[1] *Travels through Syria and Egypt in the Years 1783, 1784, and 1785*, translated from the French (London: G. G. J. and J. Robinson, 1787), I, p. 237.

[2] Gilbert J. G. de Chabrol, "Essai sur les moeurs des habitants modernes de l'Égypte," *Description de l'Égypte: État Moderne*, II, 2 (Paris, 1822), p. 364; E. F. Jomard, "Description abrégée de la ville," *op. cit.*, p. 586.

[3] F. Mengin, *Histoire de l'Égypte sous le gouvernement de Mohammed-Aly* (Paris, 1823), II, p. 317.

1835 caused a drop in the population from 300,000 to 200,000 but by 1839 it had risen to 240,000 as "this deficiency was rapidly supplied from the villages." [4] He says too that the increase was facilitated by a reduction in the army. Military service had kept many men away from their homes and others from establishing them. Although the wide range of these estimates may be accounted for in part by the difficulties of obtaining accurate statistics, the effects of famine, plague, and immigration are not to be denied. The social order must have been able to replenish its ranks in a number of ways and a degree of mobility must have been present in most segments of society.

Although the break-down of the population by the early census takers does not necessarily represent real social units in the effective sense, the divisions of their demographic reports are not irrelevant to the society they are describing. National origin, religion, and occupation stand out as major categories. The following tables have been constructed from the reports of the *Description de l'Égypte* and that of Lane:

I. *Social Groups Arranged by Special Status*

	1798 [5]	Percentage of Total Population		1839 [6]	Percentage of Total Population
Egyptian Muslims	238,000	91%	Egyptian Muslims	190,000	79%
Copts The Coptic Church under a Patriarch The Uniate Church under The Pope	10,000	3%	Copts	10,000	4%
Jews	3,000	1%	Jews	3,000-4,000	2%

---

[4] E. W. Lane, *An Account of the Manners and Customs of the Modern Egyptians* (1836), 1860 ed. (London: Everyman's Library, 1908), p. 24 n. 2. The demographic effects of plague and famine parallel those of the Mamlūk period. According to Volney, during the plague of 1783 and 1784, the number of deaths in Cairo rose to 1,500 a day. It was followed by a famine that carried off nearly as many as the plague and not a beggar could be seen in the streets (*Travels through Egypt and Syria*, I, pp. 192-193). Another report indicates that by 1831 the population had increased to 260,000 but fell to 110,000 after the plague of 1835, only to rise again to 250,000 (J. Michaud and B. Poujoulat, *Correspondence d'Orient, 1830-1831* (Paris, 1833-1835), V, p. 238).

[5] E. F. Jomard, "Description abrégée de la ville," *Description*, II, 2, p. 694.

[6] E. W. Lane, *Manners and Customs*, p. 24.

Greeks	5,000		"The Rest," "Strangers from Various Countries"		
The Greek (Orthodox) Church under a Patriarch					
The Uniate Greek Church under a Patriarch					
Syrians (Greek Catholics and Maronites)	5,000	5%		37,000-38,000	15%
Armenians	2,000				
The Armenian Church under a Patriarch					
Total	263,000		Total	240,000	

II. *Social Groups Arranged by Occupation*

	1795(?) [7]	Percentage of Total Population		1839 [8]	Percentage of Total Population
Mamlūks and Janissaries	12,000	18%	"The Remainder Consisting Chiefly of Military and Civil Servants of the Government"	15,000	19%
Landed notables and administrators	6,000		10,000 Turks		
			5,000 Bureaucrats		
Import-Export Merchants	4,000		Merchants, Petty Shopkeepers, and Artisans	30,000	
Artisans (Masters and Workers)	25,000	37%			37%
Petty Merchants	5,000				
Café Owners	2,000				
Domestics	30,000		Domestics	20,000	
Laborers and Porters	15,000	45%	Common Laborers, Porters, etc.	15,000	44%
Adult Males	99,000		Adult Males	80,000	
Women	126,000		Women and Children	160,000	
Children	75,000				
Total	300,000		Total	240,000	

[7] Gilbert J. G. de Chabrol, "Essai sur les moeurs des habitants modernes de l'Égypte," *Description*, II, 2, pp. 364-366. The figures are based upon a census made before the French expedition.

[8] E. W. Lane, *Manners and Customs*, p. 24, n. 4.

1. *The Warp of Social Structure: Special Status*

Looking at Table I, it is evident that religious differences formed the basis of the broadest divisions of the population. All foreigners as well as natives were well aware of religion as the most important determinant of status. Under the Ottoman Empire, *dhimmī* communities were called *millets* and each was governed by an official who was responsible to the state for its administration. With reference to many matters involving personal status, persons belonging to the *millets* were treated by the government as members of their respective communities and not as individuals with reference to a single inclusive system.

The figures for the eighteenth and nineteenth centuries show an overwhelming Muslim majority, a condition which had probably existed for a thousand years. Within Islam, nearly all had been Sunnī for over half that time. Serious sectarian disputes had long ceased to be a problem in Cairo, although there were local and popular movements which were tolerated if not wholeheartedly accepted by orthodox leaders. The proportionate decrease of Muslims, from 91 to 79 per cent of the total population between 1797 and 1839 that was due to the influx of foreigners, was not enough to alter the basic situation of an overwhelming Sunnī Muslim majority.

It will be noted that the proportion of native Egyptians of Coptic or Jewish faith remained very nearly the same over the four decades with which we are concerned, with perhaps an increase of only one per cent. Members of both *millets*, as payers of the *jizya*, were exempt from military service, a fact which may account for the maintenance of the size of their communities. We should remember too, however, that many of these people belonged to the fairly well-to-do middle class. [9] Lane says that:

---

[9] To say that many of them belonged to the well-to-do middle class does not deny the fact that others were impoverished. Both Lane and Clot-Bey, writing in the 1840's, call attention to the economic perils to which the Jews especially were exposed. Certainly, from earliest times, the *dhimmī* communities, like the Muslim community, included the indigent. It can be noted, however, that the *dhimmī* communities, having historically experienced relatively radical fluctuations in fortune, and possessing a fierce pride in their separate identities, were known for taking care of their own. See Antoine-Barthélemi Clot-Bey, *Aperçu général sur l'Égypte* (Paris: Fortin, Masson et Cie., 1840), II, p. 142; and also Jacob M. Landau, "The Jews in Nineteenth Century Egypt—Some Socio-economic Aspects," *Political and Social Change in Modern Egypt*, edited by P. M. Holt (London: Oxford University Press, 1968), pp. 196-208.

> Many of the Egyptian Jews are "ṣarráfs" (or bankers and money-lenders): others are ṣeyrefees and are esteemed men of strict probity. Some are goldsmiths or silversmiths; and others pursue the trades of retail grocers or fruiterers, &c. [10]

Of the Copts he writes:

> Many of the Copts are employed as secretaries or accountants ... Most of the Copts in Cairo are accountants or tradesmen: the former are chiefly employed in government offices: among the latter are many merchants, goldsmiths, silversmiths, jewellers, architects, builders, and carpenters; all of whom are generally esteemed more skilful than the Muslims. [11]

But despite the comparative prosperity of many *dhimmīs*, and the fact that many of them practiced the same occupations as Muslims, all were set aside by a number of features ranging from special forms of dress to characteristic modes of behavior resulting from the social and legal positions allocated to them. The proper turban color for non-Muslims was black, blue, grey, or light brown, and their clothes were black or of a dull hue. In the town, clear understanding of various status positions facilitated the smooth functioning of human relations in everyday situations.

The atmosphere of insecurity apparently tended to give rise to a peculiar kind of character. According to Lane the Copts, for instance, were marked by an extremely reserved disposition. [12] After so many centuries of defending their interests against tremendous odds, they had developed such a mentality of "encapsulation" that they were con-

---

10 *Manners and Customs*, p. 562.

11 *Ibid.*, p. 553.

12 In his words:

> "... So great is their aversion with which, like their illustrious ancestors, they regard all persons who are not of their own race, and so reluctant are they to admit such persons to any familiar intercourse with them, that I had almost despaired of gaining an insight into their religious, moral, and social state ... They are ... extremely avaricious, and abominable dissemblers; cringing or domineering according to circumstances ..." (*Manners and Customs*, pp. 535, 552).

It may be that this attitude developed during the early part of the nineteenth century as a result of inter-group difficulties engendered by the French occupation. Moreover it should be noted that some degree of sympathy had always existed between Muslims and Copts which exceeded that between Muslims and other groups, Lane tells us also that Muslims considered the Copts to be:

> "much more inclined than any other Christian sect to the faith of El-Islám; and this opinion has not been formed without reason; for vast numbers of them have, from time to time, and not always in consequence of persecution, become proselytes to this religion" (*Manners and Customs*, p. 552).

13. Street Scene.

scious not only of their differences with Muslims but with other Christians.

The Jews too, often led a perilous existence in the town. Like the Copts, they were very careful to avoid suspicion of their wealth and for this reason presented an unattractive picture to the outside world. The exteriors of their houses were dirty and they were accustomed to wear plain and shabby clothing in public. Such precautions, necessitated by circumstances which combined to place wealth in the hands of a group despised by the majority of the urban population, lessened the danger of intergroup conflict. Even so, Jews were frequently the victims of scapegoatism. Muslims and Jews generally regarded each other with mutual dislike. There was a saying among the former that "such a one hates me with the hate of the Jews" and it was not uncommon "to hear an Arab abuse his jaded ass, and, after applying to him various opprobrious epithets, end by calling the beast a Jew." [13]

It is an important indication for the development of urban unity that by Lane's time the friction between religious groups had become somewhat less, partly through the efforts of the government. Dress regulations had relaxed somewhat by 1839. The Jews wore the same color turban as the Christians while many Armenians, Greeks, and Syrians wore the white Muslim turban. Subjects of European powers could do the same and often adopted Turkish dress. [14] The women of *dhimmī* groups veiled themselves in public, as did the Muslims, and dressed in the same manner.

The most remarkable demographic change following the French occupation was the tremendous increase of foreigners, roughly from five to fifteen per cent according to our table. Still, it was but a trickle compared to the tidal wave that was to come in modern times. Europeans were not mentioned among the national groups listed in 1797 and perhaps there were not enough to set aside a category for them. In the eighteenth century the members of the European community belonging to the Catholic *millet* in Egypt had consisted chiefly of a few

[13] E. W. Lane, *Manners and Customs*, p. 560. Even as Savary reported that "the most reproachful epithet an Egyptian can use is the word 'Frank' which is the general denomination for Europeans" (*Letters on Egypt*, translated from the French, second edition (London: G. G. J. and J. Robinson, 1787), I, p. 79).

[14] Even the Copts were showing signs of adopting Muslim garb:

> "I find it difficult, sometimes, to perceive any difference between a Copt and a Muslim Egyptian, beyond a certain downcast and sullen expression of countenance which generally marks the former; and Muslims themselves are often deceived when they see a Copt in a white turban" (E. W. Lane, *Manners and Customs*, p. 536).

Franciscan monks, Maronites, and Uniate Copts, [15] and while certainly a number of Franks remained on the margin of society, especially the Venetians and the French, as members of capitulatory states, the merchant population had dwindled following the economic decline at the end of the Mamlūk period. Despite the fact that Lane's classification is vague, there is little doubt that by his time a relatively large number of the "strangers from various countries" were Europeans.

Part of the increase of foreigners however, resulted from the swelling of the ranks of the Syrian and Greek communities through immigration. Hundreds of refugees had fled to Egypt following the repressive measures taken against Maronites in Syria in the late eighteenth century and the Greek War of Independence in the first part of the nineteenth. As in former days, both of these groups made their living largely through commercial enterprise and, as in former days, their welfare depended in large part upon governmental policy. Many were gold- and silversmiths while others dealt in goods from the land of their origin. In the 1760's ᶜAlī-Bey, seeking to make himself independent, encouraged European trade through the special agency of Syrian traders. The latter subsequently took the monopoly of the custom houses from the Jews and further strengthened their own positions by intermarriage with European consuls and merchants. Characteristically, the minorities competed with one another for favors from the government. Savary states that:

> Their ductile cunning promotes them, occasionally, to be commissioners of the customs, and receivers of the revenues of Egypt; but their honesty may not be depended on and their arts should always be watched. Having obtained power, they employ it to oppress European Merchants, invent exactions, and shackle their commerce. [16]

Volney expresses similar sentiments regarding the Eastern Christians. [17] All of these groups, perpetually struggling to maintain their existence in the segmented society of which they were a part, were generally antagonistic toward one another. Except in limited situations, their separate legal status made real cooperation impossible.

The increase in the population of foreigners, on the other hand, indicated prosperity for these people. Life was easier for the minorities during the nineteenth century than it had been during the eighteenth.

---

[15] H. A. R. Gibb and H. Bowen, *Islamic Society and the West*, I, 2 (London: Oxford University Press, 1957), p. 260.

[16] *Letters on Egypt*, II, p. 248.

[17] *Travels through Egypt and Syria*, I, p. 231.

As foreign powers exerted more and more economic and political control, the positions of non-Muslims became somewhat more elevated. Greeks, Syrians, Armenians, and Jews, despite mutual rivalries, benefited through the relaxation of many of the restrictions that had been placed upon them as a class.

2. *The Weft of Social Structure: Class*

Turning now to Table II which shows groups listed by occupation, we notice immediately that a division of these into the broadest categories of class reveals a remarkable constancy of relative size. One would almost think that Lane had computed his estimates by using the percentages of the *Description* if there had not been such drastic changes in the constitution of some of the classes and if there were not reason to believe that he used a later census.

By Lane's time the Mamlūks and Janissaries had long disappeared and a new elite had become established. The remaining Turks and Albanians, nevertheless, had inherited the position of their predecessors and behaved much in the same way. The elite mixed least with other groups and a number of features distinguished them from the rest of the population. According to Lane, they continued to adhere to the Ḥanafī legal code and they were nearly the exclusive owners of white male slaves (mamlūks). [18] Like their predecessors also, they were rarely seen except at Cairo where they occupied governmental and military positions. Their women enjoyed much less freedom of movement than the women of the lower orders. They never went to shops but rather sent for what they required, nor were they accustomed to visit the public baths.

It is difficult to estimate the size of the elite [19] but on the basis

[18] *Manners and Customs*, p. 137.

[19] Estimates of the numbers of Mamlūks in the eighteenth century vary considerably. Some writers seem even to have included the mercenaries and camp followers as part of the Mamlūk army. George Baldwin, in a report to the British government written in 1780, stated that at the time of ᶜAlī-Bey there were more than 10,000 Mamlūks in Egypt but that in his own time there were but 4,000. Al-Jabartī, writing in the early nineteenth century, quoted 2,000 as a figure. By then, however, the sources of Mamlūks had been for some time cut off from Egypt and internecine strife as well as the French invasion had brought about a sharp decline.

Regarding the *ojāqs*, it is said that these were a force of 20,000 men at the time of the Ottoman invasion, but soon after they began to dwindle. Certainly, as time wore on most of the regimental forces were absorbed by the Mamlūks on the one hand, through the latter's purchase of positions in the corps, and on the other by the lower class through inheritance. See David Kimche, "The Political Superstructure of Egypt in the Late Eighteenth Century," *The Middle East Journal* 22 (1968), pp. 453, 460-461; David Ayalon, "Studies in al-Jabartī," pp. 164-165.

of the figure given by Lane for the number of Turks in Egypt and the virtual restriction of the elite to the leading urban center, it is safe to assume that nearly all 10,000 of them resided in Cairo. This would make the most exclusive segment of the upper class practically the same size as the earlier Mamlūk group, and the upper echelons of administrators also nearly equal. The inclusion of government servants in the upper class is especially understandable if we consider the Ottoman tendency to bureaucratize. The elite were no longer defined by a strict military ideology. Under Muḥammad ᶜAlī, even the highest ranking notable was little more than a government servant. The relative size of the upper class always depended in large part upon the share of the resources which it could command through the services of the other orders and we can readily see that the balance was maintained through tremendous changes in over-all population size and political circumstance.

With regard to the middle orders, it is somewhat more difficult to evaluate the changes that have taken place. Although the relative size of the general division appears to have remained constant, there is no way of knowing the size of the constituent groups in 1839. In the earlier period, the artisans outnumbered all others by far [20] and we may assume that they made up the largest part of Lane's category. It is also probable that the import-export merchants increased substantially by virtue of the influx of foreign population. There is no reason to think that petty merchants and café owners would have lost or gained any great number as these were always needed to supply the immediate needs of the urban center. The most interesting fact about the class as a whole is that it is nearly twice the size of the upper class even after the civil servants and petty officials have been transferred to the latter. The urban society thus was far from bifurcated, even though by far the greatest concentration of power lay with the new elite and their organization.

There may be some question as to whether the artisans who formed nearly seventy per cent of the middle class belonged with the merchants or with the laborers, that is, in the middle or lower class. It is true that in the chronicles and travelers reports we sometimes hear of "artisans and rabble" in the same breath, but it should be remembered that this is often in the context of their occasional involvement in the

[20] Taking into account the assessments of Evliya Chelebi (1660) and those of the *Description*, André Raymond concludes that half of the active population of Cairo in the eighteenth century was made up of artisans (*Artisans et commerçants au Caire,* I (Damascus: Institut Français, 1973), p. 206).

affairs of the Mamlūks where the contrast with the elite is very sharp. It is well known, on the other hand, that many craftsmen were highly respected in earlier times and Lane did not hesitate to class them with merchants of all kinds in his day. Many of the ᶜ*ulamā*ᵓ, moreover, did not disdain association with the crafts. [21]

The lowest class is the largest and, like the upper class, typically urban. Like all other groups, its relative size remained practically the same but unlike them, there seem to have been great shifts in the proportions of groups included within it. While it lost some 10,000 members, it seems that nearly all of these were domestics. Why this occurred is somewhat difficult to explain. It is commonly accepted that in time of plague, the lower orders suffer most and we saw in the previous part the sharp decline in numbers of domestics during the great plagues of the Mamlūk period. Lane tells us that the population was reconstituted to a large extent by immigration. It may be that Muḥammad ᶜAlī's policy of centralization with the institution of various governmental projects resulted in the recruitment of immigrants for common labor and industrial projects rather than private domestic service, but the information is too scanty to know for certain.

As members of the lower orders also, we should mention musicians, dancing girls, and prostitutes, as well as beggars and thieves, all socially distinct from other groups and generally marrying within their own occupational group. They also had a vocabulary peculiar to themselves, a characteristic common to those who practice disreputable professions in other places. Lane notes, however, that occasionally a dancing girl would repent and marry a respectable Arab "who is not generally considered as disgraced by such a connection." [22] Generally speaking, women of the lower orders were much less secluded than those of the upper classes. Their work frequently necessitated their visiting heavily populated sections of the city where contact with various kinds of people was most likely to occur. The "freedom" of the lower orders was thus an integral part of their low rank and in the case of women, lack of seclusion indicated questionable morality and lack of social standing. [23]

---

[21] There is also evidence, to be cited later in another context, that Janissaries did sometimes, for economic reasons, attempt to establish close formal associations with artisans, and it would be extremely unlikely that the members of the military upper class would have done so had the artisans not been of relatively high standing.

[22] *Manners and Customs*, p. 387.

[23] It is also true, however, that seclusion itself gave new opportunities of movement, for a veiled woman whose identity was unknown could go nearly everywhere

3. *The Pattern of the Social Fabric*

Socially and culturally Cairo was, like most Middle Eastern cities, heterogeneous by reason of the many disparate groups which lived within its bounds. Let us state at the outset that mutual social bonds and mobility between segments was limited. It is important to note that the emphasis placed upon formal symbols as markers of religious status were but a part of a larger scheme by which etiquette signalled social differences of all kinds. There is a sense in which the very symbols which demarcated separate personal statuses facilitated a kind of mechanical unity. That is, they facilitated certain kinds of interaction by permitting individuals who did not know one another to find a structured basis of understanding in particular contexts.

Not only special status but rank was marked by symbols and formal actions. The right to ride a horse was still reserved for the military elite, while mules were usually used by merchants, shaykhs, and noble ladies. Europeans, Eastern Christians, and Jews rode asses. [24] Clothing especially was indicative of status and rank. Even as turban color symbolized religious affiliation, so several forms of turbans represented different families or dynasties. The gown worn by persons of the lower class was typically of simple inferior materials, the poorest having only a long blue or brown shirt. Many of the women of the lower orders

---

without loss of reputation. Let us note, moreover, that observations of social life made in the last half of the nineteenth century may very well reflect a social order that had reasserted traditional mores as a response to the disorganizing impact of Western influences. There is some evidence to indicate that women in the Ottoman period were allowed much more liberty than is commonly supposed. The following quotation from the report of F. Mengin, written in the second decade of the nineteenth century is illustrative:

> "Accompanied by a slave girl who shared her secrets, she left the harem as she pleased, under the pretext of going to the baths or of making visits which could be prolonged for several days without her returning home. She was free in her actions and left undisturbed" (*Histoire de l'Égypte*, II, p. 312).

This image of the Cairene woman is much more in line with that projected by *The Thousand and One Nights*, a product of the late Mamlūk period, in which ladies hardly appear socially secluded.

[24] We have the following interesting comment from Sonnini de Manoncourt who visited Cairo in 1779:

> "it was deemed indecorous for foreign merchants, abominated on account of their religion, to ride upon animals superior even to those kept for the wives of the Beys themselves. This was sufficient to bring upon the European merchants a forced contribution, an *avanie* of four or five hundred thousand francs, which they were obliged to pay, for having kept fine donkeys" (*Travels in Upper and Lower Egypt*, tr. from the French by Henry Hunter, I (London: Printed for J. Stockdale, 1799), pp. 265-267).

never wore the veil. Naturally, patterns of deference pervaded all of social life:

> A person of the lower orders ... (salutes first) a superior ... the son kisses the hand of the father; ... and the slave, and often the free servant, that of the master. The slaves and servants of a grandee kiss their lord's sleeve, or the skirt of his clothing. [25]

Sonnini reported that in his day the French merchants

> were obliged to be attentive to the persons before and behind them. If a Mameluke, a priest, or a man in office appeared, they made way for him, alighted, placed the right hand on the breast as a token of respect, and durst not pursue their way till the rigorous and haughty Mussulman was gone by, and then only to repeat the same ceremony a few minutes afterwards. [26]

The system, while relating segments of the mosaic, did little to integrate the parts of the whole.

But if we put aside rules and regulations for a moment, and look into the deeper implications of our demographic data, we see that the fragmentation of the mosaic is only part of the picture. Corporations as legal entities remain constant but their substance often changes. Similarly, the constancy of the respective proportions of the population as a whole, while revealing some facts, tends to obscure others. Persons are not numbers on a chart, even if they do tend to replace one another in some ways. The absolute figures for each group varied considerably over the period, and with each variation, the personnel of the urban classes and status groups changed not only in number but with respect to the personal content involved. Replacement was rapid and continual. Jomard tell us that:

> If the plague does not afflict Cairo with its ravages every year, it is a rare occurrence if it does not come once every four or five years with more or less virulence ... In 1801, Cairo, lost during two months, from three to four hundred individuals a day; ... [27]

Under such conditions there must have been mechanisms for the transfer of individuals from one group to another. As disease and famine did not effect all groups equally, neither were the reconstitutive factors of natural increase and immigration equal in influence.

---

[25] E. W. Lane, *Manners and Customs*, pp. 204-205.

[26] *Travels in Upper and Lower Egypt*, I, p. 263.

[27] "Description abrégée de la ville," p. 586.

We have noted from the beginning of this work that a considerable amount of blending had taken place within the population for centuries. As Volney remarked in 1782:

> Here we see various races of inhabitants settling themselves on the same country who, adopting the same manners and interests, have sometimes united in the most intimate alliances; but more frequently we find them separated by political or religious prejudices, and remaining perpetually distinct. In the first case the different races, losing by the mixture their distinguishing characters, have formed an homogeneous people among whom it is impossible to discover any traces of the revolution. In the second, living distinct, their perpetual differences are become a monument which has outlived the ages, and which in some cases may supply the silence of history.[28]

It is impossible to know just what Volney meant by "the most intimate alliances" but in the following chapters our investigation of urban unity will particularly focus upon the problem of social mobility.

Certainly access to political and economic power were major keys to attainment of higher rank and we will in the following chapters attempt to analyze the way in which these kinds of opportunities were manipulated by specific groups. Spiritual power, however, continued to be of great significance in setting the formal framework as well as the tone of social relations. At this early stage we will postulate on the basis of historical evidence presented up to now and the preceding discussion of demography that the major factor influencing the acceptance or rejection of an individual by any social group involved his moral responsibility. The legal and ideological boundaries between special status groups were the boundaries of different moral systems and the mobility which existed between these groups was probably the least. For instance, marriage between members of various faiths was rare indeed. Within status groups, Muslim and *dhimmī*, the appurtenances of morality were an essential part of status and prestige. The term "*karīm*" meaning "generous," "beneficent," and "honorable" (person) was used also to mean "high-ranking," or "eminent" even as English speakers use the word "noble." The formal education which within Islam served as the surest road to high rank for persons of low birth was religious (moral) education. The religious and moral divisions of urban society, though not *necessarily* related to *precise* residential groupings, up until the end of the nineteenth century had

[28] *Travels through Egypt and Syria*, I, pp. 73-74.

some territorial referents. As we shall see, residence in a quarter signified moral responsibility for that community.

It is axiomatic that the mobility which occurred with respect to members of the upper class was downward and loss of rank was relatively easy. Although members of the lower classes often attained positions of higher standing through economic gains, political connections, or spiritual accomplishment, the road to achievement was difficult. The size of the elite and upper class was limited by the ability of the rest of the society to support it and great selectivity was involved. As it was easier to lose one's reputation than to make it, so it was easier to enter the lower orders than to leave them.

CHAPTER FOURTEEN

THE ECOLOGICAL MANIFESTATION: THE PLACE

The ecology of the city, from the outermost limits of its suburbs to the innermost recesses of its quarters, is inseparable from the culture and social organization of the people who inhabit it. The preceding remarks concerning general categories of the population will mean much more if we can visualize the spatial distribution of specific groups and understand the significance of urban ecological patterns for effective social relations.

1. *The Social Pattern of Residence*

The area of the city in the Turkish period was approximately the same as it had been in the Mamlūk era; that is, about three square miles. Changes on the political and economic scenes, however, in addition to sapping the city of its resources and contributing to its decay, [1] had brought about some shifts in the location of certain communities as well as the addition of new ones.

The north and northeastern sections were the focus of interest of most visitors to the city, as in many ways they represented the "nerve center" of the town, the physical site of the confrontation of various status groups and social classes; the meeting place of various economic, ideological, and political interests. Here were not just the central

---

[1] By the middle of the eighteenth century the contrast between the once glorious Cairo and European capitals was most marked. In the words of Volney:

> "When we hear of *Grand Cairo*, we are led to imagine that it must be a capital, at least, like those of Europe; but if we reflect that, even among ourselves, towns have only begun to be rendered convenient and elegant within these hundred years, we shall easily believe that, in a country where nothing has been improved since the tenth century, they must partake of the common barbarism; and, indeed, we shall find that Cairo contains none of those public or private edifices, those regular squares, or well-built streets, in which the architect displays his genius. Its environs are full of hills of dust, formed by the rubbish which is accumulating every day, while the multitude of tombs, and the stench of the common sewers, are at once offensive to the smell and the sight. Within the walls, the streets are winding and narrow; and as they are not paved, the crowds of men, camels, asses, and dogs, which press against each other, raise a very disagreeable dust; individuals often water their doors, and to this dust succeeds mud and pestiferous exhalations" (*Travels through Egypt and Syria*, I, pp. 254-255).

business districts and centers of culture and of learning, but new areas of fashionable residence. A more heterogeneous area could scarcely be found, for in close proximity were Muslim, Coptic, Maghribī, Jewish, Greek, Turkish, and European quarters. Here Christian churches rose opposite Muslim mosques. Diverse crafts clustered in the area, while merchants dealt not only in local but in foreign goods. [2]

According to a kind of natural logic residence patterns tended to follow the physical manifestations and necessities of occupational pursuits. A large proportion of the well-to-do middle class, the merchants and shaykhs, preferred to live in or near Cairo proper close to their *khān*s, colleges, and the mosque of al-Azhar. In general, the popular quarters were situated around the periphery of the agglomeration. Some of the largest of these were in the north: the Ḥusaynīya and the area west of there from the Bāb ash-Shaᶜrīya to the Bāb al-Baḥr on the road to Būlāq; and in the south near the Citadel, especially the Rumayla, Darb al-Khalīfa, and Ibn Ṭūlūn. Almost invariably the popular quarters were associated with industries that dealt with food products and the preparation of raw materials, particularly the slaughtering of animals, the pressing of oil, the tanning of skins, and the preparation and distribution of grains, legumes, and fruit. [3] It would be incorrect to say, however, that the masses were confined to these places. Residence was regulated chiefly by the demands of economic and industrial life but still there was considerable room for preference. The very economic activities of lower classes, moreover, afforded them a considerable degree of spatial mobility. At least, to dispense their goods and services many of them needed ready access to the main

---

[2] It is worth noting in passing, that well into the nineteenth century, visitors were sometimes accustomed to refer to the city as though it were still only the spatially delimited area of "Cairo proper." Lane, for instance, says:

> "(The metropolis) ... is surrounded by a wall, the gates of which are shut at night, and is commanded by a large citadel, situate at an angle of the town, near a point of the mountain" (*Manners and Customs*, p. 4).

It is clear that no wall of Cairo save that of the Fāṭimid compound ever existed and the fortifications conceived by Ṣalāḥ ad-Dīn, as they were constructed in actuality, only connected the Citadel with the northern quarters and fortified a closely delimited northern boundary. From Lane's remarks, moreover, we can see that in his time the major gates were still used to prohibit access to the urban nucleus at certain times and that the continuously occupied center of habitation, while neither geographically central nor the seat of political power, remained the most essential part of the town.

[3] See André Raymond, "Quartiers et mouvements populaires au Caire au XVIIIème siècle," *Political and Social Change in Modern Egypt*, edited by P. M. Holt (London: Oxford University Press, 1968), pp. 106-107.

arteries of town, while others resided in well-to-do quarters to serve the upper classes.

An important point to keep in mind is that with historic changes in the cultural environment centers of habitation shifted as did the placement of businesses and industries. Spatial restrictions would have been no more possible to maintain in the absolute sense than restriction of individuals to status or class, especially over long periods, but rather reflected the fluidity of social relations. André Raymond's extensive studies of residence patterns of the seventeenth and eighteenth centuries illustrate the situation very clearly. From his work we chiefly derive the following information.

As we have seen in Chapter VI, the elite frequently "pioneered" in the development of new areas. Similarly, their movements signalled changes in the pattern of land use in areas already established. Just as in Arab times the consideration of defense was of paramount concern and shifts in the locus of centers of military power indicated political as well as economic realities around which all of urban life revolved.

The defense of the city had, of course, long ceased to be a function of the old fortress. Even the Citadel was losing some of its military significance by this time. The breakdown of the "classic" Mamlūk institution had been accompanied by changes in the pattern of residence of the elite which culminated in the beginning of the nineteenth century with the establishment of new regions of political significance and fashionable habitation. Until the Ottoman conquest, the elite had favored the quarter of the Citadel and its environs for their residence. Most of their dwellings were on the right bank of the canal which divides the city from north to south. A few were in Cairo proper but most were south of there, near the fortress and the Rumayla, stretching northwards to the Bāb Zuwayla until the presence of tanneries outside the gates blocked their progress.

A number of changes occurred between 1650 and 1755. In the first place, because of the deterioration of the area, Cairo proper was totally abandoned by the beys and *kāshif*s [4] although a number of officers (Janissaries and ᶜAzabs) resided there. Concerning the residences of officers in Cairo proper, Raymond states interestingly enough that:

> The existence of a relatively large number of residences of the Officers of Ojāqs in Cairo was perhaps due to the particular relations which

[4] In this period, a *kāshif* was usually a Mamlūk freed by a bey and then delegated to govern a province.

existed between the popular classes and the military, especially the Janissaries and the ᶜAzabs. [5]

These soldiers of the pasha, who formed the lowest ranks of the aristocratic class, were organized on their own principles and, even more than the beys, lacked any roots in Egypt. It is not surprising that they often moved into regions vacated by the latter and sought support from ties with the commercial factions adjacent to their places of residence. Suffice it to say at this point that the importance of localized clienteles clustered around elite residences was nothing new. Moreover as in Mamlūk times the rulers were caught between the desire to mobilize popular movements in their interest and fear and suspicion of these forces that could easily get out of hand. [6]

In the second place, we notice a marked decline in the percentage of residences near the Citadel. To be sure, the Ottoman conquest had made the fortress the home of a new ruling group to some extent, and the presence of the pasha contributed to the prestige of the area, but we must remember that the Mamlūks soon reasserted themselves. Their virtual independence had an adverse effect upon the Citadel quarter. Since the beys had no sultan of their own, they stood apart from it. "Great Houses," [7] were set up away from the residence of

---

[5] "Essai de géographie des quartiers de résidence aristocratique au Caire aux XVIIIème siècle," *Journal of the Economic and Social History of the Orient*, VI (1963), p. 68.

[6] See André Raymond, "Quartiers et mouvements populaires au Caire," p. 111.

[7] The houses of the beys, a number of which remain to this day, can only be described as "palatial." They contained large reception halls, inner courts and gardens, and were charmingly decorated with gold arabesque, tile, and stained glass of many colors. Yet there can be no doubt that the basic consideration of the house was defense.

In domestic architecture we see nearly all the features that characterize the fortress. The typical well-built house of the eighteenth century is of two or three stories, constructed of brick or stone, and encased externally and internally to the height of the first floor with yellow limestone. The entrance is commonly "bent." One does not immediately go into the central hall but rather has first to walk through a narrow and twisting passage, the walls of which are of the same stone that reinforces the outside. The grated windows of the ground floor are placed high up so that even a person on horseback could not see into them. All windows, even those of the upper stories and those within the house itself, are latticed with *mashrafīya* work which admits considerable light and air, if used a large scale, but completely shuts off the view from the outside. Usually there was also a well of brackish water. Although in times of peace, water was brought from the Nile, this provision could be quite essential during periods when the door of the quarter was closed for several days.

Within the parts of the house, the apartments characteristically occupy different levels separated by one or two steps or perhaps by a passage which inhibits easy progress from one area to the other. Secret rooms provide hidden places for goods

the pasha. Combats in the vicinity of the fortress became so frequent that it was no longer a safe place to live. Moreover the resurgent Mamlūks saw scant advantage in exposing themselves and their property to the ravages of the quarreling Janissaries and ᶜAzabs. [8] Thus the *birkas* came to flourish at the expense of the old city and the Citadel and the neo-Mamlūk period saw the establishment of some new areas of elite residence. With the transfer of the tanneries to the Bāb al-Lūq, the way was opened for expansion into the region between the Birkat al-Fīl and the Bāb Zuwayla. By far the greatest percentage of aristocrats, including both beys and officers, had their dwellings on the right bank and almost two thirds of these surrounded the southern pond. The Quarter of Qawṣūn was most fashionable, as it was the site of the houses of the two most powerful men of the time, Ibrāḥīm-Kākhya and Riḍwān-Kākhya, [9] leaders of the Janissaries and ᶜAzabs.

The following period, 1755-1798, witnessed the ascendency of the beys, following the deaths of Ibrāḥīm-Kākhya and Riḍwān-Kākhya,

---

and persons, so essential in those times when order so often broke down and the government itself was the worst offender.

It should be mentioned also, that many dwellings, especially those of the beys, were equipped with firearms. One beside the Mosque of Ibn Ṭūlūn, the Kretlī House, said to have been inhabited by a merchant, was once equipped with cannon which were upon its roof (R. G. "John" Gayer-Anderson, translator and editor *Legends of the Bait al-Kretliya* (Ipswich, England: The East Anglian Daily Times Co., 1951), p. 54).

[8] André Raymond describes the fighting that went on in the area:

> "In 1711 the dissension between Ifrang Aḥmad, the Janissaries and the Pasha Khalīl on one side, and the six Ojāqs on the other side degenerated into armed conflict; the barracks of the ᶜAzabs were bombarded and, from April to June, violent fighting went on around Sultan Ḥasan and in the quarters situated between the Rumayla and Bāb Zuwayla, where mosques were used as fortifications. The situation got out of hand; many of the inhabitants of the region of the Citadel (Quarters of Rumayla, al-Ḥaṭṭāba, al-Maḥjar) abandoned their homes. A great number of houses were destroyed by bombardment or fire around the Rumayla" ("Essai de géographie des quartiers de résidence," pp. 70-71).

[9] Riḍwān-Kākhya had a residence on the edge of the Ezbekīya pond and a garden with many kiosks beside the canal. Al-Jabartī describes the degree of license allowed in the vicinity of this palace:

> "Riḍwān led there a life of pleasure and debauch and he hid neither his taste for drink nor the admiration he professed for beauty. Women and boys of a certain class were given, during his regime, free reign to misconduct and vicious inclinations ... The police had received orders from Riḍwān not to disturb them or their admirers. Cairo resembled then a country of gazelles or a paradise peopled with houris and darlings, its inhabitants drank avidly the cup of delight, as though no reckoning would be paid on the day of Judgment" (*ᶜAjāʾib al-Āthār*, I, p. 192; *Merveilles biographiques et historiques*, II, p. 125).

under the rule of ᶜAlī-Bey. The number of officers increased by a third but the total number of beys and their lieutenants, the *kāshifs*, increased more than three-fold. The limits of spatial expansion on the right bank of the canal were soon reached and the left bank came into its own, having 45% of aristocratic residences as opposed to only 19% in the previous period. The houses of the beys at this time were equally divided between the two sections and it is interesting that 9% of the latter had also crept back back into the old city which also claimed 20% of the *kāshifs*. A large number of these houses in the Qaṣaba, however, were in the Darb as-Saᶜāda near the canal and many of the elite dwellings in the streets and alleys of Cairo were not grand residences at all but little houses of retreat.

> Each amīr had a grand mansion (*dār kabīra*) where he lived with his family and Mamlūks, and one or two "little houses" (*dār wa dārānī ṣighār*) the location of which he kept as secret as possible and where he placed, in case the need arose, his most valuable possessions. In times of grave crises in Cairo, we see the amīrs who anticipate defeat or exile, busying themselves with the removal of their goods to their "little houses" before they themselves disappear, leaving their principal residences almost empty ... These "little houses" also served as retreats in times of difficulty. Thus the two Mamlūks of Ismāᶜīl Bey ... retired after the departure and exile of (their patron) to their little houses ...; they lived there secluded until the arrival of Ḥasan Pasha and the return of Ismāᶜīl Bey permitted them to resume their positions and great houses. [10]

Thus the enclosed quarters and narrow alleys of the most congested region of the city regularly provided some security and "insurance" for individuals who were no longer able to protect themselves and their assets, and to whom conspicuousness was a threat. As in every preceding period, the houses of the elite were visible symbols of their authority and stimulated the development of new quarters of fashionable residence but the primary consideration always remained that of defense. The insecurity of the Citadel region was the primary reason for its abandonment, while the comparative security of an inconspicuous inner quarter could provide reason enough for residence in a place which lacked prestige.

2. *Streets and Quarters*

No physical features of a city so reflect its essence as its streets. Streets are the vital arteries without which urban life would wither

[10] A. Raymond, "Essai de géographie des quartiers de résidence," pp. 84-85.

and die. They also give structure to the agglomeration. Most important, however, they create as well as solve problems, and thereby stimulate social intercourse and cultural creativity.

The function of the Cairene street was ambivalent, for streets both unified the city and divided it. All travelers remarked upon their tortuousness for the passages were often less than a yard in width.[11] One fifteen feet wide was considered large. It is said that when Muḥammed ᶜAlī consulted the *ᶜulamāᵓ* about constructing a new street through the Muskī, they replied to him that it should be able to accommodate two camels with their burdens.[12] There being little or no sense of the public domain, most inhabitants did not hesitate to encroach upon public thoroughfares with their personal properties, shops, and buildings. A common problem were the *maṣṭaba*s (stone benches) that stood before the shops. While these served to facilitate the conduct of business with clients and could prove useful as barricades in time of trouble, they seriously impeded the way. Small shops and hovels had a way of springing up along the walls of more elegant and stable edifices, ignoring the borders of the road, while new and grand buildings, symbolic of the prestige of the elite, would often block a street altogether. As Thevenot wrote in the latter part of the seventeenth century:

> There is no handsome street in Cairo, but a great many little ones that are round about; it is well known that all the houses of Cairo have been built without any plan for the town; each one takes all the space that he wants to build, without considering whether he blocks the street or not.[13]

---

[11] Many streets, in fact, had the atmosphere of retreat:
"... all of (the quarters are) traversed by innumerable streets, or rather lanes, courts, or alleys, so narrow for the most part (some not exceeding two feet and a half in width), that they exclude at all hours the rays of the sun; to effect which more completely, a succession of palm-mats is thrown across on poles, with narrow apertures here and there, to admit a certain supply of light. This custom the generality of European travelers strongly condemn; but when, after a long ride in the suburbs or surrounding country, I have returned to Cairo about the middle of the day nothing used to appear to me more delightful than to plunge out of the scorching sunshine into the cool and dusky passages, where a brisk current of air is generally felt" (J. A. St. John, *Egypt and Nubia* (London: Chapman and Hall, 1845), p. 105).

[12] A. Raymond, "Problèmes urbains et urbanisme au Caire au XVIIème et XVIIIème siècles," *Colloque international sur l'histoire du Caire* (Cairo: General Egyptian Book Organization, 1974), p. 366.

[13] *The Travels of Monsieur de Thevenot into the Levant,* translated by A. Lovell (London: H. Clark, 1686-1687), Book II, pt. 1, p. 129.

Longer streets were invariably known not by a single name but by many, each of which signified a particular section given over to a special group of persons or activity. Of course, there were some major streets, but for the total area of the city, thoroughfares connecting different regions were few. As a result these were typically the scene of heavy traffic. Two quotations are illustrative:

> Crowds of men of various nations pass through the streets, jostle one another, dispute the way with the horse of the Mameluke, the mule of the man of law ... [14]

> The number of coffee houses, public baths, and bazars is immense; the crowd which fills the latter, at all hours of the day, would not permit a woman to pass through them on foot, unless she would run the risk of losing a limb. [15]

The physical manifestation of the social order that the streets defined and structured was the quarter. Although the exact meaning of the term is difficult to define, [16] its essential implication for urban unity can readily be grasped by a glance at the map of The City of the

---

[14] Sonnini de Manoncourt, *Travels in Upper and Lower Egypt*, p. 260.

[15] W. Minutoli, *Recollections of Egypt*, translated by S. H. L. (Philadelphia: Carey, Lee, and Carey, 1827), p. 44.

[16] The quarter in fact was a vaguely defined entity depending on the one hand upon a particular cluster of streets and on the other upon the organizational unity of the special segment of society it represented. We must state at the outset that the word in the historical sources has a number of usages and that each of these was meaningful in different contexts. The variety of terms for a hierarchy of streets has relevance here. Thus the principal arteries of towns were known by the name *shāriᶜa* (avenue). The thoroughfare, however, was too grand to define a special place of residence. More important in this respect was the *darb*, an open-ended lane or alley with a number of *ᶜaṭfāt*, (s. *ᶜaṭfa*), small dead-end streets, branching from it. We also meet the terms *sikka* (side street, lane, narrower than a *shāriᶜa*) and *zuqāq* (alley, corridor). Some terms designating quarters carried social connotations, such as "*khiṭṭa*" referring to a section or district often set aside for a special purpose, as the *khiṭaṭ* of Fusṭaṭ were once set aside for separate tribal sections in the army. Residential areas composed of non-Muslim families or craft groups were frequently designated by this name but for all practical purposes the word appears to be synonymous with *ḥāra*, the term most often used to designate a street, closed off at one end, that constituted an organized, residential unit. We also find the term *ḥayy*, literally meaning "life", which denotes a block of houses or small section of a city. The writers of the *Description* list some general areas as quarters. Thus, Jomard says that the most crowded were the commercial quarters of Bāb al-Kharq, al-Muᵓayyad, al-Azhar, al-Muskī, ash-Shaᶜrāwī, al-Ḥanafī, Sayyida Zaynab, al-Ghūrī, al-Ashrafīya, as-Silāḥ, al-Afranj, al-Yahūd, ar-Rūm, an-Naṣārīya, al-Ezbekīya, etc. ("Description abrégée de la ville," *Description*, II, 2, p. 662).

The Exterior of a Private House.

The Door of a Quarter.

14. The Residential Area.

Turkish Period which shows clusters of separated alleys rather than a single network of intersecting streets. [17]

The typical quarter had its own street (*darb, sikka*, or *ḥāra*) which often carried the same name as the collection of dwellings and shops found there. These crowded in upon one another even as the people themselves lived in concentrated groupings within them. The political unity of the *ḥāra* was manifested in the physical barriers which separated it from the world outside:

> These are enclosures of houses, more or less extended, and ordinarily guarded by gates which are closed at night for the security of the city, except during Ramadan and some noctural fêtes. [18]

Although frequently the inhabitants practiced the same or related occupations, it was their residential area, cut off from the places of business by a heavy wooden door. Most *ḥāra*s with the exception of quarters of elite residence and those of well-to-do special status groups, such as those of the Franks and Christians, were in the peripheral areas mentioned above that were given over to the distribution and processing of raw materials and commestibles. [19] The commercial nature of the Qaṣaba and the great streets leading to Būlāq, the Rumayla, and the cemeteries discouraged the existence of *ḥāra*s in those areas. Generally speaking, the *ḥāra*s drew strength from a variety of kinds of social relations, whether they had their genesis in national origin, profession, religion, or even patron-client ties. [20]

Formally, the organization of the quarter was expressed in its officials, provisions for collective responsibility and defense. The *shaykh al-ḥāra*, who derived his authority more from local prestige than governmental appointment, had broad powers. Frequently he seems

---

[17] From the *Description de l'Égypte* and archival sources, André Raymond estimates that in the seventeenth and eighteenth centuries there were 63 *ḥāra*s in the city: 23 in Cairo proper, 19 in the southern region, 20 in the area west of the canal, and one in the Ḥusaynīya ("Problèmes urbains et urbanisme au Caire au XVIIème et XVIIIème siècles," p. 355).

[18] M. Jomard, "Description abrégée de la ville," p. 661.

[19] A. Raymond, "Quartiers et mouvements populaires," p. 107.

[20] Gibb and Bowen clearly describe the social basis of the *ḥāra*:

"Each *ḥâra* formed an administrative unity under its own *şeyḫ*, and was inhabited by families between whom there existed some natural tie, either of origin, occupation, or religion, thus constituting a homogeneous group. Since the number of *ḥâra*s was less than the number of separate corporations, it would appear that the *ḥâra*-system was superimposed on the corporative system, but did not conflict with it, the *şeyḫ* of the *ḥâra* having rather police (and, if necessary, military) functions" (*Islamic Society and the West*, I, 1, p. 279).

to have held a responsible position in a professional corporation or religious order as well, enforcing his rule with multiple sanctions. As an intermediary between the group of neighbors and the government, he maintained order, settled disputes, and expelled those who disturbed the neighborhood. He transmitted and supervised the carrying out of the instructions of the governmental authorities, and even took part in the administration of inheritance, receiving as compensation from two to three per cent of the total sum. [21] As time wore on the aid of the shaykhs of the *ḥāra*s was enlisted more and more by the government for the purposes of making censuses and collecting taxes. By 1803 a "shaykh of the shaykhs of the quarters" (*shaykh mashāyikh al-ḥārāt*) appears as a governmental appointee. [22]

The *ḥāra* was guarded by the *bawwāb*s (door keepers) who sometimes seem to have worked in pairs. [23] It was their duty to lock the doors at night. If anyone wished to enter after sunset he had to prove his residence there or that he was visiting a known person. Customarily the *bawwāb* collected a small fee for admitting such persons. Certainly this arrangement facilitated social control, providing the government with a means of checking upon the whereabouts of troublemakers and foreigners.

Residence in a quarter itself signified some social responsibility. Lane tells us that a man who had no relations with whom to dwell and who was not married or who had not a female slave was not allowed to rent an apartment or to reside in a quarter. [24] An indication of some degree of corporate responsibility can be seen in his statement that:

---

[21] A. Raymond, "Problèmes urbaine et urbanisme au Caire au XVIIème et XVIIIème siècles," p. 357.

[22] *Ibid.*, p. 357. Lane reported that in the middle of the nineteenth century each of the eight districts of Cairo had a shaykh, the *shaykh at-tumn* ("shaykh of the eighth") (*Manner and Customs*, p. 128).

[23] Travelers of the seventeenth century reported that in one case these were joined by means of a chain and iron collars to which the inhabitants held the key, in order to "more rigorously guard their quarter" (A. Raymond, "Problèmes urbains et urbanisme au Caire," p. 356).

[24] He relates that although he had signed a lease and made a down-payment on the rental of a house in a certain quarter, the owner subsequently informed him that the inhabitants, "mostly shereefs," objected to his living among them because he was not married, but would accept him if he would buy a female slave. Trying again in another area he did not meet such strong objections but was only asked to promise that no person wearing a hat (i.e., a European) would visit him (*Manners and Customs*, pp. 160-161).

> The price of blood is a debt incumbent on the family, tribe, or association of which the homicide is a member. It is also incumbent on the inhabitants of an enclosed quarter ... in which the body of a person killed by an unknown hand is found; unless the person has been found killed in his own house. [25]

Less formally, the spirit of the quarter could be seen on occasions when the inhabitants gave expression to their collectivity. Weddings, circumcisions and funerals all necessitated public ceremony. The birthdays (*mawlid*s) of local saints, like the Birthday of the Prophet (*Mawlid an-Nabī*) saw glorious torchlit processions embellished by colorful banners and accompanied by flutes and tambourines. The youth of the quarter tended to be particularly sensitive to the identity of their quarter, even as the gangs of *zuᶜar* were based in certain neighborhoods. Not only did these defend the *ḥāra* against aggression but upon occasion attacked rival neighborhoods. In the popular areas of the city, Ḥusaynīya, Bāb ash-Shaᶜrīya, al-Ḥaṭṭāba, and al-ᶜUtūf, the quarrels and brawls were almost ritualistic. [26]

It is instructive to consider in some detail a few of the quarters upon which we have substantial information. The Ḥusaynīya, from the time of its first establishment in the Mamlūk period, exhibited considerable character and *esprit de corps.* In the eighteenth century the butchers were exceedingly numerous, having three corporations with a total of 2,200 members. There a religious tradition was superimposed upon a powerful corporate occupational tradition: the quarter developed a new Ṣūfī order, the Bayyūmīya. We will investigate this development in a later chapter. Suffice it to say at this point that the quarter was one of the most effectively organized in town. Under Aḥmad Sālim al-Jazzār (the Butcher), the shaykh of the Bayyūmīya, the quarter rebelled twice against the impositions of Murād-Bey in 1786 and 1790; its collective strength, in conjunction with that of other popular quarters, provided a stepping stone for Muḥammad ᶜAlī to rise to power in 1805. [27]

The quarters defined by national origin also tended to represent social groups well-knit by several common concerns. While coming under the aegis of Islam, the Maghribīs were set apart by their nationality. Al-Azhar, it will be remembered, had a separate portico for Maghribī students, and they formed one of the largest of the foreign

---

[25] *Manners and Customs*, p. 108.

[26] A. Raymond, "Quartiers et mouvements populaires," pp. 110-111.

[27] *Ibid.*, pp. 110-116.

divisions. Defense was not as great a concern as it was among the elite or non-Muslim groups, but Maghribīs, like all others, sought support from friends and kinsmen in sheltered, compact, neighborhoods.

Maghribīs tended to cluster around principal mosques and commercial areas devoted to their special commodities. They had three major residential districts, the neighborhoods of al-Azhar, the Mosque of Ibn Ṭūlūn, [28] and an area west of the Ezbekīya. [29] All of these bear direct relation to the pilgrimage. In the vicinity of al-Azhar, the Sūq al-Faḥḥamīn, Sūq al-ᶜAṭṭārīn, and Sūq al-Ghūrī among others, were dominated by North Africans until the end of the eighteenth century. The Faḥḥamīn was their quarter *par excellence* where rugs, blankets, tarbushes, burnooses, etc., were sold.

The community as a whole was well known for its religious fervor and even commercial interests had religious connections. In 1699, for instance, the immigrants from Tunis and Fez strongly objected to the use of tobacco and attacked smokers at the annual procession of the *maḥmil*. The fact that many of them had come with the pilgrimage caravan led to the development of commercial activities related to supplying the needs of pilgrims, the selling of food and other articles necessary for the journey. Many Maghribīs were among the richest merchants of Cairo and, as nearly all depended upon the annual caravan as a major source of income, both with reference to supply and demand, it is difficult to separate religious and commercial aspects of their network.

Like the Maghribīs, the principal religious minorities, were not restricted to any special area of the city but were spread throughout the town and a number of fortified quarters, each having its special religious edifice where services were conducted without interference. Most of them were in Cairo proper and around the Ezbekīya but the Copts from earliest times had retained their most important center in the enclosure of Miṣr al-ᶜAtīqa or "Old Cairo" where the main church, built upon the foundations of the fortress of Babylon, had

[28] The Mosque of Ibn Ṭūlūn had been, from a very early date, perhaps the ninth or tenth century, a place of shelter for pilgrims and a commercial center for Maghribīs. In the middle of the seventeenth century, a traveler counted forty-eight shops in its environs pertaining to specialized North African goods and crafts (A. Raymond, "Tunisiens et Magrébins au Caire au dix-huitième siècle," *Cahiers de Tunisie*, 26-27 (1959), p. 358).

[29] See A. Raymond, "Tunisiens et Magrébins au Caire au dix-huitième siècle," pp. 336-371.

been in use for nearly fifteen hundred years. While the map shows a large Coptic quarter north of the Ezbekīya, there were also smaller concentrations of Christians near their churches in the Bayn as-Sūrayn (on the canal just north of the Bāb al-Kharq) and in the region of the Quarter of the Greeks (Ḥārat ar-Rūm) east of the Bāb Zuwayla. The only church of the Greeks in the main part of the city was the one in their ancient quarter but they had one other in Old Cairo, [30] evidently an area which, despite its overwhelming atmosphere of bitter historic animosity, gave shelter to Christians of various persuasions.

Of all quarters, perhaps the most isolated was that of the Franks (Ḥārat al-Afranj) established in the middle of the seventeenth century in the northwestern region between the Ezbekīya and the canal. As James Bruce, who visited it in the middle of the eighteenth century, described it:

> The part of Cairo where the French are settled is exceedingly commodious and fit for retirement. It consists of one long street, where all the merchants of that nation live together. It is shut at one end by large gates, where there is a guard, and these are kept constantly closed at the time of the plague. At the other end there is a garden tolerably kept, in which there are several pleasant walks and seats; all the enjoyment that Christians can hope for, among this vile people, reduces itself to peace and quiet; nobody seeks for more. [31]

A decade later Volney gave the following vivid description:

> (After the removal of the French Consul from Cairo in 1777 for financial reasons) the merchants ... remained at Cairo at the peril of their lives and fortunes. Their situation, which has not changed, is nearly similar to that of the Dutch at Nangazaki; that is to say, shut up in a confined place, they live among themselves, with scarcely any external communication; they even dread it, and go as little out as possible, to avoid the insults of the common people, who hate the very name of the Franks, and the insolence of the Mamlukes, who force them to dismount from their asses in the middle of the streets. In this kind of imprisonment, they tremble every instant, lest the plague should oblige them entirely to shut themselves up in their houses, or some revolt expose their quarter to be plundered; lest the chief of some party should make a pecuniary demand, or the Beys compel them to furnish them with what they want, which is always attended with no little danger. [32]

---

[30] E. F. Jomard, "Description abrégée de la ville," p. 677.

[31] *Travels to Discover the Source of the Nile in the Years 1768, 1769, 1770, 1771, 1772, and 1773* (Edinburgh: G. G. J. and J. Robinson, 1790), I, pp. 100-102.

[32] *Travels through Egypt and Syria*, I, p. 230.

The quarter was apparently divided between Europeans (principally French) and Syrians (Nestorians and Maronites) who acted as their agents. Two Catholic churches, more simply decorated than those of the Copts or Greeks, served the community. The Armenians also had their own church but Jomard says that he did not see it. [33]

The quarter of the Jews (Ḥārat al-Yahūd) was described by Lane as being "equal to a small town." [34] According to the *Description*, it was very large and populous but its main street was extremely narrow. We have already noted the shabby exteriors of the buildings which gave some protection against the cupidity of Muslim rulers, The interiors, on the other hand, were frequently "fine and well-furnished." [35] There were ten synagogues situated in its narrow streets and, although the *Description* does not mention it, another in Old Cairo which had remained in continuous use since the sixth century.

Common residence signaled the establishment of the strongest social bonds, or at least an approved status of social and economic responsibility. Although it is impossible to reconstruct the marriage patterns of the period, many travelers reported that a quarter was commonly inhabited by a group of related families, especially if the local craft involved specialized techniques or resources. Abstention from marriage with no just cause was looked upon as disreputable and a proposal of marriage was a bid for economic and political cooperation as well as the establishment of a social liaison. Endogamous marriage bonds created the basis of lasting relationships between families and formed an important part of the ties which unified the neighborhood.

3. *The City as a Whole*

The city's ecology to this point seems to reflect anything but unity. There were, of course, regions used by persons from every segment of the populace, "public" areas not given over to any single group or function. The situation, however, was not a simple case of specialized or exclusive locations as opposed to places of functional and social "integration." Rather there were a number of sites where persons of various backgrounds were wont to meet and, in each instance, one must assess the significance for urban unity with consideration of the type and extent of communication taking place.

[33] "Description abrégée de la ville," p. 678.

[34] *Cairo Fifty Years Ago*, edited by Stanley Lane-Poole (London: J. Murray, 1896), p. 39. Despite the fact that the Jews were of two sects, Talmudists and Karaites, they appear to have inhabited a single quarter.

[35] E. W. Lane, *Manners and Customs*, p. 561.

The great plazas or "squares" of Cairo were the market places near the major mosques and at the intersections of the main streets: the Rumayla, Sayyida Zaynab, al-Azhar, Bāb Zuwayla. As trade was conducted on a personalized basis, it naturally encouraged the acquaintance of persons of different stations. In this context interaction was encouraged since transactions were structured in such a way as to guard against the rise of friction and especially the disruption of social norms. Much of the business of the market place was conducted by men or persons of the lower classes but in every case the dictates of custom and markers of status indicated the bounds beyond which one should not step.

Large mosques functioned as meeting places not only for persons with religious purposes and for students, but also for those who merely wished to lounge, chat, eat, sleep, or to engage in a simple craft. Many were open from day-break until two hours after sunset. Al-Azhar remained open all night. Contacts in mosques, however, were generally restricted to Muslims, particularly men, except on special occasions. It is certain also that even in the nineteenth century, the largest were out of bounds for non-Muslims. [36]

Many local institutions catered to particular segments of the community, although they were not necessarily restricted to any special group. This was true of coffee houses frequented by men of particular neighborhoods, and also of the baths. In the eighteenth century there were nearly eighty *ḥammāms* (baths) in Cairo [37] that had different types of accommodation for people of different classes. The Ottoman period, indeed, saw the proliferation of *ḥammāms* and *sabīls* (public fountains) which, though they were erected by the amīrs for the purpose of self-glorification, substantially benefited the populace. The *ḥammāms* were, however, the location of much interaction between persons of similar social position. Frequently groups of women would hire a bath for an afternoon of enjoyment with their friends.

Continuing to be important for communication within the city were a number of large areas in which the populace gathered on feast days. Most significant in this respect were the *birkas*, from ancient times performing an essential social function. The Ezbekīya Pond, which had an area of 450,000 square feet in the 1860's, was filled with water

---

36 E. W. Lane, *Cairo Fifty Years Ago*, p. 82.

37 See André Raymond, "Les bains publics au Caire à la fin du XVIIIème siècle," *Annales Islamologiques*, VIII (Cairo. L'Institut Français d'Archéologie Orientale, 1969) pp. 132-139.

when the Nile flooded and its inundation provided entertainment for crowds who gathered to enjoy the sight of water and make pleasure trips upon it.

In the same category, strangely enough, were the cemeteries, "cities of the living" as well as "cities of the dead." Some, like the "Tombs of the Mamlūks" in the east, included shrine-mosques with schools attached. All had a number of residents including not only caretakers and their families but some small factories and craft shops. [38]

Even as the popular quarters were on the urban periphery; so the cemeteries and the outskirts of the city were particularly frequented by persons of the lower orders. Public entertainers, musicians, dancing girls, and gypsies, some of whom moved from one town to another, regularly attending all festivals and celebrations of which they were, according to Lane, "to many persons, the chief attractions." [39] Yet the separation was only general in the territorial sense and not restrictive. Water carriers (*saqqāʾīn*), paid by individual households, perpetually came and went between the Nile and the inner quarters supplying the populace with water for all domestic needs. [40] Transportation in the city was supplied by donkey men, a group associated with the lowest class, porters, pimps, and prostitutes. Mounts could be found at all the main street corners and *sūq*s to be rented for a small fee. The *ḥarāfīsh* were still found everywhere, picking up a livelihood in whatever way they could:

> A very great number of persons of both sexes among the lower orders in Cairo, ... obtain their subsistence by begging. As might be expected, not a few of these are abominable imposters. There are some whose appearance is most distressing to every humane person who sees them; but who accumulate considerable property ... [41]

---

[38] Jomard's description reminds us of Piloti's nearly four hundred years before: "We count in all three great graveyards or public cemeteries, not to speak of many burial grounds. Between these thousands of tombs and enclosures, there are kinds of streets where one can walk easily, and benches of stone upon which one may sit. The practice is to visit the tombs each Friday, at the break of day. There they pray and plant flowers, and scatter aromatic herbs. The women and children go with the men, the crowd of visitors is immense, and one can see from far the location of the necropolis. This spectacle on religious holidays, so moving and stately, must be seen many times to be appreciated" ("Description abrégée de la ville," p. 686).

[39] *Manners and Customs*, p. 388.

[40] A. Raymond, "Problèmes urbains et urbanisme au Caire au XVIIème et XVIIIème siècles," p. 362.

[41] E. W. Lane, *Manners and Customs*, p. 333. Even in Cairo today, it is commonly supposed that some of the beggars have accumulated fortunes. Thus one might gather considerable profit at a busy intersection where long line of cars stops for the red

Doubtless laborers and construction workers had temporary residence in lots adjoining their places of work as they do today.

Thus the plan of the city was indicative of both its unity and diversity. Although some quarters could, in a sense, be considered communities unto themselves, there were numerous provisions for interaction between them which increased as time went on and the city was "opened up" through the efforts of the French and Muḥammad ʿAlī. On the other hand, although physical contacts could be close, social contacts continued to be ordered in such a way as to allow limited types of communication between groups. Moreover the pattern of land use, given medieval technology, could only reflect the special niches assigned to particular divisions of the social structure.

Yet the realities of urban life, the demands for provision of goods and services and the necessities of defense called in the very least for a willingness to accommodate. It is not enough to say that no town-plan was followed. What planner could have anticipated future needs, by even a few years, in an environment so politically and economically unstable? André Raymond has described the structure of the agglomeration as regularized by social and economic phenomena that endowed it with a sort of "natural order," continually remodeled through the exigencies of circumstance and independent of any direct intervention by the local authorities. [42] The physical manifestation, like the life it followed, was not shaped by the law and institutions, rather it was shaped by the circumstances and personalities that themselves shaped the law and institutions.

---

light, even if one gets only five piasters from every twentieth car! A woman who sits on a corner in Garden City, where the author resided for a number of years, when taken into custody by the police was reported to have been discovered to have eleven thousand pounds put away in her house.

[42] A. Raymond, "Problèmes urbains et urbanisme au Caire au XVIIème et XVIIIème siècles," p. 368.

CHAPTER FIFTEEN

POLITICAL POWER AND THE STRUCTURE OF URBAN SOCIETY

Having dealt generally with the agents, the "raw materials" of Cairene society, so to speak, and the setting of social relations, we now turn to the weave of the social fabric, the ordering of relations between persons and groups, specifically with reference to the dimensions of social power. Let us first of all admit that it is difficult to extricate political power from economic and spiritual power. Control in each dimension tends to lead to influence in the other dimensions. In the intercourse of everyday life, moreover, they are inseparable since individuals only achieved their ends through a manipulation of all three.

For purposes of clarity, political power is here defined as power directly sanctioned by the military strength of the governing elite, though often mediated by agents who are motivated by economic and moral (spiritual) concerns as well. Political power originates in conquest but requires confirmation and consent. One of its most effective channels is the law. The decrees of the sultans (*qānūn*), superimposed upon the law of Islam (*sharīʿa*) formed the basis of government and administration. The law, however, served both as a standardized reference for behavior and a framework for interaction; it served as a means by which individuals and groups could achieve their ends. It is the paradox of power that conquest breeds contest, and even the legitimization of military control itself limits that control. Thus we must consider the question of political strategies, and ask not only the basic question, "What is the nature of power?" but "What were the ways of obtaining power?" and "Who succeeded in obtaining it?" We will refer not only to formal structures of law and government, but to the pervasive pattern of social control, informal as well as formal, that sprang directly from the military strength of the ruling class, and the form of administration that rested upon it.

Patently, the unified city was inseparable from centralized governmental authority. The rulers who put their force behind the legal institutions and who were the only ones really capable of instituting and maintaining public services, were in many ways the keystone of urban unity. We have seen, however, that there was even more dissension in elite ranks under the Ottoman regime than under the Mamlūk sultans. Yet, remarkably, the order of society was still maintained. [1] One could even say that under Turkish rule urban life developed a coherence and articulation that it never exhibited previously. Paradoxically, ironically, the order of Cairene society flourished in spite of and even because of the shortcomings of its rulers.

1. *The Overwhelming Power of the Elite*

Formally, the political power upon which the state rested was vested in the sultan's viceroy (the pasha), members of the military corps (*ojāqlu*), and the beys. The last named were twenty-four in number and were nominated by the pasha to fill important offices. Foremost among them were the *kākhya* (lieutenant) of the pasha who attended meetings of the Dīwān as his representative, the four captains of the naval bases of Alexandria, Damietta, Rosetta, and Suez, the *amīr al-ḥajj* (commander of the pilgrimage), the *defterdār* (register keeper and chief treasurer) who headed the fiscal administration in the country, and the *sanjaq al-khazna* who went with the caravan to Istanbul to guard the revenues of the Porte. Another appointment that came to have great importance was that of *qā'im-maqām* (acting viceroy) who exercised in full the powers of the pasha between the removal of one and the installation of another. Five beys acted as governors of important provinces: Jirjā, Sharqīya, Gharbīya, Minūfīya, and Buḥayra and were entrusted with the important duty of protecting the canals and keeping the sultan's "estate" safe from bedouin incursions. [2]

---

[1] Thus David Kimche writes:

"Not only was the everyday life of Cairo little affected by these clashes of the Mamlūks, but the state of law and security in the city seemed to have been quite satisfactory. Thus Lockroy writes: 'Cairo was as tranquil as under British domination,' while the noted traveller Niebuhr comments: 'Despite the narrow streets of Cairo, and the tyranny of its Government, one hears less of violence, of robbery and of murder among the population than one does in the large towns of Europe.'" (ref. Lockroy, *Ahmed le Boucher* (Paris, 1888), and Niebuhr, *Voyage en Egypte et en Arabie* (London, 1783), "The Political Superstructure of Egypt," p. 459).

[2] See Stanford J. Shaw, *Ottoman Egypt in the Age of the French Revolution* (Cambridge, Mass.: Harvard University Press, 1964), pp. 36-38; P. M. Holt, *Egypt and the Fertile Crescent*, p. 78.

At first Ottoman officials called *kāshif*s were appointed as governors of provinces but later it became customary for the beys to be appointed to these posts as well, hence the title "*sanjaq-bey*" became common (P. M. Holt, *Egypt and the Fertile Crescent*, p. 73; A. Raymond, *Artisans et commerçants*, I, pp. 5-6).

In theory at least, the power of the *ojāqs* balanced that of the beys. In all, there were seven corps but two of these were of outstanding importance. The Janissaries and the ᶜAzabs performed essential police functions in the town and the Citadel. The Janissar āghā [3] was the chief of Cairo police and through his executive officer controlled the *wālī* who made daily and nightly patrols, the *muḥtasib*, who policed the market, and the *amīn al-khurda* who supervised weights and measures. While the Janissaries dominated the police force, the ᶜAzabs were second only to them in that function, having the duty to police the environs of the city and the approaches to the Citadel. In return for pay from the Janissaries, they staffed the urban police stations. Both the Janissaries and the ᶜAzabs successfully laid claim to substantial resources which followed from their official duties as well as from their rapacity. [4] Moreover through their control of the most important urban tax farms (*muqāṭaᶜāt*), their military power was doubly enhanced since it led to their establishment of liaisons with popular groups and urban corporations.

The ruling bodies were the Great and Lesser Dīwāns which had legislative and administrative functions respectively. The former had "the exclusive right to enact laws on the general affairs of the country on those matters not reserved for the jurisdiction of the Porte." [5] Its membership included the *kākhya* of the pasha, the *defterdār*, the *rūznāmjī* (the administrator-general who was an Ottoman efendī) the *amīr al-ḥajj*, representatives of the regiments and the *ojāqs* as well as the principal *ᶜulamāʾ*: the *qāḍī* of Cairo (who was sent from Istanbul), the shaykhs of the *madhāhib* and the most important *muftīs* (lawyers). This council met only if convened by the pasha who also could dissolve it. However its members had to concur before the pasha could act and, even more important, it could dismiss any of its members, including the pasha, if it found such persons to be "acting against the laws and interests of the sultan." [6] The Lesser Dīwān met daily to direct the

[3] The power of the Jannisar āghā was such (he was technically commander-in-chief of the army) that he was not appointed from the corps in Egypt but sent from Istanbul. Therefore the post of his executive officer (*kākhya, kitkhudā*) was the highest to which a local Janissary could aspire (Stanford J. Shaw, *The Financial and Administrative Organization and Development of Ottoman Egypt 1517-1798* (Princeton, N. J.: Princeton University Press, 1962) (hereafter cited as S. J. Shaw, *Financial Organization*), p. 190).

[4] See Chapter XVI, pp. 316-317.

[5] M. R. X. Estève, "Memoire sur les finances de l'Égypte," *Description de l'Égypte*, I, 1 (Paris, 1809), p. 300.

[6] S. J. Shaw, *Financial Organization*, p. 2.

supervision of governmental affairs and administrate matters that did not fall under the jurisdiction of the Great Dīwān. It was composed of the *kākhya* of the pasha, his *defterdār* and *rūznāmjī*, and a representative of each of the *ojāq*s. [7]

Such were the principal officials, and such was the formal structure of government. The framework provided for a tripartite balance of power depending on the pasha, the beys, and the *ojāq*s. The system worked well enough at first. Indeed, each party could only gain its desires through alliances with one or more of the others. Although the pasha soon emerged as the weakest entity, he could, in partnership with the Janissar āghā, sometimes succeed in dominating the Dīwān until another coalition rose against them. [8]

But the "balance of power" in the sense described above was more ideal than real. Without reiterating the history and circumstances of the Mamlūk resurgence, we will simply observe that an unofficial structure continually impinged on the formal structure until, for all practical purposes, both the pasha and the *ojāq*s were obliterated.

Political power was in fact measured by the amount of military strength that the contenders could muster. It was also measured by the revenues and positions attained. The beys, through their increasing riches, strove to get their mamlūks and clients appointed to positions in the official hierarchy, succeeding most of the time in this endeavor. The pasha, usually on the defensive, feared to confront them openly and hoped only to influence the political outcome by throwing his support to one party or the other. [9] Through a special post created in the middle of the eighteenth century, that of *shaykh al-balad* ("chief of the town"), the most important bey, chosen by the Dīwān and confirmed by the pasha, was further empowered to dispense posts and favors. A contemporary account describes the power of ᶜAlī-Bey in this capacity:

---

[7] D. Kimche, "The Political Superstructure of Egypt in the Late Eighteenth Century," p. 451.

[8] *Ibid.*, p. 452.

[9] Such action frequently took the form of a declaration of "legalized plunder" whereby he would give one house the right to seize the positions and properties of a rival in return for the payment of the *ḥulwān* "inheritance tax" to the Porte (S. J. Shaw, *Financial Organization*, p. 11). More underhanded attempts to check the power of the beys would also be made, as when the representative of the Porte induced ᶜAlī-Bey's chief *kāshif* to kill him and so brought about a return to a situation of divided Mamlūk power.

> "The Beys trust him as if he were their monarch; he chooses all the officers of the Janissaries except the Janissar Agha and the Kiahya, appoints officers of the police, customs etc., can take life, pardon ..." [10]

Following the revolt of ᶜAlī-Bey in 1769-70 the Mamlūk houses progressively absorbed the revenues and positions of the Janissaries and ᶜAzabs through enrolling their own freed men in the corps. By the end of the eighteenth century most of the *ojāq*s had become legal fictions through which the Mamlūk houses received wages from the state. The corps had dissolved to the extent that if the pasha required a military force he did not call upon the officers but upon the amīrs. [11] Thus the whole military elite became part of a single Mamlūk institution. By the time Bonaparte arrived on the scene the arm of the Porte in Egypt was so paralyzed that revenues had ceased to flow to Istanbul and the new conqueror could claim he came to restore the province to the sultan. [12]

What then were the critical elements upon which the beys drew to reassert and nourish their military strength and, in particular, why were the *ojāq*s unable successfully to compete? Essentially, the situation recalls the rivalry of the Circassian Mamlūks and the Turkish and Mongol mercenaries (*wāfidīya*) four centuries earlier, with some differences. The nature of the competition between beys and officers reveals the superiority of Mamlūk institutions where military power was concerned. On the occasions when the *ojāq* leaders did dominate the scene they did so by adapting the Mamlūk institution to serve their own cause. Thus, Ibrāhīm-Kākhya, the leader of the Janissaries, and Riḍwān-Kākhya, the leader of the ᶜAzabs, established a duumvirate (1747-1754) by using their wealth to buy mamlūks and then displacing the Ottomans and dominating the *ojāq*s by giving their mamlūks the military posts. [13] The disadvantages of depending upon

---

[10] S. Lusignian, *A History of the Revolt of Aly Bey against the Ottoman Porte* (London, 1783), Ch. III, quoted by D. Kimche, "The Political Superstructure of Egypt in the Late Eighteenth Century," p. 458.

[11] S. J. Shaw, *Ottoman Egypt in the Age of the French Revolution*, p. 9; al-Jabartī, *ᶜAjāʾib al-Āthār*, IV, p. 113; *Merveilles biographiques et historiques*, VIII, pp. 252-253.

[12] Henri Dehérain, *L'Égypte turque, Histoire de la nation égyptienne*, edited by Gabriel Hanotaux, V (Paris, 1937), p. 254.

[13] We mentioned in the introduction to this part the establishment of the Qāzdughlī house by a Turkish officer and its assimilation to the Mamlūk pattern during the eighteenth century. Although Ibrāhīm-Kākhya al-Qāzdughlī attained the *riʾāsa* (supremacy) in partnership, he never entered the beylicate, while some of his mamlūks became beys. After his death and the demise of his partner, the Mamlūk supremacy had become so established that no officer ever after even contended for the *riʾāsa*.

salaried military corps were so obvious to all that as soon as the economic resources became available to them, the leaders of the *ojāqs* seized the opportunity to establish houses (*bayts*) of their own. [14]

In unbroken continuity the residences of the elite continued to serve as focal points for the activities of their mamlūks, their families, their servants, slaves, and clients. [15] Their interests in Cairo and in the provinces from which they derived much of their revenue would be supervised by their *kāshifs*, the foremost of their freed men.

Although the Mamlūks of this period differed little from their predecessors in behavior, there was an important change in their relation to the other orders of society that contributed to the social unity of the urban center. Faced with competition from a new elite from abroad, they sought to strengthen their own bonds within Egypt. It was this local support, in fact coming from all levels of society, that prevented the Ottomans from maintaining control.

By and large, the elite kept their separateness, but they could maintain themselves only by broadening their base through relaxation of some of the primary restrictions of Mamlūkdom. Ironically enough, the reestablishment of Mamlūk authority necessitated a desertion of the strict principles of recruitment and inheritance originally definitive of Mamlūk status. Whereas descent was once irrelevant and even a barrier to positions of military power, it now became an elemental factor in the right to rule. After the deposition of the pasha in 1630-31, the beys felt the necessity of legitimizing their claims and the use of genealogy, spurious or otherwise, was considered a valid means of

---

It is interesting that conversely, the political strength of a Janissary officer depended upon his remaining *within* the corps. Thus when Küchük Muḥammed seized the headquarters in 1692 he reduced two of his rivals to impotence by raising them to the beylicate where they had no support. Similarity in 1707, the opponents of the Janissary boss Afranj Aḥmad compelled him to join the beylicate (P. M. Holt, "The Pattern of Egyptian Political History from 1517 to 1798," *Political and Social Change in Modern Egypt*, p. 87; P. M. Holt, *Egypt and the Fertile Crescent*, pp. 87-88).

[14] Cf. A. Raymond, *Artisans et commerçants*, I, p. 12.

[15] As Albert Hourani has written:

> "(Local leadership) did not come either from the religious class or from the leaders of the military corps ... In the absence of local families with a tradition of leadership, the only groups which could provide the needed ᶜ*asabiyya* were the "Mamluke" households ... (cores) around which could be combined the religious leaders, the commanders of the regiments, popular guilds, and behind them the great loose combinations of Egypt, *Nisf Haram* and *Nisf Saᶜd*; and then, with this combination, to secure real power to obtain for themselves and their followers from the governor the rank of *bey* and therefore access to the great offices to which the *beys* were appointed, and to seize control of the tax farms" ("Ottoman Reform and the Politics of Notables," p. 50).

achieving this end. Most of the amīrs traced their origin through the house of Balfīya and the house of Riḍwān-Bey Ṣāḥib al-Imāra, a pious man and greatly respected *amīr al-ḥajj.* [16] It is remarkable indeed that fourth and fifth generation members of the *awlād an-nās* could now emerge to become prominent members of a neo-Mamlūk military aristocracy by appealing to a family tree for support.

No greater reversal of the former situation could be imagined. Under the Turkish regime it became customary for a *sanjaq-bey* to be succeeded by his son and not his Mamlūk. Thus the natural descendants of Mamlūks and Mamlūks' Mamlūks became blended, and intermarriage between these strengthened their bonds. For all practical purposes the terms "*bayt*" (house) and "*ᶜīla*" (colloquial of *ᶜāʾila*, family) became synonymous. [17]

There is another important sense in which the gulf between the elite and other orders of society was diminished. In the old days a Turkish name was considered necessary for membership in the elite and some rulers like Tīmūrbughā had withheld pay from "those who bore the names of the prophets and of the companions of Muḥammad." [18] Whereas almost all of the Baḥrīs and Burjīs had had Turkish, Mongol, or other non-Arab appellations, the Mamlūks of the Ottoman period bore Arab names with few exceptions. No longer expelled from the aristocracy by having names taken from the religion adopted in Egypt, instead of names acquired abroad, many now entered the elite who would have been automatically excluded in former times.

Ayalon believes that:

---

[16] A product of the Mamlūk resurgence is an interesting manuscript of the seventeenth century entitled "A Cogent Demonstration of the Lineage of the Amīrs of the Circassians and Its Connexion with Quraysh" (see P. M. Holt, "The Exalted Lineage of Ridwan Bey: Some Observations on a 17th Century Mamluk Genealogy," *Bulletin of the School of Oriental and African Studies*, 22 (1959), pp. 221-230). It attempts to establish a tie between Riḍwān-Bey al-Faqārī and the Circassian sultans, and then between the Circassians and the tribe of Quraysh. The amīr is described as the son of Janbayk ᶜAzīz and the grandson of Rustum al-Ashraf, whose ancestry is traced to Bars-Bey then to Tīmūrbughā, the father of Barqūq, then to Kīsa, ᶜAdnān, and Adam. The document places Riḍwān's religious activities in a new frame of reference. He is viewed as occupying the office of *amīr al-ḥajj* through his own hereditary right and not as a mere delegate of the Ottoman sultan who had usurped the caliph's powers.

[17] D. Ayalon, "Studies in al-Jabartī," pp. 297-299. At the end of the eighteenth century a contemporary writer spoke of "the *ṣanjaq*s who are the sons of Murād Bak and the mamlūks of their family" (Nicolas Turc, *Mudhakkirāt Niqūla Turc, Chronique d'Égypte, 1798-1804*, translated and edited by Gaston Wiet (Cairo, 1950), p. 115).

[18] D. Ayalon, "Studies in al-Jabartī," p. 152.

> If such was the state of affairs at the top of the Mamlūk hierarchy, the chances are that in the lower ranks, about which al-Jabartī and other historians supply much scantier information, the non-Mamlūk element had been represented even more strongly. [19]

While the elite remained Turko-Circassian for the most part, there seems to have been much less discrimination among them in terms of ethnic derivation than there had been in earlier times. Discord became related to family ties rather than to national origin. We have mentioned that the Bosniak and Turkish elements in the major houses had become assimilated by the eighteenth century. Even more remarkable is the fact that a few mamlūks of this time were originally Jewish, while others had been black slaves. [20]

But while some aspects of the Mamlūk institution were altered in response to the Ottoman political challenge, on the whole the modifications can be seen to be extensions and exaggerations of earlier tendencies we have seen at work in the *bayt*s of the Mamlūk sultanate. There had always been a dependence upon alliances with members of the other social orders. The strength of the bond between *khushdāshīya* (comrades in servitude and manumission) certainly was no less strong than in the previous epoch [21] and this same bond, considerably reinforced by family ties, bred loyalties and hatreds of an intensity and generational depth heretofore unrealized.

Notwithstanding the establishment of the supremacy of the beys over the other divisions of the military elite, it was only to be expected that this very intensified solidarity, centered upon each house, would sunder the elite as a whole from within. The *bayt* of the neo-Mamlūk

---

[19] "Studies in al-Jabartī," p. 157.

[20] W. G. Browne, at the end of the eighteenth century, wrote:

> "The Mamluks ... remain, as they have ever been, military slaves imported from Georgia, Circassia, and Mingrelia ... The Beys give general orders to their agents every year, and many are brought to Egypt by private merchants on speculation. When the supply proves insufficient, or many have been expended, black slaves from the interior of Africa are substituted and, if found docile, are armed and accoutred like the rest" (*Travels in Africa, Egypt, and Syria from the Year 1792 to 1798* (London: T. N. Longman and O. Rees, 1799), pp. 48-49).

[21] David Ayalon gives numerous examples. Thus the house of one amīr who was known to be destitute was crowded with people eating and drinking. When it was suggested to him that he drive them away, he retorted, "How can I drive them away while they are either the sons of my patron or my *khushdāshīya* or the sons of my *khushdāshīya*?" The *mamlūk*s of Ibrāḥīm-Kākhya rose as one against a person who for a time held the office of treasurer (*khāzindār*) in Ibrāḥīm's service, since he had been manumitted by another amīr, saying he was a "foreigner in relation to them" ("Studies in al-Jabarti," pp. 171-172).

period, even more than the *bayt* of the Mamlūk sultanate, was the center of loyalty and of conspiracy against other houses. Hatreds became so violent as to demand the absolute extermination of rival *bayts*.[22] The rivalry between the Qāsimīya and Faqārīya which began in the beginning of the Ottoman period came to an end only in 1728 when the former, whose houses were weakened by internal dissension, were wiped out by the latter. Seven years later the Faqārīya were in turn overwhelmed by the Qāzdughlīya who in a few years themselves succumbed through internal competition.

The overwhelming power of the elite depended upon their keeping their clienteles satisfied and their ranks disciplined, dual requirements that often pointed in different directions. Moreover the social weapons by which political power was grasped and maintained were double-edged. We have not yet considered the full implications of alliances with other orders of society.

The interstices in the ranks of the elite were channels for the attainment of military and political power by other classes, an essential characteristic of the weave of the social fabric. The decline of the Janissaries can be described in terms of their absorption into the lower ranks of the population.[23] The very ties through which they achieved "ground roots" control ultimately submerged them. Moreover the hereditary principle which allowed their sons to inherit their positions led to the ultimate loss of the military character of the *ojāq*s.

The Mamlūk supremacy was a relative supremacy. Although the beys also made use of the hereditary principle, they simultaneously

---

[22] The concept of "*al-bayt al-maftūḥ*" (the "open house") referred to the vitality of this instrument of political power. In the words of David Ayalon:

> "The whole conception of the *bayt maftūḥ* and the desperate fight which both rival factions usually put up either in order to preserve it or in order to destroy it have no parallel in the Mamlūk sultanate" ("Studies in al-Jabartī," p. 297).

Thus, when the Faqārīya crushed a rival house, the Iwāẓīya, the Faqārī leader tried desperately to save the life of ᶜAlī-Bey al-Hindī who had led the Iwāẓīya, as he owed ᶜAlī-Bey this favor for having saved his own life on a previous occasion. He was, however, forced to give way to the demands of his house and acquiesced saying, "Since you want to kill ᶜAlī-Bey al-Hindī, so wipe out the traces of the Qāsimīya and do not spare any one of them and do not let them have an open door." Similarly, when another of the Faqārīya tried to save the life of Muḥammad-Bey al-Jazzār, also of the Qāsimīya, he was forced to give up the attempt for it was protested that "If Muḥammad-Bey al-Jazzār remains alive, the followers of the killed amīrs will rally round him and will take us unawares, for they will still have an open house" (D. Ayalon, "Studies in al-Jabarti," p. 296).

[23] Even as under the Mamlūk sultanate the *ḥalqa* or salaried free cavalry had, by the fifteenth century, finally become largely made up of artisans and peddlars. Cf. above p. 123 n. 14.

endeavored to maintain their separation from the population through the continual importation of mamlūks. Despite the many indications that their ranks were being breached through intermarriage and inheritance, it is evident that these breaches never reached serious proportions.[24] Only when importation of mamlūks petered out, did the social "isolation" of the elite, so essential to their power, become seriously eroded.

Still, the neglect of the principle of ethnic exclusiveness, first manifest in the sixteenth century, could not but have its effect. While the membership of the beylicate remained predominantly Circassian, many amīrs were of non-Circassian or of doubtful origin. By the end of the eighteenth century the special ethnic character of the elite had melted away along with their military prowess. When the traditional sources of mamlūks were cut off and when, through the intensification of rivalry, the amīrs became too hard-pressed to undertake the training of a traditional body of followers, they finally resorted to the employment of mercenaries. At best, the ruling class consisted of relatively well-trained and disciplined Circassians, Georgians, Germans, Poles, Jews, Hungarians, Negroes, Spaniards, and Maltese. At worst they were troops such as those so vividly and tellingly described by Volney:

> The armies of the Turks and Mamlouks are nothing but a confused multitude of horsemen, without uniforms, on horses of all sizes and colours, riding without either keeping their ranks, or observing any regular order.[25]

2. *The Restraining Power of the Middle Orders*

Political power, like nature, abhors a vacuum. Normally controlled by the elite, any neglect, mismanagement, or lack on their part calls forth not only response but a degree of redistribution. To be sure, the lower orders of society, by definition, remain subordinate. Yet, by virtue of the fact that military control requires legitimization and a degree of cooperation on the part of the governed, members of the middle orders especially, frequently retain considerable capability of manipulation in the political sphere. Thus the balance of political power in the long run can be seen to hang between the military elite and the many urban notables who, by virtue of their spiritual authority

---

[24] From available evidence it appears that the children of the Mamlūks were few (D. Ayalon, "Studies in al-Jabartī," p. 157). Despite the increased importance of family, they continued to depend primarily upon recruits from abroad.

[25] *Travels through Egypt and Syria*, p. 125.

or economic power, also controlled essential threads in the urban fabric.[26]

Following the Ottoman conquest, the principal administrative and spiritual offices were filled by persons, most often sent from Istanbul, who were loyal to the sultan. Nevertheless the fact that real spiritual and moral authority cannot be imposed nor, in the last analysis, could a totally external administration be effective, meant the retention of a number of positions and real power by native *ᶜulamāʾ*. Thus among the notables as among the military elite, there was a two-fold division representing the Ottoman rulers and the Egyptian ruled. Historically, the reassertion of independence by the beys was paralleled by a reassertion on the part of the local *ᶜulamāʾ* and bureaucrats. The Ottomans were only able to retain control of the official spiritual and administrative hierarchies until the end of the seventeenth century. Especially after the revolt of ᶜAlī-Bey more and more positions of authority were held by Egyptians or Arabs, rather than by Turks.

The formal positions of political power held by the middle class were held either through official appointment (legitimization) or actual ability to control and manipulate social relations ("force"), or usually, through a combination of these factors. *In fact the power of persons holding these positions depended to a great degree upon their ability to act successfully as middlemen*[27] *without incurring alienation from either the elite or the lower orders.*

The essential importance of an independent source of political

---

[26] As Albert Hourani has written:

"... urban politics of the Ottoman provinces (at least of the Muslim provinces) cannot be understood unless we see them in terms of a 'politics of notables' or, to use Max Weber's phrase, a 'patriciate' ... The city may be subject to a monarchical power, but one on which the urban population wishes and is able to impose limits or exercise influence" ("Ottoman Reform and the Politics of Notables," p. 45).

[27] A factor that should not be forgotten in the actual conduct of political affairs is language, for language defined national allegiance to a great extent. Ottoman *qāḍī*s depended upon their *nāʾib*s (deputies) to do most of the work because they themselves did not know Arabic. Local *ᶜulamāʾ*, on the other hand, would request the ruling elite to translate because they did not know Turkish (al-Jabartī, *ᶜAjāʾib al-Āthār*, II, p. 158; *Merveilles biographiques et historiques*, V, p. 22). Both sides made use of professional translators (*tarājim*). In the Dīwān there were two, the *turjumān al-ᶜarabī*, appointed by the beys, and the *turjumān at-turkī* who was sent from Istanbul (S. J. Shaw, *Ottoman Egypt in the Age of the French Revolution*, pp. 75-76). Doubtless the linguistic gap provided many opportunities for middlemen to exploit political potentialities.

power for notables can be clearly seen in the case of the efendīs [28] who obtained their positions primarily through appointment (legitimization). These included members of the Ottoman ruling class through whom the objectives of the Porte were carried out. Under the direction of the *rūznāmjī*, the executive director of the treasury, they were organized into a scribal guild which distributed new positions and set and maintained professional standards. [29] New recruits were usually children of members. Thus the Copts who had traditionally controlled the bureaucracy were displaced and acted only as intendants and paymasters (*ṣarrāfs*) who advised Ottoman tax farmers and treasury scribes. As time wore on, however, and the actual financial administration of the country came to be carried out through the institution of tax farms that fell more and more under the control of the beys and local notables, the political power of the Ottoman efendīs progressively declined. Although for most of the period, the scribal guild maintained its independence, and with it its standards, by the last quarter of the eighteenth century the Mamlūks managed to infiltrate it through the purchase of the treasury posts that were put up for sale, or by inheritance, since many of the efendīs had sought to increase their own power by marrying into the families of the beys. [30] Even the office of the *rūznāmjī* was put up for sale. [31] Thus the political weakness of the efendī class that came from the lack of military power on the part of the Porte that appointed them was responsible for their ultimate disappearance from the scene; for with the arrival of the French at the end of the century and the defeat of the beys, they were totally isolated. The *rūznāmjī* and most of his scribes fled to Istanbul, leaving the way again open for the Copts, many of whom had continued to serve as secretaries in the houses of the amīrs, to fill their traditional positions.

---

[28] Efendī was an official Ottoman title that paralleled the titles of bey and pasha that were applied to members of the military classes. It was applied to all persons who were masters of the religious and scribal arts, lesser administrators as well as *qāḍīs* and *ᶜulamāᵓ*. The rank was assessed as "half *sanjaq-bey*" (*niṣf sanjaq*) (S. J. Shaw, *Ottoman Egypt in the Age of the French Revolution*, pp. 105-106).

[29] At first, when a post fell vacant, all qualified members bid for it and the highest bidder was appointed. Later, efendīs left their positions to their sons, who subsequently paid a fee to the *rūznāmjī* for the privilege of taking their father's position.

[30] H. A. R. Gibb and Harold Bowen, *Islamic Society and the West*, I, 2, pp. 65-69.

[31] Al-Jabartī, *ᶜAjāᵓib al-Āthār*, II, p. 156; *Merveilles biographiques et historiques*, V, p. 16.

Foremost in the official religious hierarchy were the *qāḍī* *ᶜaskar* [32] and the *qāḍī*s who headed judicial districts (s. *nāḥiya*). [33] These were appointed by the *qāḍī* *ᶜaskar* of Anatolia and came from Istanbul or elsewhere in the empire. Only occasionally were they Egyptians who had gone to the Ottoman capital for training. Usually the *qāḍī*s served for two years only before being transferred.

The courts of Cairo, Old Cairo, and Būlāq were directly under the jurisdiction of the *qāḍī* *ᶜaskar*, the city being divided into ten judicial districts each headed by a *nāᵓib* (deputy). Here again there was more continuity and ultimately more real power in the lower levels of the hierarchy, for the *nāᵓib*s, unlike the *qāḍī*s, were appointed for the most part from the Egyptian *ᶜulamāᵓ*. Especially after the revolt of ᶜAlī-Bey, Egyptian *ᶜulamāᵓ* tended to replace Turks as *qāḍī*s and with the general breakdown of Ottoman administration, local *qāḍī*s more and more assumed supervision of local government. By 1798 there were only five Ottoman *qāḍī*s in all of Egypt. [34]

As far as the official hierarchy was concerned, the native *ᶜulamāᵓ* were relegated to inferior positions. Many were *muftī*s, *faqīh*s, teachers, and scholars. Still, a few important offices were open to them and these positions, since they represented local followings, were frequently more significant bases of power than those controlled by the foreign *ᶜulamāᵓ*. The Ḥanafī, Mālikī, and Shāfiᶜī *muftī*s who ranked after the chief *qāḍī* all had positions in the Dīwān and they also represented influential groups in the population. [35] While the Ḥanafī *muftī*, as representing the Turkish persuasion, had the most prestige, the concurrence of all three *muftī*s was required for many functions of government. [36] Emerging at this time as the two most powerful popular leaders were Shaykh al-Bakrī [37] who was the head of the religious brotherhoods (*ṭuruq*) that pervaded every social class in Egypt, and

---

[32] The chief *qāḍī* was called "*qāḍī ᶜaskar*" (military *qāḍī*) because of his attachment to the conquering Ottoman army. He was called "*qāḍī* of Cairo" since Cairo had once been the seat of the caliphate (S. J. Shaw, *Ottoman Egypt in the Age of the French Revolution*, p. 95).

[33] The jurisdiction of the *qāḍī*, as we have seen, was extensive and included not only the adjudication of disputes but administration of *awqāf* and assessment and collection of taxes.

[34] S. J. Shaw, *Ottoman Egypt in the Age of the French Revolution*, pp. 95-96, 99.

[35] The Ḥanbalī *madhhab* was not prominent in Egypt.

[36] Daniel Crecelius, "The Emergence of the Shaykh al-Azhar as the Pre-eminent Religious Leader in Egypt," *Colloque international sur l'histoire du Caire* (Cairo: General Egyptian Book Oragnization, 1974), p. 113.

[37] Shaykh al-Bakrī was a descendant of the caliph Abū Bakr aṣ-Ṣiddīq.

Shaykh as-Sādāt (pl. of *sayyid*, i.e., "sharīf") who was the "family head" of the Sharīfs (descendants of the Prophet through his daughter Fāṭima and his son-in-law ᶜAlī).[38]

It is noteworthy that recruitment to all the offices that were customarily filled by native *ᶜulamā*ᵓ illustrated great social mobility. A thorough perusal of al-Jabartī's necrologies reveals that most of the religious notables of that period sprang from humble origins.[39] The famous and powerful Shaykh al-Azhar, ᶜAbdallāh ash-Sharqāwī, is said to have been so poor when a student that he often did not eat, while his rival ᶜUmar Makram seems likewise to have risen to power through ability and daring, rather than any inherited advantage. The rectorship of al-Azhar, of all positions, was the focus of the most conflict and competition since it was open to all of the native *ᶜulamā*ᵓ who were qualified by professional training, spiritual prestige, and political talents. Likewise, the positions of *muftī*, Shaykh al-Bakrī, and Shaykh as-Sādāt, while "vertically" restricted to members of certain *madhāhib*, families, or orders, were unrestricted by considerations of social class.

What then was the nature of the power of the notables? In the first place it is obvious that it had to have some basis apart from the power of the military elite with which it contrasted and that it restrained. David Ayalon has written that: "The behavior of the *ᶜulamā*ᵓ as a whole is that of people who are sure of their power and of their immunity."[40] P. M. Holt has also described their power as unquest-

---

[38] The extent to which real political influence inhered in the ability to control local followings can be seen in the developments that concerned the office of *naqīb al-ashrāf* (head of the Sharīfs) who traditionally was a Turk sent from Istanbul. The influence of this official was considerably circumscribed by Shaykh as-Sādāt. Only in 1793, when an Egyptian was appointed to the post did it gain any real significance, and it was ᶜUmar Makram who, in the troubled times at the turn of the century, gave real prominence to the office. Later, recognizing the political potential of the religious orders, Muḥammad ᶜAlī tried to centralize them by making the *naqīb al-ashrāf* head of the Sharīfs and giving the post to Shaykh al-Bakrī.

The office of shaykh al-Azhar too, did not evolve until the end of the seventeenth century. While there were heads of this institution even in Fāṭimid times, the increasing significance of al-Azhar as a national political institution in the Ottoman period saw the emergence of its rectorship as a post of some importance. If, at this time, great ceremonial significance did not attach to it directly, it was especially coveted by the native *ᶜulamā*ᵓ because of the extensive *awqāf* that fell into its domain. Al-Jabartī, in the first part of the nineteenth century, notes the competition centered upon the office (*ᶜAjā*ᵓ*ib al-Āthār*, IV, p. 7; *Merveilles biographiques et historiques*, VIII, p. 16; cf. D. Crecelius, "The Emergence of the Shaykh Al-Azhar," p. 112).

[39] D. Crecelius, "The Emergence of the Shaykh al-Azhar," p. 110.

[40] "Studies in al-Jabartī," p. 166.

ioned: "Unlike other groups in Egypt, they did not conspire or fight to secure their position—because they had no need to." [41]

The spiritual authority and influence of the *ᶜulamāᵓ* that stood behind their prestige was, ultimately, not something that could be conferred solely by appointment to official position, even though such positions were symbolic of spiritual power. Significantly, the religious leaders who played the most effective political roles were not so much the shaykhs and officials of al-Azhar as the leaders of the *ṭuruq*, the Ṣūfī orders. These claimed not only religious learning and ancestry, but also extensive local followings with the wealth and influence that could be tapped by means of such a network. Local *ᶜulamāᵓ* contrasted greatly in this respect with the efendīs who formally ranked higher than they. When *ᶜulamāᵓ* are described as "champions of the people" it is invariably locally based leaders who are meant. [42]

The power that inhered in the leadership of the Ṣūfī orders epitomizes the political power of the *ᶜulamāᵓ*. While frequently allied to one or another elite faction, the brotherhoods were completely independent of the regime. Moreover their membership encompassed every level and segment of Muslim society and they were therefore much more capable of maintaining economic and political independence than more orthodox bodies that sought official recognition and favors. Generally speaking, they stood with the Mamlūk beys against foreign invaders and against them on behalf of the people whom they oppressed.

Neither the military elite nor the Ottoman rulers could easily manipulate the shaykhs of the orders, for the leadership was held by hereditary right as well as piety, spiritual capability, and prestige. Stanford Shaw acclaims the Shaykh al-Bakrī as "the closest thing there was to a native representative leader in Ottoman times" noting that the house of the Bakrīs in the Ezbekīya was a place where people would spontaneously gather to protest exactions of the government

---

[41] "The Career of Küçük Muḥammad (1676-94)," p. 273.

[42] To quote David Ayalon:

"It is very significant that the Ottoman Qāḍīs sent to Egypt from Istanbul had been afraid of the *ᶜulamāᵓ* during the rule of the Mamluks and therefore treated the people with justice and leniency; but as soon as the Mamluks had been wiped out, they completely changed their attitude to the local population, whose money and property they robbed by all possible means, not sparing the orphans and widows" ("Studies in al-Jabartī," p. 166 n. 2).

[43] *Ottoman Egypt in the Age of the French Revolution*, p. 103.

or the excesses of the elite as well as to celebrate religious holidays.[43] The threads of the social fabric that these shaykhs controlled, moreover, were interwoven with those of the economic network, for there was a firm connection between the Ṣūfī brotherhoods and the economic corporations. The old alliance between the *ᶜulamāᵓ* and the merchants too, continued. Shaykhs not only controlled *waqf* investments but, as they had for centuries, held important interest in international trade and other commercial endeavors.[44] The Sharīfian "corporation" controlled by Shaykh as-Sadāt included merchants, religious men, artisans, and soldiers.

It would perhaps not be wrong, in the last analysis, to link the power of the local *ᶜulamāᵓ* to the actual military force that they could call up. True, military command was not the forte of these spiritual intelligentsia, and such a force most of the time could not prevail against the disciplined army that dominated the scene, but an element of military power was always latently there to fill any vacuum that might arise in the domain of force ordinarily controlled by the elite. Aḥmad Jazzār Pasha, in his report to the Ottoman Porte at the end of the eighteenth century, said that Shaykh al-Bakrī and Shaykh as-Sādāt had

> the ability to assemble in a single day a powerful military regiment of at least seventy or eighty thousand men who are docile and loyal to them.[45]

ᶜUmar Makram's power too, lay to a great degree in his ability to call up popular forces. As *naqīb al-ashrāf* he obtained funds from affluent citizens, purchased arms, and paid artisans and persons of the lower class to leave their trades and become soldiers. It was said that he could call upon nearly 40,000 armed men.[46]

---

[44] The father of al-Jabartī, one of the most highly respected *ᶜulamāᵓ* of the eighteenth century, was an expert at the art of marble inlay. He educated students not only in the religious sciences (*ᶜilm*) but also in crafts. At least once he was called upon to correct weights and measures (al-Jabartī, *ᶜAjāᵓib, al-Āthār*, I, pp. 392-399; *Merveilles biographiques et historiques*, III, pp. 181-193.)

[45] Stanford J. Shaw, *Ottoman Egypt in the Eighteenth Century* (Cambridge, Mass: The Harvard University Press, 1962), p. 23.

[46] Afaf Loutfi el-Sayed, "The Role of the *ᶜUlamāᵓ* in Egypt during the Early Nineteenth Century," *Political and Social Change in Modern Egypt*, edited by P. M. Holt (London: Oxford University Press, 1968), p. 274. Although these estimates might well be exaggerated, it is a fact that the dervishes and Sharīfs were in large part of the masses and many of them were persons like the *ḥarāfīsh* described in the previous part of this book. Both the Ottoman government and the Mamlūk elite tried a number of times to bring them effectively under their jurisdiction. During the first part of

The political power of the ᶜ*ulamā*ʾ, like political power generally, was ambivalent. A large part of the ambivalence sprang from their roles as middlemen. On the one hand they were representatives of the people, at least of their own clienteles, and on the other, they had to have access to the ruling elite not only to confirm their position but to be able to press the claims of those they represented. Their power thus fluctuated between these two poles.

Many are the instances when ᶜ*ulamā*ʾ successfully, indeed stubbornly and courageously, protected the people against the excesses of the beys. Their own "troops" could be an effective threat. Thus, when the people protested the plundering of the house of the head of the Bayyūmī order by one of the beys, the Mālikī *muftī*, Shaykh ad-Dardīr, told them to go and plunder the houses of the amīrs. A serious crisis was averted only with the intervention of the āghā of the Janissaries.[47] With the weakening of the military power of the amīrs, the ᶜ*ulamā*ʾ came progressively to the fore as popular leaders. They would even harangue the beys in the Dīwān and accuse them outrightly of injustice, tyranny, and of not acting like true Muslims.[48] In time of crisis the people would close the bazaars, the caravanserais, and the doors of the quarters and, ever looking to the ᶜ*ulamā*ʾ for leadership, would simultaneously assemble in front of al-Azhar ready to carry out whatever action the shaykhs advised.

Sometimes the amīrs retaliated by killing ᶜ*ulamā*ʾ who threatened or offended them,[49] but for the most part, they realized the value of maintaining good relations with the religious authorities. After all, both the Mamlūks and the ᶜ*ulamā*ʾ had been accustomed for cen-

---

the eighteenth century the government attempted to settle members of the orders in villages, appointing them as tax farmers of land belonging to religious foundations (S. J. Shaw, *Ottoman Egypt in the Age of the French Revolution*, pp. 104-105.) For the effectiveness of ᶜUmar Makram's troops in the rise of Muḥammad ᶜAlī, see below, p. 302, especially n. 79.

[47] Al-Jabartī, ᶜ*Ajā*ʾ*ib al-Āthār*, II, p. 17; *Merveilles biographiques et historiques*, IV, pp. 174-175. Similarly, when the tax collectors of Bilbeys complained at new impositions of tax, Shaykh ash-Sharqāwī closed al-Azhar, marshalled the ᶜ*ulamā*ʾ and the mobs, and marched with a great crowd to the house of Shaykh as-Sādāt where they presented their demands to an agent of Ibrāḥīm-Bey. Following three days of demonstrations, the amīrs, the pasha and the leading native ᶜ*ulamā*ʾ met to discuss the issues after which the *qāḍī* drafted a document in which Ibrāḥīm and Murād-Bey agreed not to impose the objectionable taxes and to henceforth follow a more just policy (al-Jabartī, ᶜ*Ajā*ʾ*ib al-Āthār*, II, p. 258; *Merveilles biographiques et historiques*, V, pp. 209-211).

[48] Nicolas Turc, *Chronique d'Égypte: 1798-1804*, pp. 193-194.

[49] Al-Jabartī, ᶜ*Ajā*ʾ*ib al-Āthār*, II, p. 17; *Merveilles biographiques et historiques*, III, pp. 267-268.

turies to cooperating in the governing of Egypt.[50] As the shaykhs on the whole depended upon the military elite for the support of their establishment, they generally tried to keep the people satisfied with their lot and to keep the amīrs persuaded that they could in fact effectively control the masses. Thus in 1785 Ibrāhīm-Bey enlisted the aid of Shaykh al-Bakrī, the Mālikī *muftī*, and another prominent shaykh in maintaining order in the city to avert possible intervention by the Porte.[51]

For all their popular ties and sentiments, the *ᶜulamāᵓ* had firm liaisons with the military elite. The family of al-Jabartī included not only bourgeoisie but *ojāqlu*.[52] Likewise the amīr ᶜAlī al-Madanī was the son-in-law of the Shaykh al-Jawharī, and one, Muḥammad Shanan al-Mālikī, Shaykh al-Azhar, who held much land in *iltizām*, even succeeded in establishing a "dynasty" of mamlūks, one of whom obtained the rank of *sanjaq*.[53] Even the great ᶜUmar Makram, re-knowned more than any other for popular leadership can be thought of as a representative of the elite, or at least an intermediary. He was, in fact, appointed to the office of *naqīb al-ashrāf* in return for successfully negotiating with the Porte for the return to Cairo of Ibrāhīm and Murād-Bey. Moreover his claim to being a Sharīf rested upon documents dated after his appointment![54]

The increasing interdependence of the beys and the *ᶜulamāᵓ* naturally led to an involvement of each group in the internal affairs of the other

---

[50] Since Arab days the local men of religion had come to terms with foreign men of war. As Afaf Loutfi el-Sayed writes:

> "by the twelfth century (the religious authorities) had learned the harsh lesson that 'necessity makes lawful what is prohibited', and developed a Sunnī tradition of submission to established authority, whenever they saw that they could not do otherwise" ("The Role of the *ᶜUlamāᵓ* in Egypt during the Early Nineteenth Century," p. 264).

[51] Al-Jabartī, *ᶜAjāᵓib al-Āthār*, II, p. 111; *Merveilles biographiques et historiques*, IV, p. 195.

[52] André Raymond, *Artisans et commerçants*, II, pp. 686-687.

Al-Jabartī describes his father as enjoying the confidence of the amīrs:

> "He occupied a prominent place in the hearts of the great and of the amīrs and of the vizīrs and of the notables. They came to him and he went to them ... and they never turned down his intercession and they were never slow in responding to his requests" (*ᶜAjāᵓib al-Āthār*, I, p. 395, quoted by David Ayalon, "The Historian al-Jabartī and his Background," *Bulletin of the School of Oriental and African Studies* XXIII (1960), p. 239).

[53] There are many examples. See André Raymond, *Artisans et commerçants*, II, p. 431.

[54] Afaf Loutfi El-Sayed, "The Role of the *ᶜUlamāᵓ* in Egypt during the Early Nineteenth Century," p. 270.

since, as we have seen in the second part of this volume, the factions and clienteles that were effective political units were not restricted to class but cross-cut society vertically. For the amīrs and the *ᶜulamāʾ*, alliances did not involve the total military and spiritual establishments; alliances rather were made between individuals, the more effectively to confront their rivals. The *ᶜulamāʾ* would negotiate Mamlūk disputes and their services in these matters became indispensible for counteracting the chronic instability of the balance of power among the military. Each was concerned for his position, but all were concerned not to let internal conflicts reach the point that would draw down Ottoman intervention. [55]

On the other side of the coin the beys played a significant role in the bargaining process through which religious officials were chosen. Thus, in the contest over the rectorship of al-Azhar, the incumbent Shaykh ᶜAbdallāh ash-Sharqāwī secured his position through the intervention of his elite patrons, although his rival claimed the support of the majority of the *ᶜulamāʾ*, ᶜUmar Makram, and Shaykh as-Sādāt. In a few instances the beys actually deposed high *ᶜulamāʾ*. [56]

Thus the situation was one characterized not as much by balance, as by fluidity; by advancing and withdrawing on the part of the elite and the notables. Certainly the *ᶜulamāʾ* were the weaker party, but since it was to the interest of the military to be able to tap their separate resources, and since, in fact, the amīrs could not themselves control the people, independence of native *ᶜulamāʾ* was maintained. Only in the nineteenth century, with the emergence of unchallenged military strength and effective centralization of resources under Muḥammad ᶜAlī, did the distribution of the highest positions of the religious establishment fall irretrievably into the hands of the ruler.

---

[55] David Ayalon notes that al-Jabartī's chronicle attests to:

"the constant participation of the *ᶜulamāʾ* and the *mashāyikh* in the councils of the rulers, ... their mediation between the quarrelling factions, ... their extremely great political power and ... the obedience of the Mamluk amirs, on many occasions, to their decisions even in matters pertaining to war and peace" ("Studies in al-Jabartī," p. 166, n. 2.)

[56] D. Crecelius, "The Emergence of the Shaykh al-Azhar," pp. 111-112. Normally the amīrs did not interpose themselves in shaykhly affairs without invitation any more than the shaykhs mediated Mamlūk disputes without the request of one or the other of the warring parties. If the *ᶜulamāʾ* had determined upon a candidate, it was practically unknown for the beys to withhold their assent. It is significant that, notwithstanding the fact that the military elite, as Ḥanafīs, would have preferred a Ḥanafī Shaykh al-Azhar, and would have been able to pressure the religious establishment into elevating such a one, they never attempted to do so (D. Crecelius, "The Emergence of Shaykh al-Azhar," p. 111) .

In its structure, if not in its essence, the power of the middle class in many ways paralleled the power of the elite. The *ᶜulamāᵓ* never really presented a united front when confronted by political challenge even as the spirit of factionalism pervaded the conduct of their internal affairs. The very universality of the religious institution, moreover, created further opportunities for the development of factions and cliques that competed for the few official positions open to them. Alignment followed not only considerations of religious interpretation, but nationality, locality, class, family, and the ties of patronage.

The official positions to which members of the middle class, as *ᶜulamāᵓ*, could aspire, were characterized by some ambiguity both with regard to the rules of recruitment and the power they implied. Daniel Crecelius writes that:

> Indeed, the methods employed in the selection of a Shaykh al-Azhar throughout the Ottoman-Mamlūk period are so varied and confusing as to suggest the total lack of any formal procedures governing the selection of a shaykh to fill this important office. [57]

Official position, rather than automatically conferring power, served as a base from which to organize and manipulate real power achieved by other means. Personalities appear to have been more important than offices, especially in time of crisis. [58] The breach in the ranks of *ᶜulamāᵓ* which had genesis in the lack of official systematization provided further opportunity for the ruling elite to interfere in their affairs. Always fearing popular leaders, the amīrs played upon factionalism in the religious establishment. Muḥammad ᶜAlī achieved the exile of ᶜUmar Makram by playing upon the jealousies of Shaykh ash-Sharqāwī, Shaykh as-Sādāt, and many others who envied the *Naqīb*'s power.

---

57 "The Emergence of the Shaykh al-Azhar," p. 110.

58 Thus in 1808, Shaykh ash-Sharqāwī, rector of al-Azhar, was arrested at the instigation of ᶜUmar Makram, *Naqīb al-Ashrāf*, and the *ᶜulamāᵓ* never protested this attack on their highest ranking official or the shift in power that resulted from it (A. Loutfi El-Sayed, "The Role of the *ᶜUlamāᵓ* in Egypt during the Early Nineteenth Century," p. 276). As Crecelius evaluates the situation:

> "... the leadership which (al-Sharqāwī and ᶜUmar Makram) gave to their nation during (the French invasion) does not truly reflect the relative importance or influence of their offices either before or after this period of crisis. With the deposition of ᶜUmar Makram in 1809, for instance, the *niqāba* lost its political importance. Successors of al-Sharqāwī were unable to preserve the influence he had enjoyed and took their place once more behind the *muftīs*, the Shaykh al-Sādāt, and the Shaykh al-Bakrī" ("The Emergence of Shaykh al-Azhar," p. 115; also p. 114, n. 22).

The law itself was an important framework for the interplay of personal contests for power, and nowhere to we see this so clearly as in the administration of justice. For more affluent groups especially, the courts represented a field for the interplay of rivalries between individuals and factions. Even in the middle of the nineteenth century, Sir John Gardner Wilkinson stated that the Cairenes were fond of litigation and that the courts were always crowded. [59] More frequently than not cases were decided on the basis of personal connections and financial resources of the participants. Lane remarks that there was never any difficulty in settling a case between a rich party and one who was poor, but only difficulty when both parties were equally rich and powerful. [60] Since the *nāʾib*s were unfamiliar with local dialects, the chief interpreter (*bash turjumān*) had considerable importance. Lane implies that he was the one to be contacted if one wished to influence a decision, for he not only acted as translator but since he, unlike the *qāḍī*s and *nāʾib*s, was a permanent official of the court, he was the one most acquainted with its procedures and the political network through which legal purposes were accomplished. [61] Customarily the loser of the case had to pay the court fees and according to available literature, bribery played a major role at every stage of the case. The poor had little chance of obtaining redress for their grievances [62] and had everything to lose by recourse to a court of law in the settlement of their disputes.

Middle class power, like elite power, depended in large part upon alliances; alliances that were strengthened by economic liaisons and intimate social bonds. As we have seen, the Ottoman period saw an

---

[59] *Handbook for Travelers in Egypt* (London: J. Murray, 1858), p. 141.

[60] E. W. Lane, *The Arabian Nights Entertainments* (London: Routledge, Warne, and Routledge, 1865), I, p. 387, n. 80. Clot-Bey presents a similar picture:

> "Often the judge lets the rank of the parties influence his decision. Sometimes he sells his decisions to the one who offers the most; the thing that is most scandalous of all is the prevalence of false witness. We have seen that the depositions of two witnesses were legal proof; the defendant or the accused found always two witnesses to buy. Before Muḥammad ᶜAlī, justice was in a worse state yet, because it was replaced by the arbitrariness of the Pachas, Beys, and of their chief subordinates who usurped the prerogatives of the judiciary" (*Aperçu général sur l'Égypte*, I, p. 256).

[61] *Manners and Customs*, p. 116.

[62] Al-Jabartī too, noted the case of a student who was at a great disadvantage in a lawsuit because he was indigent and lacked the money that "was indispensable for commissions and bribes to intermediaries and those who render judgments and to their hangers-on" (*ᶜAjāʾib al-Āthār*, IV, p. 64; *Merveilles biographiques et historiques*, VIII, p. 139).

increased involvement of the "exclusive" elite with other sections of society. Non-mamlūks who had never been able to enter the ranks of the elite could now rise to high positions. Any man of means could now buy mamlūks. Although these had not as good opportunities as mamlūks owned by the elite, some of them owned by merchants and *ᶜulamāᵓ* now became provincial governors (*sanjaq*s). Al-Jabartī's father himself owned mamlūks as well as black slaves, [63] while a rich Maghribī family of merchants, the ash-Sharāᵓibīs, owned mamlūks who entered the highest ranks in Egypt. The ash-Sharāᵓibīs married their daughters to members of the Qāzdughlīya who subsequently took up residence with them in their house in the Ezbekīya. [64] The beys felt free to go there without invitation and Riḍwān-Kākhya was accustomed to frequent it with his closest associates. [65]

But alliances, as we have seen, were double edged and although rich and prominent persons of the middle class for the most part benefited from ties with the ruling elite, such ties could and often did result in financial drain. Merchants, especially those who could not claim the protection of the religious establishment, were threatened by such encroachment on their spheres of influence.

For import-export merchants in particular, attachment to European consulates and embassies offered not only economic advantage but a measure of political security. Capitulatory states generally patronized one or several groups of merchants and businessmen. *Dhimmī*s, always beyond the pale of Muslim society, often profited by this means. The mechanism lay in the capitulatory privilege by which European consuls and vice-consuls could grant a certain number of *berāt*s, or guarantees of the consular protection, and the reduced customs rates applied to European nationals to local people who acted as translators. In return for seeing that European traders were accorded advantages in their commercial dealings and for giving them personal assistance if they should find themselves in trouble in Egyptian society, the *berātli*s claimed consular protection in the customs dīwāns. By the eighteenth

---

63 D. Ayalon, "Studies in al-Jabartī," pp. 311-312.

64 The house had twelve apartments, each forming a large dwelling in itself. The ash-Sharāᵓibīs so valued their social rank that they are said to have boasted that "their women did not leave their house except to be buried" (al-Jabartī, *ᶜAjāᵓib al-Āthār*, I, p. 204; *Merveilles biographiques et historiques*, II, pp. 143-146). The implication is that, owing to the prestige of the merchant family, the usual rule of virilocal residence was not followed even when their daughters married the beys.

65 *ᶜAjāᵓib al-Āthār*, I, pp. 204-205; *Merveilles biographiques et historiques*, II, pp. 143-146.

century the practice of granting *berāts* extended considerably beyond its originally intended limits [66] and rivalries developed between *berātlis* of different national origin paralleling European commercial rivalries. The most notable example was the contest between the Jews, whose patrons were the Venetians, and the Syrian Christians, who were leagued with the French. In the last analysis, however, the protections "guaranteed" by the *berāts* dissolved under the pressure of increasing Mamlūk demands for cash. Despite valiant attempts on the part of the Venetian consuls to protect their clients, the Jews were subjected to extortions of a severity before that time unknown and ᶜAlī-Bey, having persuaded himself that they had mismanaged the customs dīwāns, transferred control of these bureaus to the Syrians (1769-1770).

The political power of the middle class, like the power of the elite, fluctuated with the shifting center of military power. As the beys regained strength with the weakening of the representatives of the Porte, so in the eighteenth century the middle class asserted itself at the weakness of the beys. Militarily, there was some possibility of the popular orders of society coming to the fore, but there was greater likelihood of intervention by a foreign government. Reactions of the middle orders to the crises of the end of the eighteenth and beginning of the nineteenth century reflected these opportunities even as, ultimately, they reveal to us the nature of the power of the notables.

During the last decades of the eighteenth century, the *ᶜulamāʾ* had made tentative movements at filling the political vacuum that began to appear through the waning of the power of the beys. More and more their dual role as peace-makers and rabble-rousers became evident. With the advent of Napoleon on the scene, the flight of the beys, and the withdrawal of Ottoman officials, the local *ᶜulamāʾ* came into such power as was never before open to them, for the new invader, as a European power, was especially incapable of governing without their help. To legislate, to maintain order, and to mediate between the French authorities and the people, Napoleon set up councils composed of the leading religious and commercial notables. The *Dīwān al-ᶜUmūmī* (General Council) debated serious issues of national interest, from laws of inheritance and criminal justice to taxation. At the forefront in the Cairo Council were the presiding officer, Shaykh ash-Sharqāwī

[66] According to Volney, by 1785 consuls sold *berāts* for from two hundred to two hundred and fifty pounds (*Travels through Egypt and Syria*, II, p. 428). To start each ambassador had fifty *berāts* but as the gift was renewed every time an ambassador was appointed, the number of native Christian and Jewish agents continuously increased.

(Shaykh al-Azhar), Shaykh as-Sādāt, and Shaykh al-ᶜArīshī who was appointed the first Egyptian chief *qāḍī* (*qāḍī* of Cairo). [67]

The relationship of the middle orders as a whole to the invaders can best be described as ambivalent. The notables were far from united. Some showed much more readiness to collaborate than others. For the most part the *ᶜulamāᵓ* were willing to cooperate since acceptance of new military elites was no new thing, a policy of resistance offered little promise, and it was immediately evident that local officials were going to continue their important political and administrative roles. Moreover they had become disillusioned with the Mamlūks and resentful against them since they blamed them for the French occupation. [68] On the other hand, the French were a Christian power and as such were despised more than any previous invader. The impositions of the occupying army, compounded with the tactlessness and mismanagement of deputies unfamiliar with Muslim culture, soon generated expressions of resistance. As Denon wrote at the time:

> ... (The people) soon began to regret their former tyrants; and, on recovering from their first panic, they had listened to their mufti, who found means to animate them against us with a fanatic enthusiasm, and they had conspired in silence ... [69]

Thus national and collaborationist factions emerged. Shaykh as-Sādāt and ᶜUmar Makram led a series of popular revolts which finally resulted in the accession of Muḥammad ᶜAlī. Shaykh al-Bakrī, how-

---

[67] Administratively the most significant result of the occupation was the recovery by the native *ᶜulamāᵓ* of the bureaucratic positions they had lost to the Ottoman efendīs three centuries before. Only five Turkish *qāḍīs* were left to symbolize Ottoman authority. Since the *rūznāmjī* and his staff had fled. Coptic clerks and money-changers (*ṣarrāfs*) now held the vacated offices and directly administered the treasury and the tax system under the direction of a French economist (S. J. Shaw, *Ottoman Egypt in the Age of the French Revolution*, p. 25).

[68] Shaykh as-Sādāt openly accused the Mamlūks of actions leading to the Egyptian defeat (al-Jabartī, *ᶜAjāᵓib al-Āthār*, IV, p. 192; *Merveilles biographiques et historiques*, IX, p. 54). Writing in 1785, Aḥmad Jazzār Pasha reported to the Ottoman authorities that Shaykh al-Bakrī and Shaykh as-Sādāt were very badly treated by the beys and that they "very much loathe them and they constantly seek in secret those who would annihilate them and abolish their tyranny." He said also that the shaykhs of al-Azhar were in complete agreement with the above in desiring the beys' destruction (S. J. Shaw, *Ottoman Egypt in the Eighteenth Century*, p. 23). When the beys left the city upon the approach of Napoleon's troops the people took their revenge upon them by pillaging their houses (Vivant Denon, *Travels in Upper and Lower Egypt*, translated from the French by Arthur Aikin (New York, 1803), I, pp. xlix, 85).

[69] *Travels in Upper and Lower Egypt*, I, p. 151.

ever, sided with the French only to be deposed at their withdrawal. [70] Following the revolt of 1798, the General Council was dismissed, but as such a body was indispensable to the needs of the French another council was reinstituted within two months. [71]

Undoubtedly many felt that they had less to lose by associating with the invaders than by returning to a situation of anarchy in which their property and security were constantly threatened. Political alliances were cemented by the most intimate ties. Al-Jabartī tells us that the French sought marriage with the daughters of Cairene notables who, out of desire for security or opportunism, welcomed the protection of the army. [72] General ᶜAbdallāh Jacques Menou who replaced Kléber married an Egyptian woman during the occupation.

Of all the groups most willing to collaborate it would seem that the *dhimmī* communities, especially the Christian merchants, took the prize. That the military power should be in "Christian" hands presented an unparalleled opportunity to profit from the traditional pattern of alliance. Moreover Napoleon had used the "unfair treatment" of European merchants by the government of the beys as an excuse to invade the country. Syrian Christians imitated the French in manners and dress. Some even ate and drank in public during the Muslim month of fasting and used insulting language. Their behavior became so excessive that the French restored the sumptuary laws that had fallen into disuse. [73] Notably Vivant Denon compares the behavior of the middle class who resided around the Ezbekīya with that of the rest of the populace:

---

[70] His daughter was killed for consorting with the French. (al-Jabartī, *ᶜAjāᵓib al-Āthār*, III, p. 192; *Merveilles biographiques et historiques*, VII, p. 44).

[71] One class of events clearly reveals the ambivalent attitudes of the Egyptians to the French regime. Militarily, native groups were not all opposed to the occupying forces. Many were eager to achieve their ends by becoming recruits to the French army! About 2,000 Copts from Upper Egypt were organized into an infantry corps under a Coptic officer. A group of "Maghribī" soldiers who had been used by the beys as mercenaries, poorly disciplined and never allowed to join elite ranks, were also trained to fight in the European manner. Even some young mamlūks were enrolled under the French command and came to serve Napoleon loyally in the years that followed (S. J. Shaw, *Ottoman Egypt in the Age of the French Revolution*, p. 84).

[72] *ᶜAjāᵓib al-Āthār*, III, p. 162; *Merveilles biographiques et historiques*, VI, p. 305. The French would make simple profession of the Muslim faith to obtain a Muslim bride but this was generally not recognized by the orthodox as it lacked true religious conviction.

[73] Albert Hourani, "The Syrians in Egypt in the Eighteenth and Nineteenth Centuries," *Colloque international sur l'histoire du Caire* (Cairo: General Egyptian Book Organization, 1974), p. 224.

> Though the populace, the devotees, and some of the great people of Cairo, showed themselves fantastical and cruel in this revolt, the middle class (which in all countries is most accessible to reason and virtue) was perfectly humane and generous to us notwithstanding the wide differences of manners, religion, and language; whilst from the galleries of the minarets murder was devoutly preached up, whilst the streets were filled with death and carnage, all those in whose houses any Frenchmen were lodged, were eager to save them by concealment, and to supply and anticipate all their wants. [74]

The nature of middle class political power unequivocally manifests itself in the events surrounding the rise of Muḥammad ᶜAlī. At the withdrawal of the French the country was faced with economic and political chaos. It was obvious to all that the pasha and the Mamlūks were incapable of restoring order. Appealed to by the people, the *ᶜulamāᵓ* met in the house of Shaykh ash-Sharqāwī to decide what should be done. Muḥammad ᶜAlī meanwhile had approached ᶜUmar Makram and others to win their support in the deposition of Khūrshīd Pasha and the appointment of himself as viceroy. The *ᶜulamāᵓ* concurred, sent a message of deposition to the Pasha, and clothed Muḥammad ᶜAlī in the *quftān* (robe) symbolic of investiture. [75] A popular revolt led by ᶜUmar Makram followed as Khūrshīd refused to comply. In answer to his demand for an explanation. ᶜUmar Makram replied that:

> "The rulers are the *ᶜulamāᵓ* and the righteous Sultan but the Pasha is a despot and, from time immemorial, the people have deposed their rulers if they are unjust." [76]

There is no doubt that the notables, as leaders of the people, played a significant part in the rise of Muḥammad ᶜAlī to power. Certainly the *ᶜulamāᵓ* were acting as more than mediators in this case. On the other hand, to what did this power really amount? When Muḥammad ᶜAlī's position was established he swore to rule in consultation with the *ᶜulamāᵓ* and even agreed to be deposed if they should wish it. Seeing that chaos was averted, however, and relatively satisfied with the new Pasha, they told him that he was the ruler and returned to

---

74 *Travels in Upper and Lower Egypt*, I, pp. 153-154.

75 Al-Jabartī, *ᶜAjāᵓib al-Āthār*, III, p. 330; *Merveilles biographiques et historiques*, VII, p. 373.

76 Al-Jabartī, *ᶜAjāᵓib al-Āthār*, III, p. 331; *Merveilles biographiques et historiques*, VII, p. 375.

their old role of mediating between the pasha and the people,[77] a role that simply irritated Muḥammad ᶜAlī who wanted to impose new taxes. Through the insistence of the *ᶜulamā᾿* themselves, the forces of ᶜUmar Makram were disbanded. *They never really felt that they had a right to rule but only to restrain and advise.*[78] Ultimately this attitude brought about the dissolution of most of their political power, for when the new Pasha subsequently taxed them and confiscated their *waqfs*, they lost their ability to apply economic pressure and to raise an army.

Political power ultimately was seated in military power as everyone concerned well knew. Muḥammad ᶜAlī enlisted the support of the *ᶜulamā᾿* and the support of the mobs they controlled as long as his position was at all uncertain.[79] Once having attained that position, he viewed power outside of his control as a threat and lost no time in building up his own army to a fighting force which had no competitors. The sultan's validation recognized him as *de facto* ruler of the country even as it had recognized victorious amīrs before him.

Thus, although political vacua caused by temporary absences of strong military force brought forth middle class involvement in political affairs to an unprecedented degree, it is evident that *the notables never felt at ease as "representatives of the people" any more than they could tolerate being simply the tools of the elite.* No one has ever estimated their role more accurately than that military and political genius, Napoleon, when he wrote:

> "... I have preferred the ulema and the doctors of the law: first, because they are the natural leaders; secondly, because they are interpreters of the Koran ... and thirdly, because these ulema have gentle manners, love justice, and are rich and animated by good moral principles ... they are not addicted to any sort of military manoeuvring and they are ill adapted to the leadership of an armed movement."[80]

---

[77] Al-Jabartī, *ᶜAjā᾿ib al-Āthār*, III, p. 337; *Merveilles biographiques et historiques*, VII, p. 385.

[78] As P. M. Holt has written:

"ᶜUmar Makram and the *ᶜulamā᾿* were acting, as the *ᶜulamā᾿* had traditionally acted in times of political crisis, to safeguard the interests of the Muslim community by supporting the authority of the strongest contender for power. They were not in any real sense king-makers, still less spokesmen of the national will" (*Egypt and the Fertile Crescent*, p. 177).

[79] In fact, the troops that did the most fighting were the contingents of ᶜUmar Makram. Muḥammad ᶜAlī's men were relatively few, underpaid, and divided amongst themselves (A. Loutfi El-Sayed, "The Role of the *ᶜUlamā* in Egypt during the Early Nineteenth Century," p. 274).

[80] C. de la Jonquière, *L'expédition de l'Égypte* (1798-1801) (Paris, 1899-1907),

3. *The Persistent Power of the Lower Orders*

In the face of the overwhelming power of the elite and the restraining power of the notables, it would seem that the lower orders of society had little hope of real political achievement. Their voice, however, is heard as a constant murmer, if not often a thunderous roar. Two alternative modes of behavior characterized their political life, clientage or rebellion. Needless to say, the first was by far the most common.

New possibilities for persons of the lower orders to manipulate the political network opened up through the increasing neglect of the traditional rules that safeguarded elite status. Instances are rare, but it was not unknown for poor individuals to come into great wealth through patronage and then to purchase mamlūks who became amīrs. One son of a *fallāḥ*, who had been pawned by his father for the payment of a debt, through his wit and ability, accumulated a fortune and many mamlūks and slave girls whom he married to one another and set up with houses and incomes. Purchasing positions for them in the *ojāq*s, he emerged as a patron of a group of amīrs affiliated to the Qāzdughlīya known as "the group of al-Fallāḥ." Through his economic power he ultimately brought about the downfall of Ibrāḥīm-Kākhya and his house for they had borrowed from him large sums which they were unable to repay. It might be objected that, owing to his wealth he was no longer of the lower orders, but certainly he began as such and it is noteworthy that all his life he wore a modest turban and would appear in the streets riding a donkey heralded by a single servant. [81]

In another case, a poor Turkish haberdasher noticed by a bey while hawking his wares came, through the fruits of patronage, to own a large number of mamlūks, one hundred of whom became amīrs. The black mamlūk Ibrāḥīm as-Sinnārī, whose great palace in Sayyida Zaynab was later occupied by Napoleon's savants, began as a *bawwāb* (doorman, porter) in Manṣūra. At first patronized by the Mamlūks on account of his knowledge of magical arts, he spent much time in their company, adopted their dress, language, and manners, and finally

---

V, p. 597, translation quoted from F. Charles-Roux (tr. E. W. Dickes), *Bonaparte: Governor of Egypt* (London, 1937), pp. 353-354; quoted in Afaf Loutfi El-Sayed, "The Role of the *ᶜUlamāᵓ* in Egypt during the Early Nineteenth Century," p. 271.

[81] D. Ayalon, "Studies in al-Jabartī," p. 314.

came to the attention of Murād-Bey who placed great confidence in him.[82]

While cases of lower class persons acting as patrons are scarce, as clients they may often have been able to exert considerable leverage. The fighting power of the beys was to a great degree dependent upon their ability to manipulate the political bonds that crystalized around the broadly based artisan and nomad moieties, the Niṣf Saᶜd and Niṣf Ḥaram.[83] Many amīrs who in Cairo fell victim to factional struggle seem to have found refuge with artisans and tradesmen in Upper Egypt. It is a very noteworthy fact that, following the massacre of Mamlūks in the Citadel, Muḥammad ᶜAlī sought out the members of the "old houses" (*buyūt al-qadīma*). According to David Ayalon:

> On the 25th of Ṣafar sixty-four members of the *buyūt al-qadīma* were brought from Upper Egypt. Most of them were people who lived for many years in Upper Egypt and even became artisans (?) (*muḥtarifīn*). They were all executed ... Such was the fundamental method of Muḥammad ᶜAlī in his extermination of the mamluks. He did not want to take chances and killed harmless mamluks who had practically merged in the local population.[84]

Alliances between the lower orders and the elite were much more regular and common in the case of the Janissaries than in the case of

---

[82] D. Ayalon, "Studies in al-Jabartī," pp. 314-315. The decline in the exclusiveness of Mamlūk recruitment was marked also by the rise in fortune of a group of Turkish mounted servants (*sarrājūn*) who became "hatchetmen" for the beys. To quote Aḥmad Jazzār Pasha:

> "They hang daggers from their necks like amulets and attach two guns and one knife to their waists. Every *Emīr* and military officer has forty or fifty of these *sarrāces*, or more or less according to their rank" (S. J. Shaw, *Ottoman Egypt in the Eighteenth Century*, p. 24).

Ayalon notes that the servants of the Mamlūks in the time of the Mamlūk sultanate had not played such a prominent part and, in contrast, could be considered a "downtrodden element." Doubtless the intensification of rivalries between the *bayts* was an explanatory factor. See D. Ayalon, "Studies in al-Jabartī, p. 306. Bands of *sarrājūn* were much feared and came to be one of the most powerful weapons in the hands of the amīrs. Al-Jabartī claimed that most of them were Christians who used their positions to harm Muslims but the evidence concerning their origin and recruitment is inconclusive (*ᶜAjāʾib al-Āthār*, II, pp. 36-37; *Merveilles biographiques et historiques*, IV, p. 39).

[83] The Qāsimīs were leagued with the Niṣf Ḥaram and the Faqārīs with the Niṣf Saᶜd. The ᶜAzabs generally sided with the Qāsimīs and the Janissaries with the Faqārīs. Unfortunately not many details are known about these liaisons or their exact mechanism. Al-Jabartī recounts at some length the legendary history of the groupings (*ᶜAjāʾib al-Āthār*, I, pp. 21-23; *Merveilles biographiques et historiques*, I, pp. 50-54).

[84] "Studies in al-Jabartī," p. 292, n. 3.

the beys. For one thing, they developed through the framework of occupational corporations. Al-Jabartī tells us that soldiers frequently imposed their patronage upon artisans. [85] In the majority of cases this practice may have been sheer extortion, but if we recall the ancient tradition of the institutions of partnership [86] we realize that partnerships between persons of unequal social rank could well have been the rule rather than the exception. It is a matter of fact that some of the *ojāqlu* themselves became artisans rather than following military pursuits, even as artisans entered the military corps. André Raymond has pointed out that the military elite had intimate bonds with people of the crafts and cites the patronymics borne by a number of amīrs in evidence: Muḥammad-Kākhya of the Chāwīshīya, "al-Muzayyin" (the Barber); Muḥammad-Efendī "Ibn al-Bayṭār" (Son of the Veterinarian), who became a *sanjaq*; Muḥammad-Kākhya of the Janissaries, called "al-Khashshāb" (the Lumber Merchant). [87]

It might be argued that the kind of political power indicated in the examples above was negligible since, in fact, the liaisons tended to grow stronger as the power of the elite became less. On the other hand, the double edge of alliance could not but bring some advantages to both parties, however temporary.

The political power of the lower orders was most persistent in the sphere of law enforcement, for without intimate knowledge of the social web of the quarters, no one could rule them. A person needed money and connections to succeed in the courts but police affairs were of a somewhat different order. The policing of the city was, for obvious reasons, the most developed of the services provided by the central government [88] and its development was possible ultimately because of reliance upon true representatives of the people. Every night

---

[85] See above, Chapter XVI, p. 315, n. 17.

[86] See above, Chapter III, p. 63, n. 42; also Chapter XVI, pp. 337-338.

[87] *Artisans et commerçants*, II, p. 685.

[88] Specifically, the āghā of the Janissaries (*āghā mustaḥfiẓān*, "Āghā of the Guardians") was entrusted with the policing of Cairo and its suburbs. Broadly empowered where all matters of security were concerned, his authority extended to a wide range of criminal activities ranging from robbery to prostitution and public disorder. Until the decline of Janissary power with the rise of the beys, the police department functioned most effectively by virtue of the bonds the Janissaries had formed with the local corporations. The *wālī* (sometimes known by the Turkish name *ṣūbāshī*) was appointed by the āghā of the Janissaries to manage the details of police work. This official, who made regular patrols both day and night, had special jurisdiction over certain groups regarded as criminal by society, pickpockets, sellers of hashish, and prostitutes.

the streets, markets, and quarters were patrolled, not just by military guards but by private watchmen hired by merchants and residents.

Given the impossibility of effective centralization, the elite established a *modus vivendi* with criminals of all kinds. Government officials not only employed thieves as informers and plain clothesmen, thereby utilizing their special skills to their own advantage, but granted formal recognition to criminal guilds that paid tax. "If you can't beat 'em, join 'em," represented the most efficient means of controlling the criminal elements. Often the only clues detectives had were the coffee house "grape vines" and the corporations and quarters were quite capable of maintaining their semi-independence from controls imposed from the outside.

The shaykhs of urban corporations continued to hold great responsibility for the people they represented. It was they who, through economic and social sanctions, maintained discipline. When complaints against corporation members were addressed to them, redress was sure to follow. [89] The guild, [90] which we will consider in greater detail in the next chapter, could also give political unity to members of different quarters engaged in the same occupation.

When the persistent murmer of the populace became the roar of the crowd, it spoke through the voices of the shaykhs of the guilds. Ultimately the corporations most effectively tempered governmental control. Gibb and Bowen consider their typical passive resistance in the face of the frequently arbitrary governmental orders to be a natural instinct of self-preservation. [91] By the latter part of the eighteenth century their resistance was no longer passive. The chronic and tradi-

---

[89] Lane makes an interesting statement about the corporation of thieves:

> "Even the common thieves used, not many years since, to respect a superior, who was called their sheykh. He was often required to search for stolen goods, and to bring offenders to justice; which he generally accomplished. It is very remarkable that the same strange system prevailed among the ancient Egyptians" (Ref. — Diodorus Siculus, lib. i. cap. 80), (*Manners and Customs*, p. 128).

and another about the corporation of servants:

> "The servants in the metropolis are likewise under the authority of particular sheykhs. Any person in want of a servant may procure one by applying to one of these officers who, for a small fee (two or three piasters) becomes responsible for the conduct of the men whom he recommends. Should a servant so engaged rob his master, the latter gives the information to the sheykh, who, whether he can recover the stolen property or not, must indemnify the master" (*Manners and Customs*, p. 128).

[90] Although the system of guilds was of doubtful existence and hard to trace in earlier times, it was well established by the end of the second century of Ottoman rule.

[91] *Islamic Society and the West*, I, 1, p. 280.

tional pattern of demonstrations directed at economic grievances gained the semblance of political rebellion.[92] It must have been with considerable apprehension that the beys heard the signal drum that announced a crisis sound from the minaret of al-Azhar, and certainly they must have watched with fear as the people closed the *sūq*s and the "popular troops" poured out of the streets and alleys. The rulers were aware of the potential threat of organized guilds, especially when the latter were in the possession of arms, as was often the case in the eighteenth century when artisans were affiliated with the corps of Janissaries and ᶜAzabs.

In sum, the power of the people was covert rather than overt, internal rather than external, and latent most of the time surfacing only when there was some lack above. The elite both depended upon its substance and feared its eruptions. It is significant that the Porte itself, always accepting the political facts of life in its provinces, officially recognized the popular will as a sanction for the appointment of Muḥammad ᶜAlī in the firman that confirmed him in office.

92 Cf. André Raymond, "Quartiers et mouvements populaires au Caire au XVIIIème siècle," pp. 114-115.

CHAPTER SIXTEEN

ECONOMIC POWER: THE DISTRIBUTION OF RESOURCES AND ITS SOCIAL IMPLICATIONS

The social fabric, while initially delineated by political considerations, was nourished and maintained by economic power. Not only did every new regime immediately embark upon a program that would ensure for itself the country's revenues, but the urban social structure depended upon there being some regularity of redistribution. Economic power, moreover, could be seen as an index of effective political control at all levels. There was a constantly tense and shifting balance between state centralization and private control of wealth just as on the international scene the Egyptian contest itself was a vignette of a larger struggle.

The pattern is complex but coherent for a number of its threads were fixed by the loom of history. Thus, from one point of view, the developments of the first part of the nineteenth century appear radical and indeed, Muḥammad ᶜAlī's bold assertion of state control, his emphasis upon development of a market-oriented economy, and the massive introduction of foreign modes, techniques, and procedures to attain his ends signalled a new era which was to come. On the other hand, from time immemorial markets had been important and urban exchange had been heavily monetized. Every regime from the time of ᶜAmr had made a point of gathering the fruits of the land unto itself and nearly all had by special arrangements tapped the fruits of commerce as well. Moreover, from the ninth century the entrepreneurs of trade had been Cairenes of foreign origin; it was usual for merchants to play important roles when governments fell. The critical factor of the nineteenth century was that both economically and militarily Egypt was drawn into a sphere in which she could not successfully compete: the sphere dominated by Europe. Muḥammad ᶜAlī's application of the traditional pattern of rule was thus a transformation of it that, because of the expanded context, ultimately resulted in revolutionizing traditional urban economic modes.

In the interplay of economic phenomena we see the confrontation of social tendencies described in earlier chapters: considerations of special status, kinship, patronage, and the desire to override these bonds, as well as the necessity of meeting the needs of subsistence, protection, and prestige. Like social life itself, economic power does not exist without contradictions, and contentions of it never reach an other than temporary resolution. Disparities in wealth are markers of social rank, but wealth, like political power, must be used, communicated or redistributed, for its value to be realized. Moreover as we have seen, the sociopolitical fluidity of the Ottoman period emphasized the reciprocity that pertained between political, spiritual, and economic power, and ultimately produced a milieu in which quite literally, everything from military rank to spiritual authority had its price. If economic power did not destroy the hierarchy or overcome social inequality, its role in facilitating mobility within the hierarchy should not be minimized.

Basically, the social structure from the beginning of the sixteenth to the middle of the nineteenth century evinced few changes although forces at work within it, stimulated by external pressures, were to bring forth a new social order. Conquest and chronic political discord periodically dislocated networks of patronage, but still few if any Cairenes ever made important economic decisions independent of sociopolitical considerations and commitments. The substantive pattern of achieving security was too engrained. New patrons were found even if these were the state or foreign businessmen. The Ottoman, French, and "Albanian" conquests of Egypt introduced new dichotomies and corresponding economic disruption, but also showed that the traditional social matrix had vast powers of self-healing through fusion.

1. *The Control and Use of Capital: The Rulers and the Ruled*

A theme of the first two parts of this book was the interdependence of economic and political power. The waxing and waning of military strength had a profound relation to the prosperity of the nation even as it effected the affluence of rival factions within it. Conversely, wealth, because of the military support it could buy and the social control that could be exerted through economic power, was the paramount political instrument. Indeed, political struggles were focused upon control of land revenues, the food supply, and urban incomes, as well as upon the immediate attainment of military ascendancy and positions of authority.

The chief aim of the Ottoman regime, like that of every regime before it, was the provision of support particularly for the governing class, without seriously damaging the source of support itself. Subsidiary to this goal was the role of taxation as a means of social control through the control of resources; for while the immediate concern was the collection of revenue, a necessary result of taxation was the limitation of capital accumulation and hence curtailment of economic power so essential in the manipulation of social relations. By and large, however, the Porte was content to extract what it could through the offices of its agents without revolutionizing the pattern of social life in any way. [1] Cairo successfully maintained itself through the fruits of the hinterland, industry, and through trade. Despite the Mamlūk resurgence, revenue continued to flow to Istanbul until the end of the eighteenth century, an amount which represented an excess over what the local elite claimed to maintain their own establishment.

André Raymond's important work, *Artisans et commerçants au Caire*, shows that the economic developments of the Ottoman period in many respects parallel those of the Mamlūk sultanate. While, in the sixteenth century, some increase in prosperity resulted from the reestablishment of security, the depopulation that resulted from famine and plague in the seventeenth and eighteenth centuries and political rivalry could not but contribute to decline. While in the seventeenth century commerce in coffee compensated somewhat for the slackening of commerce in spices and, for a time, the Janissaries encouraged urban economic enterprise, in the long run Cairene initiative and capital were submerged by the triumph of the beys in the last part of the eighteenth century and the onslaught of European competition. [2]

Under the French regime the old administrative structure was maintained for a time, but since most of the tax farmers were Mamlūks who

---

[1] The economic policy of the Ottoman Porte was essentially related to the traditional conception of society and of the proper role of government. It was assumed that the ruler would seek to consolidate and extend his power through the increase of revenues and that the best way to do this without impairing the prosperity of the ruled who were the producers was to maintain the social hierarchy in which each class followed its proper pursuits (H. Inalcik, "The Ottoman Economic Mind and Aspects of the Ottoman Economy," *Studies in the Economic History of the Middle East*, edited by M. A. Cook (London: Oxford University Press, 1970), pp. 217-218).

[2] According to André Raymond's summary of the economic history of the Ottoman period, there was a relatively continuous period of progress from the beginning of the seventeenth century which reached an apogee about 1680. Following this a rapid succession of natural and fiscal crises gave rise to about fifty years of economic hardship. Between 1747 and 1755 (a period generally corresponding to the duumvirate of Ibrāhīm and Riḍwān-Kākhya, the chiefs of the Janissaries and ᶜAzabs), the situation was considerably ameliorated. Relative prosperity continued for another twenty years but the last two decades of the eighteenth century, which corresponded politically to the triumph of the beys and culminated in the Napoleonic invasion, were marked by the gravest problems and decline. See A. Raymond, *Artisans et commerçants*, I, p. 106; II, pp. 811-812.

had fled and few Egyptians came forward to fill their posts, the system was inoperable. Later, when it seemed to the French that they might remain, they abolished the old decentralized taxes and instituted a system of direct administration, with a single general cash tax. They also decreed that *awqāf* had to pay a land tax before their revenues could be delivered to their pious foundations. Thus, the way was prepared for Muḥammad ᶜAlī who, in proper perspective, seems hardly revolutionary, for although when the French withdrew the beys returned, the former tax farmers found that their revenues and positions had slipped away to other classes of Egyptians willing to collaborate with the occupying power. [3] By the time Muḥammad ᶜAlī massacred the Mamlūks, their households were starved of the support through which they had formerly secured their power and ambition. It was easy for the new ruler to declare a state monopoly and to end a system which had already been broken.

Muḥammad ᶜAlī made monopoly the keystone of his financial policy. While previous rulers had made wide use of the principle, [4] none chose or was able to exploit it as extensively as he. As A. E. Crouchley puts it, "The Viceroy became the sole farmer, sole manufacturer, sole landowner, and sole trader of the country." [5] From 1816-1840 he extended his control to the monopoly of all agricultural and manufactured products, requiring that such be delivered to government agencies in return for fixed prices, prices that were sometimes only half or one-third of the market value.

Setting out to reconquer an empire, his bold and massive military undertaking had to be paid for by bold and massive economic measures. At the very least the economic underpinnings of rivals at home had to be removed. As noted in the last chapter, the *ᶜulamāᵓ* and urban notables

[3] S. J. Shaw, *Ottoman Egypt in the Age of the French Revolution*, pp. 26-28.

[4] It had been usual, under the Mamlūk sultanate, for the sultans to monopolize certain strategic commodities or important export products such as metals, wood, and sugar. For the most part, however, they did not involve themselves directly in the market. (Perhaps it presented no temptation since a large amount of staples was redistributed through patronage and reciprocal arrangements.) It was not unusual either for *awqāf* (especially *waqf ahlī*, family *waqf*), to be liquidated in time of crisis (I. M. Lapidus, "The Grain Economy of Mamlūk Egypt," *Journal of the Economic and Social History of the Orient*, XII (1969), pp. 1, 4, 10). Thus, Selīm maintained *waqf khayrī* that he inherited from the former regime, but confiscated many *waqf ahlī*, especially if there was no documentary proof of their ownership (S. J. Shaw, *Financial Organization*, p. 41). Khāᵓir-Bey, the first viceroy, also seized both *waqf* and *mulk* (privately owned) lands.

[5] *The Economic Development of Modern Egypt* (London: Longmans Green & Co., 1938), p. 61.

as well as the artisans had come militarily to the fore. It should not be surprising therefore, that Muḥammad ᶜAlī's economic program manifestly swept aside all possibility of a reassertion of these independent centers of power. On the other hand, there was no new statement of principle. Like former rulers, he gathered unto himself the fruits of victory, only to redistribute to his own clientele! Enormous estates were transfered to relatives and supporters, while business agencies and new industries were put in the hands of Europeans he chose to patronize. [6] Under his rule the national product grew considerably and a greater proportion of the total collected in taxes was secured by the treasury. Yet, as we shall see, in its sociopolitical aspect, his program was far from an unqualified success. It was easier to declare a monopoly than to preserve it.

It is fitting now to look in some detail at the resources of the elite, their sources of income, and then at the pattern of investment. It will be seen that both of these aspects displayed the penetration of elite political power at all levels of society.

In basic conception, the whole of the Ottoman province of Egypt was a *muqāṭaᶜa* given in *iltizām* to the *wālī* (pasha). The imperial treasury distributed both land resources and urban wealth to which it laid claim in *amāna* (agency) or *iltizām* to agents who would exploit these properties and deliver to the government its due. Points of contact between the rulers and the ruled principally involved taxation. With the theoretical exception of the military who, in principle, were exempt from taxes, taxes penetrated every level of society. Feudalism had ostensibly come to an end and the new military establishment put emphasis upon centralized salaried infantry paid largely in cash revenues.

The operation of the treasury and its ultimate fate are illustrative of the shifts in the distribution of power. It is important to recognize that the treasury acted as a central bank for salary holders and that in

---

[6] P. M. Holt points out that even something like the *iltizām* reappeared when, in 1840, wealthy Egyptians were forced to receive villages for which they were required to pay the tax arrears and meet future liabilities (*Egypt and the Fertile Crescent*, p. 188). Thus it took Muḥammad ᶜAlī but thirty-five years to reach a point that it took the Ottoman administration nearly eighty to reach, for the efficiency of the *amīns*, their tax-collecting agents, did not deteriorate to give way to reliance upon ᶜ*āmils* or Mamlūk *multazims* until the beginning of the seventeenth century (S. J. Shaw, *Financial Organization*, p. 21). Cf. above, pp. 234-235. The loosening up of the policy of nationalization undertaken in our own time has taken only two decades.

its operation it became subject to the centripetal forces that pervaded social life. Recipients of salaries were wont to pay others who worked for them by issuing tickets indicating the transfer of a portion of their due and the treasury register would record the names of these secondary grantees alongside that of the original salary holder. [7] Payments in kind were also made from the imperial granary in Old Cairo. Theoretically each salary holder was to get a limited amount of wheat for human consumption and grain for animals a day, but in practice the *wālī* and the amīrs received up to 500 *irdabb*s [8] of wheat a day and another large amount of grain for animals. [9] By the middle of the eighteenth century the drains on the treasury were such that it had not enough cash to pay more than 80 per cent of the salaries and wages it owed. Therefore it issued tickets in place of the deficient funds which authorized the holders to collect what was due them directly from persons in arrears in payment of tax. While the military usually could manage to accomplish such a task, persons holding pension tickets often sold their tickets to *ṣarrāf*s (money changers) for less than their value and the *ṣarrāf*s collected the tax and kept the profits. [10]

It is thus easy to see that the administrative mechanism of state finances became so entangled in the social network delineated by the distribution of real political power, that effectively organized centralization could not long survive. As the beys grasped more and more of its revenues through *iltizām*s and demanded increasing wages and salaries, the surpluses originally envisioned for the Porte were whittled away as these had to be expended for the Porte's duties that did not fall into the sphere of the military administration of the country. [11] In the end the Porte abandoned the treasury to the manipulation of the beys who had succeeded in infiltrating it and acquiesced in reception of handsome *ḥulwān* ("inheritance tax") payments by the neo-Mamlūk elite in return for its acknowledgment of their right to appropriate new *muqāṭaᶜāt* or the properties of their defeated rivals.

Generally speaking, 64-63% of treasury revenues came from land tax, 20-14% of the total came from urban *muqāṭaᶜāt*, and 23-16% came from miscellaneous sources. [12] The rural revenues to which the

[7] S. J. Shaw, *Financial Organization*, p. 218.
[8] Five hundred *irdabbs* is equal to about 2,500 bushels.
[9] S. J. Shaw, *Financial Organization*, p. 221.
[10] *Ibid.*, pp. 219.
[11] S. J. Shaw, *Financial Organization*, p. 304.
[12] *Ibid.*, p. 183.

beys lay hold were the land tax revenues of groups of villages. The *multazim* would pay a sum in advance to the treasury and recoup this amount and a profit to boot. [13] For the most part land taxes were paid in kind, especially in Upper Egypt, although the use of money increased.

Urban *muqāṭaʿāt* fell into various spheres. There was the *jumruk* (customs) which taxed all import-export and transit trade, [14] there was the *shurṭa* (police) which handled not only law enforcement but also imposition of fines, and there was *iḥtisāb* through which standards were imposed and the quality of products enforced. (The *muḥtasib* supervised the markets and factories and collected a number of taxes.) Other *muqāṭaʿāt* involved the control of central, specialized warehouses (*wakālāt*) where comestibles from rural areas were received, stored, and redistributed, and the regulation of Nile and sea traffic with the use of ports and quais. [15] Generally therefore, much urban government was in the hands of holders of *muqāṭaʿāt* and this control involved economic sanctions. The practice was that the treasury would alienate such an office in return for a sum and the grantee, in turn, would collect the fees, taxes, and the costs of his administration from those who came under the jurisdiction of his office. He would deliver these sums to the treasury, keeping a certain amount as profit for which he paid another tax. [16] As can be imagined, there was considerable manipulation at every level. In the *jumruk*, treasury revenues were the result of bargaining between the merchants and those who held the customs *muqāṭaʿa* or their representatives. Moreover illegal taxes and fees were frequently invented by various officials for their own profit. The chronicles and travel reports are full of complaints against such impositions and trade decreased because of the abuses as did treasury revenues. The government, however, was usually incapable of taking effective action, even had it desired to do so.

A whole branch of revenues were protection taxes, both legal and illegal. (From earliest days, a protection tax, the *jizya*, had been paid

[13] Ostensibly for the purpose of restoring disused lands, the *multazims* also came to hold tax-free properties as estates (*waṣīya* lands), a privilege that was at first an annual tenure but evolved into a life-time and finally an inheritance grant as the *iltizāms* themselves became hereditable. (The right to corvée the *fallāḥin* of the district to labor on these estates was included). Other estates held in *waqf ahlī* were untaxable and inalienable, while tax-free *rizqa* estates would be granted by the sultan to those whom he wished to favor.

[14] The control of custom houses was so lucrative that these *muqāṭaʿāt* were among the principal stakes in the contest for power.

[15] S. J. Shaw, *Financial Organization*, p. 99.

[16] *Ibid.*, p. 100.

by *dhimmīs* to their Muslim rulers). Now the *wālī* imposed a sum on the main officers of the Dīwān in return for their appointments, symbolic of the protection of the Ottoman sovereign (*kushūfīya kabīr*), while the Porte showed itself willing to forgo confiscation of *rizqa* estates when their holders died for payment of a protection tax (*māl ḥimāya*), and the Janissaries extorted *māl ḥimāya* from the corporations whose *muqāṭaʿāt* they held.[17] Finally the beys, acting outside the scope of the treasury, took to creating new *muqāṭaʿāt* and assigning these to their own mamlūks and clients. In essence, such were often simply *māl ḥimāya* imposed on *multazims* holding official *muqāṭaʿāt* from the treasury. Stanford Shaw states that

> during (the eighteenth century) these private *Muqāṭaʿāt* came to subject almost every form of economic activity in Egypt to some form of private imposition or protection tax.[18]

Specifically, the revenues described above were distributed among the elite and upper middle class according to relative power and influence.[19] The beys not only gathered to themselves the largest portion of the rural and urban *muqāṭaʿāt* and imposed new taxes but also succeeded in maneuvering increases in old and established revenues. For instance, the sums paid to the *amīr al-ḥajj* rose 2600% from A.D. 1595 to 1760 and certainly not all of this increase was taken up by legitimate expenses of the pilgrimage caravan![20]

---

17 Al-Jabartī describes a common procedure practiced by soldiers to gain access to the resources of the artisans:

> "A soldier would enter the home of a tradesman, suspend his arms in his shop, and sketch a design on a piece of paper which he fastened to the door of the shop. This signified that the soldier had become associated with the tradesman and that he had taken him under his protection. The soldier came and went as he pleased and would sit in the shop when he desired, to ascertain the income, and lay claim to his due" (*ʿAjāʾib al-Āthār*, II, p. 115; *Merveilles biographiques et historiques*, IV, p. 209). See also S. J. Shaw, *Financial Organization*, pp. 49, 148; and A. Raymond, *Artisans et commercants*, II, pp. 668-692. When an artisan or a merchant who was under the protection of an *ojāq* died, the officers of that *ojāq* laid claim to about ten per cent of the assets of his estate (*ibid.*, pp. 696-698).

18 S. J. Shaw, *Financial Organization*, p. 138; see also lists of such taxes, *ibid.*, pp. 138-141.

19 The post of *wālī* (governor of Egypt) by the seventeenth century had ceased to be profitable and many of its occupants retired with many debts to the sultan for obligations they had not been able to fulfill. Stanford Shaw states that their only profits came from bribes given to them secretly by the beys in return for special favors and permission to violate the Ottoman law in diversion of Porte revenues (*Financial Organization*, p. 336).

20 S. J. Shaw, *Financial Organization*, pp. 247-248.

The officers, as we have seen, ultimately declined in relative power, although for a long time they were serious contenders for supremacy. By the middle of the seventeenth century, the Janissaries and ᶜAzabs had secured most of the important urban *muqāṭaᶜāt* which came to represent a greater proportion of their income than their wages. [21] Since the imperial mint was beside the Janissary Gate of the Citadel, these easily gained control of its principal offices which they exploited to a great extent, even minting coins of a greater alloy than was officially allowed and, through their control of the police force, channeling these onto the market. As guards of the imperial granary in Old Cairo, they imposed protection fees for every deposit or collection from the storehouse. [22] After 1671 they seized the customs *muqāṭaᶜāt* from the Jewish and Christian *amīns* who had administered the *jumruk* until that time [23] and gained formal recognition of possession from the *wālī* by paying him a special tax and agreeing to pay on his behalf some of the taxes he owed to the Porte. Even control of public *waqfs* fell to them when they secured its major supervisory post, while by 1734-35 they were directly entrusted with collection of the *jizya* tax from Christians and Jews. [24]

It was of essential importance that many of the *muqāṭaᶜāt* of the officers greatly enhanced their ability to establish effective liaisons with the lower orders of Cairene society. In addition to the above revenues, the Janissaries also established monopolies over the slaughterhouses as well as the processing, purchase, and sale of salt and, through their roles as policemen, secured large bribes for neglecting their official duties. [25] The ᶜAzabs received substantial revenues from their control of the largest tax farms in the city, notably those of the *khurda*

---

[21] They did, however, successfully manipulate the system of wages by forcing the *wālīs* to provide additional salaries for their mamlūks and then enrolling these in the corps. They also had wage posts established as *murattab* (equivalent to *waqf* in other revenues) on behalf of chosen beneficiaries. Thus many persons who performed no military services, children, women, and slaves, came to be officially enrolled in the corps and received salaries and pensions. In many cases the deaths of beneficiaries were not reported so the revenues continued to flow to the houses. Ultimately wage papers were sold on the open market and only rarely were held by the persons in whose names they were registered (S. J. Shaw, *Financial Organization*, pp. 208-209).

[22] S. J. Shaw, *Financial Organization*, p. 190.

[23] Jewish traders, however, continued to administer the customs dīwāns on behalf of their new owners until they were removed by ᶜAlī-Bey and the offices were taken over by Syrian Christians.

[24] S. J. Shaw, *Financial Organization*, pp. 103-191.

[25] S. J. Shaw, *Ottoman Egypt in the Age of the French Revolution*, pp. 93-94.

which was a tax on all public spectacles including the businesses of hasbish makers, drummers, tinsmiths, and ironmongers;[26] and the *simsārīya* of al-Baḥrayn, which meant the supervision of the brokers who operated at the ports of Old Cairo and Būlāq including the right to measure all grains deposited at the Būlāq warehouse and the right to tax all navigation on the river.[27]

Despite the vast holdings of the military elite, it would certainly be untrue to say that civilians were excluded from official revenue posts or major sources of income. Many *ᶜulamāʾ* possessed *iltizām*s that covered several villages.[28] The *qāḍī*s had the advantage of independence from the *wālī* and the treasury in their revenues,[29] while shaykhs of religious orders, in addition to supervision of *waqf*, had other sources of income outside the official establishment. Through patronage of the elite too, Coptic, Syrian, and Jewish merchants waxed wealthy.[30]

Despite their vulnerability to financial impositions a number of merchants built up considerable fortunes. Muḥammad ad-Dāda ash-Sharāʾibī who died in 1724 is said to have left 1,480 purses (a purse being equal to 25,000 *para*s) besides extensive holdings in urban real estate, a *khān*, and ships on the Red Sea. According to al-Jabartī, he had begun his career with only ninety purses that had been entrusted to him.[31] The Islamic prohibition against usury did not keep a number of people from increasing their riches by this means.[32] Muḥammad Chūrbajī al-Murābī (the Usurer) who died the next year left a fortune of 2,000 purses (50 million *para*s). We have noted that one Ḥājjī Ṣāliḥ al-Fallāḥ, who had risen through patronage, was responsible for

---

[26] After 1671, the *amīn al-khurda* had jurisdiction over and the power to tax all markets not under the supervision of the *muḥtasib.*

[27] S. J. Shaw, *Financial Organization*, pp. 120-121, 124, 130.

[28] Al-Jabartī, *ᶜAjāʾib al-Āthār*, IV, p. 234; *Merveilles biographiques et historiques*, IX, p. 148; see A. Raymond, *Artisans et commerçants*, II, pp. 720-722, on the exploitation of rural *muqāṭaᶜāt* by merchants.

[29] S. J. Shaw, *Ottoman Egypt in the Age of the French Revolution*, p. 96.

[30] As an index of the prosperity of these special status groups, Albert Hourani cites the amounts their religious leaders paid to the government for their annual investiture: In 1798 the Coptic patriarch paid 25,000 *para*s a year, the Greek paid 10,000, the Syrian paid 12,000, and the Jewish rabbi paid 6,750 ("The Syrians in Egypt in the Eighteenth and Nineteenth Centuries," p. 225).

[31] *ᶜAjāʾib al-Āthār*, I, p. 87; *Merveilles biographiques et historiques*, I, p. 203.

[32] According to Vansleb, the laws against usury were openly defied in the last half of the seventeenth century (quoted in A. Mez, *Renaissance*, p. 454). Lane also states that "these and several other commercial transactions of a similar kind are severely condemned; but they are not very uncommon among modern Muslims, some of whom take exorbitant interest" (*Manners and Customs*, p. 98). On the subject of interest, see also A. Raymond, *Artisans et commerçants*, I, pp. 280-281.

the financial difficulties of Ibrāḥīm-Kākhya and others to whom he lent huge sums at interest. [33]

Regardless of the gross abuses of the financial regulations, there was, therefore, considerable leeway in access to wealth. The abuses in fact gave flexibility to the system. A variety of sources of revenue could be tapped by a variety of means. Wealth was contingent upon political power but no faction succeeded in monopolizing this power for any length of time. Over the years, the balance shifted from the foreign rulers to the "native elite" and then through channels of patronage and the interstices in their ranks, what these did not absorb filtered down to lower orders of society.

With regard to the investment of wealth, two factors emerge: the priority of political considerations and the limitation of the ability of even the elite to amass capital. [34] Moreover the effects of political instability, the external drain on resources, depopulation, and insecurity brought about not only a shrinkage of the economy but produced in Cairenes of all classes a "subsistence mentality."

It is well known that a militaristic and "feudal" regime is not conducive to economic and social development, or to put it more accurately, such a regime is not conducive to the kind of social and economic development identified with modern industrial society. There is no way to know the proportion of revenue that was expended for military purposes in earlier centuries but under Muḥammad ᶜAlī who was trying to develop Egyptian industries, 60 per cent of the state budget went for the army. [35] There is little doubt that if this was the case in the middle of the nineteenth century, under the beys an even more exaggerated proportion of total revenue went for politico-military expenses.

Certainly there was emphasis upon acquisition of political positions

---

[33] Al-Jabartī, *ᶜAjāᵓib al-Āthār*, I, p. 191; *Merveilles biographiques et historiques*, II, p. 121.

[34] André Raymond notes the lack of disposable capital which was connected to the practice of selling on credit. It is a significant fact that Qāsim ibn Muḥammad ad-Dāda ash-Sharāᵓibī, a coffee merchant and one of the richest men of his time, left a legacy of 4,913,798 *paras* in negotiable merchandise but 7,166,549 *paras* in credit and mortgages, and 9,208,019 *paras* in credit with the amīrs (*Artisans et commerçants*, I, pp. 278-279).

[35] According to the Russian Consul General, "one of the great evils of Egypt is without doubt its military state, which is out of proportion to the population of the country and which absorbs more than half of its revenue" (Duhamel quoted by R. Cattaui, *La Règne de Mohamed Aly d'après les archives russe en Égypte* (Cairo and Rome, 1931-1936), II, 2, p. 420).

and favors not only by the elite but by persons throughout society as a whole. In the legal sphere, influence was obtained not only through bribery but through the purchase of judicial offices. The French tried to rid the courts of these supporters of the beys [36] but little could be done to end the system. One would purchase a position or pay a protection tax to secure other sources of revenue. The protection tax that artisans paid to Janissaries enabled them to escape the penalties that might be inflicted on them by civil authorities through appeal to the Janissar āghā. [37] In Lane's time the Jews still paid a protection tax to the *muḥtasib* to exempt their commercial quarter from his visits. Consequently they could afford to sell their goods more dearly and afford to purchase them at higher rates. [38]

Thus the Porte, in accepting *ḥulwān* payments for the transfer of holdings in lieu of regular treasury revenues, in fact had hit upon a secure and constant source of income, for if anything was sure it was that the Egyptian economic system dealt in political and social power more than any other commodity. As the tax system changed from a system whereby revenues were derived for the treasury, to a system through which the game of power was played, the Porte realized that payments for recognition of transfer of property *outside* the scope of the treasury could be quite lucrative. [39] Even at the top of the formal structure, the only way an Ottoman Pasha sustained any influence was by manipulating factions and offering positions and revenues in return for their support.

Of all the forms of investment leading to political power, the acquisition of slaves, especially mamlūks, was one of the most direct. Slaves not only provided military force and manpower, but were an important form of prestige wealth. One's rank could be assessed in the number of slaves one owned, particularly white slaves. In 1798

[36] S. J. Shaw, *Ottoman Egypt in the Age of the French Revolution*, p. 99.

[37] A. Raymond, *Artisans et commerçants*, II, p. 703. In the last years of the seventeenth century and the beginning of the eighteenth the Janissar āghā came to substitute more and more often for the *muḥtasib*, especially in time of crisis (*op. cit.*, p. 601).

[38] *Manners and Customs*, p. 559.

[39] As Stanford Shaw has put it:

> "Thus in the end the Porte found that the best means to secure for itself a share of the wealth of a country in which it lacked the authority and power necessary to enforce its administrative system was to secure it from the possessions of those who because of political impotence or death could no longer resist its claims rather than from the revenues of those currently in power, who could successfully resist any financial impositions made on them" (*Financial Organization*, pp. 9-10).

a black slave could be bought for 40 or 80 talers [40] while a Circassian might cost more than ten times as much. [41] (The price of white slaves rose astronomically so that by the nineteenth century only a few of the richest Cairenes owned them.) Slaves of any kind were an important investment and essential for the operation of commercial establishments and households. Merchant houses of necessity required armed retainers but most slaves were in domestic service. In the nineteenth century as in earlier days, black male and female slaves were so used not just by the upper crust but by physicians, merchants, shopkeepers, craftsmen, and even well-to-do *fallāḥin*. [42]

Nor should we forget to mention while considering prestige wealth, that as in the Mamlūk period, a great deal of the country's revenues were sent abroad for the sake of obtaining furs, luxurious textiles, ivory, ostrich feathers, and other goods that served to mark the rank of the upper classes. Clothing was especially important in this respect and the *wālī* and the amīrs were wont to distribute robes and fur pelisses to the high *ᶜulamāᵓ* on their accession to office or to others who pleased them.

It is difficult to assess the amount of wealth that the ruling elite and notables expended through redistribution in an effort to gain and maintain clienteles, but certainly such payments both in eash and in kind expressed personal obligations and the dependencies and loyalties that constituted the network of society. As the power of the beys became more and more diffused, they increased their patronage to *ᶜulamāᵓ* whose support and mediating services became more and more essential as well as to others whose backing might prove crucial. Given the fact that disproportionate amounts of wheat and other grains were assigned to the *wālī* and to the amīrs, and the even more obvious fact that not only the ultimate sources of supply but the warehouses were under their control, the conclusion is inescapable that a large amount of grain was distributed primarily through households and agents of the elite in accordance with political criteria and the distribution of power rather than through the operation of the market. [43]

---

[40] The Austrian taler was worth 150 *paras* in 1798.

[41] Alfī-Bey was so named because he had cost 1,000. (*Alf* means 1,000). (G. J. G. Chabrol, "Essai sur les moeurs," p. 482).

[42] G. Baer, "Social Change in Egypt," p. 150.

[43] No study has been made of the distribution of staples in the urban center but Ira Lapidus in a paper on "The Grain Economy of Mamlūk Egypt" states that "there is good reason to believe that the essential structures of the grain economy were the same in both previous and subsequent epochs" (*Journal of the Economic and Social History of the Orient*, XII (1969), pp. 2, 11).

Lastly, we should not fail to mention the great public *waqf*s as well as lesser pious foundations, often locally oriented, which were directed at gaining the support of the lower orders.

By and large the amīrs did not indulge in economic speculation except that which was likely to yield substantial and dependable returns. Thus urban industries were of little interest to them,[44] although they did invest in urban properties. The lucrative trade in coffee presented an attraction and a number of Janissaries even made commercial trips to Ḥijāz.[45]

The pattern of investment of the middle orders of society followed a similar pattern with some differences; differences which depended upon the differential of power and their special connections. Both the elite and persons of the middle orders made heavy investment in urban real estate both because such holdings could be a key to new revenue, prestige, and the political control of quarters, and because diversified holdings in real estate were less subject to confiscation or seizure in political struggles than were large scale possesions of land or of *iltizām*s.[46] The ability to successfully administer landed wealth, moreover, involved the ability to protect it from bedouin incursions as well as to have rural connections to administer it.[47]

---

[44] André Raymond draws particular attention to the neglect of industry by the elite:

> "One must count also among the principal reasons for the stagnation and industrial decline in Egypt the indifference of the political power which was scarcely interested in productive activities for the purpose of exploiting them; the sole example of the intervention of the rulers in this domain is, to our knowledge, the installation by Muḥammad bey Abū Dahab, in the enclosure of the mosque of Ibn Ṭūlūn, of an atelier for the manufacture of wool" (*Artisans et commerçants*, I, p. 212-213).

[45] See A. Raymond, *Artisans et commerçants*, II, pp. 712, 717-718. There seems, in fact, to have been considerable involvement of the military in the coffee trade. Jazzār Aḥmad Pasha mentions specifically the *sarrājūn* who were affiliated with the Janissary corps:

> "When one of these *sarrāces* has served for several years (as a mounted servant) his Āğā secures for him a place ... on the roll of a corps. He cancels his monthly allowance ... and makes him a partner (*Şerik*) of a wealthy man belonging to the guild of Cidde merchants. In this way they employ him, and then they call him *Yoldāş* ... These *Yoldāşes* travel to Cidde every year with boats from the port of Suez. They trade in coffee and other merchandise and gradually procure capital. Among them are some old ... merchants who have been able to amass as much as five hundred or one thousand purses and who have properties and households ... These (men) are also called *Tuccār* (merchants)" (S. J. Shaw, *Ottoman Egypt in the Eighteenth Century*, pp. 24-26).

[46] Afaf Loutfi al-Sayyid Marsot, "A Socio-economic Sketch of the ᶜ*Ulamā*ᵓ in the Eighteenth Century," *Colloque international sur l'histoire du Caire*, p. 317.

[47] The beys administered their rural holdings through their *kāshif*s and the only others who successfully maintained rural *iltizām*s were ᶜ*ulamā*ᵓ of peasant origin

A survey of the architectural remains of the medieval period or a walk in the older parts of Cairo even today reveals the vast amount which must have been spent in the Ottoman period in the establishment not only of mosques, but of *sabīls* (fountains), *ḥammāms* (baths), and *rab*ᶜs ("tenements"). The usual practice was first to buy one's own residence and then to acquire, if possible, other buildings and shops.[48] It is important to note that usually these shops were not of an industrial nature but that they rather sold finished wares or prepared commodities in which their owners also traded.[49] Baths were not usually managed by their owners but would be operated by lower middle class entrepreneurs who would pay monthly rent. Such tenants would not only equip the *ḥammām* but would undertake required repairs. On the whole such urban businesses could be quite lucrative for both the lessee and the owner.[50]

In the latter part of the Ottoman period the *ᶜulamāᵓ* came to the fore as investors in commerce, for the Mamlūks who in earlier times had invested in the import-export trade now found their wealth taken up by the military and political demands of their internal struggle, and other persons who had no strong political connections either foreign or domestic found it impossible to defend such investments. Thus the religious elite capitalized anew upon their role as middlemen, since for centuries they had maintained ties both with Mamlūks and with merchants.

Like the elite, the *ᶜulamāᵓ* and merchants expended substantial amounts of their riches in redistribution.[51] Shaykh as-Sādāt and

(A. Loutfi al-Sayyid Marsot, "A Socio-economic Sketch of the ᶜ*Ulamāᵓ* in the Eighteenth Century," p. 816). On the other hand André Raymond points out that the investment in rural and urban tax farms by the great merchants in the long run drew capital from the commercial speculations which had been the original and essential source of their power (*Artisans et commerçants*, II, p. 817).

[48] For instance, Shaykh ᶜAbdallāh ash-Sharqāwī's wife, who managed his money for him, bought him several houses, shops, baths, and *wakālas*, all of which paid him monthly rents (al-Jabartī, ᶜ*Ajāᵓib al-Āthār*, IV, p. 172; *Merveilles biographiques et historiques*, VIII, p. 364).

[49] Thus Shaykh Muḥammad al-Bakrī al-Kabīr who traded in grain, coffee, and indigo which he sold in both raw and manufactured form, owned flour mills, coffee houses, and buildings for the storage of indigo (A. Loutfi al-Sayyid Marsot, "A Socio-economic Sketch of the ᶜ*Ulamāᵓ* in the Eighteenth Century," p. 317).

[50] According to Chabrol, a bath could be furnished with from 9,000-90,000 *paras*, depending upon its size and elegance. Income from such ranged widely but the establishment of one bath man in 1692 gained him a small fortune of 146,198 *paras* (A. Raymond, "Les bains publics au Caire à la fin du XVIIIème siècle," p. 143).

[51] In al-Jabartī we find a succinct description of the typical pattern of investment: "In our time, the importance of a man results from the grandeur of his house,

Shaykh al-Bakrī not only managed the distribution of pious *waqfs* but were expected to provide from their own revenues the public expenses for the celebration of the great *mawlids* and feasts: the two eids, the *mawlid* of the Prophet, the *mawlid* of Sayyidna al-Ḥusayn, and the *mawlids* of Sayyida Nafīsa, Sayyida Zaynab, and the Imām ash-Shāfiᶜī. Some of these lasted for several days or nearly half a month and the populace looked forward to them with great expectation. The ash-Sharāᵓibīs especially were known for their benevolence. Sīdī Ibrāhīm, grandson of Muḥammad ad-Dāda ash-Sharāᵓibī, not only endowed *sabīls* and *kuttābs* (Qurᵓān schools), but distributed books to students who were children of the poor. [52] It was said that when the ash-Sharāᵓibīs celebrated a wedding they would give sumptuous feasts and feed Qurᵓān scholars and the poor, and that their table was always abundantly prepared to receive whatever guests might come. [53]

Last but not least were investments in *waqf*, especially *waqf ahlī* to ensure income for one's house or descendants. Private individuals could even purchase *iltizāms* and donate these, stipulating both the *nāẓir* (supervisor) and the beneficiary. Although Muḥammad ᶜAlī confiscated such *waqfs*, he did not prohibit the establishment of new ones. In 1854 Shaykh al-Bakrī who, through patronage of the ruler, had prospered, provided for his family with a *waqf* that included 10,000 Egyptian pounds worth of urban real estate and jewelry, baths, shops, *wakālas*, and other things, as well as 272 feddans of good land near Cairo. [54]

To draw together some main points, the first and most obvious conclusion is that the economic sphere was firmly tied to other spheres of endeavor in Cairene life; the returns of investment were social and political as well as economic just as the sources of wealth were tapped and secured primarily through social and political power. As in the Mamlūk period, the upper classes expended many of their resources in the acquisition of slaves, positions, and other prestige

---

the richness of his habits, and the great quantity of his rents and the great number of his servants and this importance is augmented when the person who enjoys these advantages possesses also some of those qualities which interest other men, beneficence and hospitality" (*ᶜAjāᵓib al-Āthār*, IV, p. 186; *Merveilles biographiques et historiques*, IX, p. 42).

52 Al-Jabartī, *ᶜAjāᵓib al-Āthār*, II, p. 213; *Merveilles biographiques et historiques*, V, p. 133.

53 Al-Jabartī, *ᶜAjāᵓib al-Āthār*, I, pp. 204-205; *Merveilles biographiques et historiques*, II, p. 144.

54 A. Loutfi al-Sayyid Marsot, "A Socio-economic Sketch of the *ᶜUlamāᵓ* in the Eighteenth Century," p. 318.

items. However the Ottoman period differed in an important respect. Increased political instability together with monetization meant more mobility within the hierarchy. As rank and position itself came on the market and the elite found themselves hard-pressed, they found it difficult to maintain their separateness through emphasis upon ethnic criteria and exclusive possession of prestige goods.

With the decline of the power of the elite, there was a relative increase in the economic and political power of the lower orders of society. However in an absolute sense these did not become more affluent because of the huge drains upon the economy caused by absorption of wealth in factional strife and the slipping away of revenues to foreign sources of power. There was no overturning of the hierarchy because the traditional ideas of social organization which established it were never questioned and because the political game played within its framework was regarded as inevitable.

2. *Guilds and the Structure of Work: The Articulation of the Social Hierarchy*

The social hierarchy that served as a framework for the production, distribution, and the exchange of wealth was delineated in part by the corporations of work. Materials of the Ottoman period give the first concrete evidence of occupational associations outside the sphere of the elite and the notables,[55] evidence that reflects not only formal

[55] It is not our purpose here to enter into the discussion and speculation surrounding the origin of the guilds. It is necessary, however, to consider the meaning of the term before considering the implications of such groups for the organization of society as a whole. In the first place, it would certainly be ethnocentric naiveté to expect to find guilds in Near Eastern society that paralleled European guilds in all respects, or to suppose that because such are not found, there were no guilds. In the second place, there can be no doubt that the claim that *formal* occupational corporations of any kind existed in Egypt before the middle of the sixteenth century rests upon sheer speculation. On the other hand, it is equally certain that there had always been at least an informal ranking of occupations as well as a degree of organization of persons who engaged in the same or related crafts in a single area, and that informal leadership to facilitate the solution of common problems must have emerged from time to time. That the emergence of guilds is shrouded in darkness and even the Ottoman manifestation is blurred by ambiguity should surprise no one, for it is the ambiguity that is basic and not the definition. (Note the number of Arabic terms used to designate such groupings: *ḥirfa, ṣanᶜa,* meaning "craft" or "trade," and *ṭāᵓifa*, meaning "group" were frequently used, and we also find *ṣinf*, "sort" or "kind".) The solution, in the last analysis, lies in the realization that from the sociological point of view, the concept of "corporation" entails that such a group be socially, not necessary legally, recognized. If members of a group are bound by common goals, obligations, and rights and recognize a leader or leaders, they can be considered as having corporate unity. Moreover there can be semi-corporate groups having corporate

rules of organization, but basic trends of social life in all its contradictions and exigencies of operation.

Before considering the way in which the occupational organizations fitted into the complex society with which we are dealing, it is proper to establish the prevalence of these groupings on the urban scene. In the first place it should be noted that contemporary lists of guilds differ in both the number and classification of corporations. The picture is invariably complicated by the existence of specialized subdivisions and local branches. There is, on the other hand, remarkable consistency between the list of 293 guilds made by Evliya Chelebi who visited Cairo in the 1670's and the one made by the French some 120 years later which indicated 278 corporations. [56]

The guild system embraced persons of diverse statuses and backgrounds. The whole professionally active population was organized in guilds. Even in the upper classes of society, where guilds did not exist, other organizations to some extent paralleled these associations in structure and in function; the Mamlūk *bayt*, for instance, the military corps, or the *ṭāʾifa* (group) of scholars inhabiting a section of al-Azhar. Guilds included not only artisans and performers of services but people engaged in transport, there were not only the self-employed but the privately employed and the employees of government. Some were rich, some, poor; some enjoyed high repute while others were degraded through professions of defilement, debauchery, and crime. [57]

---

attributes (see p. 3 above). There is some indication that the Ottoman regime encouraged such loose groupings and deliberately formalized them to facilitate social control through the articulation of social life. In any case it was the explicit formalization of occupational organization through the institution of guilds, rather than an ill-defined occupational structure, that was exceptional. Gabriel Baer, who has investigated the subject thoroughly, writes:

> "What happened was that at a certain juncture, apparently during the first half of the sixteenth century, there occurred a transition from free associations (i.e., *fütüvvet* and *ahi* associations) to professional guilds, probably under the auspices of the official authorities. Part of the newly established guilds, but not all of them, kept some of the traditions of the old free associations, and many of the social functions of the guilds apparently were based on these" ("Administrative, Economic, and Social Functions of Turkish Guilds," *International Journal of Middle East Studies*, I (1970), p. 49).

Regarding the initial appearance of the guilds, see also A. Raymond, *Artisans et commerçants*, II, pp. 529-538.

[56] Gabriel Baer, *Egyptian Guilds in Modern Times* (Jerusalem: The Israel Oriental Society, 1964), p. 3. Cf. A. Raymond, *Artisans et commerçants*, II, pp. 508-509.

[57] The size of guilds also varied. The largest included those who carried water on donkeys (8,000 members), makers and sellers of shoes (5,500 members), sellers of grain (3,800 members), millers (3,160 members), weavers, tailors, barbers, carpenters,

There is little question, therefore, that the institution of the guild was basic to the economic aspect of the urban network and that the relations which pertained to the system of corporations generally coincided with and reinforced most basic kinds of relationships but cross-cut others. It should be noted at the outset that the guilds cannot properly be understood apart from the organization and conditions of society as a whole. The guild organization interacted with the organization of the state on the one hand, even as it was interwoven with the organization of special status groups, families, and quarters on the other. Moreover patron-client ties shaped the guilds even as they shaped most other urban institutions.

Considering the hierarchy of social classes, there was a relatively great contrast between the import-export merchants (*tujjār*) who were closely allied to the upper ranks of the military and the artisans and small merchants who were relatively weak both politically and economically. A life in commerce, generally speaking, seems to have been more lucrative than a life spent in industry [58] but it is also true that commerce and industry were not completely divorced since usually artisans sold the products that they manufactured in their small shops. [59]

The organization of merchants seems to have involved a number of factors simultaneously: the products of trade, localization, ethnicity, and family. There were several types of corporations that were constituted of merchants. Thus the successor of the *wakīl at-tujjār* (agent of merchants) of earlier epochs was the *shāhbandar*, whose title was of Persian derivation and applied in particular to the chief of merchants who dealt in coffee and spices. This influential group, because of its

---

donkey men, and water carriers (3,000 each). The smallest guilds had but a very few members: grinders and makers of ink (6 members each), engravers of seals (3 members) and finishers of turbans (3 members). Some of the variation related to the localization of groupings as well as to the tendency toward extreme subdivision of technique (A. Raymond, *Artisans et commerçants*, II, pp. 514-515).

[58] A. Raymond, *Artisans et commerçants*, I, pp. 238-239; II, 811. From his extensive research in the archives of the Cairo *Maḥkama Sharᶜīya* (Sharīᶜa Court) André Raymond concludes that the great merchants held 93.2% of the total amount of inheritances of over 50,000 *paras* registered between 1679 and 1700, although they represented only 39% of the total number. For the period 1776-1798, 27.7% were merchants who held 88.4% of the total sum (*ibid.*, p. 401). Regarding the fortunes of artisans, in 1679-1700 and 1776-1790, the average fortune of an artisan was not more than a fifth of that of a merchant. Compared with the average fortune of a merchant excluding the great *tujjār*, the average fortune of an artisan was 72% at the end of the seventeenth century and 44% at the end of the eighteenth (A. Raymond, *Artisans et commerçants*, I, p. 238-239).

[59] A. Raymond, *Artisans et commerçants*, II, p. 521.

ties with the rulers, generally succeeded in escaping the control of the *muḥtasib* (market inspector). [60] Merchants were also grouped through the corporations of *sūqs*: the merchants of the Khān al-Khalīlī who dealt in valuable goods of the transit trade, and the merchants of the Sūq aṣ-Ṣāgha, which was the center of the gold trade. Likewise certain large *wakālas* formed their own corporations. The Wakāla al-Jallāba was the seat of a corporation of traders in black slaves. [61]

Special status also stands out as a major factor of solidarity in merchant corporations at all social levels. Merchants involved in domestic commerce as opposed to import-export merchants were often non-Muslims. Copts, Jews, Greek Orthodox and Greek Catholics were often retail merchants. These sold such things as green groceries, clothing, haberdashery, miscellaneous furnishings, and small wares and owned many shops. [62] The Turks and the Maghribīs both had large investments in commerce. The latter formed a community (*ṭāʾifa*) whose leaders (*kubarāʾ al-maghāriba*) would be called upon by the government from time to time, both for attendance at official ceremonies and for purposes of extracting "loans" and "contributions." [63]

Family ties were an essential part of corporate success. The *tujjār* of the Ottoman period, like their predecessors the Kārimīs, were connected by a multiplicity of marriage bonds. [64] The ash-Sharāʾibīs, probably the most successful merchant family in the eighteenth century, had a corporation of their own. Al-Jabartī tells us that:

> The members of the ash-Sharāʾibī family always entrusted to one of them the care of attending their affairs. That one had under his orders the clerk and the collector: he received all the revenues, rents, crops, and other things. He made a division of the profit and paid each member of the family his share including their expenses for clothes, light for summer, heavy for winter, and pocket money. At the end of the year he would prepare the balance ... This rule was observed for a long time among the family, but with the death of the elders, the younger members quarreled. Each went his own way with what he received; they separated and their prosperity left them. [65]

The relative placement of occupational corporations in hierarchical order, as well as the movement of individuals and groups within the

[60] Cf. A. Raymond, *Artisans et commerçants*, II, pp. 579, 581.

[61] A. Raymond, *Artisans et commerçants*, II, pp. 521-522.

[62] F. Mengin, *Histoire de l'Égypte*, II, pp. 271-272, 276, 282-283.

[63] André Raymond, "*Tunisiens et Maghrébins au Caire*," p. 362.

[64] A. Raymond, *Artisans et commerçants*, II, p. 412.

[65] *ʿAjāʾib al-Āthār*, I, p. 204-205; *Merveilles biographiques et historiques*, II, pp. 145-146.

hierarchy, had two principal aspects. First there were the "ideal" rules of ranking, subject of course, to interpretation, and then there were real factors of social, political, and economic power. From the formal point of view, ranking had primary relation to "religious" criteria and especially to the line of "spiritual descent" of the guild. The highest ranking guilds, according to guild lore, went back to original patrons or practitioners among the Companions of the Prophet. [66] The shaykhs of such guilds could perform the four-knot *shadd* ceremony [67] for all guilds. Other guilds that could not claim a Companion as an original founder tied only three knots symbolizing their incomplete chain of tradition. Still others were thought to fall outside the scope of Islamic tradition altogether, such as "Sāsān's guilds" [68] which supposedly had a separate spiritual basis.

On the whole, although certainly not without exception, [69] the formal ranking of guilds mirrored realistic considerations of economic power and influential connections. Persons who were entrusted with the valuable possessions of others and whose occupations required learning, physicians, barbers, weighers, druggists, and booksellers, ranked in the first category, while just after these came the wealthy guilds of corn merchants, rice merchants, and furriers, among others. Interestingly enough, saddlers were also high ranking, which can possibly be explained by the emphasis upon the equestrian arts in Mamlūk times and among Arabs generally. The lowest ranks included despised and "unclean" occupational groups, the immoral guilds, or persons who were the object of scorn and derision for other reasons. Beggars, scavengers, pickpockets, prostitutes, and rogues, as well as black slave dealers (not white slave dealers) were of this category, while cooks, bakers, butchers, porters, and dyers among others belonged to the guilds of the common people. [70]

---

[66] G. Baer, *Egyptian Guilds*, pp. 33-37.

[67] A central feature of the initiation ceremony was the ritual of the waist belt (*shadd*) of the candidate which was tied with four knots: the first in the name of his master, the second in the name of the shaykh of the guild or of his master's master, the third for the legendary patron, and the fourth for ᶜAlī.

[68] The term "Sāsān's guilds" refers to the Sāsānid dynasty of Persia overthrown by the Arabs in A.D. 640. Despite the fact that much guild tradition comes from Persian (Shīᶜī) sources, many disreputable persons including gypsies were known by the generic term "Sons of Sāsān" (*Banū Sāsān*).

[69] Thus collectors of customs, despite their affluence, were of low rank as they could not claim a patron among the Companions of the Prophet (G. Baer, *Egyptian Guilds*, pp. 33-37).

[70] For lists of guilds and their ranks during the seventeenth century, see G. Baer, *Egyptian Guilds*, pp. 35-39.

15. The Slave Market.

The internal structure of the guild formed the basis of its role in the transmission of authority. In brief, the members of the guild were theoretically graded in four ranks representing stages of occupational proficiency and degrees of acceptance into the group, from the first and second stages of apprenticeship, to the stage of worker, and finally that of master, which carried with it the license (*ijāza*) to open a shop. All personal claims against a candidate by other guild members had to be settled before the *shadd* ceremony could be performed.

The chief officers of the guild were also four in number: the shaykh; his deputy, the *naqīb*; and the two substitutes of the *naqīb*. It is significant, however, that there was a formal power hierarchy and a real power hierarchy. Masters who had attained considerable economic and social standing were known by other titles which, interestingly enough, were the same as the titles held by village heads and other local authorities. Thus the *ᶜumda* (pl. *ᶜumad*) acted in an advisory capacity to the shaykh, the *mukhtār* assisted him in his duties, and the *raʾīs* was the experienced foreman of a group of workers. These, in fact, wielded much more power than the substitutes of the *naqīb* who were his successors in office. While there seemed to be a surfeit of official duties and positions, there also was no lack of ambiguity when it came to real delegation of authority, as will become more evident as we proceed.

But we do not wish to dwell on the formalities of occupational grouping. Rather our aim is to see how the guilds operated in real life. The paramount facts that emerge from this perspective are the definitive and domineering role of government and the popular reaction, often a reaction of contestation, to this role. Egyptian guilds were not simply tools of government, although they may have been developed as such in Ottoman times, nor were they basically manifestations of communal spirit organized and given expression by the popular will. Rather with shifts in the balance of power, they seem to have fluctuated between these two poles of orientation.

Of the two highest ranking officers, the shaykh, of course, was the most important. [71] The candidate for this office had to give evidence

[71] For the most part, while he benefited from the special connections and functions of his office, the shaykh of the artisanal guild was not very wealthy. It would appear that by and large, his condition of life was not much more luxurious than that of his fellow craftsmen. In general, his economic position was determined by the nature of his craft. Between 1776 and 1798 five shaykhs left fortunes of more than 50,000 *paras* but these did not exceed that amount by very much (A. Raymond, *Artisans et commerçants*, II, p. 396).

of proficiency in theology as well as a thorough knowledge of the craft. Ideally, the most respected persons of the guild selected one of their number to occupy the office and then he was appointed by consensus of all guild members. Ordinarily the choice was subject to confirmation by the government; during much of the period, this meant the āghā and *kākhya* of the Janissaries. As time wore on, however, especially at the end of the period, the government more frequently made the nomination.[72] There was a marked tendency for shaykhs to be succeeded by their sons. The members of the guild, nevertheless, always retained the right to depose a shaykh if his conduct was not satisfactory.[73] While the shaykh's superior authority was undisputed, he consulted the *ᶜumad* on all matters of importance such as the appointment of officers, the apportionment of taxes between members, and the arbitration of disputes.

The role played by the shaykh in the maintenance of social control was probably more significant than that of any other individual in the town. He was held responsible by the authorities for the conduct of members of his corporation and consequently had considerable administrative and even judicial power.[74] He was authorized not only to close the shop of an offender and exclude him from the corporation, but also to impose fines and inflict corporal punishment. This authority, however, was established by custom and not primarily by law. Its source lay in the confidence and respect he commanded among guild members.

The most important administrative function of the guild was the collection of taxes.[75] All rulers, up until the latter part of the nine-

---

[72] During the time of Muḥammad ᶜAlī it was usual for the richest and most prominent of the guild masters to suggest his candidacy to his most respected peers and, having received their consent, to approach the government and finally receive official appointment from the Pasha (G. Baer, *Egyptian Guilds*, p. 71).

[73] Even when the government was decisive in the appointment of shaykhs, consent of guild members was required. In some cases even an annual "vote of confidence" was customary. Chabrol wrote that:

> "At the end of the year, if the artisans had no complaint against their shaykh and wanted to keep him, he could not be changed by the chief of police (*kikhyā al-mutawallī*) ... (but) when the workers were not happy with him, the *kikhyā* had to name another" ("Essai sur les moeurs," p. 553).

André Raymond, however, notes that this procedure was exceptional (*Artisans et commerçants*), II, p. 553).

[74] A. Raymond, *Artisans et commerçants*, II, p. 562.

[75] A function which, according to Baer, is considerably more evident in sources on Egyptian guilds than sources on Turkish ones ("Guilds in Middle Eastern History," *Studies in the Economic History of the Middle East*, edited by M. A. Cook, p. 20).

teenth century, realized the importance of retaining the guilds as administrative units and of controlling these cells through their respective leaders. It was the development of centralized political power that brought about the practice of governmental appointment of shaykhs.

To supervise the guilds more effectively, the rulers eventually grouped them in three general categories, each responsible to a special officer who collected their tax. The *amīn al-khurda* was in charge of the sellers of small wares (*khurda*), gardeners, and entertainers. The *muḥtasib* was in charge of the guilds of sellers of comestibles, woodworkers, and candle makers. The *miᶜmār bāshā* or chief architect supervised shaykhs of the guilds having to do with construction: builders, masons, carpenters, and architects. [76] In general, the practice seems to have been that the government would impose payment of a fixed sum upon the guild which the shaykh, in his turn, would apportion among the members. [77]

One of the effects of the development of the guild system was that it encouraged monopoly. [78] The structure of industry was already fractionated by specialization of technique and the localization of specific groups of practitioners. Sons followed fathers in the trade and artisans, like merchants, espoused their daughters to followers of their same profession. [79] To further ensure control the rulers encouraged the development of monopolistic practices. Not only was it a general rule that a shaykh had the sole right to issue licenses for the practice of the occupation, but restrictions were imposed upon the number of people exercising a given trade in a specific quarter. [80] The mechanism

In the seventeenth century the officers of the pasha's household and the *muḥtasib* competed for control of the taxes paid by the guilds. When the pasha was deposed, however, they fell under the jurisdiction of the *muḥtasib* whose office was controlled by the Janissaries.

76 G. Baer, *Egyptian Guilds*, p. 43.

77 al-Jabartī, *ᶜAjāᵓib al-Āthār*, II, pp. 151-152; *Merveilles biographiques et historiques*, V, pp. 5-6. This system was adopted by the French. In 1800 Menou levied a tax upon all the guilds, not only merchants and artisans, but tax collectors, measurers, and weighers. Muḥammad ᶜAlī's capitation tax, as well as the new professional duties instituted by him, was collected through the offices of the shaykhs of the guilds.

78 See G. Baer, "Monopolies and Restrictive Practices of Turkish Guilds," *Journal of the Economic and Social History of the Orient*, 13 (1970), pp. 145-165.

79 A. Raymond, *Artisans et commerçants*, II, p. 379.

80 The Mamlūks too, had had a practice called *taḥkīr*, which required traders, especially dealers in food stuffs, to gather in one place. This greatly facilitated supervision of the markets and gave the amīrs increased opportunity to exploit their urban properties through increasing rents on shops that they owned (I. M. Lapidus, *Muslim Cities in the Later Middle Ages*, p. 100).

which limited the expansion of local corporations was the *gedik* [81] which was the heritable right to exercise a trade in a specific shop for which the occupant paid rent. The *gedik* could be sold, but only to another person who was qualified professionally, with the consent of the shaykh of the guild. As long as the number of *gedik*s remained the same, therefore, the guild could restrict its membership, although the treasury possessed the right to create a new *gedik* for payment if the applicant proved himself capable of carrying on the craft. [82] The fractionation of technique, the encapsulation of each group, limited its horizons and generally inhibited the diffusion of new ideas. As André Raymond has observed:

> Technique was jealously guarded and transmitted within families without the risk of any innovation disturbing the natural order. [83]

Despite the fact that government control was extensive, it can be observed that in a number of respects the guilds continued to symbolize and to express popular interests. At every crack in the elite power structure, in fact, the non-elite groups seemed to assert themselves.

In the first place, guilds drew much of their strength from the fact that they were composed of individuals who knew one another, even as the shaykh's control was only effective because he knew each individually. Most of the guilds were confined to a single quarter, and if the occupation was common, practiced in all parts of the city, usually there were a number of corporations relating to separate quarters. [84] The special status of the practitioners too, was important, for ties of religion and ethnicity did much to intensify social bonds. With few exceptions, members of a guild shared ties of religion or ethnicity.

---

[81] This is a Turkish word which came to replace the Arabic term, *khilw* which appears on documents anterior to the seventeenth century (A. Raymond, *Artisans et commerçants*, I, p. 271).

[82] H. A. R. Gibb and H. Bowen, *Islamic Society and the West*, I, 1, p. 282; G. Baer, *Egyptian Guilds*, p. 107; A. Raymond, *Artisans et commerçants*, I, p. 271.

[83] *Artisans et commerçants*, II, p. 378.

[84] André Raymond, commenting on the list of the *Description*, notes that there was great variety in the territorial extension of guilds, some being limited to Cairo, Old Cairo, Giza, or to Būlāq, but others apparently pertaining to the whole agglomeration ("Une liste des corporations de métiers au Caire en 1801," *Arabica*, IV (1957), p. 154). The list mentions a number of associations which were quite specifically localized, such as the "Cloth Merchants of the Khān al-Khalīlī," the "Butchers of Sheep of the Khalīfa Quarter in Cairo," the "Grain Merchants of the Gamālīya Quarter," and the "Grave Diggers of the Cemeteries of the Quarter of the Bāb an-Naṣr." The locality of others like the "Jewelers and Goldsmiths" (*ṣāgha*),

The element of religion and "spiritual power" had essential importance where the guilds are concerned and we have already seen how the popular forces contested the power of the elite through the sanctions of religion, made articulate by the *ᶜulamāʾ*. The conceptual system by which most guilds were classified bore strong relation to the traditions of Ṣūfism as well as to the *futūwa* associations. [85] Both the content and the pattern of the initiation ceremonies of craft organizations closely paralleled those of religious orders. [86]

The persistent tendency toward autonomy of the guild can also be seen in the insistence upon assemblies and upon convening for the purpose of expressing a collective viewpoint. The author of a seventeenth century manuscript states that if a shaykh does not hold meetings or conduct them properly, he should be dismissed. [87]

It should be taken into account, when considering the importance of guild meetings, that the only evidence we have of *regular* meetings of a guild pertains to weekly congregations of the storytellers' corporation in a coffee house (1809). [88] On the other hand, many occasions called for assembly, as when members had to decide upon new admissions. [89] It is indisputable that there were frequent gatherings of guild members at feasts, festivals, and ceremonies; in short, upon nearly every occasion that had importance in the social life of the time. Guilds always figured prominently in the annual departure of the pilgrim caravan and frequently marched in procession at wed-

---

and the "Druggists" is not pinpointed by the list but we know their positions from other sources. Organizations concerned with transport, peddlers, entertainers, and those whose services involved the whole town seem to have included persons of different regions but it is evident that these too were often subdivided by locality, as were the "Water Carriers of the Bāb al-Lūq."

[85] The "four gateways," for example, are found also in Baktāshism and the Baktāshī order itself was an integral part of the Janissary organization and the few other occupational groups which belonged to it. See G. G. Arnakis," Futuwwa Traditions in the Ottoman Empire-Akhis, Bektashi Dervishes, and Craftsmen," *Journal of Near Eastern Studies*, XII (1953), pp. 232-252; also A. Raymond, *Artisans et commerçants*, II, pp. 529-533.

[86] Although there is not much evidence to indicate a regular correspondence between religious orders and guilds, as has been claimed by many writers, it is significant that the author of a seventeenth century manuscript laments the degeneration of guild traditions, the neglect of guild lore, and contemporary laxity with regard to the ceremonies of initiation (Kitāb adh-Dhakhāʾir wa at-Tuḥaf fī Bīr aṣ-Ṣanāʾiᶜ wa al-Ḥiraf, Landesbibliothek of Gotha, Arabische Handschrift No. 903).

[87] G. Baer, *Egyptian Guilds*, p. 57.

[88] *Ibid.*, p. 116.

[89] A. Raymond, *Artisans et commerçants*, II, p. 560.

dings of Cairo's elite.[90] Moreover, as members were almost always united as well by social bonds external to occupational ties, there can be no doubt that these groups were characterized by considerable solidarity, albeit a solidarity not exclusively based upon professional affiliation, and perhaps even of an informal nature. The fact that the rulers encouraged and tried to tap this solidarity in their attempts to grasp the reins of social power is ample testimony to the fact that it existed.

To summarize a few main points, it is our contention that Egyptian guilds, unlike European guilds, were never really autonomous corporate bodies with economic and social functions that set them apart from society as a whole. It is our contention that this situation pertained because of the lack of a formal concept of "corporation" in Islam, because of the character of the social fabric in which, for much of the time, there really was no stable, well-defined elite group, and finally, because of the social and economic policy of the Ottoman government toward the guilds. Theoretically, "guild-type" organizations can be arranged on a continuous scale of "corporateness" even as they can be seen to fall along a continuum between absolute autonomy and determination from above. It is historical fact that, aside from whatever potentialities for developing as autonomous organs of popular expression the guilds may have had, throughout most of the period they were controlled from above, either through Ottoman supervisors or individual patrons. Even with regard to overseeing the quality of goods produced and sold and their provision to the public (an economic function that might be assumed paramount), responsibility fell to the *muḥtasib* or other governmental officers who looked upon the leaders of corporations as their assistants.

It is of considerable interest, moreover, that despite the social power inherent in the structure of the guild, there is little evidence for economic liaisons between guild members except for partnerships between a few individuals for the pooling of capital.[91] Although many claims have been made that the guilds provided for the needs

[90] Al-Jabartī, *ᶜAjāᵓib al-Āthār*, IV, pp. 198-199: 200-201; *Merveilles biographiques et historiques*, IX, pp. 66-69; *ᶜAjāᵓib al-Āthār*, II, p. 224; *Merveilles biographiques et historiques*, V, p. 153. In the 1670's there were 30 groups of guilds that regularly marched in processions, each headed by a government officer who "protected" them and collected their taxes. Upon occasion they were even mustered to supply non-combatant support for military campaigns (al-Jabartī, *ᶜAjāᵓib al-Āthār*, III, p. 6; *Merveilles biographiques et historiques*, VI, p. 14; G. Baer, *Egyptian Guilds*, p. 19).

[91] A. Raymond, *Artisans et commerçants*, II, p. 567.

of the poor among them,[92] it is difficult to find any specific examples of such mutual assistance, aside from a single instance of the shoemakers' guild in which copper vessels presented to the shaykh as an initiation fee were rented out for celebrations and the income used to help members in distress. Upon occasion, a master of this same guild who was in need of assistance would invite his fellows to a private celebration and receive from them presents to help him through the crisis. That mutual economic cooperation between members of the same guild was not more developed is perhaps to be explained by the fact that such assistance was often supplied on the basis of religious association or even more directly, on the basis of family ties. Moreover, if we consider the guild as an institution that was shaped not only by horizontal ties between members of the same class, but also by vertical liaisons to the rest of society (i.e., the government, patrons, and clients), then further explanations emerge. The picture will become clearer as we consider first the question of mobility and then the financial arrangements of business.

In general, the question of mobility relates to the structure of the corporation, the nature of the occupation, and also to the external forces tending toward "infiltration." With regard to structure, the deficiencies or gaps in the chain of tradition or "neglect" of initiation ritual simply reflect the fact that many of the guilds of the lowest rank were those which required a short period of occupational training or little experience.[93] A large percentage of the working population was included in these organizations which comprised all of the domestic

---

[92] Nada Tomiche, "La situation des artisans et petit commerçants en Égypte de la fin du XVIIIème siècle jusqu'au milieu du XIXème," *Studia Islamica*, XII (1960), pp. 91-92.

[93] It is revealing for the question of mobility that sources of the eighteenth and nineteenth centuries do not mention the ritual or the contract that marked the beginning of apprenticeship. From Jomard's account of initiation rites in the *Description*, it would appear that the period of journeymanship was often by-passed altogether ("Description abrégée de la ville," p. 699). Another report of the 1870's states that:

> " 'each guild admits of three degrees of qualification: Moallem (master), Sanayee (Foreman) and Ashrack (Apprentice) ... these degrees are not conferred, as a rule, according to merit or seniority, but on payment of certain sums — the perquisites of the Shaykh' " (Consul Raphael Borg quoted by G. Baer, *Egyptian Guilds*, p. 59).

It may be that lack of strictness in many of the guilds of the nineteenth century was the result of progressive deterioration which began in the Ottoman period. On the other hand, there is certainly no reason to expect that guilds of porters, donkey drivers, beggars, or water carriers ever emphasized a period of learning and experience marked by a lengthy series of ritual acts that symbolized stages of competence.

servants, porters, and laborers. Many recruits to such guilds were rural-urban migrants, *fallaḥīn* and Nubians. The vagueness of some points in the ideology as well as the existence of formal ideological bonds between guilds (i.e., traditional relationship with the same patron), permitted the accommodation of new occupational groups and facilitated the recruitment of individuals across occupational and family lines.

It should also be noted that while Islamic ideology dominated the system, Christians and Jews had guilds of their own. Furthermore it appears that some guilds were "interconfessional." Both *dhimmī*s and Muslims were among the membership of guilds of goldsmiths, tailors, and joiners in particular. It is recorded in the documents of the Maḥkama Sharᶜīya at Cairo that the estates of Christian and Jewish artisans and merchants were liquidated in the presence of Muslim shaykhs of guilds.[94] Moreover some guilds seem sometimes to have had interconfessional administration: the goldsmiths had a Muslim shaykh and a Christian *naqīb*.[95] The loose conceptual structure echoed in large degree real patterns of social, economic, and administrative relations. If such had not been the case, the formal framework would never have survived over so long a period.

Entrance into a corporation or access to the benefits of a profession could be gained also by the exercise of military or economic power. It is obvious that conditions of history would not permit continued stability of the system as it was outlined ideally, if indeed such a situation ever existed. The middle and lower class corporations were especially vulnerable to such infiltration.

To understand the processes involved we must turn our attention to the assumptions underlying the peculiar knit of the social fabric and particularly to the concepts of corporation and partnership as they exist in the ideology of Islam. As stated above, strictly speaking, Islam has no concept of a legal corporation outside of the universal community of believers and we have seen that historically no social groups, with the possible and *partial* exception of elite groups, ever succeeded in maintaining any real autonomy for any length of time.

---

94 According to Elia Qoudsī, in Damascus Christians and Jews entered Muslim guilds by simply submitting themselves to the shaykh and replacing the Muslim prayers by the Pater or the recitation of the Ten Commandments ("Notice sur les corporations de Damas," *Actes du sixième Congres International des Orientalistes*, Deuxième partie, Section I: Sémitique (Leiden, 1885), pp. 29-30).

95 A. Raymond, *Artisans et commerçants*, II, pp. 524, 525.

Moreover, the Geniza material shows that during the early and High Middle Ages at least, craftsmen and workers were not united in any kinds of organizations based on horizontal ties with their social and economic peers, but rather that they tended to undertake small scale business ventures through formation of alliances or partnerships frequently with more affluent persons who would put up capital. There is less evidence concerning the mechanism of commercial ventures during the late Middle Ages but there is certainly no reason to think that there would have been a basic change in this aspect of economic life. Patronage retained its importance in the loose structure of society and basic sociopolitical instability sustained the "substantive mentality" characteristic of subsistence economy. Evidence from the Ottoman period, as far as it goes, fits in with the same essential picture: emphasis upon personal bonds and especially upon vertical ties of patronage in a social matrix outlined by considerations of ethnicity and locale.

In the first place there was no explicit concept of "corporation" to sharply delineate the guilds from the universal Islamic polity, which is doubtless one reason why they were so closely tied to the official structure of the state. In the second place, the concept of "partnership," especially the *muḍāraba*, or commenda, facilitated the establishment of vertical bonds that, because of the real elements of economic and political power they represented, tended to counteract the emergence of horizontal dependencies. In essence, the *muḍāraba* partnership was formed when one person put up capital and the other contributed his labor, [96] and they agreed to a particular division of the profits. It was an institution that contained elements of loan and employment as well as the idea of partnership. [97] Certainly the relationship was often characterized by imbalance and this seems to have been the case more often as the period drew to a close and economic stress and inequities between classes became greater. It is significant that the

---

96 While the *muḍāraba* was not valid according to the Shāfiᶜī and Mālikī interpretations of the law which reject any partnership that requires manufacturing activity on the part of the agent, it was acceptable to the Ḥanafī persuasion. We might ask then, "Since most Egyptians were Shāfiᶜī, how can it be that such commercial arrangements were common?" The answer is simply that individual Muslims, with the exception of the high *ᶜulamāᵓ* did not have to declare for one *madhhab* or the other, and a considerable amount of "switching" and rationalization went on for the sake of necessity and convenience.

97 Cf. above, p. 63. It should be noted that such partnership in Islamic law did not entail the responsibility of one partner for the obligations contracted by the other (i.e., there was no idea that a partner could bind his partners vis-à-vis an outside party). See Abraham L. Udovitch, *Partnership and Profit in Medieval Islam*, pp. 98-99.

muḍāraba was also utilized to get around the Islamic prohibition of usury. [98]

That the guilds exhibited some serious economic and political weaknesses, then, should not be surprising and, what is more, we do not have to explain these weaknesses in terms of "degeneration." Nor does the fact that they could be infiltrated necessarily indicate a breakdown of the occupational structure, although under the economic and political pressures of the Ottoman period, that was the end result in many cases.

Turning now to the factual side of mobility and economic bonds between members of different social classes, the principal examples that stand out are cases of "partnerships" between members of the military and artisans. According to Stanford Shaw:

> Many (mamlūks) were given additional revenues by being made partners (*Şerīq*) of local merchants and artisans, whom they protected in return for specified annual shares of their profits, and some of these soldiers themselves entered trade or became artisans in preference to the military pursuits of their brothers. [99]

Especially during the eighteenth century, members of the *ojāq*s often supplemented their income by establishing a relationship with artisans and craftsmen who, in turn, had some share in the distributions made to the troops. [100] Early in the eighteenth century the government attempted to prevent further disintegration of the military corps by prohibiting any liaisons between them and the guilds, but by then it was already too late to stop the infiltration. The shaykhs of the artisans responded that "the corporations were composed, for the most part, of soldiers and soldiers' sons" and the *qāḍī* subsequently ignored the order. [101] By 1784 it was no longer possible to distinguish

---

98 According to Chabrol:

"In order to elude the commands of the law which prohibit usury, we surmise the following means. A man borrows a sum of money; the lender passes as his partner, and from that takes a legitimate part of the profit that comes from the enterprise" ("Essai sur les moeurs," p. 488).

99 *Ottoman Egypt in the Age of the French Revolution*, p. 9. See also above, p. 304.

100 These distributions, however, in case of craftsmen, had little more meaning than symbolic membership in the corps. André Raymond quotes Consul De Maillet who estimated that six to eight thousand such persons were enrolled in the corps: " 'Their pay was usually spent, as they said, by the true (Janissaries)' ..." (*Artisans et commerçants*, II, p. 703).

101 Al-Jabartī, *ᶜAjāᵓib al-Āthār*, I, p. 37; *Merveilles biographiques et historiques*, I, p. 88. It should be understood, however, that the attachment of artisans and merchants to *ojāq*s was not *en bloc*, guild by guild and *ojāq* by *ojāq*. The process of infiltration was progressive but irregular. Thus the sellers of sweets (*sukkarīya*) fell under the control of the *amīn al-khurda* who was an officer of the ᶜAzabs but some

between the lower ranks of the military and civilians of low rank. In the words of Volney: "The Janissaries, the ᶜAzabs, and five other corps are only a rabble of artisans and vagabonds." [102]

While the mechanism appears to have been nothing but extortion, and al-Jabartī presents it as such, such liaisons may not always have been disadvantageous for craftsmen. Ultimately the issue depended upon the balance of power among elite factions and especially the political fortune of elite patrons. Another isolated but significant example is found in André Raymond's statement that a long established tie existed between the house of the amīr ᶜAlī-Kākhya al-Khurbaṭlī of the *Mustaḥfiẓān* (Janissaries) (d. 1769) in the quarter of Khūshqadam, and the adjacent corporation of ᶜAqqādīn ar-Rūmī (makers of silk cord). When a mamlūk of the amīr reconstructed a mosque at the entrance of the quarter, the work was supervised by the shaykh of the corporation and shops were built at the same time around the mosque. [103]

Although it must have been comparatively easy for the military to infiltrate and impose their desires upon lower class guilds, doubtless they found middle class occupational organizations harder to manipulate. Not only did such professions (i.e., physicians, booksellers, and merchants) tend to be more specialized and restricted, but as a rule they required a long period of training, frequently accomplished in the context of the family or local group. Such relatively close-knit cells probably were more successful in withstanding external pressures, but on the other hand, even these were bound to the elite by ties of alliance. According to Le Mascrier, writing in the first part of the eighteenth century:

> The principal merchants are ᶜAzabs or Janissaries, or protegés of these corps who have bought their support. [104]

In sum, the formal articulation of the guild system appears to have been in large part the result of official Ottoman policy which sought to rule more effectively through a clearly defined social hierarchy.

---

of the members of this guild were affiliated with the Janissaries, some were affiliated with the ᶜAzabs, while others were not affiliated at all (A. Raymond, *Artisans et commerçants*, II, p. 667).

102 *Travels through Egypt and Syria*, I, p. 166.

103 "Essai de géographie des quartiers de residence aristocratique," pp. 68-69; see also al-Jabartī, *ᶜAjāᵓib al-Āthār*, I, p. 168; *Merveilles biographiques et historiques*, II, p. 60.

104 *Description de l'Égypte, composée sur les mémoires du consul de Maillet* (Paris, 1735), II, p. 202. See also above, p. 321, n. 45.

The intensification of the tendency toward monopoly encouraged popular solidarities but it also contributed to the stagnation of industry. Infiltration by the military was, in the last analysis, hardly conducive to industrial growth, but monopolistic practices were equally detrimental.

Regarding the structure of society, the guilds seem to have had an ambivalent orientation, serving sometimes as instruments of popular feeling and at other times as organs of official policy. Regardless of how or when they were founded (if indeed, they can be said to have been "founded" at a particular juncture in any real sense) [105] it was inherent in their nature as organizations composed of membership of the middle and lower orders that they would at times become instruments of social conflict. Expressions of ethnic antagonism, the Egyptian and Arab ruled against the Ottoman rulers, are found in guild literature. In the Gotha manuscript (late sixteenth or early seventeenth century) there are complaints that the Ottomans discriminated against the *awlād al-ᶜArab* by destroying their *takīya*s (monasteries). [106] While on the whole, the guilds never asserted themselves strongly against the government, rumblings of discontent would be heard from time to time. Although never as powerful as the *ᶜulamāʾ*, like the *ᶜulamāʾ*, their appearance as a political force inevitably occurred with the crumbling of state control. They emerged politically when the elite were torn by factional strife, or when invasion threatened. By the time of the French occupation, the guilds had attained such importance that their shaykhs constituted a considerable number in Napoleon's Great Dīwān.

But articulation did not only mean definition but also the establishment of relationships of connection with the outstanding elements of

[105] Gabriel Baer implies that prior to the Ottoman conquest the guilds were characterized by more "vitality" and that during the seventeenth century they degenerated through official imposition of controls and infiltration of members of the military corps into the crafts. Certainly these factors strongly counteracted the tendency of the guilds toward autonomy but the sole proof he offers that they ever were in fact organizations of independent social and political power are the laments of the author of the Gotha manuscript that the guilds had seen better days. See *Egyptian Guilds*, pp. 10, 13, 57, 68. It appears rather that *the futūwa tradition degenerated with the rise of the guilds* through its incorporation in the occupational structure. André Raymond mentions interconfessionalism in the guilds as a sign of their degeneration (*Artisans et commerçants*, II, p. 543).

[106] The same manuscript magnifies the importance of the office of the *naqīb* who, more than being simply shaykh's deputy, is charged with seeing to it that the assembly was convened properly and even watching over the shaykh's behavior and judging him if he was accused of improper conduct by guild members.

the social fabric. Realities of economic and political power opened channels for occupational mobility and the personalized institution of partnership in particular, served somewhat to cushion social stresses that resulted from economic and political inequities. However as the period wore on, the brunt of the general economic decline came to be borne principally by those who were least able to defend themselves politically. The result tended to be their estrangement from the elite given ever-increasing expression in the demonstrations of the last decades of the eighteenth century. But even then no real class consciousness emerged and the lower orders simply sat by and waited to see if new elites would turn out to be more satisfactory patrons. Their position, moreover, was not strengthened by the fact that whatever autonomy they might have had had been worn largely away in the general scramble by which not only political positions but professional rights were bought and sold.

3. *The Forces of the Market: Foreign Power and Domestic Perseverance*

The market too was an important channel for the communication of resources and another, even less organized field for the contestation of power. Here too, several levels of interest were represented: not only the Ottoman rulers, the local "Turko-Circassian" elite, and the "native" ruled, but European nations which came more and more to dominate the scene as time wore on.

The rulers involved themselves in the market both directly, through investment, administration, and monopoly, and indirectly through investment with merchant-brokers. As in the Mamlūk period, those who had the power would withhold commodities (especially grain) from the market in order to force up the price, or they would force merchants and millers to purchase such things at high prices. These practices were common and caused frequent public compliants and demonstrations, but all too frequently the central authorities would not or could not do anything to remedy the situation. Official setting of price ceilings, however, was the most usual means of the state to control the market.

Although the broad sphere of private commercial activity evident in former times had shrunk considerably from absorption of wealth in politico-military preoccupations and from the loss of Egyptian supremacy, still a large part of the distribution of grain and other comestibles as well as manufactured goods was left to merchants. At their head was the *shāhbandar* (later *sartujjār*) or "provost," officially recognized by the Ottoman government to act as their representative, arbitrate their disputes, and advise the government on matters concerning commercial affairs.[107]

It is significant that successful merchants invariably had official or unofficial ties with the rulers. Since they were not represented as a political group in the governing establishment as were the *ᶜulamā*ᵓ, no mercantile families maintained their wealth without support of native or foreign elite who in many cases may have been their "silent partners." The ash-Sharāᵓibīs made not only marriage ties with holders of military and spiritual power, but came to count several amīrs and *ᶜulamā*ᵓ among their own number.[108]

State controls of the market were exercised by a number of officials who often added to their formal authority individual officiousness and rapacity. Foremost among these was the *muḥtasib*.[109] Especially concerned with the policing of the market, he had the authority to inflict the most severe punishment without trial and to chastize evil doers on the spot.[110] Despite the power of this official the *muqāṭaᶜa* of the *muḥtasib* was the least profitable of the urban *muqāṭaᶜāt*. In

---

107 At the end of the eighteenth and the beginning of the nineteenth century, members of the powerful mercantile al-Maḥrūqī family held this post for many years and received many honors from the rulers whom they served (al-Jabartī, *ᶜAjāᵓib al-Āthār*, III, pp. 225, 293; *Merveilles biographiques et historiques*, VII, pp. 120, 300; *ᶜAjāᵓib al-Āthār*, IV, p. 176; *Merveilles biographiques et historiques*, IX, p. 20). In the time of Muḥammad ᶜAlī, the increasing centralization of urban control led to the extension of the authority of the *shāhbandar* over artisans and small shopkeepers (N. Tomiche, "La situation des artisans," p. 89).

108 Yūsuf-Bey ash-Sharāᵓibī was an amīr of the Qāsimī faction (al-Jabartī, *ᶜAjāᵓib al-Āthār*, I, p. 61; *Merveilles biographiques et historiques*, I, p. 148). When Muḥammad ad-Dāda ash-Sharāᵓibī died, all the amīrs, savants, and heads of the *madhāhib*, as well as the officers of the *ojāq*s marched in the funeral procession. Huge crowds joined in, making the cortege one of the longest ever seen (al-Jabartī, *ᶜAjāᵓib al-Āthār*, I, p. 87; *Merveilles biographiques et historiques*, I, p. 204). The second son who succeeded him, ᶜAbd ar-Raḥmān, became a *chūrbajī* (commander of a company) in the corps of *Mustaḥfiẓan* (Janissaries) (al-Jabartī, *ᶜAjāᵓib al-Āthār*, I, p. 176; *Merveilles biographiques et historiques*, II, p. 81).

109 It should be noted, however, that the *muḥtasib* did not police all of the markets. Outside of his jurisdiction were others, especially those dealing in small wares and manufactured sugar sweets, supervised by the *amīn al-khurda*.

110 The *muḥtasib* would pass through the *sūq*s proceeded by a servant carrying a pair of scales and followed by a retinue of servants and executioners. Passing from shop to shop he would check the prices of various articles and the correctness of weights and measures. It was not unusual for him to stop a servant carrying food to inquire about its price and the shop from which it was purchased. Many a small merchant trembled at the thought of encountering him. For the characteristic harshness of the *muḥtasib*, see E. W. Lane, *Manners and Customs*, p. 126.

an attempt to ensure just administration it was at first given to a *qāḍī* but finally it fell under the control of the Janissaries (*Mustaḥfiẓān*) in the eighteenth century.[111]

How then did the people defend their interests against the rapacious elite when the authorities did not administer justice? There were both overt and covert methods. Of the latter means were collusion, graft, and outright theft from warehouses. Elite owners never managed their stores directly and it is difficult to estimate the percentage of their holdings that disappeared on the way from their estates to the market. Both Shaw and Lapidus seem to feel that it was high.[112]

More openly there would be shop closings, demonstrations, and revolts. Corporations of dealers in comestibles particularly would come to the fore: the butchers of Ḥusaynīya and the handlers of grains and legumes in the Rumayla. We have noted already the role these played in the rise of Muḥammād ᶜAlī.

As in the Mamlūk period, public reactions to high prices and hoarding were frequent,[113] but unavoidably they became intertwined with the political struggles of the military. The problem worsened with the progressive devaluation of the *para.* Soldiers' riots, too, became common. In 1694 when a famine ravaged the country, there was trouble as members of the corps and pensioners received pay tickets instead of the cash due them. It became more and more difficult, moreover, to separate the lower levels of the military from the artisans. Thus when Küchük Muḥammed tried to gain control of the Janissaries, he abolished many of the protection taxes which had not only fed his rivals, but as well had been an imposition upon artisans and merchants who were affiliated with the corps.[114] Certainly effectiveness of guarantees of "protection" given by the *ojāq*s was limited by the motives and foresight of the military as well as by the effectiveness

[111] S. J. Shaw, *Financial Organization,* p. 119; also A. Raymond, *Artisans et commerçants*, II, p. 589. See above, p. 319.

[112] I. M. Lapidus, "The Grain Economy of Mamlūk Egypt," p. 7; S. J. Shaw, *Financial Organization,* p. 83.

[113] As in the Mamlūk period, there was great fluctuation in the price of wheat, the principal cause of which was the erratic behavior of the Nile flood. Especially serious crises marked the years 1694, 1705, 1716, 1717, 1722, 1731, and 1783 (A. Raymond, *Artisans et commerçants*, I, pp. 55, 105). For a summary of the popular movements of the time, see A. Raymond, "Quartiers et mouvements populaires au Caire au XVIIIème siècle," pp. 104-106; also his *Artisans et commerçants*, Chs. III, XVI.

[114] P. M. Holt, *Egypt and the Fertile Crescent,* p. 87; also his "The Career of Küçük Muḥammad," pp. 269-287; and A. Raymond, *Artisans et commerçants*, II, p. 742.

of their power. The very profits of protection taxes gave rise to conflict within the corps and increased avanias.[115] When the beys achieved ascendancy over the Janissaries in the eighteenth century, the ability of the latter to protect their clients became even more seriously limited. As in previous centuries, disturbances went on only until immediate demands were satisfied. The social climate therefore was hardly conducive to the prosperity of commerce and industry and what is more, the interests of the lower classes were so entangled in the intricate web of the social fabric that no sociopolitical remedy of the situation through revolution was possible.

The rulers of Cairo found foreign trade much less easy to manipulate than the internal market. True, Egypt still played the most important role in the distribution of commodities from the Arabian Red Sea provinces and monopolized the caravan trade from the Sudan, while the passage of the pilgrims to and from the Maghrib continued to be an important commercial event. But great changes had taken place on the international scene that had disastrous consequences for the Egyptian economy. More crippling than the diversion of trade by the Cape Route were the emergence of European economic and industrial power; forces that, in combination, greatly magnified faults that for centuries had been present in the Egyptian system.

In the last half of the sixteenth century, Spanish gold and silver began to spread into the Mediterranean area. The debasement of Ottoman currency had a serious effect upon the Egyptian currency tied to it. The *para* of silver, most used by the population, became progressively more alloyed.[116] By 1584 the Egyptian *para* lost half its silver content.[117] By 1773, ninety *para*s bought one Austrian talar but by 1835 it took 800 paras to buy one. By the time of Muḥammad ᶜAlī, foreign merchants had long refused to accept Turkish coinage and, following the balance of international power, Spanish piasters, French francs, and English pounds came successively to dominate the market.[118] Additional confusion from the plurality of currencies gave even more opportunity for manipulation and fraud. Muḥammad ᶜAlī tried to impose controls through inflicting severe punishments on persons who interfered with established currency values, clipped coins, and indulged in speculation and hoarding but then he himself tampered

[115] A. Raymond, *Artisans et commerçants*, II, pp. 727-739.
[116] A. Raymond, *Artisans et commerçants*, I, pp. 35, 40-43.
[117] H. A. R. Gibb and Harold Bowen, *Islamic Society and the West*, I, 2, p. 51.
[118] A. E. Crouchley, *Economic Development*, pp. 96, 97.

with the coinage.[119] Subsequent declarations aimed at reform had but little effect, while in the end massive government investment brought about increased inflation.

The incorporation of Egypt in the Ottoman empire had provided a basis for a commercial rebirth as merchants again moved freely within secure borders and as, in the sixteenth century, the trade in coffee came to bring tremendous profits. Indeed, Egypt regained something of its former status as the principal center of redistribution on the Eastern Mediterranean. Yet in the long run, international commerce resulted in a serious drain on the country. Egypt exported raw and semi-manufactured materials[120] but generally the value of exports was very disproportionate to imports. Where imports could not be paid for by Egyptian products they were paid for in coin.[121] The Arabian and Far Eastern trade that fed the demand for luxury goods and the high consumption of spices continued to drain Egypt of gold and silver. The Dārfūr[122] and Sennār caravans too, brought to Egypt five or six thousand slaves a year, besides ivory, gum, skins, hides, and other luxury goods, while it would return loaded principally with Indian or European goods (metalware, guns, gunpowder, silk, muslin, Venetian glass, Indian mirrors, and other trinkets).

As we have shown in Chapter XI, this unfortunate situation had persisted for a long time but the eighteenth century brought an additional development. To the importation of luxury goods was added a trade in staples. Coffee,[123] sugar, and indigo of the West Indies

---

119 Since in Syria a more favorable exchange rate for some currencies was available, each month he sent his agents there with a thousand sacks of silver coins to be traded for francs. He then added three times as much copper to these and struck new silver coins (ᶜAlī al-Jiritlī, *Tārīkh aṣ-Ṣināᶜa fī Miṣr* (Cairo, 1952), pp. 101-102).

120 The principal exports in this category were rice, flax, wool, cotton thread, leather, senna, safflower, and sal-ammoniac. These constituted about 60% of the exports to Europe. The rest consisted of reexported goods of Oriental and African origin (26%) and Egyptian textiles (about 10%) (A. Raymond, *Artisans et commerçants*, I, p. 174).

121 *Ibid.*, I, pp. 136-137.

122 The Dārfūr caravan was by far the largest and consisted of 5,000 camels. From Assiut, where it was met by officials and taxed, the slaves and goods would be shipped to Cairo by boat. Its merchants would spend several months in Cairo disposing of their commodities. For information on the Dārfūr and Sennār caravans see P. S. Girard, "Mémoire sur l'agriculture, l'industrie, et le commerce de l'Égypte," *Description de l'Égypte* (Paris, 1812), II, 1, pp. 629-644.

123 See A. Raymond, *Artisans et commerçants*, I, pp. 155-156. The resulting decline in the export of Mochan coffee had serious effect upon the economy for the large amounts of European imports had been balanced by this factor (*ibid.*, I, p. 184). Moreover the coffee merchants depended upon European currency to pay for their coffee purchases in Jidda and the Yemen. As André Raymond says:

invaded the Egyptian market and European machine-made textiles fed the demand of the Cairene upper classes for satin, velvet, and other heavy fabrics. From France in the eighteenth century came woolen cloth,[124] paper, wood, metal goods, perfumes, and even tarbushes.[125] By the beginning of the nineteenth century the cotton cloth of Manchester began to displace Egyptian cotton on domestic markets.[126] The economic benefits of incorporation in the Ottoman empire depended, after all, upon the ability of that empire to defend its interests. The real problem was seated in the fact that Egypt was being drawn into a new sphere of interaction, a sphere in which both the Ottomans and the Egyptians were ill-equipped to compete.

It was also perennially true that trade was in the hands of foreigners and linked to the political power of the governments who backed them.[127] Political and military considerations even surrounded the passage of the pilgrim caravan from the Maghrib which transacted a huge amount of business. When a greedy *amīr al-ḥajj* tried to tax pilgrims[128] and seize their goods, the Maghribī sultan made an official complaint in which he threatened to withhold the caravan the next year unless justice was done. He was upheld by the Cairene *ᶜulamā᾽* and the amīr was executed.[129] Maghribī caravans, moreover, were

---

"This forwarding of specie was awaited each year with impatience by the Cairene merchants who counted on it to effectuate their indispensable expeditions to buy coffee in Jidda: the Spanish piaster and later the taler were the only current species accepted by the merchants of the Hejaz and the Yemen ..." (*Artisans et commerçants*, I, pp. 136-137).

[124] Woolen cloth was produced locally but was of poor quality.

[125] A. Raymond, *Artisans et commerçants*, I, p. 197.

[126] A. Hourani, "The Political and Social Background in the Eighteenth Century," *The Economic History of the Middle East*, 1800-1914, edited by Charles Issawi (Chicago and London: The University of Chicago Press, 1966), p. 28. As Volney observed:

> "... if we examine the channels into which this wealth is poured, if we consider that a great part of the merchandize and coffee of India passes into foreign countries, the value of which is paid in goods from Europe and Turkey; that the consumption of the country almost entirely consists of articles of luxury completely finished, and that the produce given in return is principally in raw materials, we shall perceive that all this commerce is carried on without contributing greatly to the real riches of Egypt, or the benefit of the people" (*Travels through Syria and Egypt*, I, p. 209).

[127] Cf. A. Raymond, *Artisans et commerçants*, I, pp. 201-202.

[128] In the Ottoman period pilgrims had the right of passing through Egypt without inspection or payment of duty on goods they carried (H. A. R. Gibb and H. Bowen, *Islamic Society and the West*, I, 1, p. 302).

[129] Al-Jabartī, *ᶜAjā᾽ib al-Āthār*, I, pp. 174-175; *Merveilles biographiques et historiques*, II, pp. 77-79.

usually heavily armed and Maghribīs were prone to cause trouble in the city.[130] (As noted in the previous chapter, a group of Maghribīs constituted a military element utilized peripherally by the beys and later by Napoleon.) Maghribīs were more often successful in establishing themselves as merchant families than any other Muslim group and perhaps the fact that they formed an organized community (*ṭāʾifa*) contributed to this achievement.[131]

But because of the capitulations, Venetians, Tuscans, French, and other Europeans held incontestable advantages; advantages that subsequently brushed off on Ottoman subjects who held their *berāts*.[132] Cairo's rulers flirted first with one foreign power and then with another in attempting to manipulate the balance of economic and political power. In the middle of the eighteenth century ʿAlī-Bey sent ambassadors to the governments of Europe to secure their assistance against the Porte and, to bolster the economy, he sought to open new and profitable trade relations. In removing the Jews from the custom houses and giving these to the Syrians he most certainly had in mind the prior purpose of securing the wealth of the former for his campaign.[133] Secondarily the result was favorable to the French who operated in Egypt through the agency of the Syrian Christians. By the eighth decade of the century, however, the French were groaning under the inordinate impositions imposed upon their commerce. Napoleon, aiming at securing a market for French products threatened by the cheap manufactures of England, and seeking to strike at British power in India, used as his excuse for the invasion of Egypt the insults, injuries, and losses suffered by French merchants.

Nor was the pattern of commercial alliance basically any different

---

130 A. Raymond, "Tunisiens et Maghrébins," pp. 342, 364-365. According to Aḥmad Jazzār Pasha

> "... there are in Egypt approximately forty or fifty thousand merchants of *Mağrebī* (North African) origin, who are a gunshooting people similar to Albanians ... when there is a need for more soldiers, it is their custom to hire several thousand of these *Mağrebīs* ..." (S. J. Shaw, *Ottoman Egypt in the Eighteenth Century*, p. 26).

131 Qāsim ash-Sharāʾibī is cited in a consular document as "Shaykh and Superior" of the Maghribīs of Cairo. Another, as-Sayyid Aḥmad al-Maghribī, native of Fez, gained many slaves and a great fortune through connections in Ḥijāz and was *shāhbandar* before Aḥmad al-Maḥrūqī (A. Raymond, *Artisans et commerçants*, II, p. 476; al-Jabartī, *ʿAjāʾib al-Āthār*, II, pp. 218-219; *Merveilles biographiques et historiques*, V, p. 142).

132 See above, Chapter XV, pp. 297-298.

133 See John W. Livingston, "ʿAlī Bey al-Kabīr and the Jews," *Middle East Studies*, VII (1971), pp. 221-228.

under Muḥammad ᶜAlī who, confronting the obvious fact that he needed foreign assistance in setting up and equiping his new industries, favored the establishment of European commercial houses. [134] As political interests and the greater volume of trade shifted from the Oriental to the European sphere, so the French and later their English competitors came to prosper.

With this background, it should surprise no one that the agents of subsequent economic development were foreigners. Even without the political power of Europe there was no native group which could have supplied the required leadership, the skills, or the investment. Muḥammad ᶜAlī persevered in his program of commercial and industrial development but an analysis of his failure highlights the disadvantages of the social matrix to which the program was applied, a social quagmire which made it all the more impossible to pull the economy of Egypt up by its boot straps.

In his attempt to leap a subsistence-type economy and develop an industrialized, export-oriented economy, Muḥammad ᶜAlī in 1816 monopolized existing industries and, with funds derived from his agricultural monopoly, taxation, forced "loans," and the monopoly on commerce, set up new industries with the help of foreign technicians. By 1836 there were in Egypt 14 armament factories, a well-run foundry to supply their needs and that of the arsenal, 29 factories for spinning and weaving, 12 shops for producing indigo, 4 mills for the decortication of rice, 1 tarbush factory, 3 sugar refineries and rum distilleries, 6 saltpeter works, 300 factories for pressing oil from flax, sesame, olives, and lettuce, 164 establishments for the incubation of eggs, and a national press. [135] In these factories some thirty to forty thousand persons found salaried employment. Protected administratively and by

---

[134] According to Clot-Bey writing in the third decade of the nineteenth century: "One counts today in Alexandria fourty-four European commercial houses. There were only 16 in 1822. Among these establishments are 13 French, 7 English, 9 Austrian, 8 Tuscan, 2 Sardinian, 1 Swedish, 1 Danish, 1 Prussian, one establishment of the new Greek state; there are another six Muslim merchants and 4 Levantine merchants, Greek Catholics. In Cairo, there are few merchants who work for themselves; there are found scarcely any but agents of the Alexandrian houses. We count one English establishment, 9 Austrian, 4 Tuscan, 2 Sardinian, 2 Greek, 10 Levantine, and 63 small merchants, Turks, Maghribīs and Egyptians" (*Aperçu Général*, II, p. 328).

[135] N. Tomiche, "Notes sur la hiérarchie sociale en Égypte à l'époque de Muḥammad ᶜAlī," *Political and Social Change in Modern Egypt*, edited by P. M. Holt, p. 251; C. Issawi, "The Economic Development of Modern Egypt, 1800-1960," *The Economic History of the Middle East, 1800-1914*, edited by Charles Issawi, p. 362.

government control of imports, most of the new industries appeared to prosper.

In the interests of facilitating trade, the Pasha built the Maḥmūdīya Canal to connect Alexandria with the Nile [136] and got rid of the bandits who had struck fear into the hearts of travelers. No less important was the development in transportation, for by 1850 steamships had made Egypt again a center of international commerce. Between 1830 and 1840 the voyage from England to Egypt was reduced from 40 to 14 days and Egypt was one of the first countries to be served by regular lines. [137] In 1845 an Egyptian company offered regular service between Egypt and Istanbul.

Ostensibly, the principal reason for the failure of Muḥammad ᶜAlī's grand experiment was the determination of the foreign powers to dominate the economic scene, and his inability to block them effectively in this aim. England especially felt that international prosperity resulted from national specialization and, as she already was industrialized, looked to Egypt for provision of raw materials and a market. The Porte too wished to undermine the program through which Muḥammad ᶜAlī maintained an army that could threaten Ottoman sovereignty. In 1838 the coalition between European powers and the Porte produced the Treaty of London which confirmed the right of importation of foreign goods to any part of the Ottoman dominions, Egypt specifically included, at the rate of 3% ad valorem duty and an additional 2% on retail. Additional import taxes were abrogated, while foreign merchants were to be allowed to enter freely whatever territories they desired, to buy directly from the inhabitants whatever produce or manufactured items they chose, and export them at a duty of 12%. Britain was given the status of "most favored nation." [138] For a while, the Pasha was able to defy the decree but the accumulation of economic and political strains finally became insupportable. In 1840 many of the struggling factories closed down and in 1842, the application of the Treaty dealt the death blow to his program.

But the obvious significance of the external power contest should not blind us to the less evident but equally important internal elements

---

[136] Since, with the commercial decay of the previous centuries, an older canal that had formerly been used had fallen into disrepair, travelers had had to choose between the hazardous and unpleasant alternatives of hiring camels to cross the Delta or sailing in small ships to Rosetta and gaining access to the Nile from there.

[137] A. E. Crouchley, *Economic Development*, pp. 80, 82.

[138] Ahmed Mustafa, "The Breakdown of the Monopoly System in Egypt after 1840," *Political and Social Change in Modern Egypt*, edited by P. M. Holt, p. 293.

that enmeshed the attempt to introduce a modern economic system. A detailed consideration of the factories and their management reveals more fully the nature of the industrial undertaking and the degree of its achievement. First there were the already existing industries, and then there were the industries that were newly established. With regard to the former, weaving establishments, flour mills, oil presses, saffron and indigo dye factories, saltpeter works, pottery, and other arts and crafts were simply taken over. Basically their system of production was not changed and the same machines, such as they were, were kept. The only change was that the artisans had to buy the raw materials from the government and sell to the government their finished products. The government reserved for itself also, the right to sell all manufactured goods. The state marked every piece and fixed every price. Unmarked pieces were confiscated. [139]

The succeeding stage of development saw the addition of grand new factories such as the ones for the production of wool and cotton fabric, as well as a foundry which could handle nearly every kind of iron work. Workers for these were conscripted from the country and the unemployed of the towns, and paid salaries. The machinery in these establishments was somewhat more complex but often broke down. No wonder, for it was not only that the workers lacked technical knowledge and skills but that the animals that provided nearly all the power were prone to abrupt and jerky movements! Only a few steam engines were available and coal was much more expensive than feed. [140] After the failure of the woolen factories, the cottons produced were improved by the introduction of a new strain of cotton, one of the few direct and lasting contributions of the whole program to subsequent economic development. [141]

---

[139] Al-Jabartī, *ᶜAjāᵓib al-Āthār*, IV, pp. 282-283; *Merveilles biographiques et historiques*, IX, pp. 252-253.

[140] A. E. Crouchley, *Economic Development*, p. 72.

[141] It has been pointed out that the profits of many of the new factories were largely illusory. Bookkeepers took into account only the cost of raw materials and wages without making any allowances for overhead, depreciation of equipment and buildings, rent, interest on capital, or loss of material in manufacture. When these things are included in the calculation, it appears that even factories that produced cotton goods were being operated at a loss. In 1838 Egyptian cotton cost 8.7 piasters a yard on the local market while English cotton cost 7.5 piasters. Furthermore, the breakdown of the monopoly through which raw materials were obtained at far less than their real value and the subsequent raising of the prices of these materials finally dispelled even the illusion of profit (A. E. Crouchley, *Economic Development*, pp. 73-74).

But what of the human element in this experiment? How did the lower and middle orders react to the changes it involved? In the first place, considering the entire urban working class, the workers employed in the factory system were still fewer than those in the guilds.[142] Especially those in the sphere of distribution and services, butchers, bakers, barbers, tailors, book binders, donkey drivers, shoemakers, and jewelers, etc. still went about their business. The number of artisans was only about a third of the total membership of the guilds.[143] Far from being weakened, the guild system continued to be utilized by the government for purposes of taxation and social control.[144]

In the second place, while Muḥammad ᶜAlī was trying to initiate an economic system that eventually would have raised the standard of living, and it is also true that in certain broad respects his program prepared the way for a modern diversified economy, in the short run his innovations neither raised the standard of living nor overcame the subsistence mentality.[145] Charles Issawi points out that the level of living probably even declined as the result of the inflation which resulted from frequently mismanaged investment.[146] The monopoly increased the hardships that burdened many urban dwellers. Many persons who had supplied the needs of the former elite missed the old days; the disappearance of their former patrons and the impoverishment of many of the Cairene merchants and *ᶜulamāᵓ* not only robbed them of personal support but seriously cut into the demand

---

142 G. Baer, *Egyptian Guilds*, p. 131.

143 *Ibid.*, p. 132.

144 Gabriel Baer notes that until the 1880's a ramified system of guilds existed "comprising almost the whole indigenous gainfully occupied population." When, in the 1860's, slaves were freed by the authorities, they found it very difficult to find work since labor was supplied by the guilds which monopolized the different services, crafts, and trades (*Egyptian Guilds*, p. 25; also his "Social Change in Egypt," p. 104).

145 In general, salaries were quite low. Factory workers received a little more than infantrymen in the army (20-120 piasters a month as opposed to 15 piasters a month for the infantry) but their total income was less as it did not include food, lodging, and other necessities. Moreover, often the pay was withheld to replace broken equipment, dead beasts of burden, or to compensate for flaws in workmanship. In 1821, a manager (*nāẓir*) of a copper foundry received 500 piasters a month, a salary commensurate with that of an army captain. The factories were run thus, on a pseudo-military model. In the army the low pay of the simple soldier compared with that of the captain was rationalized by the feeling that high pay for the officer would earn his devotion and hence through his effort, would secure the loyalty of his men. Moreover it was maintained that the pay of an infantryman compared favorably to the income of a *fallāḥ* prior to conscription (N. Tomiche, "Notes sur le hierarchie sociale en Égypte," pp. 252, 259, 260).

146 "The Economic Development of Egypt," p. 362.

for their services and products. Master artisans who accepted salaried employment in the factories simply became absorbed in the lower class. Moreover it was probably true that salaried workers in large factories, displaced from their accustomed ateliers, missed the comparative security offered by local patrons and felt uncomfortable having to approach a strange government official placed over them for special considerations and favors. To individuals used to a more personalized working environment, such a regime must have seemed excessively restrictive.

As might be expected there was no open revolt among the artisans but in evidence of their discontent there was much complaining, absenteeism, and general lack of cooperation. When some masons and joiners abandoned their crafts and fled, the shaykh of their corporation was required to find them and submit them to the authorities. [147] An English observer reported that:

> of the 23 or 24 cotton factories, there is not one that was not at some time or other accidentally or purposely set on fire. [148]

It is important to note, moreover, that the reticence of the workers was due to the conditions of work and the slimness of remuneration rather than to lack of readiness and apptitude for learning modern techniques. According to a French observer:

> "the promptness of their intelligence, their extreme manual address was a subject of astonishment to their instructors." [149]

As for the middle class response to Muḥammad ᶜAlī's industrial program, there does not seem to have been much involvement in it. The managers of his factories were simply salaried officials, most of whom had no driving interest in the success of the establishments they directed and were ignorant about the needs of the tasks they were called upon to do. Reports indicate that the sovereign felt it necessary to concern himself with the coordination and supervision of many detailed aspects of production. [150] The experiment therefore did not

---

[147] Al-Jabartī, *ᶜAjāᵓib al-Āthār*, IV, p. 159; *Merveilles biographiques et historiques*, VIII, p. 357.

[148] J. A. St. John, *Egypt and Mohammad Ali: or Travels in the Valley of the Nile* (London: T. N. Longman & O. Rees, 1834), II, p. 421.

[149] V. Schoelcher, *L'Égypte en 1845* (Paris, 1846), p. 52, quoted by N. Tomiche, "Notes sur le hiérarchie sociale en Égypte," p. 261.

[150] According to ᶜAlī al-Jiritlī:

> "... despite his many problems, Muḥammad ᶜAlī's assistants informed him of the contents of the reports sent by the factories, on which he commented and gave orders similar to those issued by a general manager or managing director of a

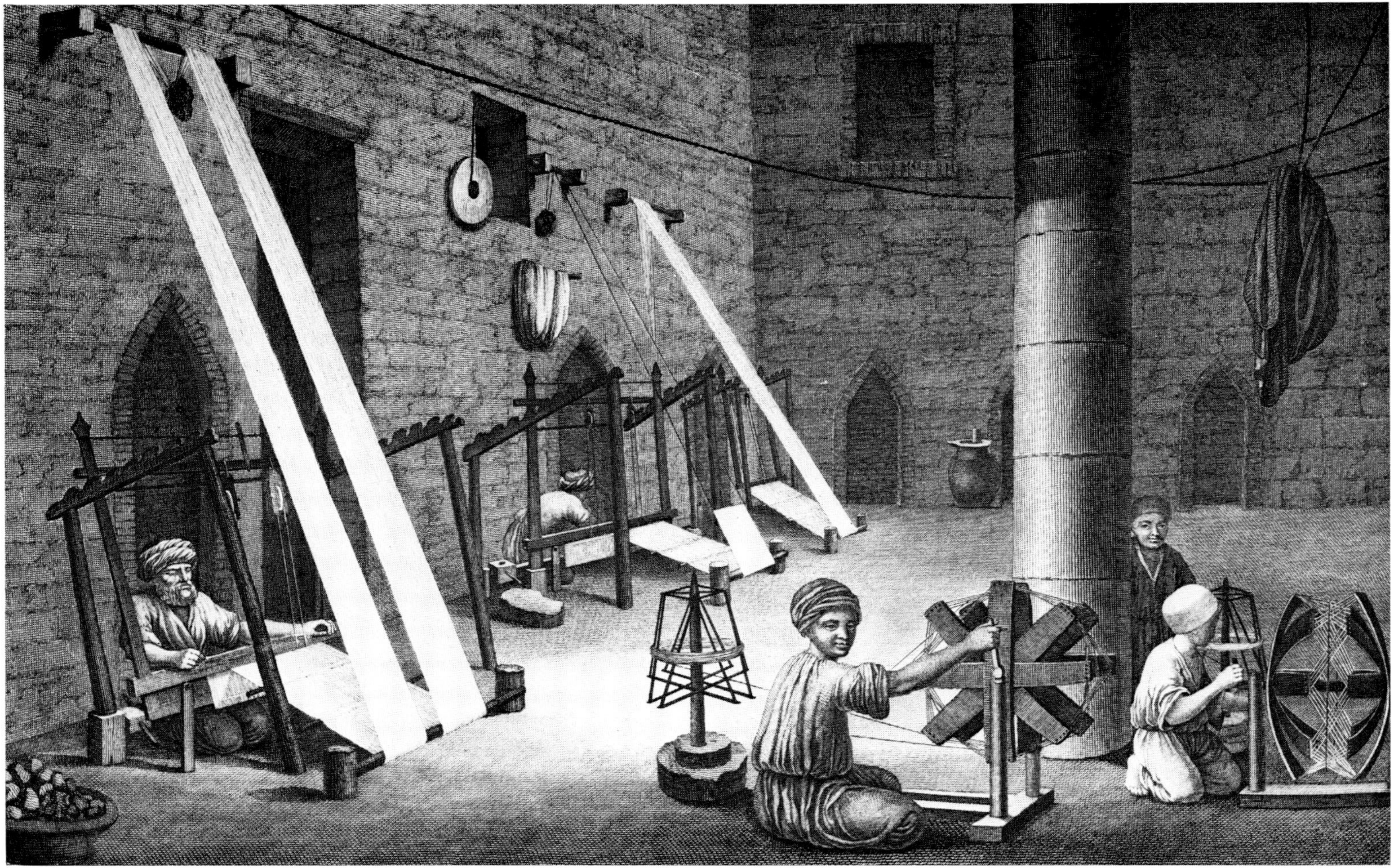

16. A Textile Factory (ca. 1800).

produce a managerial class that either felt any responsibility for the subsequent industrial development of the country or had any real financial interest in it. When the program was finally destroyed through foreign intervention, local Egyptian capitalists avoided industrial investment both because of there being no tradition for it and because of European domination of that sphere. As Girard had remarked at the turn of the century:

> It can easily be imagined that in a land which has to import wood and metals from abroad, and whose absolute government renders uncertain the enjoyment of private wealth, it is impossible to exercise advantageously any of those industrial professions which can be supported only by luxury and on which one's superfluity can be safely spent. [151]

Finally, commercial ventures were left to the initiative of foreign entrepreneurs, many of whom had already profited in the time-honored fashion through the patronage of the sovereign. [152] Even Europeans, however, tended to invest in utilities and railroads rather than in industries which had small chance of successful competition on a market dominated by European products. For all these reasons it was decades before any serious industrial development took place. Like many former conquerors of Egypt whose center of power lay elsewhere, they became interested in the land and its bounty rather than urban industrial development. To encourage agriculture, and to increase exports of raw materials to Europe, the government granted them land brought newly under cultivation tax-free for ten years, despite the capitulations which forbade foreigners to own land. [153]

---

corporation nowadays to the manager of a factory belonging to that corporation." The Pasha assessed the production goals of different machines based upon their output in well-managed factories or on general average production and then required explanations of failure. But the factory managers were not always cooperative or willing to assume responsibility. When Muḥammad ᶜAlī requested them to estimate annual needs of materials and fuels so that the government would have plenty of time to supply these, many of them did not bother to furnish this information. Others were reluctant to make relatively minute decisions; the manager of the tarbush factory even sought his advice on the mixing of different kinds of wool, to which he replied that he was not a technical expert and if the tarbushes were spoiled, he would hold the manager responsible (*Tārīkh aṣ-Ṣināᶜa fī Miṣr*, pp. 145-147).

151 "Mémoire sur l'agriculture, l'industrie, et le commerce," pp. 618-620.

152 The Treaty of 1838 did not actually come into effect in Egypt until 1842, not only because the Pasha persevered in his monopoly, but also because many merchants who had profited by patronage and speculation were loathe to bring charges against him for infractions of it.

153 An imperial decree in 1867, however, granted them this right.

By the middle of the fourth decade of the nineteenth century, nearly all that remained of Muḥammad ᶜAlī's factories were some deserted buildings and rusty and dilapidated machinery. The Pasha's vision of an Egyptian industrial revolution could not but become entangled in the internal web of habitual and deliberate popular resistance and crushed by external forces of superior economic and political power. After all, it was not so much an industrial revolution as a social and political revolution that was wanted and paradoxically, ironically, it was the last and most complete experience of foreign domination that finally brought this transformation about.

CHAPTER SEVENTEEN

SPIRITUAL POWER: POPULAR RELIGIOUS LIFE AND URBAN INTEGRATION

Of all the dimensions of social power, the spiritual dimension is, from the standpoint of our own day, the least easy to comprehend. In the modern period economic and political power have undergone fundamental changes, but spiritual power has all but vanished; its influence does not pervade our world as it pervaded the world of the medieval Cairene. Islam from the beginning was a social movement that, directly or indirectly, shaped all social institutions [1] and, on the other side of the coin, its expression in popular life reflected many major tendencies of that life, the values, contradictions, and ambiguities of social reality. Spiritual power was given expression not only in the forms of legal orthodoxy but in personalized heterodoxy; it always remained diffused and universally accessible, but was most effective in its specific and localized manifestations; it both established diversity and encouraged integration.

We have seen that, of all elements which marked divisions between groups and shaped the pattern of social relations, religious and moral precepts were most essential. It is reasonable therefore, to search for evidence of sociocultural integration in the very sphere in which, up to now, integration has seemed most lacking, for if effective unity existed at all, it must have been the result of basic liaisons between individuals which were ordered with reference to essential value systems espoused through actual behavior as well as through explicit statements of the ideal. Spiritual affiliation did not only make explicit ethnic and family allegiance but made possible the overriding of such considerations in favor of a wider sphere of social reference.

---

[1] Ernest Gellner has written:

"... it is the total manner in which Islam is a social movement which perhaps most crucially differentiates it from Christianity ... One might say that Islam is more total (than either Christianity or Judaism) in a number of dimensions: it does not restrict its appeal territorially; it does not restrict its application to some institutions only; and it does yet have a kind of independent existence in scriptural and normative record, and cannot simply be equated with the practices of the society in which it occurs" ("A Pendulum Swing Theory of Islam," *Sociology* of *Religion: Selected Readings*, edited by Roland Robertson (Baltimore, Md.: Penguin Books, 1969), p. 127).

Popular religion in particular emphasized unifying tendencies. Ṣūfism embraced a wide range of elements from ancient cults of folk religion to refined and sophisticated ideas of Islamic philosophy. To say that this religious expression was "popular" is not to say that it excluded the high ranking cadres of society. On the contrary, it was inclusive of the interests of every class and level of the hierarchy and, in the last analysis, even tended to negate the validity of the hierarchy. In brief, spiritual power, with the morality that derived from it, was instrumental in establishing social ties that formed elemental knots in the social fabric.

1. *Sunnī Orthodoxy and Ṣūfī Heterodoxy: Polar Opposites or Complementaries?*

A crucial issue in the sociology of Islam is the relation between Ṣūfism and religious orthodoxy. In theory, the relation is one of contrast and there is a dichotomy between the two. Sunnī orthodoxy insists upon strict monotheism, emphasizes scripture as the source of religious truth and the law, emphasizes rationality in interpretation, denies the possibility of personal mediation of spiritual power, and stresses puritanism and moderation in behavior. Ṣūfism, on the other hand, with its mystical, pantheistic orientation, emphasizes emotional perception of religious truth, implicitly recognizes the validity of personal revelation, the incarnation of spiritual power in individuals, objects, and symbols, and not only tolerates but encourages various types of deviant behavior under the cloak of ritual practice.

While various commentators and *ᶜulamāᵓ* continue to call attention to the dichotomy between orthodoxy and Ṣūfism's heterodox tendencies, from the standpoints of history and of social life, the gulf becomes narrowed and tends to disappear. Historically we should recall the fact that before the time of Ṣalāḥ ad-Dīn and the Sunnī "orthodox conquest" of Egypt, Fāṭimid Shīᶜism represented many of the "heterodox" tendencies that Ṣūfism implicitly incorporated. Following the Ayyūbid conquest, Shīᶜism was no longer tolerated but Ṣūfism, as a movement which had never repudiated the Sunnī orientation, remained relatively respectable.[2] Ṣalāḥ ad-Dīn and his followers established not only

---

[2] J. Spencer Trimingham outlines the early development of the Ṣūfī movement. By the eleventh century groups of individuals loosely organized convents to enhance their pursuit of a Way (*ṭarīqa*) and together sought the guidance of experienced mentors. By the end of that century Islamic legalists, through the influence of al-Ghazālī and others, had come to a qualified acceptance of Ṣūfism and a realization that the *sharīᶜa* and orthodox ritual did not satisfy all religious needs. When

madrasas to reinforce the schools of law but founded and endowed *khānqāhs* (cloisters), *ribāṭs* (religious hostels), and *zāwiyas* (Ṣūfī centers).

But although it is well known that mysticism had deep roots in Egyptian culture, and that every period of Cairene history had its non-orthodox and semi-orthodox movements, it was not until the Ottoman period that a system of disciplined mysticism spread throughout all levels of society. The rulers still relied upon the *ᶜulamāᵓ* to provide the framework of the social order, but *takīyas* and *zāwiyas* became more numerous than *madrasas*. [3] Thus schools of Ṣūfism came to have permanent centers in all of the major cities of the empire and it was usual for men in the most diverse walks of life to attach themselves to the orders (*ṭawāᵓif*). As in the case of the economic corporations, the rulers often appointed one of the shaykhs or even a *muftī* to act as a liaison between these groups and the government. [4]

The placing of *ᶜulamāᵓ* at the head of the popular orders was the final step in taking this heterodox movement under the Sunnī aegis and represented a significant step in urban integration. Islamic "sectarianism" thus fell completely within the sphere of orthodoxy and no

---

Nūr ad-Dīn and Ṣalāḥ ad-Dīn lent support to the movement with endowments and official supervision of *khānqāhs* (Ṣūfī cloisters) it gained added respectability. By the thirteenth century certain centers became regular "schools" which perpetuated the name, teaching, and rule of particular shaykhs whose *ṭarīqas* were traditionally handed down through a continuous chain (*silsila*) of spiritual heirs. Ibn Baṭṭūṭa wrote in A.D. 1326 that

> "Each *zāwiya* in Cairo is assigned to a *ṭāᵓifa* (group) of dervishes, most of whom are Persians, men of culture and trained in the Way of *taṣawwuf*" (*Mahdhab Riḥla Ibn Baṭṭūṭa*, I (Cairo, 1934), p. 27).

The headship of a *khānqāh* was obtained through appointment by governmental authorities whereas the headship of the *zāwiya* was at first a matter decided by the brotherhood and later came to be an office dominated by hereditary succession. The *zāwiya* therefore maintained an internal organizational continuity that the *khānqāh* did not have. The incorporation of the saint cult in organized Ṣūfism brought about the inclusion of numerous lay adherents and an expansion of the orders. The resultant social manifestation was characterized by considerable diversity:

> "Some (Sufi establishments) were rich and luxurious, favoured by authority, whilst others followed the strictest principles of poverty and unworldliness; some had no shaikh, others were under the authority of one leader and had become attached to one *silsila*; whilst others were governed by a council of elders. Then there were wandering dervishes such as the *qalandars*, who made use of these hostels and had their own rules and linkages but no organization" (J. Spencer Trimingham, *The Sufi Orders in Islam* (Oxford: The Clarendon Press, 1971), pp. 5-27, quotation p. 30).

[3] J. S. Trimingham, *The Sufi Orders*, p. 69.

[4] *Ibid.*, p. 242.

longer represented a serious threat outside of it. While orthodox representatives tended to become more tolerant, many Ṣūfī groups drifted towards conformity and lost some of their spontaneous religious creativity.

It has been claimed that in the Muslim town, the polar relationship of the orthodox and heterodox syndromes is a relationship of social alternatives. [5] This statement may be *relatively* true in contrast to the situation of the hinterland and its truth probably increases with the extension of literacy in modern times. On the other hand, from the contextual perspective of social life in the traditional period, how much of an option there really was for urbanites is an important question.

In the first place orthodoxy with its emphasis upon scripture and rationality depends not only upon literacy but the acquisition of enough learning to ensure an understanding of the meaning of Qurʾānic text. [6] With reference to literacy Chabrol stated that from one-third to to one-quarter of the male population of Cairo were literate. [7] Most of these were merchants, artisans, and shopkeepers who had undergone the usual elementary *kuttāb* training. The extent of their religious sophistication can be realized by recalling that the *kuttāb* pupil acquired knowledge of orthography and rote memorization of the Qurʾān but that neither grammatical analysis nor consideration of the meaning of the text was included in the syllabus. [8] Regarding the extent of university education, Lane in 1835 estimated that there were about 1,500 students at al-Azhar, but noted that some said the number was twice as large. [9]

But while many poor Cairenes and sons of *fallāḥīn* could benefit from university exposure, it should be remembered that the Ottoman period saw a marked decline in the status of learning even at al-Azhar.

---

[5] See Ernest Gellner, "A Pendulum Swing Theory of Islam," p. 136; and his *Saints of the Atlas* (Chicago: University of Chicago Press, 1969), p. 8.

[6] Gibb and Bowen go so far as to state that "the ᶜ*Ulemā* alone were thoroughly conversant with the *Şerīᶜa* and its orthodox interpretation" (*Islamic Society and the West*, I, 2, p. 185).

[7] "Essai sur les moeurs," p. 391.

[8] J. Heyworth-Dunne, *Introduction to the History of Education in Modern Egypt* (London: Luzac & Co., 1938), p. 2.

[9] *Manners and Customs*, p. 217. While many students were Turks, Maghribīs and Syrians, a large proportion came from the Egyptian countryside or were sons of townsmen who attended the University for only a couple of years and then left to practice a trade (J. Heyworth-Dunne, *Introduction to the History of Education*, p. 28). According to al-Jabartī, most of the students were poor (ᶜ*Ajāʾib al-Āthar*, I, p. 187; *Merveilles biographiques et historiques*, II, p. 112).

The conquest had resulted in the dispersal of libraries and the loss of many manuscripts. The reduction of Egypt to the status of an Ottoman province could not but effect the Egyptian religious establishment. Moreover when many of the higher posts came to be occupied by Turks, many persons rallied around native *ᶜulamāʾ*, whose spirituality and charisma was deemed more essential than education. J. Heyworth-Dunne remarked that the popular reading material of the nineteenth century

> consisted mostly of Ṣūfī tracts and literature with some Ṣūfī colouring obtainable in some kind of manuscript form from the copyists or booksellers, and judging from the quantity in libraries and still available in the book markets, the supply must have been fairly extensive. [10]

In the reality of social life, if the *ᶜulamāʾ* were to have effective contact with the people, they had to go along with Ṣūfism. As Trimingham has pointed out, the orders rather than the *sharīᶜa* mediated to the ordinary man the spiritual aspect of Islam:

> In their concern for men they played in many respects a role similar to that of the local church in Europe. They embodied in themselves the whole *mysterium fascinans* of the age, revealed, esoteric, mystical, emotional religion. [11]

Islam always lacked the institution of priesthood and there was always a tendency for personal religious influences at a local level to fall outside of the framework of formalized orthodox authority. [12] The spiritual reputation of a shaykh was often largely independent of his learning and intellectual achievements. Spiritual education meant a personal relationship with a mentor who claimed respect by virtue of his manifestation of spiritual powers rather than scholarship.

From the social as well as the spiritual angle, local mosques and *madrasa*s cannot be compared with *zāwiya*s which represented not only places of worship and study but meeting places of truly organized social groups. A man could worship in whatever mosque he chose and could patronize one *madrasa* or another according to his legal persuasion, but the *zāwiya* represented membership in a *ṭāʾifa* that entailed loyalty to a shaykh and brotherhood with comembers. The *madhāhib* never represented effective bodies in Egyptian society in this sense.

---

[10] *Introduction to the History of Education*, p. 11.

[11] *The Sufi Orders*, p. 229.

[12] It should be remembered that, from the seventh century, the issue of whether authority was ultimately seated in the *sharīᶜa* interpreted by consensus or in the personal interpretation of a (caliphal) mediary, had never been resolved.

Religious practice was thus a compromise between general conformity to performance of prayer, ritual, and formal modes of life prescribed by orthodoxy, and Ṣūfistic embellishments, interpretations, and beliefs. [13] For most people moral guidance was obtained through the Ṣūfī *ṭāʾifa* rather than from direct reference to orthodox principles.

Certainly, however, no Ṣūfī order was orthodox in the theoretical sense of Sunnī Islam and the acceptance of Ṣūfism by the *ʿulamāʾ* was a qualified acceptance. The respect for the *sharīʿa* among the upper and middle classes of society meant a ranking of the orders ranging from orthodoxy to the fringes of heresy. On one end of the scale some of the highest ranking shaykhs of al-Azhar developed their own orders, while at the other end "irregular" orders of dervishes, loose in doctrine and practice, were highly suspect of spiritual jugglery and fraud. Deviations from orthodox norms were considered polytheistic, blasphemous, superstitious, or merely degrading. The emphasis upon the miraculous often led to the manufacture of the required manifestations. As in many cultures and societies, lunatics were generally thought to be endowed with unusual powers. Prevalent among many of the orders too, was the drinking of wine and coffee, expressly forbidden or considered opposed in spirit to the nature of the law. While the orthodox attitude toward the use of narcotics was less well defined, many Ṣūfīs did not hesitate to use opium and hashish as aids to achieving mystical experience.

In urban social life the theoretical conflict between orthodoxy and heterodoxy was largely unrealized. [14] Ṣūfism was never basically opposed the the *sharīʿa* but rather represented, on a quite independent basis, both a reaction to sterile orthodox legalism and the expression

---

13 As H. J. Kissling has written:

"What good did the execrations of the orthodox do against the *d̲ikr* and music, if the masses poured into the monasteries to assist at the *d̲ikr* and listen to the music (*semāʿ*)? Of what use was it to quote ancient jurists who spoke against the cult of saints, if the people turned in their need to the tombs of saints and dervish sheikhs with votive gifts to pray for the granting of their wishes? Thus the earlier furious resistance of orthodoxy degenerated into purely academic quarrels and has remained of this nature to our times" ("The Sociological and Educational Role of the Dervish Orders in the Ottoman Empire," *Studies in Islamic Cultural History*, G. E. von Grunebaum, ed. Memoirs of the American Anthropological Association, No. 76 (April, 1954), pp. 29-30).

14 As Gibb and Bowen put it:

"... Islâm now embodied two antagonistic systems masquerading as one, the attitude to life and the conduct that one of these systems would otherwise have induced were modified by the competing prestige of the other" (*Islamic Society and the West*, I, 2, p. 203).

of local beliefs. It also brought with it an extreme flexibility. Several orders which began as "heterodox" and "suspicious" from the religious and political points of view ended up as pillars of orthodoxy, while others drifted in the opposite direction. Their ability to incorporate diverse elements of society and culture was nearly limitless. *Taṣawwuf* came to be recognized as the "science of the mystical life" and many esteemed scholars entered the orders seeking vital religious experience that was lacking in the traditional institution of learning, even as shaykhs of the orders often advised their students to go to al-Azhar to study. While some heads of the orders lacked enough formal education to qualify as *ᶜulamāᵓ*, *ᶜulamāᵓ* acquired rank from either recognized position in the orthodox hierarchy *or* in the Ṣūfī hierarchy or often in *both.*[15]

---

[15] Three examples are illustrative. Orthodox *ᶜulamāᵓ* were often widely believed to possess *baraka* (spiritual power) and were venerated on this account. Al-Jabartī speaks of

> "The great scholar, illustrious teacher, the Shaykh of Shaykhs, Muḥammad al-Qilaynī al-Azharī whose miracles are astonishing and worthy of mention. He possessed nothing, neither rent, nor salary, nor property, and was able to dispense enormous sums. He took money from no one and was wont to spend in a manner not at all in keeping with poverty. If he walked through the bazaars the poor clung to his garments, while he gave them gold and silver, and whenever he entered a bath he paid the fee for all who were present" (*ᶜAjāᵓīb al-Āthār*, I, p. 189; *Merveilles biographiques et historiques*, II, p. 117).

A respected Ṣūfī shaykh sometimes earned official recognition by the religious establishment. ᶜAlī al-Bayyūmī, founder of the popular order that bears his name, was at first strongly opposed by the *ᶜulamāᵓ* for his leadership of noisy *ḥadra*s (ritual gatherings) in Sayyidna al-Ḥusayn, but was eventually invited by the Shaykh al-Islām to occupy a chair at al-Azhar.

ᶜAbd al-Wahhāb ibn Aḥmad ash-Shaᶜrānī (A.D. 1492-1565) even more profoundly blended in his personality a meeting of the two tendencies. Trained within the Shadhilī tradition by an illuminated illiterate shaykh, he vividly described his experience of personal revelation:

> " 'My introduction (to gifted knowledge) took place on the banks of the Nile beside the houses of the Nubians and the sail-driven waterwheels. Whilst I was standing there ... I began babbling about the mysteries of the Qurᵓān and Ḥadīth, and of deriving from them the principles behind the various Islamic sciences to such a point that I believed myself able to dispense with study of the works of the scholars of the past. I filled some hundred quires with these matters. But when I showed them to my master ᶜAlī al-Khawwāṣ he told me to get rid of the lot. "This knowledge," he declared, "is contaminated with speculative matter and human acquisitions ..." ' " (Quoted by J. S. Trimingham, *Sufi Orders*, pp. 221-222).

Ash-Shaᶜrānī criticised the insensitivity of the *ᶜulamāᵓ* to the spirit of the *sharīᶜa*, likening them to "donkeys carrying books they could not comprehend," but he also strongly criticized many widely accepted orders (including the Badawīya, Rifāᶜīya, and Dasūqīya) as contravening the *sharīᶜa*. A head of the "orthodox" Khalwatī order did not regard him as a Ṣūfī, while he regarded this critic as a lax Muslim with regard to legal matters (J. S. Trimingham, *Sufi Orders*, pp. 221-223).

2. *Orders, Oscillation, and Options*

What then were the principal orders, how were they characterized, and how did they reflect social and religious options? It is interesting that all of the major *ṭarīqa*s originated outside of Egypt even though they gained considerable followings there and established numerous local branches and subbranches. Socially speaking, their most important affiliations were primarily ethnic and secondarily occupational, although of course it was their very lack of exclusiveness that accounted for their popularity and integrative function in the urban center.

The major orders in Egypt are described by Lane, although he does not give much information on their social connections. One of the most popular and most esteemed was the Rifāᶜīya. [16] It had a number of suborders in Egypt, the most notable of which were the Bāzīya, Mālikīya, Ḥabībīya, ᶜIlwānīya, and the Saᶜdīya. Members of these were generally celebrated for their performance of wonderful ritual feats such as thrusting iron spikes into themselves without injury and the handling of live venomous snakes and scorpions with impunity. Such "miracles" served to symbolize the order as did the colors of their banners and turbans which were black, dark blue, or dark green. [17]

The Qādirīya was a relatively docile order. In Egypt it had no subdivisions and most of its members were fishermen. The Qādirī banners and turbans were white and in procession they carried various colored nets on their poles. [18]

The Aḥmadīya (or Badawīya) had the largest following at the end of the eighteenth century. Founded in the thirteenth century at Ṭanṭa by Aḥmad al-Badawī who had studied at the retreat of Aḥmad ar-Rifāᶜī in Iraq, it gave rise to seventeen suborders that followed its red banner. According to Lane, the Aḥmadīya was highly respected, although it produced few great teachers or writers and tended more than others to be a people's cult. [19]

One of the most important subbranches of the Aḥmadīya was the Bayyūmīya. ᶜAlī al-Bayyūmī, born at the end of the seventeenth century in a village of Lower Egypt, studied at first in a Khalwatī *zāwiya* in Cairo but then became attached to a branch of the Aḥmadīya.

---

[16] See Ernst Bannerth, "La Rifāᶜiyya en Égypte," *Mélanges de l'Institut Dominicain des Études Orientales*, X (1970), pp. 1-35.

[17] E. W. Lane, *Manners and Customs*, p. 248; S. J. Shaw, *Ottoman Egypt in the Age of the French Revolution*, p. 101.

[18] E. W. Lane, *Manners and Customs*, p. 249.

[19] *Ibid.*, p. 249.

Establishing his own center in Ḥusaynīya, he saw himself as a reformer of the Aḥmadīya but came to be regarded as the originator of a new way on account of his charisma and institution of changes in ritual practice. After his death his tomb became a "cult" center and the new order developed a large following especially among the butchers of the Ḥusaynīya. In the last part of the eighteenth century, Aḥmad Sālim al-Jazzār (the Butcher) took up the banner, combining his role as shaykh of the Bayyūmīya with the headship of the butchers' corporation. [20] It is interesting to speculate that there may have been alliances between the Bayyūmīya and other groups represented in the quarter. André Raymond notes that the Khalwatīya (of which ᶜAlī al-Bayyūmī had been a member) continued to play an active role in the life of the Ḥusaynīya since an influential Khalwatī shaykh resided there and his brother is known to have directed the quarter in the political movement of 1792. [21]

Another founder of an Egyptian order who acquired a large following was Ibrāḥīm ad-Dasūqī, a contemporary of Aḥmad al-Badawī and like him, a product of Aḥmad ar-Rifāᶜī's teaching. His group, the Burhāmīya, was divided into two branches and was set apart by its green banners and turbans. While his center was at Dasūq, he acquired far more than local importance. [22] Together with ᶜAbd al-Qādir al-Jālānī (founder of the Qādirīya), Aḥmad ar-Rifāᶜī, and Aḥmad al-Badawī, he was believed to be one of the four "poles" (*aqṭāb*, sing. *quṭb*) which "hold up the earth." [23]

These were the principal groups in Egypt but a number of others were also well represented. Turkish and Maghribī immigrants in particular were instrumental in establishing *ṭarīqa*s. The Maghribī Abū al-Ḥasan ash-Shādhilī had, in the thirteenth century, settled in Egypt to found an important *ṭarīqa* that attracted not only a popular following but also the *ᶜulamāʾ*. Only later did his movement gain importance in his home country, but by the fifteenth century it became a significant bearer of the Maghribī *baraka* (spiritual power) concept and its traditional transmission in the saint cult. One Muḥammad ibn ᶜIsā founded a branch of the Shādhilīya and became patron saint of Meknes. Lane describes at length a *dhikr* of the ᶜIsāwīya dervishes at the *Mawlid an-*

[20] J. S. Trimingham, *The Sufi Orders*, pp. 79, 81.

[21] "Quartiers et mouvements populaires," p. 108.

[22] J. W. McPherson wrote in the middle of this century that his cult in Palestine, Syria, and some other places may exceed that in Egypt (*The Moulids of Egypt* (Cairo, 1941), p. 188-189).

[23] S. J. Shaw, *Ottoman Egypt in the Age of the French Revolution*, p. 101.

Nabī ("one of the chief attractions of the night") and remarks that these were "a class of dervishes of whom all, or almost all, are Maghrabees, or Arabs of Northern Africa, to the west of Egypt." [24]

The "Turkish" [25] orders had special significance because of their link with the ruling class. The Khalwatīya in particular had great vitality [26] not only among the elite, notables, and bureaucrats, but also among the common people. H. J. Kissling points out that in Istanbul many key positions were filled by Khalwatīs or Khalwatī sympathizers and believes that up to the middle of the seventeenth century "it played a considerable role within the state by nepotism, without exposing itself to attack." [27] The *ṭarīqa* was introduced in Cairo just before 1500 and spread through the efforts of Ibrāḥīm Gülshenī (d. 1534) and Muḥammad ad-Damirdāsh (d. 1525-26) who founded suborders in the first part of the sixteenth century. Gülshenī, originally a Turkish refugee, was welcomed in Egypt by al-Ghūrī. He settled in the Muʾayyadīya quarter where he built a *zāwiya* which enclosed his tomb. After the Ottoman conquest, he continued to teach and his son married the widow of the last Mamlūk sultan, Ṭūmān-Bey. It is said that the Janissaries so venerated him that "they were ready to fight one another in order to drink what remained of his washing water." [28] It is likely

---

[24] *Manners and Customs*, p. 466.

[25] Most of these groups had Central Asian or Anatolian origins.

[26] See Ernst Bannerth, "La Khalwatiyya en Égypte," *Mélanges de l'Institut Dominicain des Études Orientales*, VIII (Cairo, 1964-66), pp. 1-74. There were other groups as well. The Naqshabandī are mentioned by al-Jabartī and Lane and also seem to have been favored by the *ᶜulamāʾ* for their orthodox leanings (S. J. Shaw, *Ottoman Egypt in the Age of the French Revolution*, p. 101). The Baktāshīs were never numerous in Cairo although they were represented there by a beautiful *takīya* on the Muqaṭṭam from about the sixteenth century and had occupied another *takīya* in the Qaṣr al-ᶜAynī area before that. The sources of Ottoman Egypt do not say much about them, although the connection between the Baktāshīs and the Janissaries in Turkey is widely known. It is interesting that this order was known for its "irregular" heterodox tendencies. Trimingham writes that:

> "The Bektāshiyya claimed to be a Sunnī order, though in fact very unorthodox and having so strong a reverence for the House of ᶜAlī that it might well be called a Shīᶜī order" (*The Sufi Orders*, p. 80).

Its association with the Janissary corps which was officially recognized at the end of the sixteenth century, probably was instrumental in shielding it from persecution. In Istanbul, the master-general of the Order held the honorary rank of *chūrbajī* in one of the Janissary companies and eight dervishes acted as "chaplains" in the barracks (H. A. R. Gibb and H. Bowen, *Islamic Society and the West*, I, 2, p. 193). Possibly in Egypt the Khalwatīs and not the Baktāshīs played this role in the corps.

[27] "The Educational Role of the Dervish Orders," p. 31.

[28] Quoted by B. G. Martin, "A Short History of the Khalwati Order of Dervishes," *Scholars, Saints and Sufis*, edited by Nikki R. Keddie, p. 296, from Tawfīq aṭ-Ṭawīl, *at-Taṣawwuf fī Miṣr ibbān al-ᶜAṣr al-ᶜUthmānī* (Cairo, 1946), who quotes an unpublished MS of al-Munāwī's *Al-Kawākib ad-Durrīya*.

that he went himself with the Ottoman forces on campaign or sent along his representatives to bolster their morale. Significantly, he so attracted the attention and dislike of an Ottoman pasha that he was compelled to exile for a time in Istanbul. [29]

Shaykh Muḥammad ad-Damirdāsh too, founded a *zāwiya* on the outskirts of Cairo in what is now ᶜAbbāsīya and had a large following among the *ojāqs*. After his death, his family maintained his *zāwiya* and in the eighteenth century his descendants were still numbered among the prominent members of the upper classes of the city. [30]

The eighteenth century saw a renewed burst of Khalwatī activism in which even stronger links between the order and ruling bodies were forged. Muṣṭafā al-Bakrī aṣ-Ṣiddīqī (d. 1709), a Khalwatī and also a descendant of the first caliph of Islam, Abū Bakr, founded a family (Bayt aṣ-Ṣiddīq or Bayt Bakrī) whose head functioned as director and coordinator of Ṣūfī groups in Egypt from the seventeenth century until 1926. [31] According to al-Jabartī, he would mediate differences between the shaykhs of the Aḥmadīya, Rifāᶜīya, Burhāmīya, and Qādirīya *ṭarīqas*. [32] But the strongest impetus to the movement came from a Syrian shaykh, Muṣṭafā ibn Kamāl ad-Dīn al-Bakrī (d. 1749) who had studied first under a Naqshabandī guide and then under a Khalwatī in Aleppo. By means of a strong personal bond he sought to link various groups together in his own order.

The most interesting outcome of al-Bakrī's work was that several of his disciples developed the Khalwatīya within al-Azhar itself and a particular branch, the Qarbāshilīya, seems to have been "claimed as their own" by the *ᶜulamāᵓ* and shaykhs. Al-Jabartī records Shaykh al-Ḥifnāwī's initiation into it and his election as *khalīfa* and mentions the names of thirty *ᶜulamāᵓ* who were members. [33] Both al-Ḥifnāwī and ash-Sharqāwī formed Bakrīya subgroups of their own. Al-Ḥifnāwī (d. 1798) in particular, a friend and pupil of Shaykh al-Bakrī, was widely venerated and known for his concern for the people of Egypt. Al-Jabartī spoke of him as "Egypt's roof against disaster" and shows in his biography that no question of government was solved without

---

[29] B. G. Martin, "The Khalwati Order of Dervishes," p. 297.

[30] Al-Jabartī, *ᶜAjāᵓib al-Āthār*, II, p. 60; *Merveilles biographiques et historiques*, IV, p. 83.

[31] Muḥammad Tawfīq al-Bakrī, *Bayt aṣ-Ṣiddīq* (Cairo, 1905), p. 394.

[32] *ᶜAjāᵓib al-Āthār*, IV, p. 165; *Merveilles biographiques et historiques*, VIII, pp. 372-373.

[33] *ᶜAjāᵓib al-Āthār*, I, pp. 294-304; *Merveilles biographiques et historiques*, II, pp. 289-303.

acquiring his consent. He mentions also that his miracles were "too numerous to recount." [34]

In their membership, organization, and activities, the orders reflected basic tendencies in the structure of society. They also knit the social fabric, for it was through the mechanism of these popular religious organizations, by virtue of their openness, universality, and basic moral commitment, that individuals not only extended their social network but effectively reinforced their social ties.

With reference to recruitment and membership, for instance, the orders were Janus-faced, looking inward to particular social groups, families, or residents of certain quarters, but also outward to a potentially universal membership.

J. S. Trimingham states that the main factor in recruitment was the family link:

> You were, as it were, born a Shādhilī or a Khalwatī. You were associated with the local shaikh, his initiates and affiliates from infancy when an amulet made by him was hung around your neck and your mother first took you to the tomb of the *ṭāʾifa*-founder where you were offered for his blessing and intercession. If your father were of any note, on the night of your naming-ceremony a *mūlid*-recital was given in your honour; and similar recitals took place at your circumcision and on special occasions such as thanksgiving after illness or safe return from a journey. You learnt to recite the Qurʾān within the precincts of the *zāwiya*. You grew up to the sound of its songs, drum rhythms, and dances, and within the atmosphere of the protection and intercessions of its saints, on the aniversary of whose death you could let yourself go in the saturnalia of a *mūlid*. [35]

If a particular social and occupational group resided in a certain quarter, it follows that in religious association these people were pro-

[34] *ʿAjāʾib al-Āthār*, I, pp. 294-304; *Merveilles biographiques et historiques*, II, pp. 284-305. Al-Ḥifnāwī's spiritual heir, Maḥmūd al-Kūrdī (d. 1780) was supposed also to have had great charisma. According to al-Jabartī, he was able to see the Prophet at will and "had obtained many strange revelations" (*ʿAjāʾib al-Āthār*, I, p. 298; *Merveilles biographiques et historiques*, II, p. 297). Ash-Sharqāwī was a follower of al-Kūrdī.

Shaykh ad-Dardīr was another follower of al-Ḥifnāwī. He saw his own suborder as a bridge between Naqshabandī and Khalwatī movements and attempted to reconcile the differences between the two. A Mālikī from Upper Egypt, he was the chief of the Mālikī students at al-Azhar and directed their *waqf*. Known for his generosity and kindness, he also gained a great following and was known for his defense of the common people of Cairo (*ʿAjāʾib al-Āthār*, II, pp. 147-148; *Merveilles biographiques et historiques*, IV, pp. 289-291; B. G. Martin, "The Khalwati Order of Dervishes," pp. 303-304). See also above, p. 292.

[35] *The Sufi Orders*, pp. 225-226.

bably united as well. André Raymond feels that if any other type of group tends to be affiliated with the brotherhood it is the local group. [36]

But while there is little doubt that family, occupation, and locality were significantly correlated with membership, it is also true that on the whole, *there appears to have been no strict requirement, familial, occupational,* [37] *or otherwise, for recruitment.* Lack of education was no impediment to joining an order, although scholarly reknown may have facilitated entrance into some subgroups. The fact that there were inner and outer circles of devotees also facilitated accommodation of many persons as part-time practitioners. It is said that even the "orthodox" Khalwatīya, known for its association with the army, included women in its membership. [38] The military, while apparently dominated by the Khalwatīya, included representatives of all the orders. [39] Likewise, while some occupational corporations favored certain brotherhoods, it seems there never was a strict correspondence between orders and crafts. While some orders such as the Aḥmadīya and the Rifāᶜīya had more appeal among the lower classes than other orders, these also claimed many upper class adherents. [40]

Ṣūfism in practice was a means of integration, for the *ṭāᵓifa*s also provided a means of transcending hereditary limitations. Individuals could always choose their *ṭāᵓifa* and change allegiance if a new alignment of interests and relationships was called for. As Trimingham has said:

> The son of a peasant, by attaching himself to a shaikh, could exchange the confines of village life for the vast spaces of the Islamic world, sure of finding everywhere friends and the means to live and train. [41]

---

[36] *Artisans et commerçants*, II, pp. 439-440.

[37] Nearly the only evidence for definite association of occupational corporations with orders is found in Lane's statements that most of the Qādirīya were fishermen and that the water carriers called *ḥamalī*s often belonged to the Rifāᶜīya or the Bayyūmīya (*Manners and Customs*, pp. 249, 329). While we suspect that there was some kind of correlation between guilds and orders, the very isolation of these statements leads us to believe that an association which even approached strict relationship was the exception rather than the rule. André Raymond draws attention to the fact that affiliation with an order was a personal and not a collective matter and points out that many guilds had members who belonged to different orders even as the separate orders included persons who practiced different occupations (*Artisans et commerçants*, II, pp. 438-439).

[38] H. J. Kissling, "The Role of the Dervish Orders," p. 29.

[39] B. G. Martin, "The Khalwati Order of Dervishes," p. 297.

[40] A. Raymond, *Artisans et commerçants*, II, pp. 436, n. 1, 439.

[41] *The Sufi Orders*, p. 237.

It is of special importance that multiple memberships were exceedingly common. Al-Jabartī tells us that the great Khalwatī shaykh Maḥmūd al-Kūrdī continued to perform the ritual prayers of the order of ᶜAlī al-Quṣayrī to which he had belonged from his youth, even after his attainment of high position in the Khalwatīya as chief subordinate of Shaykh al-Ḥifnāwī. [42] In the sixteenth century the famous illuminate ash-Shaᶜrānī claimed he had been regularly admitted into twenty-six orders. [43] While loyalty was an essential condition of initiation [44] and on some occasions conflict might arise surrounding performance of ritual practice or belief, [45] there can be no doubt that the orders downplayed the idea of differentiation and appeal could be made to the ultimate origin of all in Qurʾānic truth and the authority of the Prophet.

Ultimately the vitality, membership, and integrative character of an order depended upon the personal influence of its shaykh. The very fact that this influence was *personal* and generally *disassociated* with family considerations meant that the brotherhood could cross-cut the strongest sociocultural boundaries. As Kissling has written:

---

[42] *ᶜAjāʾib al-Āthār*, II, p. 62; *Merveilles biographiques et historiques*, IV, pp. 89-91.

[43] Tawfīq aṭ-Ṭawīl, *At-Taṣawwuf fī Miṣr ibbān al-ᶜAṣr al-ᶜUthmānī* (Cairo, 1946), p. 75, quoting *al-Manāqib al-Kubrā*, p. 66.

[44] Lane describes the initiation ceremony or *ᶜahd* (compact) of the Damirdāshīya, which was generally similar to that of other orders:

> "Having first performed the ablution preparatory to prayer (the wuḍoó), he (the candidate) seated himself upon the ground before the sheykh, who was seated in like manner. The sheykh and he (the 'mureed,' or candidate) then clasped their right hands together in the manner which I have described as practised in making the marriage-contract: in this attitude, and with their hands covered by the sleeve of the sheykh, the candidate took the convenant; repeating, after the sheykh, the following words, commencing with the form of a common oath of repentance. 'I beg forgiveness of God, the Great' (three times); 'than whom there is no other deity; the Living, the Everlasting: I turn to Him with repentance, and beg his grace and forgiveness, and exemption from the fire.' The sheykh then said to him, 'Dost thou turn to God with repentance?' He replied, 'I do turn to God with repentance; and I return unto God; and I am grieved for what I have done (amiss); and I determine not to relapse:' and then repeated, after the sheykh, 'I beg for the favour of God, the Great, and the noble Prophet; and I take as my sheykh, my guide unto God (whose name be exalted), my master ʾAbd Er-Raḥeem Ed-Demirdáshee El-Khalwetee Er-Rifáʾee En-Nebawee; not to change, nor to separate; and God is our witness: by God, the Great!' (this oath was repeated three times). The sheykh and the mureed then recited the Fátʾḥah together; and the latter concluded the ceremony by kissing the sheykh's hand" (*Manners and Customs*, p. 250).

[45] Cf. the case of al-Kūrdī, al-Jabartī, *ᶜAjāʾib al-Āthār*, II, p. 62; *Merveilles biographiques et historiques*, IV, pp. 81-89.

> The report that many shaikhs had "revived" this or that country—*iḥyāʾ* is the term used—and had acquired in this process "thousands of disciples" is ... no exaggeration. These were the outer circle of sympathizers which often filled whole districts. [46]

The shaykh was the binding pin of the *ṭāʾifa*. He initiated members, led all ritual exercises and ceremonies, and to him unconditional obedience was due. In theory at least, his personal emanation of spiritual power was unlimited. It was commonly stated that "The dervish should be in the hands of his master like a corpse in the hands of the washer." [47] The fact that initiation was solely a matter which concerned the shaykh and the initiate greatly enhanced the social openness of the order; even the most esteemed members of the group had no part in acceptance of new candidates. The vows of the contract, moreover, involved only the most basic tenets of Islam and submission to the master. In all activities there was less emphasis upon the cooperative association of members than upon the relationship of each member to his spiritual guide.

This personal relationship with the shaykh was a relationship that could facilitate transition from one socio-religious group to another. Although it is impossible to discover from historical evidence whether common residence and economic association came before membership in an order in most cases, or vice versa, it cannot be denied that the mechanism was present for direct transition from one social group to another without previous interaction in other aspects of culture. Once *moral character* was established within the brotherhood (and it *was* evidence of moral responsibility that was required for residence in urban quarters), the way was open for the formation of more broadly based, more intimate reciprocal interactions between individual members. It would be perhaps, not far wrong to speculate that the orders generally paralleled and reinforced the clienteles in cross-cutting society.

Organizationally, Ṣūfī groups both reflected and justified the social order and corrected it with moral sanctions. Generally speaking, there was a dialectical interplay between formal rule and personal power; between the principle of election and the principle of heredity, and between the will of the rulers and the will of the ruled.

At the head of the *ṭarīqa* was the *shaykh as-sajjāda*. Since succession was spiritual, the occupant of this office was not necessarily related

[46] "The Role of the Dervish Orders," p. 29.
[47] *Ibid.*, p. 24.

to his predecessor. Often the superior designated a favorite disciple to follow him, or, if he did not do this, the brotherhood sometimes chose their leader. There was a marked tendency, however, for the headship of orders to become hereditary and this tendency grew stronger with the development of the saint cult and its associated concept of *baraka* (spiritual power) that was transmissable through the family line. Certainly the hereditary principle was an important factor in holding together groups of relatively loose organization which would have succumbed to centrifugal forces were it not for the personal magnetism of their leader. Adherence to the hereditary principle, however, may have been more characteristic at higher levels of organization than at lower levels. J. Heyworth-Dunne notes that in large "family orders" such as the Bakrīya led by Shaykh al-Bakrī and the Wafāʾīya led by Shaykh as-Sadāt, where the office of *shaykh as-sajjāda* was hereditary, it seems that "the shaykh of the order took part in the meetings and *dhikr*s only during the religious feasts and the mūlids." [48]

The *shaykh as-sajjāda* appointed *khalīfa*s to represent him at the district or town-section level. He gave these licenses (*ijāza*s) that authorized them to perform certain shaykhly functions. Especially if the order was very large, the *khalīfa*s were empowered to initiate new members, train them, and organize local gatherings. In some cases *nāʾib*s, or deputy *khalīfa*s were appointed also and the administration and finance of the *ṭāʾifa* was handled by one *khalīfa* who was appointed *wakīl* (agent). The duties of this official included not only collection of dues and contributions, but also the preparations for the *mawlid* of the patron and other celebrations. [49] Subordinate leaders usually obtained their positions through ability and appointment rather than hereditary right.

It is important to note that, while there was a hierarchy of shaykhs, *khalīfa*s, and *nāʾib*s within the order, and *khalīfa*s often instituted new lines, the genetic structure of Ṣūfī orders was not a matter of simple branching. From the historical perspective certainly, the picture was much more complex. Frequently a new luminary would emerge with innovative insights and practices (ʿAlī al-Bayyūmī from the Aḥmadīya) or would attempt to combine old *ṭarīqa*s in a new blend (Shaykh ad-Dardīr "reconciling" the Naqshabandī and Khalwatī *ṭarīqa*s). It

48 *Introduction to the History of Education*, p. 10; see the biography of Shaykh as-Sādāt in al-Jabartī, *ʿAjāʾib al-Āthār*, IV, pp. 185-196; *Merveilles biographiques et historique*, IX, pp. 38-54.

49 J. S. Trimingham, *The Sufi Orders*, p. 147.

might be hard to say whether such a one was a follower of an old way or the founder of a new one. When he established his own *zāwiya*, however, and was finally laid to rest in his tomb, the "parent" *ṭāʾifa* tended to lose its relevance for his followers. Moreover, because spiritual power was so diffuse, "saints" sometimes appeared "as from nowhere" to gain a following and to establish a shrine. Thus the orders multiplied as newly inspired or dissatisfied Ṣūfīs broke away from major lines to form *ṭarīqa*s of their own. [50]

With regard to the relationship of the orders and the ruling elite, as might be expected, it was rather ambiguous. The rulers depended upon the Ṣūfī leaders, even more than upon high ranking orthodox legalists for spiritual support. Ibn Iyās recounts how, when Sultan al-Ghūrī marched to Marj Dābiq, he surrounded himself with dervishes. [51] Following the military disaster, Ṭūmān-Bey gave a robe of honor to the son of the successor of Sayyid Aḥmad al-Badawī who had been killed by the Ottomans in the battle and "appointed him in his father's stead." [52] He also distributed one thousand dinars among the dervishes in the monasteries in and around Cairo and "gave five ardabbs of wheat to each monastery, desiring them to pray for victory to the Sulṭān and destruction to the enemy." [53] It seems, therefore, that sometimes at least, the government confirmed Ṣūfī shaykhs in office and certainly solicited their spiritual and political support.

On the other hand, if there were any bodies that maintained inde-

---

[50] *Ṭāʾifa*s, being social groups, rose and fell in the continual flux and disorder of life, but *ṭarīqa*s, being spiritual rules, had permanence as long as anyone chose to follow them. Even with respect to major ways, however, there seems to have been considerable flexibility. Depending upon its branch leaders, a *ṭarīqa* could tend toward orthodoxy or heterodoxy. We have noted above that, although there was a religiously based hierarchy of orders and a ranking according to "spiritual respectability," some *ṭarīqa*s that began as "heterodox" became "orthodox" and vice versa.

[51] "... On the right wing was the Amīr of the Faithful ... wearing a light turban and mantle, carrying an axe on his shoulder like the Sulṭān, and having over his head the Khalīfa's banner. Around the Sulṭān, borne on the heads of a body of nobles, were forty copies of the Korʾān ... There were also round him a body of dervishes, among whom was the successor of Seyyid Aḥmed al-Bedawī (founder of the Ṣūfī sect), accompanied by banners. There were also the heads of the Ḳādiriyyeh sect with their green banners, the successor of Seyyidī Aḥmed al-Rifāʿī with his banners, and Sheikh ʿAfīf al-Dīn, attendant in the mosque of Seyyidah Nefīsah with black banners" (Ibn Iyās, *An Account of the Ottoman Conquest of Egypt in the Year A.H. 922 (A.D. 1516)*, translated by W. H. Salmon (London: The Royal Asiatic Society, 1921), p. 41).

[52] *Ibid.*, p. 41.

[53] Ibn Iyās, *An Account of the Ottoman Conquest*, p. 95.

pendence, it was the Ṣūfī groups.[54] Shaykh al-Bakrī and Shaykh as-Sādāt, holding hereditary spiritual power in their own right were, apart from the elite, the two most powerful men in Cairo. Although these two contended for headship of the orders and for the office of *naqīb al-ashrāf*, an appointment which depended upon the favor of the ruling body, ultimately they can be seen as integrative forces in relation to the social system as a whole. Whenever mediation was required they came to the fore, whether the contending parties were amīrs or the rulers and the ruled. Their houses symbolized this role and provided not just a passive "neutral" meeting ground for warring parties, but places of refuge and appeal for all those who sought justice.[55]

In their activities, the *ṭāʾifa*s indicated an expansion of social consciousness with an increase in the extension and effectiveness of urban networks. J. S. Trimingham compares their *zāwiya* centers to local churches and says that the officials of the orders "approached nearer to a clergy class than any other in Islam."[56] While many local *ṭāʾifa*s centered upon the tombs of Ṣūfī saints, an establishment might be physically represented by a whole complex of buildings or even a tenement, in which case the entire household could be referred to as a *zāwiya*. Some groups did not have *zāwiya*s and communal functions took place in streets or houses of members.[57]

The shaykhs who administered such local "cells" were full members of society. For the most part they lived with their families and frequently continued to practice secular occupations. There was no conception that the dedicated life was inconsistent with the knowledge or practice of a craft or that the exercise of secular occupations conflicted with the possession of spiritual power. The spiritual mentor of ash-Shaʿrānī, ʿAlī al-Khawwāṣ, was first a trader in oils and then a palm leaf plaiter.[58] An Aḥmadīya holy man followed the occupation of a porter.[59]

---

[54] It is significant that *khānqāh*s that were supported by the state disappeared if they did not become integrated with a saint cult (J. S. Trimingham, *The Sufi Orders*, p. 69).

[55] Al-Jabartī, *ʿAjāʿib al-Āthār*, IV, p. 191; *Merveilles biographiques et historiques*, IX, p. 52.

[56] *The Sufi Orders*, pp. 71-72.

[57] *Ibid.*, pp. 174-226.

[58] *Ibid.*, p. 228.

[59] Al-Jabartī, *ʿAjāʾib al-Āthār*, I, p. 84; *Merveilles biographiques et historiques*, I, p. 197.

While there was no regular or strict relationship between the orders and the guilds, there certainly must have been some important informal ties. The idea of spiritual power was universal and no activities of any significance took place without due regard to it. Moral responsibility was an essential consideration in the acceptance of members into craft guilds, [60] but the guilds were not primarily spiritually oriented institutions. The factor of common locale was in all probability the mechanism of association. The butchers of Ḥusaynīya took advantage first of the *baraka* of ᶜAlī al-Bayyūmī and then of the leadership of the *khalīfa,* Aḥmad al-Jazzār, who was one of their own. Thus the orders consecrated secular institutions from the "lowest" to the "highest." Even the dancing girls (*ᶜawālim, ghawāzin*) were devoted to Aḥmad al-Badawī. At the end of the eighteenth century, Chabrol reported that some guilds practiced their trade inside a mosque. [61] When al-Azhar itself became a center of Ṣūfism, an organizational link was forged between the notables and the populace that greatly enhanced both mutual understanding and the possibility of united political action.

We have said that the orders were Janus-faced, looking inward to the interests of local groups and also outward to the world at large. Most people were attached to a *ṭāʾifa* from birth, but they became active initiates because of the benefits they received, benefits that pertained to vital aspects of their existence, spiritual, social, and economic. To multiply and extend these advantages, they did not hesitate to contract new memberships. To leave one's home quarter and to venture into the world at large was at best a hazardous undertaking. What better surety than the tie of brotherhood which gave one claim to hospitality, counsel, and any assistance that might be required? Thus the order not only consecrated the natural family but simultaneously created a spiritual family that in theory and practice formed a higher and wider "court of appeal."

There is another sense also in which the orientation of the orders was dual. Turning the above opposition inside out, we see that the most intense expression of their spiritual focus could result in a rejection of social ties (or, conversely, the pressures of social and family life could drive people to a life of seclusion and mysticism). While religiousity was not necessarily otherworldly for every practitioner of Ṣūfism, temporary withdrawal for training and shorter periods after-

---

[60] See above, p. 329.

[61] "Essai sur les moeurs," p. 379.

wards for the performance of exercises offered relief from the psychological stresses and strains of the outer world. [62] Individuals who sought permanent detachment could find a life of peace in *zāwiyas*, *ribāṭs*, and *khānqāhs* where the spiritual brotherhood took the place of the natural family, or even choose to adopt an existence as a hermit.

On the other side of the coin, those who used Ṣūfism as a means of escape did not entirely divest themselves of social responsibility. Rather the mode of their responsibility underwent a transformation. Dervishes of *takīyas* and monasteries fed travelers and the poor and asked no questions regarding social or religious connections. The people felt cared for by them and knew they could find refuge and support with them in any crisis, economic or political. Even the lone hermit was a source of spiritual benefit, for his *baraka* was an enhancement of his surroundings and remained a legacy when he was finally laid to rest in his tomb. [63]

The ultimate contradiction was that emphasis upon spiritual power and the application of spiritual criteria negated the social hierarchy. It did not simply ignore it. Religiously speaking, there were no classes. [64] Ash-Shaᶜrānī among others, regarded the orders as playing a vital role in Egyptian society and pointed out how many of the high *ᶜulamāʾ*, especially after the Ottoman conquest (the Turkish *ᶜulamāʾ*?),

---

[62] The exercises, although most often communally performed, were aimed at producing *personal* union with God. Common to all orders was the performance of *dhikrs*, or rhythmic repetitions (of the name of God). Sitting or standing in a circle facing each other, the dervishes would chant invocations accompanying these utterances with motions of the head, arms, and swaying of the body until almost exhausted. Frequently these performances were accompanied by flutes, drums, and tambourines, and, in the case of the Mawlawīs ("whirling dervishes"), the ritual was developed into a dance. Such practices which involved music and dancing, however, were frowned upon by the orthodox.

Some orders practiced ritual seclusion. Thus the Khalwatīs went into retreat for periods as long as forty days, fasting from daybreak until sunset in solitary cells. An Egyptian suborder, the Damirdāshīya, would go on the *mawlid* of the Shaykh ad-Damirdāsh to separate cells in his tomb-mosque in north Cairo and remain there for three days and nights, eating only a little rice and drinking a cup of sherbet in the evening. They would come out of their cells only to unite in the five daily prayers in the mosque; and would not answer anyone who spoke to them except to say "There is no deity but God" (E. W. Lane, *Manners and Customs*, p. 251).

[63] In the first part of the sixteenth century, a famous hermit and ascetic, a converted Circassian Mamlūk, lived in the Muqaṭṭam Hills for forty-seven years (J. S. Trimingham, *The Sufi Orders*, pp. 76-77).

[64] The social hierarchy in Islam, widely believed to be necessary, was a functional hierarchy. It was not reinforced by religious principles.

were detached from the life of the people. [65] A surfeit of legalistic training could blind the most well-meaning *ᶜālim* to social and moral realities, whereas for too many, the power that went with notability tended toward corruption. Venality and self-seeking hid under the aegis of official position. The people distrusted *ᶜulamā*ᵓ they did not know, especially as such were dependent for salaries and advancement upon the Ottoman and Mamlūk elite and were usually in collusion with them. [66]

It is a temptation to speculate that the efflorescence of Ṣūfism represented in part a rejection of the quest for political and economic power that seemed to dominate society. The life style of the Ṣūfīs and especially that of the dervishes generally stood in contrast to the life style of the elite, notables, and many of the high *ᶜulamā*ᵓ. Not only did Ṣūfī establishments engage in charitable activities, [67] but the fact that dervishes characteristically led lives of voluntary proverty made a deep impression upon people. Upon entering an order, respected scholars often divested themselves of their possessions and even their books, while many shaykhs were known to refuse presents, honors, and to undertake menial work. H. J. Kissling has called attention to Ṣūfism's implicit expression of socialistic ideas, noting that there is only one step from not allowing oneself any possessions to not allowing anyone else to own anything. The attitude that accompanied renouncement of material property was often an ostentatious display of scorn for persons in high places who continued to strive for the riches of this world. [68]

The effective social role of Ṣūfī orders largely depended upon the ambiguity of Ṣūfī ideology: it was the largely unrecognized but real contradictions that made resolution possible at the most comprehensive level of social structure. The dervishes had an aura of poverty but Shaykh as-Sādāt and Shaykh al-Bakrī each had more than one palace and the fullest purses in Cairo! The dervishes fed the people

---

[65] J. S. Trimingham, *The Sufi Orders*, pp. 223-224. See also above, p. 290, n. 42.

[66] B. G. Martin, "The Khalwati Order of Dervishes," p. 299, referring to Jamāl ad-Dīn ash-Shayyāl, *Muḥādarāt fī al-Ḥarakāt al-Islāḥīya wa Marākiz ath-Thaqāfa fī ash-Sharq al-Islāmī al-Ḥadīth* (Cairo, 1958), II, pp. 8, 9, 29.

[67] The Khalwatī *zāwiya* of Gülshenī near Bāb Zuwayla, for instance, emphasized the feeding of the poor. A *waqf* document cited by ᶜAlī Pasha Mubārak shows that besides having religious and supervisory personnel, and servants for the *khalwa*s, it had also a baker, a cook, and a "table-setter for the poor" (B. G. Martin, "The Khalwati Order," quoting ᶜAlī Mubārak, *Khiṭāṭ*, I, Book 3, p. 50; II, Book 6, pp. 54-55).

[68] "The Role of the Dervish Orders," pp. 28-32.

but the funds they used came not just from their own alms but from the generosity of the elite. The statement that "Riches do not matter" is ambiguous, but what really weighed in the balance was *sympathy*. The masses knew who would take their part and who would not. [69] Ṣūfī leaders, to represent the people effectively, had to have channels of power not just to the spiritual world but also to the elite, and especially to the resources of the real world. Their mainstay was their financial independence. In the last analysis it was only the surety of this support that maintained even tension in the social fabric. Only this prevented the collapse of effective networks that cross-cut classes under the one-sided pressure that emanated from the elite. The ultimate Cairene option was to downplay social conflict. Economic and political power created the social hierarchy but spiritual power, with its peculiar ambiguities, could assimilate and direct these very forces to undermine it.

3. *Saints, Symbols, and Symbiosis*

The significance of spiritual power as an integrative force cannot be fully appreciated without consideration of popular beliefs and especially of the religious symbols which gave structure and meaning to experience. Many, multidirectional, and often contradictory were the tendencies of social life. Is it any wonder then, that symbolic mechanisms, sublimely ambiguous yet so instrumental in the transmission of power, shifted into a multiplicity of gears?

Saints, not the secular authorities, were in the eyes of the people the determinants of history. Political regimes came and went but saints always remained, guarding, guiding, and generally maintaining the order of the world and of social relations.

The saints were far from shadowy figures. Everyone knew them not only from venerated tomb-shrines of pious persons long dead, and from miracles performed through the agency of these, but also by virtue of living examples. It was generally believed that a certain

---

[69] As H. J. Kissling has put it:

"The proletarian masses repudiate the 'upper classes,' whether these are men of wealth or of outstanding intellect. But such repudiation is directed only against those representatives who do not declare their solidarity with the masses. As soon as a man has been acclaimed by a socialistic group as 'leader,' although he may be boundlessly rich or a typical 'intellectual,' he will be accepted and even admired. He may do things without blame which would be strongly resisted if coming from 'others' " ("The Role of the Dervish Orders," p. 29).

constant number of saints were alive in the world at any given moment. According to popular tradition, the living saints, or *walīs*, were arranged in a hierachy under the *quṭb*, the "pole, or axis" of the world, upon whose intercession the very order of the cosmos and of social relations was thought to depend. Although the identity of the living saints was supposedly known only to themselves, the people were always on the lookout for evidence of their presence and it goes without saying that the most likely candidates for sainthood were Ṣūfī adepts.

The *ᶜulamā'* too, despite their sophisticated approach to Islam, had few doubts about the existence of saints. Indeed, many of them were candidates for sainthood. When in the fall of 1711, a well-meaning Turkish reformer, preaching in the Mosque of al-Mu'ayyad beside the Bāb Zuwayla, criticized the veneration of saints and even declared that their domes and *takīyas* be razed, he succeeded in rousing a mob to shout "Where are the saints (*awliyā'*)?" and to tear down all the rags on the gate that represented supplications of the *quṭb*. It was those "pillars of orthodoxy" the *ᶜulamā'* who issued a *fatwā* declaring that saints could perform miracles after death. The persons who had attended the preacher's sermons were punished and the miscreant was sent into exile. [70]

Like the orders, living saints came in various degrees of respect and probity. Although most people believed in saints, there was considerable difference of opinion as to who belonged to the saintly community. *Walīs* (holy men, saints) were thought to possess the highest form of magic power through their exclusive knowledge of the *ism al-ᶜaẓm* or "the greatest name of God." This magic was spiritual (*ar-rūḥānī*) as opposed to natural (*as-sīmiyā'*). Owing to the nature of the mystical state of mind, the most extreme behavioral aberrations were frequently accepted as evidence of sainthood. As long as a person did not seriously endanger the social order, he could commit the greatest enormities with no fear of reprisal. The streets were full of itinerant ascetics, idiots, and frauds who, from the appearance of mental distraction, real or pretended, were venerated by passers-by and made a living from their charity.

We do not mean to imply, however, that most of the saintly dervishes were insincere. Their way of life was accepted in Muslim society and sanctioned by the firmest religious and ethical beliefs. It is undoub-

---

[70] Al-Jabartī, *ᶜAjā'ib al-Āthār*, I, pp. 48-50; *Merveilles biographiques et historiques*, I, pp. 116-120.

tedly true that Ṣūfīs believed implicitly in the power of the shaykhs that they followed, if not in their own personal ability to produce miracles. The most mundane occurrences, moreover, might sometimes be interpreted as miraculous if motives of self-persuasion were there.

To the learned, most sophisticated Ṣūfī, a visit (*ziyāra*) to a saint's tomb was a way of honoring one whom God had honored and of focussing upon this symbolic personality as an aid to meditation. For the great mass of people, however, such visits provided not only a means of communing with a semi-divine intercessor but directly, "physically" receiving some of his *baraka*.[71] *Baraka* was a fearsome, yet a fragile thing, a thing of tenuousness and unpredictability. It was definitive of sainthood and manifest in miracles and in the charisma of Ṣūfī adepts. Increase in followers and offerings bore incontestable witness to its presence, while decrease in numbers of devotees and tributes just as strongly attested to its loss.

The symbolism of saints was amazingly integrative on different levels and in various modes. In the first place, it served to incorporate an exceedingly wide range of belief. This syncretic, unconscious fusion of ancient and un-Islamic ideas to an Islamic framework played an exceedingly important role in providing a common basis of interaction for ethnically and religiously differentiated social groups. Below the level of ideology in the abstract, this was grass roots integration: much more effective in some ways than the integration that was imposed by the governmental and legal framework, for the power of the saints was not only ideal, but incontestable, and like the power of God, but unlike that of the elite, it was imminent as well as eminent. What did it matter that a few dry academics called it "polytheism" and railed against it for its "perversion" of "true religion"? To most, it *was* the true religion. Spontaneously emergent, magically reinforced, the saint cult thrived among the people.

The world of the traditional Cairene included supernatural as well as natural forces, but he did not carefully distinguish between the two. The holy ones had their favorite haunts. The Bāb Zuwayla, that place of historical fascination and earthly retribution, frequented by the *quṭb*,[72] was the node of the spiritual network, but nearly every quarter

[71] One ritualistic way of obtaining *baraka* was to stand before the tomb and recite the *fātiḥa*. The power thus elicited was "caught" by raising the hands, palms upwards, and then passing them down in front of the face. Other methods involved touching or kissing the tomb, or acquiring pieces of its cloth covering.

[72] See above, Chapter X, pp. 177, 178, 179.

and many large houses had their own guardians. The Bayt al-Kretlīya, for instance, which stands beside the Mosque of Ibn Ṭūlūn, was protected by Sīdī Hārūn, a relative of Sayyidna al-Ḥusayn whose relics had also been brought to Cairo and deposited there by the Fāṭimids. Legends recount his many miracles, how he blinded a thief who had entered the house, and how he led to safety one of his servants who was trapped in a burning building. [73] The smallest domed tomb (*qubba*) on the narrowest street reminded every inhabitant of spiritual realities and social obligations.

Saints could exact retribution but they also offered protection. The unpredictability of spiritual power reflected the dangers of the traditional urban milieu, but the fact that it was accessible through intercession meant that it could provide a shield against all kinds of hazards. The tombs of *walī*s paralleled and intensified the function of the quarters in providing refuge from the arm of the law and from social vengeance. When sanctuary was claimed from the most widely venerated saints, this right was respected by the highest secular authorities. [74]

Other channels of *baraka* were manifest too in the practices of everyday life. The reading of the Qurʾān itself, for the popular audience, was a *baraka*-laden act and the most esteemed of all *ḥijāb*s (amulets) was a small copy of the Qurʾān (*muṣḥaf*) hung around the neck. While fortune-telling and the practice of magical arts was expressly forbidden by law, the sultan in Istanbul had his own astrologers appointed from the *ʿulamāʾ*. [75] The ability of Ṣūfī shaykhs to attract a

---

[73] See R. G. "John" Gayer-Anderson, *Legends of the Bait al-Kretliya* (Ipswich, 1951), for the stories recounted to him by the old Shaykh Sulaymān al-Kretlī who cared for Sīdī Hārūn's tomb until nearly the middle of this century and attested from personal experience to the power and miracles of the saint. It is significant too, that the house had not only an Islamic but a Pharaonic guardian, a serpent. Lane reported that each quarter "has its peculiar guardian-genius, or Agathodaemon, which (takes) the form of a serpent" (*Manners and Customs*, p. 233). In the words of Shaykh Sulaymān:

> " '... such (benevolent serpents) dwell only in these houses that are especially favoured as this one is by God's blessing, be it here in Cairo or out there among the fourteen Mudiriyas of Egypt. Such snakes are guardians that keep the place in their care allowing no other reptile to enter nor evil to harbour within its walls so that those who live here need have no fear of jinn or *afreet* and may sleep, if they will, with their doors left unlocked' " (*Legends of the Bait al-Kretliya*, p. 59).

[74] In 1768 a Mamlūk amīr, Khalīl-Bey al-Qāzdughlī, fleeing from the forces of ʿAlī-Bey, sought refuge in the tomb of Aḥmad al-Badawī at Ṭanṭa. His pursuers, not wanting to profane the sanctuary with the blood of a suppliant, spared him out of respect for the saint (al-Jabartī, *ʿAjāʾib al-Āthār*, I, pp. 317-318; *Merveilles biographiques et historiques*, III, pp. 31-32).

[75] H. A. R. Gibb and H. Bowen, *Islamic Society and the West*, I, 2, p. 205.

following was not separate from their ability not just to give sage counsel but to write effective charms. This was a carefully guarded art and the Maghribīs were reputed to be the most versed in it. Generally, this knowledge was handed down from father to son, together with collections of secret writings.[76]

Bradford G. Martin calls attention to the importance of magic in the "pastoral office" of the Khalwatī shaykh and its especial connection with his "psychiatric" and medical ministrations.[77] Even lesser *ᶜulamāᵓ* whose level of intellectual sophistication did not go beyond knowing how to write, *kuttāb* masters and *fiqīs*,[78] knew a few charms and composed amulets. Their advice was widely sought to avert the evil eye and to draw down *baraka* for the successful outcome of all sorts of enterprises.[79]

Religious celebrations, particularly *mawlids*, served to articulate the saint cult and other expressions of popular religion with the temporal order of social life. It is significant that historically *mawlids* did not become established until the thirteenth century A.D. and only gained official recognition two centuries later. Paralleling the rise of Ṣūfism, in many cases the celebration of saints' birthdays incorporated aspects of Shīᶜī and also non-Islamic celebrations.[80]

Highly esteemed scholars wrote books on a wide range of occult sciences from astrology, geomancy, and alchemy to the science of magic squares and the interpretation of dreams (J. Heyworth-Dunne, *Introduction to the History of Education*, p. 12).

[76] J. Heyworth-Dunne, *Introduction to the History of Education*, pp. 12-13.

[77] "The Khalwati Order of Dervishes," p. 294.

[78] The term "*fiqī*" is a colloquialization of "*faqīh*," meaning "jurisprudent." Popularly in Egypt it means a Qurᵓān reciter or school teacher.

[79] Especially the lovelorn solicited this kind of help. Women were concerned about retaining their husband's affections and bearing children, while men commonly sought assistance in the prevention of sterility (J. Heyworth-Dunne, *An Introduction to the History of Education*, p. 6).

It is interesting to note in passing, that the symbolism utilized in these magical arts was largely drawn from the universal substratum of lore and ancient belief and had only a thin Islamic veneer. What is more, the application of the mysteries of numerology to an already ambiguous set of symbols greatly facilitated symbolic "resolution" of paradoxes that presented dilemmas in social life. Thus the numerical values of the letters of the word "*walī*" (saint) added up to 46 and the numerical values of the letters of the word "*balīd*" (fool, idiot) also added up to 46. This result mirrored the fact that a simpleton was often thought to be a saint and the term "*walī*" became commonly used to mean "fool" (E. W. Lane, *Manners and Customs*, p. 235).

[80] The official observance of the Prophet's birthday, for instance, may originally have been intended as a compensation for the suppression of ᶜAlīd demonstrations which came to an end with the fall of the Shīᶜī regime (J. S. Trimingham, *The Sufi Orders*, p. 27).

Old hallowed places, already lore-enveloped, became resanctified by the superimposition of saints' tombs. [81] Interestingly enough, the *mawlid*s of two of the most important Egyptian saints, Aḥmad al-Badawī and Ibrāḥīm ad-Dasūqī, followed the Coptic solar calendar rather than the Islamic lunar calendar. It has been speculated that these and others incorporated a number of ancient Egyptian rituals and practices. [82]

*Mawlid*s, being an amalgam of ancient and Islamic ideology, of serious rites and more secular festivities, represented the most comprehensive and popular aspect of popular religion. [83] The Cairene populace celebrated a major *mawlid* at least once a month and of these, the Birthdays of the Prophet (*Mawlid an-Nabī*) and of Sayyidna al-Ḥusayn were the two most important. All arrangements were directed by Shaykh al-Bakrī and Shaykh as-Sādāt respectively, while the pasha and the leading beys and officers attended the opening of the festivities. [84] Such religious holidays were marked by a sharp increase in the activity of the orders and visits to the tombs of the saints. No holiday passed during which the cemeteries were not crowded from dawn until sunset and in the streets, where colorful tents were set before the mosques, the celebrations went on through the night. People would turn out in

---

[81] The Jabal Yashkūr, for instance, was not only the site of the Bayt al-Kretlīya and the tomb of Sīdī Hārūn, but according to legend was the place where Abraham had prepared to sacrifice his son, where Moses had seen the burning bush, and a number of other miracles had occurred (R. G. "John" Gayer Anderson, *Legends of the Bait al-Kretliya*, passim).

[82] J. W. McPherson, describing the *mawlid* of Aḥmad al-Badawī, wrote ...

"The Feast of Sayed el-Badawi at Tanta, is regarded by many Egyptologists as a revival of that of Shoo, the God of Sebenytus, owing some of its wonderful vogue to the mighty body and tremendous character of Ahmad suggesting subconsciously to the remote descendants of the 'Egyptian Hercules', the hero of the ancient cult" (*The Moulids of Egypt*, p. 3).

[83] As E. E. Evans-Pritchard wrote:

"... a moulid is not, and cannot be, a purely religious ceremony. It has, and must have, a secular side to it ... The secular festivities bring the people together and make the occasion a memorable one in their lives. A man remembers what he has enjoyed. The religious rites provide the festivities with a purpose and a centre round which they move. The festivities prevent the religious side from becoming a formal, lifeless, professional ritual performed by a few persons who have a local or some other exclusive interest in their maintenance. The religious rites prevent the festivities from becoming formless social gatherings, lacking the regularity and a special character of their own which alone enables them to endure" (Forward to *The Moulids of Egypt by* J. W. McPherson, pp. ix-xi).

[84] A. Lutfi al-Sayyid Marsot, "The Ulema of Cairo in the Eighteenth and Nineteenth Centuries," p. 152.

such numbers that it was not unusual for some to be trampled in the crowd. Aḥmad Chelebi reported that in 1728, seventeen people were killed in the crush at the *mawlid* of Aḥmad ar-Rifāʿī. [85]

The lesser *mawlid*s must have numbered at least two hundred. [86] Since nearly every quarter celebrated the birthday of its spiritual patron there was hardly a time, except for the months of Ramaḍān, Shawwāl, Dhū al-Qaʿda and Dhū al-Ḥijja, months which had their own spiritual activities, when these festivities were not going on in some part of Cairo. On all these occasions, there would be sports, games, singing, dancing, shadow plays, and all kinds of revelry. Coffee houses and eating places did a vast amount of business as old friends met to share holiday joy and outsiders took advantage of the free and open festive spirit to discover new dimensions of Cairene society.

Religious activities connected with *mawlid*s were both socially divisive and integrative: simultaneously they proclaimed social identities and provided a means of overriding, at least temporarily, differences in rank and status. [87] The most spectacular sights were the processions and performances of distinctive miracles by Ṣūfī brotherhoods and active participation on such occasions signified sympathy with the religious persuasion it involved. On the other hand, the fact there were various degrees of affiliation, and above all the fact that popular religion, especially the saint cult, was syncretic in nature, contributed to the blurring of distinctions of allegiance. [88] The religious celebrations in Cairo were generally unmarred by the conflict which often

---

85 André Raymond, "Quartiers et mouvements populaires," p. 109.

86 J. W. McPherson noted nearly that number in his study done during this century (*The Moulids of Egypt*, pp. 347-349).

87 In our own day J. W. McPherson noted:

> "It is a pity that of recent years rich and poor have drifted somewhat apart, at festivals and functions common to both. Typical of this is the "Cutting of the Khalig." This ceremony ... has not changed materially, but a decade or so ago, the evening celebrations, tashrifa, fireworks, and the rest were all together at the Fum el-Khalig, and there was a certain *Gemutlichkeit* about it which was quite lost when the reception tents were erected in a special enclosure on Roda Island, and the populace (was) ... only able to hear the bands and see the fireworks from the other side of the water. In the same way the intimate charm and atmosphere of friendly fellowship has gone from the Mahmal and Holy Carpet festivals to a considerable extent. This will be found very marked in the accounts of the moulids of Mohammadi (sic), Imam el-Shafei and some others" (*The Moulids of Egypt*, (Cairo, 1941), p. 11).

88 As Lane observed:

> "It is a very remarkable trait in the character of the people of Egypt and other countries of the East, that Muslims, Christians, and Jews, adopt each other's superstitions, while they abhor the leading doctrines of each other's faiths. In sickness, the Muslim sometimes employs Christian and Jewish priests to pray

took place in other parts of the Islamic world on such occasions. The religious minorities were too few in numbers to challenge the majority, and the majority by this time had long felt secure enough to tolerate and even incorporate considerable freedom of religious expression. Persons of every faith were glad of an excuse for a holiday. Even Copts were accustomed to hang lamps before their doors on the *Mawlid an-Nabī*. [89]

Periodic festivals then, gave symbolic expression to the tendencies of social life and played an important role in coordinating social relations. Generally, they gave opportunities not just for congregating but for openly making social contacts. Some regularly observed restrictions were relaxed on the occasion of celebrations. Women, for instance, seem to have participated quite prominently since they had great attachment to the cult of saints. [90] Most such contacts may, on account of their lack of "social depth," not have resulted in profound alteration of social networks but, on the other hand, any relaxation of usual restraints must have facilitated the development of symbiotic bonds even between special status groups. On the occasion of the *Mawlid* of al-ᶜAshmāwī, the same night as the *Mawlid an-Nabī*, Lane witnessed the celebrations near the tomb of this saint near the palace of Shaykh al-Bakrī beside the Ezbekīya. He mentions not only dervishes, but poets, dancing girls, and prostitutes. There was also a crowd of Copts:

> I observed many Christian black turbans here; and having seen scarcely any elsewhere this night, and heard the frequent cry of "A grain of salt in the eye of him who doth not bless the Prophet!" ejaculated by the sellers of sweetmeats, &c., which seemed to shew that Christians and Jews were at least in danger of being insulted, at a time when the zeal of the Muslims was unusually excited, I asked the reason why so many Copts should be congregated at the scene of this zikr: I was answered, that a Copt, who had become a Muslim, voluntarily paid all the expenses of this Moolid of the sheykh Darweesh ... [91]

---

for him: the Christians and Jews, in the same predicament, often call in Muslim saints for the like purpose. Many Christians are in the frequent habit of visiting certain Muslim saints here; kissing their hands; begging their prayers, counsels, or prophecies; and giving them money and other presents" (*Manners and Customs*, p. 241).

[89] E. W. Lane, *Manners and Customs*, p. 246.

[90] Lane tells us that he saw a great number of women and children, mostly of the lower classes, at the Mosque of Sayyidna al-Ḥusayn on Yawm ᶜAshūra:

"It is commonly said, by the people of Cairo, that no man goes to the mosque of the Ḥasaneyn on the day of ᵓĀshoorá but for the sake of women; that is, to be jostled among them; ..." (*Manners and Customs*, p. 436).

[91] *Manners and Customs*, pp. 450-451.

It is understandable that many Copts would be present to witness the spectacular performances of holy men, especially in the light of the fact that the Coptic quarter borders on the Ezbekīya. It is far more significant that the presence of many of them at the Prophet's birthday was in the context of the birthday of a saint with a substantial local following. Conversion to Islam, therefore, often meant membership in a special group of believers. It was not only profession of the Faith that was important, but also the establishment of one's position in a social cell.

Sprung from the social matrix like Athena from the head of Zeus, the popular cult both mirrored social tendencies and provided a focus for social movements. When saints and *walī*s unconsciously articulated the social consciousness, it was inevitable that the tongue in which these holy ones spoke should be an ambiguous, equivocal tongue, even as it expressed the simple truths of social reality.

Spiritual power was, in the broadest sense, a popular power and expressed the popular interpretation of social life in all its contradictions. Unlike political and economic power, it emanated from a level of reality beyond the sway of any ruling group or dynasty, although governments tried to manipulate it by granting official recognition to time-honored traditions and even initiating new ones. As was the case with other urban "corporations," popular religious institutions looked both inwards and outwards. Because of the strength of the ties that bound people to their shaykhs, and especially because of the emotive power these commanded, potentially the political role the orders could play was relatively great. Yet since the "orthodox" establishment had come to terms with popular religion, and under the Ottomans had even succeeded in largely incorporating it, in general religious expressions of popular feeling were regulated and kept within bounds that were consistent with economic and political realities.

Although it is true that for many, the comforts and reassurances of popular belief and mysticism were a means of escape, to relegate spiritual power to the sphere of rationalization and fatalism is to miss the main point. *The appurtenances of spirituality and morality were an essential and real part of status, rank and prestige.* In the traditional society even the elite could not ignore this essential fact of life. Respectability, trustworthiness, sympathy, generosity and especially charisma were important in the formation of clienteles. The elite could take away the estates of the *ʿulamāʾ* and curtail their right to enter into governmental decisions, but until the modern era they could not really directly control the wellsprings of popular opinion and the peculiarly emergent forms of its expression. Even when the traditional society finally disappeared under the impact of Westernization, and new cadres of administrators replaced the *ᶜulamāʾ* in many of their former capacities, for several decades the orders and the saints still remained as focal points of social feeling, while celebrations gave opportunity for articulation of social consciousness.

Because it was more fluid than political or economic power, spiritual power represented in general an element of stability in times of change and flux. Ultimately, it was integrative because on the one hand it had reference to a universal overarching ideological framework, and on the other to the ever-readjusting network of ties that constituted the social fabric. *Ideal sanctions were fixed but interpretations were variable.* This crucial fact permitted continual realignments in the dialectical interplay of social life with no explicit alteration in basic beliefs or even any conscious reappraisal of the assumptions that underpinned the entire system with its multiple transformations.

CHAPTER EIGHTEEN

CONCLUSION: THE NATURE OF URBAN UNITY

In retrospect, the history of Cairo from the foundation of its first constituent enclaves until the end of the traditional period shows not only growth, but progressive transformations of a single basic pattern. The principal developments of urban life came into existence in response to specific situations which altered the relationship of the city to the world outside and brought about changes in the alignment of networks that made up the fabric of social life. Unity was not simply characteristic of particular synchronic manifestations of the complex pattern of social relations, or even a goal toward which the whole moved. Basic unity had depth in time; it was contained in the set of "genetic" assumptions that underpinned the whole.

The elemental factors that shaped society sprang not only from an ideological framework but from the actual conditions of existence. Essentially ill-defined, in their various permutations and combinations, the basic assumptions of life represented the constant interaction of the ideal and the real.

The salient condition, the greatest problem that Cairene society faced was the gross uncertainty of its environment, natural and cultural. Even during the periods of Fāṭimid and Mamlūk efflorescence, when Cairo had no peers politically or economically, the spectre of disaster in the form of famine, plague, and political upheaval lurked in the hearts of men who, in living memory, had experienced such terrors. Intimate documents of social life and folklore as well as chronicles all attest to the fact that, despite long term affluence, relatively speaking, the short-term fluctuation of the fortunes of individuals did nothing to erase the subsistence mentality or inspire confidence in the future. The threat was not just general but specific. Every breakdown of authority and order had an immediate and obvious effect upon means of subsistence and access thereto. Moreover control of Egypt, on the crossroads of the world, was ever essential for founders of empires and the power of the Cairene elite was inevitably contested from abroad as well as from within.

The condition of everpresent threat gave rise to the leading idea that an effective military elite was necessary to existence. Even the religious notables acquiesced in a secondary political role and looked to the military for leadership. It was also realized from the start that the military elite had to maintain their separation from the rest of society both to maintain discipline and to avoid the sapping of their strength by internal forces that sought to infiltrate their ranks.

The recognition of the validity of social diversity was also a response to real conditions. It *was* a fact that Cairo, being on the crossroads of the world, came to contain many different ethnic and religious groups. It was also a fact that from the beginning, no single group was truly able to dominate all, either demographically or with respect to control of the necessary resources, military, economic, spiritual, or administrative. The combination of the environmental threat with the existence of such differences gave rise to a generally "humble" if not fatalistic attitude toward the alignment of social relations. If the medieval Cairene realized anything, he realized that change was imminent and that new configurations perpetually reappeared in the fabric of social life.

The social hierarchy was regarded as inevitable, but with the exception of the elite, the hierarchy did not refer to the true social groupings that were real in the same way that special status groups were real. Thus while one social category might, in many cases, gain ascendancy over others, the totality was not articulated primarily in terms of stratification. Ranks rather represented positions of individual attainment as the heddle of fortune opened up new interstices in the structure of power. The factions, fluid and socially heterogeneous as they were, were the real units of social action. Islamic feudalism had little in common with the feudalism of Christian Europe. It was much more "democratic." There were really only the rulers and the ruled, but the former group, being defined chiefly by its military functions, could not hope to do all of the ruling. "The ruled," therefore, included notables as well as commoners who all were at liberty to contend for resources and advantageous positions from which to manipulate the social network. For the most part the military elite were concerned with tax collection and only indirectly or secondarily involved themselves in administration and social control. A large portion of the profits from tax collection were left in the hands of the *aᶜyān*.

Of essential importance was the fact that in Islam, spiritual and economic power tended to reinforce one another. Because there was no strict division between the religious and secular life, many persons whose chief resources were spiritual were able to play prominent roles in politics and commerce. In the abstract, this bond meant more appropriate objectification of religious ideals as well as the pervasion of administration and commerce by the values of religious ideology such as trustworthiness, fairness, and willingness to accommodate. Socially, it meant the emergence of a class of notables, respected and wealthy families, who were able to curb the excesses of the elite.

The cleavage between the rulers and the ruled meant also that even as the elite had to form alliances with the subject population to attain their ends, so the latter, *recognizing the necessity of an exclusive military elite, could only deal with that elite through alliance, clientage, and "working from within."* Given the premise that special statuses were valid (and the rulers : ruled dichotomy was a form of special status), the negation of one group by the other was no longer an option. It became imperative not just to coexist but to accommodate.

Phrased in other terms, specific systems of values lay behind different special status groups and a major function of the law was to preserve the boundaries of these groups, but there was constant tension between these (restrictive) rules and the need for action. Boundaries were continually eroded by interpersonal liaisons created by the demands of accommodation. It was important that only the *minimum* of *religious* exclusiveness was set by legal rules. Custom maintained spiritual and ethnic speciality but also countenanced the blurring of borders by "traditional" patterns of alliance. Personal bonds thus to some extent compensated for the inequities of the formal system and modified the structural emphasis upon diversity. Islamic ideology proposed that "differences are valid" but ultimately this proposition implied some broader frame of reference even than Islam, the implicit system of values of a truly cosmopolitan society.

It is perhaps an inversion of the true state of affairs to begin with groups defined by the principle of diversity. [1] The bulk of the evidence presented in this book reflects a complex society that consistently

---

[1] Thus C. A. O. van Nieuwenhuijze has pointed out that Middle Eastern man, in contrast to Western man, "can afford to employ segmentation to full advantage" because he *presupposes* the holistic approach to reality (*Sociology of the Middle East*, p. 34). To Western man who represents reality as intrinsically segmented, complexity or segmentation within an ideally homogeneous state poses a problem. The Middle Easterner, on the other hand, perceives the political, economic, and religious not as separated compartments but as simultaneous aspects of unified social action. Also accepting social heterogeneity as an inevitable fact of life, the totality consists both of the intrinsic unity of reality and the reaffirmation of the validity of the segments as parts of the whole. Cf. *Sociology of the Middle East*, pp. 36, 575, 761.

struggled against a tendency of amalgamation, continually attempting to preserve and restate group boundaries rather than to eradicate them in a "melting pot" of social homogeneity. As essential as the principle of diversity was the assumption that formal ties of alliance would be supplemented by less well defined ties of personal friendship and patronage. The informal network not only bound together diverse groups but also penetrated them, for such relations concerned individuals rather than groups. Thus the scope allowed for personal initiative was directly related to the fact that the boundaries of social segments were not well defined but blurred and perpetually advanced and retreated in response to varying incentives for cooperation and restraints.

Rules of order were ever enmeshed in the formidable toils of the social network. Indeed, the ideal system was sometimes obscured completely by the real system that impinged upon it. Institutions as basic organizational forms are not of much help in understanding the social structure. [2] *They are more useful when understood as particular manifestations that result from the interplay of basic relationships, of*

---

[2] Institutional change, moreover, is more easily understood as the result of changes which took place in the pattern of interaction and alliance. The explicit framework of rules governing institutions changed infrequently over the centuries, but people and circumstances often did. Old rules were reinterpreted to fill contemporary needs. On the other side of the coin, when the rules did change, it was not unknown for old patterns of interaction to bring matters around to where they had been in the first place.

The real import of rules emerges when they seem to break down. Ordinarily the law and institutions served as a framework on which to hang the fabric of life, but all too often the social network so enveloped formal ties and so bent the rules that they appear to have lost their effectiveness completely. Almost, but not quite. The breakdown of rules in some instances seems to have generated alternative and "opposite" rules to restore tension and therefore order to social relations. It is possible to view the emergence of the Mamlūk institution with its peculiar denial of hereditary rights in favor of the "rights" of clients as an inversion of the regular mode of preserving exclusiveness through emphasis upon descent and formation of alliances with other orders of society through patron-client ties. (Kinship could reinforce solidarity but it could also weaken a group by setting up internal oppositions and especially, through generational depth, by creating a grey area of marginal persons who were neither inside nor outside the elite.) Since the formal rule of kinship had not preserved the exclusiveness of the elite, there was an attempt to substitute a special version of the "informal" patron-client relationship (significantly conceived in terms of pseudo-kinship) where the former had failed. Exclusiveness then came through patron-client ties and contributing ties with society came through the offices of relatives and *awlād an-nās*. *But the Mamlūk principle only retained effectiveness in conjunction with and in contrast to the principle of heredity.* Sultans continued to appoint their sons as successors because, despite the fact that such were constantly displaced, the original formal rule of heredity was never really abrogated.

variables of inclusion and exclusion, of variations in scale, and in the relative distribution of elements of power. Seen over a long period, institutions are nearly as fluid as the flow of life from which they emerge. Many had a marked lack of explicit formal structure until the Ottoman period. Cairene social structure emanated not as much from institutions as from much more basic and general presuppositions about human relationships and the conditions of existence.

One of the most notable things about Cairene society was that as a whole it exhibited a lack of centralization and coordination. [3] Indeed, the centrifugal forces of urban life tended to predominate to the extent that it needed repeated governmental drives to organize, regulate, centralize, and control urban institutions. The real effective units were the fluid clienteles that infiltrated and manipulated the institutions. The knots of the social fabric were personal ties derived from the debt structure of kinship, friendship, and patronage. Clienteles were made up of individuals from all walks of life and operated through chains of effective personal connections rather than by strict reference to the rules. It was because of the prevalence of the clienteles that cross-cut society that there were no effective social classes and because of them that no single group managed completely to monopolize power. Impositions tended to be erratic, individualistic, and particularistic, even as were complaints against them. Only temporarily did "class struggle" become group action. Even the elite rarely acted as a whole outside the sphere of military endeavors. More usually houses, individuals, and families struggled alone.

Yet from the very apparent disorder a kind of unity emerges, a unity which, in the last analysis had reference to the cultural majority and especially to the elite. Even as the elite were the group most set apart by their ethnicity and speciality, so they provided a counterpoint for other specialities and a structural (if not cultural) model for the units composing the society as a whole. Just so, it was the existence of the Muslim group that threw the social identities of other religious groups into relief. We have here not integration but *parallelism*, even though it should be noted that except for the contrast in a few crucial elements, overall similarities can be found in culture patterns. [4]

[3] The looseness of the social structure and the lack of emphasis upon organized institutions is clearly seen in the frequent use of the word *ṭāʾifa* (group) for all types of associations, whether organized or not. The occupational *ṭāʾifa* and the religious *ṭāʾifa* had corporate attributes but rarely seem to have been corporations in the fullest sense of the term.

[4] Cf. C. A. O. van Nieuwenhuijze, *Sociology of the Middle East*, p. 579.

The peculiar cement of urban society depended in large part upon *convergence*, convergence that had genesis in the vital role of the elite as the keystone in the mosaic of components. It was they who, by sheer force, provided secure anchor points for the development of the clienteles and factions even as it was they who stimulated economic and cultural growth both as protectors and consumers of resources. In a sense, the whole society fed upon the elite, even as the elite fed upon society.

The third type of social cement concerned the overlap of social networks, the fact that for individuals reality was of a piece. The coexistence of kinship groups, professional associations, quarters, and cross-cutting factions and clienteles precluded the possibility of disjunction or polarization on the basis of contrast or conflicting interest. Conflict of interest, rather than being ultimately disjunctive, in fact gave rise to new kinds of alliances.

Despite political and economic upheavals, change was not essentially chaotic but coherently related to the operation of basic genetic principles which in various permutations and combinations, manifested themselves in the flux of history. Successive regimes, like chambers of an involuted helix, revealed progressive variations of a single basic scheme, successively transformed by variables of scale and the distribution of power.

Changes in scale and in the orientation of the center of power significantly altered the relation of the local rulers to ruled. The increase in size with the simultaneous increase in complexity (diversity) necessitated the development of formal frameworks of interaction as well as the extension of informal chains of connection. The separatist elite both preserved diversity and promoted unity by utilizing or modifying already existent local institutions of control rather than imposing new ones wherever possible. The larger the population ruled, the less capable the rulers were of imposing their will on a society that not only expanded but became more complex and diversified. Therefore they came more often to use the modes of accommodation and "legitimization" rather than force. Thus there was always more continuity at lower levels of administration than at upper levels and urban notables played an essential role in providing stability when the elite power structure crumbled or fell. Out of the experience of social disorientation and shock a new configuration would emerge that differed from the old not as much in essential form as in degree of comprehension and complexity.

The original founding of Fusṭāṭ necessitated decisions concerning the meaning of religious allegiance and the definition of the relationship of the rulers and the ruled. The gulf between Muslims and *dhimmīs*, then recognized, was never truly bridged but the relationship of the conquerors to the conquered was over the centuries to have many and various interpretations. Under the first Arab regime, the rulers were defined not only as Muslim but as Arab. When Arabs increased in numbers and many of them, through economic and social ties, became fused to the ruled, the elite boundary was reasserted first by a substitution of Turkish or Persian ethnicity and then by a combination of ethnicity and slave status. By the Ottoman period the Mamlūk elite had come to recognize the contribution of the Egyptian base to the essence of their own identity; by the time of Muḥammad ᶜAlī, the "Turkish" elite had begun to be aware of their Egyptian nationality vis-à-vis the nations of Europe.

Yet over more than 1,500 years few basic changes in conditions or basic assumptions emerged. There were always military rulers and non-military ruled. There were always diverse groups with divergent interests. Every assertion of control by one faction was inevitably contested by another, or even by nature herself. The omnipresent threat for every group was internal as well as external. They all experienced the seeping away of their strength through the interstices in their ranks created by the very extended liaisons that nourished them. In the medieval environment what everyone knew in their hearts was that conflict and change, not harmony and equilibrium, were real. The dynamic drama of life wove a tapestry that tended to obscure its regular and fundamental underpinnings and even more importantly veiled their essential contradictions and ambiguities. Diversity did not exist without unity nor conflict without accommodation. The form of complex society that emerged was both dynamic and persistent, both flexible and stable.

Ultimately it was flexibility and the capacity for readjustment that accounted for the persistence, the very survival of a society in an environment so unstable that it could not allow the luxury of social revolution. Plague, famine, and the horrors of invasion and conquest frequently enough provided change. Society in the traditional period in fact never had opportunity to become constricted by an inflexible mold that was no longer appropriate for real conditions. On the contrary, it took real effort to assert social order, let alone maintain it in the turbulent stream of reality.

As the social hierarchy and special status served to articulate mobility, so divisiveness was the other side of unity. Contradictory functional requirements were always a problem. Rules of recruitment for every group were simultaneously rules of exclusion; exclusion meant attempts to relate to other groups through symbiotic bonds. The symbolic tapestry of deference and avoidance that asserted differentiation shielded individuals from increasing perils of interaction in a social environment that had not only expanded but which had become continuously more unpredictable by accretion of differences. Ritual and etiquette preserved speciality but at the same time prevented alienation. For the ruling elite, even more than any other group, security was seen in exclusiveness. Yet their very particular military interest made ties with clients all the more imperative. The fine roots and tendrils of the network by which they bound themselves, foreign bodies, to the social matrix nourished their houses, but in conjunction with a basic tendency of encystment, increased pressures that sundered them from within.

It is a great oversimplification, even a misstatement of the case, to say that the middle and lower orders of society simply acquiesced in the knowledge that there was no way to challenge the overwhelming military power of the elite. It has been asked why powerful secular and religious notables did not put an end to the custom of rule by an unruly military even when, as at the end of the Ottoman period, they held the reins of government in their hands. Obviously they were not capable of replacing military protectors in that role. The fact of the matter was that they *were* secular and religious notables and not military men. But there is a paradoxical truth here also. They did not want to become rulers because they already ruled. As middlemen they connected and managed the central lines of administration. They also untangled and managed the affairs of an elite whose prowess, for the most part, did not include diplomacy and who were chronically weakened by dissension, dissension that in itself added strength to the notables and further increased their opportunities for manipulation. Elite regimes came and went and elite houses came and went faster. The notables, on the other hand, went on. Notables not only had a stake in *the* military establishment but in *any* military establishment that was the prevailing one. Without such an establishment, however, there was nothing to translate, to mediate, or to manipulate. It is perhaps an ethnocentric question based on a misunderstanding of Islamic "feudalism" to ask why the middle class did not seize formal political power even when the opportunity was presented to them.

During the Ottoman period, the local elite with an ultimate interest centered upon Cairo were confronted by another dominant foreign elite, not locally oriented, that attempted to replace and exclude them. Their ranks decimated and broken, the only way to maintain themselves was to *include* local notables and others to face the common enemy. But the relation of the rulers to the ruled was fraught with friction and possible resolutions to the problem were also seen in the extension of alliance to other spheres of interaction. Some notables and merchants saw in collaboration with foreign powers a means of preserving the interests of their group. The segments that made up urban society then achieved an informal unity previously unknown but also a degree of disorder not before in evidence. Pressures on Egyptian resources emanating from abroad increased conflicts and pressures already at work. By the end of the eighteenth century the panicky rapacity of feuding houses, the venality of officials, and general interference with comfortable traditional usages heralded a new crisis.

A disciplined and capable central government was a keystone in the structure of urban life. Without such a keystone there was unity but this unity lacked coordination. Moreover the centrifugal forces that increasing size, diversity, and density engendered were no longer balanced by any strong centripetal pull that normally preserved the tension necessary for the weaving of the social fabric.

Political and economic power shifted their center of gravity as conquest bred contest but spiritual power provided an important key to urban unity as it underwent major transformations in the passage of time. From the start, ideology was expressed at different levels of social structure and the locus of spiritual power was ambiguous. In the early settlements, orthodox religion was a mechanism of social differentiation rather than an encouragement to unity. Even the Islamic recognition of the "People of the Book" by which these people were granted a form of acceptance in Muslim society made this acceptance conditional upon the retention of special and mutually exclusive status. In the area of everyday life, on the other hand, popular beliefs and practices continually fermented to produce a common outlook and basic understandings that no official dogma could erase. The extension of the "orthodox umbrella" over the most diverse manifestations of spirituality, moreover, signalled the emergence of a religious establishment with the greatest integrating powers. Al-Azhar in fact was, in microcosm, an image of the larger society. While excluding *dhimmīs*, it was a community that included every type of Muslim in Cairene society regardless of rank or ethnic derivation.

The ultimate transformation in the realm of spiritual power is seen in the development over the centuries of a more *inclusive moral order.* The Ottoman developments through which orthodoxy and heterodoxy were fused can be translated not just in religious terms but in terms of developing social sophistication and broadmindedness. It is entirely possible that the attempts of the Ottoman government to articulate social life sprang not simply from a desire to control through centralization, but a realization that group boundaries, even those traditionally supported by ideology, were breaking down. Spirituality had lost none of its power to specify and differentiate but developed into the most important mechanism for coordination of social life.

If traditional Cairene society was anything it was a cosmopolitan society. It developed through the ramification of its international ties as diverse groups with diverse interests converged upon a limited space and competed for limited resources. There was much cause for conflict but less for agreement. *The problem was solved not so much by facing it directly through formal allocation of spheres of interest but rather by avoiding explicit delineation of boundaries beyond a minimum that was not to be trespassed.* Chronic dissension and shifts in the balance of power gave rise to social mobility, but most important, experience of conflict and instability made for flexibility, social sophistication, and the ability to accommodate. Through manipulation of reciprocal ties of alliance, patronage, and friendship, the ambiguous but undeniable debt structure of favors, the inhabitants of Cairo continually and patiently coped with basic and often unpredictable challenges to existence. By avoidance of confrontation or rather, *by acceptance of the inevitability of confrontation and subsequent manipulation of it*, the social fabric progressively absorbed a wide range of incongruent and even contradictory elements and successfully incorporated them into its own design. Continual reinterpretation preserved the elemental framework with its essential underpinnings of original premises.

Social movements crystalized around the policies of particular regimes but, because of a constancy in basic assumptions and principles, the specific configurations that emerged tended to fall into a repetitious pattern. The drama of Cairene history tended to obscure the fact that there were no true social revolutions. Drama rather added intensity to essential delineation of social relationships and etched more deeply the interlockings of a single elastic arabesque, an arabesque that was basically constituted of a few simple motifs, but which evolved an infinitely involuted and nearly endless series of transformations on different levels. A fine network of interpersonal ties threw into relief the formal design, sometimes contributing substance to ideal forms, sometimes calling attention to ideal forms through negativity and contrast.

Integration was characteristic of the malleable ideology that permitted symbiotic readjustment rather than the objectification of that adjustment. In the dimension of the real, the ultimate contradiction was that the warp of special status and the weft of the social hierarchy were maintained as mobility in all directions increased. The loose symbiotic knots, weaving a union that was no union, produced a social mobility that stimulated the continual reassertion of structural differentiation. Islamic acceptance of differences established a kind of ideal social unity that extended far beyond the borders of Cairo and of Egypt. The ultimate ideological contradiction was implied in the assertion that "differences are valid," a statement that can be transformed through a change in emphasis into an even more ambiguous proposition that "differences do not matter." Formal frameworks that contained implicit contradictions provided the tension necessary for the weaving of the social fabric, but only the ambiguity of even more basic principles gave the required flexibility as a continually more comprehensive, yet ever more involuted, social tapestry was worked on the loom of history.

EPILOGUE

MODERN CAIRO: TRANSFORMATION OF THE TRADITIONAL PATTERN

There can be no doubt that the city of the present, in outward form and inner working, manifests tremendous changes. The modern distribution of variables of power and especially the vast alterations in scale that have taken place over the past centuries have combined to produce transformations hitherto undreamed. A totally new aspect pervades the nature and role of government, and major shifts in the keystone have had impact on the whole. Socially, old collectivities have broken up and stratification has received new impetus with the advent of environmental stability and the emergence of more broadly based social groupings. It would seem a simple matter to state that the traditional pattern is no more and go unchallenged. Yet logic as well as fact protests that this is too simple. The statement "it changed" itself implies that something basic is ongoing. Understanding demands that we probe contemporary manifestations in terms of the broadest generalizations derived from the past, and in so doing, meet head-on the nature of change itself with what it might bring for the future.

The principal aspect of the transformation of the social fabric is reflected in the vastly greater emphasis upon the whole rather than its social components. This tendency, heralded by Muḥammad ᶜAlī's decimation of notables and of the landlords who had previously mediated the relationship between the elite and lower orders, has now been reinforced to the point of non-return by technological developments that enable the government to control more directly popular social movements. By closing the major channels of popular opposition, Muḥammad ᶜAlī created huge gaps in the weave of the social fabric that have not been completely filled until now. It is only in our own day and age that we can again speak of "politics" that involves levels of society other than the highest echelons of military and the educated upper class. Muḥammad ᶜAlī's institution of an all pervasive governmentally appointed hierarchy, however, made way for the modern order by linking each citizen directly to the state. Major shifts in the modes of military and economic power together with essential changes in the framework of government ultimately gave rise to the possibility of revolution in social goals as well in methods of achieving them.

Most of the major threads that give structure to the social fabric still lead to a military elite but the leaders as well as the army now represent national rather than foreign interests. The elite, still largely defined as military elite, determine the objectives of the development process, if not the details of its implementation. The 1952 revolution even more than the "revolution" of Muḥammad ᶜAlī represents the threshhold of modernity. Yet, it is only fair to ask "How revolutionary is the revolution?" Certainly ᶜAbd an-Nāṣir, like Ṣalāḥ ad-Dīn and Muḥammad ᶜAlī before him, strove primarily to make Egypt competitive among the nations of the world and to make Cairo a capital to rival the greatest seats of political, ideological, and economic power. There is considerable doubt, however, that there ever was, or yet is, any thought of transforming the social fabric by replacing the underlying system of values and attitudes manifest in personalized networks with formal mechanistic modes of getting things done. True, there is realization that some social attitudes must be modified, but modified only to the point at which they no longer interfere with the attainment of development goals. "Social revolution" in the deepest sociological sense, never has been a goal. Moreover there is yet no consensus as to what "development" and "modernization" mean, let alone a sophisticated sociological realization on the part of the social managers that the traditional pattern of relations might not in the last analysis be consistent with the needs of full technological development. The new elite like the old elite, and like most Egyptians, take the social structure for granted. They are too practical, too realistic, and too intelligent to cut away their base and the base upon which the success of specific development projects depends by destroying the fabric of social reciprocities and patron-client ties that has made Egyptian society viable over the centuries.

In any case, development generally does not depend primarily upon the elite and their perspectives, even though they may initiate it. It depends upon the interaction between the lower orders and the power structure and especially upon those who, at the local level, shoulder its burden. The nation-state has been established. The long arm of government reaches into economy, polity, religion, and even into family. Even so, in the Middle East even more than in the impersonalized, technocratized West, where most "independent" internal structures have long ago been eroded, the state cannot be everything to everybody. In form, governments may appear more totalitarian, but in operation they are not. In the old days the elite struggled to keep their distance but were forced to compromise themselves to control the threads of the social fabric. Nowadays they have squarely faced the fact that they must depend not so much upon exclusiveness as upon effective ties with their support base. The social trappings of the elite still make them conspicuous, but even more than in the most "liberal" eras of the past, the phenomenon of government is pervaded by the two-fold tendency of the elite to enlist the aid of the middle orders and of the latter to become established amidst the elite.

The crux of the question of the nature and extent of societal transformation really lies in the structure of the lower orders even more than in the structure of the elite or the outward forms of government. It should be noted in the first place that the middle orders never were more than roughly defined as a class. Indeed, it was their very "residuality" that formed the basis of their potential in mediation. The implementation of the 1952 revolution saw another decimation of notables in the religious institution and the business community and the virtual removal of the great landlords as a power group. The bureaucracy, however, of necessity has not only continued but expanded.

To some degree the centralization of resources under government control, and especially progressive industrialization, seems to have brought about the emergence of a variety of "middle class" that resembles the middle layer of Western society. Since it is by no means alienated from the elite, however, it remains to be seen whether it will fully emerge as a well-defined entity. Moreover the character of any social class depends upon the entire system of "stratification." In Cairene society, now as traditionally, the lowest levels of the masses that are likely to present the most problems are not made up of persons directly and regularly involved in urban institutions but rather a subproletariat of those who have not succeeded in finding places in the structure of the labor market. Unemployment is a serious problem; in the long run, industrialization may make it more rather than less.

While the government has sought to strengthen its positions by circumventing the traditional mediators and appealing directly to commoners, its success in this aim depends upon the degree to which it can politically awaken the common man and mold his outlook into a reliable support base. At least now the masses are becoming sensitized to their role in public affairs through government sponsored organizations and through the media. Indeed, it *is* something of a revolution that we can now speak meaningfully of a public domain that is something other than a "free-for-all" or a no-man's land.

Ultimately major revolution in the social fabric can only come about through change in the mode of making social linkages and in the values and attitudes that form the essential underpinnings of social relations. A key to this is communication of information as well as of authority. Much has been claimed for the impact of the transistor radio upon the popular mentality and certainly the mass media are essential channels of government-disseminated information. On the other hand, no careful study has ever been made of the context of reception and it is exceedingly doubtful if the rumor-opinion network is any less effective than it ever was. Much listening and viewing is a matter of group participation and local opinion leaders still shape the end result. Moreover there is considerable evidence that, as traditionally, official reports tend to be taken with more than a grain of salt.

With regard to the transmission of authority, urban officials are still appointed by the central government, which still uses the local social network to check on people's comings and goings. Even in Garden City, the *shaykh al-ḥāra* and the *bawwāb*s play central roles in maintaining order. Ostentatiously, large bureaucratic offices have multiplied and uneasy petitioners find themselves entangled in more official red tape than ever before. Yet, as anyone who has lived in Cairo knows, the way into the office is through the back door rather than the front. It is still a contest between clients for the fruits of patronage rather than an "automated" and "impartial" distribution of privilege. The idea is to manipulate formality if possible rather than to use it to increase efficiency. Technical efficiency is not an end, or even seen as the preferable method of obtaining results. Social relations are still valued *per se*, and even conflict plays a positive role. How many times has the author been advised by her Egyptian friends, when applying for some simple privilege that Westerners would take for granted: "You *must* quarrel with him!" Essentially such an attitude has basis in lack of assurance about the dependability of political and economic stability. The governing elite themselves, still unsure of their support base, would not risk altering the pattern rigorously. In any case alienation would be more likely to result from an unrelieved dependance upon technical formality than a continuance of traditional mores.

In an era in which change seems paramount, it is instructive to try to relate the character and prospects of modern Cairo to the character of change in the world at large. The impact of technological advance is beyond doubt the primary factor. Ecologically speaking, the technological revolution has directly or indirectly given rise to disorientation and to urban blight. For instance, the whole concept of the street has changed. The physical framework of the old city assumed human interaction, a slow-moving pedestrian traffic, rather than hundreds of thousands of cars, trucks, and buses rushing past and tending generally to ignore the cultural content along the way in their sole concern to reach a destination. Most foreign visitors to the city are struck by the dilapidation of all but the newest areas and the congestion that has resulted from the staggering rate of population growth and the influx of refugees from the canal cities devastated by war.

Certainly the contrast between the new and old architecture and the new and old style of life indicates a contest between spurious and genuine culture, at most a depressing frustration of spiritual coherence, at least a challenge to the search for cultural identity. It is a mistake, however, to overlook the temporal context of these manifestations of change. It may be that the challenge is now greater than ever before, but there has never been a time when dilapidated and crumbling properties did not stand beside modern ones, when major streets were not so crowded that the pedestrian ran the risk of being crushed, and when the most dramatic reshuffling of allegiances and values was not called for. The central government always did act as a keystone and now a new kind of coherence is being achieved as its even more penetrating authority is complemented by the increasing participation of other social components. In any case it is necessary to interpret the so-called "urban blight" with reference to deep principles of social structure rather than simply to accept the visible "Westernized," "secularized" façade of "modernity" as definitive.

Ultimately the shape of Cairo's future, even more than the shape of its past, depends upon the world context. It is change in scale more than any other factor that is central to the issue. The configuration of internal components has always been responsive to the international distribution of power, but now the unprecedented rate of change combined with the confrontation of major value systems calls for a basic reappraisal.

Of essential relevance is the confrontation of the Oriental and Western conceptions of change. [1] The latter combines a directional flow with the comparatively recent assumption that technological advance is the principal causative factor. It is both ethnocentric and tem-

---

[1] C. A. O. van Nieuwenhuijze, *Sociology of the Middle East* (Leiden: E. J. Brill, 1971), pp. 38, 682, 690.

porocentric. Our own experience of the past two centuries confirms our faith in the inevitability of technocracy and the resulting crumbling of religious and humanistic values. The future is seen to depend upon the concrete present rather than upon the lessons of long past experience. The Oriental idea, on the other hand, is that eternal ideal norms have equal relevance for any of the infinitely varied manifestations of concrete reality. Separate transformations are deviations from the norm, but still stand in more direct necessary relation to it than to each other. In other words, the future is in the hand of God and no matter how obvious the characteristics of the present situation may appear, their inevitability for the future is looked upon with some skepticism and doubt. Thus, the "fatalism" of the "Oriental attitude" is a kind of humility born of chronic instability and experience of change. Security is found under the elastic umbrella of ideology rather than faith in the as yet unfulfilled promise of technology.

Bearing in mind this traditional conception of change, it is entirely possible to view the developments of the past two centuries in Egypt as attempts at restoration and revitalization rather than true revolution. Muḥammad ᶜAlī and Jamāl ᶜAbd an-Nāṣir, like Ṣalāḥ ad-Dīn were primarily concerned to breathe new life into the sociocultural and political entity to enable it to face the challenge of the West. Western modes were adopted not to further the development of Westernization, but rather to eliminate its impact. It is, of course, entirely probable, even most inevitable, that the sum total of piecemeal borrowings of Western culture, spurious as they now appear, may eventually add up to major changes in the operational modes of social life. The general lack of direct attack upon the attitudinal underpinnings of the traditional pattern, however, facilitates accommodation of change by the elastic traditional ideology.

One mistake Western interpreters of change on the Middle Eastern scene are prone to make is the result of their own culture-biased view of the general phenomenon. They tend to think in terms of dichotomies, that is, ideology : technology, religious : secular, past : future, to say nothing of circumscribing Islam in very narrow limits. As we have seen in traditional Cairo, a man's religion did not just delimit his social sphere but as *dīn*, with reference to general attributes of respectability, trustworthiness, and reliability, gave him access to social groups beyond his own even as it pervaded all of his activities.

In the broad sense, ideology is nothing more or less than fundamental perceptions of the nature of reality and the way in which it operates. Socially, ideology refers especially to perceptions of the meaning of differences, whether they be religious, ethnic, political, or economic. All change, even change in the technocratic world, involves a reordering of older concepts; shifting emphases, changing priorities, making "relative" things "absolute" and "absolute" things "relative." New transformations are nothing more or less than the result of such manipulation. The conceptual content of Islam still provides nearly unlimited possibilities for reinterpretation, a fact certainly not lost upon the elite who steer the course of social action. Religious sanctions even stand behind the Egyptian elaboration of socialism. Thus, "democracy" and "social justice" relate to the concept of *umma* or community of believers and to the idea of consultation and consensus that goes back to the early days of Islam. The strict and regular observation of religious ritual and the other-world reference has weakened in many circles, but the government sees to it that a considerable amount of television and radio time is given over to religious observances and subsidizes trips to Mecca. Even as Islam incorporated many ideas even older and more deeply rooted than itself, so it can stimulate and incorporate new interpretations through the perpetual interaction of the ideal and the real. No new cultural integration, no new assertion of identity is likely to emerge apart from it. In the political context, development results from the manner in which the followers follow, not simply how the leaders lead. Moreover the leaders have no desire to overturn the ideological foundations of their own social matrix.

In the last analysis, we should ask "How inevitable are the values of a technocratic society for the world of the future?" and "What are the central challenges that Egyptian society, as part of human society, will face?" With regard to the first question, while it is highly probable that technological development will proceed at a more and more rapid pace, the inevitability of the implicit system of values that lies behind "technocratic culture" is seriously open to question. Not a few sociologists, scientists, and novelists have for a long time now, decried the lack of social and moral sophistication to parallel development in the technical sphere. Now there are signs that the Western "man in the street" is beginning to realize the naiveté of the assumption that more technology is the whole answer to his problems. The present and threatening energy crisis at least encourages a more humble attitude and less arrogant stance vis-à-vis value systems that emphasize human and personal considerations rather than efficiency. Already "liberation" movements in Western culture have reasserted the value of ethnic and racial identities and masses of youth, feeling the lack of humanizing influence in technocratic civilization, have gone off to establish their own communes.

With regard to the second question, the modern change in scale has brought us to the point at which it is even more appropriate to speak of complex societies rather than cities. The international balance of power plays an even more direct role in shaping the future of component entities. The key to the problems that Egypt faces today lies not just in the nature of her own polity but in the nature of the polity of human society and the relationship between them. If world catastrophy from a lack of social, moral, and political development does not occur, man may be able to benefit from a restoration of the "world balance of power." Even as it was through historical accident that the complex of Western industrialism was able to impose itself upon the world and, for two centuries, overwhelm "preindustrial" civilization, so the very extension of technological improvement and industrialization to "the developing world" may bring about a restoration of the balance. The attitudes and values of Western technocracy may, in the long run, turn out to be based upon short-term affluence.

If, in the future, social perspectives continue to broaden to human society as a whole, then the Cairene experience of urbanism may indeed present a more relevant model than the Western technocratic one in all its overwhelming glory. With respect to the critical factor of the confrontation of ethnic groups, the situation much more nearly parallels the confrontation of nations in the contemporary period. It is highly unlikely, given the nature of human beings to assert their special identities as well as to strive for connections, that the community of nations will become fused in a melting pot.

Cairene society, with its perennial experience of conquest and fusion, of all societies has the social sophistication to meet the challenge of the new age. It is accommodation that is most needed when the social stresses to which technology gives rise, surpass the ability of rigid formal structures to contain them. In the Cairene context conflict has never signalled the eradication of differences. Conflict rather has signalled the positive search for new adjustments, new transformations, in which the components find more comfortable relations between themselves and to the whole. It is perhaps not irrelevant that Anwār as-Sādāt who steers the present course is of the family of Shaykh Anwār as-Sādāt who successfully mediated conflicts of two centuries ago.

On the Cairene scene, participation is more and more coming to modify one-sided authority as formal communication channels between elite and commoners complement the informal networks that have always been there to redistribute more evenly the variables of power. To a considerable degree the aloofness between the majority and minorities is being eroded. The differences between the past and the future, however, are of degree rather than kind. Technology may be recent but experience with social crisis is far from new. It is certain that a new cement is being forged to assert the primacy of the social composite over components, but it is equally certain that through increasing internationalism, the problem is even now being reborn at another level. When it appears in the full glory of its challenge the victorious city, as ever at the center of the world, will be ready.

SELECTED BIBLIOGRAPHY

I. PRIMARY SOURCES

Adler, Elkan N., ed. *Jewish Travelers.* London: George Routledge and Sons, 1930.

Breydenbach, Bernard de. *Les saintes pérégrinations de Bernard de Breydenbach.* Translated by F. Larrivaz. Cairo, 1904.

Browne, W. G. *Travels in Africa, Egypt and Syria from the Year 1792 to 1798.* London: T. N. Longman and O. Rees, 1799.

Bruce, James. *Travels to Discover the Source of the Nile in the Years 1768, 1769, 1770, 1771, 1772, and 1773.* Vol. I. Edinburgh: G. G. J. and J. Robinson, 1790.

Burton, Richard F., translator and editor. *The Book of a Thousand Nights and a Night.* 10 vols. Benares (= Stoke Newington), 1885; *Supplemental Nights.* 6 vols. Benares (= Stoke Newington), 1886-1888.

Clot-Bey, Antoine-Barthélemi. *Aperçu général sur l'Égypte.* 2 vols. Paris: Fortin, Masson et Cie., 1840.

Chabrol, Gilbert J. G. de. "Essai sur les moeurs des habitants modernes de l'Égypte." *Description de l'Égypte, État moderne.* Vol. II, 2, pp. 361-526. Paris: L'Imprimerie Royale, 1822.

Denon, Vivant. *Travels in Upper and Lower Egypt During the Campaignes of General Bonaparte in the Country.* Translated from the French by Arthur Aikin. 2 vols. New York, 1803.

Estève, M. R. X. "Mémoire sur les finances de l'Égypte depuis la conquête de ce pays par le Sultan Selim Ier jusqu'à celle du Général en chef Bonaparte." *Description de l'Égypte, État moderne.* Vol. I, 1, pp. 299-398. Paris: L'Imprimerie Impériale, 1809.

Gayer-Anderson, R. G. "John", translator and editor. *Legends of the Bait al-Kretliya.* Ipswich, England: The East Anglian Daily Times Co., 1951.

Girard, P. S. "Mémoire sur l'agriculture, l'industrie, et le commerce de l'Égypte." *Description de l'Égypte, État moderne.* Vol. II, 1, pp. 491-714. Paris: L'Imprimerie Royale, 1812.

Ibn al-Athīr. *Al-Kāmil fī at-Tārīkh.* Edited by C. J. Tornberg. 12 vols. Leiden: E. J. Brill, 1851-1876.

Ibn Baṭṭūṭa. *Mahdhab Riḥla ibn Baṭṭūṭa.* 2 vols. Cairo, 1934, 1939.

——. *The Travels of Ibn Baṭṭūṭa (A.D. 1325-1354).* Translated and selected by H. A. R. Gibb. 2 vols. Cambridge, Eng.: The Cambridge University Press, 1958-1961.

Ibn Duqmāq. *Kitāb al-Intiṣār li-Wāsiṭāt ᶜIqd al-Amṣār (Description de l'Égypte).* Edited by Karl Vollers. Cairo: Imprimerie Nationale, 1893.

Ibn Ḥawqal. *Kitāb Ṣūrat al-Arḍ.* 2 parts in 1 vol. Leiden: E. J. Brill, 1938.

——. *Configuration de la terre* (a translation of *Kitāb Ṣūrat al-Arḍ*). Introduced and translated by J. H. Kramers and G. Wiet. 2 vols. Beirut: Commission Internationale Pour La Traduction des Chefs D'Oeuvres, 1964.

Ibn Iyās. *Badāʾiᶜ az-Zuhūr fī Waqāʾiᶜ ad-Duhūr.* 2 vols. Cairo (Būlāq), 1892. Vols. IV-V. 2nd edition edited by Muḥammad Muṣṭafā. Cairo, 1960-1961.

——. *Badāʾiᶜ az-Zuhūr fī Waqāʾiᶜ ad-Duhūr.* Edited by P. Kahle, M. Muṣṭafā, and M. Soberneim. Vols. III-V. *Bibliotheca Islamica* 5/c to f. Istanbul, 1931-1936.

——. *An Account of the Ottoman Conquest of Egypt in the Year A.H. 922 (A.D. 1516)* (a partial translation of *Badāʾiᶜ az-Zuhūr*). Translated by W. H. Salmon. London: The Royal Asiatic Society, 1921.

——. *Histoire des mamlouks circassiens* (a partial translation of *Badāʾiʿ az-Zuhūr*). Translated by Gaston Wiet. Vol. II. Cairo: Imprimerie de l'Institut Français d'Archéologie Orientale, 1945.

——. *Journal d'un bourgeois du Caire; chronique d'Ibn Iyās* (a partial translation of *Badāʾiʿ az-Zuhūr*). Translated by Gaston Wiet. 2 vols. Paris: A. Colin, 1955, 1960.

Ibn Jubayr. *Riḥlat Ibn Jubayr*. Beirut: Dār Ṣādir, 1959.

——. *The Travels of Ibn Jubayr*. Translated by R. J. C. Broadhurst. London: Jonathan Cape, 1952.

Ibn Khaldūn. *The Muqaddimah, an Introduction to History*. Translated by Franz Rosenthal. 3 vols. New York: Pantheon Books, 1958.

——. *At-Taʿrīf bi-Ibn Khaldūn wa Riḥlatuhu Gharban wa Sharqan*. Edited by Muḥammad ibn Tāwīt aṭ-Ṭanjī. Cairo, 1951.

Ibn Khallikān. *Kitāb Wafayāt al-Aʿyān (Ibn Khallikān's Biographical Dictionary)*. Translated into English by M. de Slane. 4 vols. Paris: 1843-1871.

Ibn Taghrī-Birdī. *Ḥawādith ad-Duhūr fī Madā al-Ayyām wa ash-Shuhūr*. Edited by William Popper. *University of California Publications in Semitic Philology*, Vol. VIII. Berkeley: University of California Press, 1930-1931.

——. *Al-Manhal aṣ-Ṣāfī*. Vol. I. Cairo, 1957.

——. *An-Nujūm az-Zāhira fī Mulūk Miṣr wa al-Qāhira*. Edited by William Popper. *University of California Publications in Semitic Philology*. Vols. V-VII, XIII, XIV, XVII-XIX, XXII. Berkeley: University of California Press, 1915-1960.

——. *History of Egypt, 1382-1469 A.D.* Translated by William Popper. 7 vols. Berkeley: University of California Press, 1954-1960.

al-ʿIrāqī. Adh-Dhayl ʿala Kitāb al-ʿIbar. MS Dār al-Kutub al-Miṣrīya, Cairo, no. 5615.

al-Jabartī. *ʿAjāʾib al-Āthār fī Tarājim wa al-Akhbār*. 4 vols. Cairo (Būlāq): Imprimerie Nationale, 1880.

——. *Merveilles biographiques et historiques ou chroniques du cheikh Abd-el-Rahman el-Djabarti*. Translated by Chefik Mansour Bey et al. 9 vols. Cairo: Imprimerie Nationale, 1888-1896.

al-Jazarī. Jawāhir as-Sulūk fī Khulafāʾi wa al-Mulūk. MS Dār al-Kutub al-Miṣrīya, Cairo, no. 7575.

John, Bishop of Nikiu. *The Chronicle of John, Bishop of Nikiu*. Translated from Zotenberg's Ethiopic text by R. H. Charles. Oxford, 1916.

Jomard, E. F. "Description abrégée de la ville et de la citadelle du Kaire." *Description de l'Égypte, État moderne*. Vol. II, 2, pp. 579-778. Paris: L'Imprimerie Royale, 1822.

al-Kindī. *Kitāb al-Wulāh wa Kitāb al-Quḍāh*. Edited by Rhuvon Guest. Leiden: E. J. Brill, 1912.

Kitāb adh-Dhakāʾir wa at-Tuḥaf fī Bīr aṣ-Ṣanāʾiʿ wa al-Ḥiraf. MS Landesbibliothek of Gotha, Arabische Handschrift no. 903.

Lane, Edward W. *An Account of the Manners and Customs of the Modern Egyptians* (1836). 1860 edition. London: Everyman's Library, 1908.

——. *The Arabian Nights Entertainments*. 3 vols. London: Routledge, Warne, and Routledge, 1865.

——. *Cairo Fifty Years Ago*. Edited by Stanley Lane-Poole. London: J. Murray, 1896.

Le Mascrier, Jean Baptiste. *Description de l'Égypte... composée sur les mémoires du consul de Maillet*. Paris, 1735.

al-Maqrīzī. *Ighāthat al-Umma bi-Kashf al-Ghumma*. Edited by Jamāl ad-Dīn Muḥammad ash-Shayyāl and Muḥammad Muṣṭafā Ziyāda. Cairo, 1940.

——. "Le traité des famines de Maqrīzī" (a translation of *Ighātha*). Translated by Gaston Wiet. *Journal of the Economic and Social History of the Orient*, V (1962), pp. 1-90.

——. *Itti^cāẓ al-Hunafā^ɔ bi-Akhbār al-A^cimma al-Fāṭimīyūn al-Khulafā^ɔ*. Edited by H. Bunz. Jerusalem, 1909.
——. *Kitāb al-Mawā^ciẓ wa al-I^ctibār bi-Dhikr al-Khiṭaṭ wa al-Āthār.* 2 vols. Cairo (Būlāq), 1854.
——. *Kitāb as-Sulūk li-Ma^crifat Duwal al-Mulūk.* Edited by M. Muṣṭafā Ziyāda. 6 vols. Cairo, 1934-1958.
——. *Histoire d'Égypte* (a partial translation of *Sulūk*). Translated by E. Blochet. Paris, 1908.
al-Mas^cūdī. *Kitāb at-Tanbīh. Bibliotheca Geographorum Arabicorum.* Edited by M. J. De Goeje. Vol. VIII. Leiden: E. J. Brill, 1893.
——. *Murūj adh-Dhahab.* 4 vols. in 2 Cairo, 1958.
——. *Les prairies d'or* (a translation of *Murūj*). Translated by Barbier de Meynard and Pavet de Courteille, revised and corrected by Charles Pellat. 2 vols. Paris: Société Asiatique, 1965.
Mengin, Felix. *Histoire de l'Égypte sous le gouvernement de Mohammed-Aly.* 2 vols. Paris: A. Bertrand, 1823.
Michaud, Joseph F. and B. Poujoulat. *Correspondence d'Orient, 1830-1831.* 8 vols. in 4. Paris, 1833-1835.
Minutoli, Wolfradine (von der Schulenburg) von Watzdorf. *Recollections of Egypt.* Translated by S. H. L. Philadelphia: Carey, Lea and Carey, 1827.
Mufaḍḍal ibn Abī al-Faḍā^ɔil. *An-Najh as-Sadīd wa ad-Darr al-Farīd.* Edited and translated by E. Blochet. "Histoire des sultans mamlouks." *Patrologia Orientalis*, XII (Paris, 1919), pp. 345-550; XIV (1920), pp. 375-672; XX (1929), pp. 1-270.
al-Mu^ɔminī. Futūḥ an-Naṣr fī Tārīkh Mulūk Miṣr. MS Dār al-Kutub al-Miṣrīya, Cairo, no. 2399.
al-Muqaddasī. *Kitāb Aḥsan at-Taqāsīm fī Ma^crifat al-Aqālīm.* Edited by M. J. De Goeje. Leiden: E. J. Brill, 1967.
Nāṣir-i Khusraw. *Sefer Nameh. Relation du voyage.* Translated from the Persian by Charles Schefer. Paris: E. Leroux, 1881.
Piloti de Crete, Emmanuel. *L'Égypte au commencement du quinzième siècle.* Edited with introduction and notes by P.-H. Dopp. Cairo: Cairo University Press, 1950.
al-Qalqashandī. *Aṣ-Ṣubḥ al-A^cshā.* 14 vols. Cairo, 1914-1928.
——. *Al-Qalqashandī: Les institutions des Faṭimides en Égypte.* Edited by Marius Canard. Algiers: La Maison des Livres, 1957.
St. John. James Augustus. *Egypt and Mohammed Ali: or Travels in the Valley of the Nile.* 2 vols. London: T. N. Longman and O. Rees, 1834.
——. *Egypt and Nubia.* London: Chapman and Hall, 1845.
as-Sakhāwī. *Aḍ-Ḍaw^c al-Lāmi^c.* 12 vols. Cairo, 1934-1935.
——. *At-Tibr al-Masbūk fī Dhayl as-Sulūk.* Cairo (Būlāq), 1896.
Savary, Claude Etienne. *Letters on Egypt.* Translated from the French. 2nd edition. London: G. G. J. and J. Robinson, 1787.
Sāwīrus ibn al-Muqaffa^c (Severus of Ushmunayn). *Historia Patriarcharum Alexandrinorum.* Edited by C. F. Seybold. *Corpus Scriptorum Christianorum Orientalium.* Scr. Ar. Ser. III, tom. 9 fasc. 1, 2. Beirut, 1904-1910.
——. *History of the Patriarchs of the Coptic Church of Alexandria.* Translated by B. Evetts. *Patrologia Orientalis*, vols. V, pp. 1-215, X, pp. 357-551. Paris, 1904-1915.
Sonnini de Manoncourt, Charles Nicholas Sigisbert. *Travels in Upper Lower Egypt.* Translated from the French by Henry Hunter. London: Printed for J. Stockdale, 1799.
as-Suyūṭī. *Ḥusn al-Muḥāḍara fī Tārīkh Miṣr wa al-Qāhira.* 2 vols. Cairo, 1967-1968.
Thenaud, Jean, and Domenico Trevisan. *Le voyage d'Outre-mer de Jean Thenaud*

suivi de la relation de l'Ambassade de Domenico Trevisan auprès du Soudan d'Égypte. 2nd edition. Edited and annotated by Charles Schefer. Paris: E. Leroux, 1884.

Thevenot, Jean de. *The Travels of Monsieur de Thevenot into the Levant.* Translated by A. Lovell. 3 vols. in 1. London: H. Clark, 1686-1687.

Turc, Nicolas. *Mudhakkirāt Niqūla Turc, Chronique d'Égypte, 1798-1804.* Translated and edited by Gaston Wiet. Cairo, 1950.

Volney, Constantin-François Chasseboeuf. *Travels through Egypt and Syria in the Years 1783, 1784, and 1785.* Translated from the French. 2 vols. London: G. G. J. and J. Robinson, 1787.

Wilkinson, John Gardner. *Handbook for Travelers in Egypt.* London: J. Murray, 1858.

——. *Modern Egypt and Thebes.* London: J. Murray, 1867.

William of Tyre. *Historia rerum in partibus transmarinis gestarum, Recueil des historiens des croissades: historiens occidentaux.* Vol. I, chapters 19, 20. Paris, 1844.

al-Ya^c^qūbī. *Kitāb al-Buldān. Bibliotheca Geographorum Arabicorum.* Edited by M. J. De Goeje. Vol. VII. Leiden: E. J. Brill, 1967.

——. *Livre de les pays* (a translation of *Kitāb al-Buldān*). Translated by Gaston Wiet. Cairo: Imprimerie de l'Institut Français d'Archéologie Orientale, 1937.

aẓ-Ẓāhirī, Khalīl. *Kitāb Zubda Kashf al-Mamālik.* Edited by P. Ravaisse. Paris, 1894.

——. *La Zubda Kachf al-Mamâlik de Khalīl az-Zāhirī* (a translation of *Kitāb Zubda*). Edited by Jean Gaulmier. Beirut, 1950.

II. SECONDARY SOURCES

Abbott, Nabia. *The Ḳurrah Papyri from Aphrodite in the Oriental Institut.* Chicago Ill.: The University of Chicago Press, 1938.

Abu-Lughod, Janet L. *Cairo: 1001 Years of the City Victorious.* Princeton, N.J.: Princeton University Press, 1971.

Arnakis, G. G. "Futuwwa Traditions in the Ottoman Empire Akhis, Bektashi Dervishes, and Craftsmen." *Journal of Near Eastern Studies,* XII (1953), pp. 232-252.

Ashtor, Eli. "Le coût de la vie dans l'Égypt médiévale." *Journal of the Economic and Social History of the Orient,* III (1960), pp. 56-77.

——. "L'évolution des prix dans la Proche-Orient à la basse-époque." *Journal of the Economic and Social History of the Orient,* IV (1961), pp. 15-46.

——. "The Kārimī Merchants." *Journal of the Royal Asiatic Society,* 1956, pp. 45-56.

Ayalon, David. "The Circassians in the Mamluk Kingdom." *Journal of the American Oriental Society,* LXIX (1949), pp. 135-147.

——. *L'esclavage du Mamelouk.* Jerusalem: The Israel Oriental Society, 1951.

——. *Gunpowder and Firearms in the Mamluk Kingdom: A Challenge to Medieval Society.* London: Vallentine, Mitchell, 1956.

——. "The Historian al-Jabartī and his Background." *Bulletin of the School of Oriental and African Studies,* XXIII (1960), pp. 217-250.

——. "Studies in al-Jabartī I: Notes on the Transformation of Mamlūk Society in Egypt under the Ottomans." *Journal of the Economic and Social History of the Orient,* III (1960), pp. 148-174; pp. 275-325.

——. "Studies on the Structure of the Mamluk Army." *Bulletin of the School of Oriental and African Studies,* XV (1953), pp. 203-228, 448-476; XIV (1954), pp. 57-90.

——. "Studies on the Transfer of the ^c^Abbāsid Caliphate from Baghdād to Cairo." *Arabica,* 7 (1960), pp. 41-59.

——. "The Wafidiya in the Mamluk Kingdom." *Islamic Culture,* XXV (1951), pp. 89-104.

Baer, Gabriel. "Administrative, Economic, and Social Functions of Turkish Guilds." *International Journal of Middle East Studies*, 1 (1970), pp. 28-50.

——. *Egyptian Guilds in Modern Times.* Jerusalem: The Israel Oriental Society, 1964.

——. "'Guilds in Middle Eastern History." *Studies in the Economic History of the Middle East*, pp. 11-30. Edited by M. A. Cook, London: Oxford University Press, 1970.

——. "Monopolies and Restrictive Practices of Turkish Guilds." *Journal of the Economic and Social History of the Orient*, 13 (1970), pp. 145-165.

——. "Social Change in Egypt: 1800-1914." *Political and Social Change in Modern Egypt*, pp. 135-161. Edited by P. M. Holt. London: Oxford University Press, 1968.

al-Bakrī, Muḥammad Tawfīq. *Bayt aṣ-Ṣiddīq.* Cairo, 1905.

Bannerth, Ernst. "La Khalwatiyya en Égypte." *Mélanges de l'Institut Dominicain des Études Orientales*, VIII (Cairo, 1964-66), pp. 1-74.

——. "La Rifāᶜiyya en Égypte." *Mélanges de l'Institut Dominicain des Études Orientales*, X (Cairo, 1970), pp. 1-35.

Barkan, Ömer Lutfi. "Quelques observations sur l'organisation économique et sociale des villes Ottomanes." *La Ville*, VII, pp. 289-311. Société Jean Bodin. Brussels, 1955.

Becker, C. H. "Cairo." *Encyclopaedia of Islam.* Leiden, 1913.

——. "Egypt." *Encyclopaedia of Islam.* Leiden, 1913.

Bell, H. I. "The Administration of Egypt under the Umayyad Khalifs." *Byzantinische Zeitschrift*, 28 (1928), pp. 278-286.

Boissevain, Jeremy. "The Place of Non-Groups in the Social Sciences." *Man*, 3 (1968), pp. 542-556.

Bosworth, C. E. "Christian and Jewish Religious Dignitaries in Mamlūk Egypt and Syria: Qalqashandī's Information on Their Hierarchy, Titulature, and Appointment." *International Journal of Middle East Studies*, 3 (1972), pp. 59-74; pp. 199-216.

Brinner, William M. "The Significance of the Ḥarāfīsh and Their 'Sultan'." *Journal of the Economic and Social History of the Orient*, 6 (1963), pp. 190-215.

Butler, Alfred J. *The Arab Conquest of Egypt.* Oxford: The Clarendon Press, 1902.

——. *Babylon of Egypt.* Oxford: The Clarendon Press, 1914.

Cahen, Claude. "Les marchands étrangers au Caire sous les Fāṭimides et les Ayyūbides." *Colloque international sur l'histoire du Caire*, pp. 97-101. Cairo: General Egyptian Book Organization, 1974.

——. "Mouvements populaires et autonomisme urbain dans l'Asie musulmane de moyen âge." *Arabica*, V (1958), pp. 225-50; VI (1959), pp. 25-26, 223-265.

——. "Y a-t-il eu des corporations professionelles dans le monde musulman classique?" *The Islamic City*, pp. 51-63. Edited by A. H. Hourani and S. M. Stern. Oxford: Bruno Cassirer, 1970.

Canard, Marius. "L'impérialisme des Fatimides et leur propagande." *Annales de l'Institut d'Études Orientales*, 6 (1942-1947), pp. 156-193.

——. "Notes sur les Arméniens en Égypte à l'époque fâṭimite." *Annales de l'Institut d'Études Orientales*, 13 (1955), pp. 143-157.

——. "Un vizir chretien à l'époque fâṭimite: l'Arménien Bahrâm." *Annales de l'Institut d'Études Orientales*, 12 (1954), pp. 84-113.

Casanova, Paul. *Essai de reconstitution topographique de la ville d'al-Fousṭāṭ ou Miṣr.* Mémoires publiés par les membres de l'Institut Français d'Archéologie Orientale au Caire, XXXV, etc. Cairo, 1919.

——. *Histoire et description de la citadelle du Caire.* Mémoires publiés par les membres de la Mission Archaéologique Française au Caire, VI (Paris, 1894-97), pp. 509-780.

Casson, L. "Tax Collection Problems in Early Arab Egypt." *Transactions and Proceedings of the American Philological Association*, 69 (1938), pp. 274-291.

Cattaui, René. *La règne de Mohamed Aly d'après les archives russes en Égypte.* 3 vols. Cairo-Rome, 1931-1936.

Christie, A. H. "Islamic Minor Arts and Their Influence upon European Work." *The Legacy of Islam,* pp. 108-151. Edited by Sir Thomas Arnold and Alfred Guillaume. London: Oxford University Press, 1931.

Clerget, Marcel. *Le Caire. Étude de géographie urbaine et d'histoire économique.* 2 vols. Cairo: E. and R. Schindler, 1934.

Cohen, Hayyim J. "The Economic Background and Secular Occupations of Muslim Jurisprudents and Traditionalists in the Classical Period of Islam." *Journal of the Economic and Social History of the Orient,* XIII (1970), pp. 16-61.

Cohen, Ronald. "Power, Authority, and Personal Success in Islam and Bornu." *Political Anthropology,* pp. 129-139. Edited by Marc J. Swartz, et al. Chicago: Aldine, 1966.

Crecelius, Daniel. "The Emergence of the Shaykh al-Azhar as the Pre-eminent Religious Leader in Egypt." *Colloque international sur l'histoire du Caire,* pp. 109-123. Cairo: General Egyptian Book Organization, 1974.

Creswell, K. A. C. "Fortification in Islam before A.D. 1250." *Proceedings of the British Academy,* 38 (1952), pp. 89-125.

Crouchley, A. E. "The Development of Commerce in the Reign of Mohamed Ali." *L'Égypte Contemporaine,* 28 (1937), pp. 305-368.

——. *The Economic Development of Modern Egypt.* London: Longmans Green & Co., 1938.

Dehérain, Henri. *L'Égypte turque. Histoire de la nation égyptienne,* V. Edited by Gabriel Hanotaux. Paris, 1937.

Dodge, Bayard. *Al-Azhar: A Millennium of Muslim Learning.* Washington, D.C.: The Middle East Institute, 1961.

Dols, Michael. "Ibn al-Wardī's *Risālah al-Nabaʾ ʿan al-Wabaʾ*, a Translation of a Major Source for the History of the Black Death in the Middle East." *Near Eastern Numismatics, Iconography, Epigraphy, and History: Studies in Honor of George C. Miles,* pp. 443-455. Edited by Dickran K. Kouymjian. Beirut: American University of Beirut Press, 1974.

Dopp, P.-H. "Le Caire: Vu par les voyageurs occidentaux du Moyen Âge." *Bulletin de la Société Royale de Géographie d'Égypte,* XXIII (1950), pp. 117-149; XXIV (1951), pp. 115-162.

Ebers, Georg. *Aegypten in Bild und wort.* 2 vols. Stuttgart: Hallberger, 1878-1880.

Fischel, Walter J. "The City in Islam." *Middle Eastern Affairs,* 7 (1956), pp. 227-232.

——. "Ibn Khaldūn's Activities in Mamlūk Egypt (1382-1406)." *Semitic and Oriental Studies,* pp. 103-123. Edited by Walter J. Fischel. Berkeley: University of California Press, 1951.

——. *Jews in the Economic and Political Life of Medieval Islam.* London: The Royal Asiatic Society of Great Britain and Ireland, 1937.

——. "The Spice Trade in Mamluk Egypt." *Journal of the Economic and Social History of the Orient,* I (1958), pp. 157-174.

Forand, Paul G. "The Relation of the Slave and Client to the Master or Patron in Medieval Islam." *International Journal of Middle East Studies,* 2 (1971), pp. 59-66.

Gellner, Ernest. "A Pendulum Swing Theory of Islam." *Sociology of Religion: Selected Readings,* pp. 127-138. Edited by Roland Robertson. Baltimore, Md.: Penguin Books, 1969.

Gibb, H. A. R. "The Achievement of Saladin." *Bulletin of the John Rylands Library,* 35 (Manchester, 1952) pp. 44-60. Reprinted in H. A. R. Gibb. *Studies on the Civilization of Islam,* pp. 90-107. Edited by Stanford J. Shaw and W. R. Polk. Boston: The Beacon Press, 1962.

——. "The Evolution of Government in Early Islam." *Studia Islamica*, IV (1955), pp. 1-17. Reprinted in H. A. R. Gibb, *Studies on the Civilization of Islam*, pp. 34-46. Edited by Stanford J. Shaw and W. R. Polk. Boston: The Beacon Press, 1962.

——. *Mohammedanism.* London: Oxford University Press, 1949.

Gibb, H. A. R. and Harold Bowen. *Islamic Society and the West.* 1 vol. in 2 parts. I: *Islamic Society in the Eighteenth Century.* London: Oxford University Press, 1950, 1957.

Goitein, S. D. "Bankers' Accounts from the Eleventh Century A.D." *Journal of the Economic and Social History of the Orient*, 9 (1966), pp. 28-68.

——. "Cairo: An Islamic City in the Light of the Geniza Documents." *Middle Eastern Cities*, pp. 80-96. Edited by Ira M. Lapidus. Berkeley: University of California Press, 1969.

——. "Evidence on the Muslim Poll-Tax from Non-Muslim Sources." *Journal of the Economic and Social History of the Orient*, 6 (1963), pp. 278-295.

——. *A Mediterranean Society.* I: *Economic Foundations.* II: *The Community.* Berkeley: University of California Press, 1967, 1971.

——. "The Mentality of the Middle Class in Medieval Islam." *Studies in Islamic History and Institutions*, pp. 242-254. S. D. Goitein. Leiden: E. J. Brill, 1966.

——. "New Light on the Beginnings of the Kārim Merchants." *Journal of the Economic and Social History of the Orient*, I (1958), pp. 175-184.

——. "Petitions to Fatimid Caliphs from the Cairo Geniza." *Jewish Quarterly Review*, N.S. 45 (1954-1955), pp. 30-38.

——. "The Rise of the Middle-Eastern Bourgeoisie in Early Islamic Times." *Studies in Islamic History and Institutions*, pp. 217-241. S. D. Goitein. Leiden: E. J. Brill, 1966.

——. "Slaves and Slave Girls in the Cairo Geniza Records." *Arabica*, IX (1962), pp. 1-20.

Gottschalk, H. *Die Mādarā'ijjūn. Studien zur Geschichte und Kultur des islamischen Orients*, 6. Heft. Berlin and Leipzig: W. de Gruyter & Co., 1931.

Guest, A. R. "Cairene Topography: El Qarafa According to Ibn Ez-Zaiyat." *Journal of the Royal Asiatic Society*, 1926, pp. 57-61.

——. "The Foundation of Fustat and the Khittahs of that Town." *Journal of the Royal Asiatic Society*, 1907, pp. 49-83.

Ḥasan, Ḥasan Ibrāḥīm. *Al-Fāṭimīyūn fī Miṣr.* Cairo, 1932.

Heyd, W. *Histoire du commerce du Levant au moyen-âge.* Translated by F. Reynaud. II. Amsterdam: Adolph M. Hakkert, 1959.

Heyworth-Dunne, J. *An Introduction to the History of Education in Modern Egypt.* London: Luzac & Co., 1938.

Holt, P. M. "The Career of Küçük Muḥammad (1676-94)." *Bulletin of the School of Oriental and African Studies*, XXVI (1963), pp. 269-287.

——. "Dhu'l-Faḳāriyya." *Encyclopaedia of Islam*, 1960.

——. *Egypt and the Fertile Crescent*, 1516-1922. London: Longmans, Green & Co., 1966.

——. "The Exalted Lineage of Riḍwān Bey: Some Observations on a 17th Century Mamlūk Genealogy." *Bulletin of the School of Oriental and African Studies*, 22 (1959), pp. 221-230.

——. "The Pattern of Egyptian Political History from 1517-1798." *Political and Social Change in Modern Egypt*, pp. 79-90. Edited by P. M. Holt. London: Oxford University Press, 1968.

Hourani, Albert H. "The Islamic City in the Light of Recent Research." *The Islamic City*, pp. 9-24. Edited by A. H. Hourani and S. M. Stern. Oxford: Bruno Cassirer, 1970.

——. "Ottoman Reform and the Politics of Notables." *Beginnings of Modernization in the Middle East: The Nineteenth Century*, pp. 41-68. Edited by William R. Polk and Richard L. Chambers. Chicago: The University of Chicago Press, 1968.

——. "The Political and Social Background in the Nineteenth Century." *The Economic History of the Middle East, 1800-1914*, pp. 23-29. Edited by Charles Issawi. Chicago and London: The University of Chicago Press, 1966.

——. "The Syrians in Egypt in the Eighteenth and Nineteenth Centuries." *Colloque international sur l'histoire du Caire*, pp. 221-233. Cairo: General Egyptian Book Organization, 1974.

Humphreys, R. Stephen. "The Political Role of the ᶜUlamāᵓ in the Age of the Ayyūbids." A paper delivered at the Middle East Studies Association Annual Meeting. Toronto, Canada, November, 1969.

Inalcik, H. "The Ottoman Economic Mind and Aspects of the Ottoman Economy." *Studies in the Economic History of the Middle East*, pp. 207-218. Edited by M. A. Cook. London: Oxford University Press, 1970.

Issawi, Charles. "The Decline of Middle Eastern Trade, 1100-1850." *Islam and the Trade of Asia*, pp. 245-266. Edited by Donald S. Richards. Oxford: Bruno Cassirer, 1970.

——. "The Economic Development of Modern Egypt, 1800-1960." *The Economic History of the Middle East 1800-1914*, pp. 359-374. Edited by Charles Issawi. Chicago and London: The University of Chicago Press, 1966.

Ivanow, W. "The Organization of the Fatimid Propaganda." *Journal of the Bombay Branch of the Royal Asiatic Society*, N.S. 15 (1938), pp. 1-35.

al-Jiritlī, ᶜAlī. *Tārīkh aṣ-Ṣināᶜa fī Miṣr*. Cairo, 1952.

Kahle, Paul. "The Arabic Shadow Play in Egypt." *Opera Minora*, pp. 297-306. Paul Kahle. Leiden: E. J. Brill, 1956.

Kimche, David. "The Political Superstructure of Egypt in the Late Eighteenth Century." *The Middle East Journal*, 22 (1968), pp. 448-462.

Kissling, Hans Joachim. "The Sociological and Educational Role of the Dervish Orders in the Ottoman Empire." *Studies in Islamic Cultural History*, pp. 23-35. Edited by G. E. von Grunebaum. Memoirs of the American Anthropological Association, no. 76 (April, 1954).

Kramers, J. H. "Geography and Commerce." *The Legacy of Islam*, pp. 79-107. Edited by Sir Thomas Arnold and Alfred Guillaume. London:: The Oxford University Press, 1931.

Labīb, Subḥī. "Egyptian Commercial Policy in the Middle Ages." *Studies in the Economic History of the Middle East*, pp. 63-77. Edited by M. A. Cook. London: Oxford University Press, 1970.

——. *Handelsgeschichte Ägyptens im Spätmittelalter* (1171-1517). Wiesbaden, 1965.

Landau, Jacob M. "The Jews in Nineteenth-century Egypt—Some Socio-economic Aspects." *Political and Social Change in Modern Egypt*, pp. 196-208. Edited by P. M. Holt. London: Oxford University Press, 1968.

Lane, F. C. "The Mediterranean Spice Trade." *American Historical Review*, XLV (1940), pp. 581-590.

——. "Venetian Shipping during the Commercial Revolution." *American Historical Review*, XXXVIII (1933), pp. 219-237.

Lane-Poole, Stanley. *Cairo, Sketches of Its History, Monuments, and Social Life*. London, 1895.

——. *A History of Egypt in the Middle Ages. History of Egypt*, VI. London: Methuen & Co., 1901.

——. *Saladin and the Fall of the Kingdom of Jerusalem*. New York: G. P. Putnam's Sons, 1898.

——. *Social Life in Egypt: A Description of the Country and Its People. A Supplement to Picturesque Palestine.* Edited by Col. Wilson. London: n.d. (1884?).
——. *The Story of Cairo.* London: J. M. Dent & Co., 1902.
Lapidus, Ira M. "Ayyūbid Religious Policy and the Development of the Schools of Law in Cairo." *Colloque international sur l'histoire du Caire*, pp. 279-286. Cairo: General Egyptian Book Organization, 1974.
——. "The Grain Economy of Mamlūk Egypt." *Journal of the Economic and Social History of the Orient*, XII (1969), pp. 1-15.
——. *Muslim Cities in the Later Middle Ages.* Cambridge, Mass.: Harvard University Press, 1967.
Livingston, John W. "ᶜAlī Bey al-Kabīr and the Jews." *Middle East Studies*, VII (1971), pp. 221-228.
Lopez, R. et al. "England to Egypt, 1350-1500: Long-term Trends and Long-distance Trade." *Studies in the Economic History of the Middle East.* pp. 93-128. Edited by M. A. Cook. London: Oxford University Press, 1970.
Loutfi el-Sayed, Afaf. "The Role of the *ᶜUlamāʾ* in Egypt during the Early Nineteenth Century." *Political and Social Change in Modern Egypt*, pp. 264-280. Edited by P. M. Holt. London: Oxford University Press, 1968.
Lybyer, Albert H. "The Ottoman Turks and the Routes of Oriental Trade." *English Historical Review*, 30 (1915), pp. 577-588.
McPherson, J. W. *The Moulids of Egypt.* Cairo, 1941.
Mann, Jacob. *The Jews in Egypt and in Palestine under the Fatimid Caliphs.* 2 vols. London: Humphrey Milford, 1920-1922.
Margoliouth, D. S. *Cairo, Jerusalem and Damascus.* London: Chatto and Windus, 1907.
Marsot, Afaf Lutfi al-Sayyid. "A Socio-economic Sketch of the *ᶜUlamāʾ* in the Eighteenth Century." *Colloque international sur l'histoire du Caire*, pp. 313-319. Cairo: General Egyptian Book Oragnization, 1974.
——. "The Ulema of Cairo in the Eighteenth and Nineteenth Centuries." *Scholars, Saints and Sufis*, pp. 149-165. Edited by Nikki R. Keddie. Los Angeles: University of California Press, 1972.
Martin, Bradford G. "A Short History of the Khalwati Order of Dervishes." *Scholars, Saints and Sufis*, pp. 275-305. Edited by Nikki R. Keddie. Los Angeles: University of California Press, 1972.
Massignon, L. "Explication du plan de Baṣra (Irak)." *Westöstliche Abhandlungen R. Tschudi*, pp. 155-174. Wiesbaden, 1954.
——. "Explication du plan de Qufa (Iraq)." *Mélanges Maspéro*, III, pp. 337-360. Extraits de la Mémoires de l'Institut Française d'Archéologie Orientale, Cairo, 1935.
Mayer, L. A. *Saracenic Heraldry.* Oxford, 1933.
Mez, Adam. *Die Renaissance des Islams.* Edited by H. Rechendorf. Heidelberg: C. Winter, 1922.
Mubārak, ᶜAlī Pasha. *Al-Khiṭaṭ at-Tawfīqīya al-Jadīda li-Miṣr al-Qāhira.* 20 vols. in 5. Cairo (Būlāq), 1888.
Muir, William. *The Mameluke or Slave Dynasty of Egypt 1260-1517.* London: Smith, Elder, and Co., 1896.
Mustafa, Ahmed. "The Breakdown of the Monopoly System in Egypt after 1840." *Political and Social Change in Modern Egypt*, pp. 291-307. Edited by P. M. Holt. London: Oxford University Press, 1968.
Neustadt, David (David Ayalon). "The Plague and Its Effects upon the Mamlūk Army." *Journal of the Royal Asiatic Society*, 1946, pp. 67-73.
O'Leary, De Lacy E. *A Short History of the Fatimid Califate.* London: K. Paul, Trench, and Trubner, 1923.
Pedersen, John. "Masdjid." *Encyclopaedia of Islam.* Leiden, 1913.

Perlmann, Moshe. "Notes on Anti-Christian Propaganda in the Mamlūk Empire." *Bulletin of the School of Oriental and African Studies*, X (1940-1942), pp. 843-861.

Petry, Carl. "The Geographic Origins and Residence Patterns of the ᶜUlemaᵓ of Cairo during the Fifteenth Century." A paper delivered at the annual meeting of the Middle East Studies Association. Milwaukee, Wisconsin, November, 1973.

Poliak, A. N. "Le charactere colonial de l'état mamelouk dans ses rapports avec la Horde d'or." *Revue des Études Islamiques*, 9 (1935), pp. 231-248.

——. *Feudalism in Egypt, Syria, Palestine and the Lebanon 1250-1900*. London: The Royal Asiatic Society, 1939.

——. "The Influence of Chingiz-Khan's Yāsa upon the General Organization of the Mamluk State." *Bulletin of the School of Oriental and African Studies*, X (1942), pp. 862-876.

——. "Les révoltes populaires en Égypt à l'époque des mamelouks et leurs causes économiques." *Revue des Études Islamiques*, VIII (1934), pp. 251-273.

——. "Some Notes on the Feudal System of the Mamlūks." *Journal of the Royal Asiatic Society*, 1937, pp. 97-107.

Popper, William. *Egypt and Syria under the Circassian Sultans 1382-1468 A.D.* University of California Publications in Semitic Philology, XV, XVI. Berkeley and Los Angeles: University of California Press, 1955, 1957.

Qoudsī, Elia. "Notice sur les corporations de Damas." *Actes du sixième Congrès International des Orientalistes*, Deuxième partie, Section 1: Sémitique, Leiden, 1885.

Rabie, Hassanein. "The Size and Value of the *Iqṭāᶜ* in Egypt, 564-741 A.H. 1169-1341 A.D." *Studies in the Economic History of the Middle East*, pp. 129-138. Edited by M. A. Cook. London: Oxford University Preass, 1970.

Raymond, André. *Artisans et commerçants au Caire*. 2 vols. Damascus: Institut Français, 1973, 1974.

——. "Les bains publics au Caire à la fin du XVIIIe siècle." *Annales Islamologiques*, VIII, pp. 129-150. Cairo: L'Institut Français d'Archéologie Orientale, 1969.

——. "Essai de géographie des quartiers de résidence aristocratique au Caire aux XVIIIᵉ siècle." *Journal of the Economic and Social History of the Orient*, VI (1963), pp. 58-103.

——. "Une liste des corporations de métiers au Caire en 1801." *Arabica*, IV (1957), pp. 150-163.

——. "Problèmes urbains et urbanisme au Caire au XVIIème et XVIIIème siècles." *Colloque international sur l'histoire du Caire*, pp. 353-372. Cairo: General Egyptian Book Organization, 1974.

——. "Quartiers et mouvements populaires au Caire au XVIIIème siècle." *Political and Social Change in Modern Egypt*, pp. 104-116. Edited by P. M. Holt. London: Oxford University Press, 1968.

——. "Tunisiens et Magrébins au Caire au dix-huitième siècle." *Cahiers de Tunisie*, 26-27 (1959), pp. 336-371.

Reitemeyer, Else. *Die Städtegründungen der Araber im Islām nach den arabischen Historikern und Geographen*. Munich, 1912.

Richards, Donald. "The Coptic Bureaucracy under the Mamlūks." *Colloque international sur l'histoire du Caire*, pp. 373-381. Cairo: General Egyptian Book Organization, 1974.

Richmond, Ernest. "The Significance of Cairo." *Journal of the Royal Asiatic Society*, 1913, pp. 23-40.

Rodinson, Maxime. "Histoire économique et histoire des classes sociales dans le monde musulman." *Studies in the Economic History of the Middle East*, pp. 139-155. Edited by M. A. Cook. London: Oxford University Press, 1970.

——. *Islam et capitalisme*. Paris: Editions du Seuil, 1966.

Russell, Dorothea. *Medieval Cairo and the Monasteries of the Wādi Natrūn*. London: Weidenfeld and Nicolson, 1962.

Salama, Ibrahim. *L'enseignement islamique en Égypte*. Cairo, 1938.

Sanger, William. "The Black Death." *Scientific American*, 210 (1964), pp. 114-121.

Scanlon, George T. "Fustat Expedition: Preliminary Report 1965, Part I." *Journal of the American Research Center in Egypt*, V (1966), pp. 83-112.

——. "Housing and Sanitation: Some Aspects of Medieval Public Service." *The Islamic City*, pp. 179-194. Edited by A. H. Hourani and S. M. Stern. Oxford: Bruno Cassirer, 1969.

Schacht, Joseph. *An Introduction to Islamic Law*. Oxford: The Clarendon Press, 1964.

——. "Sharīᶜa." *Encyclopaedia of Islam*. Leiden, 1913.

Schäfer, B. *Beiträge zur Mamlukischen Historiographie nach dem Tode al-Malik an-Nasirs mit einem Teiledition der Chronik Šems ad-Din aš-Šugais*. Freiburg im Breisgau, 1971.

Shaw, Stanford J. *The Financial and Administrative Organization and Development of Ottoman Egypt 1517-1798*. Princeton, N.J.: Princeton University Press, 1962.

——. "Landholding and Land-tax Revenues in Ottoman Egypt." *Political and Social Change in Modern Egypt*, pp. 91-103. Edited by P. M. Holt. London: Oxford University Press, 1968.

——. *Ottoman Egypt in the Age of the French Revolution* by Ḥuseyn Efendī. Translated from the original Arabic with introduction and notes. Cambridge, Mass.: The Harvard University Press for the Center for Middle Eastern Studies, 1964.

——. *Ottoman Egypt in the Eighteenth Century*, The *Niẓāmnāme-i Miṣir* of Cezzār Aḥmed Pasha. Edited and translated from the original Turkish. Cambridge, Mass.: The Harvard University Press for the Center for Middle Eastern Studies, 1962.

el-Shayyal, Gamal al-Din. "Some Aspects of Intellectual and Social Life in Eighteenth-century Egypt." *Political and Social Change in Modern Egypt*, pp. 117-132. Edited by P. M. Holt. London: Oxford University Press, 1968.

ash-Shayyāl, Jamāl ad-Dīn. *Muḥādarāt fī al-Ḥarakāt al-Islāḥīya wa Marākiz ath-Thaqāfa fī ash-Sharq al-Islāmī al-Ḥadīth*. 2 vols. Cairo, 1958.

Soberneim, M. "Mamlūks." *Encyclopaedia of Islam*. Leiden, 1913.

Spuler, Bertold. *The Muslim World: A Historical Survey*. Part II: *The Mongol Period*. Translated by F. R. C. Bagley. Leiden: E. J. Brill, 1960.

Stern, S. M. "The Constitution of the Islamic City." *The Islamic City*, pp. 25-50. Edited by A. H. Hourani and S. M. Stern. Oxford: Bruno Cassirer, 1970.

Strauss, Eli (Eli Ashtor). "Prix et salaires à l'époque mamlouke. Une étude sur l'état économique de l'Égypte et de la Syrié à la fin du moyen âge." *Revue des Études Islamiques*, 1949, pp. 49-94.

aṭ-Ṭawīl, Tawfīq. *At-Taṣawwuf fī Miṣr ibbān al-ᶜAṣr al-ᶜUthmānī*. Cairo, 1946.

Tomiche, Nada. "Notes sur la hiérarchie sociale en Égypte à l'époque de Muḥammad ᶜAlī." *Political and Social Change in Modern Egypt*, pp. 249-263. Edited by P. M. Holt. London: Oxford University Press, 1968.

——. "La situation des artisans et petite commerçants en Égypte de la fin du XVIIIᵉ siècle jusqu'au milieu du XIXᵉ." *Studia Islamica* XII (1960), pp. 79-98.

Trimingham, J. Spencer. *The Sufi Orders in Islam*. Oxford: The Clarendon Press, 1971.

Tritton, Arthur S. *Materials on Muslim Education in the Middle Ages*. London: Luzac & Co., 1957.

Tyan, Emile. *Histoire de l'organisation judiciare en pays d'Islam*. 2nd edition. Leiden: E. J. Brill, 1960.

Udovitch, Abraham L. *Partnership and Profit in Medieval Islam*. Princeton, N.J.: Princeton University Press, 1970.

van Nieuwenhuijze, C. A. O. *Sociology of the Middle East*. Leiden: E. J. Brill, 1971.

Vatikiotis, P. J. "The Rise of Extremist Sects and the Dissolution of Fatimid Empire in Egypt." *Islamic Culture*, 31 (1957), pp. 17-26.

Vollers, K. "Al-Azhar." *Encyclopaedia of Islam*. Leiden, 1913.

von Grunebaum, G. E. "The Structure of the Muslim Town." *Islam: Essays in the Nature and Growth of a Cultural Tradition*, pp. 141-158. Memoirs of the American Anthropological Association, no. 81 (1955).

Wansbrough, John. "A Mamluk Ambassador to Venice in 913/1507." *Bulletin of the School of Oriental and African Studies*, XXVI (1963), pp. 501-530.

Wiet, Gaston. *Cairo: City of Art and Commerce*. Translated by Seymour Feiler. The Centers of Civilization Series. Norman, Oklahoma: The University of Oklahoma Press, 1964.

——. "Les Communications en Égypte au Moyen Âge." *L'Égypte Contemporaine*, 24 (1933), pp. 241-264.

——. *L'Égypte arabe, Histoire de la nation égyptienne*. Edited by Gabriel Hanotaux. IV. Paris, 1937.

——. *L'Égypte musulmane. Précis de l'histoire d'Égypte*, III. Cairo, 1932.

——. "Les marchands d'épices sous les sultans mamlouks." *Cahiers d'Histoire Égyptienne*, VII (1955), pp. 81-147.

——. "Personnes déplacées." *Revue des Études Islamiques*, 27 (1959), pp. 9-21.

Wilson, Col., ed. *Picturesque Palestine, Sinai and Egypt*. 4 vols. with 1. New York: D. Appleton Co., 1883.

Wolf, Eric R. "Kinship, Friendship, and Patron-Client Relations in Complex Societies," *The Social Anthropology of Complex Societies*, pp. 1-22. Edited by Michael Banton. A.S.A. Monograph, no. 4. London: Tavistock Publications, 1966.

INDEX

Ibrāhīm-Bey al-Kabīr, Mamlūk, 238, 239, 292, 293
Ibrāhīm ad-Dasūqī, founder of Ṣūfī order, 363; *mawlid*, 381
Ibrāhīm Gülshenī, founder of Ṣūfī order, 364-365; *zāwiya* of, 364, 375
Ibrāhīm-Kākhya al-Qāzdughlī, officer of Janissaries, 237, 262, 280, 283, 303, 310, 318
Ibrāhīm ash-Sharāᵓibī, merchant, 323
Ibrāhīm as-Sinnārī, black Mamlūk, 303
Ideology, political: Arab, 17, 18, 22, 25, 27, 28, 29, 30; Ayyūbid, 84, 85, 86, 88, 96; Fāṭimid, 51, 76, 91; in modern times, 402-403; Ottoman, 233-234, 307
Ijmāᶜ (consensus), 90
Ikhshīd, *see* Muḥammad ibn Ṭughj
Ikhshīdids, 44, 47, 48, 50
*Iltizām*s (tax farms), *see* Taxes
ᶜIlwānīya, Ṣūfī order, 362
Imām (Shīᶜī leader), 51, 52, 53, 76, 91
Immigrants: from the Eastern Arab lands, 46, 67; Europeans, 229, 249; *fallāḥīn*, 208, 245, 253, 336; Greeks, 250; Maghribīs, 67, 74, 270, 363; Mamlūks as, 120-122, 133; Syrians, 250; *wāfidīya* (refugees from Mongol invasions), 112, 114, 115, 119, 122, 123, 160
Imports, *see* Trade
Īnāl, Burjī sultan, 110, 203, 209
India, 45, 105, 163, 165, 167, 168, 204, 345
Indian Ocean, 163, 167
Industries: associated with popular quarters, 259; competition from Europe, 204, 344-346; decline, Ottoman period, 321, 332, 340; development program of Muḥammad ᶜAlī, 241, 348-354; heavy, 23, 24, 114; lack of investment in, 207, 321; textiles, 34, 346, 350 (*illus.*). *See also* Crafts; *names of specific industries*
Informality (in social relations and specification of duties), 64, 131, 137, 140, 150, 295. *See also* Ambiguity; Flexibility
Inheritance: administration of, 268, 315, 330; legal only within groups defined by religious status, 35; among Mamlūks, 126, 132, 133, 135, 235; among merchants, 171; of the office of shaykh of the guild, 330; within the *ojāq*s, 284; during the plague, 196, 198, 203; of profession, 62. *See also* Hereditary principle
Insecurity, of economic environment, 2, 195, 199, 386
Institution, institutionalization: lack of, 90; limitations of the concept, 389-390. *See also* Corporation; Formal rules
Integration: facilitated by Ṣūfism, 367-369; relation to value systems, 355; through symbolism and ideology, 378-385, 396
Intelligentsia, 67, 69, 85, 96, 134, 139, 141, 144-146, 148, 154. *See also* ᶜ*Ulamā*ᵓ
Interest, taking of, 35, 153. *See also* Money lending; Usury
Intolerance, 21, 71, 151-154, 249. *See also* Persecution
Invasions: Arab, 16-19; Crusaders, 67; Hilāl and Sulaym, 67; Mongol, 103, 139; Ottoman, 105, 229, 231-234. *See also* Conquest, of Egypt
Investiture: of Mamlūk sultans, 102; of Muḥammad ᶜAlī, 301
Investment: in commerce, 46-47, 129, 148, 169, 321, 322; in crafts and industries, 207, 321, 337, 339, 353; discouraged by confiscation, 205, 206; al-Jabartī on, 322-323; in military concerns, 318; through patronage of partnership, 63, 337, 339; typical pattern 318-324; in urban real estate, 59, 322
*Iqṭāᶜ*s (fiefs), 20, 103, 121, 234. *See also* Fiefs
Iran, *see* Persia
Iraq, 46, 67, 139; Ṣūfism in, 362. *See also specific place names*
Irdabb, measure of, 156
Irrigation systems, 2, 77
Islam: encouragement of social mobility, 155; as framework of society, 2, 3, 4, 34, 91; instruction in, 68, *see also* Education; law of, *see Sharīᶜa*; popular traditions of, 32, 33, *see also* Folk culture; relation to modern socialistic ideology, 403; on slavery, 183; as a social movement, 355; territory of, 2-4, 45, 102, 164. *See also* Orthodoxy; Shīᶜa; Ṣūfism; Sunnī Islam
Ismāᶜīl, Khedive, 229
Ismāᶜīl, Ṣafavid Shāh, 210
Ismāᶜīlī movement, 50
Istanbul, 233, 234, 277, 278, 280, 286,